ABSOLUTE C++

WALTER SAVITCH

University of California, San Diego

Addison
Wesley

Boston San Francisco New York London
Toronto Sydney Tokyo Singapore Madrid Mexico City
Munich Paris Cape Town Hong Kong Montreal

Executive Editor	Susan Hartman Sullivan
Editorial Assistant	Galia Shokry
Executive Marketing Manager	Michael Hirsch
Project Management	Argosy Publishing
Composition and Art	Argosy Publishing
Copyeditor	Cindy Kogut
Proofreader	Bob LaRoche
Indexer	Larry Sweazy
Text and Cover Design	Leslie Haimes
Cover Photo	Renee Lynn/Stone by Getty Images
Design Manager	Gina Hagen Kolenda
Prepress and Manufacturing	Caroline Fell

Access the latest information about Addison-Wesley titles from our World Wide Web site:
http://www.aw.com/cs

Library of Congress Cataloging-in-Publication Data
Savitch, Walter J., 1943-
    Absolute C++ / Walter Savitch
        p. cm.
    ISBN 0-201-70927-9 (pbk.)
    1. C++ (Computer program language) I. Title.
  QA76.73.C153 S279 2002
  005.13'3--dc212001046383

Reprinted with corrections.

Chapter Opener Image: © 2002 PhotoDisc, Inc.

ISBN 0-201-70927-9
45678910-DOC-0403

Preface

This book is designed to be a textbook and reference for programming in the C++ language. Although it does include programming techniques, it is organized around the features of the C++ language rather than any particular curriculum of programming techniques. The main audience I had in mind when writing this book was undergraduate students who have not had extensive programming experience with the C++ language. As such, it would be a suitable C++ text or reference for a second or later computer science course that uses C++; it could even be used for a first programming course. This book is designed to accommodate a wide range of users. The beginning chapters are written at a level that is accessible to beginners, while the boxed sections of those chapters serve to quickly introduce more experienced programmers to basic C++ syntax. Later chapters are still designed to be accessible, but are written at a level suitable for students who have progressed to these more advanced topics. (For those who want a beginning textbook with more pedagogical material and more on very basic programming technique, I suggest another book I wrote that is more along these lines.)[1]

This book also includes an introduction to patterns and the Unified Modeling Language (UML). Since many computer science curricula postpone recursions to a second computer science course, the book includes a full chapter on recursion.

The C++ coverage in this book is very complete, going well beyond what a beginner needs to know. In particular, there is extensive coverage of inheritance, polymorphism, and exception handling in C++. There is also extensive material on the Standard Template Library (STL), as well as an introduction to patterns and the Unified Modeling Language (UML). Since many computer science curricula postpone recursion to a second computer science course, the book includes a full chapter on recursion.

SPECIAL FEATURES

ANSI/ISO C++ STANDARD

This book was written to conform to the new ANSI/ISO C++ standard.

STANDARD TEMPLATE LIBRARY

The Standard Template Library is an extensive library collection of preprogrammed data structure classes and important algorithms. The STL is perhaps as big a topic as the core C++ language. This book contains a very substantial introduction to the STL. There is a full chapter on the general topic of templates and a full chapter on the particulars of the STL, as well as other material on or related to the STL at other points in the text.

---

[1] Walter Savitch, *Problem Solving with C++: The Object of Programming,* Third Edition, Addison-Wesley Pub. Co., 2001, ISBN# 0-201-70390-4. Also, available in a Visual C++ package.

OBJECT-ORIENTED PROGRAMMING

This book is organized around the structure of the C++ language. As such, the earlier chapters, which cover aspects of C++ that are common to almost all high-level programming languages, are not particularly oriented toward object-oriented programming (OOP). This makes sense for a reference book and a book for learning a second language. However, I do consider C++ to be an OOP language. If you are really programming in C++ and not C, then you must avail yourself of the OOP features of C++. This book gives extensive coverage of encapsulation, inheritance, and polymorphism as realized in the C++ language. The final chapter on patterns and UML gives additional coverage of OOP-related material.

FLEXIBILITY IN TOPIC ORDERING

This book allows instructors wide latitude in reordering the material. This is important if a book is to serve as a reference. It is also in keeping with my philosophy of writing books that accommodate themselves to an instructor's style, rather than tieing the instructor to an author's personal preference of topic ordering. With this in mind, each chapter introduction explains what material must be covered before doing each section of the chapter.

ACCESSIBLE TO STUDENTS

It is not enough for a book to present the right topics in the right order. It is not even enough for it be clear and correct when read by an instructor or other expert. The material needs to be presented in a way that is accessible to the person who does not yet know the material. Like my other textbooks that have proved to be very popular with students, this book was written to be friendly and accessible to the student.

Summary Boxes

Each major point is summarized in a boxed section. These boxed sections are spread throughout each chapter. They serve as summaries of the material, as a quick reference source, and a way to quickly learn the C++ syntax for features the reader knows about in general but for which he or she needs to know the C++ particulars.

Self-Test Exercises

Each chapter contains numerous Self-Test Exercises at strategic points in the chapter. Complete answers for all the Self-Test Exercises are given at the end of each chapter.

Other Features

Pitfall sections, programming technique sections, and examples of complete programs with sample I/O are given throughout each chapter. Each chapter ends with a summary section and a collection of programming projects suitable to assign to students.

SUPPORT MATERIAL

Each book comes with a free copy of the Microsoft Visual C++ 6.0 Introductory Edition. In addition, the following supplements are available on the book's companion website at http://www.aw.com/savitch/:

- Source code from the book
- PowerPoint slides

The following resources are available to qualified instructors only. Please contact your local sales representative or send e-mail to aw.cse@awl.com for access information:

- Instructor's manual
- Computerized testbank

ACKNOWLEDGMENTS

Numerous individuals have contributed invaluable help and support in making this book happen. Frank Ruggirello and my editor Susan Hartman at Addison-Wesley are the ones who first conceived of the idea for this book. Susan Hartman, Galia Shokry, Lisa Kalner, Patty Mahtani, and the other fine people at Addison-Wesley were a continuing source of support and encouragement in getting the book reviewed, revised, and out the door.

Cindy Kogut did an incredibly thorough job of copyediting. Sally Boylan and others at Argosy Publishing did great work under rushed conditions in converting the manuscript to typeset pages.

David Teague deserves special acknowledgment. I very much appreciate his hard work, good insights, and careful researching for this book.

I thank my good friend Mario Lopez for the many helpful conversations we had about C++.

The following reviewers provided corrections and suggestions that contributed greatly to the final product. I thank them all. In random order they are Kenrick Mock, University of Alaska, Anchorage; Richard Albright, University of Delaware; H. E. Dunsmore, Purdue University; Christopher E. Cramer; Drue Coles, Boston University; Evan Golub, University of Maryland; Stephen Corbesero, Moravian College; Fredrick H. Colclough, Colorado Technical University; Joel Weinstein, Northeastern University; Stephen P. Leach, Florida State University; Alvin S. Lim, Auburn University; and Martin Dulberg, North Carolina State University.

I thank Fred Colclough for doing an excellent job of preparing the PowerPoint slides. I again thank David Teague—this time for his excellent work in preparing the instructor's guide.

Finally, I thank Christina for putting up with my working late on the book and even offering encouragement instead of complaining.

Walter Savitch
http://www-cse.ucsd.edu/users/savitch/
wsavitch@ucsd.edu

Contents

Chapter 9   Strings 349

Chapter 15   Polymorphism and Virtual Functions 627

Chapter 16   Templates 653

1 CHAPTER

C++ Basics

1 C++ Basics

The Analytical Engine has no pretensions whatever to originate anything.
It can do whatever we know how to order it to perform. It can follow
analysis; but it has no power of anticipating any analytical relations or
truths. Its province is to assist us in making available what we are already
acquainted with.

Ada Augusta, Countess of Lovelace

INTRODUCTION

This chapter introduces the C++ language and gives enough detail to allow you to handle simple programs involving expression, assignments, and console input/output (I/O). The details of assignment and expressions are similar to those of most other high-level languages. Every language has its own console I/O syntax, so if you are not familiar with C++, that may look new and different to you.

1.1 Introduction to C++

Language is the only instrument of science.

Samuel Johnson

This section gives an overview of the C++ programming language.

ORIGINS OF THE C++ LANGUAGE

The C++ programming languages can be thought of as the C programming language with classes (and other modern features added). The C programming language was developed by Dennis Ritchie of AT&T Bell Laboratories in the 1970s. It was first used for writing and maintaining the UNIX operating system. (Up until that time, UNIX systems programs were written either in assembly language or in a language called B, a language developed by Ken Thompson, the originator of UNIX.) C is a general-purpose language that can be used for writing any sort of program, but its success and popularity are closely tied to the UNIX operating system. If you wanted to maintain your UNIX system, you needed to use C. C and UNIX fit together so well that soon not just systems programs but almost all commercial programs that ran under UNIX were written in the C language. C became so popular that versions of the language were written for other popular operating systems; its use is thus not limited to computers that use UNIX. However, despite its popularity, C was not without its shortcomings.

The C language is peculiar because it is a high-level language with many of the features of a low-level language. C is somewhere in between the two extremes of a very high-level language and a low-level language, and therein lies both its strengths and its weaknesses. Like (low-level) assembly language, C language programs can directly manipulate the computer's memory. On the other hand, C has the features of a high-level language, which makes it easier to read and write than assembly language. This makes C an excellent choice for writing systems programs, but for other programs (and in some sense even for systems programs) C is not as easy to understand as other languages; also, it does not have as many automatic checks as some other high-level languages.

To overcome these and other shortcomings of C, Bjarne Stroustrup of AT&T Bell Laboratories developed C++ in the early 1980s. Stroustrup designed C++ to be a better C. Most of C is a subset of C++, and so most C programs are also C++ programs. (The reverse is not true; many C++ programs are definitely not C programs.) Unlike C, C++ has facilities for classes and so can be used for object-oriented programming.

C++ AND OBJECT-ORIENTED PROGRAMMING

Object-oriented programming (OOP) is a currently popular and powerful programming technique. The main characteristics of OOP are encapsulation, inheritance, and polymorphism. Encapsulation is a form of information hiding or abstraction. Inheritance has to do with writing reusable code. Polymorphism refers to a way that a single name can have multiple meanings in the context of inheritance. Having made those statements, we must admit that they will hold little meaning for readers who have not heard of OOP before. However, we will describe all these terms in detail later in this book. C++ accommodates OOP by providing classes, a kind of data type combining both data and algorithms. C++ is not what some authorities would call a "pure OOP language." C++ tempers its OOP features with concerns for efficiency and what some might call "practicality." This combination has made C++ currently the most widely used OOP language, although not all of its usage strictly follows the OOP philosophy.

THE CHARACTER OF C++

C++ has classes that allow it to be used as an object-oriented language. It allows for overloading of functions and operators. (All these terms will be explained eventually, so do not be concerned if you do not fully understand some terms.) C++'s connection to the C language gives it a more traditional look than newer object-oriented languages, yet it has more powerful abstraction mechanisms than many other currently popular languages. C++ has a template facility that allows for full and direct implementation of algorithm abstraction. C++ templates allow you to code using parameters for types. The newest C++ standard, and most C++ compilers, allow multiple namespaces to accommodate more reuse of class and function names. The exception handling facilities in C++ are similar to what you would find in other programming languages. Memory management in C++ is similar to that in C. The programmer must allocate his or her own memory and handle his or her own garbage collection. Most compilers will allow you to do C-style memory management in C++, since C is essentially a subset of C++. However, C++ also has its own syntax for a C++ style of memory management, and you are advised to use the C++ style of memory management when coding in C++. This book uses only the C++ style of memory management.

■ C++ TERMINOLOGY

functions

program

All procedure-like entities are called **functions** in C++. Things that are called *procedures, methods, functions,* or *subprograms* in other languages are all called *functions* in C++. As we will see in the next subsection, a C++ **program** is basically just a function called main; when you run a program, the run-time system automatically invokes the function named main. Other C++ terminology is pretty much the same as most other programming languages, and in any case, will be explained when each concept is introduced.

■ A SAMPLE C++ PROGRAM

Display 1.1 contains a simple C++ program and two possible screen displays that might be generated when a user runs the program. A C++ program is really a function definition for a function named main. When the program is run, the function named main is invoked. The body of the function main is enclosed in braces, {}. When the program is run, the statements in the braces are executed.

The following two lines set up things so that the libraries with console input and output facilities are available to the program. The details concerning these two lines and related topics are covered in Section 1.3 and in Chapters 9, 11, and 12.

```
#include <iostream>
using namespace std;
```

int main()

The following line says that main is a function with no parameters that returns an int (integer) value:

```
int main( )
```

Some compilers will allow you to omit the int or replace it with void, which indicates a function that does not return a value. However, the above form is the most universally accepted way to start the main function of a C++ program.

return 0;

The program ends when the following statement is executed:

```
return 0;
```

This statement ends the invocation of the function main and returns 0 as the function's value. According to the ANSI/ISO C++ standard, this statement is not required, but many compilers still require it. Chapter 3 covers all these details about C++ functions.

Display 1.1   A Sample C++ Program

```
1    #include <iostream>
2    using namespace std;

3    int main( )
4    {
5        int numberOfLanguages;

6        cout << "Hello reader.\n"
7             << "Welcome to C++.\n";

8        cout << "How many programming languages have you used? ";
9        cin >> numberOfLanguages;

10       if (numberOfLanguages < 1)
11           cout << "Read the preface. You may prefer\n"
12                << "a more elementary book by the same author.\n";
13       else
14           cout << "Enjoy the book.\n";

15       return 0;
16   }
```

SAMPLE DIALOGUE 1

```
Hello reader.
Welcome to C++.
How many programming languages have you used? 0 ◄──────── User types in 0 on the keyboard.
Read the preface. You may prefer
a more elementary book by the same author.
```

SAMPLE DIALOGUE 2

```
Hello reader.
Welcome to C++.
How many programming languages have you used? 1 ◄──────── User types in 1 on the keyboard.
Enjoy the book
```

Variable declarations in C++ are similar to what they are in other programming languages. The following line from Display 1.1 declares the variable numberOfLanguages:

```
int numberOfLanguages;
```

The type int is one of the C++ types for whole numbers (integers).

If you have not programmed in C++ before, then the use of `cin` and `cout` for console I/O is likely to be new to you. That topic is covered a little later in this chapter, but the general idea can be observed in this sample program. For example, consider the following two lines from Display 1.1:

```
cout << "How many programming languages have you used? ";
cin >> numberOfLanguages;
```

The first line outputs the text within the quotation marks to the screen. The second line reads in a number that the user enters at the keyboard and sets the value of the variable `numberOfLanguages` to this number.

The lines

```
cout << "Read the preface. You may prefer\n"
     << "a more elementary book by the same author.\n";
```

output two strings instead of just one string. The details are explained in Section 1.3 later in this chapter, but this brief introduction will be enough to allow you to understand the simple use of `cin` and `cout` in the examples that precede Section 1.3. The symbolism \n is the newline character, which instructs the computer to start a new line of output.

Although you may not yet be certain of the exact details of how to write such statements, you can probably guess the meaning of the `if–else` statement. The details will be explained in the next chapter.

(By the way, if you have not had at least some experience with some programming languages, you should read the preface to see if you might not prefer the more elementary book discussed in this program. You need not have had any experience with C++ to read this book, but some minimal programming experience is strongly suggested.)

1.2 Variables, Expressions, and Assignment Statements

Once a person has understood the way variables are used in programming, he has understood the quintessence of programming.

E. W. Dijkstra, *Notes on Structured Programming*

Variables, expressions, and assignments in C++ are similar to those in most other general-purpose languages.

IDENTIFIERS

identifier

The name of a variable (or other item you might define in a program) is called an **identifier**. A C++ identifier must start with either a letter or the underscore symbol, and all the rest of the characters must be letters, digits, or the underscore symbol. For example, the following are all valid identifiers:

```
x x1 x_1 _abc ABC123z7 sum RATE count data2 bigBonus
```

All the above names are legal and would be accepted by the compiler, but the first five are poor choices for identifiers because they are not descriptive of the identifier's use. None of the following are legal identifiers, and all would be rejected by the compiler:

```
12  3X  %change  data-1  myfirst.c  PROG.CPP
```

The first three are not allowed because they do not start with a letter or an underscore. The remaining three are not identifiers because they contain symbols other than letters, digits, and the underscore symbol.

Although it is legal to start an identifier with an underscore, you should avoid doing so, because identifiers starting with an underscore are informally reserved for system identifiers and standard libraries.

C++ is a **case-sensitive** language; that is, it distinguishes between uppercase and lowercase letters in the spelling of identifiers. Hence, the following are three distinct identifiers and could be used to name three distinct variables:

> case sensitive

```
rate  RATE  Rate
```

However, it is not a good idea to use two such variants in the same program, since that might be confusing. Although it is not required by C++, variables are usually spelled with their first letter in lowercase. The predefined identifiers, such as main, cin, cout, and so forth, must be spelled in all lowercase letters. The convention that is now becoming universal in object-oriented programming is to spell variable names with a mix of upper- and lowercase letters (and digits), to always start a variable name with a lowercase letter, and to indicate "word" boundaries with an uppercase letter, as illustrated by the following variable names:

```
topSpeed, bankRate1, bankRate2, timeOfArrival
```

This convention is not as common in C++ as in some other object-oriented languages, but is becoming more widely used and is a good convention to follow.

A C++ identifier can be of any length, although some compilers will ignore all characters after some (large) specified number of initial characters.

IDENTIFIERS

A C++ identifier must start with either a letter or the underscore symbol, and the remaining characters must all be letters, digits, or the underscore symbol. C++ identifiers are case sensitive and have no limit to their length.

keyword or reserved word

There is a special class of identifiers, called **keywords** or **reserved words**, that have a predefined meaning in C++ and cannot be used as names for variables or anything else. In the code displays of this book keywords are shown in a different color. A complete list of keywords is given in Appendix 1.

Some predefined words, such as cin and cout, are not keywords. These predefined words are not part of the core C++ language, and you are allowed to redefine them. Although these predefined words are not keywords, they are defined in libraries required by the C++ language standard. Needless to say, using a predefined identifier for anything other than its standard meaning can be confusing and dangerous and thus should be avoided. The safest and easiest practice is to treat all predefined identifiers as if they were keywords.

VARIABLES

declare

Every variable in a C++ program must be *declared* before it is used When you **declare** a variable you are telling the compiler—and, ultimately, the computer—what kind of data you will be storing in the variable. For example, the following are two definitions that might occur in a C++ program:

```
int numberOfBeans;
double oneWeight, totalWeight;
```

The first defines the variable numberOfBeans so that it can hold a value of type int, that is, a whole number. The name int is an abbreviation for "integer." The type int is one of the types for whole numbers. The second definition declares oneWeight and total-Weight to be variables of type double, which is one of the types for numbers with a decimal point (known as **floating-point numbers**). As illustrated here, when there is more than one variable in a definition, the variables are separated by commas. Also, note that each definition ends with a semicolon.

floating-point number

Every variable must be declared before it is used; otherwise, variables may be declared any place. Of course, they should always be declared in a location that makes the program easier to read. Typically, variables are declared either just before they are used or at the start of a block (indicated by an opening brace, {). Any legal identifier, other than a reserved word, may be used for a variable name.[1]

C++ has basic types for characters, integers, and floating-point numbers (numbers with a decimal point). Display 1.2 lists the basic C++ types. The commonly used type

---

[1] C++ makes a distinction between *declaring* and *defining* an identifier. When an identifier is declared, the name is introduced. When it is defined, storage for the named item is allocated. For the kind of variables we discuss in this chapter, and for much more of the book, what we are calling a *variable declaration* both declares the variable and defines the variable, that is, allocates storage for the variable. Many authors blur the distinction between variable definition and variable declaration, The difference between declaring and defining an identifier is more important for other kinds of identifiers, which we will encounter in later chapters.

Display 1.2   **Simple Types**

TYPE NAME	MEMORY USED	SIZE RANGE	PRECISION
short (also called short int)	2 bytes	−32,767 to 32,767	Not applicable
int	4 bytes	−2,147,483,647 to 2,147,483,647	Not applicable
long (also called long int)	4 bytes	−2,147,483,647 to 2,147,483,647	Not applicable
float	4 bytes	approximately 10^{-38} to 10^{38}	7 digits
double	8 bytes	approximately 10^{-308} to 10^{308}	15 digits
long double	10 bytes	approximately 10^{-4932} to 10^{4932}	19 digits
char	1 byte	All ASCII characters (Can also be used as an integer type, although we do not recommend doing so.)	Not applicable
bool	1 byte	true, false	Not applicable

The values listed here are only sample values to give you a general idea of how the types differ. The values for any of these entries may be different on your system. *Precision* refers to the number of meaningful digits, including digits in front of the decimal point. The ranges for the types float, double, and long double are the ranges for positive numbers. Negative numbers have a similar range, but with a negative sign in front of each number.

for integers is int. The type char is the type for single characters. The type char can be treated as an integer type, but we do not encourage you to do so. The commonly used type for floating-point numbers is double, and so you should use double for floating-point numbers unless you have a specific reason to use one of the other floating-point types. The type bool (short for *Boolean*) has the values true and false. It is not an integer type, but to accommodate older code, you can convert back and forth between bool and any of the integer types. In addition, the standard library named string provides the type string, which is used for strings of characters. The programmer can define types for arrays, classes, and pointers, all of which are discussed in later chapters of this book.

unsigned

Each of the integer types has an **unsigned** version that includes only nonnegative values. These types are unsigned short, unsigned int, and unsigned long. Their ranges do not exactly correspond to the ranges of the positive values of the types short, int, and long, but are likely to be larger (since they use the same storage as their corresponding types short, int, or long, but need not remember a sign). You are unlikely to need these types, but may run into them in specifications for predefined functions in some of the C++ libraries, which we discuss in Chapter 3.

ASSIGNMENT STATEMENTS

assignment statement

The most direct way to change the value of a variable is to use an **assignment statement**. In C++ the equal sign is used as the assignment operator. An assignment statement always consists of a variable on the left-hand side of the equal sign and an expression on the right-hand side. An assignment statement ends with a semicolon. The expression on the right-hand side of the equal sign may be a variable, a number, or a more complicated expression made up of variables, numbers, operators, and function invocations. An assignment statement instructs the computer to evaluate (that is, to compute the value of) the expression on the right-hand side of the equal sign and to set the value of the variable on the left-hand side equal to the value of that expression. The following are examples of C++ assignment statements:

```
totalWeight = oneWeight * numberOfBeans;
temperature = 98.6;
count = count + 2;
```

The first assignment statement sets the value of totalWeight equal to the number in the variable oneWeight multiplied by the number in numberOfBeans. (Multiplication is expressed using the asterisk, *, in C++.) The second assignment statement sets the value of temperature to 98.6. The third assignment statement increases the value of the variable count by 2.

In C++, assignment statements can be used as expressions. When used as an expression, an assignment statement returns the value assigned to the variable. For example, consider

```
n = (m = 2);
```

The subexpression (m = 2) both changes the value of m to 2 and returns the value 2. Thus, this sets both n and m equal to 2. As you will see when we discuss precedence of operators in detail in Chapter 2, you can omit the parentheses, so the assignment statement under discussion can be written as

```
n = m = 2;
```

We advise you not to use an assignment statement as an expression, but you should be aware of this behavior because it will help you understand certain kinds of coding errors. For one thing, it will explain why you will not get an error message when you mistakenly write

```
n = m = 2;
```

when you meant to write

```
n = m + 2;
```

(This is an easy mistake to make since = and + are on the same keyboard key.)

UNINITIALIZED VARIABLES

uninitialized
variable

A variable has no meaningful value until a program gives it one. For example, if the variable min-imumNumber has not been given a value either as the left-hand side of an assignment statement or by some other means (such as being given an input value with a cin statement), then the following is an error:

```
desiredNumber = minimumNumber + 10;
```

This is because minimumNumber has no meaningful value, and so the entire expression on the right-hand side of the equal sign has no meaningful value. A variable like minimumNumber that has not been given a value is said to be **uninitialized**. This situation is, in fact, worse than it would be if minimumNumber had no value at all. An uninitialized variable, like minimumNumber, will simply have some garbage value. The value of an uninitialized variable is determined by whatever pattern of zeros and ones was left in its memory location by the last program that used that portion of memory.

One way to avoid an uninitialized variable is to initialize variables at the same time they are declared. This can be done by adding an equal sign and a value, as follows:

```
int minimumNumber = 3;
```

This both declares minimumNumber to be a variable of type int and sets the value of the variable minimumNumber equal to 3. You can use a more complicated expression involving operations such as addition or multiplication when you initialize a variable inside the declaration in this way. As another example, the following declares three variables and initializes two of them:

```
double rate = 0.07, time, balance = 0.00;
```

C++ allows an alternative notation for initializing variables when they are declared. This alternative notation is illustrated by the following, which is equivalent to the preceding declaration:

```
double rate(0.07), time, balance(0.00);
```

INITIALIZING VARIABLES IN DECLARATIONS

You can initialize a variable (that is, give it a value) at the time that you declare the variable.

SYNTAX

```
Type_Name  Variable_Name_1 = Expression_for_Value_1,
           Variable_Name_2 = Expresssion_for_Value_2,...;
```

EXAMPLES

```
int count = 0, limit = 10, fudgeFactor = 2;
double distance = 999.99;
```

SYNTAX

Alternative syntax for initializing in declarations:

Type_Name Variable_Name_1 (Expression_for_Value_1),
      Variable_Name_2 (Expression_for_Value_2),...;

EXAMPLES

```
int count(0), limit(10), fudgeFactor(2);
double distance(999.99);
```

Tip

USE MEANINGFUL NAMES

Variable names and other names in a program should at least hint at the meaning or use of the thing they are naming. It is much easier to understand a program if the variables have meaningful names. Contrast

```
x = y * z;
```

with the more suggestive

```
distance = speed * time;
```

The two statements accomplish the same thing, but the second is easier to understand.

MORE ASSIGNMENT STATEMENTS

A shorthand notation exists that combines the assignment operator (=) and an arithmetic operator so that a given variable can have its value changed by adding, subtracting, multiplying by, or dividing by a specified value. The general form is

Variable Operator = Expression

which is equivalent to

Variable = Variable Operator (Expression)

The *Expression* can be another variable, a constant, or a more complicated arithmetic expression. The following list gives examples.

EXAMPLE	EQUIVALENT TO
count += 2;	count = count + 2;
total -= discount;	total = total - discount;
bonus *= 2;	bonus = bonus * 2;
time /= rushFactor;	time = time/rushFactor;
change %= 100;	change = change % 100;
amount *= cnt1 + cnt2;	amount = amount * (cnt1 + cnt2);

Self-Test Exercises

1. Give the declaration for two variables called feet and inches. Both variables are of type int and both are to be initialized to zero in the declaration. Give both initialization alternatives.

2. Give the declaration for two variables called count and distance. count is of type int and is initialized to zero. distance is of type double and is initialized to 1.5. Give both initialization alternatives.

3. Write a program that contains statements that output the values of five or six variables that have been defined, but not initialized. Compile and run the program. What is the output? Explain.

ASSIGNMENT COMPATIBILITY

As a general rule, you cannot store a value of one type in a variable of another type. For example, most compilers will object to the following:

```
int intVariable;
intVariable = 2.99;
```

The problem is a type mismatch. The constant 2.99 is of type double, and the variable intVariable is of type int. Unfortunately, not all compilers will react the same way to the above assignment statement. Some will issue an error message, some will give only a warning message, and some compilers will not object at all. Even if the compiler does allow you to use the above assignment, it will give intVariable the int value 2, not the value 3. Since you cannot count on your compiler accepting the above assignment, you should not assign a double value to a variable of type int.

Even if the compiler will allow you to mix types in an assignment statement, in most cases you should not. Doing so makes your program less portable, and it can be confusing.

There are some special cases in which it is permitted to assign a value of one type to a variable of another type. It is acceptable to assign a value of an integer type, such as int, to a variable of a floating-point type, such as type double. For example, the following is both legal and acceptable style:

assigning int **values to** double **variables**

```
double doubleVariable;
doubleVariable = 2;
```

The above will set the value of the variable named doubleVariable equal to 2.0.

Although it is usually a bad idea to do so, you can store an int value such as 65 in a variable of type char and you can store a letter such as 'Z' in a variable of type int. For many purposes, the C language considers characters to be small integers, and perhaps unfortunately, C++ inherited this from C. The reason for allowing this is that variables of type char consume less memory than variables of type int; thus, doing arithmetic with variables of type char can save some memory. However, it is clearer to use the type int when you are dealing with integers and to use the type char when you are dealing with characters.

The general rule is that you cannot place a value of one type in a variable of another type—though it may seem that there are more exceptions to the rule than there are cases that follow the rule. Even if the compiler does not enforce this rule very strictly, it is a good rule to follow. Placing data of one type in a variable of another type can cause problems because the value must be changed to a value of the appropriate type and that value may not be what you would expect.

mixing types

Values of type bool can be assigned to variables of an integer type (short, int, long), and integers can be assigned to variables of type bool. However, it is poor style to do this. For completeness and to help you read other people's code, here are the details: When assigned to a variable of type bool, any nonzero integer will be stored as the value true. Zero will be stored as the value false. When assigning a bool value to an integer variable, true will be stored as 1, and false will be stored as 0.

integers and Booleans

■ LITERALS

A **literal** is a name for one specific value. Literals are often called **constants** in contrast to variables. Literals or constants do not change value; variables can change their values. Integer constants are written in the way you are used to writing numbers. Constants of type int (or any other integer type) must not contain a decimal point. Constants of type double may be written in either of two forms. The simple form for double constants is like the everyday way of writing decimal fractions. When written in this form a double constant must contain a decimal point. No number constant (either integer or floating-point) in C++ may contain a comma.

literal constant

scientific
notation or
floating-
point
notation

A more complicated notation for constants of type double is called **scientific notation** or **floating-point notation** and is particularly handy for writing very large numbers and very small fractions. For instance, 3.67×10^{17}, which is the same as

```
367000000000000000.0
```

is best expressed in C++ by the constant 3.67e17. The number 5.89×10^{-6}, which is the same as 0.00000589, is best expressed in C++ by the constant 5.89e-6.   The e stands for *exponent* and means "multiply by 10 to the power that follows." The e may be either uppercase or lowercase.

Think of the number after the e as telling you the direction and number of digits to move the decimal point. For example, to change 3.49e4 to a numeral without an e, you move the decimal point four places to the right to obtain 34900.0, which is another way of writing the same number. If the number after the e is negative, you move the decimal point the indicated number of spaces to the left, inserting extra zeros if need be. So, 3.49e-2 is the same as 0.0349.

The number before the e may contain a decimal point, although it is not required. However, the exponent after the e definitely must *not* contain a decimal point.

WHAT IS DOUBLED?

Why is the type for numbers with a fractional part called double? Is there a type called "single" that is half as big? No, but something like that is true. Many programming languages traditionally used two types for numbers with a fractional part. One type used less storage and was very imprecise (that is, it did not allow very many significant digits). The second type used double the amount of storage and so was much more precise; it also allowed numbers that were larger (although programmers tend to care more about precision than about size). The kind of numbers that used twice as much storage were called *double-precision* numbers; those that used less storage were called *single precision*. Following this tradition, the type that (more or less) corresponds to this double-precision type was named double in C++. The type that corresponds to single precision in C++ was called float. C++ also has a third type for numbers with a fractional part, which is called long double.

Constants of type char are expressed by placing the character in single quotes, as illustrated in what follows:

```
char symbol = 'Z';
```

Note that the left and right single quote symbol are the same symbol.

Constants for strings of characters are given in double quotes, as illustrated by the following line taken from Display 1.1:

```
cout << "How many programming languages have you used? ";
```

Be sure to notice that string constants are placed inside double quotes, while constants of type char are placed inside single quotes. The two kinds of quotes mean different things. In particular, 'A' and "A" mean different things. 'A' is a value of type char and can be stored in a variable of type char. "A" is a string of characters. The fact that the string happens to contain only one character does *not* make "A" a value of type char. Also notice that for both strings and characters, the left and right quotes are the same.

quotes

Strings in double quotes, like "Hello", are often called **C-strings**. In Chapter 9 we will see that C++ has more than one kind of string, and this particular kind happens to be called C-strings.

C-string

The type bool has two constants, true and false. These two constants may be assigned to a variable of type bool or used anyplace else an expression of type bool is allowed. They must be spelled with all lowercase letters.

ESCAPE SEQUENCES

A backslash, \ , preceding a character tells the compiler that the sequence following the backslash does not have the same meaning as the character appearing by itself. Such a sequence is called an **escape sequence**. The sequence is typed in as two characters with no space between the symbols. Several escape sequences are defined in C++.

escape sequence

If you want to put a backslash, \, or a quote symbol, ", into a string constant, you must escape the ability of the " to terminate a string constant by using \", or the ability of the \ to escape, by using \\. The \\ tells the compiler you mean a real backslash, \, not an escape sequence; the \" tells it you mean a real quote, not the end of a string constant.

A stray \, say \z, in a string constant will have different effects on different compilers. One compiler may simply give back a z; another might produce an error. The ANSI/ISO standard states that unspecified escape sequences have undefined behavior. This means a compiler can do anything its author finds convenient. The consequence is that code that uses undefined escape sequences is not portable. You should not use any escape sequences other than those provided by the C++ standard. These C++ control characters are listed in Display 1.3.

NAMING CONSTANTS

Numbers in a computer program pose two problems. The first is that they carry no mnemonic value. For example, when the number 10 is encountered in a program, it gives no hint of its significance. If the program is a banking program, it might be the number of branch offices or the number of teller windows at the main office. To

Display 1.3   Some Escape Sequences

SEQUENCE	MEANING
\n	New line
\r	Carriage return (Positions the cursor at the start of the current line. You are not likely to use this very much.)
\t	(Horizontal) Tab (Advances the cursor to the next tab stop.)
\a	Alert (Sounds the alert noise, typically a bell.)
\\	Backslash (Allows you to place a backslash in a quoted expression.)
\'	Single quote (Mostly used to place a single quote inside single quotes.)
\"	Double quote (Mostly used to place a double quote inside a quoted string.)
The following are not as commonly used, but we include them for completeness:	
\v	Vertical tab
\b	Backspace
\f	Form feed
\?	Question mark

understand the program, you need to know the significance of each constant. The second problem is that when a program needs to have some numbers changed, the changing tends to introduce errors. Suppose that 10 occurs twelve times in a banking program—four of the times it represents the number of branch offices, and eight of the times it represents the number of teller windows at the main office. When the bank opens a new branch and the program needs to be updated, there is a good chance that some of the 10s that should be changed to 11 will not be, or some that should not be changed will be. The way to avoid these problems is to name each number and use the name instead of the number within your program. For example, a banking program might have two constants with the names BRANCH_COUNT and WINDOW_COUNT. Both these numbers might have a value of 10, but when the bank opens a new branch, all you need do to update the program is change the definition of BRANCH_COUNT.

How do you name a number in a C++ program? One way to name a number is to initialize a variable to that number value, as in the following example:

```
int BRANCH_COUNT = 10;
int WINDOW_COUNT = 10;
```

There is, however, one problem with this method of naming number constants: You might inadvertently change the value of one of these variables. C++ provides a way of marking an initialized variable so that it cannot be changed. If your program tries to change one of these variables, it produces an error condition. To mark a variable declaration so that the value of the variable cannot be changed, precede the declaration with the word const (which is an abbreviation of *constant*). For example: const

```
const int BRANCH_COUNT = 10;
const int WINDOW_COUNT = 10;
```

If the variables are of the same type, it is possible to combine the above lines into one declaration, as follows:

```
const int BRANCH_COUNT = 10, WINDOW_COUNT = 10;
```

However, most programmers find that placing each name definition on a separate line is clearer. The word const is often called a **modifier**, because it modifies (restricts) the variables being declared. modifier

A variable declared using the const modifier is often called a **declared constant**. Writing declared constants in all uppercase letters is not required by the C++ language, but it is standard practice among C++ programmers. declared
constant

Once a number has been named in this way, the name can then be used anywhere the number is allowed, and it will have exactly the same meaning as the number it names. To change a named constant, you need only change the initializing value in the const variable declaration. The meaning of all occurrences of BRANCH_COUNT, for instance, can be changed from 10 to 11 simply by changing the initializing value of 10 in the declaration of BRANCH_COUNT.

Display 1.4 contains a simple program that illustrates the use of the declaration modifier const.

ARITHMETIC OPERATORS AND EXPRESSIONS

As in most other languages, C++ allows you to form expressions using variables, constants, and the arithmetic operators: + (addition), - (subtraction), * (multiplication), / (division), and % (modulo, remainder). These expressions can be used anyplace it is legal to use a value of the type produced by the expression.

All the arithmetic operators can be used with numbers of type int, numbers of type double, and even with one number of each type. However, the type of the value produced and the exact value of the result depend on the types of the numbers being combined. If both operands (that is, both numbers) are of type int, then the result of combining them with an arithmetic operator is of type int. If one or both of the operands are of type double, then the result is of type double. For example, if the variables baseAmount and increase are of type int, then the number produced by the following expression is of type int: mixing
types

```
baseAmount + increase
```

Display 1.4 Named Constant

```
1   #include <iostream>
2   using namespace std;
3
4   int main( )
5   {
6       const double RATE = 6.9;
7       double deposit;
8
8       cout << "Enter the amount of your deposit $";
9       cin >> deposit;
10
10      double newBalance;
11      newBalance = deposit + deposit*(RATE/100);
12      cout << "In one year, that deposit will grow to\n"
13           << "$" << newBalance << " an amount worth waiting for.\n";
14
14      return 0;
15  }
```

SAMPLE DIALOGUE

```
Enter the amount of your deposit $100
In one year, that deposit will grow to
$106.9 an amount worth waiting for.
```

However, if one or both of the two variables are of type double, then the result is of type double. This is also true if you replace the operator + with any of the operators -, *, or /.

More generally, you can combine any of the arithmetic types in expressions. If all the types are integer types, the result will be the integer type. If at least one of the sub-expressions is of a floating-point type, the result will be a floating-point type. C++ tries its best to make the type of an expression either int or double, but if the value produced by the expression is not of one of these types because of the value's size, a suitable different integer or floating-point type will be produced.

precedence rules

You can specify the order of operations in an arithmetic expression by inserting parentheses. If you omit parentheses, the computer will follow rules called **precedence rules** that determine the order in which the operations, such as addition and multiplication, are performed. These precedence rules are similar to rules used in algebra and other mathematics classes. For example:

```
x + y * z
```

is evaluated by first doing the multiplication and then the addition. Except in some standard cases, such as a string of additions or a simple multiplication embedded inside

---

NAMING CONSTANTS WITH THE const MODIFIER

When you initialize a variable inside a declaration, you can mark the variable so that the program is not allowed to change its value. To do this, place the word const in front of the declaration, as described below:

SYNTAX

const *Type_Name Variable_Name = Constant*;

EXAMPLES

```
const int MAX_TRIES = 3;
const double PI = 3.14159;
```

---

an addition, it is usually best to include the parentheses, even if the intended order of operations is the one dictated by the precedence rules. The parentheses make the expression easier to read and less prone to programmer error.   A complete set of C++ precedence rules is given in Appendix 2.

INTEGER AND FLOATING-POINT DIVISION

When used with one or both operands of type double, the division operator, /, behaves as you might expect. However, when used with two operands of type int, the division operator yields the integer part resulting from division. In other words, integer division discards the part after the decimal point. So, 10/3 is 3 (not 3.3333...), 5/2 is 2 (not 2.5), and 11/3 is 3 (not 3.6666...). Notice that the number *is not rounded*; the part after the decimal point is discarded no matter how large it is.

integer division

The operator % can be used with operands of type int to recover the information lost when you use / to do division with numbers of type int. When used with values of type int, the two operators / and % yield the two numbers produced when you perform the long division algorithm you learned in grade school. For example, 17 divided by 5 yields 3 with a remainder of 2. The / operation yields the number of times one number "goes into" another. The % operation gives the remainder. For example, the statements

the % operator

```
cout << "17 divided by 5 is " << (17/5) << "\n";
cout << "with a remainder of " << (17%5) << "\n";
```

yield the following output:

```
17 divided by 5 is 3
with a remainder of 2
```

When used with negative values of type int, the result of the operators / and % can be different for different implementations of C++. Thus, you should use / and % with int values only when you know that both values are nonnegative.

negative integers in division

DIVISION WITH WHOLE NUMBERS

When you use the division operator / on two integers, the result is an integer. This can be a problem if you expect a fraction. Moreover, the problem can easily go unnoticed, resulting in a program that looks fine but is producing incorrect output without you even being aware of the problem. For example, suppose you are a landscape architect who charges $5,000 per mile to landscape a highway, and suppose you know the length of the highway you are working on in feet. The price you charge can easily be calculated by the following C++ statement:

```
totalPrice = 5000 * (feet/5280.0);
```

This works because there are 5,280 feet in a mile. If the stretch of highway you are landscaping is 15,000 feet long, this formula will tell you that the total price is

```
5000 * (15000/5280.0)
```

Your C++ program obtains the final value as follows: 15000/5280.0 is computed as 2.84. Then the program multiplies 5000 by 2.84 to produce the value 14200.00. With the aid of your C++ program, you know that you should charge $14,200 for the project.

Now suppose the variable feet is of type int, and you forget to put in the decimal point and the zero, so that the assignment statement in your program reads

```
totalPrice = 5000 * (feet/5280);
```

It still looks fine, but will cause serious problems. If you use this second form of the assignment statement, you are dividing two values of type int, so the result of the division feet/5280 is 15000/5280, which is the int value 2 (instead of the value 2.84 that you think you are getting). The value assigned to totalPrice is thus 5000*2, or 10000.00. If you forget the decimal point, you will charge $10,000. However, as we have already seen, the correct value is $14,200. A missing decimal point has cost you $4,200. Note that this will be true whether the type of totalPrice is int or double; the damage is done before the value is assigned to totalPrice.

Self-Test Exercises

4. Convert each of the following mathematical formulas to a C++ expression.

$$3x \qquad 3x + y \qquad \frac{x+y}{7} \qquad \frac{3x+y}{z+2}$$

5. What is the output of the following program lines when they are embedded in a correct program that declares all variables to be of type char?

```
a = 'b';
b = 'c';
c = a;
cout << a << b << c << 'c';
```

6. What is the output of the following program lines when they are embedded in a correct program that declares number to be of type int?

```
number = (1/3) * 3;
cout << "(1/3) * 3 is equal to " << number;
```

7. Write a complete C++ program that reads two whole numbers into two variables of type int and then outputs both the whole number part and the remainder when the first number is divided by the second. This can be done using the operators / and %.

8. Given the following fragment that purports to convert from degrees Celsius to degrees Fahrenheit, answer the following questions:

```
double c = 20;
double f;
f = (9/5) * c + 32.0;
```

a. What value is assigned to f?

b. Explain what is actually happening, and what the programmer likely wanted.

c. Rewrite the code as the programmer intended.

TYPE CASTING

A **type cast** is a way of changing a value of one type to a value of another type. A type cast is a kind of function that takes a value of one type and produces a value of another type that is C++'s best guess of an equivalent value. C++ has four to six different kinds of casts, depending on how you count them. There is an older form of type cast that has two notations for expressing it, and there are four new kinds of type casts introduced with the latest standard. The new kinds of type casts were designed as replacements for the older form; in this book, we will use the newer kinds. However, C++ retains the older kind(s) of cast along with the newer kinds, so we will briefly describe the older kind as well.

type cast

Let's start with the newer kinds of type casts. Consider the expression 9/2. In C++ this expression evaluates to 4 because when both operands are of an integer type, C++ performs integer division. In some situations, you might want the answer to be the double value 4.5. You can get a result of 4.5 by using the "equivalent" floating-point value 2.0 in place of the integer value 2, as in 9/2.0, which evaluates to 4.5. But what if the 9 and the 2 are the values of variables of type int named n and m? Then, n/m yields 4. If you want floating-point division in this case, you must do a type cast from int to double (or another floating-point type), such as in the following:

```
double ans = n/static_cast<double>(m);
```

The expression

```
static_cast<double>(m)
```

is a type cast. The expression static_cast<double> is like a function that takes an int argument (actually, an argument of almost any type) and returns an "equivalent" value of type double. So, if the value of m is 2, the expression static_cast<double>(m) returns the double value 2.0.

Note that static_cast<double>(n) does not change the value of the variable n. If n has the value 2 before this expression is evaluated, then n still has the value 2 after the expression is evaluated. (If you know what a function is in mathematics or in some programming language, you can think of static_cast<double> as a function that returns an "equivalent" value of type double.)

You may use any type name in place of double to obtain a type cast to another type. We said this produces an "equivalent" value of the target type. The word equivalent is in quotes because there is no clear notion of equivalent that applies between any two types. In the case of a type cast from an integer type to a floating-point type, the effect is to add a decimal point and a zero. The type cast in the other direction, from a floating-point type to an integer type, simply deletes the decimal point and all digits after the decimal point. Note that when type casting from a floating-point type to an integer type, the number is truncated, not rounded. static_cast<int>(2.9) is 2; it is not 3.

This static_cast is the most common kind of type cast and the only one we will use for some time. For completeness and reference value, we list all four kinds of type casts. Some may not make sense until you reach the relevant topics. If some or all of the remaining three kinds do not make sense to you at this point, do not worry. The four kinds of type cast are as follows:

```
static_cast<Type>(Expression)
const_cast<Type>(Expression)
dynamic_cast<Type>(Expression)
reinterpret_cast<Type>(Expression)
```

We have already discussed static_cast. It is a general-purpose type cast that applies in most "ordinary" situations. The const_cast is used to cast away constantness. The dynamic_cast is used for safe downcasting from one type to a descendent type in an inheritance hierarchy. The reinterpret_cast is an implementation-dependent cast that we will not discuss in this book and that you are unlikely to need. (These descriptions may not make sense until you cover the appropriate topics, where they will be discussed further. For now, we only use static_cast.)

The older form of type casting is approximately equivalent to the static_cast kind of type casting but uses a different notation. One of the two notations uses a type name as if it were a function name. For example int(9.3) returns the int value 9; double(42) returns the value 42.0. The second, equivalent, notation for the older form of type casting would write (double)42 instead of double(42). Either notation can be used with variables or other more complicated expressions instead of just with constants.

Although C++ retains this older form of type casting, you are encouraged to use the newer form of type casting. (Someday, the older form may go away, although there is, as yet, no such plan for its elimination.)

As we noted earlier, you can always assign a value of an integer type to a variable of a floating-point type, as in

```
double d = 5;
```

In such cases C++ performs an automatic type cast, converting the 5 to 5.0 and placing 5.0 in the variable d. You cannot store the 5 as the value of d without a type cast, but sometimes C++ does the type cast for you. Such an automatic conversion is sometimes called a **type coercion**.

type coercion

■ INCREMENT AND DECREMENT OPERATORS

The ++ in the name of the C++ language comes from the increment operator, ++. The **increment operator** adds 1 to the value of a variable. The **decrement operator**, --, subtracts 1 from the value of a variable. They are usually used with variables of type int, but they can be used with any numeric type. If n is a variable of a numeric type, then n++ increases the value of n by 1 and n-- decreases the value of n by 1. So n++ and n-- (when followed by a semicolon) are executable statements. For example, the statements

increment operator decrement operator

```
int n = 1, m = 7;
n++;
cout << "The value of n is changed to " << n << "\n";
m--;
cout << "The value of m is changed to " << m << "\n";
```

yield the following output:

```
The value of n is changed to 2
The value of m is changed to 6
```

An expression like n++ returns a value as well as changing the value of the variable n, so n++ can be used in an arithmetic expression such as

```
2*(n++)
```

The expression n++ first returns the value of the variable n, and *then* the value of n is increased by 1. For example, consider the following code:

```
int n = 2;
int valueProduced = 2*(n++);
cout << valueProduced << "\n";
cout << n << "\n";
```

This code will produce the output:

```
4
3
```

Notice the expression 2*(n++). When C++ evaluates this expression, it uses the value that number has *before* it is incremented, not the value that it has after it is incremented. Thus, the value produced by the expression n++ is 2, even though the increment operator changes the value of n to 3. This may seem strange, but sometimes it is just what you want. And, as you are about to see, if you want an expression that behaves differently, you can have it.

v++ **versus**
++v
The expression n++ evaluates to the value of the variable n, and *then* the value of the variable n is incremented by 1. If you reverse the order and place the ++ in front of the variable, the order of these two actions is reversed. The expression ++n first increments the value of the variable n and then returns this increased value of n. For example, consider the following code:

```
int n = 2;
int valueProduced = 2*(++n);
cout << valueProduced << "\n";
cout << n << "\n";
```

This code is the same as the previous piece of code except that the ++ is before the variable, so this code will produce the following output:

```
6
3
```

Notice that the two increment operators in n++ and ++n have the same effect on a variable n: They both increase the value of n by 1. But the two expressions evaluate to different values. Remember, if the ++ is *before* the variable, the incrementing is done *before* the value is returned; if the ++ is *after* the variable, the incrementing is done *after* the value is returned.

Everything we said about the increment operator applies to the decrement operator as well, except that the value of the variable is decreased by 1 rather than increased by 1. For example, consider the following code:

```
int n = 8;
int valueProduced = n--;
cout << valueProduced << "\n";
cout << n << "\n";
```

This produces the output

```
8
7
```

On the other hand, the code

```
int n = 8;
int valueProduced = --n;
cout << valueProduced << "\n";
cout << n << "\n";
```

produces the output

```
7
7
```

n–– returns the value of n and then decrements n; on the other hand, ––n first decrements n and then returns the value of n.

You cannot apply the increment and decrement operators to anything other than a single variable. Expressions such as (x + y)++, ––(x + y), 5++, and so forth, are all illegal in C++.

The increment and decrement operators can be dangerous when used inside more complicated expressions, as explained in the Pitfall.

Pitfall

ORDER OF EVALUATION

For most operators, the order of evaluation of subexpressions is not guaranteed. In particular, you normally cannot assume that the order of evaluation is left to right. For example, consider the following expression:

```
n + (++n)
```

Suppose n has the value 2 before the expression is evaluated. Then, if the first expression is evaluated first, the result is 2 + 3. If the second expression is evaluated first, the result is 3 + 3. Since C++ does not guarantee the order of evaluation, the expression could evaluate to either 5 or 6. The moral is that you should not program in a way that depends on order of evaluation, except for the operators discussed in the next paragraph.

Some operators do guarantee that their order of evaluation of subexpressions is left to right. For the operators && (and), || (or), and the comma operator (which is discussed in Chapter 2), C++ guarantees that the order of evaluations is left to right. Fortunately, these are the operators for which you are most likely to want a predicable order of evaluation. For example, consider

```
(n <– 2) && (++n > 2)
```

Suppose n has the value 2, before the expression is evaluated. In this case you know that the subexpression (n <= 2) is evaluated before the value of n is incremented. You thus know that (n <= 2) will evaluate to true and so the entire expression will evaluate to true.

Do not confuse order of operations (by precedence rules) with order of evaluation. For example,

```
(n + 2) * (++n) + 5
```

always means

```
((n + 2) * (++n)) + 5
```

> However, it is not clear whether the ++n is evaluated before or after the n + 2. Either one could be evaluated first.
>
> Now you know why we said that it is usually a bad idea to use the increment (++) and decrement (−−) operators as subexpressions of larger expressions.
>
> If this is too confusing, just follow the simple rule of not writing code that depends on the order of evaluation of subexpressions.

1.3 Console Input/Output

Garbage in means garbage out.

Programmer's saying

Simple console input is done with the objects cin, cout, and cerr, all of which are defined in the library iostream. In order to use this library, your program should contain the following near the start of the file containing your code:

```
#include <iostream>
using namespace std;
```

OUTPUT USING cout

cout

The values of variables as well as strings of text may be output to the screen using cout. Any combination of variables and strings can be output. For example, consider the following from the program in Display 1.1:

```
cout << "Hello reader.\n"
     << "Welcome to C++.\n";
```

This statement outputs two strings, one per line. Using cout, you can output any number of items, each either a string, variable, or more complicated expression. Simply insert a << before each thing to be output.

As another example, consider the following:

```
cout << numberOfGames << " games played.";
```

This statement tells the computer to output two items: the value of the variable numberOfGames and the quoted string " games played.".

Notice that you do not need a separate copy of the object cout for each item output. You can simply list all the items to be output, preceding each item to be output with the arrow symbols <<. The previous single cout statement is equivalent to the following two cout statements:

```
cout << numberOfGames;
cout << " games played.";
```

You can include arithmetic expressions in a cout statement, as shown by the following example, where price and tax are variables:

```
cout << "The total cost is $" << (price + tax);
```

expression in a cout **statement**

Parentheses around arithmetic expressions, such as price + tax, are required by some compilers, so it is best to include them.

The two < symbols should be typed without any space between them. The arrow notation << is often called the **insertion operator**. The entire cout statement ends with a semicolon.

Notice the spaces inside the quotes in our examples. The computer does not insert any extra space before or after the items output by a cout statement, which is why the quoted strings in the examples often start or end with a blank. The blanks keep the various strings and numbers from running together. If all you need is a space and there is no quoted string where you want to insert the space, then use a string that contains only a space, as in the following:

spaces in output

```
cout << firstNumber << " " << secondNumber;
```

NEW LINES IN OUTPUT

As noted in the subsection on escape sequences, \n tells the computer to start a new line of output. Unless you tell the computer to go to the next line, it will put all the output on the same line. Depending on how your screen is set up, this can produce anything from arbitrary line breaks to output that runs off the screen. Notice that the \n goes inside the quotes. In C++, going to the next line is considered to be a special character, and the way you spell this special character inside a quoted string is \n, with no space between the two symbols in \n. Although it is typed as two symbols, C++ considers \n to be a single character that is called the **newline character**.

newline character

If you wish to insert a blank line in the output, you can output the newline character \n by itself:

```
cout << "\n";
```

Another way to output a blank line is to use endl, which means essentially the same thing as "\n". So you can also output a blank line as follows:

```
cout << endl;
```

Although "\n" and endl mean the same thing, they are used slightly differently; \n must always be inside quotes, and endl should not be placed in quotes.

A good rule for deciding whether to use \n or endl is the following: If you can include the \n at the end of a longer string, then use \n, as in the following:

```
cout << "Fuel efficiency is "
     << mpg << " miles per gallon\n";
```

On the other hand, if the \n would appear by itself as the short string "\n", then use endl instead:

```
cout << "You entered " << number << endl;
```

STARTING NEW LINES IN OUTPUT

To start a new output line, you can include \n in a quoted string, as in the following example:

```
cout << "You have definitely won\n"
     << "one of the following prizes:\n";
```

Recall that \n is typed as two symbols with no space in between the two symbols.

Alternatively, you can start a new line by outputting endl. An equivalent way to write the above cout statement is as follows:

```
cout << "You have definitely won" << endl
     << "one of the following prizes:" << endl;
```

Tip

END EACH PROGRAM WITH \n OR endl

It is a good idea to output a newline instruction at the end of every program. If the last item to be output is a string, then include a \n at the end of the string; if not, output an endl as the last output action in your program. This serves two purposes. Some compilers will not output the last line of your program unless you include a newline instruction at the end. On other systems, your program may work fine without this final newline instruction, but the next program that is run will have its first line of output mixed with the last line of the previous program. Even if neither of these problems occurs on your system, putting a newline instruction at the end will make your programs more portable.

■ FORMATTING FOR NUMBERS WITH A DECIMAL POINT

When the computer outputs a value of type double, the format may not be what you would like. For example, the following simple cout statement can produce any of a wide range of outputs:

```
cout << "The price is $" << price << endl;
```

If `price` has the value 78.5, the output might be

```
The price is $78.500000
```

or it might be

```
The price is $78.5
```

or it might be output in the following notation (which was explained in the subsection entitled **Literals**):

```
The price is $7.850000e01
```

It is extremely unlikely that the output will be the following, however, even though this is the format that makes the most sense:

```
The price is $78.50
```

To ensure that the output is in the form you want, your program should contain some sort of instructions that tell the computer how to output the numbers.

There is a "magic formula" that you can insert in your program to cause numbers that contain a decimal point, such as numbers of type `double`, to be output in everyday notation with the exact number of digits after the decimal point that you specify. If you want two digits after the decimal point, use the following magic formula:

magic formula

```
cout.setf(ios::fixed);
cout.setf(ios::showpoint);
cout.precision(2);
```

If you insert the preceding three statements in your program, then any `cout` statements that follow these statements will output values of any floating-point type in ordinary notation, with exactly two digits after the decimal point. For example, suppose the following `cout` statement appears somewhere after this magic formula and suppose the value of `price` is 78.5.

outputting money amounts

```
cout << "The price is $" << price << endl;
```

The output will then be as follows:

```
The price is $78.50
```

You may use any other nonnegative whole number in place of 2 to specify a different number of digits after the decimal point. You can even use a variable of type `int` in place of the 2.

We will explain this magic formula in detail in Chapter 12. For now, you should think of this magic formula as one long instruction that tells the computer how you want it to output numbers that contain a decimal point.

If you wish to change the number of digits after the decimal point so that different values in your program are output with different numbers of digits, you can repeat the magic formula with some other number in place of 2. However, when you repeat the magic formula, you only need to repeat the last line of the formula. If the magic formula has already occurred once in your program, then the following line will change the number of digits after the decimal point to five for all subsequent values of any floating-point type that are output:

```
cout.precision(5);
```

OUTPUTTING VALUES OF TYPE double

If you insert the following "magic formula" in your program, then all numbers of type double (or any other type of floating-point number) will be output in ordinary notation with two digits after the decimal point:

```
cout.setf(ios::fixed);
cout.setf(ios::showpoint);
cout.precision(2);
```

You can use any other nonnegative whole number in place of the 2 to specify a different number of digits after the decimal point. You can even use a variable of type int in place of the 2.

OUTPUT WITH cerr

cerr

The object cerr is used in the same way as cout. The object cerr sends its output to the standard error output stream, which normally is the console screen. This gives you a way to distinguish two kinds of output: cout for regular output, and cerr for error message output. If you do nothing special to change things, then cout and cerr will both send their output to the console screen, so there is no difference between them.

On some systems you can redirect output from your program to a file. This is an operating system instruction, not a C++ instruction, but it can be useful. On systems that allow for output redirection, cout and cerr may be redirected to different files.

INPUT USING cin

cin

You use cin for input more or less the same way you use cout for output. The syntax is similar, except that cin is used in place of cout and the arrows point in the opposite direction. For example, in the program in Display 1.1, the variable numberOfLanguages was filled by the following cin statement:

```
cin >> numberOfLanguages;
```

You can list more than one variable in a single cin statement, as illustrated by the following:

```
cout << "Enter the number of dragons\n"
     << "followed by the number of trolls.\n";
cin >> dragons >> trolls;
```

If you prefer, the above cin statement can be written on two lines, as follows:

```
cin >> dragons
    >> trolls;
```

Notice that, as with the cout statement, there is just one semicolon for each occurrence of cin.

When a program reaches a cin statement, it waits for input to be entered from the keyboard. It sets the first variable equal to the first value typed at the keyboard, the second variable equal to the second value typed, and so forth. However, the program does not read the input until the user presses the Return key. This allows the user to backspace and correct mistakes when entering a line of input.

how cin **works**

Numbers in the input must be separated by one or more spaces or by a line break. When you use cin statements, the computer will skip over any number of blanks or line breaks until it finds the next input value. Thus, it does not matter whether input numbers are separated by one space or several spaces or even a line break.

separate numbers with spaces

You can read in integers, floating-point numbers, or characters using cin. Later in this book we will discuss the reading in of other kinds of data using cin.

---

cin STATEMENTS

A cin statement sets variables equal to values typed in at the keyboard.

SYNTAX

```
cin >> Variable_1 >> Variable_2 >>...;
```

EXAMPLES

```
cin >> number >> size;
cin >> timeLeft
    >> pointsNeeded;
```

LINE BREAKS IN I/O

It is possible to keep output and input on the same line, and sometimes it can produce a nicer interface for the user. If you simply omit a \n or endl at the end of the last prompt line, then the user's input will appear on the same line as the prompt. For example, suppose you use the following prompt and input statements:

```
cout << "Enter the cost per person: $";
cin >> costPerPerson;
```

When the cout statement is executed, the following will appear on the screen:

```
Enter the cost per person: $
```

When the user types in the input, it will appear on the same line, like this:

```
Enter the cost per person: $1.25
```

Self-Test Exercises

9. Give an output statement that will produce the following message on the screen.
```
The answer to the question of
Life, the Universe, and Everything is 42.
```

10. Give an input statement that will fill the variable theNumber (of type int) with a number typed in at the keyboard. Precede the input statement with a prompt statement asking the user to enter a whole number.

11. What statements should you include in your program to ensure that when a number of type double is output, it will be output in ordinary notation with three digits after the decimal point?

12. Write a complete C++ program that writes the phrase Hello world to the screen. The program does nothing else.

13. Give an output statement that produces the letter 'A', followed by the newline character, followed by the letter 'B', followed by the tab character, followed by the letter 'C'.

1.4 Program Style

> *In matters of grave importance, style, not sincerity, is the vital thing.*
>
> Oscar Wilde, *The Importance of Being Earnest*

C++ programming style is similar to that used in other languages. The goal is to make your code easy to read and easy to modify. We will say a bit about indenting in the next chapter. We have already discussed defined constants. Most, if not all, literals in a program should be defined constants. Choice of variable names and careful indenting should eliminate the need for very many comments, but any points that still remain unclear deserve a comment.

COMMENTS

There are two ways to insert comments in a C++ program. In C++, two slashes, //, are used to indicate the start of a comment. All the text between the // and the end of the line is a comment. The compiler simply ignores anything that follows // on a line. If you want a comment that covers more than one line, place a // on each line of the comment. The symbols // do not have a space between them.

Another way to insert comments in a C++ program is to use the symbol pairs /* and */. Text between these symbols is considered a comment and is ignored by the compiler. Unlike the // comments, which require an additional // on each line, the /*-to-*/ comments can span several lines, like so:

```
/*This is a comment that spans
three lines. Note that there is no comment
symbol of any kind on the second line.*/
```

Comments of the /* */ type may be inserted anywhere in a program that a space or line break is allowed. However, they should not be inserted anywhere except where they are easy to read and do not distract from the layout of the program. Usually, comments are placed at the ends of lines or on separate lines by themselves.

Opinions differ regarding which kind of comment is best to use. Either variety (the // kind or the /* */ kind) can be effective if used with care. One approach is to use the // comments in final code and reserve the /**/-style comments for temporarily commenting out code while debugging.

It is difficult to say just how many comments a program should contain. The only correct answer is "just enough," which of course conveys little to the novice programmer. It will take some experience to get a feel for when it is best to include a comment.

when to comment

Whenever something is important and not obvious, it merits a comment. However, too many comments are as bad as too few. A program that has a comment on each line will be so buried in comments that the structure of the program is hidden in a sea of obvious observations. Comments like the following contribute nothing to understanding and should not appear in a program:

```
distance = speed * time; //Computes the distance traveled.
```

1.5 Libraries and Namespaces

C++ comes with a number of standard libraries. These libraries place their definitions in a *namespace*, which is simply a name given to a collection of definitions. The techniques for including libraries and dealing with namespaces will be discussed in detail later in this book. This section discusses enough details to allow you to use the standard C++ libraries.

■ LIBRARIES AND include DIRECTIVES

#include

C++ includes a number of standard libraries. In fact, it is almost impossible to write a C++ program without using at least one of these libraries. The normal way to make a library available to your program is with an include directive. An include directive for a standard library has the form:

```
#include <Library_Name>
```

For example, the library for console I/O is iostream. So, most of our demonstration programs will begin

```
#include <iostream>
```

Compilers (preprocessors) can be very fussy about spacing in include directives. Thus, it is safest to type an include directive with no extra space: no space before the #, no space after the #, and no spaces inside the <>.

An include directive is simply an instruction to include the text found in a file at the location of the include directive. A library name is simply the name of a file that includes all the definition of items in the library. We will eventually discuss using include directives for things other than standard libraries, but for now we only need include directives for standard C++ libraries. A list of some standard C++ libraries is given in Appendix 4.

preprocessor

C++ has a **preprocessor** that handles some simple textual manipulation before the text of your program is given to the compiler. Some people will tell you that include directives are not processed by the compiler but are processed by a **preprocessor**. They're right, but the difference is more of a word game than anything that need concern you. On almost all compilers, the preprocessor is called automatically when you compile your program.

Technically speaking only part of the library definition is given in the header file. However, at this stage, that is not an important distinction, since using the `include` directive with the header file for a library will (on almost all systems) cause C++ to automatically add the rest of the library definition.

■ NAMESPACES

A **namespace** is a collection of name definitions. One name, such as a function name, can be given different definitions in two namespaces. A program can then use one of these namespaces in one place and the other in another location. We will discuss namespaces in detail later in this book. For now, we only need to discuss the namespace `std`. All the standard libraries we will be using place their definitions in the `std` (standard) namespace. To use any of these definitions in your program, you must insert the following `using` directive:

namespace

```
using namespace std;
```

Thus, a simple program that uses console I/O would begin

using namespace

```
#include <iostream>
using namespace std;
```

If you want to make some, but not all, names in a namespace available to your program, there is a form of the `using` directive that makes just one name available. For example, if you only want to make the name `cin` from the `std` namespace available to your program, you could use the following `using` directive:

```
using std::cin;
```

Thus, if the only names from the `std` namespace that your program uses are `cin`, `count`, and `endl`, you might start your program with the following:

```
#include <iostream>
using std::cin;
using std::cout;
using std::endl;
```

instead of

```
#include <iostream>
using namespace std;
```

Older C++ header files for libraries did not place their definitions in the `std` namespace, so if you look at older C++ code, you will probably see that the header file names are spelled slightly differently and the code does not contain any `using` directive. This is allowed for backward compatibility. However, you should use the newer library header files and the `std` namespace directive.

Pitfall

PROBLEMS WITH LIBRARY NAMES

The C++ language is currently in transition. A new standard has come out with, among other things, new names for libraries. If you are using a compiler that has not yet been revised to meet the new standard, then you will need to use different library names.

If the following does not work

```
#include <iostream>
```

use

```
#include <iostream.h>
```

Similarly, other library names are different for older compilers. Appendix 5 gives the correspondence between older and newer library names. This book always uses the new compiler names. If a library name does not work with your compiler, try the corresponding older library name. In all probability, either all the new library names will work or you will need to use all old library names. It is unlikely that only some of the library names have been made up to date on your system.

If you use the older library names (the ones that end in .h), you do *not* need the using directive

```
using namespace std;
```

Chapter Summary

- C++ is case sensitive. For example, count and COUNT are two different identifiers.
- Use meaningful names for variables.
- Variables must be declared before they are used. Other than following this rule, a variable declaration may appear anyplace.
- Be sure that variables are initialized before the program attempts to use their value. This can be done when the variable is declared or with an assignment statement before the variable is first used.
- You can assign a value of an integer type, like int, to a variable of a floating-point type, like double, but not vice versa.
- Almost all number constants in a program should be given meaningful names that can be used in place of the numbers. This can be done by using the modifier const in a variable declaration.
- Use enough parentheses in arithmetic expressions to make the order of operations clear.
- The object cout is used for console output.
- A \n in a quoted string or an endl sent to console output starts a new line of output.

- The object cerr is used for error messages. In a typical environment, cerr behaves the same as cout.
- The object cin is used for console input.
- In order to use cin, cout, or cerr, you should place the following directives near the beginning of the file with your program:

```
#include <iostream>
using namespace std;
```

- There are two forms of comments in C++: Everything following // on the same line is a comment, and anything enclosed in * and *\ is a comment.
- Do not overcomment.

ANSWERS TO SELF-TEST EXERCISES

1. ```
int feet = 0, inches = 0;
int feet(0), inches(0);
```

2. ```
int count = 0;
double distance = 1.5;

int count(0);
double distance(1.5);
```

3. The actual output from a program such as this is dependent on the system and the history of the use of the system.

```
#include <iostream>
using namespace std;

int main( )
{
  int first, second, third, fourth, fifth;
  cout << first << " " << second << " " << third
       << " " << fourth << " " << fifth << "\n";
  return 0;
}
```

4. ```
3*x
3*x + y
(x + y)/7   Note that x + y/7 is not correct.
(3*x + y)/(z + 2)
```

5. bcbc

6. ```
(1/3) * 3 is equal to 0
```

Since 1 and 3 are of type int, the / operator performs integer division, which discards the remainder, so the value of 1/3 is 0, not 0.3333.... This makes the value of the entire expression 0 * 3, which of course is 0.

7.
```cpp
#include <iostream>
using namespace std;

int main( )
{
    int number1, number2;

    cout << "Enter two whole numbers: ";
    cin >> number1 >> number2;
    cout << number1 << " divided by " << number2
         << " equals " << (number1/number2) << "\n"
         << "with a remainder of " << (number1%number2)
         << "\n";
    return 0;
}
```

8. a. 52.0

   b. 9/5 has int value 1. Since the numerator and denominator are both int, integer division is done; the fractional part is discarded. The programmer probably wanted floating-point division, which does not discard the part after the decimal point.

   c. f = (9.0/5) * c + 32.0;
   or
   f = 1.8 * c + 32.0;

9.
```cpp
cout << "The answer to the question of\n"
     << "Life, the Universe, and Everything is 42.\n";
```

10.
```cpp
cout << "Enter a whole number and press Return: ";
cin >> theNumber;
```

11.
```cpp
cout.setf(ios::fixed);
cout.setf(ios::showpoint);
cout.precision(3);
```

12.
```cpp
#include <iostream>
using namespace std;

int main( )
{
    cout << "Hello world\n";
    return 0;
}
```

13.
```cpp
cout << 'A' << endl << 'B' << '\t' << 'C';
```

   Other answers are also correct. For example, the letters could be in double quotes instead of single quotes. Another possible answer is the following:

```cpp
cout << "A\nB\tC";
```

PROGRAMMING PROJECTS

1. A metric ton is 35,273.92 ounces. Write a program that will read the weight of a package of breakfast cereal in ounces and output the weight in metric tons as well as the number of boxes needed to yield one metric ton of cereal.

2. A government research lab has concluded that an artificial sweetener commonly used in diet soda will cause death in laboratory mice. A friend of yours is desperate to lose weight but cannot give up soda. Your friend wants to know how much diet soda it is possible to drink without dying as a result. Write a program to supply the answer. The input to the program is the amount of artificial sweetener needed to kill a mouse, the weight of the mouse, and the weight of the dieter. To ensure the safety of your friend, be sure the program requests the weight at which the dieter will stop dieting, rather than the dieter's current weight. Assume that diet soda contains one-tenth of 1% artificial sweetener. Use a variable declaration with the modifier `const` to give a name to this fraction. You may want to express the percentage as the `double` value `0.001`.

3. Workers at a particular company have won a 7.6% pay increase retroactive for six months. Write a program that takes an employee's previous annual salary as input and outputs the amount of retroactive pay due the employee, the new annual salary, and the new monthly salary. Use a variable declaration with the modifier `const` to express the pay increase.

4. Negotiating a consumer loan is not always straightforward. One form of loan is the discount installment loan, which works as follows. Suppose a loan has a face value of $1,000, the interest rate is 15%, and the duration is 18 months. The interest is computed by multiplying the face value of $1,000 by 0.15, yielding $150. That figure is then multiplied by the loan period of 1.5 years to yield $225 as the total interest owed. That amount is immediately deducted from the face value, leaving the consumer with only $775. Repayment is made in equal monthly installments based on the face value. So the monthly loan payment will be $1,000 divided by 18, which is $55.56. This method of calculation may not be too bad if the consumer needs $775 dollars, but the calculation is a bit more complicated if the consumer needs $1,000. Write a program that will take three inputs: the amount the consumer needs to receive, the interest rate, and the duration of the loan in months. The program should then calculate the face value required in order for the consumer to receive the amount needed. It should also calculate the monthly payment.

5. Write a program that determines whether a meeting room is in violation of fire law regulations regarding the maximum room capacity. The program will read in the maximum room capacity and the number of people to attend the meeting. If the number of people is less than or equal to the maximum room capacity, the program announces that it is legal to hold the meeting and tells how many additional people may legally attend. If the number of people exceeds the maximum room capacity, the program announces that the meeting cannot be held as planned due to fire regulations and tells how many people must be excluded in order to meet the fire regulations.

6. An employee is paid at a rate of $16.78 per hour for regular hours worked in a week. Any hours over that are paid at the overtime rate of one and one-half times that. From the worker's gross pay, 6% is withheld for Social Security tax, 14% is withheld for federal

income tax, 5% is withheld for state income tax, and $10 per week is withheld for union dues. If the worker has three or more dependents, then an additional $35 is withheld to cover the extra cost of health insurance beyond what the employer pays. Write a program that will read in the number of hours worked in a week and the number of dependents as input and that will then output the worker's gross pay, each withholding amount, and the net take-home pay for the week.

2 CHAPTER

Flow of Control

2 Flow of Control

"Would you tell me, please, which way I ought to go from here?"
"That depends a good deal on where you want to get to," said
the Cat.

Lewis Carroll, *Alice in Wonderland*

INTRODUCTION

As in most programming languages, C++ handles flow of control with branching and looping statements. C++ branching and looping statements are similar to branching and looping statements in other languages. They are the same as in the C language and very similar to what they are in the Java programming language. Exception handling is also a way to handle flow of control. Exception handling is covered in Chapter 18.

2.1 Boolean Expressions

He who would distinguish the true from the false must have an
adequate idea of what is true and false.

Benedict Spinoza, *Ethics*

Boolean
expression

Most branching statements are controlled by Boolean expressions. A **Boolean expression** is any expression that is either true or false. The simplest form for a Boolean expression consists of two expressions, such as numbers or variables, that are compared with one of the comparison operators shown in Display 2.1. Notice that some of the operators are spelled with two symbols, for example, ==, !=, <=, >=. Be sure to notice that you use a double equal == for the equal sign and that you use the two symbols != for not equal. Such two-symbol operators should not have any space between the two symbols.

BUILDING BOOLEAN EXPRESSIONS

&& means
"and"

You can combine two comparisons using the "and" operator, which is spelled && in C++. For example, the following Boolean expression is true provided x is greater than 2 *and* x is less than 7:

    (2 < x) && (x < 7)

When two comparisons are connected using a &&, the entire expression is true, provided both of the comparisons are true; otherwise, the entire expression is false.

THE "AND" OPERATOR, &&

You can form a more elaborate Boolean expression by combining two simpler Boolean expressions using the "and" operator, &&.

SYNTAX FOR A BOOLEAN EXPRESSION USING &&

(Boolean_Exp_1) && (Boolean_Exp_2)

EXAMPLE (WITHIN AN if-else STATEMENT)

```
if ( (score > 0) && (score < 10) )
    cout << "score is between 0 and 10.\n";
else
    cout << "score is not between 0 and 10.\n";
```

If the value of score is greater than 0 and the value of score is also less than 10, then the first cout statement will be executed; otherwise, the second cout statement will be executed. (if-else statements are covered a bit later in this chapter, but the meaning of this simple example should be intuitively clear.)

You can also combine two comparisons using the "or" operator, which is spelled || in C++. For example, the following is true provided y is less than 0 *or* y is greater than 12:

|| means "or"

(y < 0) || (y > 12)

When two comparisons are connected using a ||, the entire expression is true provided that one or both of the comparisons are true; otherwise, the entire expression is false.

You can negate any Boolean expression using the ! operator. If you want to negate a Boolean expression, place the expression in parentheses and place the ! operator in front of it. For example, !(x < y) means "x is *not* less than y." The ! operator can usually be avoided. For example, !(x < y) is equivalent to x >= y. In some cases you can safely omit the parentheses, but the parentheses never do any harm. The exact details on omitting parentheses are given in the subsection entitled **Precedence Rules**.

Pitfall

STRINGS OF INEQUALITIES

Do not use a string of inequalities such as x < z < y. If you do, your program will probably compile and run, but it will undoubtedly give incorrect output. Instead, you must use two inequalities connected with an &&, as follows:

(x < z) && (z < y)

Display 2.1 Comparison Operators

MATH SYMBOL	ENGLISH	C++ NOTATION	C++ SAMPLE	MATH EQUIVALENT
=	Equal to	==	x + 7 == 2*y	x + 7 = 2y
≠	Not equal to	!=	ans != 'n'	ans ≠ 'n'
<	Less than	<	count < m + 3	count < m + 3
≤	Less than or equal to	<=	time <= limit	time ≤ limit
>	Greater than	>	time > limit	time > limit
≥	Greater than or equal to	>=	age >= 21	age ≥ 21

THE "OR" OPERATOR, ||

You can form a more elaborate Boolean expression by combining two simpler Boolean expressions using the "or" operator, ||.

SYNTAX FOR A BOOLEAN EXPRESSION USING ||

(Boolean_Exp_1) || (Boolean_Exp_2)

EXAMPLE WITHIN AN if-else STATEMENT

```
if ( (x == 1) || (x == y) )
    cout << "x is 1 or x equals y.\n";
else
    cout << "x is neither 1 nor equal to y.\n";
```

If the value of x is equal to 1 or the value of x is equal to the value of y (or both), then the first cout statement will be executed; otherwise, the second cout statement will be executed. (if-else statements are covered a bit later in this chapter, but the meaning of this simple example should be intuitively clear.)

■ EVALUATING BOOLEAN EXPRESSIONS

As you will see in the next two sections of this chapter, Boolean expressions are used to control branching and looping statements. However, a Boolean expression has an independent identity apart from any branching or looping statement you might use it in. A variable of type `bool` can store either of the values `true` or `false`. Thus, you can set a variable of type `bool` equal to a boolean expression. For example:

```
bool result = (x < z) && (z < y);
```

A Boolean expression can be evaluated in the same way that an arithmetic expression is evaluated. The only difference is that an arithmetic expression uses operations such as +, *, and / and produces a number as the final result, whereas a Boolean expression uses relational operations such as == and < and Boolean operations such as &&, ||, and ! and produces one of the two values `true` or `false` as the final result. Note that =, !=, <, <=, and so forth, operate on pairs of any built-in type to produce a Boolean value `true` or `false`.

First let's review evaluating an arithmetic expression. The same technique will work to evaluate Boolean expressions. Consider the following arithmetic expression:

```
(x + 1) * (x + 3)
```

Assume that the variable x has the value 2. To evaluate this arithmetic expression, you evaluate the two sums to obtain the numbers 3 and 5, and then you combine these two numbers 3 and 5 using the * operator to obtain 15 as the final value. Notice that in performing this evaluation, you do not multiply the expressions (x + 1) and (x + 3). Instead, you multiply the values of these expressions. You use 3; you do not use (x + 1). You use 5; you do not use (x + 3).

The computer evaluates Boolean expressions the same way. Subexpressions are evaluated to obtain values, each of which is either `true` or `false`. These individual values of `true` or `false` are then combined according to the rules in the tables shown in Display 2.2. For example, consider the Boolean expression

truth tables

```
!( ( y < 3) || (y > 7) )
```

which might be the controlling expression for an `if-else` statement. Suppose the value of y is 8. In this case (y < 3) evaluates to `false` and (y > 7) evaluates to `true`, so the above Boolean expression is equivalent to

```
!( false || true )
```

Consulting the tables for || (which is labeled OR), the computer sees that the expression inside the parentheses evaluates to `true`. Thus, the computer sees that the entire expression is equivalent to

```
!(true)
```

Consulting the tables again, the computer sees that `!(true)` evaluates to `false`, and so it concludes that `false` is the value of the original Boolean expression.

Display 2.2   Truth Tables

AND

Exp_1	Exp_2	Exp_1 && Exp_2
true	true	true
true	false	false
false	true	false
false	false	false

NOT

Exp	!(Exp)
true	false
false	true

OR

Exp_1	Exp_2	Exp_1 || Exp_2
true	true	true
true	false	true
false	true	true
false	false	false

THE BOOLEAN (bool) VALUES ARE true AND false

true and false are predefined constants of type bool. (They must be written in lowercase.) In C++, a Boolean expression evaluates to the bool value true when it is satisfied and to the bool value false when it is not satisfied.

◼ PRECEDENCE RULES

parentheses

Boolean expressions (and arithmetic expressions) need not be fully parenthesized. If you omit parentheses, the default precedence is as follows: Perform ! first, then perform relational operations such as <, then &&, and then ||. However, it is a good practice to include most parentheses to make the expression easier to understand. One place where parentheses can safely be omitted is a simple string of &&'s or ||'s (but not a mixture of the two). The following expression is acceptable in terms of both the C++ compiler and readability:

```
(temperature > 90) && (humidity > 0.90) && (poolGate == OPEN)
```

Since the relational operations > and == are performed before the && operation, you could omit the parentheses in the above expression and it would have the same meaning, but including some parentheses makes the expression easier to read.

When parentheses are omitted from an expression, the compiler groups items according to rules known as **precedence rules**. Most of the precedence rules for C++ are given in Display 2.3. The table includes a number of operators that are not discussed until later in this book, but they are included for completeness and for those who may already know about them.

precedence rules

Display 2.3   Precedence of Operators *(part 1 of 2)*

`::`	Scope resolution operator	*Highest precedence (done first)*
`.`	Dot operator	
`->`	Member selection	
`[]`	Array indexing	
`( )`	Function call	
`++`	Postfix increment operator (placed after the variable)	
`--`	Postfix decrement operator (placed after the variable)	
`++`	Prefix increment operator (placed before the variable)	
`--`	Prefix decrement operator (placed before the variable)	
`!`	Not	
`-`	Unary minus	
`+`	Unary plus	
`*`	Dereference	
`&`	Address of	
`new`	Create (allocate memory)	
`delete`	Destroy (deallocate)	
`delete[]`	Destroy array (deallocate)	
`sizeof`	Size of object	
`( )`	Type cast	
`*`	Multiply	
`/`	Divide	
`%`	Remainder (modulo)	
`+`	Addition	
`-`	Subtraction	
`<<`	Insertion operator (console output)	*Lower precedence (done later)*
`>>`	Extraction operator (console input)	

Display 2.3   Precedence of Operators *(part 2 of 2)*

All operators in part 2 are of lower precedence than those in part 1.

<	Less than
>	Greater than
<=	Less than or equal to
>=	Greater than or equal to
==	Equal
!=	Not equal
&&	And
||	Or
=	Assignment
+=	Add and assign
-=	Subtract and assign
*=	Multiply and assign
/=	Divide and assign
%=	Modulo and assign
? :	Conditional operator
throw	Throw an exception
,	Comma operator

Lowest precedence (done last)

If one operation is performed before another, the operation that is performed first is said to have **higher precedence**. All the operators in a given box in Display 2.3 have the same precedence. Operators in higher boxes have higher precedence than operators in lower boxes.

higher precedence

When operators have the same precedences and the order is not determined by parentheses, then unary operations are done right to left. The assignment operations are also done right to left. For example, x = y = z means x = (y = z). Other binary operations that have the same precedences are done left to right. For example, x+y+z means (x+y)+z.

Notice that the precedence rules include both arithmetic operators such as + and * as well as Boolean operators such as && and ||. This is because many expressions combine arithmetic and Boolean operations, as in the following simple example:

```
(x + 1) > 2 || (x + 1) < -3
```

If you check the precedence rules given in Display 2.2, you will see that this expression is equivalent to:

```
((x + 1) > 2) || ((x + 1) < -3)
```

because > and < have higher precedence than ||. In fact, you could omit all the parentheses in the previous expression and it would have the same meaning, although it would be harder to read. Although we do not advocate omitting all the parentheses, it might be instructive to see how such an expression is interpreted using the precedence rules. Here is the expression without any parentheses:

```
x + 1 > 2 || x + 1 < -3
```

The precedences rules say first apply the unary –, then apply the +'s, then the > and the <, and finally apply the ||, which is exactly what the fully parenthesized version says to do.

The previous description of how a Boolean expression is evaluated is basically correct, but in C++, the computer actually takes an occasional shortcut when evaluating a Boolean expression. Notice that in many cases you need to evaluate only the first of two subexpressions in a Boolean expression. For example, consider the following:

```
(x >= 0) && (y > 1)
```

If x is negative, then (x >= 0) is false. As you can see in the tables in Display 2.1, when one subexpression in an && expression is false, then the whole expression is false, no matter whether the other expression is true or false. Thus, if we know that the first expression is false, there is no need to evaluate the second expression. A similar thing happens with || expressions. If the first of two expressions joined with the || operator is true, then you know the entire expression is true, no matter whether the second expression is true or false. The C++ language uses this fact to sometimes save itself the trouble of evaluating the second subexpression in a logical expression connected with an && or ||. C++ first evaluates the leftmost of the two expressions joined by an && or ||. If that gives it enough information to determine the final value of the expression (independent of the value of the second expression), then C++ does not bother to evaluate the second expression. This method of evaluation is called **short-circuit evaluation**.

short-circuit evaluation

Some languages other than C++ use **complete evaluation**. In complete evaluation, when two expressions are joined by an && or ||, both subexpressions are always evaluated and then the truth tables are used to obtain the value of the final expression.

complete evaluation

Both short-circuit evaluation and complete evaluation give the same answer, so why should you care that C++ uses short-circuit evaluation? Most of the time you need not care. As long as both subexpressions joined by the && or the || have a value, the two methods yield the same result. However, if the second subexpression is undefined, you might be happy to know that C++ uses short-circuit evaluation. Let's look at an example that illustrates this point. Consider the following statement:

```
if ( (kids != 0) && ((pieces/kids) >= 2) )
    cout << "Each child may have two pieces!";
```

If the value of kids is not zero, this statement involves no subtleties. However, suppose the value of kids is zero; consider how short-circuit evaluation handles this case. The expression (kids != 0) evaluates to false, so there would be no need to evaluate the second expression. Using short-circuit evaluation, C++ says that the entire expression is false, without bothering to evaluate the second expression. This prevents a run-time error, since evaluating the second expression would involve dividing by zero.

INTEGER VALUES CAN BE USED AS BOOLEAN VALUES

integers convert to bool

C++ sometimes uses integers as if they were Boolean values and bool values as if they were integers. In particular, C++ converts the integer 1 to true and converts the integer 0 to false, and vice versa. The situation is even a bit more complicated than simply using 1 for true and 0 for false. The compiler will treat any nonzero number as if it were the value true and will treat 0 as if it were the value false. As long as you make no mistakes in writing Boolean expressions, this conversion causes no problems. However, when you are debugging, it might help to know that the compiler is happy to combine integers using the Boolean operators &&, ||, and !.

For example, suppose you want a Boolean expression that is true provided that time has not yet run out (in some game or process). You might use the following:

```
!time > limit
```

This sounds right if you read it out loud: "not time greater than limit." The Boolean expression is wrong, however, and unfortunately, the compiler will not give you an error message. The compiler will apply the precedence rules from Display 2.3 and interpret your Boolean expression as the following:

```
(!time) > limit
```

This looks like nonsense, and intuitively it is nonsense. If the value of time is, for example, 36, what could possibly be the meaning of (!time)? After all, that is equivalent to "not 36." But in C++, any nonzero integer converts to true and 0 is converted to false. Thus, !36 is interpreted as "not true" and so it evaluates to false, which is in turn converted back to 0 because we are comparing to an int.

What we want as the value of this Boolean expression and what C++ gives us are not the same. If time has a value of 36 and limit has a value of 60, you want the above displayed Boolean expression to evaluate to true (because it is *not* true that time > limit). Unfortunately, the Boolean expression instead evaluates as follows: (!time) evaluates to false, which is converted to 0, so the entire Boolean expression is equivalent to

```
0 > limit
```

That in turn is equivalent to 0 > 60, because 60 is the value of limit, and that evaluates to false. Thus, the above logical expression evaluates to false, when you want it to evaluate to true.

There are two ways to correct this problem. One way is to use the ! operator correctly. When using the operator !, be sure to include parentheses around the argument. The correct way to write the above Boolean expression is

```
!(time > limit)
```

Another way to correct this problem is to completely avoid using the ! operator. For example, the following is also correct and easier to read:

```
if (time <= limit)
```

You can almost always avoid using the ! operator, and some programmers advocate avoiding it as much as possible.

Self-Test Exercises

1. Determine the value, true or false, of each of the following Boolean expressions, assuming that the value of the variable count is 0 and the value of the variable limit is 10. Give your answer as one of the values true or false.

    a. (count == 0) && (limit < 20)

    b. count == 0 && limit < 20

    c. (limit > 20) || (count < 5)

    d. !(count == 12)

    e. (count == 1) && (x < y)

    f. (count < 10) || (x < y)

    g. !(((count < 10) || (x < y)) && (count >= 0))

    h. ((limit/count) > 7) || (limit < 20)

    i. (limit < 20) || ((limit/count) > 7)

    j. ((limit/count) > 7) && (limit < 0)

    k. (limit < 0) && ((limit/count) > 7)

    l. (5 && 7) + (!6)

2. You sometimes see numeric intervals given as
   2 < x < 3

   In C++ this interval does not have the meaning you may expect. Explain and give the correct C++ Boolean expression that specifies that x lies between 2 and 3.

3. Consider a quadratic expression, say

   $x^2 - x - 2$

Describing where this quadratic is positive (that is, greater than 0) involves describing a set of numbers that are either less than the smaller root (which is −1) or greater than the larger root (which is 2). Write a C++ Boolean expression that is true when this formula has positive values.

4. Consider the quadratic expression

$$x^2 - 4x + 3$$

Describing where this quadratic is negative involves describing a set of numbers that are simultaneously greater than the smaller root (1) and less than the larger root (3). Write a C++ Boolean expression that is true when the value of this quadratic is negative.

2.2 Branching Mechanisms

When you come to a fork in the road, take it.

Attributed to Yogi Berra

■ if-else STATEMENTS

if-else
statement

An **if-else statement** chooses between two alternative statements based on the value of a Boolean expression. For example, suppose you want to design a program to compute a week's salary for an hourly employee. Assume the firm pays an overtime rate of one-and-one-half times the regular rate for all hours after the first 40 hours worked. When the employee works 40 or more hours, the pay is then equal to

```
rate*40 + 1.5*rate*(hours - 40)
```

However, if the employee works less than 40 hours, the correct pay formula is simply

```
rate*hours
```

The following if-else statement computes the correct pay for an employee whether the employee works less than 40 hours or works 40 or more hours,

```
if (hours > 40)
    grossPay = rate*40 + 1.5*rate*(hours - 40);
else
    grossPay = rate*hours;
```

The syntax for an if-else statement is given in the accompanying box. If the Boolean expression in parentheses (after the if) evaluates to true, then the statement before the else is executed. If the Boolean expression evaluates to false, the statement after the else is executed.

if-else STATEMENT

The if-else statement chooses between two alternative actions based on the value of a Boolean expression. The syntax is shown below. Be sure to note that the Boolean expression must be enclosed in parentheses.

SYNTAX: A SINGLE STATEMENT FOR EACH ALTERNATIVE

```
if (Boolean_Expression)
    Yes_Statement
else
    No_Statement
```

If the *Boolean_Expression* evaluates to true, then the *Yes_Statement* is executed. If the *Boolean_Expression* evaluates to false, then the *No_Statement* is executed.

SYNTAX: A SEQUENCE OF STATEMENTS FOR EACH ALTERNATIVE

```
if (Boolean_Expression)
{
    Yes_Statement_1
    Yes_Statement_2
      . . .
    Yes_Statement_Last
}
else
{
    No_Statement_1
    No_Statement_2
      . . .
    No_Statement_Last
}
```

EXAMPLE

```
if (myScore > yourScore)
{
    cout << "I win!\n";
    wager = wager + 100;
}
else
{
    cout << "I wish these were golf scores.\n";
    wager = 0;
}
```

Notice that an `if-else` statement has smaller statements embedded in it. Most of the statement forms in C++ allow you to make larger statements out of smaller statements by combining the smaller statements in certain ways.

Remember that when you use a Boolean expression in an `if-else` statement, the Boolean expression must be enclosed in parentheses.

■ COMPOUND STATEMENTS

You will often want the branches of an `if-else` statement to execute more than one statement each. To accomplish this, enclose the statements for each branch between a pair of braces, { and }, as indicated in the second syntax template in the box entitled **if-else Statement**. A list of statements enclosed in a pair of braces is called a **compound statement**. A compound statement is treated as a single statement by C++ and may be used anywhere that a single statement may be used. (Thus, the second syntax template in the box entitled `if-else` Statement. is really just a special case of the first one.)

There are two commonly used ways of indenting and placing braces in `if-else` statements, which are illustrated below:

```cpp
if (myScore > yourScore)
{
    cout << "I win!\n";
    wager = wager + 100;
}
else
{
    cout << "I wish these were golf scores.\n";
    wager = 0;
}
```

and

```cpp
if (myScore > yourScore){
    cout << "I win!\n";
    wager = wager + 100;
} else {
    cout << "I wish these were golf scores.\n";
    wager = 0;
}
```

The only differences are the placement of braces. We find the first form easier to read and therefore prefer it. The second form saves lines, and so some programmers prefer the second form or some minor variant of it.

Pitfall

USING = IN PLACE OF ==

Unfortunately, you can write many things in C++ that you would think are incorrectly formed C++ statements but which turn out to have some obscure meaning. This means that if you mistakenly write something that you would expect to produce an error message, you may find that the program compiles and runs with no error messages but gives incorrect output. Since you may not realize you wrote something incorrectly, this can cause serious problems. For example, consider an if–else statement that begins as follows:

```
if (x = 12)
    Do_Something
else
    Do_Something_Else
```

Suppose you wanted to test to see if the value of x is equal to 12, so that you really meant to use == rather than =. You might think the compiler would catch your mistake. The expression

```
x = 12
```

is not something that is satisfied or not. It is an assignment statement, so surely the compiler will give an error message. Unfortunately, that is not the case. In C++ the expression x = 12 is an expression that returns a value, just like x + 12 or 2 + 3. An assignment expression's value is the value transferred to the variable on the left. For example, the value of x = 12 is 12. We saw in our discussion of Boolean value compatibility that nonzero int values are converted to true. If you use x = 12 as the Boolean expression in an if–else statement, the Boolean expression will always evaluate to true.

This error is very hard to find, because it looks right. The compiler can find the error without any special instructions if you put the 12 on the left side of the comparison: 12 == x will produce no error message, but 12 = x will generate an error message.

Self-Test Exercises

5. Does the following sequence produce division by zero?

```
j = -1;
if ((j > 0) && (1/(j+1) > 10))
    cout << i << endl;
```

6. Write an if–else statement that outputs the word High if the value of the variable score is greater than 100 and Low if the value of score is at most 100. The variable score is of type int.

7. Suppose `savings` and `expenses` are variables of type `double` that have been given values. Write an `if-else` statement that outputs the word `Solvent`, decreases the value of `savings` by the value of `expenses`, and sets the value of `expenses` to zero provided that `savings` is at least as large as `expenses`. If, however, `savings` is less than `expenses`, the `if-else` statement simply outputs the word `Bankrupt` and does not change the value of any variables.

8. Write an `if-else` statement that outputs the word `Passed` provided the value of the variable `exam` is greater than or equal to 60 and also the value of the variable `programsDone` is greater than or equal to 10. Otherwise, the `if-else` statement outputs the word `Failed`. The variables `exam` and `programsDone` are both of type `int`.

9. Write an `if-else` statement that outputs the word `Warning` provided that either the value of the variable `temperature` is greater than or equal to 100, or the value of the variable `pressure` is greater than or equal to 200, or both. Otherwise, the `if-else` statement outputs the word `OK`. The variables `temperature` and `pressure` are both of type `int`.

10. What is the output of the following? Explain your answers.

a.
```
if(0)
   cout << "0 is true";
else
   cout << "0 is false";
cout << endl;
```

b.
```
if(1)
   cout << "1 is true";
else
   cout << "1 is false";
cout << endl;
```

c.
```
if(-1)
   cout << "-1 is true";
else
   cout << "-1 is false";
cout << endl;
```

Note: This is an exercise only. This is *not* intended to illustrate programming style you should follow.

■ OMITTING THE `else`

Sometimes you want one of the two alternatives in an `if-else` statement to do nothing at all. In C++ this can be accomplished by omitting the `else` part. These sorts of statements are referred to as **if statements** to distinguish them from if-else statements. For example, the first of the following two statements is an if statement:

```
if (sales >= minimum)
    salary = salary + bonus;
cout << "salary = $" << salary;
```

If the value of sales is greater than or equal to the value of minimum, the assignment statement is executed and then the following cout statement is executed. On the other hand, if the value of sales is less than minimum, then the embedded assignment statement is not executed. Thus, the if statement causes no change (that is, no bonus is added to the base salary), and the program proceeds directly to the cout statement.

NESTED STATEMENTS

As you have seen, if-else statements and if statements contain smaller statements within them. Thus far we have used compound statements and simple statements such as assignment statements as these smaller substatements, but there are other possibilities. In fact, any statement at all can be used as a subpart of an if-else statement or of other statements that have one or more statements within them.

When nesting statements, you normally indent each level of nested substatements, although there are some special situations (such as a multiway if-else branch) where this rule is not followed.

MULTIWAY if-else STATEMENT

The multiway if-else statement is not really a different kind of C++ statement. It is simply an ordinary if-else statement nested inside if-else statements, but it is thought of as a kind of statement and is indented differently from other nested statements so as to reflect this thinking.

The syntax for a multiway if-else statement and a simple example are given in the accompanying box. Note that the Boolean expressions are aligned with one another, and their corresponding actions are also aligned with each other. This makes it easy to see the correspondence between Boolean expressions and actions. The Boolean expressions are evaluated in order until a true Boolean expression is found. At that point the evaluation of Boolean expressions stops, and the action corresponding to the first true Boolean expression is executed. The final else is optional. If there is a final else and all the Boolean expressions are false, the final action is executed. If there is no final else and all the Boolean expressions are false, then no action is taken.

MULTIWAY if–else STATEMENT

SYNTAX

```
if (Boolean_Expression_1)
    Statement_1
else if (Boolean_Expression_2)
    Statement_2
          .
          .
          .
else if (Boolean_Expression_n)
    Statement_n
else
    Statement_For_All_Other_Possibilities
```

EXAMPLE

```
if ((temperature < -10) && (day == SUNDAY))
    cout << "Stay home.";
else if (temperature < -10) //and day != SUNDAY
    cout << "Stay home, but call work.";
else if (temperature <= 0) //and temperature >= -10
    cout << "Dress warm.";
else //temperature > 0
    cout << "Work hard and play hard.";
```

The Boolean expressions are checked in order until the first true Boolean expression is encountered, and then the corresponding statement is executed. If none of the Boolean expressions is true, then the Statement_For_All_Other_Possibilities is executed.

Self-Test Exercises

11. What output will be produced by the following code?

```
int x = 2;
cout << "Start\n";
if (x <= 3)
    if (x != 0)
        cout << "Hello from the second if.\n";
    else
        cout << "Hello from the else.\n";
cout << "End\n";

cout << "Start again\n";
if (x > 3)
    if (x != 0)
```

```
                cout << "Hello from the second if.\n";
        else
                cout << "Hello from the else.\n";
    cout << "End again\n";
```

12. What output will be produced by the following code?

```
int extra = 2;
if (extra < 0)
    cout << "small";
else if (extra == 0)
    cout << "medium";
else
    cout << "large";
```

13. What would be the output in Self-Test Exercise 12 if the assignment were changed to the following?

```
int extra = -37;
```

14. What would be the output in Self-Test Exercise 12 if the assignment were changed to the following?

```
int extra = 0;
```

15. Write a multiway if-else statement that classifies the value of an int variable n into one of the following categories and writes out an appropriate message.

```
n < 0 or 0 ≤ n ≤ 100 or n > 100
```

■ THE switch STATEMENT

The **switch statement** is the only other kind of C++ statement that implements multiway branches. Syntax for a switch statement and a simple example are shown in the accompanying box.

When a switch statement is executed, one of a number of different branches is executed. The choice of which branch to execute is determined by a **controlling expression** given in parentheses after the keyword switch. The controlling expression for a switch statement must always return either a bool value, an enum constant (discussed later in this chapter), one of the integer types, or a character. When the switch statement is executed, this controlling expression is evaluated and the computer looks at the constant values given after the various occurrences of the case identifiers. If it finds a constant that equals the value of the controlling expression, it executes the code for that case. You cannot have two occurrences of case with the same constant value after them because that would create an ambiguous instruction.

switch
statement

controlling
expression

switch STATEMENT

SYNTAX

```
switch (Controlling_Expression)
{
    case Constant_1:
        Statement_Sequence_1
        break;
    case Constant_2:
        Statement_Sequence_2
        break;
                .
                .
                .
    case Constant_n:
        Statement_Sequence_n
        break;
    default:
        Default_Statement_Sequence
}
```

You need not place a break statement in each case. If you omit a break, that case continues until a break (or the end of the switch statement) is reached.

EXAMPLE

```
int vehicleClass;
double toll;
cout << "Enter vehicle class: ";
cin >> vehicleClass;

switch (vehicleClass)
{
    case 1:
        cout << "Passenger car.";
        toll = 0.50;
        break;
    case 2:
        cout << "Bus.";
        toll = 1.50;
        break;
    case 3:
        cout << "Truck.";
        toll = 2.00;
        break;
    default:
        cout << "Unknown vehicle class!";
    }
```

If you forget this break, then passenger cars will pay $1.50.

The `switch` statement ends when either a `break` statement is encountered or the end of the `switch` statement is reached. A **break statement** consists of the keyword `break` followed by a semicolon. When the computer executes the statements after a `case` label, it continues until it reaches a `break` statement. When the computer encounters a `break` statement, the `switch` statement ends. If you omit the `break` statements, then after executing the code for one `case`, the computer will go on to execute the code for the next `case`.

break statement

Note that you can have two `case` labels for the same section of code, as in the following portion of a `switch` statement:

```
case 'A':
case 'a':
    cout << "Excellent. "
        << "You need not take the final.\n";
    break;
```

Since the first `case` has no `break` statement (in fact, no statement at all), the effect is the same as having two labels for one `case`, but C++ syntax requires one keyword `case` for each label, such as `'A'` and `'a'`.

If no `case` label has a constant that matches the value of the controlling expression, then the statements following the `default` label are executed. You need not have a `default` section. If there is no `default` section and no match is found for the value of the controlling expression, then nothing happens when the `switch` statement is executed. However, it is safest to always have a `default` section. If you think your `case` labels list all possible outcomes, then you can put an error message in the `default` section.

default

Pitfall

FORGETTING A break IN A switch STATEMENT

If you forget a `break` in a `switch` statement, the compiler will not issue an error message. You will have written a syntactically correct `switch` statement, but it will not do what you intended it to do. Notice the annotation in the example in the box entitled **switch Statement**.

Tip

USE switch STATEMENTS FOR MENUS

The multiway `if-else` statement is more versatile than the `switch` statement, and you can use a multiway `if-else` statement anywhere you can use a `switch` statement. However, sometimes the `switch` statement is clearer. For example, the `switch` statement is perfect for implementing menus. Each branch of the `switch` statement can be one menu choice.

▪ ENUMERATION TYPES

enumeration
type

An **enumeration type** is a type whose values are defined by a list of constants of type int. An enumeration type is very much like a list of declared constants. Enumeration types can be handy for defining a list of identifiers to use as the case labels in a switch statement.

When defining an enumeration type, you can use any int values and can define any number of constants. For example, the following enumeration type defines a constant for the length of each month:

```
enum MonthLength { JAN_LENGTH = 31, FEB_LENGTH = 28,
    MAR_LENGTH = 31, APR_LENGTH = 30, MAY_LENGTH = 31,
    JUN_LENGTH = 30, JUL_LENGTH = 31, AUG_LENGTH = 31,
    SEP_LENGTH = 30, OCT_LENGTH = 31, NOV_LENGTH = 30,
    DEC_LENGTH = 31 };
```

As this example shows, two or more named constants in an enumeration type can receive the same int value.

If you do not specify any numeric values, the identifiers in an enumeration type definition are assigned consecutive values beginning with 0. For example, the type definition

```
enum Direction { NORTH = 0, SOUTH = 1, EAST = 2, WEST = 3 };
```

is equivalent to

```
enum Direction { NORTH, SOUTH, EAST, WEST };
```

The form that does not explicitly list the int values is normally used when you just want a list of names and do not care about what values they have.

Suppose you initialize an enumeration constant to some value, say

```
enum MyEnum { ONE = 17, TWO, THREE, FOUR = -3, FIVE };
```

then ONE takes the value 17; TWO takes the next int value, 18; THREE takes the next value, 19; FOUR takes -3; and FIVE takes the next value, -2. In short, the default for the first enumeration constant is 0. The rest increase by 1 unless you set one or more of the enumeration constants.

Although the constants in an enumeration type are give as int values and can be used as integers in many contexts, remember that an enumeration type is a separate type and treat it as a type different from the type int. Use enumeration types as labels and avoid doing arithmetic with variables of an enumerations type.

▪ THE CONDITIONAL OPERATOR

conditional
operator

It is possible to embed a conditional inside an expression by using a ternary operator know as the **conditional operator** (also called the *ternary operator* or *arithmetic if*). Its use is reminiscent of an older programming style, and we do not advise using it. It is included here for the sake of completeness (and in case you disagree with our programming style).

The conditional operator is a notational variant on certain forms of the `if-else` statement. This variant is illustrated below. Consider the statement

```
if (n1 > n2)
    max = n1;
else
    max = n2;
```

This can be expressed using the conditional operator as follows:

```
max = (n1 > n2) ? n1 : n2;
```

The expression on the right-hand side of the assignment statement is the **conditional operator expression**:

```
(n1 > n2) ? n1 : n2
```

conditional operator expression

The ? and : together form a ternary operator know as the conditional operator. A conditional operator expression starts with a Boolean expression followed by a ? and then followed by two expressions separated with a colon. If the Boolean expression is `true`, then the first of the two expressions is returned; otherwise, the second of the two expressions is returned.

Self-Test Exercises

16. Given the following declaration and output statement, assume that this has been embedded in a correct program and is run. What is the output?

```
enum Direction { N, S, E, W };
// ...
cout << W << " " << E << " " << S << " " << N << endl;
```

17. Given the following declaration and output statement, assume that this has been embedded in a correct program and is run. What is the output?

```
enum Direction { N = 5, S = 7, E = 1, W };
// ...
cout << W << " " << E << " " << S << " " << N << endl;
```

2.3 Loops

*It is not true that life is one damn thing after another—It's one
damn thing over and over.*

> Edna St. Vincent Millay,
> Letter to Arthur Darison Ficke, October 24, 1930

Looping mechanisms in C++ are similar to those in other high-level languages. The
three C++ loop statements are the while statement, the do-while statement, and the
for statement. The same terminology is used with C++ as with other languages. The
code that is repeated in a loop is called the **loop body**. Each repetition of the loop body
is called an **iteration** of the loop.

while **and**
do-while
compared

■ THE while AND do-while STATEMENTS

The syntax for the while statement and its variant, the do-while statement, is given in
the accompanying box. In both cases, the multistatement body syntax is a special case
of the syntax for a loop with a single-statement body. The multistatement body is a single compound statement. Examples of a while statement and a do-while statement are
given in Displays 2.4 and 2.5.

SYNTAX FOR while AND do-while STATEMENTS

A while STATEMENT WITH A SINGLE STATEMENT BODY

```
while (Boolean_Expression)
    Statement
```

A while STATEMENT WITH A MULTISTATEMENT BODY

```
while (Boolean_Expression)
{
    Statement_1
    Statement_2
      .
      .
      .
    Statement_Last
}
```

A do–while Statement with a Single-Statement Body

```
do
    Statement
while (Boolean_Expression);
```

A do–while Statement with a Multistatement Body

```
do
{
    Statement_1
    Statement_2
        .
        .
        .
    Statement_Last
} while (Boolean_Expression);
```

Do not forget the final semicolon.

Display 2.4   Example of a while Statement *(part 1 of 2)*

```
1   #include <iostream>
2   using namespace std;

3   int main( )
4   {
5       int countDown;

6       cout << "How many greetings do you want? ";
7       cin >> countDown;

8       while (countDown > 0)
9       {
10          cout << "Hello ";
11          countDown = countDown - 1;
12      }

13      cout << endl;
14      cout << "That's all!\n";

15      return 0;
16  }
```

Display 2.4   Example of a while Statement *(part 2 of 2)*

SAMPLE DIALOGUE 1

```
How many greetings do you want? 3
Hello Hello Hello
That's all!
```

SAMPLE DIALOGUE 2

```
How many greetings do you want? 0

That's all!
```
                                          The loop body is executed
                                          zero times

Display 2.5   Example of a do–while Statement *(part 1 of 2)*

```
1    #include <iostream>
2    using namespace std;

3    int main( )
4    {
5        int countDown;

6        cout << "How many greetings do you want? ";
7        cin >> countDown;

8        do
9        {
10           cout << "Hello ";
11           countDown = countDown - 1;
12       }while (countDown > 0);

13       cout << endl;
14       cout << "That's all!\n";

15       return 0;
16   }
```

SAMPLE DIALOGUE 1

```
How many greetings do you want? 3
Hello Hello Hello
That's all!
```

Display 2.5   Example of a do-while Statement *(part 2 of 2)*

SAMPLE DIALOGUE 2

```
How many greetings do you want? 0
Hello          ←————————————————————————           The loop body
That's all!                                          is always executed at least once.
```

The important difference between the while and do-while loops involves *when* the controlling Boolean expression is checked. With a while statement, the Boolean expression is checked *before* the loop body is executed. If the Boolean expression evaluates to false, the body is not executed at all. With a do-while statement, the body of the loop is executed first and the Boolean expression is checked *after* the loop body is executed. Thus, the do-while statement always executes the loop body at least once. After this start-up, the while loop and the do-while loop behave the same. After each iteration of the loop body, the Boolean expression is again checked; if it is true, the loop is iterated again. If it has changed from true to false, the loop statement ends.

The first thing that happens when a while loop is executed is that the controlling Boolean expression is evaluated. If the Boolean expression evaluates to false at that point, the body of the loop is never executed. It may seem pointless to execute the body of a loop zero times, but that is sometimes the desired action. For example, a while loop is often used to sum a list of numbers, but the list could be empty. To be more specific, a checkbook balancing program might use a while loop to sum the values of all the checks you have written in a month—but you might take a month's vacation and write no checks at all. In that case, there are zero numbers to sum and so the loop is iterated zero times.

executing the body zero times

INCREMENT AND DECREMENT OPERATORS REVISITED

In general, we discourage the use of the increment and decrement operators in expressions. However, many programmers like to use them in the controlling Boolean expression of a while or do-while statement. If done with care, this can work out satisfactorily. An example is given in Display 2.6. Be sure to notice that in count++ <= numberOfItems, the value returned by count++ is the value of count before it is incremented.

Display 2.6   The Increment Operator in an Expression

```
1    #include <iostream>
2    using namespace std;

3    int main( )
4    {
5        int numberOfItems, count,
6            caloriesForItem, totalCalories;

7        cout << "How many items did you eat today? ";
8        cin >> numberOfItems;

9        totalCalories = 0;
10       count = 1;
11       cout << "Enter the number of calories in each of the\n"
12           << numberOfItems << " items eaten:\n";

13       while (count++ <= numberOfItems)
14       {
15           cin >> caloriesForItem;
16           totalCalories = totalCalories
17                           + caloriesForItem;
18       }

19       cout << "Total calories eaten today = "
20           << totalCalories << endl;
21       return 0;
22   }
```

SAMPLE DIALOGUE

```
How many items did you eat today? 7
Enter the number of calories in each of the
7 items eaten:
300 60 1200 600 150 1 120
Total calories eaten today = 2431
```

Self-Test Exercises

18. What is the output of the following?

```
int count = 3;
while (count-- > 0)
    cout << count << " ";
```

19. What is the output of the following?

```
int count = 3;
while (--count > 0)
    cout << count << " ";
```

20. What is the output of the following?

```
int n = 1;
do
    cout << n << " ";
while (n++ <= 3);
```

21. What is the output of the following?

```
int n = 1;
do
    cout << n << " ";
while (++n <= 3);
```

22. What is the output produced by the following? (x is of type int.)

```
int x = 10;
while (x > 0)
{
    cout << x << endl;
    x = x - 3;
}
```

23. What output would be produced in the previous exercise if the > sign were replaced with <?

24. What is the output produced by the following? (x is of type int.)

```
int x = 10;
do
{
    cout << x << endl;
    x = x - 3;
} while (x > 0);
```

25. What is the output produced by the following? (x is of type int.)

```
int x = -42;
do
{
    cout << x << endl;
    x = x - 3;
} while (x > 0);
```

26. What is the most important difference between a while statement and a do-while statement?

THE COMMA OPERATOR

comma
operator

The **comma operator** is a way of evaluating a list of expressions and returning the value of the last expression. It is sometimes handy to use in a for loop, as indicated in our discussion of the for loop in the next subsection. We do not advise using it in other contexts, but it is legal to use it in any expression.

The comma operator is illustrated by the following assignment statement:

```
result = (first = 2, second = first + 1);
```

The comma operator is the comma shown. The **comma expression** is the expression on the right-hand side of the assignment operator. The comma operator has two expressions as operands. In this case the two operands are

```
first = 2 and second = first + 1
```

The first expression is evaluated, and then the second expression is evaluated. As you may recall from Chapter 1, the assignment statement when used as an expression returns the new value of the variable on the left side of the assignment operator. So, this comma expression returns the final value of the variable second, which means that the variable result is set equal to 3.

Since only the value of the second expression is returned, the first expression is evaluated solely for its side effects. In the above example, the side effect of the first expression is to change the value of the variable first.

You may have a longer list of expressions connected with commas, but you should only do so when the order of evaluation is not important. If the order of evaluation is important, you should use parentheses. For example:

```
result = ((first = 2, second = first + 1), third = second + 1);
```

sets the value of result equal to 4. However, the value that the following gives to result is unpredictable, because it does not guarantee that the expressions are evaluated in order:

```
result = (first = 2, second = first + 1, third = second + 1);
```

For example, third = second + 1 might be evaluated before second = first + 1.[1]

THE for STATEMENT

The third and final loop statement in C++ is the **for statement**. The for statement is most commonly used to step through some integer variable in equal increments. As we will see in Chapter 5, the for statement is often used to step through an array. The for statement is, however, a completely general looping mechanism that can do anything that a while loop can do.

for statement

For example, the following for statement sums the integers 1 through 10:

```
sum = 0;
for (n = 1; n <= 10; n++)
    sum = sum + n;
```

A for statement begins with the keyword for followed by three things in parentheses that tell the computer what to do with the controlling variable. The beginning of a for statement looks like the following:

```
for (Initialization_Action; Boolean_Expression; Update_Action)
```

The first expression tells how the variable, variables, or other things are initialized; the second gives a Boolean expression that is used to check for when the loop should end; and the last expression tells how the loop control variable is updated after each iteration of the loop body.

The three expressions at the start of a for statement are separated by two—and only two—semicolons. Do not succumb to the temptation to place a semicolon after the third expression. (The technical explanation is that these three things are expressions, not statements, and so do not require a semicolon at the end.)

A for statement often uses a single int variable to control loop iteration and loop ending. However, the three expressions at the start of a for statement may be any C++ expressions; therefore, they may involve more (or even fewer) than one variable, and the variables may be of any type.

---

[1] The C++ standard does specify that the expressions joined by commas should be evaluated left to right. However, our experience has been that not all compilers conform to the standard in this regard.

Using the comma operator, you can add multiple actions to either the first or the last (but normally not the second) of the three items in parentheses. For example, you can move the initialization of the variable sum inside the for loop to obtain the following, which is equivalent to the for statement code we showed earlier:

```
for (sum = 0, n = 1; n <= 10; n++)
    sum = sum + n;
```

Although we do not advise doing so because it is not as easy to read, you can move the entire body of the for loop into the third item in parentheses. The previous for statement is equivalent to the following:

```
for (sum = 0, n = 1; n <= 10; sum = sum + n, n++);
```

Display 2.7 shows the syntax of a for statement and also describes the action of the for statement by showing how it translates into an equivalent while statement. Notice that in a for statement, as in the corresponding while statement, the stopping condition is tested before the first loop iteration. Thus, it is possible to have a for loop whose body is executed zero times.

The body of a for statement may be, and commonly is, a compound statement, as in the following example:

```
for (number = 100; number >= 0; number--)
{
    cout << number
         << " bottles of beer on the shelf.\n";
    if (number > 0)
        cout << "Take one down and pass it around.\n";
}
```

The first and last expressions in parentheses at the start of a for statement may be any C++ expression and thus may involve any number of variables and may be of any type.

In a for statement, a variable may be declared at the same time as it is initialized. For example:

```
for (int n = 1; n < 10; n++)
    cout << n << endl;
```

Compilers may vary in how they handle such declarations within a for statement. This is discussed in Chapter 3 in the subsection entitled "Variables Declared in a for Loop". It might be wise to avoid such declarations within a for statement until you reach Chapter 3, but we mention it here for reference value.

Display 2.7   for Statement

___

for STATEMENT SYNTAX

for (*Initialization_Action*; *Boolean_Expression*; *Update_Action*)
    Body_Statement

EXAMPLE

```
for (number = 100; number >= 0; number--)
    cout << number
        << " bottles of beer on the shelf.\n";
```

EQUIVALENT while LOOP SYNTAX

Initialization_Action;
while (*Boolean_Expression*)
{
    Body_Statement
    Update_Action;
}

EQUIVALENT EXAMPLE

```
number = 100;
while (number >= 0)
{
    cout << number
        << " bottles of beer on the shelf.\n";
    number--;
}
```

SAMPLE DIALOGUE

```
100 bottles of beer on the shelf.
99 bottles of beer on the shelf.
            .
            .
            .
0 bottles of beer on the shelf.
```

for STATEMENT

SYNTAX

```
for (Initialization_Action; Boolean_Expression; Update_Action)
    Body_Statement
```

EXAMPLE

```
for (sum = 0, n = 1; n <= 10; n++)
    sum = sum + n;
```

See Display 2.7 for an explanation of the action of a for statement.

Tip

REPEAT-*N*-TIMES LOOPS

A for statement can be used to produce a loop that repeats the loop body a predetermined number of times. For example, the following is a loop body that repeats its loop body three times:

```
for (int count = 1; count <= 3; count++)
    cout << "Hip, Hip, Hurray\n";
```

The body of a for statement need not make any reference to a loop control variable, such as the variable count.

Pitfall

EXTRA SEMICOLON IN A for STATEMENT

You normally do not place a semicolon after the parentheses at the beginning of a for loop. To see what can happen, consider the following for loop:

```
for (int count = 1; count <= 10; count++);    ◄——— Problem semicolon
    cout << "Hello\n";
```

If you did not notice the extra semicolon, you might expect this for loop to write Hello to the screen ten times. If you do notice the semicolon, you might expect the compiler to issue an error message. Neither of those things happens. If you embed this for loop in a complete program, the compiler will not complain. If you run the program, only one Hello will be output instead of ten Hellos. What is happening? To answer that question, we need a little background.

One way to create a statement in C++ is to put a semicolon after something. If you put a semicolon after x++, you change the expression

```
x++
```

into the statement

```
x++;
```

If you place a semicolon after nothing, you still create a statement. Thus, the semicolon by itself is a statement, which is called the **empty statement** or the **null statement**. The empty statement performs no action, but it still is a statement. Therefore, the following is a complete and legitimate for loop, whose body is the empty statement:

```
for (int count = 1; count <= 10; count++);
```

This for loop is indeed iterated ten times, but since the body is the empty statement, nothing happens when the body is iterated. This loop does nothing, and it does nothing ten times!

This same sort of problem can arise with a while loop. Be careful not to place a semicolon after the closing parenthesis that encloses the Boolean expression at the start of a while loop. A do–while loop has just the opposite problem. You must remember always to end a do–while loop with a semicolon.

Pitfall

INFINITE LOOPS

A while loop, do–while loop, or for loop does not terminate as long as the controlling Boolean expression is true. This Boolean expression normally contains a variable that will be changed by the loop body, and usually the value of this variable is changed in a way that eventually makes the Boolean expression false and therefore terminates the loop. However, if you make a mistake and write your program so that the Boolean expression is always true, then the loop will run forever. A loop that runs forever is called an **infinite loop**.

Unfortunately, examples of infinite loops are not hard to come by. First let's describe a loop that does terminate. The following C++ code will write out the positive even numbers less than 12. That is, it will output the numbers 2, 4, 6, 8, and 10, one per line, and then the loop will end.

```
x = 2;
while (x != 12)
{
    cout << x << endl;
    x = x + 2;
}
```

The value of x is increased by 2 on each loop iteration until it reaches 12. At that point, the Boolean expression after the word while is no longer true, so the loop ends.

Now suppose you want to write out the odd numbers less than 12, rather than the even numbers. You might mistakenly think that all you need do is change the initializing statement to

```
x = 1;
```

But this mistake will create an infinite loop. Because the value of x goes from 11 to 13, the value of x is never equal to 12; thus, the loop will never terminate.

This sort of problem is common when loops are terminated by checking a numeric quantity using == or !=. When dealing with numbers, it is always safer to test for passing a value. For example, the following will work fine as the first line of our while loop:

```
while (x < 12)
```

With this change, x can be initialized to any number and the loop will still terminate.

A program that is in an infinite loop will run forever unless some external force stops it. Since you can now write programs that contain an infinite loop, it is a good idea to learn how to force a program to terminate. The method for forcing a program to stop varies from system to system. The keystrokes Control-C will terminate a program on many systems. (To type Control-C, hold down the Control key while pressing the C key.)

In simple programs, an infinite loop is almost always an error. However, some programs are intentionally written to run forever (in principle), such as the main outer loop in an airline reservation program, which just keeps asking for more reservations until you shut down the computer (or otherwise terminate the program in an atypical way).

Self-Test Exercises

27. What is the output of the following (when embedded in a complete program)?

```
for (int count = 1; count < 5; count++)
    cout << (2 * count) << " ";
```

28. What is the output of the following (when embedded in a complete program)?

```
for (int n = 10; n > 0; n = n - 2)
{
    cout << "Hello ";
        cout << n << endl;
}
```

29. What is the output of the following (when embedded in a complete program)?

```
for (double sample = 2; sample > 0; sample = sample - 0.5)
    cout << sample << " ";
```

30. Rewrite the following loops as for loops.

a.

```
int i = 1;
while(i <= 10)
{
```

```
      if (i < 5 && i != 2)
          cout << 'X';
      i++;
}
```

b.

```
int i = 1;
while(i <=10)
{
   cout << 'X';
   i = i + 3;
}
```

c.

```
long n = 100;
do
{
   cout << 'X';
   n = n + 100;
} while(n < 1000);
```

31. What is the output of this loop? Identify the connection between the value of n and the value of the variable `log`.

```
int n = 1024;
int log = 0;
for (int i = 1; i < n; i = i * 2)
    log++;
cout << n << " " << log << endl;
```

32. What is the output of this loop? Comment on the code. (This is not the same as the previous exercise.)

```
int n = 1024;
int log = 0;
for (int i = 1; i < n; i = i * 2);
    log++;
cout << n << " " << log << endl;
```

33. What is the output of this loop? Comment on the code. (This is not the same as either of the two previous exercises.)

```
int n = 1024;
int log = 0;
for (int i = 0; i < n; i = i * 2);
    log++;
cout << n << " " << log << endl;
```

34. For each of the following situations, tell which type of loop (`while`, `do-while`, or `for`) would work best.

    a. Summing a series, such as 1/2 + 1/3 + 1/4 + 1/5 + . . . + 1/10.

    b. Reading in the list of exam scores for one student.

    c. Reading in the number of days of sick leave taken by employees in a department.

    d. Testing a function to see how it performs for different values of its arguments.

35. What is the output produced by the following? (`x` is of type `int`.)

```cpp
int x = 10;
while (x > 0)
{
    cout << x << endl;
    x = x + 3;
}
```

THE break AND continue STATEMENTS

In previous subsections, we have described the basic flow of control for the `while`, `do-while`, and `for` loops. This is how the loops should normally be used and is the way they are usually used. However, you can alter the flow of control in two ways, which in rare cases can be a useful and safe technique. The two ways of altering the flow of control are to insert a `break` or `continue` statement. The `break` statement ends the loop. The `continue` statement ends the current iteration of the loop body. The `break` statement can be used with any of the C++ loop statements.

We described the `break` statement when we discussed the `switch` statement. The `break` statement consists of the keyword `break` followed by a semicolon. When executed, the `break` statement ends the nearest enclosing `switch` or loop statement. Display 2.8 contains an example of a `break` statement that ends a loop when inappropriate input is entered.

continue
statement

The **continue statement** consists of the keyword `continue` followed by a semicolon. When executed, the `continue` statement ends the current loop body iteration of the nearest enclosing loop statement. Display 2.9 contains an example of a loop that contains a `continue` statement.

One point that you should note when using the `continue` statement in a `for` loop is that the `continue` statement transfers control to the update expression. So, any loop control variable will be updated immediately after the `continue` statement is executed.

Note that a `break` statement completely ends the loop. In contrast, a `continue` statement merely ends one loop iteration; the next iteration (if any) continues the loop. You will find it instructive to compare the details of the programs in Displays 2.8 and 2.9. Pay particular attention to the change in the controlling Boolean expression.

Display 2.8   A break Statement in a Loop

```
1    #include <iostream>
2    using namespace std;

3    int main( )
4    {
5        int number, sum = 0, count = 0;
6        cout << "Enter 4 negative numbers:\n";

7        while (++count <= 4)
8        {
9            cin >> number;

10           if (number >= 0)
11           {
12               cout << "ERROR: positive number"
13                    << " or zero was entered as the\n"
14                    << count << "th number! Input ends "
15                    << "with the " << count << "th number.\n"
16                    << count << "th number was not added in.\n";
17               break;
18           }

19           sum = sum + number;
20       }

21       cout << sum << " is the sum of the first "
22            << (count - 1) << " numbers.\n";

23       return 0;
24   }
```

SAMPLE DIALOGUE

```
Enter 4 negative numbers:
-1 -2 3 -4
ERROR: positive number or zero was entered as the
3rd number! Input ends with the 3rd number.
3rd number was not added in
-3 is the sum of the first 2 numbers.
```

Display 2.9   A continue Statement in a Loop

```
1    #include <iostream>
2    using namespace std;

3    int main( )
4    {
5        int number, sum = 0, count = 0;
6        cout << "Enter 4 negative numbers, ONE PER LINE:\n";

7        while (count < 4)
8        {
9            cin >> number;

10           if (number >= 0)
11           {
12               cout << "ERROR: positive number (or zero)!\n"
13                   << "Reenter that number and continue:\n";
14               continue;
15           }

16           sum = sum + number;
17           count++;
18       }

19       cout << sum << " is the sum of the "
20           << count << " numbers.\n";
21       return 0;
22   }
```

SAMPLE DIALOGUE

```
Enter 4 negative numbers, ONE PER LINE:
1
ERROR: positive number (or zero)!
Reenter that number and continue:
-1
-2
3
ERROR: positive number!
Reenter that number and continue:
-3
-4
-10 is the sum of the 4 numbers.
```

Note that you never absolutely need a break or continue statement. The programs in Displays 2.8 and 2.9 can be rewritten so that neither uses either a break or continue statement. The continue statement can be particularly tricky and can make your code hard to read. It may be best to avoid the continue statement completely or at least use it only on rare occasions.

NESTED LOOPS

It is perfectly legal to nest one loop statement inside another loop statement. When doing so, remember that any break or continue statement applies to the innermost loop (or switch) statement containing the break or continue statement. It is best to avoid nested loops by placing the inner loop inside a function definition and placing a function invocation inside the outer loop. Functions are introduced in Chapter 3.

Self-Test Exercises

36. What does a break statement do? Where is it legal to put a break statement?

37. Predict the output of the following nested loops:
```
int n, m;
for (n = 1; n <= 10; n++)
    for (m = 10; m >= 1; m--)
        cout << n << " times " << m
             << " = " << n*m << endl;
```

Chapter Summary

- Boolean expressions are evaluated similar to the way arithmetic expressions are evaluated.

- The C++ branching statements are the if-else statement and the switch statement.

- A switch statement is a multiway branching statement. You can also form multiway branching statements by nesting if-else statements to form a multiway if-else statement.

- A switch statement is a good way to implement a menu for the user of your program.

- The C++ loop statements are the while, do-while, and for statements.

- A do-while statement always iterates their loop body at least one time. Both a while statement and a for statement might iterate their loop body zero times.

- A for loop can be used to obtain the equivalent of the instruction "repeat the loop body n times."

- A loop can be ended early with a break statement. A single iteration of a loop body may be ended early with a continue statement. It is best to use break statements sparingly. It is best to completely avoid using continue statements, although some programmers do use them on rare occasions.

ANSWERS TO SELF-TEST EXERCISES

1. a. true.

   b. true. Note that expressions a and b mean exactly the same thing. Because the operators == and < have higher precedence than &&, you do not need to include the parentheses. The parentheses do, however, make it easier to read. Most people find the expression in a easier to read than the expression in b, even though they mean the same thing.

   c. true.

   d. true.

   e. false. Since the value of the first subexpression, (count == 1), is false, you know that the entire expression is false without bothering to evaluate the second subexpression. Thus, it does not matter what the values of x and y are. This is *short-circuit evaluation*.

   f. true. Since the value of the first subexpression, (count < 10), is true, you know that the entire expression is true without bothering to evaluate the second subexpression. Thus, it does not matter what the values of x and y are. This is *short-circuit evaluation*.

   g. false. Notice that the expression in g includes the expression in f as a subexpression. This subexpression is evaluated using short-circuit evaluation as we described for f. The entire expression in g is equivalent to

   ```
   !( (true || (x < y)) && true )
   ```

   which in turn is equivalent to !(true && true), and that is equivalent to !(true), which is equivalent to the final value of false.

   h. This expression produces an error when it is evaluated because the first subexpression, ((limit/count) > 7), involves a division by zero.

   i. true. Since the value of the first subexpression, (limit < 20), is true, you know that the entire expression is true without bothering to evaluate the second subexpression. Thus, the second subexpression,

   ```
   ((limit/count) > 7)
   ```

   is never evaluated, and so the fact that it involves a division by zero is never noticed by the computer. This is *short-circuit evaluation*.

   j. This expression produces an error when it is evaluated because the first subexpression, ((limit/count) > 7), involves a division by zero.

k. **false**. Since the value of the first subexpression, (limit < 0), is **false**, you know that the entire expression is **false** without bothering to evaluate the second subexpression. Thus, the second subexpression,

```
((limit/count) > 7)
```

is never evaluated, and so the fact that it involves a division by zero is never noticed by the computer. This is *short-circuit evaluation*.

l. If you think this expression is nonsense, you are correct. The expression has no intuitive meaning, but C++ converts the **int** values to **bool** and then evaluates the **&&** and **!** operations. Thus, C++ will evaluate this mess. Recall that in C++, any nonzero integer converts to **true** and 0 converts to **false**, so C++ will evaluate

```
(5 && 7) + (!6)
```

as follows. In the expression (5 && 7), the 5 and 7 convert to **true**; **true** && **true** evaluates to **true**, which C++ converts to 1. In the expression (!6) the 6 is converted to **true**, so !(true) evaluates to **false**, which C++ converts to 0. Thus, the entire expression evaluates to 1 + 0, which is 1. The final value is thus 1. C++ will convert the number 1 to **true**, but the answer has little intuitive meaning as **true**; it is perhaps better to just say the answer is 1. There is no need to become proficient at evaluating these nonsense expressions, but doing a few will help you to understand why the compiler does not give you an error message when you make the mistake of mixing numeric and Boolean operators in a single expression.

2. The expression 2 < x < 3 is legal. However, it does not mean

```
(2 < x) && (x < 3)
```

as many would wish. It means (2 < x) < 3. Since (2 < x) is a Boolean expression, its value is either **true** or **false** and is thus converted to either 0 or 1, either of which is less than 3. So, 2 < x < 3 is always true. The result is **true** regardless of the value of x.

3. (x < -1 || (x > 2)

4. (x > 1 && (x < 3)

5. No. In the Boolean expression, (j > 0) is **false** (j was just assigned −1). The && uses short-circuit evaluation, which does not evaluate the second expression if the truth value can be determined from the first expression. The first expression is **false**, so the second does not matter.

6. ```
if (score > 100)
    cout << "High";
else
    cout << "Low";
```

You may want to add \n to the end of the above quoted strings, depending on the other details of the program.
```

```
7. if (savings >= expenses)
   {
       savings = savings - expenses;
       expenses = 0;
       cout << "Solvent";
   }
   else
   {
       cout << "Bankrupt";
   }
```

You may want to add \n to the end of the above quoted strings, depending on the other details of the program.

```
8. if ( (exam >= 60) && (programsDone >= 10) )
       cout << "Passed";
   else
       cout << "Failed";
```

You may want to add \n to the end of the above quoted strings, depending on the other details of the program.

```
9. if ( (temperature >= 100) || (pressure >= 200) )
       cout << "Warning";
   else
       cout << "OK";
```

You may want to add \n to the end of the above quoted strings, depending on the other details of the program.

10. All nonzero integers are converted to `true`; 0 is converted to `false`.
    a. 0 is false
    b. 1 is true
    c. -1 is true

```
11. Start
    Hello from the second if.
    End
    Start again
    End again
```

12. `large`

13. `small`

14. `medium`

15. Both of the following are correct:
```
    if (n < 0)
        cout << n << " is less than zero.\n";
```

```
else if ((0 <= n) && (n <= 100))
    cout << n << " is between 0 and 100 (inclusive).\n";
else if (n >100)
    cout << n << " is larger than 100.\n";
```

and

```
if (n < 0)
    cout << n << " is less than zero.\n";
else if (n <= 100)
    cout << n << " is between 0 and 100 (inclusive).\n";
else
    cout << n << " is larger than 100.\n";
```

16. 3 2 1 0

17. 2 1 7 5

18. 2 1 0

19. 2 1

20. 1 2 3 4

21. 1 2 3

22. 10
    7
    4
    1

23. There would be no output; the loop is iterated zero times.

24. 10
    7
    4
    1

25. −42

26. With a do−while statement, the loop body is always executed at least once. With a while statement, there can be conditions under which the loop body is not executed at all.

27. 2 4 6 8

28. Hello 10
    Hello 8
    Hello 6
    Hello 4
    Hello 2

29. 2.000000 1.500000 1.000000 0.500000

30. a. for (int i = 1; i <= 10; i++)
       if (i < 5 && i != 2)
          cout << 'X';

    b. for (int i = 1; i <= 10; i = i + 3)

          cout << 'X';

    c. cout << 'X'// necessary to keep output the same. Note

       // also the change in initialization of n
       for (long n = 200; n < 1000; n = n + 100)
          cout << 'X';

31. The output is 1024 10. The second number is the base 2 log of the first number. (If the first number is not a power of 2, then only an approximation to the base 2 log is produced.)

32. The output is 1024 1. The semicolon after the first line of the for loop is probably a pitfall error.

33. This is an infinite loop. Consider the update expression, i = i * 2. It cannot change i because its initial value is 0, so it leaves i at its initial value, 0. It gives no output because of the semicolon after the first line of the for loop.

34. a. A for loop

    b. and c.   Both require a while loop because the input list might be empty.

    d. A do–while loop can be used because at least one test will be performed.

35. This is an infinite loop. The first few lines of output are as follows:

    10
    13
    16
    19
    21

36. A break statement is used to exit a loop (a while, do–while, or for statement) or to terminate a switch statement. A break statement is not legal anywhere else in a C++ program. Note that if the loops are nested, a break statement only terminates one level of the loop.

37. The output is too long to reproduce here. The pattern is as follows:

    1 times 10 = 10
    1 times 9 = 9
       .
       .
       .

```
1 times 1 = 1
2 times 10 = 20
2 times 9 = 18

    .
    .
    .

2 times 1 = 2
3 times 10 = 30

    .
    .
    .
```

PROGRAMMING PROJECTS

1. It is difficult to make a budget that spans several years, because prices are not stable. If your company needs 200 pencils per year, you cannot simply use this year's price as the cost of pencils two years from now. Because of inflation the cost is likely to be higher than it is today. Write a program to gauge the expected cost of an item in a specified number of years. The program asks for the cost of the item, the number of years from now that the item will be purchased, and the rate of inflation. The program then outputs the estimated cost of the item after the specified period. Have the user enter the inflation rate as a percentage, such as 5.6 (percent). Your program should then convert the percentage to a fraction, such as 0.056, and should use a loop to estimate the price adjusted for inflation. (*Hint:* Use a loop.)

2. You have just purchased a stereo system that cost $1000 on the following credit plan: no down payment, an interest rate of 18% per year (and hence 1.5% per month), and monthly payments of $50. The monthly payment of $50 is used to pay the interest, and whatever is left is used to pay part of the remaining debt. Hence, the first month you pay 1.5% of $1000 in interest. That is $15 in interest. The remaining $35 is deducted from your debt, which leaves you with a debt of $965.00. The next month you pay interest of 1.5% of $965.00, which is $14.48. Hence, you can deduct $35.52 (which is $50 - $14.48) from the amount you owe.

   Write a program that will tell you how many months it will take you to pay off the loan, as well as the total amount of interest paid over the life of the loan. Use a loop to calculate the amount of interest and the size of the debt after each month. (Your final program need not output the monthly amount of interest paid and remaining debt, but you may want to write a preliminary version of the program that does output these values.) Use a variable to count the number of loop iterations and hence the number of months until the debt is zero. You may want to use other variables as well. The last payment may be less than $50 if the debt is small, but do not forget the interest. If you owe $50, then your monthly payment of $50 will not pay off your debt, although it will come close. One month's interest on $50 is only 75 cents.

3 CHAPTER

Function Basics

3 Function Basics

Good things come in small packages.

Common saying

INTRODUCTION

If you have programmed in some other language, then the contents of this chapter will be familiar to you. You should still scan this chapter to see the C++ syntax and terminology for the basics of functions. Chapter 4 contains the material on functions that might be different in C++ than in other languages.

A program can be thought of as consisting of subparts such as obtaining the input data, calculating the output data, and displaying the output data. C++, like most programming languages, has facilities to name and code each of these subparts separately. In C++ these subparts are called *functions*. Most programming languages have functions or something similar to functions, although they are not always called by that name in other languages. The terms *procedure*, *subprogram*, and *method*, which you may have heard before, mean essentially the same thing as *function*. In C++ a function may return a value (produce a value) or may perform some action without returning a value, but whether the subpart returns a value or not, it is still called a function in C++. This chapter presents the basic details about C++ functions. Before telling you how to write your own functions, we will first tell you how to use some predefined C++ functions.

3.1 Predefined Functions

Do not reinvent the wheel.

Common saying

C++ comes with libraries of predefined functions that you can use in your programs. There are two kinds of functions in C++: functions that return (produce) a value and functions that do not return a value. Functions that do not return a value are called **void functions**. We first discuss functions that return a value and then discuss void functions.

void
function

■ PREDEFINED FUNCTIONS THAT RETURN A VALUE

We will use the sqrt function to illustrate how you use a predefined function that returns a value. The sqrt function calculates the square root of a number.

(The square root of a number is that number which when multiplied by itself will produce the number you started out with. For example, the square root of 9 is 3 because 3^2 is equal to 9.) The function sqrt starts with a number, such as 9.0, and computes its square root, in this case 3.0. The value the function starts out with is called its **argument**. The value it computes is called the **value returned.** Some functions may have more than one argument, but no function has more than one value returned.

argument
value
returned

The syntax for using functions in your program is simple. To set a variable named theRoot equal to the square root of 9.0, you can use the following assignment statement:

```
theRoot = sqrt(9.0);
```

The expression sqrt(9.0) is known as a **function call** or **function invocation**. An argument in a function call can be a constant, such as 9.0, a variable, or a more complicated expression. A function call is an expression that can be used like any other expression. For example, the value returned by sqrt is of type double; therefore, the following is legal (although perhaps stingy):

function
call or
function
invocation

```
bonus = sqrt(sales)/10;
```

sales and bonus are variables that would normally be of type double. The function call sqrt(sales) is a single item, just as if it were enclosed in parentheses. Thus, the above assignment statement is equivalent to

```
bonus = (sqrt(sales))/10;
```

You can use a function call wherever it is legal to use an expression of the type specified for the value returned by the function.

Display 3.1 contains a complete program that uses the predefined function sqrt. The program computes the size of the largest square doghouse that can be built for the amount of money the user is willing to spend. The program asks the user for an amount of money and then determines how many square feet of floor space can be purchased for that amount. That calculation yields an area in square feet for the floor of the doghouse. The function sqrt yields the length of one side of the doghouse floor.

The cmath library contains the definition of the function sqrt and a number of other mathematical functions. If your program uses a predefined function from some library, then it must contain an include directive that names that library. For example, the program in Display 3.1 uses the sqrt function and so it contains

#include
directive

```
#include <cmath>
```

This particular program has two include directives. It does not matter in what order you give these two include directives. include directives were discussed in Chapter 1.

Definitions for predefined functions normally place these functions in the std namespace and so also require the following using directive, as illustrated in Display 3.1:

```
using namespace std;
```

Display 3.1   A Predefined Function That Returns a Value

```
1    //Computes the size of a doghouse that can be purchased
2    //given the user's budget.
3    #include <iostream>
4    #include <cmath>
5    using namespace std;

6    int main( )
7    {
8        const double COST_PER_SQ_FT = 10.50;
9        double budget, area, lengthSide;

10       cout << "Enter the amount budgeted for your doghouse $";
11       cin >> budget;

12       area = budget/COST_PER_SQ_FT;
13       lengthSide = sqrt(area);

14       cout.setf(ios::fixed);
15       cout.setf(ios::showpoint);
16       cout.precision(2);
17          cout << "For a price of $" << budget << endl
18             << "I can build you a luxurious square doghouse\n"
19             << "that is " << lengthSide
20             << " feet on each side.\n";

21       return 0;
22   }
```

SAMPLE DIALOGUE

```
Enter the amount budgeted for your doghouse $25.00
For a price of $25.00
I can build you a luxurious square doghouse
that is 1.54 feet on each side.
```

#include
may not be
enough

Usually, all you need do to use a library is to place an `include` directive and a `using` directive for that library in the file with your program. If things work with just these directives, you need not worry about doing anything else. However, for some libraries on some systems you may need to give additional instructions to the compiler or explicitly run a linker program to link in the library. The details vary from one system to another; you will have to check your manual or a local expert to see exactly what is necessary.

abs and labs

A few predefined functions are described in Display 3.2. More predefined functions are described in Appendix 4. Notice that the absolute value functions abs and labs are

---

FUNCTIONS THAT RETURN A VALUE

For a function that returns a value, a function call is an expression consisting of the function name followed by arguments enclosed in parentheses. If there is more than one argument, the arguments are separated by commas. If the function call returns a value, then the function call is an expression that can be used like any other expression of the type specified for the value returned by the function.

SYNTAX

```
Function_Name(Argument_List)
```
where the *Argument_List* is a comma-separated list of arguments:
Argument_1, *Argument_2*,. . ., *Argument_Last*

EXAMPLES

```
side = sqrt(area);
cout << "2.5 to the power 3.0 is "
     << pow(2.5, 3.0);
```

---

in the library with header file cstdlib, so any program that uses either of these functions must contain the following directive:

```
#include <cstdlib>
```

Also notice that there are three absolute value functions. If you want to produce the absolute value of a number of type int, use abs; if you want to produce the absolute value of a number of type long, use labs; and if you want to produce the absolute value of a number of type double, use fabs. To complicate things even more, abs and labs are in the library with header file cstdlib, whereas fabs is in the library with header file cmath. fabs is an abbreviation for *floating-point absolute value*. Recall that numbers with a fraction after the decimal point, such as numbers of type double, are often called *floating-point numbers*.

fabs

Another example of a predefined function is pow, which is in the library with header file cmath. The function pow can be used to do exponentiation in C++. For example, if you want to set a variable result equal to x^y, you can use the following:

pow

```
result = pow(x, y);
```

Hence, the following three lines of program code will output the number 9.0 to the screen, because $(3.0)^{2.0}$ is 9.0:

```
double result, x = 3.0, y = 2.0;
result = pow(x, y);
cout << result;
```

Display 3.2 Some Predefined Functions

NAME	DESCRIPTION	TYPE OF ARGUMENTS	TYPE OF VALUE RETURNED	EXAMPLE	VALUE	LIBRARY HEADER
sqrt	Square root	double	double	sqrt(4.0)	2.0	cmath
pow	Powers	double	double	pow(2.0,3.0)	8.0	cmath
abs	Absolute value for int	int	int	abs(−7) abs(7)	7 7	cstdlib
labs	Absolute value for long	long	long	labs(−70000) labs(70000)	70000 70000	cstdlib
fabs	Absolute value for double	double	double	fabs(−7.5) fabs(7.5)	7.5 7.5	cmath
ceil	Ceiling (round up)	double	double	ceil(3.2) ceil(3.9)	4.0 4.0	cmath
floor	Floor (round down)	double	double	floor(3.2) floor(3.9)	3.0 3.0	cmath
exit	End program	int	void	exit(1);	None	cstdlib
rand	Random number	None	int	rand( )	Varies	cstdlib
srand	Set seed for rand	unsigned int	void	srand(42);	None	cstdlib

All these predefined functions require using namespace std; as well as an include directive.

arguments have a type

Notice that the previous call to pow returns 9.0, not 9. The function pow always returns a value of type double, not of type int. Also notice that the function pow requires two arguments. A function can have any number of arguments. Moreover, every argument position has a specified type, and the argument used in a function call should be of that type. In many cases, if you use an argument of the wrong type, some automatic type conversion will be done for you by C++. However, the results may not be what you intended. When you call a function, you should use arguments of the type specified for that function. One exception to this caution is the automatic conversion of arguments from type int to type double. In many situations, including calls to the

> ### void FUNCTIONS
>
> A void function performs some action, but does not return a value. For a void function, a function call is a statement consisting of the function name followed by arguments enclosed in parentheses and then terminated with a semicolon. If there is more than one argument, the arguments are separated by commas. For a void function, a function invocation (function call) is a statement that can be used like any other C++ statement.
>
> ### SYNTAX
>
> ```
> Function_Name(Argument_List);
> ```
> where the *Argument_List* is a comma-separated list of arguments:
> *Argument_1*, *Argument_2*, . . . , *Argument_Last*
>
> ### EXAMPLE
>
> ```
> exit(1);
> ```

function pow, you can safely use an argument of type int (or other integer type) when an argument of type double (or other floating-point type) is specified.

Many implementations of pow have a restriction on what arguments can be used. In these implementations, if the first argument to pow is negative, then the second argument must be a whole number. It might be easiest and safest to use pow only when the first argument is nonnegative.

restrictions on pow

PREDEFINED void FUNCTIONS

A void function performs some action, but does not return a value. Since it performs an action, a void function invocation is a statement. The function call for a void function is written similar to a function call for a function that returns a value, except that it is terminated with a semicolon and is used as a statement rather than as an expression. Predefined void functions are handled in the same way as predefined functions that return a value. Thus, to use a predefined void function, your program must have an include directive that gives the name of the library that defines the function.

For example, the function exit is defined in the library cstdlib, and so a program that uses that function must contain the following at (or near) the start of the file:

exit

```
#include <cstdlib>
using namespace std;
```

The following is a sample invocation (sample call) of the function exit:

```
exit(1);
```

THE exit FUNCTION

The exit function is a predefined void function that takes one argument of type int. Thus, an invocation of the exit function is a statement written as follows:

```
exit(Integer_Value);
```

When the exit function is invoked (that is, when the above statement is executed), the program ends immediately. Any *Integer_Value* may be used, but by convention, 1 is used for a call to exit that is caused by an error, and 0 is used in other cases.

The exit function definition is in the library cstdlib and it places the exit function in the std namespace. Therefore, any program that uses the exit function must contain the following two directives:

```
#include <cstdlib>
using namespace std;
```

An invocation of the exit function ends the program immediately. Display 3.3 contains a toy program that demonstrates the exit function.

Note that the function exit has one argument, which is of type int. The argument is given to the operating system. As far as your C++ program is concerned, you can use

Display 3.3   A Function Call for a Predefined void Function

```
 1    #include <iostream>
 2    #include <cstdlib>
 3    using namespace std;

 4    int main( )
 5    {
 6        cout << "Hello Out There!\n";
 7        exit(1);

 8        cout << "This statement is pointless,\n"
 9             << "because it will never be executed.\n"
10             << "This is just a toy program to illustrate exit.\n";

11        return 0;
12    }
```

This is just a toy example. It would produce the same output if you omitted these lines.

SAMPLE DIALOGUE

```
Hello Out There!
```

any int value as the argument, but by convention, 1 is used for a call to exit that is caused by an error, and 0 is used in other cases.

A void function can have any number of arguments. The details on arguments for void functions are the same as they were for functions that return a value. In particular, if you use an argument of the wrong type, then, in many cases, some automatic type conversion will be done for you by C++. However, the results may not be what you intended.

Self-Test Exercises

1. Determine the value of each of the following arithmetic expressions.

sqrt(16.0)	sqrt(16)	pow(2.0, 3.0)
pow(2, 3)	pow(2.0, 3)	pow(1.1, 2)
abs(3)	abs(-3)	abs(0)
fabs(-3.0)	fabs(-3.5)	fabs(3.5)
ceil(5.1)	ceil(5.8)	floor(5.1)
floor(5.8)	pow(3.0, 2)/2.0	pow(3.0, 2)/2
7/abs(-2)	(7 + sqrt(4.0))/3.0	sqrt(pow(3, 2))

2. Convert each of the following mathematical expressions to a C++ arithmetic expression.

a. $\sqrt{x+y}$ b. x^{y+7} c. $\sqrt{area + fudge}$

d. $\dfrac{\sqrt{time + tide}}{nobody}$ e. $\dfrac{-b + \sqrt{b^2 - 4ac}}{2a}$ f. $|x - y|$

3. Write a complete C++ program to compute and output the square roots of the whole numbers from 1 to 10.

4. What is the function of the int argument to the void function exit?

■ A RANDOM NUMBER GENERATOR

A random number generator is a function that returns a "randomly chosen" number. It is unlike the functions we have seen so far in that the value returned is not determined by the arguments (of which there are usually none) but rather by some global conditions. Since you can think of the value returned as being a random number, you can use a random number generator to simulate random events, such as the result of throwing dice or flipping a coin. In addition to simulating games of chance, random number generators can be used to simulate things that strictly speaking may not be random but that appear to us to be random, such as the amount of time between the arrival of cars at a toll booth.

The C++ library with header file `<cstdlib>` contains a random number function named rand. This function has no arguments. When your program invokes rand, the function returns an integer in the range 0 to RAND_MAX, inclusive. (The number generated might be equal to 0 or RAND_MAX.) RAND_MAX is a defined integer constant whose definition is also in the library with header file `<cstdlib>`. The exact value of RAND_MAX is system-dependent but will always be at least 32767 (the maximum two-byte positive integer). For example, the following outputs a list of ten "random" numbers in the range 0 to RAND_MAX:

```
int i;
for (i = 0; i < 10; i++)
    cout << rand( ) << endl;
```

You are more likely to want a random number in some smaller range, such as the range 0 to 10. To ensure that the value is in the range 0 to 10 (including the end points), you can use

```
rand( ) % 11
```

This is called **scaling**. The following outputs ten "random" integers in the range 0 to 10 (inclusive):

```
int i;
for (i = 0; i < 10; i++)
    cout << (rand( ) % 11) << endl;
```

Random number generators, such as the function rand, do not generate truly random numbers. (That's the reason for all the quotes around "random.") A sequence of calls to the function rand (or almost any random number generator) will produce a sequence of numbers (the values returned by rand) that appear to be random. However, if you could return the computer to the state it was in when the sequence of calls to rand began, you would get the same sequence of "random numbers." Numbers that appear to be random but really are not, such as a sequence of numbers generated by calls to rand, are called **pseudorandom numbers**.

A sequence of pseudorandom numbers is usually determined by one number known as the **seed**. If you start the random number generator with the same seed, over and over, then each time it will produce the same (random-looking) sequence of numbers. You can use the function srand to set the seed for the function rand. The void function srand takes one (positive) integer argument, which is the seed. For example, the following will output two identical sequences of ten pseudorandom numbers:

```
int i;
srand(99);
for (i = 0; i < 10; i++)
    cout << (rand( ) % 11) << endl;
srand(99);
for (i = 0; i < 10; i++)
    cout << (rand( ) % 11) << endl;
```

There is nothing special about the number 99, other than the fact that we used the same number for both calls to srand.

Note that the sequence of pseudorandom numbers produced for a given seed might be system-dependent. If rerun on a different system with the same seed, the sequence of pseudorandom numbers might be different on that system. However, as long as you are on the same system using the same implementation of C++, the same seed will produce the same sequence of pseudorandom numbers.

PSEUDORANDOM NUMBERS

The function rand takes no arguments and returns a pseudorandom integer in the range 0 to RAND_MAX (inclusive). The void function srand takes one argument, which is the seed for the random number generator rand. The argument to srand is of type unsigned int, so the argument must be nonnegative. The functions rand and srand, as well as the defined constant RAND_MAX, are defined in the library cstdlib, so programs that use them must contain the following directives:

```
#include <cstdlib>
using namespace std;
```

These pseudorandom numbers are close enough to true random numbers for most applications. In fact, they are often preferable to true random numbers. A pseudorandom number generator has one big advantage over a true random number generator: The sequence of numbers it produces is repeatable. If run twice with the same seed value, it will produce the same sequence of numbers. This can be very handy for a number of purposes. When an error is discovered and fixed, the program can be rerun with the same sequence of pseudorandom numbers as those that exposed the error. Similarly, a particularly interesting run of the program can be repeated, provided a pseudorandom number generator is used. With a true random number generator every run of the program is likely to be different.

Display 3.4 shows a program that uses the random number generator rand to "predict" the weather. In this case the prediction is random, but some people think that is about as good as weather prediction gets. (Weather prediction can actually be very accurate, but this program is just a game to illustrate pseudorandom numbers.)

Note that in Display 3.4, the seed value used for the argument of srand is the month times the day. That way if the program is rerun and the same date is entered, the same prediction will be made. (Of course, this program is still pretty simple. The prediction for the day after the 14th may or may not be the same as the 15th, but this program will do as a simple example.)

Probabilities are usually expressed as a floating-point number in the range 0.0 to 1.0. Suppose you want a random probability instead of a random integer. This can be

floating-point random numbers

Display 3.4   A Function Using a Random Number Generator (part 1 of 2)

```
1   #include <iostream>
2   #include <cstdlib>
3   using namespace std;

4   int main( )
5   {
6       int month, day;
7       cout << "Welcome to your friendly weather program.\n"
8            << "Enter today's date as two integers for the month and the day:\n";
9       cin >> month;
10      cin >> day;
11      srand(month*day);
12      int prediction;
13      char ans;
14      cout << "Weather for today:\n";
15      do
16      {
17          prediction = rand( ) % 3;
18          switch (prediction)
19          {
20              case 0:
21                  cout << "The day will be sunny!!\n";
22                  break;
23              case 1:
24                  cout << "The day will be cloudy.\n";
25                  break;
26              case 2:
27                  cout << "The day will be stormy!\n";
28                  break;
29              default:
30                  cout << "Weather program is not functioning properly.\n";
31          }
32          cout << "Want the weather for the next day?(y/n): ";
33          cin >> ans;
34      } while (ans == 'y' || ans == 'Y');
35      cout << "That's it from your 24-hour weather program.\n";
36      return 0;
37  }
```

produced by another form of scaling. The following generates a pseudorandom floating-point value between 0.0 and 1.0:

```
rand( )/static_cast<double>(RAND_MAX)
```

The type cast is made so that we get floating-point division rather than integer division.

Display 3.4   A Function Using a Random Number Generator *(part 2 of 2)*

SAMPLE DIALOGUE

```
Welcome to your friendly weather program.
Enter today's date as two integers for the month and the day:
2  14
Weather for today:
The day will be cloudy.
Want the weather for the next day?(y/n): y
The day will be cloudy.
Want the weather for the next day?(y/n): y
The day will be stormy!
Want the weather for the next day?(y/n): y
The day will be stormy!
Want the weather for the next day?(y/n): y
The day will be sunny!!
Want the weather for the next day?(y/n): n
That's it from your 24-hour weather program.
```

Self-Test Exercises

5. Give an expression to produce a pseudorandom integer number in the range 5 to 10 (inclusive).

6. Write a complete program that asks the user for a seed and then outputs a list of ten random numbers based on that seed. The numbers should be floating-point numbers in the range 0.0 to 1.0 (inclusive).

3.2   Programmer-Defined Functions

A custom-tailored suit always fits better than one off the rack.

My uncle, the tailor

The previous section told you how to use predefined functions. This section tells you how to define your own functions.

DEFINING FUNCTIONS THAT RETURN A VALUE

You can define your own functions, either in the same file as the main part of your program or in a separate file so that the functions can be used by several different programs.

The definition is the same in either case, but for now we will assume that the function definition will be in the same file as the main part of your program. This subsection discusses only functions that return a value. A later subsection tells you how to define void functions.

Display 3.5 contains a sample function definition in a complete program that demonstrates a call to the function. The function is called totalCost and takes two arguments—the price for one item and the number of items for a purchase. The function returns the total cost, including sales tax, for that many items at the specified price. The function is called in the same way a predefined function is called. The definition of the function, which the programmer must write, is a bit more complicated.

The description of the function is given in two parts. The first part is called the **function declaration** or **function prototype**. The following is the function declaration (function prototype) for the function defined in Display 3.5:

function declaration or function prototype

```
double totalCost(int numberParameter, double priceParameter);
```

type for value returned

The first word in a function declaration specifies the type of the value returned by the function. Thus, for the function totalCost, the type of the value returned is double. Next, the function declaration tells you the name of the function; in this case, totalCost. The function declaration tells you (and the compiler) everything you need to know in order to write and use a call to the function. It tells you how many arguments the function needs and what type the arguments should be; in this case, the function totalCost takes two arguments, the first one of type int and the second one of type double. The identifiers numberParameter and priceParameter are called **formal parameters**, or **parameters** for short. A formal parameter is used as a kind of blank, or placeholder, to stand in for the argument. When you write a function declaration, you do not know what the arguments will be, so you use the formal parameters in place of the arguments. Names of formal parameters can be any valid identifiers. Notice that a function declaration ends with a semicolon.

formal parameter

Although the function declaration tells you all you need to know to write a function call, it does not tell you what value will be returned. The value returned is determined by the function definition. In Display 3.3 the function definition is in lines 24 to 30 of the program. A **function definition** describes how the function computes the value it returns. A function definition consists of a *function header* followed by a *function body*. The **function header** is written similar to the function declaration, except that the header does *not* have a semicolon at the end. The value returned is determined by the statements in the *function body*.

function definition

function header

The **function body** follows the function header and completes the function definition. The function body consists of declarations and executable statements enclosed within a pair of braces. Thus, the function body is just like the body of the main part of a program. When the function is called, the argument values are plugged in for the formal parameters, and then the statements in the body are executed. The value returned by the function is determined when the function executes a return *statement*. (The details of this "plugging in" will be discussed in Chapter 4.)

function body

Display 3.5   A Function Using a Random Number Generator (part 1 of 2)

```
1    #include <iostream>
2    using namespace std;

3    double totalCost(int numberParameter, double priceParameter);
4    //Computes the total cost, including 5% sales tax,
5    //on numberParameter items at a cost of priceParameter each.

6    int main( )
7    {
8        double price, bill;
9        int number;

10       cout << "Enter the number of items purchased: ";
11       cin >> number;
12       cout << "Enter the price per item $";
13       cin >> price;

14       bill = totalCost(number, price);

15       cout.setf(ios::fixed);
16       cout.setf(ios::showpoint);
17       cout.precision(2);
18       cout << number << " items at "
19            << "$" << price << " each.\n"
20            << "Final bill, including tax, is $" << bill
21            << endl;

22       return 0;
23   }

24   double totalCost(int numberParameter, double priceParameter)
25   {
26       const double TAXRATE = 0.05; //5% sales tax
27       double subtotal;

28       subtotal = priceParameter * numberParameter;
29       return (subtotal + subtotal*TAXRATE);
30   }
```

Function declaration; also called the function prototype

Function call

Function head

Function body

Function definition

SAMPLE DIALOGUE

```
Enter the number of items purchased: 2
Enter the price per item: $10.10
2 items at  $10.10 each.
Final bill, including tax, is $21.21
```

A **return statement** consists of the keyword `return` followed by an expression. The function definition in Display 3.5 contains the following `return` statement:

```
return (subtotal + subtotal*TAXRATE);
```

When this `return` statement is executed, the value of the following expression is returned as the value of the function call:

```
(subtotal + subtotal*TAXRATE)
```

The parentheses are not needed. The program will run the same if the parentheses are omitted. However, with longer expressions, the parentheses make the `return` statement easier to read. For consistency, some programmers advocate using these parentheses even with simple expressions. In the function definition in Display 3.3 there are no statements after the `return` statement, but if there were, they would not be executed. When a `return` statement is executed, the function call ends.

Note that the function body can contain any C++ statements and that the statements will be executed when the function is called. Thus, a function that returns a value may do any other action as well as return a value. In most cases, however, the main purpose of a function that returns a value is to return that value.

Either the complete function definition or the function declaration (function prototype) must appear in the code before the function is called. The most typical arrangement is for the function declaration and the `main` part of the program to appear in one or more files, with the function declaration before the `main` part of the program, and for the function definition to appear in another file. We have not yet discussed dividing a program across more than one file, and so we will place the function definitions after the `main` part of the program. If the full function definition is placed before the `main` part of the program, the function declaration can be omitted.

ALTERNATE FORM FOR FUNCTION DECLARATIONS

You are not required to list formal parameter names in a function declaration (function prototype). The following two function declarations are equivalent:

```
double totalCost(int numberParameter, double priceParameter);
```

and

```
double totalCost(int, double);
```

We will usually use the first form so that we can refer to the formal parameters in the comment that accompanies the function declaration. However, you will often see the second form in manuals.

This alternate form applies only to function declarations. *A function definition must always list the formal parameter names.*

Pitfall

ARGUMENTS IN THE WRONG ORDER

When a function is called, the computer substitutes the first argument for the first formal parameter, the second argument for the second formal parameter, and so forth. Although the computer checks the type of each argument, it does not check for reasonableness. If you confuse the order of the arguments, the program will not do what you want it to do. If there is a type violation due to an argument of the wrong type, then you will get an error message. If there is no type violation, your program will probably run normally but produce an incorrect value for the value returned by the function.

Pitfall

USE OF THE TERMS *PARAMETER* AND *ARGUMENT*

The use of the terms *formal parameter* and *argument* that we follow in this book is consistent with common usage, but people also often use the terms *parameter* and *argument* interchangeably. When you see the terms *parameter* and *argument,* you must determine their exact meaning from context. Many people use the term *parameter* for both what we call *formal parameters* and what we call *arguments*. Other people use the term *argument* both for what we call *formal parameters* and what we call *arguments*. Do not expect consistency in how people use these two terms. (In this book we sometimes use the term *parameter* to mean *formal parameter*, but this is more of an abbreviation than a true inconsistency.)

FUNCTIONS CALLING FUNCTIONS

A function body may contain a call to another function. The situation for these sorts of function calls is the same as if the function call had occurred in the main part of the program; the only restriction is that the function declaration (or function definition) must appear before the function is used. If you set up your programs as we have been doing, this will happen automatically, since all function declarations come before the main part of the program and all function definitions come after the main part of the program. Although you may include a function *call* within the definition of another function, you cannot place the *definition* of one function within the body of another function definition.

Example

A ROUNDING FUNCTION

The table of predefined functions (Display 3.2) does not include any function for rounding a number. The functions ceil and floor are almost, but not quite, rounding functions. The function ceil always returns the next-highest whole number (or its argument if it happens to be a whole number). So, ceil(2.1) returns 3.0, not 2.0. The function floor always returns the nearest whole number less than (or equal to) the argument. So, floor(2.9) returns 2.0, not round

3.0. Fortunately, it is easy to define a function that does true rounding. The function is defined in Display 3.6. The function round rounds its argument to the nearest integer. For example, round(2.3) returns 2, and round(2.6) returns 3.

To see that round works correctly, let's look at some examples. Consider round(2.4). The value returned is the following (converted to an int value):

```
floor(2.4 + 0.5)
```

which is floor(2.9), or 2.0. In fact, for any number that is greater than or equal to 2.0 and strictly less than 2.5, that number plus 0.5 will be less than 3.0, and so floor applied to that number plus 0.5 will return 2.0. Thus, round applied to any number that is greater than or equal to 2.0 and strictly less than 2.5 will return 2. (Since the function declaration for round specifies that the type for the value returned is int, we have type cast the computed value to the type int.)

Now consider numbers greater than or equal to 2.5; for example, 2.6. The value returned by the call round(2.6) is the following (converted to an int value):

```
floor(2.6 + 0.5)
```

which is floor(3.1), or 3.0. In fact, for any number that is greater than 2.5 and less than or equal to 3.0, that number plus 0.5 will be greater than 3.0. Thus, round called with any number that is greater than 2.5 and less than or equal to 3.0 will return 3.

Thus, round works correctly for all arguments between 2.0 and 3.0. Clearly, there is nothing special about arguments between 2.0 and 3.0. A similar argument applies to all nonnegative numbers. So, round works correctly for all nonnegative arguments.

Display 3.6   The Function round (part 1 of 2)

```
1   #include <iostream>                        Testing program for
2   #include <cmath>                            the function round
3   using namespace std;

4   int round(double number);
5   //Assumes number >= 0.
6   //Returns number rounded to the nearest integer.

7   int main( )
8   {
9       double doubleValue;
10      char ans;

11      do
12      {
13          cout << "Enter a double value: ";
14          cin >> doubleValue;
```

Display 3.6   The Function round *(part 2 of 2)*

```
15            cout << "Rounded that number is " << round(doubleValue) << endl;
16            cout << "Again? (y/n): ";
17            cin >> ans;
18        }while (ans == 'y' || ans == 'Y');
19        cout << "End of testing.\n";

20        return 0;
21    }

22    //Uses cmath:
23    int round(double number)
24    {
25        return static_cast<int>(floor(number + 0.5));
26    }
```

SAMPLE DIALOGUE

```
Enter a double value: 9.6
Rounded, that number is 10
Again? (y/n): y
Enter a double value: 2.49
Rounded, that number is 2
Again? (y/n): n
End of testing.
```

Self-Test Exercises

7. What is the output produced by the following program?

```
#include <iostream>
using namespace std;

char mystery(int firstParameter, int secondParameter);

int main( )
{
    cout << mystery(10, 9) << "ow\n";
    return 0;
}
char mystery(int firstParameter, int secondParameter)
{
    if (firstParameter >= secondParameter)
        return 'W';
    else
        return 'H';
}
```

8. Write a function declaration (function prototype) and a function definition for a function that takes three arguments, all of type int, and that returns the sum of its three arguments.

9. Write a function declaration and a function definition for a function that takes one argument of type double. The function returns the character value 'P' if its argument is positive and returns 'N' if its argument is zero or negative.

10. Can a function definition appear inside the body of another function definition?

11. List the similarities and differences between how you invoke (call) a predefined (that is, library) function and a user-defined function.

FUNCTIONS THAT RETURN A BOOLEAN VALUE

The returned type for a function can be the type bool. A call to such a function returns one of the values true or false and can be used anywhere that a Boolean expression is allowed. For example, it can be used in a Boolean expression to control an if-else statement or to control a loop statement. This can often make a program easier to read. By means of a function declaration, you can associate a complex Boolean expression with a meaningful name. For example, the statement

```
if (((rate >= 10) && (rate < 20)) || (rate == 0))
{
    ...
}
```

can be made to read

```
if (appropriate(rate))
{
    ...
}
```

provided that the following function has been defined:

```
bool appropriate(int rate)
{
    return (((rate >= 10) && (rate < 20)) || (rate == 0));
}
```

Self-Test Exercises

12. Write a function definition for a function called inOrder that takes three arguments of type int. The function returns true if the three arguments are in ascending order; otherwise, it returns false. For example, inOrder(1, 2, 3) and inOrder(1, 2, 2) both return true, whereas inOrder(1, 3, 2) returns false.

13. Write a function definition for a function called even that takes one argument of type int and returns a bool value. The function returns true if its one argument is an even number; otherwise, it returns false.

14. Write a function definition for a function isDigit that takes one argument of type char and returns a bool value. The function returns true if the argument is a decimal digit; otherwise, it returns false.

■ DEFINING void FUNCTIONS

In C++ a void function is defined in a way similar to that of functions that return a value. For example, the following is a void function that outputs the result of a calculation that converts a temperature expressed in degrees Fahrenheit to a temperature expressed in degrees Celsius. The actual calculation would be done elsewhere in the program. This void function implements only the subtask for outputting the results of the calculation.

```
void showResults(double fDegrees, double cDegrees)
{
    cout.setf(ios::fixed);
    cout.setf(ios::showpoint);
    cout.precision(1);
    cout << fDegrees
         << " degrees Fahrenheit is equivalent to\n"
         << cDegrees << " degrees Celsius.\n";
}
```

As the above function definition illustrates, there are only two differences between a function definition for a void function and for a function that returns a value. One difference is that we use the keyword void where we would normally specify the type of the value to be returned. This tells the compiler that this function will not return any value. The name void is used as a way of saying "no value is returned by this function." The second difference is that a void function definition does not require a return statement. The function execution ends when the last statement in the function body is executed.

void function definition

A void function call is an executable statement. For example, the above function showResults might be called as follows:

void function call

```
showResults(32.5, 0.3);
```

If the above statement were executed in a program, it would cause the following to appear on the screen:

```
32.5 degrees Fahrenheit is equivalent to
0.3 degrees Celsius.
```

Notice that the function call ends with a semicolon, which tells the compiler that the function call is an executable statement.

When a void function is called, the arguments are substituted for the formal parameters, and the statements in the function body are executed. For example, a call to the void function showResults, which we gave earlier in this section, will cause some output to be written to the screen. One way to think of a call to a void function is to imagine that the body of the function definition is copied into the program in place of the function call. When the function is called, the arguments are substituted for the formal parameters, and then it is just as if the body of the function were lines in the program. (Chapter 4 describes the process of substituting arguments for formal parameters in detail. Until then, we will use only simple examples that should be clear enough without a formal description of the substitution process.)

functions with no arguments

It is perfectly legal, and sometimes useful, to have a function with no arguments. In that case there simply are no formal parameters listed in the function declaration and no arguments are used when the function is called. For example, the void function initializeScreen, defined below, simply sends a newline command to the screen:

```
void initializeScreen( )
{
    cout << endl;
}
```

If your program includes the following call to this function as its first executable statement, then the output from the previously run program will be separated from the output for your program:

```
initializeScreen( );
```

Be sure to notice that even when there are no parameters to a function, you still must include the parentheses in the function declaration and in a call to the function.

Placement of the function declaration (function prototype) and the function definition is the same for void functions as what we described for functions that return a value.

return STATEMENTS IN void FUNCTIONS

void functions and return statements

Both void functions and functions that return a value can have return statements. In the case of a function that returns a value, the return statement specifies the value returned. In the case of a void function, the return statement does not include any expression for a value returned. A return statement in a void function simply ends the function call. Every function that returns a value must end by executing a return statement. However, a void function need not contain a return statement. If it does not contain a return statement, it will end after executing the code in the function body. It is as if there were an implicit return statement just before the final closing brace, }, at the end of the function body.

FUNCTION DECLARATION (FUNCTION PROTOTYPE)

A function declaration (function prototype) tells you all you need to know to write a call to the function. A function declaration (or the full function definition) must appear in your code prior to a call to the function. Function declarations are normally placed before the main part of your program.

SYNTAX

Do not forget this semicolon.

```
Type_Returned_Or_void   FunctionName(Parameter_List);
```

where the *Parameter_List* is a comma-separated list of parameters:

```
Type_1 Formal_Parameter_1, Type_2 Formal_Parameter_2,...
                    ..., Type_Last Formal_Parameter_Last
```

EXAMPLES

```
double totalWeight(int number, double weightOfOne);
//Returns the total weight of number items that
//each weigh weightOfOne.

void showResults(double fDegrees, double cDegrees);
//Displays a message saying fDegrees Fahrenheit
//is equivalent to cDegrees Celsius.
```

The fact that there is an implicit `return` statement before the final closing brace in a function body does not mean that you never need a `return` statement in a `void` function. For example, the function definition in Display 3.7 might be used as part of a restaurant-management program. That function outputs instructions for dividing a given amount of ice cream among the people at a table. If there are no people at the table (that is, if `number` equals 0), then the `return` statement within the `if` statement terminates the function call and avoids a division by zero. If `number` is not 0, then the function call ends when the last `cout` statement is executed at the end of the function body.

PRECONDITIONS AND POSTCONDITIONS

One good way to write a function declaration comment is to break it down into two kinds of information called the *precondition* and the *postcondition*. The **precondition** states what is assumed to be true when the function is called. The function should not be used and cannot be expected to perform correctly unless the precondition holds. The **postcondition** describes the effect of the function call; that is, the postcondition tells what will be true after the function is executed in a situation in which the precondition holds. For a function that returns a value, the postcondition will describe the value

precondition

post-
condition

Display 3.7   Use of return in a void Function

```
1    #include <iostream>
2    using namespace std;

3    void iceCreamDivision(int number, double totalWeight);
4    //Outputs instructions for dividing totalWeight ounces of ice cream among
5    //number customers. If number is 0, only an error message is output.

6    int main( )
7    {
8        int number;
9        double totalWeight;

10       cout << "Enter the number of customers: ";
11       cin >> number;
12       cout << "Enter weight of ice cream to divide (in ounces): ";
13       cin >> totalWeight;

14       iceCreamDivision(number, totalWeight);

15       return 0;
16   }

17   void iceCreamDivision(int number, double totalWeight)
18   {
19       double portion;

20       if (number == 0)
21       {
22           cout << "Cannot divide among zero customers.\n";
23           return;  ◄─────────────────────── If number is 0, then the
24       }                                      function execution ends here.
25       portion = totalWeight/number;
26       cout << "Each one receives "
27           << portion << " ounces of ice cream." << endl;
28   }
```

SAMPLE DIALOGUE

```
Enter the number of customers: 0
Enter weight of ice cream to divide (in ounces): 12
Cannot divide among zero customers.
```

returned by the function. For a function that changes the value of some argument variables, the postcondition will describe all the changes made to the values of the arguments.

For example, the following is a function declaration with precondition and postcondition:

```
void showInterest(double balance, double rate);
//Precondition: balance is a nonnegative savings account balance.
//rate is the interest rate expressed as a percentage, such as 5 for 5%.
//Postcondition: The amount of interest on the given balance
//at the given rate is shown on the screen.
```

You do not need to know the definition of the function showInterest in order to use this function. All that you need to know in order to use this function is given by the precondition and postcondition.

When the only postcondition is a description of the value returned, programmers usually omit the word Postcondition, as in the following example:

```
double celsius(double fahrenheit);
//Precondition: fahrenheit is a temperature in degrees Fahrenheit.
//Returns the equivalent temperature expressed in degrees Celsius.
```

Some programmers choose not to use the words *precondition* and *postcondition* in their function comments. However, whether you use the words or not, you should always think in terms of precondition and postcondition when designing a function and when deciding what to include in the function comment.

main IS A FUNCTION

As we already noted, the main part of a program is actually the definition of a function called main. When the program is run, the function main is automatically called; it, in turn, may call other functions. Although it may seem that the return statement in the main part of a program should be optional, practically speaking it is not. The C++ standard says that you can omit the return 0 statement in the main part of the program, but many compilers still require it and almost all compilers allow you to include it. For the sake of portability, you should include return 0 statement in the main function. You should consider the main part of a program to be a function that returns a value of type int and thus requires a return statement. Treating the main part of your program as a function that returns an integer may sound strange, but that's the tradition which many compilers enforce.

Although some compilers may allow you to get away with it, you should not include a call to main in your code. Only the system should call main, which it does when you run your program.

■ **RECURSIVE FUNCTIONS**

C++ does allow you to define recursive functions. Recursive functions are covered in Chapter 13. If you do not know what recursive functions are, there is no need to be concerned until you reach that chapter. If you want to read about recursive functions early, you can read Sections 13.1 and 13.2 of Chapter 13 after you complete Chapter 4. Note that the main function should not be called recursively.

Self-Test Exercises

15. What is the output of the following program?

```cpp
#include <iostream>
using namespace std;

void friendly( );

void shy(int audienceCount);
int main( )
{
    friendly( );
    shy(6);
    cout << "One more time:\n";
    shy(2);
    friendly( );
    cout << "End of program.\n";
    return 0;
}

void friendly( )
{
    cout << "Hello\n";
}

void shy(int audienceCount)
{
    if (audienceCount < 5)
        return;
    cout << "Goodbye\n";
}
```

16. Suppose you omitted the return statement in the function definition for iceCreamDivision in Display 3.7. What effect would it have on the program? Would the program compile? Would it run? Would the program behave any differently?

17. Write a definition for a void function that has three arguments of type int and that outputs to the screen the product of these three arguments. Put the definition in a complete program that reads in three numbers and then calls this function.

18. Does your compiler allow `void main( )` and `int main( )`? What warnings are issued if you have `int main( )` and do not supply a `return 0;` statement? To find out, write several small test programs and perhaps ask your instructor or a local guru.

19. Give a precondition and a postcondition for the predefined function `sqrt`, which returns the square root of its argument.

3.3 Scope Rules

Let the end be legitimate, let it be within the scope of the constitution, . . .

John Marshall, Chief Justice U.S. Supreme Court,
McCulloch v. Maryland (1803)

Functions should be self-contained units that do not interfere with other functions—or any other code for that matter. To achieve this you often need to give the function variables of its own that are distinct from any other variables that are declared outside the function definition and that may have the same names as the variables that belong to the function. These variables that are declared in a function definition are called *local variables* and are the topic of this section.

▨ LOCAL VARIABLES

Look back at the program in Display 3.1. It includes a call to the predefined function sqrt. We did not need to know anything about the details of the function definition for sqrt in order to use this function. In particular, we did not need to know what variables were declared in the definition of sqrt. A function that you define is no different. Variable declarations within a function definition are the same as if they were variable declarations in a predefined function or in another program. If you declare a variable in a function definition and then declare another variable of the same name in the main function of the program (or in the body of some other function definition), then these two variables are two different variables, even though they have the same name. Let's look at an example.

The program in Display 3.8 has two variables named averagePea; one is declared and used in the function definition for the function estimateOfTotal, and the other is declared and used in the main function of the program. The variable averagePea in the function definition for estimateOfTotal and the variable averagePea in the main function are two different variables. It is the same as if the function estimateOfTotal were a predefined function. The two variables named averagePea will not interfere with each other any more than two variables in two completely different programs would.

Display 3.8 Local Variables *(part 1 of 2)*

```
1    //Computes the average yield on an experimental pea growing patch.
2    #include <iostream>
3    using namespace std;

4    double estimateOfTotal(int minPeas, int maxPeas, int podCount);
5    //Returns an estimate of the total number of peas harvested.
6    //The formal parameter podCount is the number of pods.
7    //The formal parameters minPeas and maxPeas are the minimum
8    //and maximum number of peas in a pod.

9    int main( )
10   {
11       int maxCount, minCount, podCount;
12       double averagePea, yield;
```
This variable named averagePea is local to the main function.
```
13       cout << "Enter minimum and maximum number of peas in a pod: ";
14       cin >> minCount >> maxCount;
15       cout << "Enter the number of pods: ";
16       cin >> podCount;
17       cout << "Enter the weight of an average pea (in ounces): ";
18       cin >> averagePea;

19       yield =
20               estimateOfTotal(minCount, maxCount, podCount) * averagePea;

21       cout.setf(ios::fixed);
22       cout.setf(ios::showpoint);
23       cout.precision(3);
24       cout << "Min number of peas per pod = " << minCount << endl
25            << "Max number of peas per pod = " << maxCount << endl
26            << "Pod count = " << podCount << endl
27            << "Average pea weight = "
28            << averagePea << " ounces" << endl
29            << "Estimated average yield = " << yield << " ounces"
30            << endl;

31       return 0;
32   }

33
34   double estimateOfTotal(int minPeas, int maxPeas, int podCount)
35   {
36       double averagePea;
```
This variable named averagePea is local to the function estimateOfTotal.
```
37       averagePea = (maxPeas + minPeas)/2.0;
38       return (podCount * averagePea);
39   }
```

Display 3.8   Local Variables (part 2 of 2)

SAMPLE DIALOGUE

```
Enter minimum and maximum number of peas in a pod: 4 6
Enter the number of pods: 10
Enter the weight of an average pea (in ounces): 0.5
Min number of peas per pod = 4
Max number of peas per pod = 6
Pod count = 10
Average pea weight = 0.500 ounces
Estimated average yield = 25.000 ounces
```

When the variable averagePea is given a value in the function call to estimateOfTotal, this does not change the value of the variable in the main function that is also named averagePea.

Variables that are declared within the body of a function definition are said to be **local** to that function or to have that function as their **scope**. If a variable is local to some function, we sometimes simply call it a *local variable*, without specifying the function.

local variable scope

Another example of local variables can be seen in Display 3.5. The definition of the function totalCost in that program begins as follows:

```
double totalCost(int numberParameter, double priceParameter)
{
    const double TAXRATE = 0.05; //5% sales tax
    double subtotal;
```

The variable subtotal is local to the function totalCost. The named constant TAXRATE is also local to the function totalCost. (A named constant is in fact nothing but a variable that is initialized to a value and that cannot have that value changed.)

LOCAL VARIABLES

Variables that are declared within the body of a function definition are said to be *local to that function* or to have that function as their *scope*. If a variable is local to a function, then you can have another variable (or other kind of item) with the same name that is declared in another function definition; these will be two different variables, even though they have the same name. (In particular, this is true even if one of the functions is the main function.)

■ PROCEDURAL ABSTRACTION

A person who uses a program should not need to know the details of how the program is coded. Imagine how miserable your life would be if you had to know and remember the code for the compiler you use. A program has a job to do, such as compiling your program or checking the spelling of words in your paper. You need to know *what* the program's job is so that you can use the program, but you do not (or at least should not) need to know *how* the program does its job. A function is like a small program and should be used in a similar way. A programmer who uses a function in a program needs to know *what* the function does (such as calculate a square root or convert a temperature from degrees Fahrenheit to degrees Celsius), but should not need to know *how* the function accomplishes its task. This is often referred to as treating the function like a *black box.*

black box

Calling something a **black box** is a figure of speech intended to convey the image of a physical device that you know how to use but whose method of operation is a mystery because it is enclosed in a black box that you cannot see inside of (and cannot pry open). If a function is well designed, the programmer can use the function as if it were a black box. All the programmer needs to know is that if he or she puts appropriate arguments into the black box, then it will take some appropriate action. Designing a function so that it can be used as a black box is sometimes called **information hiding** to emphasize the fact that the programmer acts as if the body of the function were hidden from view.

information
hiding

procedural
abstraction

Writing and using functions as if they were black boxes is also called **procedural abstraction**. When programming in C++ it might make more sense to call it *functional abstraction.* However, *procedure* is a more general term than *function* and computer scientists use it for all "function-like" sets of instructions, and so they prefer the

PROCEDURAL ABSTRACTION

When applied to a function definition, the principle of *procedural abstraction* means that your function should be written so that it can be used like a black box. This means that the programmer who uses the function should not need to look at the body of the function definition to see how the function works. The function declaration and the accompanying comment should be all the programmer needs to know in order to use the function. To ensure that your function definitions have this important property, you should strictly adhere to the following rules:

HOW TO WRITE A BLACK-BOX FUNCTION DEFINITION

- The function declaration comment should tell the programmer any and all conditions that are required of the arguments to the function and should describe the result of a function invocation.
- All variables used in the function body should be declared in the function body. (The formal parameters do not need to be declared, because they are listed in the function heading.)

term *procedural abstraction*. The term *abstraction* is intended to convey the idea that when you use a function as a black box, you are abstracting away the details of the code contained in the function body. You can call this technique the *black box principle* or the *principle of procedural abstraction* or *information hiding*. The three terms mean the same thing. Whatever you call this principle, the important point is that you should use it when designing and writing your function definitions.

■ GLOBAL CONSTANTS AND GLOBAL VARIABLES

As we noted in Chapter 1, you can and should name constant values using the `const` modifier. For example, in Display 3.5 we used the `const` modifier to give a name to the rate of sales tax with the following declaration:

```
const double TAXRATE = 0.05; //5% sales tax
```

If this declaration is inside the definition of a function, as in Display 3.5, then the name `TAXRATE` is local to the function definition, which means that outside the definition of the function that contains the declaration, you can use the name `TAXRATE` for another named constant, or variable, or anything else.

On the other hand, if this declaration were to appear at the beginning of your program, outside the body of all the functions (and outside the body of the `main` part of your program), then the named constant is said to be a **global named constant** and the named constant can be used in any function definition that follows the constant declaration.

global
named
constant

Display 3.9 shows a program with an example of a global named constant. The program asks for a radius and then computes both the area of a circle and the volume of a sphere with that radius, using the following formulas:

$$area = \pi \times (radius)^2$$
$$volume = (4/3) \times \pi \times (radius)^3$$

Both formulas include the constant π, which is approximately equal to 3.14159. The symbol π is the Greek letter called "pi." The program thus uses the following global named constant:

```
const double PI = 3.14159;
```

which appears outside the definition of any function (including outside the definition of `main`).

The compiler allows you wide latitude in where you place the declarations for your global named constants. To aid readability, however, you should place all your `include` directives together, all your global named constant declarations together in another group, and all your function declarations (function prototypes) together. We will follow standard practice and place all our global named constant declarations after our `include` and `using` directives and before our function declarations.

Display 3.9   A Global Named Constant *(part 1 of 2)*

```
1    //Computes the area of a circle and the volume of a sphere.
2    //Uses the same radius for both calculations.
3    #include <iostream>
4    #include <cmath>
5    using namespace std;

6    const double PI = 3.14159;

7    double area(double radius);
8    //Returns the area of a circle with the specified radius.

9    double volume(double radius);
10   //Returns the volume of a sphere with the specified radius.

11   int main( )
12   {
13       double radiusOfBoth, areaOfCircle, volumeOfSphere;

14       cout << "Enter a radius to use for both a circle\n"
15            << "and a sphere (in inches): ";
16       cin >> radiusOfBoth;

17       areaOfCircle = area(radiusOfBoth);
18       volumeOfSphere = volume(radiusOfBoth);

19       cout << "Radius = " << radiusOfBoth << " inches\n"
20            << "Area of circle = " << areaOfCircle
21            << " square inches\n"
22            << "Volume of sphere = " << volumeOfSphere
23            << " cubic inches\n";

24       return 0;
25   }
26
27   double area(double radius)
28   {
29       return (PI * pow(radius, 2));
30   }

31   double volume(double radius)
32   {
33       return ((4.0/3.0) * PI * pow(radius, 3));
34   }
```

Display 3.9 A Global Named Constant *(part 2 of 2)*

SAMPLE DIALOGUE

```
Enter a radius to use for both a circle
and a sphere (in inches): 2
Radius = 2 inches
Area of circle = 12.5664 square inches
Volume of sphere = 33.5103 cubic inches
```

Placing all named constant declarations at the start of your program can aid readability even if the named constant is used by only one function. If the named constant might need to be changed in a future version of your program, it will be easier to find if it is at the beginning of your program. For example, placing the constant declaration for the sales tax rate at the beginning of an accounting program will make it easy to revise the program should the tax rate change.

It is possible to declare ordinary variables, without the const modifier, as **global variables**, which are accessible to all function definitions in the file. This is done similar to the way it is done for global named constants, except that the modifier const is not used in the variable declaration. However, there is seldom any need to use such global variables. Moreover, global variables can make a program harder to understand and maintain, so we urge you to avoid using them.

global variable

Self-Test Exercises

20. If you use a variable in a function definition, where should you declare the variable? In the function definition? In the main function? Any place that is convenient?

21. Suppose a function named function1 has a variable named sam declared within the definition of function1, and a function named function2 also has a variable named sam declared within the definition of function2. Will the program compile (assuming everything else is correct)? If the program will compile, will it run (assuming that everything else is correct)? If it runs, will it generate an error message when run (assuming everything else is correct)? If it runs and does not produce an error message when run, will it give the correct output (assuming everything else is correct)?

22. What is the purpose of the comment that accompanies a function declaration?

23. What is the principle of procedural abstraction as applied to function definitions?

24. What does it mean when we say the programmer who uses a function should be able to treat the function like a black box? (This question is very closely related to the previous question.)

■ BLOCKS

A variable declared inside a compound statement (that is, inside a pair of braces) is local to the compound statement. The name of the variable can be used for something else, such as the name of a different variable, outside the compound statement.

block

A compound statement with declarations is usually called a **block**. Actually, *block* and *compound statement* are two terms for the same thing. However, when we focus on variables declared within a compound statement, we normally use the term *block* rather than *compound statement* and we say that the variables declared within the block are *local to the block*.

If a variable is declared in a block, then the definition applies from the location of the declaration to the end of the block. This is usually expressed by saying that the *scope* of the declaration is from the location of the declaration to the end of the block. So if a variable is declared at the start of a block, its scope is the entire block. If the variable is declared part way through the block, the declaration does not take effect until the program reaches the location of the declaration (see Self-Test Exercise 25).

Notice that the body of a function definition is a block. Thus, a variable that is local to a function is the same thing as a variable that is local to the body of the function definition (which is a block).

BLOCKS

A *block* is some C++ code enclosed in braces. The variables declared in a block are local to the block, and so the variable names can be used outside the block for something else (such as being reused as the names for different variables).

■ NESTED SCOPES

Suppose you have one block nested inside another block, and suppose that one identifier is declared as a variable in each of these two blocks. These are two different variables with the same name. One variable exists only within the inner block and cannot be accessed outside that inner block. The other variable exists only in the outer block and cannot be accessed in the inner block. The two variables are distinct, so changes made to one of these variables will have no effect on the other of these two variables.

SCOPE RULE FOR NESTED BLOCKS

If an identifier is declared as a variable in each of two blocks, one within the other, then these are two different variables with the same name. One variable exists only within the inner block and cannot be accessed outside of the inner block. The other variable exists only in the outer block and cannot be accessed in the inner block. The two variables are distinct, so changes made to one of these variables will have no effect on the other of these two variables.

Tip

USE FUNCTION CALLS IN BRANCHING AND LOOP STATEMENTS

The switch statement and the if-else statement allow you to place several different statements in each branch. However, doing so can make the switch statement or if-else statement difficult to read. Rather than placing a compound statement in a branching statement, it is usually preferable to convert the compound statement to a function definition and place a function call in the branch. Similarly, if a loop body is large, it is preferable to convert the compound statement to a function definition and make the loop body a function call.

VARIABLES DECLARED IN A for LOOP

A variable may be declared in the heading of a for statement so that the variable is both declared and initialized at the start of the for statement. For example,

```
for (int n = 1; n <= 10; n++)
        sum = sum + n;
```

The ANSI/ISO C++ standard requires that a C++ compiler that claims compliance with the standard treat any declaration in a for loop initializer as if it were local to the body of the loop. Earlier C++ compilers did not do this. You should determine how your compiler treats variables declared in a for loop initializer. If portability is critical to your application, you should not write code that depends on this behavior. Eventually, all widely used C++ compilers will likely comply with this rule, but compilers presently available may or may not comply.

25. Though we urge you not to program using this style, we are providing an exercise that uses nested blocks to help you understand the scope rules. State the output that this code fragment would produce if embedded in an otherwise complete, correct program.

```
{
    int x = 1;
    cout << x << endl;
    {
        cout << x << endl;
        int x = 2;
        cout << x << endl;
        {
            cout << x << endl;
            int x = 3;
            cout << x << endl;
        }
        cout << x << endl;
    }
    cout << x << endl;
}
```

Chapter Summary

- There are two kinds of functions in C++: functions that return a value and void functions.

- A function should be defined so that it can be used as a black box. The programmer who uses the function should not need to know any details about how the function is coded. All the programmer should need to know is the function declaration and the accompanying comment that describes the value returned. This rule is sometimes called the principle of procedural abstraction.

- A good way to write a function declaration comment is to use a precondition and a postcondition. The precondition states what is assumed to be true when the function is called. The postcondition describes the effect of the function call; that is, the postcondition tells what will be true after the function is executed in a situation in which the precondition holds.

- A variable that is declared in a function definition is said to be local to the function.

- A formal parameter is a kind of placeholder that is filled in with a function argument when the function is called. The details on this "filling in" process are covered in Chapter 4.

ANSWERS TO SELF-TEST EXERCISES

1. 4.0   4.0   8.0
   8.0   8.0   1.21
   3   3   0
   3.0   3.5   3.5
   6.0   6.0   5.0
   5.0   4.5   4.5
   3   3.0   3.0

2. a. sqrt(x + y)

   b. pow(x, y + 7)

   c. sqrt(area + fudge)

   d. sqrt(time+tide)/nobody

   e. (-b + sqrt(b*b - 4*a*c))/(2*a)

   f. abs(x - y) or labs(x - y) or fabs(x - y)

3.
```
#include <iostream>
#include <cmath>
using namespace std;
int main( )
{
    int i;
    for (i = 1; i <= 10; i++)
    cout << "The square root of  " << i
        << " is " << sqrt(i) << endl;
    return 0;
}
```

4. The argument is given to the operating system. As far as your C++ program is concerned, you can use any int value as the argument. By convention, however, 1 is used for a call to exit that is caused by an error, and 0 is used in other cases.

5. (5 + (rand( ) % 6))

6.
```
#include <iostream>
#include <cstdlib>
using namespace std;

int main( )
{
  cout << "Enter a nonnegative integer to use as the\n"
      << "seed for the random number generator: ";
  unsigned int seed;
  cin >> seed;
  srand(seed);

  cout << "Here are ten random probabilities:\n";
```

```cpp
    int i;
    for (i = 0; i < 10; i++)
    cout << ((RAND_MAX - rand( ))/static_cast<double>(RAND_MAX))
        << endl;

    return 0;
}
```

7. Wow

8. The function declaration is

```cpp
int sum(int n1, int n2, int n3);
//Returns the sum of n1, n2, and n3.
```

The function definition is

```cpp
int sum(int n1, int n2, int n3)
{
    return (n1 + n2 + n3);
}
```

9. The function declaration is

```cpp
char positiveTest(double number);
//Returns 'P' if number is positive.
//Returns 'N' if number is negative or zero.
```

The function definition is

```cpp
char positiveTest(double number)
{
    if (number > 0)
        return 'P';
    else
        return 'N';
}
```

10. No, a function definition cannot appear inside the body of another function definition.

11. Predefined functions and user-defined functions are invoked (called) in the same way.

12.
```cpp
bool inOrder(int n1, int n2, int n3)
{
    return ((n1 <= n2) && (n2 <= n3));
}
```

13.
```cpp
bool even(int n)
{
    return ((n % 2) == 0);
}
```

14.
```cpp
bool isDigit(char ch)
{
    return ('0' <= ch) && (ch <= '9');
}
```

15.
```
Hello
Goodbye
One more time:
Hello
End of program.
```

16. If you omitted the `return` statement in the function definition for `iceCreamDivision` in Display 3.7, the program would compile and run. However, if you input zero for the number of customers, then the program would produce a run-time error because of a division by zero.

17.
```cpp
#include <iostream>
using namespace std;
void productOut(int n1, int n2, int n3);

int main( )
{
    int num1, num2, num3;
    cout << "Enter three integers: ";
    cin >> num1 >> num2 >> num3;
    productOut(num1, num2, num3);
    return 0;
}

void productOut(int n1, int n2, int n3)
{
    cout << "The product of the three numbers "
         << n1 << ", " << n2 << ", and "
         << n3 << " is " << (n1*n2*n3) << endl;
}
```

18. These answers are system-dependent.

19.
```cpp
double sqrt(double n);
//Precondition: n >= 0.
//Returns the square root of n.
```

You can rewrite the second comment line as the following if you prefer, but the version above is the usual form used for a function that returns a value:

```cpp
//Postcondition: Returns the square root of n.
```

20. If you use a variable in a function definition, you should declare the variable in the body of the function definition.

21. Everything will be fine. The program will compile (assuming everything else is correct). The program will run (assuming that everything else is correct). The program will not generate an error message when run (assuming everything else is correct). The program will give the correct output (assuming everything else is correct).

22. The comment explains what action the function takes, including any value returned, and gives any other information that you need to know in order to use the function.

23. The principle of procedural abstraction says that a function should be written so that it can be used like a black box. This means that the programmer who uses the function need not look at the body of the function definition to see how the function works. The function declaration and accompanying comment should be all the programmer needs in order to use the function.

24. When we say that the programmer who uses a function should be able to treat the function like a black box, we mean the programmer should not need to look at the body of the function definition to see how the function works. The function declaration and accompanying comment should be all the programmer needs in order to use the function.

25. It helps to slightly change the code fragment to understand to which declaration each usage resolves. The code has three different variables named x. In the following we have renamed these three variables x1, x2, and x3. The output is given in the comments.

```
{
    int x1 = 1;// output in this column
    cout << x1 << endl;// 1<new line>
    {
        cout << x1 << endl;// 1<new line>
        int x2 = 2;
        cout << x2 << endl;// 2<new line>
        {
            cout << x2 << endl;// 2<new line>
            int x3 = 3;
            cout << x3 << endl;// 3<new line>
        }
        cout << x2 << endl;// 2<new line>
    }
    cout << x1 << endl;// 1<new line>
}
```

PROGRAMMING PROJECTS

1. A liter is 0.264179 gallons. Write a program that will read in the number of liters of gasoline consumed by the user's car and the number of miles traveled by the car and will then output the number of miles per gallon the car delivered. Your program should allow the user to repeat this calculation as often as the user wishes. Define a function to compute the

number of miles per gallon. Your program should use a globally defined constant for the number of gallons per liter.

2. Write a program to gauge the rate of inflation for the past year. The program asks for the price of an item (such as a hot dog or a one-carat diamond) both one year ago and today. It estimates the inflation rate as the difference in price divided by the year-ago price. Your program should allow the user to repeat this calculation as often as the user wishes. Define a function to compute the rate of inflation. The inflation rate should be a value of type double giving the rate as a percentage, for example 5.3 for 5.3%.

3. Enhance your program from the previous exercise by having it also print out the estimated price of the item in one and in two years from the time of the calculation. The increase in cost over one year is estimated as the inflation rate times the price at the start of the year. Define a second function to determine the estimated cost of an item in a specified number of years, given the current price of the item and the inflation rate as arguments.

4. The gravitational attractive force between two bodies with masses m_1 and m_2 separated by a distance d is given by the following formula:

$$F = \frac{G m_1 m_2}{d^2}$$

where G is the universal gravitational constant:

$$G = 6.673 \times 10^{-8} \text{ cm}^3/(\text{g} \bullet \sec^2)$$

Write a function definition that takes arguments for the masses of two bodies and the distance between them and returns the gravitational force between them. Since you will use the above formula, the gravitational force will be in dynes. One dyne equals a

$$\text{g} \bullet \text{cm/sec}^2$$

You should use a globally defined constant for the universal gravitational constant. Embed your function definition in a complete program that computes the gravitational force between two objects given suitable inputs. Your program should allow the user to repeat this calculation as often as the user wishes.

5. Write a program that asks for the user's height, weight, and age, and then computes clothing sizes according to the following formulas.

- Hat size = weight in pounds divided by height in inches and all that multiplied by 2.9.
- Jacket size (chest in inches) = height times weight divided by 288 and then adjusted by adding one-eighth of an inch for each 10 years over age 30. (Note that the adjustment only takes place after a full 10 years. So, there is no adjustment for ages 30 through 39, but one-eighth of an inch is added for age 40.)
- Waist in inches = weight divided by 5.7 and then adjusted by adding one-tenth of an inch for each 2 years over age 28. (Note that the adjustment only takes place after a full 2 years. So, there is no adjustment for age 29, but one-tenth of an inch is added for age 30.)

Use functions for each calculation. Your program should allow the user to repeat this calculation as often as the user wishes.

6. Write a function that computes the average and standard deviation of four scores. The standard deviation is defined to be the square root of the average of the four values: $(s_i - a)^2$, where a is the average of the four scores s_1, s_2, s_3, and s_4. The function will have six parameters and will call two other functions. Embed the function in a program that allows you to test the function again and again until you tell the program you are finished.

7. In cold weather, meteorologists report an index called the *wind chill factor*, which takes into account the wind speed and the temperature. The index provides a measure of the chilling effect of wind at a given air temperature. Wind chill may be approximated by the following formula:

$$W = 13.12 + 0.6215 * t - 11.37 * v^{0.16} + 0.3965 * t * v^{0.016}$$

where

   v = wind speed in m/sec

   t = temperature in degrees Celsius: $t <= 10$

   W = wind chill index (in degrees Celsius)

Write a function that returns the wind chill index. Your code should ensure that the restriction on the temperature is not violated. Look up some weather reports in back issues of a newspaper in your library and compare the wind chill index you calculate with the result reported in the newspaper.

4 CHAPTER
Parameters and Overloading

4 Parameters and Overloading

Just fill in the blanks.

Common Instruction

INTRODUCTION

This chapter discusses the details of the mechanisms used by C++ for plugging in arguments for parameters in function calls. It also discusses overloading, which is a way to give two (or more) different function definitions to the same function name. Finally, it goes over some basic techniques for testing functions.

4.1 Parameters

You can't put a square peg in a round hole.

Common saying

This section describes the details of the mechanisms used by C++ for plugging in an argument for a formal parameter when a function is invoked. There are two basic kinds of parameters and therefore two basic plugging-in mechanisms in C++. The two basic kinds of parameters are *call-by-value parameters* and *call-by-reference parameters*. All the parameters that appeared before this point in the book were call-by-value parameters. With **call-by-value parameters**, only the value of the argument is plugged in. With **call-by-reference parameters**, the argument is a variable and the variable itself is plugged in; therefore, the variable's value can be changed by the function invocation. A call-by-reference parameter is indicated by appending the ampersand sign, &, to the parameter type, as illustrated by the following function declarations:

call-by-value parameter

call-by-reference parameter

```
void getInput(double& variableOne, int& variableTwo);
```

A call-by-value parameter is indicated by not using the ampersand. The details on call-by-value and call-by-reference parameters are given in the following subsections.

■ CALL-BY-VALUE PARAMETERS

Call-by-value parameters are more than just blanks that are filled in with the argument values for the function. A call-by-value parameter is actually a local variable. When the function is invoked, the value of a call-by-value argument is computed and the corresponding call-by-value parameter, which is a local variable, is initialized to this value.

In most cases, you can think of a call-by-value parameter as a kind of blank, or placeholder, that is filled in by the value of its corresponding argument in the function invocation. However, in some cases it is handy to use a call-by-value parameter as a local variable and change the value of the parameter within the body of the function definition. For example, the program in Display 4.1 illustrates a call-by-value parameter used as a local variable whose value is changed in the body of the function definition. Notice the formal parameter minutesWorked in the definition of the function fee. It is used as a variable and has its value changed by the following line, which occurs within the function definition:

```
minutesWorked = hoursWorked*60 + minutesWorked;
```

Display 4.1   Formal Parameter Used as a Local Variable *(part 1 of 2)*

```
1   //Law office billing program.
2   #include <iostream>
3   using namespace std;

4   const double RATE = 150.00; //Dollars per quarter hour.

5   double fee(int hoursWorked, int minutesWorked);
6   //Returns the charges for hoursWorked hours and
7   //minutesWorked minutes of legal services.

8   int main( )
9   {
10      int hours, minutes;
11      double bill;

12      cout << "Welcome to the law office of\n"
13           << "Dewey, Cheatham, and Howe.\n"
14           << "The law office with a heart.\n"
15           << "Enter the hours and minutes"
16           << " of your consultation:\n";
17      cin >> hours >> minutes;

18      bill = fee(hours, minutes);

19      cout.setf(ios::fixed);
20      cout.setf(ios::showpoint);
21      cout.precision(2);
22      cout << "For " << hours << " hours and " << minutes
23           << " minutes, your bill is $" << bill << endl;

24      return 0;
25  }
```

The value of minutes is not changed by the call to fee.

Display 4.1   Formal Parameter Used as a Local Variable *(part 2 of 2)*

```
26   double fee(int hoursWorked, int minutesWorked)      minutesWorked is a local
27   {                                                    variable initialized to the
28       int quarterHours;                                value of minutes.

29       minutesWorked = hoursWorked*60 + minutesWorked;
30       quarterHours = minutesWorked/15;
31       return (quarterHours*RATE);
32   }
```

SAMPLE DIALOGUE

```
Welcome to the law office of
Dewey, Cheatham, and Howe.
The law office with a heart.
Enter the hours and minutes of your consultation:
5  46
For 5 hours and 46 minutes, your bill is $3450.00
```

Call-by-value parameters are local variables just like the variables you declare within the body of a function. However, you should not add a variable declaration for the formal parameters. Listing the formal parameter minutesWorked in the function heading also serves as the variable declaration. The following is the *wrong way* to start the function definition for fee because it declares minutesWorked twice:

```
double fee(int hoursWorked, int minutesWorked)
{
    int quarterHours;                   Do not do this when minutesWorked
    int minutesWorked;   ←              is a parameter!
         . . .
```

Self-Test Exercises

1. Carefully describe the call-by-value parameter mechanism.

2. The following function is supposed to take as arguments a length expressed in feet and inches and to return the total number of inches in that many feet and inches. For example, totalinches(1, 2) is supposed to return 14, because 1 foot and 2 inches is the same as 14 inches. Will the following function perform correctly? If not, why not?
```
double totalInches(int feet, int inches)
{
    inches = 12*feet + inches;
    return inches;
}
```

A FIRST LOOK AT CALL-BY-REFERENCE PARAMETERS

The call-by-value mechanism that we used until now is not sufficient for all tasks you might want a function to perform. For example, one common task for a function is to obtain an input value from the user and set the value of an argument variable to this input value. With the call-by-value formal parameters that we have used until now, a corresponding argument in a function call can be a variable, but the function takes only the value of the variable and does not change the variable in any way. With a call-by-value formal parameter only the *value* of the argument is substituted for the formal parameter. For an input function, you want the *variable* (not the value of the variable) to be substituted for the formal parameter. The call-by-reference mechanism works in just this way. With a call-by-reference formal parameter, the corresponding argument in a function call must be a variable, and this argument variable is substituted for the formal parameter. It is almost as if the argument variable were literally copied into the body of the function definition in place of the formal parameter. After the argument is substituted in, the code in the function body is executed and can change the value of the argument variable.

A call-by-reference parameter must be marked in some way so that the compiler will know it from a call-by-value parameter. The way that you indicate a call-by-reference parameter is to attach the **ampersand sign, &,** to the end of the type name in the for- *ampersand,* mal parameter list. This is done in both the function declaration (function prototype) *&* and the header of the function definition. For example, the following function definition has one formal parameter, `receiver`, which is a call-by-reference parameter:

```
void getInput(double& receiver)
{
    cout << "Enter input number:\n";
    cin >> receiver;
}
```

In a program that contains this function definition, the following function call will set the `double` variable `inputNumber` equal to a value read from the keyboard:

```
getInput(inputNumber);
```

C++ allows you to place the ampersand either with the type name or with the parameter name, so you will sometimes see

```
void getInput(double &receiver);
```

which is equivalent to

```
void getInput(double& receiver);
```

Display 4.2 demonstrates call-by-reference parameters. The program reads in two numbers and writes the same numbers out, but in the reverse order. The parameters in

Display 4.2   Call-by-Reference Parameters *(part 1 of 2)*

```
1    //Program to demonstrate call-by-reference parameters.
2    #include <iostream>
3    using namespace std;

4    void getNumbers(int& input1, int& input2);
5    //Reads two integers from the keyboard.

6    void swapValues(int& variable1, int& variable2);
7    //Interchanges the values of variable1 and variable2.

8    void showResults(int output1, int output2);
9    //Shows the values of variable1 and variable2, in that order.

10   int main( )
11   {
12       int firstNum, secondNum;

13       getNumbers(firstNum, secondNum);
14       swapValues(firstNum, secondNum);
15       showResults(firstNum, secondNum);
16       return 0;
17   }

18   void getNumbers(int& input1, int& input2)
19   {
20       cout << "Enter two integers: ";
21       cin >> input1
22           >> input2;
23   }

24   void swapValues(int& variable1, int& variable2)
25   {
26       int temp;

27       temp = variable1;
28       variable1 = variable2;
29       variable2 = temp;
30   }
31
32   void showResults(int output1, int output2)
33   {
34       cout << "In reverse order the numbers are: "
35            << output1 << " " << output2 << endl;
36   }
```

Display 4.2   **Call-by-Reference Parameters** *(part 2 of 2)*

SAMPLE DIALOGUE

```
Enter two integers: 5 6
In reverse order the numbers are: 6 5
```

the functions getNumbers and swapValues are call-by-reference parameters. The input is performed by the function call

```
getNumbers(firstNum, secondNum);
```

The values of the variables firstNum and secondNum are set by this function call. After that, the following function call reverses the values in the two variables firstNum and secondNum:

```
swapValues(firstNum, secondNum);
```

The next few subsections describe the call-by-reference mechanism in more detail and also explain the particular functions used in Display 4.2.

CALL-BY-REFERENCE PARAMETERS

To make a formal parameter a call-by-reference parameter, append the ampersand sign, &, to its type name. The corresponding argument in a call to the function should then be a variable, not a constant or other expression. When the function is called, the corresponding variable argument (not its value) will be substituted for the formal parameter. Any change made to the formal parameter in the function body will be made to the argument variable when the function is called. The exact details of the substitution mechanisms are given in the text of this chapter.

EXAMPLE

```
void getData(int& firstInput, double& secondInput);
```

CALL-BY-REFERENCE MECHANISM IN DETAIL

In most situations the call-by-reference mechanism works as if the name of the variable given as the function argument were literally substituted for the call-by-reference formal parameter. However, the process is a bit more subtle than that. In some situations, this subtlety is important, so we need to examine more details of this call-by-reference substitution process.

Program variables are implemented as memory locations. Each memory location has a unique **address** that is a number. The compiler assigns one memory location to each variable. For example, when the program in Display 4.2 is compiled, the variable `firstNum` might be assigned location 1010, and the variable `secondNum` might be assigned 1012. For all practical purposes, these memory locations are the variables.

For example, consider the following function declaration from Display 4.2:

```
void getNumbers(int& input1, int& input2);
```

The call-by-reference formal parameters `input1` and `input2` are placeholders for the actual arguments used in a function call.

Now consider a function call like the following from the same program:

```
getNumbers(firstNum, secondNum);
```

When the function call is executed, the function is not given the argument names `firstNum` and `secondNum`. Instead, it is given a list of the memory locations associated with each name. In this example, the list consists of the locations

```
1010
1012
```

which are the locations assigned to the argument variables `firstNum` and `secondNum`, *in that order*. It is these memory locations that are associated with the formal parameters. The first memory location is associated with the first formal parameter, the second memory location is associated with the second formal parameter, and so forth. Diagrammatically, in this case the correspondence is

```
firstNum  ───────► 1010 ───────► input1
secondNum ───────► 1012 ───────► input2
```

When the function statements are executed, whatever the function body says to do to a formal parameter is actually done to the variable in the memory location associated with that formal parameter. In this case, the instructions in the body of the function `getNumbers` say that a value should be stored in the formal parameter `input1` using a `cin` statement, and so that value is stored in the variable in memory location 1010 (which happens to be the variable `firstNum`). Similarly, the instructions in the body of the function `getNumbers` say that another value should then be stored in the formal parameter `input2` using a `cin` statement, and so that value is stored in the variable in memory location 1012 (which happens to be the variable `secondNum`). Thus, whatever the function instructs the computer to do to `input1` and `input2` is actually done to the variables `firstNum` and `secondNum`.

It may seem that there is an extra level of detail, or at least an extra level of verbiage. If `firstNum` is the variable with memory location 1010, why do we insist on saying "the variable at memory location 1010" instead of simply saying "`firstNum`"? This extra level of detail is needed if the arguments and formal parameters contain some confusing coincidence of names. For example, the function getNumbers has formal parameters named input1 and input2. Suppose you want to change the program in Display 4.2 so that it uses the function getNumbers with arguments that are also named input1 and input2, and suppose that you want to do something less than obvious. Suppose you want the first number typed in to be stored in a variable named input2, and the second number typed in to be stored in the variable named input1—perhaps because the second number will be processed first or because it is the more important number. Now, let's suppose that the variables input1 and input2, which are declared in the main part of your program, have been assigned memory locations 1014 and 1016. The function call could be as follows:

```
int input1, input2;
getNumbers(input2, input1);        Notice the order
                                   of the arguments.
```

In this case if you say "input1," we do not know whether you mean the variable named input1 that is declared in the main part of your program or the formal parameter input1. However, if the variable input1 declared in the main function of your program is assigned memory location 1014, the phrase "the variable at memory location 1014" is unambiguous. Let's go over the details of the substitution mechanisms in this case.

In this call the argument corresponding to the formal parameter input1 is the variable input2, and the argument corresponding to the formal parameter input2 is the variable input1. This can be confusing to us, but it produces no problem at all for the computer, since the computer never does actually "substitute input2 for input1" or "substitute input1 for input2." The computer simply deals with memory locations. The computer substitutes "the variable at memory location 1016" for the formal parameter input1, and "the variable at memory location 1014" for the formal parameter input2.

Example

THE swapValues FUNCTION

The function swapValues defined in Display 4.2 interchanges the values stored in two variables. The description of the function is given by the following function declaration and accompanying comment:

```
void swapValues(int& variable1, int& variable2);
//Interchanges the values of variable1 and variable2.
```

To see how the function is supposed to work, assume that the variable firstNum has the value 5 and the variable secondNum has the value 6 and consider the following function call:

```
swapValues(firstNum, secondNum);
```

After this function call, the value of firstNum will be 6 and the value of secondNum will be 5.

As shown in Display 4.2, the definition of the function `swapValues` uses a local variable called `temp`. This local variable is needed. You might be tempted to think the function definition could be simplified to the following:

```
void swapValues(int& variable1, int& variable2)
{
    variable1 = variable2;
    variable2 = variable1;              This does not work!
}
```

To see that this alternative definition cannot work, consider what would happen with this definition and the function call

```
swapValues(firstNum, secondNum);
```

The variables `firstNum` and `secondNum` would be substituted for the formal parameters `variable1` and `variable2` so that with this incorrect function definition, the function call would be equivalent to the following:

```
firstNum = secondNum;
secondNum = firstNum;
```

This code does not produce the desired result. The value of `firstNum` is set equal to the value of `secondNum`, just as it should be. But then, the value of `secondNum` is set equal to the changed value of `firstNum`, which is now the original value of `secondNum`. Thus, the value of `secondNum` is not changed at all. (If this is unclear, go through the steps with specific values for the variables `firstNum` and `secondNum`.) What the function needs to do is save the original value of `firstNum` so that value is not lost. This is what the local variable `temp` in the correct function definition is used for. That correct definition is the one in Display 4.2. When that correct version is used and the function is called with the arguments `firstNum` and `secondNum`, the function call is equivalent to the following code, which works correctly:

```
temp = firstNum;
firstNum = secondNum;
secondNum = temp;
```

▦ CONSTANT REFERENCE PARAMETERS

We place this subsection here for reference value. If you are reading this book in order, you may as well skip this section. The topic is explained in more detail later in the book.

If you place a const before a call-by-reference parameter's type, you get a call-by-reference parameter that cannot be changed. For the types we have seen so far, this has no advantages. However, it will turn out to be an aid to efficiency with array and class type parameters. We will discuss these constant parameters when we discuss arrays and when we discuss classes.

Tip	**THINK OF ACTIONS, NOT CODE**

Although we can explain how a function call works in terms of substituting code for the function call, that is not the way you should normally think about a function call. You should instead think of a function call as an action. For example, consider the function swapValues in Display 4.2 and an invocation such as

```
swapValues(firstNum, secondNum);
```

It is easier and clearer to think of this function call as the action of swapping the values of its two arguments. It is much less clear to think of it as the code

```
temp = firstNum;
firstNum = secondNum;
secondNum = temp;
```

Self-Test Exercises

3. What is the output of the following program?

```cpp
#include <iostream>
using namespace std;

void figureMeOut(int& x, int y, int& z);

int main( )
{
    int a, b, c;
    a = 10;
    b = 20;
    c = 30;
    figureMeOut(a, b, c);
    cout << a << " " << b << " " << c << endl;
    return 0;
}

void figureMeOut(int& x, int y, int& z)
{
    cout << x << " " << y << " " << z << endl;
    x = 1;
    y = 2;
    z = 3;
    cout << x << " " << y << " " << z << endl;
}
```

4. What would be the output of the program in Display 4.2 if you omitted the ampersands (&) from the first parameter in the function declaration and function heading of swapValues? The ampersand is not removed from the second parameter. Assume the user enters numbers as in the sample dialogue in Display 4.2.

5. Write a void function definition for a function called zeroBoth that has two call-by-reference parameters, both of which are variables of type int, and sets the values of both variables to 0.

6. Write a void function definition for a function called addTax. The function addTax has two formal parameters: taxRate, which is the amount of sales tax expressed as a percentage; and cost, which is the cost of an item before tax. The function changes the value of cost so that it includes sales tax.

▪ MIXED PARAMETER LISTS

Whether a formal parameter is a call-by-value parameter or a call-by-reference parameter is determined by whether there is an ampersand attached to its type specification. If the ampersand is present, the formal parameter is a call-by-reference parameter. If there is no ampersand associated with the formal parameter, it is a call-by-value parameter.

PARAMETERS AND ARGUMENTS

All the different terms that have to do with parameters and arguments can be confusing. However, if you keep a few simple points in mind, you will be able to easily handle these terms.

1. The *formal parameters* for a function are listed in the function declaration and are used in the body of the function definition. A formal parameter (of any sort) is a kind of blank or placeholder that is filled in with something when the function is called.

2. An *argument* is something that is used to fill in a formal parameter. When you write down a function call, the arguments are listed in parentheses after the function name. When the function call is executed, the arguments are plugged in for the formal parameters.

3. The terms *call-by-value* and *call-by-reference* refer to the mechanism that is used in the plugging-in process. In the *call-by-value* method only the value of the argument is used. In this call-by-value mechanism, the formal parameter is a local variable that is initialized to the value of the corresponding argument. In the *call-by-reference* mechanism the argument is a variable and the entire variable is used. In the call-by-reference mechanism the argument variable is substituted for the formal parameter so that any change that is made to the formal parameter is actually made to the argument variable.

It is perfectly legitimate to mix call-by-value and call-by-reference formal parameters in the same function. For example, the first and last of the formal parameters in the following function declaration are call-by-reference formal parameters, and the middle one is a call-by-value parameter:

```
void goodStuff(int& par1, int par2, double& par3);
```

Call-by-reference parameters are not restricted to void functions. You can also use them in functions that return a value. Thus, a function with a call-by-reference parameter could both change the value of a variable given as an argument and return a value.

mixing call-by-reference and call-by-value parameters

Tip

WHAT KIND OF PARAMETER TO USE

Display 4.3 illustrates the differences between how the compiler treats call-by-value and call-by-reference formal parameters. The parameters par1Value and par2Ref are both assigned a value inside the body of the function definition. Because they are different kinds of parameters, however, the effect is different in the two cases.

par1Value is a call-by-value parameter, so it is a local variable. When the function is called as follows,

```
doStuff(n1, n2);
```

the local variable par1Value is initialized to the value of n1. That is, the local variable par1Value is initialized to 1 and the variable n1 is then ignored by the function. As you can see from the sample dialogue, the formal parameter par1Value (which is a local variable) is set to 111 in the function body, and this value is output to the screen. However, the value of the argument n1 is not changed. As shown in the sample dialogue, n1 has retained its value of 1.

On the other hand, par2Ref is a call-by-reference parameter. When the function is called, the variable argument n2 (not just its value) is substituted for the formal parameter par2Ref. So when the following code is executed,

```
par2Ref = 222;
```

it is the same as if the following were executed:

```
n2 = 222;
```

Thus, the value of the variable n2 is changed when the function body is executed, so, as the dialogue shows, the value of n2 is changed from 2 to 222 by the function call.

If you keep in mind the lesson of Display 4.3, it is easy to decide which parameter mechanism to use. If you want a function to change the value of a variable, then the corresponding formal parameter must be a call-by-reference formal parameter and must be marked with the ampersand sign, &. In all other cases, you can use a call-by-value formal parameter.

Display 4.3 Comparing Argument Mechanisms

```
1   //Illustrates the difference between a call-by-value
2   //parameter and a call-by-reference parameter.
3   #include <iostream>
4   using namespace std;

5   void doStuff(int par1Value, int& par2Ref);
6   //par1Value is a call-by-value formal parameter and
7   //par2Ref is a call-by-reference formal parameter.

8   int main( )
9   {
10      int n1, n2;

12      n1 = 1;
13      n2 = 2;
14      doStuff(n1, n2);
15      cout << "n1 after function call = " << n1 << endl;
16      cout << "n2 after function call = " << n2 << endl;
17      return 0;
18  }

19  void doStuff(int par1Value, int& par2Ref)
20  {
21      par1Value = 111;
22      cout << "par1Value in function call = "
23              << par1Value << endl;
24      par2Ref = 222;
25      cout << "par2Ref in function call = "
26              << par2Ref << endl;
27  }
```

SAMPLE DIALOGUE

```
par1Value in function call = 111
par2Ref in function call = 222
n1 after function call = 1
n2 after function call = 222
```

Pitfall   **INADVERTENT LOCAL VARIABLES**

If you want a function to change the value of a variable, the corresponding formal parameter must be a call-by-reference parameter and therefore must have the ampersand, &, attached to its type. If you carelessly omit the ampersand, the function will have a call-by-value parameter where you meant to have a call-by-reference parameter. When the program is run, you will discover that the function call does not change the value of the corresponding argument, because a formal call-by-value parameter is a local variable. If the parameter has its value changed in the function, then, as with any local variable, that change has no effect outside the function body. This is an error that can be very difficult to see because the code *looks* right.

For example, the program in Display 4.4 is similar to the program in Display 4.2 except that the ampersands were mistakenly omitted from the function swapValues. As a result, the formal parameters variable1 and variable2 are local variables. The argument *variables* firstNum and secondNum are never substituted in for variable1 and variable2; variable1 and variable2 are instead initialized to *the values of* firstNum and secondNum. Then, the values of variable1 and variable2 are interchanged, but the values of firstNum and secondNum are left unchanged. The omission of two ampersands has made the program completely wrong, yet it looks almost identical to the correct program and will compile and run without any error messages.

Tip

CHOOSING FORMAL PARAMETER NAMES

Functions should be self-contained modules that are designed separately from the rest of the program. On large programming projects, different programmers may be assigned to write different functions. The programmer should choose the most meaningful names he or she can find for formal parameters. The arguments that will be substituted for the formal parameters may well be variables in another function or in the main function. These variables should also be given meaningful names, often chosen by someone other than the programmer who writes the function definition. This makes it likely that some or all arguments will have the same names as some of the formal parameters. This is perfectly acceptable. No matter what names are chosen for the variables that will be used as arguments, these names will not produce any confusion with the names used for formal parameters.

Example

BUYING PIZZA

The large "economy" size of an item is not always a better buy than the smaller size. This is particularly true when buying pizzas. Pizza sizes are given as the diameter of the pizza in inches. However, the quantity of pizza is determined by the area of the pizza, and the area is not proportional to the diameter. Most people cannot easily estimate the difference in area between a ten-inch pizza and a twelve-inch pizza and so cannot easily determine which size is the best buy—that is, which size has the lowest price per square inch. Display 4.5 shows a program that a consumer can use to determine which of two sizes of pizza is the better buy.

Note that the functions getData and giveResults have the same parameters, but since getData will change the values of its arguments, its parameters are call-by-reference. On the other hand, giveResults only needs the values of its arguments, and so its parameters are call-by-value.

Also note that giveResults has two local variables and that its function body includes calls to the function unitPrice. Finally, note that the function unitPrice has both local variables and a locally defined constant.

Display 4.4   Inadvertent Local Variable

```
1    //Program to demonstrate call-by-reference parameters.
2    #include <iostream>
3    using namespace std;

4    void getNumbers(int& input1, int& input2);
5    //Reads two integers from the keyboard.          Forgot the & here

6    void swapValues(int variable1, int variable2);
7    //Interchanges the values of variable1 and variable2.

8    void showResults(int output1, int output2);
9    //Shows the values of variable1 and variable2, in that order.

10   int main( )
11   {
12       int firstNum, secondNum;

13       getNumbers(firstNum, secondNum);
14       swapValues(firstNum, secondNum);
15       showResults(firstNum, secondNum);        Forgot the & here
16       return 0;
17   }

18   void swapValues(int variable1, int variable2)
19   {
20       int temp;
                                              Inadvertent
21       temp = variable1;                    local variables
22       variable1 = variable2;
23       variable2 = temp;
24   }
25           The definitions of getNumbers and
26                  showResults are the same as in Display 4.2.
```

SAMPLE DIALOGUE

```
Enter two integers: 5 6                    Error due to
In reverse order the numbers are: 5 6      inadvertent local
                                           variables
```

Display 4.5 Buying Pizza *(part 1 of 2)*

```
1    //Determines which of two pizza sizes is the best buy.
2    #include <iostream>
3    using namespace std;

4    void getData(int& smallDiameter, double& priceSmall,
5                 int& largeDiameter, double& priceLarge);

6    void giveResults(int smallDiameter, double priceSmall,
7                     int largeDiameter, double priceLarge);

8    double unitPrice(int diameter, double price);
9    //Returns the price per square inch of a pizza.
10   //Precondition: The diameter parameter is the diameter of the pizza
11   //in inches. The price parameter is the price of the pizza.

12   int main( )
13   {
14       int diameterSmall, diameterLarge;
15       double priceSmall, priceLarge;

16       getData(diameterSmall, priceSmall, diameterLarge, priceLarge);
17       giveResults(diameterSmall, priceSmall, diameterLarge, priceLarge);

18       return 0;
19   }

20   void getData(int& smallDiameter, double& priceSmall,
21                int& largeDiameter, double& priceLarge)
22   {
23       cout << "Welcome to the Pizza Consumers Union.\n";
24       cout << "Enter diameter of a small pizza (in inches): ";
25       cin >> smallDiameter;
26       cout << "Enter the price of a small pizza: $";
27       cin >> priceSmall;
28       cout << "Enter diameter of a large pizza (in inches): ";
29       cin >> largeDiameter;
30       cout << "Enter the price of a large pizza: $";
31       cin >> priceLarge;
32   }

34   void giveResults(int smallDiameter, double priceSmall,
35                    int largeDiameter, double priceLarge)
36   {
37       double unitPriceSmall, unitPriceLarge;

38       unitPriceSmall = unitPrice(smallDiameter, priceSmall);
39       unitPriceLarge = unitPrice(largeDiameter, priceLarge);
```

The variables diameterSmall, diameterLarge, priceSmall, and priceLarge are used to carry data from the function getData to the function giveResults.

One function called within another function

Display 4.5   Buying Pizza *(part 2 of 2)*

```
40        cout.setf(ios::fixed);
41        cout.setf(ios::showpoint);
42        cout.precision(2);
43        cout << "Small pizza:\n"
44             << "Diameter = " << smallDiameter << " inches\n"
45             << "Price = $" << priceSmall
46             << " Per square inch = $" << unitPriceSmall << endl
47             << "Large pizza:\n"
48             << "Diameter = " << largeDiameter << " inches\n"
49             << "Price = $" << priceLarge
50             << " Per square inch = $" << unitPriceLarge << endl;
51        if (unitPriceLarge < unitPriceSmall)
52            cout << "The large one is the better buy.\n";
53        else
54            cout << "The small one is the better buy.\n";
55        cout << "Buon Appetito!\n";
56    }

57    double unitPrice(int diameter, double price)
58    {
59        const double PI = 3.14159;
60        double radius, area;

61        radius = diameter/static_cast<double>(2);
62        area = PI * radius * radius;
63        return (price/area);
64    }
```

SAMPLE DIALOGUE

```
Welcome to the Pizza Consumers Union.
Enter diameter of a small pizza (in inches): 10
Enter the price of a small pizza: $7.50
Enter diameter of a large pizza (in inches): 13
Enter the price of a large pizza: $14.75
Small pizza:
Diameter = 10 inches
Price = $7.50 Per square inch = $0.10
Large pizza:
Diameter = 13 inches
Price = $14.75 Per square inch = $0.11
The small one is the better buy.
Buon Appetito!
```

7. What would be the output of the program in Display 4.3 if you changed the function declaration for the function doStuff to the following and you changed the function header to match, so that the formal parameter par2Ref were changed to a call-by-value parameter?

```
void doStuff(int par1Value, int par2Ref);
```

4.2   Overloading and Default Arguments

> *"...and that shows that there are three hundred and sixty-four days when you might get un-birthday presents—"*
> *"Certainly," said Alice.*
> *"And only one for birthday presents, you know. There's glory for you!"*
> *"I don't know what you mean by 'glory,' " Alice said.*
> *Humpty Dumpty smiled contemptuously, "Of course you don't—till I tell you. I mean 'there's a nice knock-down argument for you!' "*
> *"But 'glory' doesn't mean 'a nice knock-down argument,' " Alice objected.*
> *"When I use a word," Humpty Dumpty said, in rather a scornful tone, "it means just what I choose it to mean—neither more nor less."*
> *"The question is," said Alice, "whether you can make words mean so many different things."*
> *"The question is," said Humpty Dumpty, "which is to be master—that's all."*
>
> Lewis Carroll, *Through the Looking-Glass*

C++ allows you to give two or more different definitions to the same function name, which means you can reuse names that have strong intuitive appeal across a variety of situations. For example, you could have three functions called max: one that computes the largest of two numbers, another that computes the largest of three numbers, and yet another that computes the largest of four numbers. Giving two (or more) function definitions for the same function name is called **overloading** the function name.   overloading

▪ INTRODUCTION TO OVERLOADING

Suppose you are writing a program that requires you to compute the average of two numbers. You might use the following function definition:

```
double ave(double n1, double n2)
{
    return ((n1 + n2)/2.0);
}
```

Now suppose your program also requires a function to compute the average of three numbers. You might define a new function called ave3 as follows:

```
double ave3(double n1, double n2, double n3)
{
    return ((n1 + n2 + n3)/3.0);
}
```

This will work, and in many programming languages you have no choice but to do something like this. However, C++ overloading allows for a more elegant solution. In C++ you can simply use the same function name ave for both functions. In C++ you can use the following function definition in place of the function definition ave3:

```
double ave(double n1, double n2, double n3)
{
    return ((n1 + n2 + n3)/3.0);
}
```

so that the function name ave then has two definitions. This is an example of overloading. In this case we have overloaded the function name ave. Display 4.6 embeds these two function definitions for ave into a complete sample program. Be sure to notice that each function definition has its own declaration (prototype).

The compiler can tell which function definition to use by checking the number and types of the arguments in a function call. In the program in Display 4.6, one of the functions called ave has two arguments and the other has three arguments. When there are two arguments in a function call, the first definition applies. When there are three arguments in a function call, the second definition applies.

Overloading a Function Name

If you have two or more function definitions for the same function name, that is called *overloading*. When you overload a function name, the function definitions must have different numbers of formal parameters or some formal parameters of different types. When there is a function call, the compiler uses the function definition whose number of formal parameters and types of formal parameters match the arguments in the function call.

---

determining
which
definition
applies

Whenever you give two or more definitions to the same function name, the various function definitions must have different specifications for their arguments; that is, any two function definitions that have the same function name must use different numbers of formal parameters or have one or more parameters of different types (or both). Notice that when you overload a function name, the declarations for the two different definitions must differ in their formal parameters. *You cannot overload a function name by giving two definitions that differ only in the type of the value returned.* Nor can you

Display 4.6   Overloading a Function Name

```
1    //Illustrates overloading the function name ave.
2    #include <iostream>
3    using namespace std;

4    double ave(double n1, double n2);
5    //Returns the average of the two numbers n1 and n2.
6
7    double ave(double n1, double n2, double n3);
8    //Returns the average of the three numbers n1, n2, and n3.

9    int main( )
10   {
11       cout << "The average of 2.0, 2.5, and 3.0 is "
12            << ave(2.0, 2.5, 3.0) << endl;

13       cout << "The average of 4.5 and 5.5 is "
14            << ave(4.5, 5.5) << endl;

15       return 0;
16   }                                              Two arguments

17   double ave(double n1, double n2)
18   {
19       return ((n1 + n2)/2.0);
20   }                                              Three arguments

21   double ave(double n1, double n2, double n3)
22   {
23       return ((n1 + n2 + n3)/3.0);
24   }
```

SAMPLE DIALOGUE

```
The average of 2.0, 2.5, and 3.0 is 2.5
The average of 4.5 and 5.5 is 5.0
```

overload based on any difference other than the number or types of parameters. You cannot overload based solely on const or solely on call-by-value versus call-by-reference parameters.[1]

----

[1] Some compilers will, in fact, allow you to overload on the basis of const versus no const, but you should not count on this. The C++ standard says it is not allowed.

You already saw a kind of overloading in Chapter 1 (reviewed here) with the division operator, /. If both operands are of type int, as in 13/2, then the value returned is the result of integer division, in this case, 6. On the other hand, if one or both operands are of type double, then the value returned is the result of regular division; for example, 13/2.0 returns the value 6.5. There are two definitions for the division operator, /, and the two definitions are distinguished not by having different numbers of operands but rather by requiring operands of different types. The only difference between overloading of / and overloading function names is that the C++ language designers have already done the overloading of /, whereas you must program the overloading of your function names yourself. Chapter 8 discusses how to overload operators such as +, -, and so on.

SIGNATURE

A function's **signature** is the function's name with the sequence of types in the parameter list, not including the const keyword and not including the ampersand, &. When you overload a function name, the two definitions of the function name must have different signatures using this definition of signature. (Some authorities include the const and/or ampersand as part of the signature, but we wanted a definition that works for explaining overloading.)

Pitfall   AUTOMATIC TYPE CONVERSION AND OVERLOADING

Suppose that the following function definition occurs in your program and that you have *not* overloaded the function name mpg (so this is the only definition of a function called mpg).

```
double mpg(double miles, double gallons)
//Returns miles per gallon.
{
    return (miles/gallons);
}
```

If you call the function mpg with arguments of type int, then C++ will automatically convert any argument of type int to a value of type double. Hence, the following will output 22.5 miles per gallon to the screen:

```
cout << mpg(45, 2) << " miles per gallon";
```

C++ converts the 45 to 45.0 and the 2 to 2.0 and then performs the division 45.0/2.0 to obtain the value returned, which is 22.5.

interaction of overloading and type conversion

If a function requires an argument of type double and you give it an argument of type int, C++ will automatically convert the int argument to a value of type double. This is so useful and natural that we hardly give it a thought. However, overloading can interfere with this automatic type conversion. Let's look at an example.

Suppose you had (foolishly) overloaded the function name mpg so that your program contained the following definition of mpg as well as the one previous:

```
int mpg(int goals, int misses)
//Returns the Measure of Perfect Goals
//which is computed as (goals - misses).
{
    return (goals - misses);
}
```

In a program that contains both of these definitions for the function name mpg, the following will (unfortunately) output 43 miles per gallon (since 43 is 45 – 2):

```
cout << mpg(45, 2) << " miles per gallon";
```

When C++ sees the function call mpg(45, 2), which has two arguments of type int, C++ *first* looks for a function definition of mpg that has two formal parameters of type int. If it finds such a function definition, C++ uses that function definition. C++ does not convert an int argument to a value of type double unless that is the only way it can find a matching function definition.

The mpg example illustrates one more point about overloading: You should not use the same function name for two unrelated functions. Such careless use of function names is certain to eventually produce confusion.

Self-Test Exercises

8. Suppose you have two function definitions with the following declarations:

```
double score(double time, double distance);
int score(double points);
```

Which function definition would be used in the following function call and why would it be the one used? (x is of type double.)

```
double finalScore = score(x);
```

9. Suppose you have two function definitions with the following declarations:

```
double theAnswer(double data1, double data2);
double theAnswer(double time, int count);
```

Which function definition would be used in the following function call and why would it be the one used? (x and y are of type double.)

```
x = theAnswer(y, 6.0);
```

■ RULES FOR RESOLVING OVERLOADING

If you use overloading to produce two definitions of the same function name with similar (but not identical) parameter lists, then the interaction of overloading and automatic type conversion can be confusing. The rules that the compiler uses for resolving which of multiple overloaded definitions of a function name to apply to a given function call are as follows:

1. *Exact match:* If the number and types of arguments exactly match a definition (without any automatic type conversion), then that is the definition used.

2. *Match using automatic type conversion:* If there is no exact match but there is a match using automatic type conversion, then that match is used.

If two matches are found at stage 1 or if no matches are found at stage 1 and two matches are found at stage 2, then there is an ambiguous situation and an error message will be issued.

For example, the following overloading is dubious style, but is perfectly valid:

```
void f(int n, double m);
void f(double n, int m);
```

However, if you also have the invocation

```
f(98, 99);
```

then the compiler does not know which of the two int arguments to convert to a value of type double, and an error message is generated.

To see how confusing and dangerous the situation can be, suppose you add the following third overloading:

```
void f(int n, int m);
```

With this third overloading added, you no longer get an error message, since there is now an exact match. Obviously, such confusing overloading is to be avoided.

The above two rules will work in almost all situations. In fact, if you need more precise rules, you should rewrite your code to be more straightforward. However, the exact rules are even a bit more complicated. For reference value, we give the exact rules below. Some of the terms may not make sense until you read more of this book, but do not be concerned. The simple two rules given above will serve you well until you do understand the more complete rules.

1. Exact match as described earlier.

2. Matches using promotion within integer types or within floating-point types, such as short to int or float to double. (Note that bool-to-int and char-to-int conversions are considered promotions within integer types.)

3. Matches using other conversions of predefined types, such as int to double.

4. Matches using conversions of user-defined types (see Chapter 8).

5. Matches using ellipses ... (This is not covered in this book, and if you do not use it, it will not be an issue.)

If two matches are found at the first stage that a match is found, then there is an ambiguous situation and an error message will be issued.

Example

REVISED PIZZA-BUYING PROGRAM

The Pizza Consumers Union has been very successful with the program that we wrote for it in Display 4.5. In fact, now everybody always buys the pizza that is the best buy. One disreputable pizza parlor used to make money by fooling consumers into buying the more expensive pizza, but our program has put an end to its evil practices. However, the owners wish to continue their despicable behavior and have come up with a new way to fool consumers. They now offer both round pizzas and rectangular pizzas. They know that the program we wrote cannot deal with rectangularly shaped pizzas, so they hope they can again confuse consumers. Display 4.7 is another version of our program that compares a round pizza and a rectangular pizza. Note that the function name unitPrice has been overloaded so that it applies to both round and rectangular pizzas.

Display 4.7   Revised Pizza Program (part 1 of 3)

```
1    //Determines whether a round pizza or a rectangular pizza is the best buy.
2    #include <iostream>
3    using namespace std;

4    double unitPrice(int diameter, double price);
5    //Returns the price per square inch of a round pizza.
6    //The formal parameter named diameter is the diameter of the pizza
7    //in inches. The formal parameter named price is the price of the pizza.

8    double unitPrice(int length, int width, double price);
9    //Returns the price per square inch of a rectangular pizza
10   //with dimensions length by width inches.
11   //The formal parameter price is the price of the pizza.

12   int main( )
13   {
14       int diameter, length, width;
15       double priceRound, unitPriceRound,
16               priceRectangular, unitPriceRectangular;

17       cout << "Welcome to the Pizza Consumers Union.\n";
18       cout << "Enter the diameter in inches"
19            << " of a round pizza: ";
20       cin >> diameter;
21       cout << "Enter the price of a round pizza: $";
```

Display 4.7   Revised Pizza Program *(part 2 of 3)*

```
22        cin >> priceRound;
23        cout << "Enter length and width in inches\n"
24            << "of a rectangular pizza: ";
25        cin >> length >> width;
26        cout << "Enter the price of a rectangular pizza: $";
27        cin >> priceRectangular;

28        unitPriceRectangular =
29                    unitPrice(length, width, priceRectangular);
30        unitPriceRound = unitPrice(diameter, priceRound);

31        cout.setf(ios::fixed);
32        cout.setf(ios::showpoint);
33        cout.precision(2);
34        cout << endl
35            << "Round pizza: Diameter = "
36            << diameter << " inches\n"
37            << "Price = $" << priceRound
38            << " Per square inch = $" << unitPriceRound
39            << endl
40            << "Rectangular pizza: Length = "
41            << length << " inches\n"
42            << "Rectangular pizza: Width = "
43            << width << " inches\n"
44            << "Price = $" << priceRectangular
45            << " Per square inch = $" << unitPriceRectangular
46            << endl;

47        if (unitPriceRound < unitPriceRectangular)
48            cout << "The round one is the better buy.\n";
49        else
50            cout << "The rectangular one is the better buy.\n";
51        cout << "Buon Appetito!\n";

52        return 0;
53    }

54    double unitPrice(int diameter, double price)
55    {
56        const double PI = 3.14159;
57        double radius, area;
58
59        radius = diameter/double(2);
60        area = PI * radius * radius;
61        return (price/area);
62    }
```

Display 4.7   Revised Pizza Program (part 3 of 3)

```
63   double unitPrice(int length, int width, double price)
64   {
65       double area = length * width;
66       return (price/area);
67   }
```

SAMPLE DIALOGUE

```
Welcome to the Pizza Consumers Union.
Enter the diameter in inches of a round pizza: 10
Enter the price of a round pizza: $8.50
Enter length and width in inches
of a rectangular pizza: 6 4
Enter the price of a rectangular pizza: $7.55

Round pizza: Diameter = 10 inches
Price = $8.50 Per square inch = $0.11
Rectangular pizza: Length = 6 inches
Rectangular pizza: Width = 4 inches
Price = $7.55 Per square inch = $0.31
The round one is the better buy.
Buon Appetito!
```

DEFAULT ARGUMENTS

You can specify a **default argument** for one or more call-by-value parameters in a function. If the corresponding argument is omitted, then it is replaced by the default argument. For example, the function volume in Display 4.8 computes the volume of a box from its length, width, and height. If no height is given, the height is assumed to be 1. If neither a width nor a height is given, they are both assumed to be 1.

default argument

Note that in Display 4.8 the default arguments are given in the function declaration but not in the function definition. A default argument is given the first time the function is declared (or defined, if that occurs first). Subsequent declarations or a following definition should not give the default arguments again because some compilers will consider this an error even if the arguments given are consistent with the ones given previously.

You may have more than one default argument, but all the default argument positions must be in the rightmost positions. Thus, for the function volume in Display 4.8, we could have given default arguments for the last one, last two, or all three parameters, but any other combinations of default arguments are not allowed.

Display 4.8   Default Arguments

```
1                                              Default arguments
2    #include <iostream>
3    using namespace std;

4    void showVolume(int length, int width = 1, int height = 1);
5    //Returns the volume of a box.
6    //If no height is given, the height is assumed to be 1.
7    //If neither height nor width is given, both are assumed to be 1.

8    int main( )
9    {
10       showVolume(4, 6, 2);                   A default argument should not
11       showVolume(4, 6);                      be given a second time.
12       showVolume(4);

13       return 0;
14   }

15   void showVolume(int length, int width, int height)
16   {
17       cout << "Volume of a box with \n"
18            << "Length = " << length << ", Width = " << width << endl
19            << "and Height = " << height
20            << " is " << length*width*height << endl;
21   }
```

SAMPLE DIALOGUE

```
Volume of a box with
Length = 4, Width = 6
and Height = 2 is 48
Volume of a box with
Length = 4, Width = 6
and Height = 1 is 24
Volume of a box with
Length = 4, Width = 1
and Height = 1 is 4
```

If you have more than one default argument, then when the function is invoked, you must omit arguments starting from the right. For example, note that in Display 4.8 there are two default arguments. When only one argument is omitted, it is assumed to be the last argument. There is no way to omit the second argument in an invocation of volume without also omitting the third argument.

Default arguments are of limited value, but sometimes they can be used to reflect your way of thinking about arguments. Default arguments can only be used with call-by-value parameters. They do not make sense for call-by-reference parameters. Anything you can do with default arguments can be done using overloading, although the default argument version will probably be shorter than the overloading version.

Self-Test Exercises

10. This question has to do with the programming example entitled **Revised Pizza-Buying Program**. Suppose the evil pizza parlor that is always trying to fool customers introduces a square pizza. Can you overload the function unitPrice so that it can compute the price per square inch of a square pizza as well as the price per square inch of a round pizza? Why or why not?

4.3 Testing and Debugging Functions

I beheld the wretch—the miserable monster whom I had created.

Mary Wollstonecraft Shelley, *Frankenstein*

This section reviews some general guidelines for testing programs and functions.

THE assert MACRO

An **assertion** is a statement that is either true or false. Assertions are used to document and check the correctness of programs. Preconditions and postconditions, which we discussed in Chapter 3, are examples of assertions. When expressed precisely and in the syntax of C++, an assertion is simply a Boolean expression. If you convert an assertion to a Boolean expression, then the predefined macro assert can be used to check whether or not your code satisfies the assertion. (A **macro** is very similar to an inline function and is used just like a function is used.)

assertion

macro

The assert macro is used like a void function that takes one call-by-value parameter of type bool. Since an assertion is just a Boolean expression, this means that the argument to assert is an assertion. When the assert macro is invoked, its assertion argument is evaluated. If it evaluates to true, then nothing happens. If the argument evaluates to false, then the program ends and an error message is issued. Thus, calls to the assert macro are a compact way to include error checks within your program.

For example, the following function declaration is taken from Programming Project 3:

```
void computeCoin(int coinValue, int& number, int& amountLeft);
//Precondition: 0 < coinValue < 100; 0 <= amountLeft < 100.
//Postcondition: number has been set equal to the maximum number
```

```
//of coins of denomination coinValue cents that can be obtained
//from amountLeft cents. amountLeft has been decreased by the
//value of the coins, that is, decreased by number*coinValue.
```

You can check that the precondition holds for a function invocation, as shown by the following example:

```
assert((0 < currentCoin) && (currentCoin < 100)
    && (0 <= currentAmountLeft) && (currentAmountLeft < 100));
computeCoin(currentCoin, number, currentAmountLeft);
```

If the precondition is not satisfied, your program will end and an error message will be output.

The assert macro is defined in the library cassert, so any program that uses the assert macro must contain the following:

```
#include <cassert>
```

turning off assert

One advantage of using assert is that you can turn assert invocations off. You can use assert invocations in your program to debug your program, and then turn them off so that users do not get error messages that they might not understand. Doing so reduces the overhead performed by your program. To turn off all the #define NDEBUG assertions in your program, add #define NDEBUG before the include directive, as follows:

#define NDEBUG

```
#define NDEBUG
#include <cassert>
```

Thus, if you insert #define NDEBUG in your program after it is fully debugged, all assert invocations in your program will be turned off. If you later change your program and need to debug it again, you can turn the assert invocations back on by deleting the #define NDEBUG line (or commenting it out).

Not all comment assertions can easily be translated into C++ Boolean expressions. Preconditions are more likely to translate easily than postconditions are. Thus, the assert macro is not a cure-all for debugging your functions, but it can be very useful.

■ **STUBS AND DRIVERS**

driver program

Each function should be designed, coded, and tested as a separate unit from the rest of the program. When you treat each function as a separate unit, you transform one big task into a series of smaller, more manageable tasks. But how do you test a function outside the program for which it is intended? One way is to write a special program to do the testing. For example, Display 4.9 shows a program to test the function unit-Price that was used in the program in Display 4.5. Programs like this one are called **driver programs**. These driver programs are temporary tools and can be quite minimal. They need not have fancy input routines. They need not perform all the calculations the final program will perform. All they need do is obtain reasonable values for

Display 4.9   Driver Program (part 1 of 2)

```
1
2    //Driver program for the function unitPrice.
3    #include <iostream>
4    using namespace std;

5    double unitPrice(int diameter, double price);
6    //Returns the price per square inch of a pizza.
7    //Precondition: The diameter parameter is the diameter of the pizza.
8    //in inches. The price parameter is the price of the pizza.

9    int main( )
10   {
11       double diameter, price;
12       char ans;

13       do
14       {
15           cout << "Enter diameter and price:\n";
16           cin >> diameter >> price;

17           cout << "unit Price is $"
18                << unitPrice(diameter, price) << endl;

19           cout << "Test again? (y/n)";
20           cin >> ans;
21           cout << endl;
22       } while (ans == 'y' || ans == 'Y');

23       return 0;
24   }

25
26   double unitPrice(int diameter, double price)
27   {
28       const double PI = 3.14159;
29       double radius, area;

30       radius = diameter/static_cast<double>(2);
31       area = PI * radius * radius;
32       return (price/area);
33   }
```

Display 4.9   Driver Program (part 2 of 2)

SAMPLE DIALOGUE

```
Enter diameter and price:
13 14.75
Unit price is: $0.111126
Test again? (y/n): y

Enter diameter and price:
2 3.15
Unit price is: $1.00268
Test again? (y/n): n
```

the function arguments in as simple a way as possible—typically from the user—then execute the function and show the result. A loop, as in the program shown in Display 4.9, will allow you to retest the function on different arguments without having to rerun the program.

If you test each function separately, you will find most of the mistakes in your program. Moreover, you will find out which functions contain the mistakes. If you were to test only the entire program, you would probably find out if there were a mistake, but you may have no idea where the mistake is. Even worse, you may think you know where the mistake is, but be wrong.

Once you have fully tested a function, you can use it in the driver program for some other function. Each function should be tested in a program in which it is the only untested function. However, it's fine to use a fully tested function when testing some other function. If a bug is found, you know the bug is in the untested function.

It is sometimes impossible or inconvenient to test a function without using some other function that has not yet been written or has not yet been tested. In this case, you can use a simplified version of the missing or untested function. These simplified functions are called **stubs**. These stubs will not necessarily perform the correct calculation, but they will deliver values that suffice for testing, and they are simple enough that you can have confidence in their performance. For example, the following is a possible stub for the function unitPrice:

stub

```
//A stub. The final function definition must still be written.
double unitPrice(int diameter, double price)
{
    return (9.99);//Not correct but good enough for a stub.
}
```

Using a program outline with stubs allows you to test and then flesh out the basic program outline, rather than write a completely new program to test each function. For this reason, a program outline with stubs is usually the most efficient method of testing. A common approach is to use driver programs to test some basic functions, such as input and output, and then use a program with stubs to test the remaining functions. The stubs are replaced by functions one at a time: One stub is replaced by a complete function and tested; once that function is fully tested, another stub is replaced by a full function definition, and so forth, until the final program is produced.

THE FUNDAMENTAL RULE FOR TESTING FUNCTIONS

Every function should be tested in a program in which every other function in that program has already been fully tested and debugged.

Self-Test Exercises

11. What is the fundamental rule for testing functions? Why is this a good way to test functions?

12. What is a driver program?

13. What is a stub?

14. Write a stub for the function whose declaration is given below. Do not write a whole program, only the stub that would go in a program. (*Hint:* It will be very short.)

```
double rainProb(double pressure, double humidity, double temp);
//Precondition: pressure is the barometric pressure in inches of mercury,
//humidity is the relative humidity as a percentage, and
//temp is the temperature in degrees Fahrenheit.
//Returns the probability of rain, which is a number between 0 and 1.
//(0 means no chance of rain, 1 means rain is 100% certain..)
```

Chapter Summary

- A formal parameter is a kind of placeholder that is filled in with a function argument when the function is called. In C++, there are two methods of performing this substitution, call by value and call by reference, and so there are two basic kinds of parameters: call-by-value parameters and call-by-reference parameters.

- A call-by-value formal parameter is a local variable that is initialized to the value of its corresponding argument when the function is called. Occasionally, it is useful to use a formal call-by-value parameter as a local variable.

- In the call-by-reference substitution mechanism, the argument should be a variable, and the entire variable is substituted for the corresponding argument.

- The way to indicate a call-by-reference parameter in a function definition is to attach the ampersand sign, &, to the type of the formal parameter. (A call-by-value parameter is indicated by the absence of an ampersand.)

- An argument corresponding to a call-by-value parameter cannot be changed by a function call. An argument corresponding to a call-by-reference parameter can be changed by a function call. If you want a function to change the value of a variable, then you must use a call-by-reference parameter.

- You can give multiple definitions to the same function name, provided that the different functions with the same name have different numbers of parameters or some parameter position with differing types, or both. This is called overloading the function name.

- You can specify a default argument for one or more call-by-value parameters in a function. Default arguments are always in the rightmost argument positions.

- The assert macro can be used to help debug your program by checking whether or not assertions hold.

- Every function should be tested in a program in which every other function in that program has already been fully tested and debugged.

ANSWERS TO SELF-TEST EXERCISES

1. A call-by-value parameter is a local variable. When the function is invoked, the value of a call-by-value argument is computed and the corresponding call-by-value parameter (which is a local variable) is initialized to this value.

2. The function will work fine. That is the entire answer, but here is some additional information: The formal parameter inches is a call-by-value parameter and, as discussed in the text, is therefore a local variable. Thus, the value of the argument will not be changed.

3. 10 20 30
   1 2 3
   1 20 3

4. Enter two integers: **5 10**
   In reverse order the numbers are: 5 5

5. void zeroBoth(int& n1, int& n2)
   {
       n1 = 0;
       n2 = 0;
   }

6.
```
void addTax(double taxRate, double& cost)
{
    cost = cost + (taxRate/100.0)*cost;
}
```

The division by 100 is to convert a percentage to a fraction. For example, 10% is 10/100.0, or one-tenth of the cost.

7.
```
par1Value in function call = 111
par2Ref in function call = 222
n1 after function call = 1
n2 after function call = 2  ◄──────── Different
```

8. The one with one parameter would be used because the function call has only one parameter.

9. The first one would be used because it is an exact match, namely, two parameters of type `double`.

10. This cannot be done (at least not in any nice way). The natural ways to represent a square and a round pizza are the same. Each is naturally represented as one number, which is the radius for a round pizza and the length of a side for a square pizza. In either case the function `unitPrice` would need to have one formal parameter of type `double` for the price and one formal parameter of type `int` for the size (either radius or side). Thus, the two function declarations would have the same number and types of formal parameters. (Specifically, they would both have one formal parameter of type `double` and one formal parameter of type `int`.) Thus, the compiler would not be able to decide which definition to use. You can still defeat this evil pizza parlor's strategy by defining two functions, but they will need to have different names.

11. The fundamental rule for testing functions is that every function should be tested in a program in which every other function in that program has already been fully tested and debugged. This is a good way to test a function because if you follow this rule, then when you find a bug, you will know which function contains the bug.

12. A driver program is a program written for the sole purpose of testing a function.

13. A stub is a simplified version of a function that is used in place of the function so that other functions can be tested.

14.
```
//THIS IS JUST A STUB.
double rainProb(double pressure,
                double humidity, double temp)
{
    return 0.25; //Not correct,
                 //but good enough for some testing.
}
```

PROGRAMMING PROJECTS

1. Write a program that converts from 24-hour notation to 12-hour notation. For example, it should convert 14:25 to 2:25 P.M. The input is given as two integers. There should be at least three functions: one for input, one to do the conversion, and one for output. Record the A.M./P.M. information as a value of type char, 'A' for A.M. and 'P' for P.M. Thus, the function for doing the conversions will have a call-by-reference formal parameter of type char to record whether it is A.M. or P.M. (The function will have other parameters as well.) Include a loop that lets the user repeat this computation for new input values again and again until the user says he or she wants to end the program.

2. The area of an arbitrary triangle can be computed using the formula

$$area = \sqrt{s(s-a)(s-b)(s-c)}$$

   where a, b, and c are the lengths of the sides, and s is the semiperimeter.

$$s = (a+b+c)/2$$

   Write a void function that uses five parameters: three value parameters that provide the lengths of the edges, and two reference parameters that compute the area and perimeter (*not the semiperimeter*). Make your function robust. Note that not all combinations of a, b, and c produce a triangle. Your function should produce correct results for legal data and reasonable results for illegal combinations.

3. Write a program that tells what coins to give out for any amount of change from 1 cent to 99 cents. For example, if the amount is 86 cents, the output would be something like the following:

```
86 cents can be given as
3 quarter(s) 1 dime(s) and 1 penny(pennies)
```

   Use coin denominations of 25 cents (quarters), 10 cents (dimes), and 1 cent (pennies). Do not use nickel and half-dollar coins. Your program will use the following function (among others):

```
void computeCoin(int coinValue, int& number, int& amountLeft);
//Precondition: 0 < coinValue < 100; 0 <= amountLeft < 100.
//Postcondition: number has been set equal to the maximum number
//of coins of denomination coinValue cents that can be obtained
//from amountLeft cents. amountLeft has been decreased by the
//value of the coins, that is, decreased by number*coinValue.
```

   For example, suppose the value of the variable amountLeft is 86. Then, after the following call, the value of number will be 3 and the value of amountLeft will be 11 (because if you take three quarters from 86 cents, that leaves 11 cents):

```
computeCoins(25, number, amountLeft);
```

Include a loop that lets the user repeat this computation for new input values until the user says he or she wants to end the program. (*Hint:* Use integer division and the % operator to implement this function.)

4. Write a program that will read in a length in feet and inches and output the equivalent length in meters and centimeters. Use at least three functions: one for input, one or more for calculating, and one for output. Include a loop that lets the user repeat this computation for new input values until the user says he or she wants to end the program. There are 0.3048 meters in a foot, 100 centimeters in a meter, and 12 inches in a foot.

5. Write a program like that of the previous exercise that converts from meters and centimeters into feet and inches. Use functions for the subtasks.

6. (You should do the previous two programming projects before doing this one.) Write a program that combines the functions in the previous two programming projects. The program asks the user if he or she wants to convert from feet and inches to meters and centimeters or from meters and centimeters to feet and inches. The program then performs the desired conversion. Have the user respond by typing the integer 1 for one type of conversion and 2 for the other conversion. The program reads the user's answer and then executes an if-else statement. Each branch of the if-else statement will be a function call. The two functions called in the if-else statement will have function definitions that are very similar to the programs for the previous two programming projects. Thus, they will be fairly complicated function definitions that call other functions. Include a loop that lets the user repeat this computation for new input values until the user says he or she wants to end the program.

7. Write a program that will read in a weight in pounds and ounces and will output the equivalent weight in kilograms and grams. Use at least three functions: one for input, one or more for calculating, and one for output. Include a loop that lets the user repeat this computation for new input values until the user says he or she wants to end the program. There are 2.2046 pounds in a kilogram, 1000 grams in a kilogram, and 16 ounces in a pound.

8. Write a program like that of the previous exercise that converts from kilograms and grams into pounds and ounces. Use functions for the subtasks.

9. (You should do the previous two programming projects before doing this one.) Write a program that combines the functions of the previous two programming projects. The program asks the user if he or she wants to convert from pounds and ounces to kilograms and grams or from kilograms and grams to pounds and ounces. The program then performs the desired conversion. Have the user respond by typing the integer 1 for one type of conversion and 2 for the other. The program reads the user's answer and then executes an if-else statement. Each branch of the if-else statement will be a function call. The two functions called in the if-else statement will have function definitions that are very similar to the programs for the previous two programming projects. Thus, they will be fairly complicated function definitions that call other functions in their function bodies. Include a loop that lets the user repeat this computation for new input values until the user says he or she wants to end the program.

10. (You should do Programming Projects 6 and 9 before doing this programming project.) Write a program that combines the functions of Programming Projects 6 and 9. The program asks the user if he or she wants to convert lengths or weights. If the user chooses lengths, then the program asks the user if he or she wants to convert from feet and inches to meters and centimeters or from meters and centimeters to feet and inches. If the user chooses weights, a similar question about pounds, ounces, kilograms, and grams is asked. The program then performs the desired conversion. Have the user respond by typing the integer 1 for one type of conversion and 2 for the other. The program reads the user's answer and then executes an if-else statement. Each branch of the if-else statement will be a function call. The two functions called in the if-else statement will have function definitions that are very similar to the programs for Programming Projects 6 and 9. Thus, these functions will be fairly complicated function definitions that call other functions; however, they will be very easy to write by adapting the programs you wrote for Programming Projects 6 and 9. Notice that your program will have if-else statements embedded inside of if-else statements, but only in an indirect way. The outer if-else statement will include two function calls, as its two branches. These two function calls will each in turn include an if-else statement, but you need not think about that. They are just function calls and the details are in a black box that you create when you define these functions. If you try to create a four-way branch, you are probably on the wrong track. You should only need to think about two-way branches (even though the entire program does ultimately branch into four cases). Include a loop that lets the user repeat this computation for new input values until the user says he or she wants to end the program.

5 CHAPTER

Arrays

5 Arrays

It is a capital mistake to theorize before one has data.

Sir Arthur Conan Doyle, *Scandal in Bohemia* (Sherlock Holmes)

INTRODUCTION

An *array* is used to process a collection of data all of which is of the same type, such as a list of temperatures or a list of names. This chapter introduces the basics of defining and using arrays in C++ and presents many of the basic techniques used when designing algorithms and programs that use arrays.

You may skip this chapter and read Chapter 6 and most of Chapter 7, which cover classes, before reading this chapter. The only material in those chapters that uses material from this chapter is Section 7.3, which introduces vectors.

5.1 Introduction to Arrays

Suppose we wish to write a program that reads in five test scores and performs some manipulations on these scores. For instance, the program might compute the highest test score and then output the amount by which each score falls short of the highest. The highest score is not known until all five scores are read in. Hence, all five scores must be retained in storage so that after the highest score is computed each score can be compared with it. To retain the five scores, we will need something equivalent to five variables of type int. We could use five individual variables of type int, but five variables are hard to keep track of, and we may later want to change our program to handle 100 scores; certainly, 100 variables are impractical. An array is the perfect solution. An **array** behaves like a list of variables with a uniform naming mechanism that can be declared in a single line of simple code. For example, the names for the five individual variables we need might be score[0], score[1], score[2], score[3], and score[4]. The part that does not change, in this case score, is the name of the array. The part that can change is the integer in the square brackets, [].

array

DECLARING AND REFERENCING ARRAYS

In C++, an array consisting of five variables of type int can be declared as follows:

```
int score[5];
```

This declaration is like declaring the following five variables to all be of type int:

```
score[0], score[1], score[2], score[3], score[4]
```

These individual variables that together make up the array are referred to in a variety of different ways. We will call them **indexed variables**, though they are also sometimes called **subscripted variables** or **elements** of the array. The number in square brackets is called an **index** or a **subscript**. In C++, *indexes are numbered starting with 0, not starting with 1 or any other number except 0*. The number of indexed variables in an array is called the **declared size** of the array, or sometimes simply the **size** of the array. When an array is declared, the size of the array is given in square brackets after the array name. The indexed variables are then numbered (also using square brackets), starting with 0 and ending with the integer that is one less than the size of the array.

indexed variable, subscripted variable, or element

index or subscript

declared size

In our example, the indexed variables were of type int, but an array can have indexed variables of any type. For example, to declare an array with indexed variables of type double, simply use the type name double instead of int in the declaration of the array. All the indexed variables for one array, however, are of the same type. This type is called the **base type** of the array. Thus, in our example of the array score, the base type is int.

base type

You can declare arrays and regular variables together. For example, the following declares the two int variables next and max in addition to the array score:

```
int next, score[5], max;
```

An indexed variable such as score[3] can be used anyplace that an ordinary variable of type int can be used.

Do not confuse the two ways to use the square brackets, [], with an array name. When used in a declaration, such as

```
int score[5];
```

the number enclosed in the square brackets specifies how many indexed variables the array has. When used anywhere else, the number enclosed in the square brackets tells which indexed variable is meant. For example, score[0] through score[4] are indexed variables of the array declared above.

The index inside the square brackets need not be given as an integer constant. You can use any expression in the square brackets as long as the expression evaluates to one of the integers ranging from 0 through the integer one less than the size of the array. For example, the following will set the value of score[3] equal to 99:

```
int n = 2;
score[n + 1] = 99;
```

Although they may look different, score[n + 1] and score[3] are the same indexed variable in the above code, because n + 1 evaluates to 3.

The identity of an indexed variable, such as score[i], is determined by the value of its index, which in this instance is i. Thus, you can write programs that say things like "do such and such to the ith indexed variable," where the value of i is computed by the program. For example, the program in Display 5.1 reads in scores and processes them in the way described at the start of this chapter.

Display 5.1   Program Using an Array

```
1    //Reads in five scores and shows how much each
2    //score differs from the highest score.
3    #include <iostream>
4    using namespace std;

5    int main( )
6    {
7        int i, score[5], max;

8        cout << "Enter 5 scores:\n";
9        cin >> score[0];
10       max = score[0];
11       for (i = 1; i < 5; i++)
12       {
13           cin >> score[i];
14           if (score[i] > max)
15               max = score[i];
16           //max is the largest of the values score[0],..., score[i].
17       }
18       cout << "The highest score is " << max << endl
19            << "The scores and their\n"
20            << "differences from the highest are:\n";
21       for (i = 0; i < 5; i++)
22           cout << score[i] << " off by "
23                << (max - score[i]) << endl;

24       return 0;
25   }
```

SAMPLE DIALOGUE

```
Enter 5 scores:
5 9 2 10 6
The highest score is 10
The scores and their
differences from the highest are:
5 off by 5
9 off by 1
2 off by 8
10 off by 0
6 off by 4
```

Tip

USE for LOOPS WITH ARRAYS

The second for loop in Display 5.1 illustrates a common way to step through an array

```
for (i = 0; i < 5; i++)
    cout << score[i] << " off by "
         << (max - score[i]) << endl;
```

The for statement is ideally suited to array manipulations.

Pitfall

ARRAY INDEXES ALWAYS START WITH ZERO

The indexes of an array always start with 0 and end with the integer that is one less than the size of the array.

Tip

USE A DEFINED CONSTANT FOR THE SIZE OF AN ARRAY

Look again at the program in Display 5.1. It only works for classes that have exactly five students. Most classes do not have exactly five students. One way to make a program more versatile is to use a defined constant for the size of each array. For example, the program in Display 5.1 could be rewritten to use the following defined constant:

```
const int NUMBER_OF_STUDENTS = 5;
```

The line with the array declaration would then be

```
int i, score[NUMBER_OF_STUDENTS], max;
```

Of course, all places in the program that have a 5 for the size of the array should also be changed to have NUMBER_OF_STUDENTS instead of 5. If these changes are made to the program (or better still, if the program had been written this way in the first place), then the program can be revised to work for any number of students by simply changing the one line that defines the constant NUMBER_OF_STUDENTS.

Note that you *cannot* use a variable for the array size, such as the following:

```
cout << "Enter number of students:\n";
cin >> number;
int score[number]; //ILLEGAL ON MANY COMPILERS!
```

Some but not all compilers will allow you to specify an array size with a variable in this way. However, for the sake of portability you should not do so, even if your compiler permits it. (In Chapter 10 we will discuss a different kind of array whose size can be determined when the program is run.)

ARRAY DECLARATION

SYNTAX

Type_Name Array_Name[*Declared_Size*];

EXAMPLES

```
int bigArray[100];
double a[3];
double b[5];
char grade[10], oneGrade;
```

An array declaration of the form shown above will define *Declared_Size* index variables, namely, the indexed variables *Array_Name*[0] through *Array_Name*[*Declared_Size*–1]. Each index variable is a variable of type *Type_Name*.

The array a consists of the indexed variables a[0], a[1], and a[2], all of type double. The array b consists of the indexed variables b[0], b[1], b[2], b[3], and b[4], also all of type double. You can combine array declarations with the declaration of simple variables, such as the variable oneGrade shown above.

ARRAYS IN MEMORY

address

Before discussing how arrays are represented in a computer's memory, let's first see how a simple variable, such as a variable of type int or double, is represented in the computer's memory. A computer's memory consists of a list of numbered locations called *bytes*.[1] The number of a byte is known as its **address**. A simple variable is implemented as a portion of memory consisting of some number of consecutive bytes. The number of bytes is determined by the type of the variable. Thus, a simple variable in memory is described by two pieces of information: an address in memory (giving the location of the first byte for that variable) and the type of the variable, which tells how many bytes of memory the variable requires. When we speak of the *address of a variable*, it is this address we are talking about. When your program stores a value in the variable, what really happens is that the value (coded as zeros and ones) is placed in those bytes of memory that are assigned to that variable. Similarly, when a variable is given as a (call-by-reference) argument to a function, it is the address of the variable that is actually given to the calling function. Now let's move on to discuss how arrays are stored in memory.

arrays in memory

Array indexed variables are represented in memory the same way as ordinary variables, but with arrays there is a little more to the story. The locations of the various

---

[1] A byte consists of eight bits, but the exact size of a byte is not important to this discussion.

array indexed variables are always placed next to one another in memory. For example, consider the following:

```
int a[6];
```

When you declare this array, the computer reserves enough memory to hold six variables of type int. Moreover, the computer always places these variables one after the other in memory. The computer then remembers the address of indexed variable a[0], but it does not remember the address of any other indexed variable. When your program needs the address of some other indexed variable in this array, the computer calculates the address for this other indexed variable from the address of a[0]. For example, if you start at the address of a[0] and count past enough memory for three variables of type int, then you will be at the address of a[3]. To obtain the address of a[3], the computer starts with the address of a[0] (which is a number). The computer then adds the number of bytes needed to hold three variables of type int to the number for the address of a[0]. The result is the address of a[3]. This implementation is diagrammed in Display 5.2. Many of the peculiarities of arrays in C++ can only be understood in terms of these details about memory. For example, in the next pitfall section, we use these details to explain what happens when your program uses an illegal array index.

Pitfall

ARRAY INDEX OUT OF RANGE

The most common programming error made when using arrays is attempting to reference a non-existent array index. For example, consider the following array declaration:

```
int a[6];
```

When using the array a, every index expression must evaluate to one of the integers 0 through 5. For example, if your program contains the indexed variable a[i], the i must evaluate to one of the six integers 0, 1, 2, 3, 4, or 5. If i evaluates to anything else, that is an error. When an index expression evaluates to some value other than those allowed by the array declaration, the index is said to be **out of range** or simply **illegal**. On most systems, the result of an illegal array index is that your program will simply do something wrong, possibly disastrously wrong, and will do so without giving you any warning.

illegal
array index

For example, suppose your system is typical, the array a is declared as above, and your program contains the following:

```
a[i] = 238;
```

Now, suppose the value of i, unfortunately, happens to be 7. The computer proceeds as if a[7] were a legal indexed variable. The computer calculates the address where a[7] would be (if only there were an a[7]) and places the value 238 in that location in memory. However, there is no indexed variable a[7] and the memory that receives this 238 probably belongs to some other variable, maybe a variable named moreStuff. So the value of moreStuff has been unintentionally changed. This situation is illustrated in Display 5.2.

Array indexes most commonly get out of range at the first or last iteration of a loop that processes the array. Thus, it pays to carefully check all array processing loops to be certain that they begin and end with legal array indexes.

Display 5.2   An Array in Memory

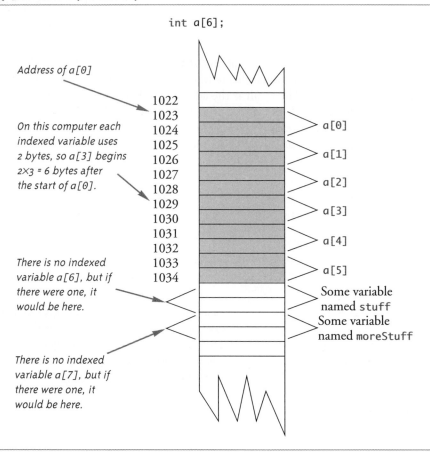

int a[6];

Address of a[0]

On this computer each
indexed variable uses
2 bytes, so a[3] begins
2×3 = 6 bytes after
the start of a[0].

There is no indexed
variable a[6], but if
there were one, it
would be here.

There is no indexed
variable a[7], but if
there were one, it
would be here.

1022
1023
1024
1025
1026
1027
1028
1029
1030
1031
1032
1033
1034

a[0]
a[1]
a[2]
a[3]
a[4]
a[5]
Some variable
named stuff
Some variable
named moreStuff

INITIALIZING ARRAYS

An array can be initialized when it is declared. When initializing the array, the values for the various indexed variables are enclosed in braces and separated with commas. For example:

```
int children[3] = {2, 12, 1};
```

The previous declaration is equivalent to the following code:

```
int children[3];
children[0] = 2;
children[1] = 12;
children[2] = 1;
```

If you list fewer values than there are indexed variables, those values will be used to initialize the first few indexed variables, and the remaining indexed variables will be initialized to a zero of the array base type. In this situation, indexed variables not provided with initializers are initialized to zero. However, arrays with no initializers and other variables declared within a function definition, including the `main` function of a program, are not initialized. Although array indexed variables (and other variables) may sometimes be automatically initialized to zero, you cannot and should not count on it.

If you initialize an array when it is declared, you can omit the size of the array, and the array will automatically be declared to have the minimum size needed for the initialization values. For example, the following declaration

```
int b[] = {5, 12, 11};
```

is equivalent to

```
int b[3] = {5, 12, 11};
```

Self-Test Exercises

1. Describe the difference in the meaning of `int a[5];` and the meaning of `a[4]`. What is the meaning of the `[5]` and `[4]` in each case?

2. In the array declaration

   ```
   double score[5];
   ```

   identify the following:

   a. The array name

   b. The base type

   c. The declared size of the array

   d. The range of values an index accessing this array can have

   e. One of the indexed variables (or elements) of this array

3. Identify any errors in the following array declarations.

   a. `int x[4] = { 8, 7, 6, 4, 3 };`

   b. `int x[] = { 8, 7, 6, 4 };`

c.
```
const int SIZE = 4;

    int x[SIZE];
```

4. What is the output of the following code?

```
char symbol[3] = {'a', 'b', 'c'};
for (int index = 0; index < 3; index++)
    cout << symbol[index];
```

5. What is the output of the following code?

```
double a[3] = {1.1, 2.2, 3.3};
cout << a[0] << " " << a[1] << " " << a[2] << endl;
a[1] = a[2];
cout << a[0] << " " << a[1] << " " << a[2] << endl;
```

6. What is the output of the following code?

```
int i, temp[10];
for (i = 0; i < 10; i++)
    temp[i] = 2*i;
for (i = 0; i < 10; i++)
    cout << temp[i] << " ";
cout << endl;
for (i = 0; i < 10; i = i + 2)
    cout << temp[i] << " ";
```

7. What is wrong with the following piece of code?

```
int sampleArray[10];
for (int index = 1; index <= 10; index++)
    sampleArray[index] = 3*index;
```

8. Suppose we expect the elements of the array a to be ordered so that

$$a[0] \leq a[1] \leq a[2] \leq ...$$

However, to be safe we want our program to test the array and issue a warning in case it turns out that some elements are out of order. The following code is supposed to output such a warning, but it contains a bug. What is it?

```
double a[10];
    <Some code to fill the array a goes here.>
for (int index = 0; index < 10; index++)
    if (a[index] > a[index + 1])
        cout << "Array elements " << index << " and "
             << (index + 1) << " are out of order.";
```

9. Write some C++ code that will fill an array *a* with 20 values of type int read in from the keyboard. You need not write a full program, just the code to do this, but do give the declarations for the array and for all variables.

10. Suppose you have the following array declaration in your program:

```
int yourArray[7];
```

Also, suppose that in your implementation of C++, variables of type int use two bytes of memory. When you run your program, how much memory will this array consume? Suppose that, when you run your program, the system assigns the memory address 1000 to the indexed variable yourArray[0]. What will be the address of the indexed variable yourArray[3]?

5.2 Arrays in Functions

You can use both array indexed variables and entire arrays as arguments to functions. We first discuss array indexed variables as arguments to functions.

INDEXED VARIABLES AS FUNCTION ARGUMENTS

An indexed variable can be an argument to a function in exactly the same way that any variable of the array base type can be an argument. For example, suppose a program contains the following declarations:

```
double i, n, a[10];
```

If myFunction takes one argument of type double, then the following is legal:

```
myFunction(n);
```

Since an indexed variable of the array *a* is also a variable of type double, just like n, the following is equally legal:

```
myFunction(a[3]);
```

An indexed variable can be a call-by-value argument or a call-by-reference argument.

One subtlety applies to indexed variables used as arguments, however. For example, consider the following function call:

```
myFunction(a[i]);
```

If the value of i is 3, then the argument is a[3]. On the other hand, if the value of i is 0, then this call is equivalent to the following:

```
myFunction(a[0]);
```

The indexed expression is evaluated in order to determine exactly which indexed variable is given as the argument.

Self-Test Exercises

11. Consider the following function definition:

```
void tripler(int& n)
{
    n = 3*n;
}
```

Which of the following are acceptable function calls?

```
int a[3] = {4, 5, 6}, number = 2;
tripler(a[2]);
tripler(a[3]);
tripler(a[number]);
tripler(a);
tripler(number);
```

12. What (if anything) is wrong with the following code? The definition of tripler is given in Self-Test Exercise 11.

```
int b[5] = {1, 2, 3, 4, 5};
for (int i = 1; i <= 5; i++)
    tripler(b[i]);
```

ENTIRE ARRAYS AS FUNCTION ARGUMENTS

array parameter

A function can have a formal parameter for an entire array so that when the function is called, the argument that is plugged in for this formal parameter is an entire array. However, a formal parameter for an entire array is neither a call-by-value parameter nor a call-by-reference parameter; it is a new kind of formal parameter referred to as an **array parameter**. Let's start with an example.

The function defined in Display 5.3 has one array parameter, a, which will be replaced by an entire array when the function is called. It also has one ordinary call-by-value parameter (size) that is assumed to be an integer value equal to the size of the array. This function fills its array argument (that is, fills all the array's indexed variables)

Display 5.3   Function with an Array Parameter

FUNCTION DECLARATION

```
void fillUp(int a[], int size);
//Precondition: size is the declared size of the array a.
//The user will type in size integers.
//Postcondition: The array a is filled with size integers
//from the keyboard.
```

FUNCTION DEFINITION

```
void fillUp(int a[], int size)
{
    cout << "Enter " << size << " numbers:\n";
    for (int i = 0; i < size; i++)
        cin >> a[i];
    cout << "The last array index used is " << (size - 1) << endl;
}
```

---

with values typed in from the keyboard; the function then outputs a message to the screen telling the index of the last array index used.

The formal parameter int a[] is an array parameter. The square brackets, with no index expression inside, are what C++ uses to indicate an array parameter. An array parameter is not quite a call-by-reference parameter, but for most practical purposes it behaves very much like a call-by-reference parameter. Let's go through this example in detail to see how an array argument works in this case. (An **array argument** is, of course, an array that is plugged in for an array parameter, such as a[].)

array argument

When the function fillUp is called, it must have two arguments: The first gives an array of integers, and the second should give the declared size of the array. For example, the following is an acceptable function call:

```
int score[5], numberOfScores = 5;
fillUp(score, numberOfScores);
```

This call to fillUp will fill the array score with five integers typed in at the keyboard. Notice that the formal parameter a[] (which is used in the function declaration and the heading of the function definition) is given with square brackets but no index expression. (You may insert a number inside the square brackets for an array parameter, but the compiler will simply ignore the number, so we will not use such numbers in this book.) On the other hand, the argument given in the function call (score, in this example) is given without any square brackets or any index expression.

when to use []

What happens to the array argument score in this function call? Very loosely speaking, the argument score is plugged in for the formal array parameter a in the body of the function, and then the function body is executed. Thus, the function call

```
fillUp(score, numberOfScores);
```

is equivalent to the following code:

```
{
    size = 5;  ◄────────── 5 is the value of
                            numberOfScores
    cout << "Enter " << size << " numbers:\n";
    for (int i = 0; i < size; i++)
        cin >> score[i];
    cout << "The last array index used is " << (size - 1) << endl;
}
```

The formal parameter a is a different kind of parameter from the ones we have seen before now. The formal parameter a is merely a placeholder for the argument score. When the function fillUp is called with score as the array argument, the computer behaves as if a were replaced with the corresponding argument score. When an array is used as an argument in a function call, any action that is performed on the array parameter is performed on the array argument, so the values of the indexed variables of the array argument can be changed by the function. If the formal parameter in the function body is changed (for example, with a cin statement), then the array argument will be changed.

So far it looks as if an array parameter is simply a call-by-reference parameter for an array. That is close to being true, but an array parameter is slightly different from a call-by-reference parameter. To help explain the difference, let's review some details about arrays.

arrays in memory

Recall that an array is stored as a contiguous chunk of memory. For example, consider the following declaration for the array score:

```
int score[5];
```

When you declare this array, the computer reserves enough memory to hold five variables of type int, which are stored one after the other in the computer's memory. The computer does not remember the addresses of each of these five indexed variables; it remembers only the address of indexed variable score[0]. The computer also remembers that score has a total of five indexed variables, all of type int. It does not remember the address in memory of any indexed variable other than score[0]. For example, when your program needs score[3], the computer calculates the address of score[3] from the address of score[0]. The computer knows that score[3] is located three int variables past score[0]. Thus, to obtain the address of score[3], the computer takes the address of score[0] and adds a number that represents the amount of memory used by three int variables; the result is the address of score[3].

Viewed this way, an array has three parts: the address (location in memory) of the first indexed variable, the base type of the array (which determines how much memory each indexed variable uses), and the size of the array (that is, the number of indexed variables). When an array is used as an array argument to a function, only the first of these three parts is given to the function. When an array argument is plugged in for its corresponding formal parameter, all that is plugged in is the address of the array's first indexed variable. The base type of the array argument must match the base type of the formal parameter, so the function also knows the base type of the array. *However, the array argument does not tell the function the size of the array.* When the code in the function body is executed, the computer knows where the array starts in memory and how much memory each indexed variable uses, but (unless you make special provisions) it does not know how many indexed variables the array has. That is why it is critical that you always have another int argument telling the function the size of the array. (That is also why an array parameter is *not* the same as a call-by-reference parameter. You can think of an array parameter as a weak form of call-by-reference parameter in which everything about the array is told to the function except for the size of the array.)[2]

These array parameters may seem a little strange, but they have at least one very nice property as a direct result of their seemingly strange definition. This advantage is best illustrated by again looking at our example of the function fillUp given in Display 5.3. *That same function can be used to fill an array of any size*, as long as the base type of the array is int. For example, suppose you have the following array declarations:

```
int score[5], time[10];
```

The first of the following calls to fillUp fills the array score with five values, and the second fills the array time with ten values:

```
fillUp(score, 5);
fillUp(time, 10);
```

You can use the same function for array arguments of different sizes, because the size is a separate argument.

Different size array arguments can be plugged in for the same array parameter

THE const PARAMETER MODIFIER

When you use an array argument in a function call, the function can change the values stored in the array. This is usually fine. However, in a complicated function definition, you might write code that inadvertently changes one or more of the values stored in an array even though the array should not be changed at all. As a precaution, you can tell the compiler that you do not intend to change the array argument, and the computer will then check to make sure your code does not inadvertently change any of the values in the array. To tell the compiler that an array argument should not be changed by your function, insert the modifier const before the array parameter for that argument

const

---

[2] If you have heard of pointers, this will sound like pointers and indeed an array augment is passed by passing a pointer to its first (zeroth) index variable. We will discuss this in Chapter 10. If you have not yet learned about pointers, you can safely ignore this footnote.

ARRAY FORMAL PARAMETERS AND ARGUMENTS

An argument to a function may be an entire array, but an argument for an entire array is neither a call-by-value argument nor a call-by-reference argument. It is a new kind of argument known as an *array argument*. When an array argument is plugged in for an *array parameter*, all that is given to the function is the address in memory of the first indexed variable of the array argument (the one indexed by 0). The array argument does not tell the function the size of the array. Therefore, when you have an array parameter to a function, you normally must also have another formal parameter of type int that gives the size of the array (as in the example below).

An array argument is like a call-by-reference argument in the following way: If the function body changes the array parameter, then when the function is called, that change is actually made to the array argument. Thus, a function can change the values of an array argument (that is, can change the values of its indexed variables).

The syntax for a function declaration with an array parameter is as follows.

SYNTAX

Type_Returned Function_Name(..., *Base_Type Array_Name*[],...);

EXAMPLE

```
void sumArray(double& sum, double a[], int size);
```

constant array
parameter

position. An array parameter that is modified with a const is called a **constant array parameter**.

For example, the following function outputs the values in an array but does not change the values in the array:

```
void showTheWorld(int a[], int sizeOfa)
//Precondition: sizeOfa is the declared size of the array a.
//All indexed variables of a have been given values.
//Postcondition: The values in a have been written to the screen.
{
    cout << "The array contains the following values:\n";
    for (int i = 0; i < sizeOfa; i++)
        cout << a[i] << " ";
    cout << endl;
}
```

This function will work fine. However, as an added safety measure, you can add the modifier const to the function heading as follows:

```
void showTheWorld(const int a[], int sizeOfa)
```

With the addition of this modifier const, the computer will issue an error message if your function definition contains a mistake that changes any of the values in the array argument. For example, the following is a version of the function showTheWorld that contains a mistake that inadvertently changes the value of the array argument. Fortunately, this version of the function definition includes the modifier const, so that an error message will tell us that the array a has been changed. This error message will help to explain the mistake:

```
void showTheWorld(const int a[], int sizeOfa)
//Precondition: sizeOfa is the declared size of the array a.
//All indexed variables of a have been given values.
//Postcondition: The values in a have been written to the screen.
{
    cout << "The array contains the following values:\n";
    for (int i = 0; i < sizeOfa; a[i]++)
        cout << a[i] << " ";          Mistake, but the compiler
    cout << endl;                     will not catch it unless you
}                                     use the const modifier.
```

If we had not used the const modifier in the above function definition and if we made the mistake shown, the function would compile and run with no error messages. However, the code would contain an infinite loop that continually increments a[0] and writes its new value to the screen.

The problem with this incorrect version of showTheWorld is that the wrong item is incremented in the for loop. The indexed variable a[i] is incremented, but it should be the index i that is incremented. In this incorrect version, the index i starts with the value 0 and that value is never changed. But a[i], which is the same as a[0], is incremented. When the indexed variable a[i] is incremented, that changes a value in the array, and since we included the modifier const, the computer will issue a warning message. That error message should serve as a clue to what is wrong.

You normally have a function declaration in your program in addition to the function definition. When you use the const modifier in a function definition, you must also use it in the function declaration so that the function heading and the function declaration are consistent.

The modifier const can be used with any kind of parameter, but it is normally used only with array parameters and call-by-reference parameters for classes, which are discussed in Chapters 6 and 7.

Pitfall   **INCONSISTENT USE OF const PARAMETERS**

The const parameter modifier is an all-or-nothing proposition. If you use it for one array parameter of a particular type, then you should use it for every other array parameter that has that type and that is not changed by the function. The reason has to do with function calls within function calls. Consider the definition of the function showDifference, which is given below along with the declaration of a function used in the definition:

```
double computeAverage(int a[], int numberUsed);
//Returns the average of the elements in the first numberUsed
//elements of the array a. The array a is unchanged.

void showDifference(const int a[], int numberUsed)
{
    double average = computeAverage(a, numberUsed);
    cout << "Average of the " << numberUsed
         << " numbers = " << average << endl
         << "The numbers are:\n";
    for (int index = 0; index < numberUsed; index++)
        cout << a[index] << " differs from average by "
             << (a[index] - average) << endl;
}
```

The above code will give an error message or warning message with most compilers. The function computeAverage does not change its parameter a. However, when the compiler processes the function definition for showDifference, it will think that computeAverage does (or at least might) change the value of its parameter a. This is because when it is translating the function definition for showDifference, all the compiler knows about the function computeAverage is the function declaration for computeAverage, which does not contain a const to tell the compiler that the parameter a will not be changed. Thus, if you use const with the parameter a in the function showDifference, then you should also use the modifier const with the parameter a in the function computeAverage. The function declaration for computeAverage should be as follows:

```
double computeAverage(const int a[], int numberUsed);
```

FUNCTIONS THAT RETURN AN ARRAY

A function may not return an array in the same way that it returns a value of type int or double. There is a way to obtain something more or less equivalent to a function that returns an array. The thing to do is return a pointer to the array. We will discuss this topic when we discuss the interaction of arrays and pointers in Chapter 10. Until you learn about pointers, you have no way to write a function that returns an array.

Example

PRODUCTION GRAPH

Display 5.4 contains a program that uses an array and a number of array parameters. This program for the Apex Plastic Spoon Manufacturing Company displays a bar graph showing the productivity of each of its four manufacturing plants for any given week. Plants keep separate production figures for each department, such as the teaspoon department, soup spoon department, plain cocktail spoon department, colored cocktail spoon department, and so forth. Moreover, each of the four plants has a different number of departments.

As you can see from the sample dialogue in Display 5.4, the graph uses one asterisk for each 1000 production units. Since output is in units of 1000, it must be scaled by dividing it by 1000. This presents a problem because the computer must display a whole number of asterisks. It cannot display 1.6 asterisks for 1600 units. We therefore round to the nearest thousand. Thus, 1600 will be the same as 2000 and will produce two asterisks.

The array production holds the total production for each of the four plants. In C++, array indexes always start with 0. But since the plants are numbered 1 through 4, rather than 0 through 3, we have placed the total production for plant number n in indexed variable production [n−1]. The total output for plant number 1 will be held in production[0], the figures for plant 2 will be held in production[1], and so forth.

Since the output is in thousands of units, the program will scale the values of the array elements. If the total output for plant number 3 is 4040 units, then the value of production[2] will initially be set to 4040. This value of 4040 will then be scaled to 4 so that the value of production[2] is changed to 4 and four asterisks will be output to represent the output for plant number 3. This scaling is done by the function scale, which takes the entire array production as an argument and changes the values stored in the array.

The function round rounds its argument to the nearest integer. For example, round(2.3) returns 2, and round(2.6) returns 3. The function round was discussed in Chapter 3, in the programming example entitled "A Rounding Function".

round

Display 5.4   **Production Graph Program** *(part 1 of 4)*

```
1   //Reads data and displays a bar graph showing productivity for each plant.
2   #include <iostream>
3   #include <cmath>
4   using namespace std;
5   const int NUMBER_OF_PLANTS = 4;

6   void inputData(int a[], int lastPlantNumber);
7   //Precondition: lastPlantNumber is the declared size of the array a.
8   //Postcondition: For plantNumber = 1 through lastPlantNumber:
9   //a[plantNumber−1] equals the total production for plant number plantNumber.

10  void scale(int a[], int size);
11  //Precondition: a[0] through a[size−1] each has a nonnegative value.
12  //Postcondition: a[i] has been changed to the number of 1000s (rounded to
13  //an integer) that were originally in a[i], for all i such that 0 <= i <= size−1.
```

Display 5.4   Production Graph Program *(part 2 of 4)*

```
14   void graph(const int asteriskCount[], int lastPlantNumber);
15   //Precondition: a[0] through a[lastPlantNumber-1] have nonnegative values.
16   //Postcondition: A bar graph has been displayed saying that plant
17   //number N has produced a[N-1] 1000s of units, for each N such that
18   //1 <= N <= lastPlantNumber

19   void getTotal(int& sum);
20   //Reads nonnegative integers from the keyboard and
21   //places their total in sum.

22   int round(double number);
23   //Precondition: number >= 0.
24   //Returns number rounded to the nearest integer.

25   void printAsterisks(int n);
26   //Prints n asterisks to the screen.

27   int main( )
28   {
29       int production[NUMBER_OF_PLANTS];

30       cout << "This program displays a graph showing\n"
31           << "production for each plant in the company.\n";

32       inputData(production, NUMBER_OF_PLANTS);
33       scale(production, NUMBER_OF_PLANTS);
34       graph(production, NUMBER_OF_PLANTS);
35       return 0;
36   }

37   void inputData(int a[], int lastPlantNumber)
38   {
39       for (int plantNumber = 1;
40                   plantNumber <= lastPlantNumber; plantNumber++)
41       {
42           cout << endl
43               << "Enter production data for plant number "
44               << plantNumber << endl;
45           getTotal(a[plantNumber - 1]);
46       }
47   }

48   void getTotal(int& sum)
49   {
```

Display 5.4   **Production Graph Program** *(part 3 of 4)*

```
50          cout << "Enter number of units produced by each department.\n"
51              << "Append a negative number to the end of the list.\n";

52      sum = 0;
53      int next;
54      cin >> next;
55      while (next >= 0)
56      {
57          sum = sum + next;
58          cin >> next;
59      }

60      cout << "Total = " << sum << endl;
61  }
62
63  void scale(int a[], int size)
64  {
65      for (int index = 0; index < size; index++)
66          a[index] = round(a[index]/1000.0);
67  }

68  int round(double number)
69  {
70      return static_cast<int>(floor(number + 0.5));
71  }

72  void graph(const int asteriskCount[], int lastPlantNumber)
73  {
74      cout << "\nUnits produced in thousands of units:\n";
75      for (int plantNumber = 1;
76              plantNumber <= lastPlantNumber; plantNumber++)
77      {
78          cout << "Plant #" << plantNumber << " ";
79          printAsterisks(asteriskCount[plantNumber - 1]);
80          cout << endl;
81      }
82  }

83  void printAsterisks(int n)
84  {
85      for (int count = 1; count <= n; count++)
86          cout << "*";
87  }
```

Display 5.4   Production Graph Program *(part 4 of 4)*

SAMPLE DIALOGUE

```
This program displays a graph showing
production for each plant in the company.

Enter production data for plant number 1
Enter number of units produced by each department.
Append a negative number to the end of the list.
2000 3000 1000 -1
Total = 6000

Enter production data for plant number 2
Enter number of units produced by each department.
Append a negative number to the end of the list.
2050 3002 1300 -1
Total = 6352

Enter production data for plant number 3
Enter number of units produced by each department.
Append a negative number to the end of the list.
5000 4020 500 4348 -1
Total = 13868

Enter production data for plant number 4
Enter number of units produced by each department.
Append a negative number to the end of the list.
2507 6050 1809 -1
Total = 10366

Units produced in thousands of units:

Plant #1 ******
Plant #2 ******
Plant #3 **************
Plant #4 **********
```

Self-Test Exercises

13. Write a function definition for a function called oneMore, which has a formal parameter for an array of integers and increases the value of each array element by 1. Add any other formal parameters that are needed.

14. Consider the following function definition:

```
void too2(int a[], int howMany)
{
    for (int index = 0; index < howMany; index++)
        a[index] = 2;
}
```

Which of the following are acceptable function calls?

```
int myArray[29];
too2(myArray, 29);
too2(myArray, 10);
too2(myArray, 55);
"Hey too2. Please come over here."
int yourArray[100];
too2(yourArray, 100);
too2(myArray[3], 29);
```

15. Insert **const** before any of the following array parameters that can be changed to constant array parameters.

```
void output(double a[], int size);
//Precondition: a[0] through a[size - 1] have values.
//Postcondition: a[0] through a[size - 1] have been written out.


void dropOdd(int a[], int size);
//Precondition: a[0] through a[size - 1] have values.
//Postcondition: All odd numbers in a[0] through a[size - 1]
//have been changed to 0.
```

16. Write a function named outOfOrder that takes as parameters an array of double and an int parameter named size and returns a value of type int. This function will test this array for being out of order, meaning that the array violates the following condition:

```
a[0] <= a[1] <= a[2] <= ...
```

The function returns –1 if the elements are not out of order; otherwise, it will return the index of the first element of the array that is out of order. For example, consider the declaration

```
double a[10] = {1.2, 2.1, 3.3, 2.5, 4.5,
                7.9, 5.4, 8.7, 9.9, 1.0};
```

In the array above, a[2] and a[3] are the first pair out of order and a[3] is the first element out of order, so the function returns 3. If the array were sorted, the function would return -1.

5.3 Programming with Arrays

*Never trust to general impressions, my boy, but concentrate
yourself upon details.*

Sir Arthur Conan Doyle, *A Case of Identity* (Sherlock Holmes)

This section discusses partially filled arrays and gives a brief introduction to sorting and searching of arrays. This section includes no new material about the C++ language, but does include more practice with C++ array parameters.

PARTIALLY FILLED ARRAYS

Often the exact size needed for an array is not known when a program is written, or the size may vary from one run of the program to another. One common and easy way to handle this situation is to declare the array to be of the largest size the program could possibly need. The program is then free to use as much or as little of the array as is needed.

Partially filled arrays require some care. The program must keep track of how much of the array is used and must not reference any indexed variable that has not been given a value. The program in Display 5.5 illustrates this point. The program reads in a list of golf scores and shows how much each score differs from the average. This program will work for lists as short as one score, as long as ten scores, and of any length in between. The scores are stored in the array score, which has ten indexed variables, but the program uses only as much of the array as it needs. The variable numberUsed keeps track of how many elements are stored in the array. The elements (that is, the scores) are stored in positions score[0] through score[numberUsed - 1]. The details are very similar to what they would be if numberUsed were the declared size of the array and the entire array were used. In particular, the variable numberUsed usually must be an argument to any function that manipulates the partially filled array. Since the argument numberUsed (when used properly) can often ensure that the function will not reference an illegal array index, this sometimes (but not always) eliminates the need for an argument that gives the declared size of the array. For example, the functions showDifference and computeAverage use the argument numberUsed to ensure that only legal array indexes are used. However, the function fillArray needs to know the maximum declared size for the array so that it does not overfill the array.

Tip

DO NOT SKIMP ON FORMAL PARAMETERS

Notice the function fillArray in Display 5.5. When fillArray is called, the declared array size MAX_NUMBER_SCORES is given as one of the arguments, as shown in the following function call from Display 5.5:

```
fillArray(score, MAX_NUMBER_SCORES, numberUsed);
```

You might protest that MAX_NUMBER_SCORES is a globally defined constant and so it could be used in the definition of fillArray without the need to make it an argument. You would be correct, and if we did not use fillArray in any program other than the one in Display 5.5, we could get by without making MAX_NUMBER_SCORES an argument to fillArray. However, fillArray is a generally useful function that you may want to use in several different programs. We do in fact also use the function fillArray in the program in Display 5.6, discussed in the next subsection. In the program in Display 5.6 the argument for the declared array size is a different named global constant. If we had written the global constant MAX_NUMBER_SCORES into the body of the function fillArray, we would not have been able to reuse the function in the program in Display 5.6.

Even if we used fillArray in only one program, it can still be a good idea to make the declared array size an argument to fillArray. Displaying the declared size of the array as an argument reminds us that the function needs this information in a critically important way.

Display 5.5   Partially Filled Array *(part 1 of 3)*

```
1   //Shows the difference between each of a list of golf scores and their average.
2   #include <iostream>
3   using namespace std;
4   const int MAX_NUMBER_SCORES = 10;

5   void fillArray(int a[], int size, int& numberUsed);
6   //Precondition: size is the declared size of the array a.
7   //Postcondition: numberUsed is the number of values stored in a.
8   //a[0] through a[numberUsed-1] have been filled with
9   //nonnegative integers read from the keyboard.

10  double computeAverage(const int a[], int numberUsed);
11  //Precondition: a[0] through a[numberUsed-1] have values; numberUsed > 0.
12  //Returns the average of numbers a[0] through a[numberUsed-1].

13  void showDifference(const int a[], int numberUsed);
14  //Precondition: The first numberUsed indexed variables of a have values.
15  //Postcondition: Gives screen output showing how much each of the first
16  //numberUsed elements of the array a differs from their average.

17  int main( )
18  {
19      int score[MAX_NUMBER_SCORES], numberUsed;

20      cout << "This program reads golf scores and shows\n"
21           << "how much each differs from the average.\n";

22      cout << "Enter golf scores:\n";
```

Display 5.5 Partially Filled Array *(part 2 of 3)*

```
23          fillArray(score, MAX_NUMBER_SCORES, numberUsed);
24          showDifference(score, numberUsed);

25          return 0;
26      }

27      void fillArray(int a[], int size, int& numberUsed)
28      {
29          cout << "Enter up to " << size << " nonnegative whole numbers.\n"
30              << "Mark the end of the list with a negative number.\n";
31          int next, index = 0;
32          cin >> next;
33          while ((next >= 0) && (index < size))
34          {
35              a[index] = next;
36              index++;
37              cin >> next;
38          }
39          numberUsed = index;
40      }

41      double computeAverage(const int a[], int numberUsed)
42      {
43          double total = 0;
44          for (int index = 0; index < numberUsed; index++)
45              total = total + a[index];
46          if (numberUsed > 0)
47          {
48              return (total/numberUsed);
49          }
50          else
51          {
52              cout << "ERROR: number of elements is 0 in computeAverage.\n"
53                  << "computeAverage returns 0.\n";
54              return 0;
55          }
56      }

57      void showDifference(const int a[], int numberUsed)
58      {
59          double average = computeAverage(a, numberUsed);
60          cout << "Average of the " << numberUsed
61              << " scores = " << average << endl
62              << "The scores are:\n";
```

Display 5.5 Partially Filled Array *(part 3 of 3)*

```
63        for (int index = 0; index < numberUsed; index++)
64        cout << a[index] << " differs from average by "
65              << (a[index] - average) << endl;
66    }
```

SAMPLE DIALOGUE

```
This program reads golf scores and shows
how much each differs from the average.
Enter golf scores:
Enter up to 10 nonnegative whole numbers.
Mark the end of the list with a negative number.
69 74 68 -1
Average of the 3 scores = 70.3333
The scores are:
69 differs from average by -1.33333
74 differs from average by 3.66667
68 differs from average by -2.33333
```

Example **SEARCHING AN ARRAY**

A common programming task is to search an array for a given value. For example, the array may contain the student numbers for all students in a given course. To tell whether a particular student is enrolled, the array is searched to see if it contains the student's number. The simple program in Display 5.6 fills an array and then searches the array for values specified by the user. A real application program would be much more elaborate, but this shows all the essentials of the sequential search algorithm. The **sequential search** is the most straightforward searching algorithm you could imagine: The program looks at the array elements in order, first to last, to see if the target number is equal to any of the array elements.

In Display 5.6 the function search is used to search the array. When searching an array, you often want to know more than simply whether or not the target value is in the array. If the target value is in the array, you often want to know the index of the indexed variable holding that target value, since the index may serve as a guide to some additional information about the target value. Therefore, we designed the function search to return an index giving the location of the target value in the array, provided the target value is, in fact, in the array. If the target value is not in the array, search returns -1. Let's look at the function search in a little more detail.

The function search uses a while loop to check the array elements one after the other to see whether any of them equals the target value. The variable found is used as a flag to record whether or not the target element has been found. If the target element is found in the array, found is set to true, which in turn ends the while loop.

sequential search

Display 5.6 Searching an Array *(part 1 of 2)*

```
1    //Searches a partially filled array of nonnegative integers.
2    #include <iostream>
3    using namespace std;
4    const int DECLARED_SIZE = 20;

5    void fillArray(int a[], int size, int& numberUsed);
6    //Precondition: size is the declared size of the array a.
7    //Postcondition: numberUsed is the number of values stored in a.
8    //a[0] through a[numberUsed−1] have been filled with
9    //nonnegative integers read from the keyboard.

10   int search(const int a[], int numberUsed, int target);
11   //Precondition: numberUsed is <= the declared size of a.
12   //Also, a[0] through a[numberUsed −1] have values.
13   //Returns the first index such that a[index] == target,
14   //provided there is such an index; otherwise, returns −1.

15   int main( )
16   {
17       int arr[DECLARED_SIZE], listSize, target;

18       fillArray(arr, DECLARED_SIZE, listSize);

19       char ans;
20       int result;
21       do
22       {
23           cout << "Enter a number to search for: ";
24           cin >> target;

25           result = search(arr, listSize, target);
26           if (result == −1)
27               cout << target << " is not on the list.\n";
28           else
29               cout << target << " is stored in array position "
30                       << result << endl
31                       << "(Remember: The first position is 0.)\n";

32           cout << "Search again?(y/n followed by Return): ";
33           cin >> ans;
34       } while ((ans != 'n') && (ans != 'N'));
35       cout << "End of program.\n";
36       return 0;
37   }

38   void fillArray(int a[], int size, int& numberUsed)
39   <The rest of the definition of fillArray is given in Display 5.5>
```

Display 5.6 Searching an Array *(part 2 of 2)*

```
40    int search(const int a[], int numberUsed, int target)
41    {
42        int index = 0;
43        bool found = false;
44        while ((!found) && (index < numberUsed))
45        if (target == a[index])
46            found = true;
47        else
48            index++;

49        if (found)
50            return index;
51        else
52            return -1;
53    }
```

SAMPLE DIALOGUE

```
Enter up to 20 nonnegative whole numbers.
Mark the end of the list with a negative number.
10 20 30 40 50 60 70 80 -1
Enter a number to search for: 10
10 is stored in array position 0
(Remember: The first position is 0.)
Search again?(y/n followed by Return): y
Enter a number to search for: 40
40 is stored in array position 3
(Remember: The first position is 0.)
Search again?(y/n followed by Return): y
Enter a number to search for: 42
42 is not on the list.
Search again?(y/n followed by Return): n
End of program.
```

Example   **SORTING AN ARRAY**

One of the most widely encountered programming tasks, and certainly the most thoroughly studied, is sorting a list of values, such as a list of sales figures that must be sorted from lowest to highest or from highest to lowest, or a list of words that must be sorted into alphabetical order. This example describes a function called sort that will sort a partially filled array of numbers so that they are ordered from smallest to largest.

The procedure sort has one array parameter, a. The array a will be partially filled, so there is an additional formal parameter called numberUsed that tells how many array positions are used. Thus, the declaration and precondition for the function sort are as follows:

```
void sort(int a[], int numberUsed);
//Precondition: numberUsed <= declared size of the array a.
//The array elements a[0] through a[numberUsed-1] have values.
```

The function sort rearranges the elements in array a so that after the function call is completed the elements are sorted as follows:

$$a[0] \leq a[1] \leq a[2] \leq \ldots \leq a[numberUsed - 1]$$

The algorithm we use to do the sorting is called *selection sort*. It is one of the easiest of the sorting algorithms to understand.

selection sort

One way to design an algorithm is to rely on the definition of the problem. In this case the problem is to sort an array a from smallest to largest. That means rearranging the values so that $a[0]$ is the smallest, $a[1]$ the next smallest, and so forth. That definition yields an outline for the **selection sort** algorithm:

```
for (int index = 0; index < numberUsed; index++)
      Place the indexth smallest element in a[index]
```

There are many ways to realize this general approach. The details could be developed using two arrays and copying the elements from one array to the other in sorted order, but one array should be both adequate and economical. Therefore, the function sort uses only the one array containing the values to be sorted. The function sort rearranges the values in the array a by interchanging pairs of values. Let us go through a concrete example so that you can see how the algorithm works.

Consider the array shown in Display 5.7. The algorithm will place the smallest value in $a[0]$. The smallest value is the value in $a[3]$, so the algorithm interchanges the values of $a[0]$ and $a[3]$. The algorithm then looks for the next-smallest element. The value in $a[0]$ is now the smallest element, and so the next-smallest element is the smallest of the remaining elements $a[1]$, $a[2]$, $a[3], \ldots, a[9]$. In the example in Display 5.7 the next-smallest element is in $a[5]$, so the algorithm interchanges the values of $a[1]$ and $a[5]$. This positioning of the second-smallest element is illustrated in the fourth and fifth array pictures in Display 5.7. The algorithm then positions the third-smallest element, and so forth. As the sorting proceeds, the beginning array elements are set equal to the correct sorted values. The sorted portion of the array grows by adding elements one after the other from the elements in the unsorted end of the array. Notice that the algorithm need not do anything with the value in the last indexed variable, $a[9]$. Once the other elements are positioned correctly, $a[9]$ must also have the correct value. After all, the correct value for $a[9]$ is the smallest value left to be moved, and the only value left to be moved is the value that is already in $a[9]$.

The definition of the function sort, included in a demonstration program, is given in Display 5.8. sort uses the function indexOfSmallest to find the index of the smallest element in the unsorted end of the array, and then it does an interchange to move this next-smallest element down into the sorted part of the array.

The function swapValues, shown in Display 5.8, is used to interchange the values of indexed variables. For example, the following call will interchange the values of a[0] and a[3]:

```
swapValues(a[0], a[3]);
```

The function swapValues was explained in Chapter 4.

Display 5.7   Selection Sort

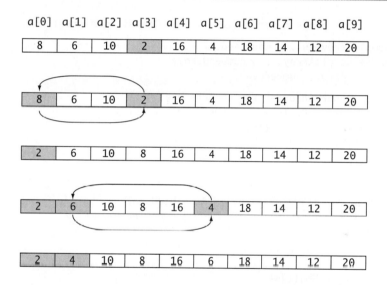

Display 5.8   Sorting an Array (part 1 of 3)

```
1   //Tests the procedure sort.
2   #include <iostream>
3   using namespace std;

4   void fillArray(int a[], int size, int& numberUsed);
5   //Precondition: size is the declared size of the array a.
6   //Postcondition: numberUsed is the number of values stored in a.
7   //a[0] through a[numberUsed - 1] have been filled with
8   //nonnegative integers read from the keyboard.
9   void sort(int a[], int numberUsed);
10  //Precondition: numberUsed <= declared size of the array a.
```

Display 5.8   Sorting an Array *(part 2 of 3)*

```
11    //The array elements a[0] through a[numberUsed – 1] have values.
12    //Postcondition: The values of a[0] through a[numberUsed – 1] have
13    //been rearranged so that a[0] <= a[1] <= ... <= a[numberUsed – 1].

14    void swapValues(int& v1, int& v2);
15    //Interchanges the values of v1 and v2.

16    int indexOfSmallest(const int a[], int startIndex, int numberUsed);
17    //Precondition: 0 <= startIndex < numberUsed. Reference array elements
18    //have values. Returns the index i such that a[i] is the smallest of the
19    //values a[startIndex], a[startIndex + 1], ..., a[numberUsed – 1].

20    int main( )
21    {
22        cout << "This program sorts numbers from lowest to highest.\n";

23        int sampleArray[10], numberUsed;
24        fillArray(sampleArray, 10, numberUsed);
25        sort(sampleArray, numberUsed);

26        cout << "In sorted order the numbers are:\n";
27        for (int index = 0; index < numberUsed; index++)
28            cout << sampleArray[index] << " ";
29        cout << endl;

30        return 0;
31    }

32    void fillArray(int a[], int size, int& numberUsed)
33                    <The rest of the definition of fillArray is given in Display 5.5.>


34    void sort(int a[], int numberUsed)
35    {
36        int indexOfNextSmallest;
37        for (int index = 0; index < numberUsed – 1; index++)
38        {//Place the correct value in a[index]:
39            indexOfNextSmallest =
40                        indexOfSmallest(a, index, numberUsed);
41            swapValues(a[index], a[indexOfNextSmallest]);
42            //a[0] <= a[1] <=...<= a[index] are the smallest of the original array
43            //elements. The rest of the elements are in the remaining positions.
44        }
45    }

46    void swapValues(int& v1, int& v2)
47    {
48        int temp;
49        temp = v1;
50        v1 = v2;
```

Display 5.8 **Sorting an Array** *(part 3 of 3)*

```
51        v2 = temp;
52   }
53

54   int indexOfSmallest(const int a[], int startIndex, int numberUsed)
55   {
56        int min = a[startIndex],
57            indexOfMin = startIndex;
58        for (int index = startIndex + 1; index < numberUsed; index++)
59            if (a[index] < min)
60            {
61                min = a[index];
62                indexOfMin = index;
63                //min is the smallest of a[startIndex] through a[index]
64            }

65        return indexOfMin;
66   }
```

SAMPLE DIALOGUE

```
This program sorts numbers from lowest to highest.
Enter up to 10 nonnegative whole numbers.
Mark the end of the list with a negative number.
80 30 50 70 60 90 20 30 40 -1
In sorted order the numbers are:
20 30 30 40 50 60 70 80 90
```

Self-Test Exercises

17. Write a program that will read up to ten nonnegative integers into an array called **number-Array** and then write the integers back to the screen. For this exercise you need not use any functions. This is just a toy program and can be very minimal.

18. Write a program that will read up to ten letters into an array and write the letters back to the screen in the reverse order. For example, if the input is

    abcd.

    then the output should be

    dcba

Use a period as a sentinel value to mark the end of the input. Call the array letterBox. For this exercise you need not use any functions. This is just a toy program and can be very minimal.

19. Below is the declaration for an alternative version of the function search defined in Display 5.6. In order to use this alternative version of the search function we would need to rewrite the program slightly, but for this exercise all you need do is write the function definition for this alternative version of search.

```
bool search(const int a[], int numberUsed,
                           int target, int& where);
//Precondition: numberUsed is <= the declared size of the
//array a. Also, a[0] through a[numberUsed -1] have values.
//Postcondition: If target is one of the elements a[0]
//through a[numberUsed - 1], then this function returns
//true and sets the value of where so that a[where] ==
//target; otherwise, this function returns false and the
//value of where is unchanged.
```

5.4 Multidimensional Arrays

C++ allows you to declare arrays with more than one index. This section describes these multidimensional arrays.

MULTIDIMENSIONAL ARRAY BASICS

array declarations indexed variables

It is sometimes useful to have an array with more than one index, and this is allowed in C++. The following declares an array of characters called page. The array page has two indexes: The first index ranges from 0 to 29 and the second from 0 to 99.

```
char page[30][100];
```

The indexed variables for this array each have two indexes. For example, page[0][0], page[15][32], and page[29][99] are three of the indexed variables for this array. Note that each index must be enclosed in its own set of square brackets. As was true of the one-dimensional arrays we have already seen, each indexed variable for a multidimensional array is a variable of the base type.

An array may have any number of indexes, but perhaps the most common number of indexes is two. A two-dimensional array can be visualized as a two dimensional display with the first index giving the row and the second index giving the column. For example, the array indexed variables of the two-dimensional array page can be visualized as follows:

```
page[0][0], page[0][1], ..., page[0][99]
page[1][0], page[1][1], ..., page[1][99]
page[2][0], page[2][1], ..., page[2][99]
            .
            .
            .
page[29][0], page[29][1], ..., page[29][99]
```

You might use the array page to store all the characters on a page of text that has thirty lines (numbered 0 through 29) and 100 characters on each line (numbered 0 through 99).

In C++, a two-dimensional array, such as page, is actually an array of arrays. The array page above is actually a one-dimensional array of size 30, whose base type is a one-dimensional array of characters of size 100. Normally, this need not concern you, and you can usually act as if the array page were actually an array with two indexes (rather than an array of arrays, which is harder to keep track of). There is, however, at least one situation in which a two-dimensional array looks very much like an array of arrays, namely, when you have a function with an array parameter for a two-dimensional array, which is discussed in the next subsection.

MULTIDIMENSIONAL ARRAY DECLARATION

SYNTAX

Type Array_Name[*Size_Dim_1*][*Size_Dim_2*]...[*Size_Dim_Last*];

EXAMPLES

```
char page[30][100];
int matrix[2][3];
double threeDPicture[10][20][30];
```

An array declaration of the form shown above will define one indexed variable for each combination of array indexes. For example, the second of the above sample declarations defines the following six indexed variables for the array matrix:

```
matrix[0][0], matrix[0][1], matrix[0][2],
matrix[1][0], matrix[1][1], matrix[1][2]
```

■ MULTIDIMENSIONAL ARRAY PARAMETERS

The following declaration of a two-dimensional array actually declares a one-dimensional array of size 30 whose base type is a one-dimensional array of characters of size 100.

```
char page[30][100];
```

Viewing a two-dimensional array as an array of arrays will help you to understand how C++ handles parameters for multidimensional arrays.

For example, the following is a function that takes an array, like page, and prints it to the screen:

```cpp
void displayPage(const char p[][100], int sizeDimension1)
{
    for (int index1 = 0; index1 < sizeDimension1; index1++)
    {//Printing one line:
        for (int index2 = 0; index2 < 100; index2++)
            cout << p[index1][index2];
        cout << endl;
    }
}
```

Notice that with a two-dimensional array parameter, the size of the first dimension is not given, so we must include an int parameter to give the size of this first dimension. (As with ordinary arrays, the compiler will allow you to specify the first dimension by placing a number within the first pair of square brackets. However, such a number is only a comment; the compiler ignores the number.) The size of the second dimension (and all other dimensions if there are more than two) is given after the array parameter, as shown for the parameter

```cpp
const char p[][100]
```

If you realize that a multidimensional array is an array of arrays, then this rule begins to make sense. Since the two-dimensional array parameter

```cpp
const char p[][100]
```

is a parameter for an array of arrays, the first dimension is really the index of the array and is treated just like an array index for an ordinary, one-dimensional array. The second dimension is part of the description of the base type, which is an array of characters of size 100.

MULTIDIMENSIONAL ARRAY PARAMETERS

When a multidimensional array parameter is given in a function heading or function declaration, the size of the first dimension is not given, but the remaining dimension sizes must be given in square brackets. Since the first dimension size is not given, you usually need an additional parameter of type int that gives the size of this first dimension. Below is an example of a function declaration with a two-dimensional array parameter p:

```cpp
void getPage(char p[][100], int sizeDimension1);
```

Example

TWO-DIMENSIONAL GRADING PROGRAM

Display 5.9 contains a program that uses a two-dimensional array named grade to store and then display the grade records for a small class. The class has four students, and the records include three quizzes. Display 5.10 illustrates how the array grade is used to store data. The first array index is used to designate a student, and the second array index is used to designate a quiz. Since the students and quizzes are numbered starting with 1 rather than 0, we must subtract 1 from the student number and subtract 1 from the quiz number to obtain the indexed variable that stores a particular quiz score. For example, the score that student number 4 received on quiz number 1 is recorded in grade[3][0].

Our program also uses two ordinary one-dimensional arrays. The array stAve will be used to record the average quiz score for each of the students. For example, the program will set stAve[0] equal to the average of the quiz scores received by student 1, stAve[1] equal to the average of the quiz scores received by student 2, and so forth. The array quizAve will be used to record the average score for each quiz. For example, the program will set quizAve[0] equal to the average of all the student scores for quiz 1, quizAve[1] will record the average score for quiz 2, and so forth. Display 5.10 illustrates the relationship between the arrays grade, stAve, and quizAve. This display shows some sample data for the array grade. These data, in turn, determine the values that the program stores in stAve and in quizAve. Display 5.11 also shows these values, which the program computes for stAve and quizAve.

The complete program for filling the array grade and then computing and displaying both the student averages and the quiz averages is shown in Display 5.9. In that program we have declared array dimensions as global named constants. Since the procedures are particular to this program and could not be reused elsewhere, we have used these globally defined constants in the procedure bodies, rather than having parameters for the size of the array dimensions. Since it is routine, the display does not show the code that fills the array.

Display 5.9   Two-Dimensional Array *(part 1 of 3)*

```
1   //Reads quiz scores for each student into the two-dimensional array grade (but the input
2   //code is not shown in this display). Computes the average score for each student and
3   //the average score for each quiz. Displays the quiz scores and the averages.
4   #include <iostream>
5   #include <iomanip>
6   using namespace std;
7   const int NUMBER_STUDENTS = 4, NUMBER_QUIZZES = 3;

8   void computeStAve(const int grade[][NUMBER_QUIZZES], double stAve[]);
9   //Precondition: Global constants NUMBER_STUDENTS and NUMBER_QUIZZES
10  //are the dimensions of the array grade. Each of the indexed variables
11  //grade[stNum-1, quizNum-1] contains the score for student stNum on quiz quizNum.
12  //Postcondition: Each stAve[stNum-1] contains the average for student number stNum.
13
```

Display 5.9   Two-dimensional Array *(part 2 of 3)*

```
14   void computeQuizAve(const int grade[][NUMBER_QUIZZES], double quizAve[]);
15   //Precondition: Global constants NUMBER_STUDENTS and NUMBER_QUIZZES
16   //are the dimensions of the array grade. Each of the indexed variables
17   //grade[stNum-1, quizNum-1] contains the score for student stNum on quiz quizNum.
18   //Postcondition: Each quizAve[quizNum-1] contains the average for quiz numbered
19   //quizNum.

20   void display(const int grade[][NUMBER_QUIZZES],
21                            const double stAve[], const double quizAve[]);
22   //Precondition: Global constants NUMBER_STUDENTS and NUMBER_QUIZZES are the
23   //dimensions of the array grade. Each of the indexed variables grade[stNum-1,
24   //quizNum-1] contains the score for student stNum on quiz quizNum. Each
25   //stAve[stNum-1] contains the average for student stNum. Each quizAve[quizNum-1]
26   //contains the average for quiz numbered quizNum.
27   //Postcondition: All the data in grade, stAve, and quizAve have been output.

28   int main( )
29   {
30       int grade[NUMBER_STUDENTS][NUMBER_QUIZZES];
31       double stAve[NUMBER_STUDENTS];
32       double quizAve[NUMBER_QUIZZES];
33
34           <The code for filling the array grade goes here, but is not shown.>
35
36       computeStAve(grade, stAve);
37       computeQuizAve(grade, quizAve);
38       display(grade, stAve, quizAve);
39       return 0;
40   }

41   void computeStAve(const int grade[][NUMBER_QUIZZES], double stAve[])
42   {
43       for (int stNum = 1; stNum <= NUMBER_STUDENTS; stNum++)
44       {//Process one stNum:
45           double sum = 0;
46           for (int quizNum = 1; quizNum <= NUMBER_QUIZZES; quizNum++)
47               sum = sum + grade[stNum-1][quizNum-1];
48           //sum contains the sum of the quiz scores for student number stNum.
49           stAve[stNum-1] = sum/NUMBER_QUIZZES;
50           //Average for student stNum is the value of stAve[stNum-1]
51       }
52   }

53   void computeQuizAve(const int grade[][NUMBER_QUIZZES], double quizAve[])
```

Display 5.9   Two-dimensional Array *(part 3 of 3)*

```
54   {
55        for (int quizNum = 1; quizNum <= NUMBER_QUIZZES; quizNum++)
56        {//Process one quiz (for all students):
57            double sum = 0;
58            for (int stNum = 1; stNum <= NUMBER_STUDENTS; stNum++)
59                sum = sum + grade[stNum-1][quizNum-1];
60            //sum contains the sum of all student scores on quiz number quizNum.
61            quizAve[quizNum-1] = sum/NUMBER_STUDENTS;
62            //Average for quiz quizNum is the value of quizAve[quizNum-1]
63        }
64   }

65   void display(const int grade[][NUMBER_QUIZZES],
66                             const double stAve[], const double quizAve[])
67   {
68        cout.setf(ios::fixed);
69        cout.setf(ios::showpoint);
70        cout.precision(1);

71        cout << setw(10) << "Student"
72             << setw(5) << "Ave"
73             << setw(15) << "Quizzes\n";
74        for (int stNum = 1; stNum <= NUMBER_STUDENTS; stNum++)
75        {//Display for one stNum:
76            cout << setw(10) << stNum
77                 << setw(5) << stAve[stNum-1] << " ";
78            for (int quizNum = 1; quizNum <= NUMBER_QUIZZES; quizNum++)
79                cout << setw(5) << grade[stNum-1][quizNum-1];
80            cout << endl;
81        }

82        cout << "Quiz averages = ";
83        for (int quizNum = 1; quizNum <= NUMBER_QUIZZES; quizNum++)
84            cout << setw(5) << quizAve[quizNum-1];
85        cout << endl;
86   }
```

SAMPLE DIALOGUE

```
<The dialogue for filling the array grade is not shown.>
Student     Ave         Quizzes
      1     10.0        10    10    10
      2      1.0         2     0     1
      3      7.7         8     6     9
      4      7.3         8     4    10
Quiz Average =          7.0   5.0   7.5
```

Display 5.10   The Two-Dimensional Array grade

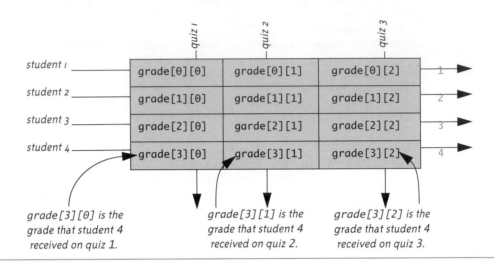

grade[3][0] is the
grade that student 4
received on quiz 1.

grade[3][1] is the
grade that student 4
received on quiz 2.

grade[3][2] is the
grade that student 4
received on quiz 3.

Display 5.11   The Two-Dimensional Array grade

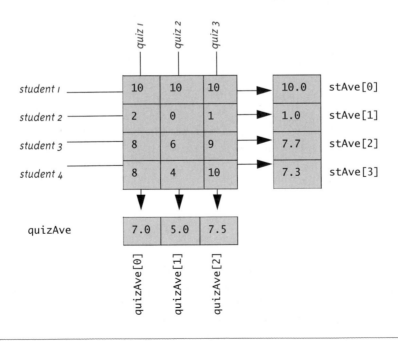

Self-Test Exercises

20. What is the output produced by the following code?

```
int myArray[4][4], index1, index2;
for (index1 = 0; index1 < 4; index1++)
    for (index2 = 0; index2 < 4; index2++)
        myArray[index1][index2] = index2;
for (index1 = 0; index1 < 4; index1++)
{
    for (index2 = 0; index2 < 4; index2++)
        cout << myArray[index1][index2] << " ";
    cout << endl;
}
```

21. Write code that will fill the array a (declared below) with numbers typed in at the keyboard. The numbers will be input five per line, on four lines (although your solution need not depend on how the input numbers are divided into lines).

```
int a[4][5];
```

22. Write a function definition for a void function called echo such that the following function call will echo the input described in Self-Test Exercise 21, and will echo it in the same format as we specified for the input (that is, four lines of five numbers per line):

```
echo(a, 4);
```

Chapter Summary

- An array can be used to store and manipulate a collection of data that is all of the same type.

- The indexed variables of an array can be used just like any other variables of the base type of the array.

- A for loop is a good way to step through the elements of an array and perform some program action on each indexed variable.

- The most common programming error made when using arrays is attempting to access a nonexistent array index. Always check the first and last iterations of a loop that manipulates an array to make sure it does not use an index that is illegally small or illegally large.

- An array formal parameter is neither a call-by-value parameter nor a call-by-reference parameter, but a new kind of parameter. An array parameter is similar to a call-by-reference parameter in that any change that is made to the formal parameter in the body of the function will be made to the array argument when the function is called.

- The indexed variables for an array are stored next to each other in the computer's memory so that the array occupies a contiguous portion of memory. When the array is passed as an argument to a function, only the address of the first indexed variable (the one numbered 0) is given to the calling function. Therefore, a function with an array parameter usually needs another formal parameter of type int to give the size of the array.

- When using a partially filled array, your program needs an additional variable of type int to keep track of how much of the array is being used.

- To tell the compiler that an array argument should not be changed by your function, you can insert the modifier const before the array parameter for that argument position. An array parameter that is modified with a const is called a constant array parameter.

- If you need an array with more than one index, you can use a multidimensional array, which is actually an array of arrays.

ANSWERS TO SELF-TEST EXERCISES

1. The statement int a[5]; is a declaration, in which 5 is the number of array elements. The expression a[4] is an access into the array defined by the previous statement. The access is to the element having index 4, which is the fifth (and last) array element.

2. a. score

   b. double

   c. 5

   d. 0 through 4

   e. Any of score[0], score[1], score[2], score[3], score[4]

3. a. One too many initializers

   b. Correct. The array size is 4.

   c. Correct. The array size is 4.

4. abc

5. 1.1 2.2 3.3
   1.1 3.3 3.3

   (Remember that the indexes start with 0, not 1.)

6. 0 2 4 6 8 10 12 14 16 18
   0 4 8 12 16

7. The indexed variables of sampleArray are sampleArray[0] through sampleArray[9], but this piece of code tries to fill sampleArray[1] through sampleArray[10]. The index 10 in sampleArray[10] is out of range.

8. There is an index out of range. When `index` is equal to 9, `index + 1` is equal to 10, so `a[index + 1]`, which is the same as `a[10]`, has an illegal index. The loop should stop with one fewer iteration. To correct the code, change the first line of the `for` loop to

```
for (int index = 0; index < 9; index++)
```

9.
```
int i, a[20];
cout << "Enter 20 numbers:\n";
for (i = 0; i < 20; i++)
    cin >> a[i];
```

10. The array will consume 14 bytes of memory. The address of the indexed variable `yourArray[3]` is 1006.

11. The following function calls are acceptable:

```
tripler(a[2]);
tripler(a[number]);
tripler(number);
```

The following function calls are incorrect:

```
tripler(a[3]);
tripler(a);
```

The first one has an illegal index. The second has no indexed expression at all. You cannot use an entire array as an argument to `tripler`, as in the second call. The section **Entire Arrays as Function Arguments** discusses a different situation in which you can use an entire array as an argument.

12. The loop steps through indexed variables `b[1]` through `b[5]`, but 5 is an illegal index for the array `b`. The indexes are 0, 1, 2, 3, and 4. The correct version of the code is given below:

```
int b[5] = {1, 2, 3, 4, 5};
for (int i = 0; i < 5; i++)
    tripler(b[i]);
```

13.
```
void oneMore(int a[], int size)
//Precondition: size is the declared size of the array a.
//a[0] through a[size-1] have been given values.
//Postcondition: a[index] has been increased by 1
//for all indexed variables of a.
{
    for (int index = 0; index < size; index++)
        a[index] = a[index] + 1;
}
```

14. The following function calls are all acceptable:

```
too2(myArray, 29);
too2(myArray, 10);
too2(yourArray, 100);
```

The call

```
too2(myArray, 10);
```

is legal, but will fill only the first ten indexed variables of myArray. If that is what is desired, the call is acceptable.

The following function calls are all incorrect:

```
too2(myArray, 55);
"Hey too2. Please come over here."
too2(myArray[3], 29);
```

The first of these is incorrect because the second argument is too large, the second because it is missing a final semicolon (and for other reasons), and the third because it uses an indexed variable for an argument where it should use the entire array.

15. You can make the array parameter in output a constant parameter, since there is no need to change the values of any indexed variables of the array parameter. You cannot make the parameter in dropOdd a constant parameter because it may have the values of some of its indexed variables changed.

```
void output(const double a[], int size);
//Precondition: a[0] through a[size – 1] have values.
//Postcondition: a[0] through a[size – 1] have been written out.

void dropOdd(int a[], int size);
//Precondition: a[0] through a[size – 1] have values.
//Postcondition: All odd numbers in a[0] through a[size – 1]
//have been changed to 0.
```

16.
```
int outOfOrder(double array[], int size)
{
    for(int i = 0; i < size – 1; i++)
        if (array[i] > array[i+1])//fetch a[i+1] for each i.
            return i+1;
    return –1;
}
```

17.
```
#include <iostream>
using namespace std;
const int DECLARED_SIZE = 10;

int main( )
```

```
    {
        cout << "Enter up to ten nonnegative integers.\n"
             << "Place a negative number at the end.\n";
        int numberArray[DECLARED_SIZE], next, index = 0;
        cin >> next;
        while ( (next >= 0) && (index < DECLARED_SIZE) )
        {
            numberArray[index] = next;
            index++;
            cin >> next;
        }

        int numberUsed = index;
        cout << "Here they are back at you:";
        for (index = 0; index < numberUsed; index++)
            cout << numberArray[index] << " ";
        cout << endl;
        return 0;
    }

18. #include <iostream>
    using namespace std;
    const int DECLARED_SIZE = 10;

    int main( )
    {
        cout << "Enter up to ten letters"
             << " followed by a period:\n";
        char letterBox[DECLARED_SIZE], next;
        int index = 0;
        cin >> next;
        while ( (next != '.') && (index < DECLARED_SIZE) )
        {
            letterBox[index] = next;
            index++;
            cin >> next;
        }

        int numberUsed = index;
        cout << "Here they are backwards:\n";
        for (index = numberUsed-1; index >= 0; index--)
            cout << letterBox[index];
        cout << endl;
        return 0;
    }
```

19.
```
bool search(const int a[], int numberUsed,
                         int target, int& where)
{
    int index = 0;
    bool found = false;
    while ((!found) && (index < numberUsed))
    if (target == a[index])
        found = true;
    else
        index++;
    //If target was found, then
    //found == true and a[index] == target.

    if (found)
        where = index;
    return found;
}
```

20.
```
0 1 2 3
0 1 2 3
0 1 2 3
0 1 2 3
```

21.
```
int a[4][5];
int index1, index2;
for (index1 = 0; index1 < 4; index1++)
    for (index2 = 0; index2 < 5; index2++)
        cin >> a[index1][index2];
```

22.
```
void echo(const int a[][5], int sizeOfa)
//Outputs the values in the array a on sizeOfa lines
//with 5 numbers per line.
{
    for (int index1 = 0; index1 < sizeOfa; index1++)
    {
        for (int index2 = 0; index2 < 5; index2++)
            cout << a[index1][index2] << " ";
        cout << endl;
    }
}
```

PROGRAMMING PROJECTS

1. Write a program that reads in the average monthly rainfall for a city for each month of the year and then reads in the actual monthly rainfall for each of the previous 12 months. The program then prints out a nicely formatted table showing the rainfall for each of the previous 12 months as well as how much above or below average the rainfall was for each month. The average monthly rainfall is given for the months January, February, and so

forth, in order. To obtain the actual rainfall for the previous 12 months, the program first asks what the current month is and then asks for the rainfall figures for the previous 12 months. The output should correctly label the months.

There are a variety of ways to deal with the month names. One straightforward method is to code the months as integers and then do a conversion before doing the output. A large `switch` statement is acceptable in an output function. The month input can be handled in any manner you wish, as long as it is relatively easy and pleasant for the user.

After you have completed the above program, produce an enhanced version that also outputs a graph showing the average rainfall and the actual rainfall for each of the previous 12 months. The graph should be similar to the one shown in Display 5.4, except that there should be two bar graphs for each month and they should be labeled as the average rainfall and the rainfall for the most recent month. Your program should ask the user whether she or he wants to see the table or the bar graph, and then should display whichever format is requested. Include a loop that allows the user to see either format as often as the user wishes until the user requests that the program end.

2. Write a function called `deleteRepeats` that has a partially filled array of characters as a formal parameter and that deletes all repeated letters from the array. Since a partially filled array requires two arguments, the function will actually have two formal parameters: an array parameter and a formal parameter of type `int` that gives the number of array positions used. When a letter is deleted, the remaining letters are moved forward to fill in the gap. This will create empty positions at the end of the array so that less of the array is used. Since the formal parameter is a partially filled array, a second formal parameter of type `int` will tell how many array positions are filled. This second formal parameter will be a call-by-reference parameter and will be changed to show how much of the array is used after the repeated letters are deleted. For example, consider the following code:

```
char a[10];
a[0] = 'a';
a[1] = 'b';
a[2] = 'a';
a[3] = 'c';
int size = 4;
deleteRepeats(a, size);
```

After this code is executed, the value of `a[0]` is `'a'`, the value of `a[1]` is `'b'`, the value of `a[2]` is `'c'`, and the value of `size` is `3`. (The value of `a[3]` is no longer of any concern, since the partially filled array no longer uses this indexed variable.) You may assume that the partially filled array contains only lowercase letters. Embed your function in a suitable test program.

3. The standard deviation of a list of numbers is a measure of how much the numbers deviate from the average. If the standard deviation is small, the numbers are clustered close to the average. If the standard deviation is large, the numbers are scattered far from the average. The standard deviation, S, of a list of N numbers x_i is defined as follows:

$$S = \sqrt{\frac{\sum_{i=1}^{N} (x_i - \bar{x})^2}{N}}$$

where $\bar{x}$ is the average of the N numbers x_1, x_2, ... Define a function that takes a partially filled array of numbers as its argument and returns the standard deviation of the numbers in the partially filled array. Since a partially filled array requires two arguments, the function will actually have two formal parameters: an array parameter and a formal parameter of type `int` that gives the number of array positions used. The numbers in the array will be of type `double`. Embed your function in a suitable test program.

4. Write a program that reads in an array of type `int`. You may assume that there are fewer than 50 entries in the array. Your program determines how many entries are used. The output is to be a two-column list. The first column is a list of the distinct array elements; the second column is the count of the number of occurrences of each element. The list should be sorted on entries in the first column, largest to smallest.

For the array values:

```
-12 3 -12 4 1 1 -12 1 -1 1 2 3 4 2 3 -12
```

the output should be

```
N     Count
4     2
3     3
2     2
1     4
-1    1
-12   4
```

5. An array can be used to store large integers one digit at a time. For example, the integer 1234 could be stored in the array `a` by setting `a[0]` to 1, `a[1]` to 2, `a[2]` to 3, and `a[3]` to 4. However, for this exercise you might find it more useful to store the digits backward, that is, place 4 in `a[0]`, 3 in `a[1]`, 2 in `a[2]`, and 1 in `a[3]`. In this exercise you will write a program that reads in two positive integers that are 20 or fewer digits in length and then outputs the sum of the two numbers. Your program will read the digits as values of type `char` so that the number 1234 is read as the four characters '1', '2', '3', and '4'. After they are read into the program, the characters are changed to values of type `int`. The digits will be read into a partially filled array, and you might find it useful to reverse the order of the elements in the array after the array is filled with data from the keyboard. (Whether or not you reverse the order of the elements in the array is up to you. It can be done either way, and each way has its advantages and disadvantages.) Your program will perform the addition by implementing the usual paper-and-pencil addition algorithm. The result of the addition is stored in an array of size 20 and the result is then written to the screen. If the result of the addition is an integer with more than the maximum number of digits (that is,

more than 20 digits), then your program should issue a message saying that it has encountered "integer overflow." You should be able to change the maximum length of the integers by changing only one globally defined constant. Include a loop that allows the user to continue to do more additions until the user says the program should end.

6. Write a program that will allow two users to play tic-tac-toe. The program should ask for moves alternately from player X and player O. The program displays the game positions as follows:

```
1  2  3
4  5  6
7  8  9
```

The players enter their moves by entering the position number they wish to mark. After each move, the program displays the changed board. A sample board configuration is as follows:

```
X  X  0
4  5  6
0  8  9
```

7. Write a program to assign passengers seats in an airplane. Assume a small airplane with seat numbering as follows:

```
1    A B  C D
2    A B  C D
3    A B  C D
4    A B  C D
5    A B  C D
6    A B  C D
7    A B  C D
```

The program should display the seat pattern, with an 'X' marking the seats already assigned. For example, after seats 1A, 2B, and 4C are taken, the display should look like this:

```
1    X B  C D
2    A X  C D
3    A B  C D
4    A B  X D
5    A B  C D
6    A B  C D
7    A B  C D
```

After displaying the seats available, the program prompts for the seat desired, the user types in a seat, and then the display of available seats is updated. This continues until all seats are filled or until the user signals that the program should end. If the user types in a seat that is already assigned, the program should say that that seat is occupied and ask for another choice.

8. Write a program that accepts input like the program in Display 5.4 and that outputs a bar graph like the one in that program, except that your program will output the bars vertically rather than horizontally. A two-dimensional array may be useful.

9. The mathematician John Horton Conway invented the "Game of Life." Though not a "game" in any traditional sense, it provides interesting behavior that is specified with only a few rules. This project asks you to write a program that allows you to specify an initial configuration. The program follows the rules of Life (listed shortly) to show the continuing behavior of the configuration.

LIFE is an organism that lives in a discrete, two-dimensional world. While this world is actually unlimited, we don't have that luxury, so we restrict the array to 80 characters wide by 22 character positions high. If you have access to a larger screen, by all means use it.

This world is an array with each cell capable of holding one LIFE cell. Generations mark the passing of time. Each generation brings births and deaths to the LIFE community. The births and deaths follow this set of rules:

1. We define each cell to have eight neighbor cells. The neighbors of a cell are the cells directly above, below, to the right, to the left, diagonally above to the right and left, and diagonally below, to the right and left.

2. If an occupied cell has zero or one neighbor, it dies of loneliness. If an occupied cell has more than three neighbors, it dies of overcrowding.

3. If an empty cell has exactly three occupied neighbor cells, there is a birth of a new cell to replace the empty cell.

4. Births and deaths are instantaneous and occur at the changes of generation. A cell dying for whatever reason may help cause birth, but a newborn cell cannot resurrect a cell that is dying, nor will a cell's death prevent the death of another, say, by reducing the local population.

```
                          *
Examples:   *** becomes   *  then becomes  ***  again, and so on.
                          *
```

Notes: Some configurations grow from relatively small starting configurations. Others move across the region. It is recommended that for text output you use a rectangular char array with 80 columns and 22 rows to store the LIFE world's successive generations. Use an * to indicate a living cell and use a blank to indicate an empty (or dead) cell. If you have a screen with more rows than that, by all means make use of the whole screen.

Suggestions: Look for stable configurations. That is, look for communities that repeat patterns continually. The number of configurations in the repetition is called the *period*. There are configurations that are fixed, that is, that continue without change. A possible project is to find such configurations.

Hints: Define a void function named generation that takes the array we call world, an 80-column by 22-row array of type char, which contains the initial configuration. The function scans the array and modifies the cells, marking the cells with births and deaths in accord with the rules listed previously. This involves examining each cell in turn and either killing the cell, letting it live, or, if the cell is empty, deciding whether a cell should be born. There should be a function `display` that accepts the array `world` and displays the array on the screen. Some sort of time delay is appropriate between calls to `generation` and `display`. To do this, your program should generate and display the next generation when you press Return. You are at liberty to automate this, but automation is not necessary for the program.

6 CHAPTER

Structures and Classes

6

Structures and Classes

'The time has come,' the Walrus said,
'To talk of many things:
Of shoes—and ships—and sealing wax—
Of cabbages—and kings.'

Lewis Carroll, *Through the Looking Glass*

INTRODUCTION

Classes are perhaps the single most significant feature that separates the C++ language from the C language. A *class* is a type whose values are called *objects*. Objects have both data and member functions. The member functions have special access to the data of their object. These objects are the objects of object-oriented programming, a very popular and powerful programming philosophy.

structure

We will introduce classes in two steps. We first tell you how to give a type definition for a structure. A **structure** (of the kind discussed here) can be thought of as an object without any member functions.[1] The important property of structures is that the data in a structure can be a collection of data items of diverse types. After you learn about structures it will be a natural extension to define classes.

You do not need the material on arrays given in Chapter 5 in order to read Chapter 6, and most of Chapters 7 and 8, which cover classes.

6.1 Structures

I don't care to belong to any club that will accept me as a member.

Groucho Marx, *The Groucho Letters*

Sometimes it is useful to have a collection of values of different types and to treat the collection as a single item. For example, consider a bank certificate of deposit, which is often called a CD. A CD is a bank account that does not allow withdrawals for a specified number of months. A CD naturally has three

---

[1] A structure actually can have member functions in C++, but that is not the approach we will take. This detail is explained later in the chapter. This footnote is only to let readers who feel they have found an error know that we are aware of the official definition of a structure. Most readers should ignore this footnote.

pieces of data associated with it: the account balance, the interest rate for the account, and the term, which is the number of months until maturity. The first two items can be represented as values of type double, and the number of months can be represented as a value of type int. Display 6.1 shows the definition of a structure called CDAccountV1 that can be used for this kind of account. (The V1 stands for version 1. We will define an improved version later in this chapter.)

Display 6.1   A Structure Definition (part 1 of 2)

```
1   //Program to demonstrate the CDAccountV1 structure type.
2   #include <iostream>
3   using namespace std;

4   //Structure for a bank certificate of deposit:
5   struct CDAccountV1
6   {
7       double balance;
8       double interestRate;
9       int term;//months until maturity
10  };
```

An improved version of this structure will be given later in this chapter.

```
11  void getData(CDAccountV1& theAccount);
12  //Postcondition: theAccount.balance, theAccount.interestRate, and
13  //theAccount.term have been given values that the user entered at the keyboard.

14  int main( )
15  {
16      CDAccountV1 account;
17      getData(account);

18      double rateFraction, interest;
19      rateFraction = account.interestRate/100.0;
20      interest = account.balance*(rateFraction*(account.term/12.0));
21      account.balance = account.balance + interest;

22      cout.setf(ios::fixed);
23      cout.setf(ios::showpoint);
24      cout.precision(2);
25      cout << "When your CD matures in "
26          << account.term << " months,\n"
27          << "it will have a balance of $"
28          << account.balance << endl;

29      return 0;
30  }
```

Display 6.1   A Structure Definition *(part 2 of 2)*

```
31    //Uses iostream:
32    void getData(CDAccountV1& theAccount)
33    {
34        cout << "Enter account balance: $";
35        cin >> theAccount.balance;
36        cout << "Enter account interest rate: ";
37        cin >> theAccount.interestRate;
38        cout << "Enter the number of months until maturity: ";
39        cin >> theAccount.term;
40    }
```

SAMPLE DIALOGUE

```
Enter account balance: $100.00
Enter account interest rate: 10.0
Enter the number of months until maturity: 6
When your CD matures in 6 months,
it will have a balance of $105.00
```

STRUCTURE TYPES

The structure definition in Display 6.1 is as follows:

```
struct CDAccountV1
{
    double balance;
    double interestRate;
    int term;//months until maturity
};
```

struct

structure tag

member name

The keyword `struct` announces that this is a structure type definition. The identifier `CDAccountV1` is the name of the structure type, which is known as the **structure tag**. The structure tag can be any legal identifier that is not a keyword. Although this is not required by the C++ language, structure tags are usually spelled starting with an upper-case letter. The identifiers declared inside the braces, {}, are called **member names**. As illustrated in this example, a structure type definition ends with both a brace, }, and a semicolon.

where to place a structure definition

A structure definition is usually placed outside any function definition (in the same way that globally defined constant declarations are placed outside all function definitions). The structure type is then a global definition that is available to all the code that follows the structure definition.

Once a structure type definition has been given, the structure type can be used just like the predefined types `int`, `char`, and so forth. Note that in Display 6.1 the structure type CDAccountV1 is used to declare a variable in the function main and is used as the name of the parameter type for the function getData.

A structure variable can hold values just like any other variable can. A **structure value** is a collection of smaller values called **member values**. There is one member value for each member name declared in the structure definition. For example, a value of the type CDAccountV1 is a collection of three member values, two of type double and one of type int. The member values that together make up the structure value are stored in member variables, which we discuss next.

structure
value
member
value

Each structure type specifies a list of member names. In Display 6.1 the structure CDAccountV1 has three member names: balance, interestRate, and term. Each of these member names can be used to pick out one smaller variable that is a part of the larger structure variable. These smaller variables are called **member variables**. Member variables are specified by giving the name of the structure variable followed by a dot and then the member name. For example, if account is a structure variable of type CDAccountV1 (as declared in Display 6.1), then the structure variable account has the following three member variables:

member
variable

```
account.balance
account.interestRate
account.term
```

The first two member variables are of type double, and the last is of type int. As illustrated in Display 6.1, these member variables can be used just like any other variables of those types. For example, the following line from the program in Display 6.1 will add the value contained in the member variable account.balance and the value contained in the ordinary variable interest and will then place the result in the member variable account.balance:

```
account.balance = account.balance + interest;
```

Two or more structure types may use the same member names. For example, it is perfectly legal to have the following two type definitions in the same program:

reusing
member
names

```
struct FertilizerStock
{
    double quantity;
    double nitrogenContent;
};
```

and

```
struct CropYield
{
    int quantity;
    double size;
};
```

THE DOT OPERATOR

The **dot operator** is used to specify a member variable of a structure variable.

Syntax ———————— *Dot operator*

Structure_Variable_Name.Member_Variable_Name

EXAMPLES

```
struct StudentRecord
{
    int studentNumber;
    char grade;
};

int main( )
{
    StudentRecord yourRecord;
    yourRecord.studentNumber = 2001;
    yourRecord.grade = 'A';
```

Some writers call the dot operator the *structure member access operator*, although we will not use that term.

This coincidence of names will produce no problems. For example, if you declare the following two structure variables:

```
FertilizerStock superGrow;
CropYield apples;
```

then the quantity of `superGrow` fertilizer is stored in the member variable `super-Grow.quantity` and the quantity of apples produced is stored in the member variable `apples.quantity`. The dot operator and the structure variable specify which `quantity` is meant in each instance.

A structure value can be viewed as a collection of member values. A structure value can also be viewed as a single (complex) value (that just happens to be made up of member values). Since a structure value can be viewed as a single value, structure values and structure variables can be used in the same ways that you use simple values and simple variables of the predefined types such as `int`. In particular, you can assign struc-ture values using the equal sign. For example, if `apples` and `oranges` are structure vari-ables of the type `CropYield` defined earlier, then the following is perfectly legal:

structure variables in assignment statements

```
apples = oranges;
```

The previous assignment statement is equivalent to

```
apples.quantity = oranges.quantity;
apples.size = oranges.size;
```

SIMPLE STRUCTURE TYPES

You define a structure type as shown below. The *Structure_Tag* is the name of the structure type.

SYNTAX

```
struct Structure_Tag
{
    Type_1  Member_Variable_Name_1;
    Type_2  Member_Variable_Name_2;
            ⋮
    Type_Last  Member_Variable_Name_Last;
};  ←——————— Do not forget this semicolon.
```

EXAMPLE

```
struct Automobile
{
    int year;
    int doors;
    double horsePower;
    char model;
};
```

Although we will not use this feature, you can combine member names of the same type into a single list separated by commas. For example, the following is equivalent to the above structure definition:

```
struct Automobile
{
    int year, doors;
    double horsePower;
    char model;
};
```

Variables of a structure type can be declared in the same way as variables of other types. For example:

```
Automobile myCar, yourCar;
```

The member variables are specified using the dot operator. For example: myCar.year, myCar.doors, myCar.horsePower, and myCar.model.

FORGETTING A SEMICOLON IN A STRUCTURE DEFINITION

When you add the final brace, }, to a structure definition, it feels like the structure definition is finished, but it is not. You must also place a semicolon after that final brace. There is a reason for this, even though the reason is a feature that we will have no occasion to use. A structure definition is more than a definition. It can also be used to declare structure variables. You are allowed to list structure variable names between that final brace and that final semicolon. For example, the following defines a structure called WeatherData and declares two structure variables, dataPoint1 and dataPoint2, both of type WeatherData:

```
struct WeatherData
{
    double temperature;
    double windVelocity;
} dataPoint1, dataPoint2;
```

STRUCTURES AS FUNCTION ARGUMENTS

structure arguments

A function can have call-by-value parameters of a structure type or call-by-reference parameters of a structure type, or both. The program in Display 6.1, for example, includes a function named getData that has a call-by-reference parameter with the structure type CDAccountV1.

functions can return structures

A structure type can also be the type for the value returned by a function. For example, the following defines a function that takes one argument of type CDAccountV1 and returns a different structure of type CDAccountV1. The structure returned will have the same balance and term as the argument, but will pay double the interest rate that the argument pays.

```
CDAccountV1 doubleInterest(CDAccountV1 oldAccount)
{
    CDAccountV1 temp;
    temp = oldAccount;
    temp.interestRate = 2*oldAccount.interestRate;
    return temp;
}
```

Notice the local variable temp of type CDAccountV1; temp is used to build up a complete structure value of the desired kind, which is then returned by the function. If myAccount is a variable of type CDAccountV1 that has been given values for its member variables, then the following will give yourAccount values for an account with double the interest rate of myAccount:

```
CDAccountV1 yourAccount;
yourAccount = doubleInterest(myAccount);
```

Tip

USE HIERARCHICAL STRUCTURES

Sometimes it makes sense to have structures whose members are themselves smaller structures. For example, a structure type called `PersonInfo` that can be used to store a person's height, weight, and birth date can be defined as follows:

```
struct Date
{
    int month;
    int day;
    int year;
};

struct PersonInfo
{
    double height;//in inches
    int weight;//in pounds
    Date birthday;
};
```

A structure variable of type `PersonInfo` is declared in the usual way:

```
PersonInfo person1;
```

If the structure variable `person1` has had its value set to record a person's birth date, then the year the person was born can be output to the screen as follows:

```
cout << person1.birthday.year;
```

The way to read such expressions is left to right, and very carefully. Starting at the left end, `person1` is a structure variable of type `PersonInfo`. To obtain the member variable with the name `birthday`, you use the dot operator as follows:

```
person1.birthday
```

This member variable is itself a structure variable of type `Date`. Thus, this member variable itself has member variables. A member variable of the structure variable `person1.birthday` is obtained by adding a dot and the member variable name, such as `year`, which produces the expression `person1.birthday.year` shown above.

In Display 6.2 we have rewritten the class for a certificate of deposit from Display 6.1. This new version has a member variable of the structure type `Date` that holds the date of maturity. We have also replaced the single `balance` member variable with two new member variables giving the initial balance and the balance at maturity.

Display 6.2   A Structure with a Structure Member *(part 1 of 2)*

```
 1   //Program to demonstrate the CDAccount structure type.
 2   #include <iostream>
 3   using namespace std;

 4   struct Date
 5   {
 6       int month;
 7       int day;
 8       int year;
 9   };
```

This is an improved version of the structure CDAccountV1 defined in Display 6.1.

```
10   //Improved structure for a bank certificate of deposit:
11   struct CDAccount
12   {
13       double initialBalance;
14       double interestRate;
15       int term;//months until maturity
16       Date maturity; //date when CD matures
17       double balanceAtMaturity;
18   };

19   void getCDData(CDAccount& theAccount);
20   //Postcondition: theAccount.initialBalance, theAccount.interestRate,
21   //theAccount.term, and theAccount.maturity have been given values
22   //that the user entered at the keyboard.

24   void getDate(Date& theDate);
25   //Postcondition: theDate.month, theDate.day, and theDate.year
26   //have been given values that the user entered at the keyboard.

27   int main( )
28   {
29       CDAccount account;
30       cout << "Enter account data on the day account was opened:\n";
31       getCDData(account);
32       double rateFraction, interest;
33       rateFraction = account.interestRate/100.0;
34       interest = account.initialBalance*(rateFraction*(account.term/12.0));
35       account.balanceAtMaturity = account.initialBalance + interest;

36       cout.setf(ios::fixed);
37       cout.setf(ios::showpoint);
38       cout.precision(2);
39       cout << "When the CD matured on "
40            << account.maturity.month << "-" << account.maturity.day
```

Display 6.2   A Structure with A Structure Member (part 2 of 2)

```
41              << "-" << account.maturity.year << endl
42              << "it had a balance of $"
43              << account.balanceAtMaturity << endl;
44        return 0;
45    }

46    //uses iostream:
47    void getCDData(CDAccount& theAccount)
48    {
49        cout << "Enter account initial balance: $";
50        cin >> theAccount.initialBalance;
51        cout << "Enter account interest rate: ";
52        cin >> theAccount.interestRate;
53        cout << "Enter the number of months until maturity: ";
54        cin >> theAccount.term;
55        cout << "Enter the maturity date:\n";
56        getDate(theAccount.maturity);
57    }

58    //uses iostream:
59    void getDate(Date& theDate)
60    {
61        cout << "Enter month: ";
62        cin >> theDate.month;
63        cout << "Enter day: ";
64        cin >> theDate.day;
65        cout << "Enter year: ";
66        cin >> theDate.year;
67    }
```

SAMPLE DIALOGUE

```
Enter account data on the day account was opened:
Enter account initial balance: $100.00
Enter account interest rate: 10.0
Enter the number of months until maturity: 6
Enter the maturity date:
Enter month: 2
Enter day: 14
Enter year: 1899
When the CD matured on 2-14-1899
it had a balance of $105.00
```

■ INITIALIZING STRUCTURES

You can initialize a structure at the time that it is declared. To give a structure variable a value, follow it by an equal sign and a list of the member values enclosed in braces. For example, the following definition of a structure type for a date was given in the previous subsection:

```
struct Date
{
    int month;
    int day;
    int year;
};
```

Once the type Date is defined, you can declare and initialize a structure variable called dueDate as follows:

```
Date dueDate = {12, 31, 2003};
```

The initializing values must be given in the order that corresponds to the order of member variables in the structure type definition. In this example, dueDate.month receives the first initializing value of 12, dueDate.day receives the second value of 31, and dueDate.year receives the third value of 2003.

It is an error if there are more initializer values than struct members. If there are fewer initializer values than struct members, the provided values are used to initialize data members, in order. Each data member without an initializer is initialized to a zero value of an appropriate type for the variable.

Self-Test Exercises

1. Given the following structure and structure variable declaration,

```
struct CDAccountV2
{
    double balance;
    double interestRate;
    int term;
    char initial1;
    char initial2;
};
CDAccountV2 account;
```

what is the type of each of the following? Mark any that are not correct.

a. account.balance

b. account.interestRate

c. `CDAccountV1.term`

d. `account.initial2`

e. `account`

2. Consider the following type definition:

```
struct ShoeType
{
    char style;
    double price;
};
```

Given the above structure type definitions, what will be the output produced by the following code?

```
ShoeType shoe1, shoe2;
shoe1.style ='A';
shoe1.price = 9.99;
cout << shoe1.style << " $" << shoe1.price << endl;
shoe2 = shoe1;

shoe2.price = shoe2.price/9;
cout << shoe2.style << " $" << shoe2.price << endl;
```

3. What is the error in the following structure definition?

```
struct Stuff
{
    int b;
    int c;
}

int main( )
{
    Stuff x;
    // other code
}
```

4. Given the following `struct` definition,

```
struct A
{
    int member b;
    int member c;
};
```

declare x to have this structure type. Initialize the members of x, member b and member c, to the values 1 and 2, respectively.

5. Here is an initialization of a structure type. State what happens with each initialization. Note any problems with these initializations.

```
struct Date
{
    int month;
    int day;
    int year;
};
```

a. `Date dueDate = {12, 21};`

b. `Date dueDate = {12, 21, 1995};`

c. `Date dueDate = {12, 21, 19, 95};`

6. Write a definition for a structure type for records consisting of a person's wage rate, accrued vacation (which is some whole number of days), and status (which is either hourly or salaried). Represent the status as one of the two `char` values `'H'` and `'S'`. Call the type `EmployeeRecord`.

7. Give a function definition corresponding to the following function declaration. (The type `ShoeType` is given in Self-Test Exercise 2.)

```
void readShoeRecord(ShoeType& newShoe);
//Fills newShoe with values read from the keyboard.
```

8. Give a function definition corresponding to the following function declaration. (The type `ShoeType` is given in Self-Test Exercise 2.)

```
ShoeType discount(ShoeType oldRecord);
//Returns a structure that is the same as its argument,
//but with the price reduced by 10%.
```

6.2 Classes

We all know—the Times *knows—but we pretend we don't.*

Virginia Woolf, *Monday or Tuesday*

A class is basically a structure with member functions as well as member data. Classes are central to the programming methodology known as *object-oriented programming*.

■ DEFINING CLASSES AND MEMBER FUNCTIONS

class

A **class** is a type that is similar to a structure type, but a class type normally has member functions as well as member variables. An overly simple, but illustrative, example of a class called `DayOfYear` is given in Display 6.3. This class has one member function named output, as well as the two member variables month and day. The term public: is called an access specifier. It simply means that there are no restrictions on the members that follow. We will discuss public: and its alternatives after going through this simple example. The type DayOfYear defined in Display 6.3 is a class definition for objects whose values are dates, such as January 1 or July 4.

Display 6.3 Class with a Member Function (part 1 of 2)

```
1    //Program to demonstrate a very simple example of a class.
2    //A better version of the class DayOfYear will be given in Display 6.4.
3    #include <iostream>
4    using namespace std;

5    class DayOfYear
6    {
7    public:
8        void output( );
9        int month;
10       int day;
11   };

12   int main( )
13   {
14       DayOfYear today, birthday;
15       cout << "Enter today's date:\n";
16       cout << "Enter month as a number: ";
17       cin >> today.month;
18       cout << "Enter the day of the month: ";
19       cin >> today.day;
20       cout << "Enter your birthday:\n";
21       cout << "Enter month as a number: ";
22       cin >> birthday.month;
23       cout << "Enter the day of the month: ";
24       cin >> birthday.day;

25       cout << "Today's date is ";
26       today.output( );
27       cout << endl;
28       cout << "Your birthday is ";
29       birthday.output( );
30       cout << endl;

31       if (today.month == birthday.month && today.day == birthday.day)
32           cout << "Happy Birthday!\n";
33       else
34           cout << "Happy Unbirthday!\n";
35       return 0;
36   }
```

Normally, member variables are private and not public, as in this example. This is discussed a bit later in this chapter.

← *Member function declaration*

← *Calls to the member function output*

Display 6.3 Class with a Member Function *(part 2 of 2)*

```
37    //Uses iostream:
38    void DayOfYear::output( )
39    {
40        switch (month)
41        {
42            case 1:
43                cout << "January "; break;
44            case 2:
45                cout << "February "; break;
46            case 3:
47                cout << "March "; break;
48            case 4:
49                cout << "April "; break;              ⟵——— Member function definition
50            case 5:
51                cout << "May "; break;
52            case 6:
53                cout << "June "; break;
54            case 7:
55                cout << "July "; break;
56            case 8:
57                cout << "August "; break;
58            case 9:
59                cout << "September "; break;
60            case 10:
61                cout << "October "; break;
62            case 11:
63                cout << "November "; break;
64            case 12:
65                cout << "December "; break;
66            default:
67                cout << "Error in DayOfYear::output. Contact software vendor.";
68        }
69
70        cout << day;
71    }
```

SAMPLE DIALOGUE

```
Enter today's date:
Enter month as a number: 10
Enter the day of the month: 15
Enter your birthday:
Enter month as a number: 2
Enter the day of the month: 21
Today's date is October 15
Your birthday is February 21
Happy Unbirthday!
```

The value of a variable of a class type is called an **object** (therefore, when speaking loosely, a variable of a class type is also often called an *object*). An object has both data members and function members. When programming with classes, a program is viewed as a collection of interacting objects. The objects can interact because they are capable of actions, namely, invocations of member functions. Variables of a class type hold objects as values. Variables of a class type are declared in the same way as variables of the predefined types and in the same way as structure variables.

For the moment ignore the word public: shown in Display 6.3. The rest of the definition of the class DayOfYear is very much like a structure definition, except that it uses the keyword class instead of struct and it lists the member function output (as well as the member variables month and day). Notice that the member function output is listed by giving its declaration (prototype). A class definition normally contains only the declaration for its member functions. The definitions for the member functions are usually given elsewhere. In a C++ class definition, you can intermix the ordering of the member variables and member functions in any way you wish, but the style we will follow has a tendency to list the member functions before the member variables.

Member variables for an object of a class type are specified using the dot operator in the same way that the dot operator is used to specify member variables of a structure. For example, if today is a variable of the class type DayOfYear defined in Display 6.3, then today.month and today.day are the two member variables of the object today.

Member functions for classes that you define are invoked using the dot operator in a way that is similar to how you specify a member variable. For example, the program in Display 6.3 declares two objects of type DayOfYear in the following way:

```
DayOfYear today, birthday;
```

The member function output is called with the object today as follows:

```
today.output( );
```

and the member function output is called with the object birthday as follows:

```
birthday.output( );
```

When a member function is defined, the definition must include the class name because there may be two or more classes that have member functions with the same name. In Display 6.3 there is only one class definition, but in other situations you may have many class definitions, and more than one class may have member functions with the same name. The definition for the member function output of the class DayOfYear is shown in part 2 of Display 6.3. The definition is similar to an ordinary function definition except that you must specify the class name in the heading of the function definition.

The heading of the function definition for the member function output is as follows:

```
void DayOfYear::output( )
```

The operator :: is called the **scope resolution operator** and serves a purpose similar to that of the dot operator. Both the dot operator and the scope resolution operator are used

object

member function

calling member functions

defining member functions

scope resolution operator

to tell what a member function is a member of. However, the scope resolution operator : : is used with a class name, whereas the dot operator is used with objects (that is, with class variables). The scope resolution operator consists of two colons with no space between them. The class name that precedes the scope resolution operator is often called a **type qualifier**, because it specializes ("qualifies") the function name to one particular type.

type qualifier

member variables in function definitions

Look at the definition of the member function DayOfYear::output given in Display 6.3. Notice that in the function definition of DayOfYear::output, we used the member names month and day by themselves without first giving the object and dot operator. That is not as strange as it may at first appear. At this point we are simply defining the member function output. This definition of output will apply to all objects of type DayOfYear, but at this point we do not know the names of the objects of type DayOfYear that we will use, so we cannot give their names. When the member function is called, as in

```
today.output( );
```

all the member names in the function definition are specialized to the name of the calling object. So, the above function call is equivalent to the following:

```
{
    switch (today.month)
    {
        case 1:
            .
            .
            .
    }

    cout << today.day;
}
```

Member Function Definition

A member function is defined similar to any other function except that the *Class_Name* and the scope resolution operator, : :, are given in the function heading.

Syntax

```
Returned_Type Class_Name::Function_Name(Parameter_List)
{
    Function_Body_Statements
}
```

Example

See Display 6.3. Note that the member variables (month and day) are not preceded by an object name and dot when they occur in a member function definition.

In the function definition for a member function, you can use the names of all members of that class (both the data members and the function members) without using the dot operator.

THE DOT OPERATOR AND THE SCOPE RESOLUTION OPERATOR

Both the dot operator and the scope resolution operator are used with member names to specify of what thing they are a member. For example, suppose you have declared a class called DayOf-Year and you declare an object called today as follows:

```
DayOfYear today;
```

You use the dot operator to specify a member of the object today. For example, output is a member function for the class DayOfYear (defined in Display 6.3), and the following function call will output the data values stored in the object today:

```
today.output( );
```

You use the scope resolution operator, ::, to specify the class name when giving the function definition for a member function. For example, the heading of the function definition for the member function output would be as follows:

```
void DayOfYear::output( )
```

Remember, the scope resolution operator, ::, is used with a class name, whereas the dot operator is used with an object of that class.

A CLASS IS A FULL-FLEDGED TYPE

A class is a type just like the types int and double. You can have variables of a class type, you can have parameters of a class type, a function can return a value of a class type, and more generally, you can use a class type like any other type.

Self-Test Exercises

9. Below we have redefined the class DayOfYear from Display 6.3 so that it now has one additional member function called input. Write an appropriate definition for the member function input.

```
class DayOfYear
{
public:
```

```
        void input( );
        void output( );
        int month;
        int day;

};
```

10. Given the following class definition, write an appropriate definition for the member function set.

```
class Temperature
{
public:
    void set(double newDegrees, char newScale);
    //Sets the member variables to the values given as
    //arguments.
    double degrees;
    char scale; //'F' for Fahrenheit or 'C' for Celsius.

};
```

11. Carefully distinguish between the meaning and use of the dot operator and the scope resolution operator, ::.

ENCAPSULATION

data types and abstract data types

A data type, such as the type int, has certain specified values, such as 0, 1, −1, 2, and so forth. You tend to think of the data type as being these values, but the operations on these values are just as important as the values. Without the operations, you could do nothing of interest with the values. The operations for the type int consist of +, −, *, /, %, and a few other operators and predefined library functions. You should not think of a data type as being simply a collection of values. A **data type** consists of a collection of values *together with* a set of basic operations defined on these values. A data type is called an **abstract data type** (abbreviated **ADT**) if the programmers who use the type do not have access to the details of how the values and operations are implemented. The predefined types, such as int, are abstract data types (ADTs). You do not know how the operations, such as + and *, are implemented for the type int. Even if you did know, you could not use this information in any C++ program. Classes, which are programmer-defined types, should also be ADTs; that is, the details of how the "operations" are implemented should be hidden from, or at least irrelevant to, any programmer who uses the class. The operations of a class are the (public) member functions of the class. A programmer who uses a class should not need to even look at the definitions of the member functions. The member function declarations, given in the class definition, and a few comments should be all the programmer needs in order to use the class.

A programmer who uses a class also should not need to know how the data of the class is implemented. The implementation of the data should be as hidden as the implementation of the member functions. In fact, it is close to impossible to distinguish between hiding the implementation of the member functions and the implementation of the data. To a programmer, the class DayOfYear (Display 6.3) has dates as data, not numbers. The programmer should not know or care whether the month March is implemented as the int value 3, the quoted string "March", or in some other way.

Defining a class so that the implementation of the member functions and the implementation of the data in objects are not known, or is at least irrelevant, to the programmer who uses the class is known by a number of different terms. The most common terms used are **information hiding**, **data abstraction**, and **encapsulation**, each of which means that the details of the implementation of a class are hidden from the programmer who uses the class. This principle is one of the main tenets of object-oriented programming (OOP). When discussing OOP, the term that is used most frequently is *encapsulation*. One of the ways to apply this principle of encapsulation to your class definitions is to make all member variables private, which is what we discuss in the next subsection.

encapsulation

PUBLIC AND PRIVATE MEMBERS

Look back at the definition of the type DayOfYear given in Display 6.3. In order to use that class, you need to know that there are two member variables of type int that are named month and day. This violates the principle of encapsulation (information hiding) that we discussed in the previous subsection. Display 6.4 is a rewritten version of the class DayOfYear that better conforms to this encapsulation principle.

Notice the words private: and public: in Display 6.4. All the items that follow the word private: (in this case the member variables month and day) are said to be **private**, which means that they cannot be referenced by name anyplace except within the definitions of the member functions of the class DayOfYear. For example, with this changed definition of the class DayOfYear, the following two assignments and other indicated code are no longer permitted in the main function of the program and are not permitted in any other function definition, except for member functions of the class DayOfYear:

private:

private member variable

```
DayOfYear today; //This line is OK.
today.month = 12;//ILLEGAL
today.day = 25;//ILLEGAL
cout << today.month;//ILLEGAL
cout << today.day;//ILLEGAL
if (today.month == 1) //ILLEGAL
    cout << "January";
```

Once you make a member variable a private member variable, there is no way to change its value (or to reference the member variable in any other way) except by using one of the member functions. That means that the compiler will enforce the hiding of

Display 6.4   Class with Private Members (part 1 of 3)

```
1   #include <iostream>
2   #include <cstdlib>
3   using namespace std;                        This is an improved version
                                                of the class DayOfYear that we gave
4   class DayOfYear                             in Display 6.3.
5   {
6   public:
7       void input( );
8       void output( );
9       void set(int newMonth, int newDay);
10      //Precondition: newMonth and newDay form a possible date.

11      void set(int newMonth);
12      //Precondition: 1 <= newMonth <= 12
13      //Postcondition: The date is set to the first day of the given month.

14      int getMonthNumber( ); //Returns 1 for January, 2 for February, etc.
15      int getDay( );
16  private:
17      int month;                      Private members
18      int day;
19  };

20  int main( )
21  {
22      DayOfYear today, bachBirthday;
23      cout << "Enter today's date:\n";
24      today.input( );
25      cout << "Today's date is ";
26      today.output( );
27      cout << endl;

28      bachBirthday.set(3, 21);
29      cout << "J. S. Bach's birthday is ";
30      bachBirthday.output( );
31      cout << endl;
32      if ( today.getMonthNumber( ) == bachBirthday.getMonthNumber( ) &&
33              today.getDay( ) == bachBirthday.getDay( ) )
34          cout << "Happy Birthday Johann Sebastian!\n";
35      else
36          cout << "Happy Unbirthday Johann Sebastian!\n";
37
38      return 0;
39  }

40  //Uses iostream and cstdlib:
41  void DayOfYear::set(int newMonth, int newDay)
```

Note that the function name set is overloaded. You can overload a member function just like you can overload any other function.

Display 6.4   Class with Private Members (part 2 of 3)

```
42   {
43       if ((newMonth >= 1) && (newMonth <= 12))
44           month = newMonth;
45       else
46       {
47           cout << "Illegal month value! Program aborted.\n";
48           exit(1);
49       }
50       if ((newDay >= 1) && (newDay <= 31))
51           day = newDay;
52       else
53       {
54           cout << "Illegal day value! Program aborted.\n";
55           exit(1);
56       }
57   }

58   //Uses iostream and cstdlib:
59   void DayOfYear::set(int newMonth)
60   {
61       if ((newMonth >= 1) && (newMonth <= 12))
62           month = newMonth;
63       else
64       {
65           cout << "Illegal month value! Program aborted.\n";
66           exit(1);
67       }
68       day = 1;
69   }
70
71   int DayOfYear::getMonthNumber( )
72   {
73       return month;
74   }

75   int DayOfYear::getDay( )
76   {
77       return day;
78   }

79   //Uses iostream and cstdlib:
80   void DayOfYear::input( )
81   {
82       cout << "Enter the month as a number: ";
83       cin >> month;
84       cout << "Enter the day of the month: ";
85       cin >> day;
```

Mutator functions

Accessor functions

Private members may be used in member function definitions (but not elsewhere).

Display 6.4   Class with Private Members *(part 3 of 3)*

```
86          if ((month < 1) || (month > 12) || (day < 1) || (day > 31))
87          {
88              cout << "Illegal date! Program aborted.\n";
89              exit(1);
90          }
91      }

92      void DayOfYear::output( )
93          <The rest of the definition of DayOfYear::output is given in Display 6.3. >
```

SAMPLE DIALOGUE

```
Enter today's date:
Enter the month as a number: 3
Enter the day of the month: 21
Today's date is March 21
J. S. Bach's birthday is March 21
Happy Birthday Johann Sebastian!
```

the implementation of the data for the class DayOfYear. If you look carefully at the program in Display 6.4, you will see that the only place the member variable names month and day are used is in the definitions of the member functions. There is no reference to today.month, today.day, bachBirthday.month, or bachBirthday.day anyplace outside the definitions of member functions.

public:

All the items that follow the word public: (in this case the member functions) are said to be **public**, which means that they can be referenced by name anyplace. There are no restrictions on the use of public members.

public member variable

Any member variables can be either public or private. Any member functions can be public or private. However, normal good programming practices require that *all* member variables be private and that typically most member functions be public.

You can have any number of occurrences of public and private access specifiers in a class definition. Every time you insert the label

    public:

the list of members changes from private to public. Every time you insert the label

    private:

the list of members changes back to being private members. You need not have just one public and one private group of members. However, it is common to have just one public section and one private section.

There is no universal agreement about whether the public members should be listed first or the private members should be listed first. The majority seem to prefer listing the public members first. This allows for easy viewing of the portions programmers using the class actually get to use. You can make your own decision on what you wish to place first, but the examples in the book will go along with the majority and list the public members before the private members.

In one sense C++ seems to favor placing the private members first. If the first group of members has neither the `public:` nor the `private:` specifier, then members of that group will automatically be private. You will see this default behavior used in code and should be familiar with it. However, we will not use it in this book.

ACCESSOR AND MUTATOR FUNCTIONS

You should always make all member variables in a class private. You may sometimes need to do something with the data in a class object, however. The member functions will allow you to do many things with the data in an object, but sooner or later you will want or need to do something with the data for which there is no member function. How can you do anything new with the data in an object? The answer is that you can do anything you might reasonably want, provided you equip your classes with suitable accessor and mutator functions. These are member functions that allow you to access and change the data in an object in a very general way. **Accessor functions** allow you to read the data. In Display 6.4, the member functions `getMonthNumber` and `getDay` are accessor functions. The accessor functions need not literally return the values of each member variable, but they must return something equivalent to those values. For example, for a class like `DayOfYear`, you might have an accessor function return the name of the month as some sort of string value, rather than return the month as a number.

accessor function

Mutator functions allow you to change the data. In Display 6.4, the two functions named `set` are mutator functions. It is traditional to use names that include the word `get` for accessor functions and names that include the word `set` for mutator functions. (The functions `input` and `output` in Display 6.4 are really mutator and accessor functions, respectively, but I/O is such a special case that they are usually just called *I/O functions* rather than accessor or mutator functions.)

mutator function

Your class definitions should always provide an adequate collection of accessor and mutator functions.

It may seem that accessor and mutator functions defeat the purpose of making member variables private, but that is not so. Notice the mutator function `set` in Display 6.4. It will not allow you to set the `month` member variable to 13 or to any number that does not represent a month. Similarly, it will not allow you to set the `day` member variable to any number that is not in the range 1 to 31 (inclusive). If the variables were public you could set the data to values that do not make sense for a date. (As it is, you can still set the data to values that do not represent a real date, such as February 31, but it would be easy to exclude these dates as well. We did not exclude these dates to keep the example simple.) With mutator functions, you can control and filter changes to the data.

Self-Test Exercises

12. Suppose your program contains the following class definition,

```
class Automobile
{
public:
    void setPrice(double newPrice);
    void setProfit(double newProfit);
    double getPrice( );
private:
    double price;
    double profit;
    double getProfit( );
};
```

and suppose the main function of your program contains the following declaration and that the program somehow sets the values of all the member variables to some values:

```
Automobile hyundai, jaguar;
```

Which of the following statements are then allowed in the main function of your program?

```
hyundai.price = 4999.99;
jaguar.setPrice(30000.97);
double aPrice, aProfit;
aPrice = jaguar.getPrice( );
aProfit = jaguar.getProfit( );
aProfit = hyundai.getProfit( );
hyundai = jaguar;
```

13. Suppose you change Self-Test Exercise 12 so that in the definition of the class Automobile all member variables are public instead of private. How would this change your answer to the question in Self-Test Exercise 12?

14. Explain what public: and private: mean in a class definition.

15. a. How many public: sections are required in a class for the class to be useful?

b. How many private: sections are required in a class?

Tip

SEPARATE INTERFACE AND IMPLEMENTATION

The principle of encapsulation says that you should define classes so that a programmer who uses the class need not be concerned with the details of how the class is implemented. The programmer who uses the class need only know the rules for how to use the class. The rules for how to use the class are known as the **interface** or **API**. There is some disagreement on exactly what the initials API stand for, but it is generally agreed that they stand for something like *application programmer*

interface

API

interface or *abstract programming interface* or something similar. In this book we will call these rules the *interface* for the class. It is important to keep in mind a clear distinction between the interface and the implementation of a class. If your class is well designed, then any programmer who uses the class need only know the interface for the class and need not know any details of the implementation of the class. A class whose interface and implementation are separated in this way is sometimes called an *abstract data type (ADT)* or a nicely encapsulated class. In Chapter 11 we will show you how to separate the interface and implementation by placing them in different files, but the important thing is to keep them conceptually separated.

For a C++ class, the **interface** consists of two sorts of things: the comments, usually at the beginning of the class definition, that tell what the data of the object is supposed to represent, such as a date or bank account or state of a simulated car wash; and the public member functions of the class along with the comments that tell how to use these public member functions. In a well-designed class, the interface of the class should be all you need to know in order to use the class in your program.

The **implementation** of a class tells how the class interface is realized as C++ code. The implementation consists of the private members of the class and the definitions of both the public and private member functions. Although you need the implementation in order to run a program that uses the class, you should not need to know anything about the implementation in order to write the rest of a program that uses the class; that is, you should not need to know anything about the implementation in order to write the `main` function of the program and to write any nonmember functions or other classes used by the `main` function.

implemen-
tation

The most obvious benefit you derive from cleanly separating the interface and implementation of your classes is that you can change the implementation without having to change the other parts of your program. On large programming projects this division between interface and implementation will facilitate dividing the work among different programmers. If you have a well-designed interface, then one programmer can write the implementation for the class while other programmers write the code that uses the class. Even if you are the only programmer working on a project, you have divided one larger task into two smaller tasks, which makes your program easier to design and to debug.

Tip

A TEST FOR ENCAPSULATION

If your class definition produces an ADT (that is, if it properly separates the interface and the implementation), then you can change the implementation of the class (that is, change the data representation and/or change the implementation of some member functions) without needing to change any (other) code for any program that uses the class definition. This is a sure test for whether you have defined an ADT or just some class that is not properly encapsulated.

For example, you can change the implementation of the class DayOfYear in Display 6.4 to the following and no program that uses this class definition would need any changes:

```
class DayOfYear
{
```

```
    public:
        void input( );
        void output( );

        void set(int newMonth, int newDay);
        //Precondition: newMonth and newDay form a possible date.
        //Postcondition: The date is reset according to the arguments.

        void set(int newMonth);
        //Precondition: 1 <= newMonth <= 12
        //Postcondition: The date is set to first day of the month.

        int getMonthNumber( );
        //Returns 1 for January, 2 for February, etc.

        int getDay( );
    private:
        char firstLetter;//of month
        char secondLetter;//of month
        char thirdLetter;//of month
        int day;
    };
```

In this version, a month is represented by the first three letters in its name, such as 'J', 'a', and 'n' for January. The member functions should also be rewritten, of course, but they can be rewritten to behave *exactly* as they did before. For example, the definition of the function get-MonthNumber might start as follows:

```
    int DayOfYear::getMonthNumber( )
    {
        if (firstLetter == 'J' && secondLetter == 'a'
                && thirdLetter == 'n')
            return 1;
        if (firstLetter == 'F' && secondLetter == 'e'
                && thirdLetter == 'b')
            return 2;
            . . .
```

This would be rather tedious, but not difficult.

■ STRUCTURES VERSUS CLASSES

Structures are normally used with all member variables public and with no member functions. However, in C++ a structure can have private member variables and both public and private member functions. Aside from some notational differences, a C++ structure can do anything a class can do. Having said this and satisfied the "truth in advertising" requirement, we advocate that you forget this technical detail about structures. If

CLASSES AND OBJECTS

A class is a type whose variables can have both member variables and member functions. The syntax for a class definition is given below.

SYNTAX

```
class Class_Name
{

             .
public:
      Member_SpecificationN+1
      Member_SpecificationN+2                    > Public members
             .
             .
             .
private:
      Member_Specification_1
      Member_Specification_2
             .                                   > Private members
             .
             .
      Member_SpecificationN
};              ——————— Do not forget this semicolon.
```

Each *Member_Specification_i* is either a member variable declaration or a member function declaration (prototype).

Additional public: and private: sections are permitted. If the first group of members does not have either a public: or a private: label, then it is the same as if there were a private: before the first group.

EXAMPLE

```
class Bicycle
{
public:
      char getColor( );
      int numberOfSpeeds( );
      void set(int theSpeeds, char theColor);
private:
      int speeds;
      char color;
};
```

Once a class is defined, an object variable (variable of the class type) can be declared in the same way as variables of any other type. For example, the following declares two object variables of type Bicycle:

```
Bicycle myBike, yourBike;
```

you take this technical detail seriously and use structures in the same way that you use classes, then you will have two names (with different syntax rules) for the same concept. On the other hand, if you use structures as we described them, then you will have a meaningful difference between structures (as you use them) and classes; and your usage will be the same as that of most other programmers.

One difference between a structure and a class is that they differ in how they treat an initial group of members that has neither a public nor a private access specifier. If the first group of members in a definition is not labeled with either public: or private:, then a structure assumes the group is public, whereas a class would assume the group is private.

Tip

THINKING OBJECTS

If you have not programmed with classes before, it can take a little while to get the feel of programming with them. When you program with classes, data rather than algorithms takes center stage. It is not that there are no algorithms. However, the algorithms are made to fit the data, as opposed to designing the data to fit the algorithms. It's a difference in point of view. In the extreme case, which is considered by many to be the best style, you have no global functions at all, only classes with member functions. In this case, you define objects and how the objects interact, rather than algorithms that operate on data. We will discuss the details of how you accomplish this throughout this book. Of course, you can ignore classes completely or relegate them to a minor role, but then you are really programming in C, not C++.

Self-Test Exercises

16. When you define a C++ class, should you make the member variables public or private? Should you make the member functions public or private?

17. When you define a C++ class, what items are considered part of the interface? What items are considered part of the implementation?

Chapter Summary

- A structure can be used to combine data of different types into a single (compound) data value.
- A class can be used to combine data and functions into a single (compound) object.
- A member variable or a member function for a class can be either public or private. If it is public, it can be used outside the class. If it is private, it can be used only in the definition of a member function.

- A function can have formal parameters of a class or structure type. A function can return values of a class or structure type.

- A member function for a class can be overloaded in the same way as ordinary functions are overloaded.

- When defining a C++ class, you should separate the interface and implementation so that any programmer who uses the class need only know the interface and need not even look at the implementation. This is the principle of encapsulation.

ANSWERS TO SELF-TEST EXERCISES

1. a. `double`

   b. `double`

   c. illegal—cannot use a structure tag instead of a structure variable

   d. `char`

   e. `CDAccountV2`

2. `A $9.99`
   `A $1.11`

3. A semicolon is missing from the end of the definition of `Stuff`.

4. `A x = {1,2};`

5. a. Too few initializers; not a syntax error. After initialization, `month==12`, `day==21`, and `year==0`. Member variables not provided an initializer are initialized to a zero of the appropriate type.

   b. Correct after initialization. `12==month`, `21==day`, and `1995==year`.

   c. Error: too many initializers.

6.
```
struct EmployeeRecord
{
    double wageRate;
    int vacation;
    char status;
};
```

7.
```
void readShoeRecord(ShoeType& newShoe)
{
    cout << "Enter shoe style (one letter): ";
    cin >> newShoe.style;
    cout << "Enter shoe price $";
    cin >> newShoe.price;
}
```

8.
```
ShoeType discount(ShoeType oldRecord)
{
    ShoeType temp;
    temp.style = oldRecord.style;
    temp.price = 0.90*oldRecord.price;
    return temp;
}
```

9.
```
void DayOfYear::input( )
{
    cout << "Enter month as a number: ";
    cin >> month;
    cout << "Enter the day of the month: ";
    cin >> day;
}
```

10.
```
void Temperature::set(double newDegrees, char newScale)
{
    degrees = newDegrees;
    scale = newScale;
}
```

11. Both the dot operator and the scope resolution operator are used with member names to specify of what class or structure the member name is a member. If `class DayOfYear` is as defined in Display 6.3 and `today` is an object of the class `DayOfYear`, then the member `month` may be accessed with the dot operator: `today.month`. When we give the definition of a member function, the scope resolution operator is used to tell the compiler that this function is the one declared in the class.

12.
```
hyundai.price = 4999.99; //ILLEGAL. price is private.
jaguar.setPrice(30000.97); //LEGAL
double aPrice, aProfit;//LEGAL
aPrice = jaguar.getPrice( );//LEGAL
aProfit = jaguar.getProfit( );//ILLEGAL. getProfit is
                                        //private.
aProfit = hyundai.getProfit( );//ILLEGAL. getProfit is
                                        // private.
hyundai = jaguar;//LEGAL
```

13. After the change, they would all be legal.

14. All members (member variables and member functions) that are marked `private:` can only be accessed by name in the definitions of member functions (both public and private) of the same class. Members marked `public:` have no restrictions on where they can be used.

15. a. Only one. The compiler warns if you have no `public:` members in a class (or `struct`, for that matter).

    b. None, but we normally expect to find at least one `private:` section in a class.

16. The member variables should all be private. The member functions that are part of the interface should be public. You may also have auxiliary (helping) functions that are only used in the definitions of other member functions. These auxiliary functions should be private.

17. All the declarations of private member variables are part of the implementation. (There should be no public member variables.) All the declarations for public member functions of the class (which are listed in the class definitions), as well as the explanatory comments for these declarations, are parts of the interface. All the declarations for private member functions are parts of the implementation. All member function definitions (whether the function is public or private) are parts of the implementation.

PROGRAMMING PROJECTS

1. Write a grading program for a class with the following grading policies.

   a. There are two quizzes, each graded on the basis of 10 points.

   b. There is one midterm exam and one final exam, each graded on the basis of 100 points.

   c. The final exam counts for 50% of the grade, the midterm counts for 25%, and the two quizzes together count for a total of 25%. (Do not forget to normalize the quiz scores. They should be converted to a percentage before they are averaged in.)

   Any grade of 90 or more is an A, any grade of 80 or more (but less than 90) is a B, any grade of 70 or more (but less than 80) is a C, any grade of 60 or more (but less than 70) is a D, and any grade below 60 is an F. The program will read in the student's scores and output the student's record, which consists of two quiz and two exam scores as well as the student's average numeric score for the entire course and final letter grade. Define and use a structure for the student record.

2. Define a class for a type called `CounterType`. An object of this type is used to count things, so it records a count that is a nonnegative whole number. Include a mutator function that sets the counter to a count given as an argument. Include member functions to increase the count by one and to decrease the count by one. Be sure that no member function allows the value of the counter to become negative. Also, include a member function that returns the current count value and one that outputs the count. Embed your class definition in a test program.

3. The type `Point` is a fairly simple data type, but under another name (the template class `pair`) this data type is defined and used in the C++ Standard Template Library, although you need not know anything about the Standard template Library to do this exercise. Write a definition of a class named `Point` that might be used to store and manipulate the location

of a point in the plane. You will need to declare and implement the following member functions:

a. a member function `set` that sets the private data after an object of this class is created.

b. a member function to move the point by an amount along the vertical and horizontal directions specified by the first and second arguments.

c. a member function to rotate the point by 90 degrees clockwise around the origin.

d. two `const` inspector functions to retrieve the current coordinates of the point.

Document these functions with appropriate comments. Embed your class in a test program that requests data for several points from the user, creates the points, then exercises the member functions.

4. Write the definition for a class named `GasPump` to be used to model a pump at an automobile service station. Before you go further with this programming exercise, write down the behavior you expect from a gas pump from the point of view of the purchaser.

Below are listed things a gas pump might be expected to do. If your list differs, and you think your list is as good or better than these, then consult your instructor. You and your instructor should jointly decide what behavior you are to implement. Then implement and test the agreed upon design for a gas pump class.

a. A display of the amount dispensed,

b. A display of the amount charged for the amount dispensed

d. A display of the cost per gallon, liter, or other unit of volume that is used where you reside.

e. Before use, the gas pump must reset the amount dispensed and amount charged to zero.

f. Actual behavior of the gas pump is, once started, it dispenses as long as you hold the nozzle lever. Peculiarities of console I/O make it difficult to continue to dispense while waiting for signal to stop. One solution is to model this behavior by having the user repeatedly press the return (enter) key, dispensing a quantum of fuel and recomputing the amount charged, say 0.1 gallons at each press.

g. A stop dispensing control of some kind is needed.

Implement the behavior of the gas pump as declarations of member functions of the gas pump class, then write implementations of these member functions. You will have to decide if there is data the gas pump has to keep track of that the user of the pump should not have access to. If so, make these private member variables.

7 CHAPTER

Constructors and Other Tools

7 Constructors and Other Tools

Give us the tools and, and we will finish the job.

Winston Churchill, Radio broadcast (February 9, 1941)

INTRODUCTION

This chapter presents a number of important tools to use when programming with classes. The most important of these tools are class constructors, a kind of function used to initialize objects of the class.

Section 7.3 introduces *vectors* as an example of classes and as a preview of the Standard Template Library (STL). Vectors are similar to arrays but can grow and shrink in size. The STL is an extensive library of predefined classes. Section 7.3 may be covered now or later. The material in Chapters 8 through 18 does not require the material in Section 7.3, so you may postpone covering vectors (Section 7.3) if you wish.

Sections 7.1 and 7.2 do not use the material in Chapter 5 but do use the material in Chapter 6. Section 7.3 requires Chapters 1 through 6 as well as Section 7.1.

7.1 Constructors

Well begun is half done.

Proverb

Often you want to initialize some or all the member variables for an object when you declare the object. As we will see later in this book, there are other initializing actions you might also want to take, but initializing member variables is the most common sort of initialization. C++ includes special provisions for such initializations. When you define a class you can define a special

constructor

kind of member function known as a **constructor**. A constructor is a member function that is automatically called when an object of that class is declared. A constructor is used to initialize the values of some or all member variables and to do any other sort of initialization that may be needed.

CONSTRUCTOR DEFINITIONS

You define a constructor the same way that you define any other member function, except for two points:

1. A constructor must have the same name as the class. For example, if the class is named BankAccount, then any constructor for this class must be named BankAccount.

2. A constructor definition cannot return a value. Moreover, no type, not even void, can be given at the start of the function declaration or in the function header.

For example, suppose we wanted to add a constructor for initializing the month and day for objects of type DayOfYear, which we gave in Display 6.4 and redefine in what follows so it includes a constructor. (We have omitted some of the comments to save space, but they should be included in an actual program.)

```
class DayOfYear
{
public:
    DayOfYear(int monthValue, int dayValue);  ◄──── Constructor
    //Initializes the month and day to arguments.

    void input( );
    void output( );
    void set(int newMonth, int newDay);
    void set(int newMonth);
    int getMonthNumber( );
    int getDay( );
private:
    int month;
    int day;
};
```

Notice that the constructor is named DayOfYear, which is the name of the class. Also notice that the declaration (prototype) for the constructor DayOfYear does not start with void or any other type name. Finally, notice that the constructor is placed in the public section of the class definition. Normally, you should make your constructors public member functions. If you were to make all your constructors private members, then you would not be able to declare any objects of that class type, which would make the class completely useless.

With the redefined class DayOfYear, two objects of type DayOfYear can be declared and initialized as follows:

```
DayOfYear date1(7, 4), date2(5, 5);
```

Assuming that the definition of the constructor performs the initializing action that we promised, the above declaration will declare the object date1, set the value of date1.month to 7, and set the value of date1.day to 4. Thus, the object date1 is initialized so that it represents the date July 4. Similarly, date2 is initialized so that it represents the date May 5. What happens is that the object date1 is declared, and then the constructor DayOfYear is called with the two arguments 7 and 4. Similarly, date2 is declared, and then the constructor DayOfYear is called with the arguments 5 and 5. The result is conceptually equivalent to the following (although you cannot write it this way in C++):

```
DayOfYear date1, date2; //PROBLEMS--BUT FIXABLE
date1.DayOfYear(7, 4); //VERY ILLEGAL
date2.DayOfYear(5, 5); //VERY ILLEGAL
```

As the comments indicate, you cannot place the above three lines in your program. The first line can be made to be acceptable, but the two calls to the constructor DayOfYear are illegal. A constructor cannot be called in the same way as an ordinary member function is called. Still, it is clear what we want to happen when we write the above three lines, and that happens automatically when you declare the objects date1 and date2 as follows:

```
DayOfYear date1(7, 4), date2(5, 5);
```

The definition of a constructor is given in the same way as any other member function. For example, if you revise the definition of the class DayOfYear by adding the constructor just described, you need to also add a definition of the constructor, which might be as follows:

```
DayOfYear::DayOfYear(int monthValue, int dayValue)
{
    month = monthValue;
    day = dayValue;
}
```

Since the class and the constructor function have the same name, the name DayOfYear occurs twice in the function heading; the DayOfYear before the scope resolution operator :: is the name of the class, and the DayOfYear after the scope resolution operator is the name of the constructor function. Also notice that no return type is specified in the heading of the constructor definition, not even the type void. Aside from these points, a constructor can be defined in the same way as an ordinary member function.

CONSTRUCTOR

A **constructor** is a member function of a class that has the same name as the class. A constructor is called automatically when an object of the class is declared. Constructors are used to initialize objects. A constructor must have the same name as the class of which it is a member.

As we just illustrated, a constructor can be defined just like any other member function. However, there is an alternative way of defining constructors that is preferable to use. The previous definition of the constructor DayOfYear is completely equivalent to the following version:

```
DayOfYear::DayOfYear(int monthValue, int dayValue)
                              : month(monthValue), day(dayValue)
{/*Body intentionally empty*/}
```

The new element shown on the second line of the constructor definition is called the **initialization section**. As this example shows, the initialization section goes after the parenthesis that ends the parameter list and before the opening brace of the function body. The initialization section consists of a colon followed by a list of some or all the member variables separated by commas. Each member variable is followed by its initializing value in parentheses. Notice that the initializing values can be given in terms of the constructor parameters.

initialization section

The function body in a constructor definition with an initialization section need not be empty as in the above example. For example, the following improved version of the constructor definition checks to see that the arguments are appropriate:

```
DayOfYear::DayOfYear(int monthValue, int dayValue)
                                  : month(monthValue), day(dayValue)
{
    if ((month < 1) || (month > 12))
    {
        cout << "Illegal month value!\n";
        exit(1);
    }
    if ((day < 1) || (day > 31))
    {
        cout << "Illegal day value!\n";
        exit(1);
    }
}
```

You can overload a constructor name like DayOfYear::DayOfYear, just as you can overload any other member function name. In fact, constructors usually are overloaded so that objects can be initialized in more than one way. For example, in Display 7.1 we have redefined the class DayOfYear so that it has three versions of its constructor. This redefinition overloads the constructor name DayOfYear so that it can have two arguments (as we just discussed), one argument, or no arguments.

Notice that in Display 7.1, two constructors call the member function testDate to check that their initialized values are appropriate. The member function testDate is private since it is only intended to be used by other member functions and so is part of the hidden implementation details.

We have omitted the member function set from this revised class definition of DayOfYear. Once you have a good set of constructor definitions, there is no need for any other member functions to set the member variables of the class. You can use the constructor DayOfYear in Display 7.1 for the same purposes that you would use the

Display 7.1   Class with Constructors *(part 1 of 2)*

```
1    #include <iostream>
2    #include <cstdlib> //for exit
3    using namespace std;
```
This definition of DayOfYear is an improved version of the class DayOfYear given in Display 6.4.

```
4    class DayOfYear
5    {
6    public:
7        DayOfYear(int monthValue, int dayValue);
8        //Initializes the month and day to arguments.

9        DayOfYear(int monthValue);
10       //Initializes the date to the first of the given month.

11       DayOfYear( );◄───────────────────── default constructor
12       //Initializes the date to January 1.

13       void input( );
14       void output( );
15       int getMonthNumber( );
16       //Returns 1 for January, 2 for February, etc.

17       int getDay( );
18   private:
19       int month;
20       int day;
21       void testDate( );
22   };
```
This causes a call to the default constructor. Notice that there are no parentheses.

```
23   int main( )
24   {
25       DayOfYear date1(2, 21), date2(5), date3;
26       cout << "Initialized dates:\n";
27       date1.output( ); cout << endl;
28       date2.output( ); cout << endl;
29       date3.output( ); cout << endl;
30       date1 = DayOfYear(10, 31);
31       cout << "date1 reset to the following:\n";
32       date1.output( ); cout << endl;
33       return 0;
34   }
35
36   DayOfYear::DayOfYear(int monthValue, int dayValue)
37                          : month(monthValue), day(dayValue)
38   {
39       testDate( );
40   }
```
an explicit call to the constructor DayOfYear::DayOfYear

Display 7.1   Class with Constructors *(part 2 of 2)*

```
41   DayOfYear::DayOfYear(int monthValue) : month(monthValue), day(1)
42   {
43       testDate( );
44   }

45   DayOfYear::DayOfYear( ) : month(1), day(1)
46   {/*Body intentionally empty.*/}

47   //uses iostream and cstdlib:
48   void DayOfYear::testDate( )
49   {
50       if ((month < 1) || (month > 12))
51       {
52           cout << "Illegal month value!\n";
53           exit(1);
54       }
55       if ((day < 1) || (day > 31))
56       {
57           cout << "Illegal day value!\n";
58           exit(1);
59       }                                    <Definitions of the other member
60   }                                        functions are the same as in Display 6.4.>
```

SAMPLE DIALOGUE

```
Initialized dates:
February 21
May 1
January 1
date1 reset to the following:
October 31
```

member function set (which we included in the old version of the class shown in Display 6.4).

Pitfall   **CONSTRUCTORS WITH NO ARGUMENTS**

It is important to remember not to use any parentheses when you declare a class variable and want the constructor invoked with no arguments. For example, consider the following line from Display 7.1:

```
DayOfYear date1(2, 21), date2(5), date3;
```

The object `date1` is initialized by the constructor that takes two arguments, the object `date2` is initialized by the constructor that takes one argument, and the object `date3` is initialized by the constructor that takes no arguments.

It is tempting to think that empty parentheses should be used when declaring a variable for which you want the constructor with no arguments invoked, but there is a reason why this is not done. Consider the following, which seems like it should declare the variable `date3` and invoke the constructor with no arguments:

```
DayOfYear date3( );//PROBLEM! Not what you might think it is.
```

The problem with this is that although you may mean it as a declaration and constructor invocation, the compiler sees it as a declaration (prototype) of a function named `date3` that has no parameters and that returns a value of type `DayOfYear`. Since a function named `date3` that has no parameters and that returns a value of type `DayOfYear` is perfectly legal, this notation always has that meaning. A different notation (without parentheses) is used when you want to invoke a constructor with no arguments.

CALLING A CONSTRUCTOR

A constructor is called automatically when an object is declared, but you must give the arguments for the constructor when you declare the object. A constructor can also be called explicitly, but the syntax is different from what is used for ordinary member functions.

SYNTAX FOR AN OBJECT DECLARATION WHEN YOU HAVE CONSTRUCTORS

Class_Name Variable_Name(Arguments_for_Constructor);

EXAMPLE

```
DayOfYear holiday(7, 4);
```

SYNTAX FOR AN EXPLICIT CONSTRUCTOR CALL

Variable = Constructor_Name(Arguments_For_Constructor);

EXAMPLE

```
holiday = DayOfyear(10, 31);
```

A constructor must have the same name as the class of which it is a member. Thus, in the above syntax descriptions, *Class_Name* and *Constructor_Name* are the same identifier.

■ EXPLICIT CONSTRUCTOR CALLS

A constructor is called automatically whenever you declare an object of the class type, but it can also be called again after the object has been declared. This allows you to conveniently set all the members of an object. The technical details are as follows. Calling the constructor creates an anonymous object with new values. An anonymous object is an object that is not named (as yet) by any variable. The anonymous object can be assigned to the named object. For example, the following is a call to the constructor DayOfYear that creates an anonymous object for the date May 5. This anonymous object is assigned to the variable holiday (which has been declared to be of type DayOf-Year) so that holiday also represents the date May 5.[1]

```
holiday = DayOfYear(5, 5);
```

(As you might guess from the notation, a constructor sometimes behaves like a function that returns an object of its class type.)

Note that when you explicitly invoke a constructor with no arguments, you *do* include parentheses as follows:

```
holiday = DayOfYear( );
```

The parentheses are only omitted when you declare a variable of the class type and want to invoke a constructor with no arguments as part of the declaration.

Tip

ALWAYS INCLUDE A DEFAULT CONSTRUCTOR

A constructor that takes no arguments is called a **default constructor**. This name can be misleading because sometimes it is generated by default (that is, automatically) and sometimes it is not. Here is the full story. If you define a class and include absolutely no constructors of any kind, then a default constructor will be automatically created. This default constructor does not do anything, but it does give you an uninitialized object of the class type, which can be assigned to a variable of the class type. If your class definition includes one or more constructors of any kind, no constructor is generated automatically. So, for example, suppose you define a class called SampleClass. If you include one or more constructors that each takes one or more arguments, but you do not include a default constructor in your class definition, then there is no default constructor and any declaration like the following will be illegal:

```
SampleClass aVariable;
```

The problem with the above declaration is that it asks the compiler to invoke the default constructor, but there is no default constructor in this case.

default
constructor

---

[1] Note that this process is more complicated than simply changing the values of member variables. For efficiency reasons, therefore, you may wish to retain the member functions named set to use in place of an explicit call to a constructor.

To make this concrete, suppose you define a class as follows:

```
class SampleClass
{
public:
    SampleClass(int parameter1, double parameter2);
    void doStuff( );
private:
    int data1;
    double data2;
};
```

You should recognize the following as a legal way to declare an object of type SampleClass and call the constructor for that class:

```
SampleClass myVariable(7, 7.77);
```

However, the following is illegal:

```
SampleClass yourVariable;
```

The compiler interprets the above declaration as including a call to a constructor with no arguments, but there is no definition for a constructor with zero arguments. You must either add two arguments to the declaration of yourVariable or else add a constructor definition for a constructor with no arguments.

If you redefine the class SampleClass as follows, then the above declaration of yourVariable would be legal:

```
class SampleClass
{
public:
    SampleClass(int parameter1, double parameter2);
    SampleClass( );  ←———— Default constructor
    void doStuff( );
private:
    int data1;
    double data2;
};
```

To avoid this sort of confusion, you should always include a default constructor in any class you define. If you do not want the default constructor to initialize any member variables, you can simply give it an empty body when you implement it. The following constructor definition is perfectly legal. It does nothing but create an uninitialized object:

```
SampleClass::SampleClass( )
{/*Do nothing.*/}
```

CONSTRUCTORS WITH NO ARGUMENTS

A constructor that takes no arguments is called a **default constructor**. When you declare an object and want the constructor with zero arguments to be called, you do not include any parentheses. For example, to declare an object and pass two arguments to the constructor, you might do the following:

```
DayOfYear date1(12, 31);
```

However, if you want the constructor with zero arguments to be used, you declare the object as follows:

```
DayOfYear date2;
```

You do *not* declare the object as follows:

```
DayOfYear date2();//PROBLEM!
```

(The problem is that this syntax declares a function that returns a DayOfYear object and has no parameters.)

You do, however, include the parentheses when you explicitly invoke a constructor with no arguments, as shown below:

```
date1 = DayOfYear( );
```

Self-Test Exercises

1. Suppose your program contains the following class definition (along with definitions of the member functions):

```
class YourClass
{
public:
    YourClass(int newInfo, char moreNewInfo);
    YourClass( );
    void doStuff( );
private:
    int information;
    char moreInformation;
};
```

Which of the following are legal?

```
YourClass anObject(42, 'A');
YourClass anotherObject;
```

```
YourClass yetAnotherObject( );
anObject = YourClass(99, 'B');
anObject = YourClass( );
anObject = YourClass;
```

2. What is a default constructor. Does every class have a default constructor?

Example

BankAccount CLASS

Display 7.2 contains the definition of a class representing a simple bank account embedded in a small demonstration program. A bank account of this form has two pieces of data: the account balance and the interest rate. Note that we have represented the account balance as two values of type int, one for the dollars and one for the cents. This illustrates the fact that the internal representation of the data need not be simply a member variable for each conceptual piece of data. It may seem that the balance should be represented as a value of type double, rather than two int values. However, an account contains an exact number of dollars and cents, and a value of type double is, practically speaking, an approximate quantity. Moreover, a balance such as $323.52 is not a dollar sign in front of a floating-point value. The $323.52 cannot have any more or fewer than two digits after the decimal point. You cannot have a balance of $323.523, and a member variable of type double would allow such a balance. It is not impossible to have an account with fractional cents. It is just not what we want for a bank account.

Note that the programmer who is using the class BankAccount can think of the balance as a value of type double or as two values of type int (for dollars and cents). The accessor and mutator functions allow the programmer to read and set the balance as either a double or two ints. The programmer who is using the class need not and should not think of any underlying member variables. That is part of the implementation that is "hidden" from the programmer using the class.

Note that the mutator function setBalance, as well as the constructor names, are overloaded. Also note that all constructors and mutator functions check values to make sure they are appropriate. For example, an interest rate cannot be negative. A balance can be negative, but you cannot have a positive number of dollars and a negative number of cents.

This class has four private member functions: dollarsPart, centsPart, round, and fraction. These member functions are made private because they are only intended to be used in the definitions of other member functions.

Display 7.2 BankAccount Class *(part 1 of 5)*

```
1    #include <iostream>
2    #include <cmath>
3    #include <cstdlib>
4    using namespace std;

5    //Data consists of two items: an amount of money for the account balance
6    //and a percentage for the interest rate.
7    class BankAccount
8    {
9    public:
10       BankAccount(double balance, double rate);
11       //Initializes balance and rate according to arguments.

12       BankAccount(int dollars, int cents, double rate);
13       //Initializes the account balance to $dollars.cents. For a negative balance both
14       //dollars and cents must be negative. Initializes the interest rate to rate percent.

15       BankAccount(int dollars, double rate);
16       //Initializes the account balance to $dollars.00 and
17       //initializes the interest rate to rate percent.

18       BankAccount( );
19       //Initializes the account balance to $0.00 and the interest rate to 0.0%.

20       void update( );
21       //Postcondition: One year of simple interest has been added to the account.
22       void input( );
23       void output( );
24       double getBalance( );
25       int getDollars( );
26       int getCents( );
27       double getRate( );//Returns interest rate as a percentage.

28       void setBalance(double balance);
29       void setBalance(int dollars, int cents);
30       //Checks that arguments are both nonnegative or both nonpositive.

31       void setRate(double newRate);
32       //If newRate is nonnegative, it becomes the new rate. Otherwise, abort program.
33
34   private:                                                    Private members
35       //A negative amount is represented as negative dollars and negative cents.
36       //For example, negative $4.50 sets accountDollars to −4 and accountCents to −50.
37       int accountDollars; //of balance
38       int accountCents; //of balance
39       double rate;//as a percent
```

Display 7.2   BankAccount Class *(part 2 of 5)*

```
40        int dollarsPart(double amount);
41        int centsPart(double amount);
42        int round(double number);

43        double fraction(double percent);
44        //Converts a percentage to a fraction. For example, fraction(50.3) returns 0.503.
45    };
```

This declaration causes a call to the default constructor. Notice that there are no parentheses.

```
46    int main( )
47    {
48        BankAccount account1(1345.52, 2.3), account2;
49        cout << "account1 initialized as follows:\n";
50        account1.output( );
51        cout << "account2 initialized as follows:\n";
52        account2.output( );

53        account1 = BankAccount(999, 99, 5.5);
54        cout << "account1 reset to the following:\n";
55        account1.output( );

56        cout << "Enter new data for account 2:\n";
57        account2.input( );
58        cout << "account2 reset to the following:\n";
59        account2.output( );

60        account2.update( );
61        cout << "In one year account2 will grow to:\n";
62        account2.output( );

63        return 0;
64    }
```

an explicit call to the constructor BankAccount::BankAccount

```
65    BankAccount::BankAccount(double balance, double rate)
66      : accountDollars(dollarsPart(balance)), accountCents(centsPart(balance))
67    {
68        setRate(rate);
69    }

70    BankAccount::BankAccount(int dollars, int cents, double rate)
71    {
72        setBalance(dollars, cents);
73        setRate(rate);
74    }
```

These functions check that the data is appropriate.

```
75    BankAccount::BankAccount(int dollars, double rate)
76                                    : accountDollars(dollars), accountCents(0)
77    {
78        setRate(rate);
```

Display 7.2   BankAccount Class *(part 3 of 5)*

```
79   }

80   BankAccount::BankAccount( ): accountDollars(0), accountCents(0), rate(0.0)
81   {/*Body intentionally empty.*/}

82   void BankAccount::update( )
83   {
84       double balance = accountDollars + accountCents*0.01;
85       balance = balance + fraction(rate)*balance;
86       accountDollars = dollarsPart(balance);
87       accountCents = centsPart(balance);
88   }

89   //Uses iostream:
90   void BankAccount::input( )
91   {
92       double balanceAsDouble;
93       cout << "Enter account balance $";
94       cin >> balanceAsDouble;
95       accountDollars = dollarsPart(balanceAsDouble);
96       accountCents = centsPart(balanceAsDouble);
97       cout << "Enter interest rate (NO percent sign): ";
98       cin >> rate;
99       setRate(rate);
100   }
101   //Uses iostream and cstdlib:
102   void BankAccount::output( )
103   {
104       int absDollars = abs(accountDollars);
105       int absCents = abs(accountCents);
106       cout << "Account balance: $";
107       if (accountDollars < 0)
108           cout << "-";
109       cout << absDollars;
110       if (absCents >= 10)
111           cout << "." << absCents << endl;
112       else
113           cout << "." << '0' << absCents << endl;

114       cout << "Rate: " << rate << "%\n";
115   }

116   double BankAccount::getBalance( )
117   {
118       return (accountDollars + accountCents*0.01);
119   }
```

For a better definition of BankAccount::input see Self-Test Exercise 3.

Display 7.2   Bank Account Class *(part 4 of 5)*

```
120   int BankAccount::getDollars( )
121   {
122       return accountDollars;
123   }
```
The programmer using the class does not care if the balance is stored as one real or two ints.

```
124   int BankAccount::getCents( )
125   {
126       return accountCents;
127   }

128   double BankAccount::getRate( )
129   {
130       return rate;
131   }

132   void BankAccount::setBalance(double balance)
133   {
134       accountDollars = dollarsPart(balance);
135       accountCents = centsPart(balance);
136   }

137   //Uses cstdlib:
138   void BankAccount::setBalance(int dollars, int cents)
139   {
140       if ((dollars < 0 && cents > 0) || (dollars > 0 && cents < 0))
141       {
142           cout << "Inconsistent account data.\n";
143           exit(1);
144       }
145       accountDollars = dollars;
146       accountCents = cents;
147   }

148   //Uses cstdlib:
149   void BankAccount::setRate(double newRate)
150   {
151       if (newRate >= 0.0)
152           rate = newRate;
153       else
154       {
155           cout << "Cannot have a negative interest rate.\n";
156           exit(1);
157       }
158   }
```
This could be a regular function rather than a member function, but as a member functions we were able to make it private.

```
159   int BankAccount::dollarsPart(double amount)
160   {
```

Display 7.2 Bank Account Class *(part 5 of 5)*

```
161        return static_cast<int>(amount);
162    }
163    //Uses cmath:
164    int BankAccount::centsPart(double amount)
165    {
166        double doubleCents = amount*100;
167        int intCents = (round(fabs(doubleCents)))%100;//% can misbehave on negatives
168        if (amount < 0)
169            intCents = -intCents;
170        return intCents;
171    }
```

These could be regular functions rather than member functions, but as member functions we were able to make them private.

```
172    //Uses cmath:
173    int BankAccount::round(double number)
174    {
175        return static_cast<int>(floor(number + 0.5));
176    }
```

if this does not seem clear, see the discussion of round in Chapter 3, Section 3.2.

```
177    double BankAccount::fraction(double percent)
178    {
179        return (percent/100.0);
180    }
```

SAMPLE DIALOGUE

```
account1 initialized as follows:
Account balance: $1345.52
Rate: 2.3%
account2 initialized as follows:
Account balance: $0.00
Rate: 0%
account1 reset to the following:
Account balance: $999.99
Rate: 5.5%
Enter new data for account 2:
Enter account balance $100.00
Enter interest rate (NO percent sign): 10
account2 reset to the following:
Account balance: $100
Rate: 10%
In one year account2 will grow to:
Account balance: $110
Rate: 10%
```

Self-Test Exercises

3. The function `BankAccount::input` in Display 7.2 reads the balance of the account as a value of type `double`. When the value is stored in the computer's memory in binary form, this can create a slight error. It would normally not be noticed and the function is good enough for the demonstration class `BankAccount`. Spending too much time on numerical analysis would detract from the message at hand. Still, this input function is not good enough for banking. Rewrite the function `BankAccount::input` so it reads an amount such as `78.96` as the `int` `76` and the three `char` values `'.'`, `'9'`, and `'6'`. You can assume the user always enters two digits for the cents in an amount, such as `99.00` instead of just `99` and nothing more. *Hint:* The following formula will convert a digit to the corresponding `int` value, such as `'6'` to 6:

```
static_cast<int>(digit) - static_cast<int>('0')
```

■ **CLASS TYPE MEMBER VARIABLES**

A class may have a member variable whose type is that of another class. By and large there is nothing special that you need to do to have a class member variable, but there is a special notation to allow for the invocation of the member variable's constructor within the constructor of the outer class. An example is given in Display 7.3.

The class `Holiday` in Display 7.3 might be used by some city police department to help keep track of which holidays will have parking enforcement (of things such as parking meters and one hour parking zones). It's a highly simplified class. A real class would have more member functions, but the class `Holiday` is complete enough to illustrate our points.

The class `Holiday` has two member variables. The member variable `parkingEnforcement` is an ordinary member variable of the simple type `bool`. The member variable `date` is of the class type `DayOfYear`.

Below we have reproduced one constructor definition from Display 7.3:

```
Holiday::Holiday(int month, int day, bool theEnforcement)
        : date(month, day), parkingEnforcement(theEnforcement)
{/*Intentionally empty*/}
```

Notice that we have set the member variable `parkingEnforcement` in the initialization section in the usual way, namely, with

```
parkingEnforcement(theEnforcement)
```

The member variable `date` is a member of the class type `DayOfYear`. To initialize `date`, we need to invoke a constructor from the class `DayOfYear` (the type of `date`). This is done in the initialization section with the similar notation

```
date(month, day)
```

Display 7.3   A Class Member Variable *(part 1 of 3)*

```
1    #include <iostream>
2    #include<cstdlib>
3    using namespace std;

4    class DayOfYear
5    {
6    public:
7        DayOfYear(int monthValue, int dayValue);
8        DayOfYear(int monthValue);
9        DayOfYear( );
10       void input( );
11       void output( );
12       int getMonthNumber( );
13       int getDay( );
14   private:
15       int month;
16       int day;
17       void testDate( );
18   };

19   class Holiday
20   {
21   public:
22       Holiday( );//Initializes to January 1 with no parking enforcement
23       Holiday(int month, int day, bool theEnforcement);
24       void output( );
25   private:
26       DayOfYear date;
27       bool parkingEnforcement;//true if enforced
28   };

29   int main( )
30   {
31       Holiday h(2, 14, true);
32       cout << "Testing the class Holiday.\n";
33       h.output( );

34       return 0;
35   }
36
37   Holiday::Holiday( ) : date(1, 1), parkingEnforcement(false)
38   {/*Intentionally empty*/}

39   Holiday::Holiday(int month, int day, bool theEnforcement)
40                      : date(month, day), parkingEnforcement(theEnforcement)
41   {/*Intentionally empty*/}
```

The class DayOfYear is the same as in Display 7.1, but we have repeated all the details you need for this discussion.

member variable of a class type

Invocations of constructors from the class DayOfYear.

Display 7.3   A Class Member Variable *(part 2 of 3)*

```
42   void Holiday::output( )
43   {
44       date.output( );
45       cout << endl;
46       if (parkingEnforcement)
47           cout << "Parking laws will be enforced.\n";
48       else
49           cout << "Parking laws will not be enforced.\n";
50   }

51   DayOfYear::DayOfYear(int monthValue, int dayValue)
52                           : month(monthValue), day(dayValue)
53   {
54       testDate( );
55   }

56   //uses iostream and cstdlib:
57   void DayOfYear::testDate( )
58   {
59       if ((month < 1) || (month > 12))
60       {
61           cout << "Illegal month value!\n";
62           exit(1);
63       }
64       if ((day < 1) || (day > 31))
65       {
66           cout << "Illegal day value!\n";
67           exit(1);
68       }
69   }
70
71   //Uses iostream:
72   void DayOfYear::output( )
73   {
74       switch (month)
75       {
76           case 1:
77               cout << "January "; break;
78           case 2:
79               cout << "February "; break;
80           case 3:
81               cout << "March "; break;
                 .
                 .
                 .
```

The omitted lines are in Display 6.3, but they are obvious enough that you should not have to look there.

Display 7.3   A Class Member Variable *(part 3 of 3)*

```
82              case 11:
83                  cout << "November "; break;
84              case 12:
85                  cout << "December "; break;
86              default:
87                  cout << "Error in DayOfYear::output. Contact software vendor.";
88          }

89          cout << day;
90      }
```

SAMPLE DIALOGUE

```
Testing the class Holiday.
February 14
Parking laws will be enforced.
```

The notation date(month, day) is an invocation of the constructor for the class DayOf-Year with arguments month and day to initialize the member variables of date. Notice that this notation is analogous to how you would declare a variable date of type Day-OfYear. Also notice that the parameters of the larger class constructor Holiday can be used in the invocation of the constructor for the member variable.

7.2   More Tools

Intelligence . . . is the facility of making artificial objects, especially tools to make tools.

Henri Bergson, *Creative Evolution*

This section discusses three topics that, although important, did not fit easily before here. The three topics are const parameters for classes, inline functions, and static class members.

THE const PARAMETER MODIFIER

A call-by-reference parameter is more efficient than a call-by-value parameter. A call-by-value parameter is a local variable that is initialized to the value of its argument, so when the function is called there are two copies of the argument. With a call-by-reference parameter, the parameter is just a placeholder that is replaced by the argument, so there is only one copy of the argument. For parameters of simple types, such as int or dou-ble, the difference in efficiency is negligible, but for class parameters the difference in

constant
parameter

efficiency can sometimes be important. Thus, it can make sense to use a call-by-reference parameter rather than a call-by-value parameter for a class, even if the function does not change the parameter.

If you are using a call-by-reference parameter and your function does not change the value of the parameter, you can mark the parameter so that the compiler knows that the parameter should not be changed. To do so, place the modifier const before the parameter type. The parameter is then called a **constant parameter** or **constant call-by-reference parameter**. For example, in Display 7.2 we defined a class named BankAccount for simple bank accounts. In some program you might want to write a Boolean-valued function to test which of two accounts has the larger balance. The definition of the function might be as follows:

```
bool isLarger(BankAccount account1, BankAccount account2)
//Returns true if the balance in account1 is greater than that
//in account2. Otherwise returns false.
{
    return(account1.getBalance( ) > account2.getBalance( ));
}
```

This is perfectly legal. The two parameters are call-by-value parameters. However, it would be more efficient and is more common to make the parameters constant call-by-reference parameters, as follows:

```
bool isLarger(const BankAccount& account1,
                     const BankAccount& account2)
//Returns true if the balance in account1 is greater than that
//in account2. Otherwise, returns false.
{
    return(account1.getBalance( ) > account2.getBalance( ));
}
```

Note that the only difference is that we made the parameter call-by-reference by adding & and we added the const modifiers. If there is a function declaration, then the same change must be made to the parameters in the function declaration.

Constant parameters are a form of automatic error checking. If your function definition contains a mistake that causes an inadvertent change to the constant parameter, the compiler will issue an error message.

The parameter modifier const can be used with any kind of parameter; however, it is normally used only for call-by-reference parameters for classes (and for certain other parameters whose corresponding arguments are large, such as arrays).

Suppose you invoke a member function for an object of a class, such as the class BankAccount in Display 7.2. For example:

```
BankAccount myAccount;
myAccount.input( );
myAccount.output( );
```

The invocation of the member function input changes the values of the member variables in the calling object myAccount. So the calling object behaves sort of like a call-by-reference parameter; the function invocation can change the calling object. Sometimes, you do not want to change the member variables of the calling object. For example, the member function output should not change the values of the calling object's member variables. You can use the const modifier to tell the compiler that a member function invocation should not change the calling object.

The modifier const applies to calling objects in the same way that it applies to parameters. If you have a member function that should not change the value of a calling object, you can mark the function with the const modifier; the computer will then issue an error message if your function code inadvertently changes the value of the calling object. In the case of a member function, the const goes at the end of the function declaration, just before the final semicolon, as shown below:

const with member functions

```
class BankAccount
{
public:
        . . .
    void output( ) const;
        . . .
```

The modifier const should be used in both the function declaration and the function definition, so the function definition for output would begin as follows:

```
void BankAccount::output( ) const
{
    . . .
```

The remainder of the function definition would be the same as in Display 7.2.

Pitfall

INCONSISTENT USE OF const

Use of the const modifier is an all-or-nothing proposition. If you use const for one parameter of a particular type, then you should use it for every other parameter that has that type and that is not changed by the function call. Moreover, if the type is a class type, then you should also use the const modifier for every member function that does not change the value of its calling object. The reason has to do with function calls within function calls. For example, consider the following definition of the function welcome:

```
void welcome(const BankAccount& yourAccount)
{
    cout << "Welcome to our bank.\n"
         << "The status of your account is:\n";
    yourAccount.output( );
}
```

If you do *not* add the const modifier to the function declaration for the member function out-put, then the function welcome will produce an error message. The member function welcome does not change the calling object price. However, when the compiler processes the function definition for welcome, it will think that welcome does (or at least might) change the value of

const PARAMETER MODIFIER

If you place the modifier const before the type for a call-by-reference parameter, the parameter is called a **constant parameter.** When you add the const you are telling the compiler that this parameter should not be changed. If you make a mistake in your definition of the function so that it does change the constant parameter, then the compiler will give an error message. Parameters of a class type that are not changed by the function ordinarily should be constant call-by-reference parameters rather than call-by-value parameters.

If a member function does not change the value of its calling object, then you can mark the function by adding the const modifier to the function declaration. If you make a mistake in your definition of the function so that it does change the calling object and the function is marked with const, the computer will give an error message. The const is placed at the end of the function declaration, just before the final semicolon. The heading of the function definition should also have a const so that it matches the function declaration.

EXAMPLE

```
class Sample
{
public:
    Sample( );
    void input( );
    void output( ) const;
private:
    int stuff;
    double moreStuff;
};

int compare(const Sample& s1, const Sample& s2);
```

Use of the const modifier is an all or nothing proposition. You should use the const modifier whenever it is appropriate for a class parameter and whenever it is appropriate for a member function of the class. If you do not use const every time that it is appropriate for a class, then you should never use it for that class.

yourAccount. This is because when it is translating the function definition for welcome, all that the compiler knows about the member function output is the function declaration for output. If the function declaration does not contain a const that tells the compiler that the calling object will not be changed, then the compiler assumes that the calling object will be changed. Thus, if you use the modifier const with parameters of type BankAccount, then you should also use const with all BankAccount member functions that do not change the values of their calling objects. In particular, the function declaration for the member function output should include a const.

In Display 7.4 we have rewritten the definition of the class BankAccount given in Display 7.2, but this time we have used the const modifier where appropriate. In Display 7.4 we have also added the two functions isLarger and welcome, which we discussed earlier and which have constant parameters.

Self-Test Exercises

4. Why would it be incorrect to add the modifier const, as shown below, to the declaration for the member function input of the class BankAccount given in Display 7.2?

```
class BankAccount
{
public:
    void input( ) const;
        ...
```

5. What are the differences and the similarities between a call-by-value parameter and a constant call-by-reference parameter? Declarations that illustrate these follow.

```
void callByValue(int x);
void callByConstReference(const int& x);
```

6. Given the definitions

```
const int x = 17;
class A
{
public:
    A( );
    A(int n);
    int f( )const;
    int g(const A& x);
private:
    int i;
};
```

Each of the three const keywords is a promise to the compiler that the compiler will enforce. What is the promise in each case?

Display 7.4   The const Parameter Modifier *(part 1 of 3)*

```
1   #include <iostream>
2   #include <cmath>
3   #include <cstdlib>
4   using namespace std;

5   //Data consists of two items: an amount of money for the account balance
6   //and a percentage for the interest rate.
7   class BankAccount
8   {
9   public:
10      BankAccount(double balance, double rate);
11      //Initializes balance and rate according to arguments.

12      BankAccount(int dollars, int cents, double rate);
13      //Initializes the account balance to $dollars.cents. For a negative balance both
14      //dollars and cents must be negative. Initializes the interest rate to rate percent.

15      BankAccount(int dollars, double rate);
16      //Initializes the account balance to $dollars.00 and
17      //initializes the interest rate to rate percent.

18      BankAccount( );
19      //Initializes the account balance to $0.00 and the interest rate to 0.0%.

20      void update( );
21      //Postcondition: One year of simple interest has been added to the account.
22      void input( );
23      void output( ) const;
24      double getBalance( ) const;
25      int getDollars( ) const;
26      int getCents( ) const;
27      double getRate( ) const;//Returns interest rate as a percentage.

28      void setBalance(double balance);
29      void setBalance(int dollars, int cents);
30      //Checks that arguments are both nonnegative or both nonpositive.

31      void setRate(double newRate);
32      //If newRate is nonnegative, it becomes the new rate. Otherwise, abort program.
33
34  private:
35      //A negative amount is represented as negative dollars and negative cents.
36      //For example, negative $4.50 sets accountDollars to -4 and accountCents to -50.
37      int accountDollars; //of balance
38      int accountCents; //of balance
39      double rate;//as a percent
```

This is class from Display 7.2 rewritten using the const modifier.

Display 7.4   The const Parameter Modifier *(part 2 of 3)*

```
40       int dollarsPart(double amount) const;
41       int centsPart(double amount) const;
42       int round(double number) const;

43       double fraction(double percent) const;
44       //Converts a percentage to a fraction. For example, fraction(50.3) returns 0.503.
45    };

46    //Returns true if the balance in account1 is greater than that
47    //in account2. Otherwise returns false.
48    bool isLarger(const BankAccount& account1, const BankAccount& account2);

49    void welcome(const BankAccount& yourAccount);

50    int main( )
51    {
52        BankAccount account1(6543.21, 4.5), account2;
53        welcome(account1);
54        cout << "Enter data for account 2:\n";
55        account2.input( );
56        if (isLarger(account1, account2))
57            cout << "account1 is larger.\n";
58        else
59            cout << "account2 is at least as large as account1.\n";

60            return 0;
61    }
62
63    bool isLarger(const BankAccount& account1, const BankAccount& account2)
64    {
65        return(account1.getBalance( ) > account2.getBalance( ));
66    }

67    void welcome(const BankAccount& yourAccount)
68    {
69        cout << "Welcome to our bank.\n"
70             << "The status of your account is:\n";
71        yourAccount.output( );
72    }

73    //Uses iostream and cstdlib:
74    void BankAccount::output( ) const
75        <The rest of the function definition is the same as in Display 7.2.>


76        <Other function definitions are the same as in Display 7.2, except that
77            const is added where needed to match the function declaration.>
```

Display 7.4   The const Parameter Modifier (part 3 of 3)

SAMPLE DIALOGUE

```
Welcome to our bank.
The status of your account is:
Account balance: $6543.21
Rate: 4.5%
Enter data for account 2:
Enter account balance $100.00
Enter interest rate (NO percent sign): 10
account1 is larger.
```

INLINE FUNCTIONS

inline function

You can give the complete definition of a member function within the definition of its class. Such definitions are called **inline function definitions**. These inline definitions are typically used for very short function definitions. Display 7.5 shows the class in Display 7.4 rewritten with a number of inline functions.

Inline functions are more than just a notational variant of the kind of member function definitions we have already seen. The compiler treats an inline function in a special way. The code for an inline function declaration is inserted at each location where the function is invoked. This saves the overhead of a function invocation.

All other things being equal, an inline function should be more efficient and hence presumably preferable to a function defined in the usual way. However, all other things are seldom, if ever, equal. Inline functions have the disadvantage of mixing the interface and implementation of a class and so go against the principle of encapsulation. And, so the usual arguments go back and forth.

It is generally believed that only very short function definitions should be defined inline. For long function definitions, the inline version can actually be less efficient, because a large piece of code is repeated frequently. Beyond that general rule, you will have to decide for yourself whether to use inline functions.

Any function can be defined to be an inline function. To define a nonmember function to be inline, just place the keyword `inline` before the function declaration and function definition. We will not use, or further discuss, inline nonmember functions in this book.

Self-Test Exercises

7. Rewrite the definition of the class DayOfYear given in Display 7.3 so that the functions getMonthNumber and getDay are defined inline.

Display 7.5   Inline Function Definitions

```
1    #include <iostream>            This is Display 7.4 rewritten using inline member functions.
2    #include <cmath>
3    #include <cstdlib>
4    using namespace std;

5    class BankAccount
6    {
7     public:
8         BankAccount(double balance, double rate);
9         BankAccount(int dollars, int cents, double rate);
10        BankAccount(int dollars, double rate);
11        BankAccount( );
12        void update( );
13        void input( );
14        void output( ) const;

15        double getBalance( ) const { return (accountDollars + accountCents*0.01);}

16        int getDollars( ) const { return accountDollars; }

17        int getCents( ) const { return accountCents; }

18        double getRate( ) const { return rate; }

19        void setBalance(double balance);
20        void setBalance(int dollars, int cents);
21        void setRate(double newRate);
22     private:
23        int accountDollars; //of balance
24        int accountCents; //of balance
25        double rate;//as a percentage

26        int dollarsPart(double amount) const { return static_cast<int>(amount); }

27        int centsPart(double amount) const;

28        int round(double number) const
29        { return static_cast<int>(floor(number + 0.5)); }

30        double fraction(double percent) const { return (percent/100.0); }
31    };
```

<Inline functions have no further definitions. Other function definitions are as in Display 7.4.>

■ STATIC MEMBERS

static variable

Sometimes you want to have one variable that is shared by all the objects of a class. For example, you might want one variable to count the number of times a particular member function is invoked by all objects of the class. Such variables are called **static variables** and can be used for objects of the class to communicate with each other or coordinate their actions. Such variables allow some of the advantages of global variables without opening the flood gates to all the abuses that true global variables invite. In particular, a static variable can be private so that only objects of the class can directly access it.

If a function does not access the data of any object and yet you want the function to be a member of the class, you can make it a static function. Static functions can be invoked in the normal way, using a calling object of the class. However, it is more common and clearer to invoke a static function using the class name and scope resolution operator, as in the following example:

```
Server::getTurn( )
```

Because a static function does not need a calling object, the definition of a static function cannot use anything that depends on a calling object. A static function definition cannot use any nonstatic variables or nonstatic member functions, unless the nonstatic variable or function has a calling object that is a local variable or some object otherwise created in the definition. If that last sentence seems hard to understand, just use the simpler rule that the definition of a static function cannot use anything that depends on a calling object.

Display 7.6 is a demonstration program that uses both static variables and static functions. Note that static variables are indicated by the qualifying keyword `static` at the start of their declaration. Also notice that all the static variables are initialized as follows:

initializing
static
member
variables

```
int Server::turn = 0;
int Server::lastServed = 0;
bool Server::nowOpen = true;
```

Such initialization requires a bit of explanation. Every static variable must be initialized outside the class definition. Also, a static variable cannot be initialized more than once. As in Display 7.6, private static variables—in fact, all static variables—are initialized outside the class. This may seem to be contrary to the notion of private. However, the author of a class is expected to do the initializations, typically in the same file as the class definition. In that case, no programmer who uses the class can initialize the static variables, since a static variable cannot be initialized a second time.

Notice that the keyword `static` is used in the member function declaration but is not used in the member function definition.

Display 7.6   Static Members *(part 1 of 2)*

```
1   #include <iostream>
2   using namespace std;

3   class Server
4   {
5   public:
6       Server(char letterName);
7       static int getTurn( );
8       void serveOne( );
9       static bool stillOpen( );
10  private:
11      static int turn;
12      static int lastServed;
13      static bool nowOpen;
14      char name;
15  };

16  int Server:: turn = 0;
17  int Server:: lastServed = 0;
18  bool Server::nowOpen = true;

19  int main( )
20  {
21      Server s1('A'), s2('B');
22      int number, count;
23      do
24      {
25          cout << "How many in your group? ";
26          cin >> number;
27          cout << "Your turns are: ";
28          for (count = 0; count < number; count++)
29              cout << Server::getTurn( ) << ' ';
30          cout << endl;
31          s1.serveOne( );
32          s2.serveOne( );
33      } while (Server::stillOpen( ));

34      cout << "Now closing service.\n";

35      return 0;
36  }

37
38  Server::Server(char letterName) : name(letterName)
39  {/*Intentionally empty*/}

40  int Server::getTurn( )
41  {
42      turn++;
43      return turn;
44  }
```

Since getTurn is static, only static members can be referenced in here.

Display 7.6   Static Members *(part 2 of 2)*

```
45    bool Server::stillOpen( )
46    {
47        return nowOpen;
48    }

49    void Server::serveOne( )
50    {
51        if (nowOpen && lastServed < turn)
52        {
53            lastServed++;
54            cout << "Server " << name
55                << " now serving " << lastServed << endl;
56        }

57        if (lastServed >= turn) //Everyone served
58            nowOpen = false;
59    }
```

SAMPLE DIALOGUE

```
How many in your group? 3
Your turns are: 1 2 3
Server A now serving 1
Server B now serving 2
How many in your group? 2
Your turns are: 4 5
Server A now serving 3
Server B now serving 4
How many in your group? 0
Your turns are:
Server A now serving 5
Now closing service.
```

The program in Display 7.6 is the outline of a scenario that has one queue of clients waiting for service and two servers to service this single queue. You can come up with a number of system programming scenarios to flesh this out to a realistic example. For a simple minded model just to learn the concepts, think of the numbers produced by getTurn as those little slips of paper handed out to customers in a delicatessen or ice cream shop. The two servers are then two clerks who wait on customers. One perhaps peculiar detail of this shop is that customers arrive in groups but are waited on one at a time (perhaps to order their own particular kind of sandwich or ice cream flavor).

Self-Test Exercises

8. Could the function defined as follows be added to the class `Server` in Display 7.6 as a static function? Explain your answer.
```
void Server::showStatus( )
{
    cout << "Currently serving " << turn << endl;
    cout << "server name " << name << endl;
}
```

▪ NESTED AND LOCAL CLASS DEFINITIONS

The material in this section is included for reference value and, except for a brief passing reference in Chapter 17, is not used elsewhere in this book.

You can define a class within a class. Such a class within a class is called a **nested class**. The general layout is obvious:

nested class

```
class OuterClass
{
public:
    ...
private:
    class InnerClass
    {
        ...
    };
    ...
};
```

A nested class can be either public or private. If it is private, as in our sample layout, then it cannot be used outside of the outer class. Whether the nested class is public or private, it can be used in member function definitions of the outer class.

Since the nested class is in the scope of the outer class, the name of the nested class, like `InnerClass` in our sample layout, may be used for something else outside of the outer class. If the nested class is public, the nested class can be used as a type outside of the outer class. However, outside of the outer class, the type name of the nested class is `OuterClass::InnerClass`.

We will not have occasion to use such nested class definitions in this book. However, in Chapter 17 we do suggest one possible application for nested classes.[2]

A class definition can also be defined within a function definition. In such cases the class is called a **local class**, since its meaning is confined to the function definition. A

local class

---

[2] The suggestion is in the subsection of Chapter 17 entitled "Friend Classes and Similar Alternatives."

local class may not contain static members. We will not have occasion to use local classes in this book.

7.3 Vectors—A Preview of the Standard Template Library

"Well, I'll eat it," said Alice, "and if it makes me grow larger, I can reach the key; and if it makes me grow smaller, I can creep under the door; so either way I'll get into the garden."

Lewis Carroll, *Alice's Adventures in Wonderland*

vector

Vectors can be thought of as arrays that can grow (and shrink) in length while your program is running. In C++, once your program creates an array, it cannot change the length of the array. Vectors serve the same purpose as arrays except that they can change length while the program is running.

Vectors are formed from a template class in the Standard Template Library (STL). We discuss templates in Chapter 16 and discuss the STL in Chapter 19. However, it is easy to learn some basic uses of vectors before you learn about templates and the STL in detail. You do not need to know a great deal about classes to use vectors. You can cover this section on vectors after reading Chapter 6. You need not have read the previous sections of this chapter before covering this section.

▨ VECTOR BASICS

Like an array, a vector has a base type, and like an array, a vector stores a collection of values of its base type. However, the syntax for a vector type and a vector variable declaration is different from the syntax for arrays.

declaring a
vector
variable

You declare a variable, v, for a vector with base type int as follows:

```
vector<int> v;
```

template class

The notation vector<*Base_Type*> is a **template class**, which means you can plug in any type for *Base_Type* and that will produce a class for vectors with that base type. You can simply think of this as specifying the base type for a vector in the same sense as you specify a base type for an array. You can use any type, including class types, as the base type for a vector. The notation vector<int> is a class name and so the previous declaration of v as a vector of type vector<int> includes a call to the default constructor for the class vector<int> that creates a vector object that is empty (has no elements).

v[i]

Vector elements are indexed starting with 0, the same as arrays. The square brackets notation can be used to read or change these elements, just as with an array. For example, the following changes the value of the ith element of the vector v and then outputs that changed value. (i is an int variable.)

```
v[i] = 42;
cout << "The answer is " << v[i];
```

There is, however, a restriction on this use of the square brackets notation with vectors that is unlike the same notation used with arrays. You can use v[i] to change the value of the ith element. However, you cannot initialize the ith element using v[i]; you can only change an element that has already been given some value. To add an element to a vector for the first time, you normally use the member function push_back.

You add elements to a vector in order of positions, first at position 0, then position 1, then 2, and so forth. The member function push_back adds an element in the next available position. For example, the following gives initial values to elements 0, 1, and 2 of the vector sample:

push_back

```
vector<double> sample;
sample.push_back(0.0);
sample.push_back(1.1);
sample.push_back(2.2);
```

The number of elements in a vector is called the **size** of the vector. The member function size can be used to determine how many elements are in a vector. For example, after the previously shown code is executed, sample.size( ) returns 3. You can write out all the elements currently in the vector sample as follows:

size

```
for (int i = 0; i < sample.size( ); i++)
    cout << sample[i] << endl;
```

The function size returns a value of type unsigned int, not a value of type int. This returned value should be automatically converted to type int when it needs to be of type int, but some compiler may warn you that you are using an unsigned int where an int is required. If you want to be very safe, you can always apply a type cast to convert the returned unsigned int to an int, or in cases like this for loop, use a loop control variable of type unsigned int as follows:

size
unsigned
int

```
for (unsigned int i = 0; i < sample.size( ); i++)
    cout << sample[i] << endl;
```

A simple demonstration illustrating some basic vector techniques is given in Display 7.7.

There is a vector constructor that takes one integer argument and will initialize the number of positions given as the argument. For example, if you declare v as follows:

```
vector<int> v(10);
```

then the first ten elements are initialized to 0 and v.size( ) would return 10. You can then set the value of the ith element using v[i] for values of i equal to 0 through 9. In particular, the following could immediately follow the declaration:

```
for (unsigned int i = 0; i < 10; i++)
    v[i] = i;
```

Display 7.7   Using a Vector

```
1   #include <iostream>
2   #include <vector>
3   using namespace std;

4   int main( )
5   {
6       vector<int> v;
7       cout << "Enter a list of positive numbers.\n"
8            << "Place a negative number at the end.\n";

9       int next;
10      cin >> next;
11      while (next > 0)
12      {
13          v.push_back(next);
14          cout << next << " added. ";
15          cout << "v.size( ) = " << v.size( ) << endl;
16          cin >> next;
17      }

18      cout << "You entered:\n";
19      for (unsigned int i = 0; i < v.size( ); i++)
20          cout << v[i] << " ";
21      cout << endl;

22      return 0;
23  }
```

SAMPLE DIALOGUE

```
Enter a list of positive numbers.
Place a negative number at the end.
2 4 6 8 -1
2 added. v.size = 1
4 added. v.size = 2
6 added. v.size = 3
8 added. v.size = 4
You entered:
2 4 6 8
```

To set the ith element for i greater than or equal to 10, you would use push_back.

When you use the constructor with an integer argument, vectors of numbers are initialized to the zero of the number type. If the vector base type is a class type, the default constructor is used for initialization.

The vector definition is given in the library vector, which places it in the std namespace. Thus, a file that uses vectors would include the following (or something similar):

```
#include <vector>
using namespace std;
```

VECTORS

Vectors are used very much like arrays, but a vector does not have a fixed size. If it needs more capacity to store another element, its capacity is automatically increased. Vectors are defined in the library vector, which places them in the std namespace. Thus, a file that uses vectors would include the following lines:

```
#include <vector>
using namespace std;
```

The vector class for a given *Base_Type* is written vector<*Base Type*>. Two sample vector declarations are as follows:

```
vector<int> v; //default constructor producing an empty vector.
vector<AClass> record(20); //vector constructor uses the
    //default constructor for AClass to initialize 20 elements.
```

Elements are added to a vector using the member function push_back, as illustrated below:

```
v.push_back(42);
```

Once an element position has received its first element, either with push_back or with a constructor initialization, that element position can then be accessed using square bracket notation, just like an array element.

Pitfall | USING SQUARE BRACKETS BEYOND THE VECTOR SIZE

If v is a vector and i is greater than or equal to v.size( ), then the element v[i] does not yet exits and needs to be created by using push_back to add elements up to and including position i. If you try to set v[i] for i greater than or equal to v.size( ), as in

```
v[i] = n;
```

then you may or may not get an error message, but your program will undoubtedly misbehave at some point.

Tip	**VECTOR ASSIGNMENT IS WELL BEHAVED**

The assignment operator with vectors does an element-by-element assignment to the vector on the left-hand side of the assignment operator (increasing capacity if needed and resetting the size of the vector on the left-hand side of the assignment operator). Thus, provided the assignment operator on the base type makes an independent copy of an element of the base type, then the assignment operator on the vector will make an independent copy, not an alias, of the vector on the right-hand side of the assignment operator.

Note that for the assignment operator to produce a totally independent copy of the vector on the right-hand side of the assignment operator requires that the assignment operator on the base type make completely independent copies. The assignment operator on a vector is only as good (or bad) as the assignment operator on its base type.

EFFICIENCY ISSUES

capacity

At any point in time a vector has a **capacity**, which is the number of elements for which it currently has memory allocated. The member function capacity( ) can be used to find out the capacity of a vector. Do not confuse the capacity of a vector with the size of a vector. The size is the number of elements in a vector, whereas the capacity is the number of elements for which there is memory allocated. Typically the capacity is larger than the size, and the capacity is always greater than or equal to the size.

Whenever a vector runs out of capacity and needs room for an additional member, the capacity is automatically increased. The exact amount of the increase is implementation dependent, but always allows for more capacity than is immediately needed. A commonly used implementation scheme is for the capacity to double whenever it needs to increase. Because increasing capacity is a complex task, this approach of reallocating capacity in large chunks is more efficient than allocating numerous small chunks.

You can completely ignore the capacity of a vector and that will have no effect on what your program does. However, if efficiency is an issue, you may want to manage capacity yourself and not simply accept the default behavior of doubling capacity whenever more is needed. You can use the member function reserve to explicitly increase the capacity of a vector. For example,

```
v.reserve(32);
```

sets the capacity to at least 32 elements, and

```
v.reserve(v.size( ) + 10);
```

sets the capacity to at least 10 more than the number of elements currently in the vector. Note that you can rely on v.reserve to increase the capacity of a vector, but it does not necessarily decrease the capacity of a vector if the argument is smaller than the current capacity.

You can change the size of a vector using the member function `resize`. For example, the following resizes a vector to 24 elements:

```
v.resize(24);
```

If the previous size were less than 24, then the new elements are initialized as we described for the constructor with an integer argument. If the previous size were greater than 24, then all but the first 24 elements are lost. The capacity is automatically increased if need be. Using `resize` and `reserve`, you can shrink the size and capacity of a vector when there is no longer any need for some elements or some capacity.

SIZE AND CAPACITY

The **size** of a vector is the number of elements in the vector. The **capacity** of a vector is the number of elements for which it currently has memory allocated. For a vector v, the size and capacity can be recovered with the member functions v.size( ) and v.capacity( ).

Self-Test Exercises

9. Is the following program legal? If so, what is the output?
```
#include <iostream>
#include <vector>
using namespace std;

int main( )
{
    vector<int> v(10);
    int i;

    for (i = 0; i < v.size( ); i++)
        v[i] = i;

    vector<int> copy;
    copy = v;
    v[0] = 42;

    for (i = 0; i < copy.size( ); i++)
        cout << copy[i] << " ";
    cout << endl;

    return 0;
}
```

10. What is the difference between the size and the capacity of a vector?

Chapter Summary

■ A **constructor** is a member function of a class that is called automatically when an object of the class is declared. A constructor must have the same name as the class of which it is a member.

■ A **default constructor** is a constructor with no parameters. You should always define a default constructor for your classes.

■ A member variable for a class may itself be of a class type. If a class has a class member variable, then the member variable constructor can be invoked in the initialization section of the outer class constructor.

■ A constant call-by-reference parameter is more efficient than a call-by-value parameter for class type parameters.

■ Making very short function definitions inline can improve the efficiency of your code.

■ Static member variables are variables that are shared by all objects of a class.

■ Vector classes have objects that behave very much like arrays whose capacity to hold elements will automatically increase if more capacity is needed.

ANSWERS TO SELF-TEST EXERCISES

1. ```
YourClass anObject(42, 'A'); //LEGAL
YourClass anotherObject; //LEGAL
YourClass yetAnotherObject( ); //PROBLEM
anObject = YourClass(99, 'B'); //LEGAL
anObject = YourClass( ); //LEGAL
anObject = YourClass; //ILLEGAL
```

   The statement marked //PROBLEM is not strictly illegal, but it does not mean what you might think it means. If you mean this to be a declaration of an object called yetAnotherObject, then it is wrong. It is a correct declaration for a function called yetAnotherObject that takes zero arguments and that returns a value of type YourClass, but that is not usually the intended meaning. As a practical matter, you can probably consider it illegal. The correct way to declare an object called yetAnotherObject so that it will be initialized with the default constructor is as follows:

   ```
YourClass yetAnotherObject;
```

2. A default constructor is a constructor that takes no arguments. Not every class has a default constructor. If you define absolutely no constructors for a class, then a default constructor will be automatically provided. On the other hand, if you define one or more constructors but do not define a default constructor, then your class will have no default constructor.
```

3. The definition is easier to give if you also add a private helping function named `BankAc-count::digitToInt`, as below, to the class `BankAccount`.

```
//Uses iostream:
void BankAccount::input( )
{
    int dollars;
    char point, digit1, digit2;
    cout <<
        "Enter account balance (include cents even if .00) $";
    cin >> dollars;
    cin >> point >> digit1 >> digit2;
    accountDollars = dollars;
    accountCents = digitToInt(digit1)*10 + digitToInt(digit2);
    if (accountDollars < 0)
        accountCents = -accountCents;
    cout << "Enter interest rate (NO percent sign): ";
    cin >> rate;
    setRate(rate);
}


int BankAccount::digitToInt(char digit)
{
    return (static_cast<int>(digit) - static_cast<int>('0'));
}
```

4. The member function `input` changes the value of its calling object, and so the compiler will issue an error message if you add the `const` modifier.

5. Similarities: Each parameter call method protects the caller's argument from change. Differences: If the type is a large structure or class object, a call by value makes a copy of the caller's argument and thus uses more memory than a call by constant reference.

6. In `const int x = 17;`, the `const` keyword promises the compiler that code written by the author will not change the value of `x`.

   In the `int f( ) const;` declaration, the `const` keyword is a promise to the compiler that code written by the author to implement function `f` will not change anything in the calling object.

   In `int g(const A& x);`, the `const` keyword is a promise to the compiler that code written by the class author will not change the argument plugged in for `x`.

7. ```
class DayOfYear
{
public:
    DayOfYear(int monthValue, int dayValue);
    DayOfYear(int monthValue);
    DayOfYear( );
```
```

```
      void input( );
      void output( );
      int getMonthNumber( ) { return month; }
      int getDay( ) { return day; }
  private:
      int month;
      int day;
      void testDate( );
  };
```

8. No, it cannot be a static member function because it requires a calling object for the member variable `name`.

9. The program is legal. The output is

```
0 1 2 3 4 5 6 7 8 9
```

Note that changing v does not change `copy`. A true independent copy is made with the assignment.

```
copy = v;
```

10. The size is the number of elements in a vector, while the capacity is number of elements for which there is memory allocated. Typically the capacity is larger than the size.

PROGRAMMING PROJECTS

1. Define a class called `Month` that is an abstract data type for a month. Your class will have one member variable of type `int` to represent a month (1 for January, 2 for February, and so forth). Include all the following member functions: a constructor to set the month using the first three letters in the name of the month as three arguments, a constructor to set the month using an integer as an argument (1 for January, 2 for February, and so forth), a default constructor, an input function that reads the month as an integer, an input function that reads the month as the first three letters in the name of the month, an output function that outputs the month as an integer, an output function that outputs the month as the first three letters in the name of the month, and a member function that returns the next month as a value of type `Month`. Embed your class definition in a test program.

2. Redefine the implementation of the class `Month` described in Programming Project 1. (or do the definition for the first time, but do the implementation as described here). This time the month is implemented as three member variables of type `char` that store the first three letters in the name of the month. Embed your definition in a test program.

3. My mother always took a little red counter to the grocery store. The counter was used to keep tally of the amount of money she would have spent so far on that visit to the store if she bought everything in the basket. The counter had a four-digit display, increment buttons for each digit, and a reset button. An overflow indicator came up red if more money was entered than the $99.99 it would register. (This was a *long* time ago.)

Write and implement the member functions of a class Counter that simulates and slightly generalizes the behavior of this grocery store counter. The constructor should create a Counter object that can count up to the constructor's argument. That is, Counter(9999) should provide a counter that can count up to 9999. A newly constructed counter displays a reading of 0. The member function void reset( ); sets the counter's number to 0. The member function void incr1( ); increments the units digits by 1, void incr10( ); increments the tens digit by 1, and void incr100( ); and void incr1000( ); increment the next two digits, respectively. Accounting for any carrying when you increment should require no further action than adding an appropriate number to the private data member. A member function bool overflow( ); detects overflow. (Overflow is the result of incrementing the counter's private data member beyond the maximum entered at counter construction.)

Use this class to provide a simulation of my mother's little red clicker. Even though the display is an integer, in the simulation, the rightmost (lower order) two digits are always thought of as cents and tens of cents, the next digit is dollars, and the fourth digit is tens of dollars.

Provide keys for cents, dimes, dollars, and tens of dollars. Unfortunately, no choice of keys seems particularly mnemonic. One choice is to use the keys asdfo: a for cents, followed by a digit 1 to 9; s for dimes, followed by a digit 1 to 9; d for dollars, followed by a digit 1 to 9; and f for tens of dollars, again followed by a digit 1 to 9. Each entry (one of asdf followed by 1 to 9) is followed by pressing the Return key. Any overflow is reported after each operation. Overflow can be requested by pressing the o key.

8 CHAPTER

Operator Overloading, Friends, and References

8
Operator Overloading, Friends, and References

Eternal truths will be neither true nor eternal unless they have fresh meaning for every new social situation.

Franklin D. Roosevelt, Address at the University of Pennsylvania
[September 20, 1940]

INTRODUCTION

This chapter discusses a number of tools to use when defining classes. The first tool is operator overloading, which allows you to overload operators, such as + and ==, so that they apply to objects of the classes you define. The second tool is the use of friend functions which are functions that are not members of a class but still have access to the private members of the class. This chapter also discusses how to provide automatic type conversion from other data types to the classes you define.

If you have not yet covered arrays (Chapter 5), you should skip the subsection of 8.3 entitled **Overloading the Array Operator [ ]**. It covers a topic that may not make sense unless you know about array basics.

8.1 Basic Operator Overloading

He's a smooth operator.

Line from a song by Sade (written by Sade Adu and Ray St. John)

operators and functions

operand

syntactic sugar

Operators such as +, –, %, ==, and so forth are nothing but functions that are used with a slightly different syntax. We write x + 7 rather than +(x, 7), but the + operator is a function that takes two arguments (often called **operands** rather than arguments) and returns a single value. As such, operators are not really necessary. We could make do with +(x, 7) or even add(x, 7). Operands are an example of what is often called **syntactic sugar**, meaning a slightly different syntax that people like. However, people are very comfortable with the usual operator syntax, x + 7, that C++ uses for types such as int and double. And one way to view a high-level language, such as C++, is as a way to make people comfortable with programming computers. Thus, this syntactic sugar is probably a good idea; at the least, it is a well-entrenched idea. In C++ you can overload the operators, such as + and ==, so that they work with operands in the classes you define. The way to overload an operator is very similar to the way you overload a function name. The details are best explained through an example.

OVERLOADING BASICS

Display 8.1 contains the definition of a class whose values are amounts of U.S. money, such as $9.99 or $1567.29. The class has a lot in common with the `BankAccount` class we defined in Display 7.2. It represents amounts of money in the same way, as two `int`s for the dollars and cents parts. It has the same private helping functions. Its constructors and accessor and mutator functions are similar to those of the class `BankAccount`. What is truly new about this `Money` class is that we have overloaded the plus sign and the minus sign so they can be used to add or subtract two objects of the class `Money`, and we have overloaded the `==` sign so it can be used to compare two objects of the class `Money` to see if they represent the same amount of money. Let's look at these overloaded operators.

You can overload the operator `+` (and many other operators) so that it will accept arguments of a class type. The difference between overloading the `+` operator and defining an ordinary function involves only a slight change in syntax: You use the symbol `+` as the function name and precede the `+` with the keyword `operator`. The operator declaration (function declaration) for the plus sign is as follows:

how to overload an operator

```
const Money operator +(const Money& amount1, const Money& amount2);
```

The operands (arguments) are both constant reference parameters of type `Money`. The operands can be of any type, as long as at least one is a class type. In the general case, operands may be call-by-value or call-by-reference parameters and may have the `const` modifier or not. However, for efficiency reasons, constant call by reference is usually used in place of call by value for classes. In this case the value returned is of type `Money`, but in the general case the value returned can be of any type, including `void`. The `const` before the returned type `Money` will be explained later in this chapter. For now, you can safely ignore that `const`.

Note that the overloaded binary operators `+` and `-` are not member operators (member functions) of the class `Money` and therefore do not have access to the private members of the class `Money`. That is why the definition for the overloaded operators uses accessor and mutator functions. Later in this chapter we will see other ways of overloading an operand, including overloading it as a member operator. Each of the different ways of overloading an operator has its advantages and disadvantages.

The definitions of the overloaded binary operators `+` and `-` are perhaps a bit more complicated than you might expect. The extra details are there to cope with the fact that amounts of money can be negative.

The unary minus sign operator `-` is discussed in the subsection **Overloading Unary Operators**, later in this chapter.

The operator `==` is also overloaded so that it can be used to compare two objects of the class `Money`. Note that the type returned is `bool` so that `==` can be used to make comparisons in the usual ways, such as in an `if–else` statement.

Display 8.1   Operator Overloading *(part 1 of 5)*

```
1   #include <iostream>
2   #include <cstdlib>
3   #include <cmath>
4   using namespace std;

5   //Class for amounts of money in U.S. currency
6   class Money
7   {
8   public:
9       Money( );
10      Money(double amount);
11      Money(int theDollars, int theCents);
12      Money(int theDollars);
13      double getAmount( ) const;
14      int getDollars( ) const;
15      int getCents( ) const;
16      void input( ); //Reads the dollar sign as well as the amount number.
17      void output( ) const;
18  private:
19      int dollars; //A negative amount is represented as negative dollars and
20      int cents; //negative cents. Negative $4.50 is represented as -4 and -50.

21      int dollarsPart(double amount) const;
22      int centsPart(double amount) const;
23      int round(double number) const;
24  };

25  const Money operator +(const Money& amount1, const Money& amount2);

26  const Money operator -(const Money& amount1, const Money& amount2);

27  bool operator ==(const Money& amount1, const Money& amount2);

28  const Money operator -(const Money& amount);

29  int main( )
30  {
31      Money yourAmount, myAmount(10, 9);
32      cout << "Enter an amount of money: ";
33      yourAmount.input( );
34      cout << "Your amount is ";
35      yourAmount.output( );
36      cout << endl;
37      cout << "My amount is ";
38      myAmount.output( );
39      cout << endl;
```

This is a unary operator and is discussed in the subsection **Overloading Unary Operators.**

For an explanation of a const *on a returned type see the subsection* **Returning by** const **Value.**

Display 8.1   Operator Overloading *(part 2 of 5)*

```
40        if (yourAmount == myAmount)
41            cout << "We have the same amounts.\n";
42        else
43            cout << "One of us is richer.\n";

44        Money ourAmount = yourAmount + myAmount;
45        yourAmount.output( ); cout << " + "; myAmount.output( );
46        cout << " equals "; ourAmount.output( ); cout << endl;

47        Money diffAmount = yourAmount - myAmount;
48        yourAmount.output( ); cout << " - "; myAmount.output( );
49        cout << " equals "; diffAmount.output( ); cout << endl;

50        return 0;
51    }
```

Note that we need to use accessor and mutator functions.

```
52    const Money operator +(const Money& amount1, const Money& amount2)
53    {
54        int allCents1 = amount1.getCents( ) + amount1.getDollars( )*100;
55        int allCents2 = amount2.getCents( ) + amount2.getDollars( )*100;
56        int sumAllCents = allCents1 + allCents2;
57        int absAllCents = abs(sumAllCents); //Money can be negative.
58        int finalDollars = absAllCents/100;
59        int finalCents = absAllCents%100;

60        if (sumAllCents < 0)
61        {
62            finalDollars = -finalDollars;
63            finalCents = -finalCents;
64        }

65        return Money(finalDollars, finalCents);
66    }
67    //Uses cstdlib:
68    const Money operator -(const Money& amount1, const Money& amount2)
69    {
70        int allCents1 = amount1.getCents( ) + amount1.getDollars( )*100;
71        int allCents2 = amount2.getCents( ) + amount2.getDollars( )*100;
72        int diffAllCents = allCents1 - allCents2;
73        int absAllCents = abs(diffAllCents);
74        int finalDollars = absAllCents/100;
75        int finalCents = absAllCents%100;

76        if (diffAllCents < 0)
77        {
78            finalDollars = -finalDollars;
```

*If the return statements puzzle you, see the tip entitled **A Constructor Can Return an Object**.*

Display 8.1   Operator Overloading *(part 3 of 5)*

```
79              finalCents = -finalCents;
80         }

81      return Money(finalDollars, finalCents);
82  }

83  bool operator ==(const Money& amount1, const Money& amount2)
84  {
85      return ((amount1.getDollars( ) == amount2.getDollars( ))
86             && (amount1.getCents( ) == amount2.getCents( )));
87  }

88  const Money operator -(const Money& amount)
89  {
90      return Money(-amount.getDollars( ), -amount.getCents( ));
91  }
```

```
92  Money::Money( ): dollars(0), cents(0)
93  {/*Body intentionally empty.*/}
```

If you prefer, you could make these short constructor definitions inline function definitions as discussed in Chapter 7.

```
94  Money::Money(double amount)
95                  : dollars(dollarsPart(amount)), cents(centsPart(amount))
96  {/*Body intentionally empty*/}

97  Money::Money(int theDollars)
98                  : dollars(theDollars), cents(0)
99  {/*Body intentionally empty*/}
100
101 //Uses cstdlib:
102 Money::Money(int theDollars, int theCents)
103 {
104     if ((theDollars < 0 && theCents > 0) || (theDollars > 0 && theCents < 0))
105     {
106         cout << "Inconsistent money data.\n";
107         exit(1);
108     }
109     dollars = theDollars;
110     cents = theCents;
111 }

112 double Money::getAmount( ) const
113 {
114     return (dollars + cents*0.01);
115 }

116 int Money::getDollars( ) const
```

Display 8.1   Operator Overloading *(part 4 of 5)*

```
117    {
118        return dollars;
119    }

120    int Money::getCents( ) const
121    {
122        return cents;
123    }

124    //Uses iostream and cstdlib:
125    void Money::output( ) const
126    {
127        int absDollars = abs(dollars);
128        int absCents = abs(cents);
129        if (dollars < 0 || cents < 0)//accounts for dollars == 0 or cents == 0
130            cout << "$-";
131        else
132            cout << '$';
133        cout << absDollars;
134
135        if (absCents >= 10)
136            cout << '.' << absCents;
137        else
138            cout << '.' << '0' << absCents;
139    }

140    //Uses iostream and cstdlib:
141    void Money::input( )
142    {
143        char dollarSign;
144        cin >> dollarSign; //hopefully
145        if (dollarSign != '$')
146        {
147            cout << "No dollar sign in Money input.\n";
148            exit(1);
149        }

150        double amountAsDouble;
151        cin >> amountAsDouble;
152        dollars = dollarsPart(amountAsDouble);
153        cents = centsPart(amountAsDouble);
154    }

155    int Money::dollarsPart(double amount) const
156        <The rest of the definition is the same as BankAccount::dollarsPart in Display 7.2.>
```

For a better definition of the input function, see Self-Test Exercise 3 in Chapter 7.

Display 8.1   Operator Overloading *(part 5 of 5)*

```
157    int Money::centsPart(double amount) const
158          <The rest of the definition is the same as BankAccount::centsPart in Display 7.2.>

159    int Money::round(double number) const
160          <The rest of the definition is the same as BankAccount::round in Display 7.2.>
```

SAMPLE DIALOGUE

```
Enter an amount of money: $123.45
Your amount is $123.45
My amount is $10.09.
One of us is richer.
$123.45 + $10.09 equals $133.54
$123.45 - $10.09 equals $113.36
```

If you look at the `main` function in the demonstration program in Display 8.1, you will see that the overloaded binary operators +, -, and == are used with objects of the class Money in the same way that +, -, and == are used with the predefined types, such as int and double.

You can overload most but not all operators. One major restriction on overloading an operator is that at least one operand must be of a class type. So, for example, you can overload the % operator to apply to two objects of type Money or to an object of type Money and a double, but you cannot overload % to combine two doubles.

OPERATOR OVERLOADING

A (binary) operator, such as +, -, /, %, and so forth, is simply a function that is called using a different syntax for listing its arguments. With a binary operator, the arguments are listed before and after the operator; with a function the arguments are listed in parentheses after the function name. An operator definition is written similar to a function definition, except that the operator definition includes the reserved word `operator` before the operator name. The predefined operators, such as +, -, and so forth, can be overloaded by giving them a new definition for a class type. An example of overloading the +, -, and == operators is given in Display 8.1.

Tip

A CONSTRUCTOR CAN RETURN AN OBJECT

We often think of a constructor as if it were a `void` function. However, constructors are special functions with special properties, and sometimes it makes more sense to think of them as returning a value. Notice the `return` statement in the definition of the overloaded + operator in Display 8.1, which we repeat below:

```
return Money(finalDollars, finalCents);
```

The expression that is returned is an invocation of the constructor for Money. Although we sometimes think of a constructor as a void function, a constructor constructs an object and can also be thought of as returning an object of the class. If you feel uncomfortable with this use of the constructor, it may help to know that this return statement is equivalent to the following, more cumbersome and less efficient, code:

```
Money temp;
temp = Money(finalDollars, finalCents);
return temp;
```

An expression, such as Money(finalDollars, finalCents), is sometimes called an **anonymous object**, since it is not named by any variable. However, it is still a full-fledged object. You can even use it as a calling object, as in the following:

```
Money(finalDollars, finalCents).getDollars( )
```

The previous expression returns the int value of finalDollars.

anonymous object

Self-Test Exercises

1. What is the difference between a (binary) operator and a function?

2. Suppose you wish to overload the operator < so that it applies to the type Money defined in Display 8.1. What do you need to add to the definition of Money given in Display 8.1?

3. Is it possible using operator overloading to change the behavior of + on integers? Why or why not?

RETURNING BY const VALUE

Notice the returned types in the declarations for overloaded operators for the class Money in Display 8.1. For example, the following is the declaration for the overloaded plus operator as it appears in Display 8.1:

```
const Money operator +(const Money& amount1, const Money& amount2);
```

This subsection explains the const at the start of the line. But before we discuss that first const, let's make sure we understand all the other details about returning a value. So, let's first consider the case where that const does not appear in either the declaration or definition of the overloaded plus operator. Let's suppose that the declaration reads as follows:

```
Money operator +(const Money& amount1, const Money& amount2);
```

and let's see what we can do with the value returned.

When an object is returned, for example, (m1 + m2), where m1 and m2 are of type Money, the object can be used to invoke a member function, which may or may not change the value of the member variables in the object (m1 + m2). For example,

```
(m1 + m2).output( );
```

is perfectly legal. In this case, it does not change the object (m1 + m2). However, if we omitted the const before the type returned for the plus operator, then the following would be legal and would change the values of the member variables of the object (m1 + m2):

```
(m1 + m2).input( );
```

So, objects can be changed, even when they are not associated with any variable. One way to make sense of this is to note that objects have member variables and thus have some kinds of variables that can be changed.

Now let's assume that everything is as shown in Display 8.1; that is, there is a const before the returned type of each operator that returns an object of type Money. For example, below is the declaration for the overloaded plus operator as it appears in Display 8.1:

```
const Money operator +(const Money& amount1, const Money& amount2);
```

return by constant value

The first const on the line is a new use of the const modifier. This is called **returning a value as const** or **returning by const value** or **returning by constant value**. What the const modifier means in this case is that the returned object cannot be changed. For example, consider the following code:

```
Money m1(10.99), m2(23.57);
(m1 + m2).output( );
```

The invocation of output is perfectly legal because it does not change the object (m1 + m2). However, with that const before the returned type, the following will produce a compiler error message:

```
(m1 + m2).input( );
```

Why would you want to return by const value? It provides a kind of automatic error checking. When you construct (m1 + m2), you do not want to inadvertently change it.

At first this protection from changing an object may seem like too much protection, since you can have

```
Money m3;
m3 = (m1 + m2);
```

and you very well may want to change m3. No problem—the following is perfectly legal:

```
m3 = (m1 + m2);
m3.input( );
```

The values of m3 and (m1 + m2) are two different objects. The assignment operator does not make m3 the same as the object (m1 + m2). Instead, it copies the values of the member variables of (m1 + m2) into the member variables of m3. *With objects of a class, the default assignment operator does not make the two objects the same object, it only copies values of member variables from one object to another object.*

This distinction is subtle but important. It may help you understand the details if you recall that a variable of a class type and an object of a class type are not the same thing. An object is a value of a class type and may be stored in a variable of a class type, but the variable and the object are not the same thing. In the code

```
m3 = (m1 + m2);
```

the variable m3 and its value (m1 + m2) are different things, just as n and 5 are different things in

```
int n = 5;
```

or in

```
int n = (2 + 3);
```

It may take you a while to become comfortable with this notion of return by const value. In the meantime, a good rule of thumb is to always return class types by const value unless you have an explicit reason not to do so. For most simple programs this will have no effect on your program other than to flag some subtle errors.

Note that although it is legal, it is pointless to return basic types, such as int, by const value. The const has no effect in the case of basic types. When a function or operator returns a value of one of the basic types, such as int, double, or char, it returns the value, such as 5, 5.5, or 'A'. It does not return a variable or anything like a variable.[1] Unlike a variable, the value cannot be changed—you cannot change 5. Values of a basic type cannot be changed whether there is a const before the returned type or not. On the other hand, values of a class type—that is, objects—can be changed, since they have member variables, and so the const modifier has an effect on the object returned.

---

[1] Unless the value returned is returned by reference, but return by reference is a topic covered later in this chapter. Here we assume the value is not returned by reference.

Tip

RETURNING MEMBER VARIABLES OF A CLASS TYPE

When returning a member variable of a class type, in almost all cases it is important to return the member value by const value. To see why, suppose you do not, as in the example outlined in what follows:

```
class Employee
{
public:
    Money getSalary( ) { return salary; }
    . . .
private:
    Money salary;
    . . .
};
```

In this example, salary is a private member variable that should not be changeable except by using some accessor function of the class Employee. However, this privateness is easily circumvented as follows:

```
Employee joe;
(joe.getSalary( )).input( );
```

The lucky employee named joe can now enter any salary she wishes!

On the other hand, suppose getSalary returns its value by const value, as follows:

```
class Employee
{
public:
    const Money getSalary( ) { return salary; }
    . . .
private:
    Money salary;
    . . .
};
```

In this case, the following will give a compiler error message.

```
(joe.getSalary( )).input( );
```

(The declaration for getSalary should ideally be

```
const Money getSalary( ) const { return salary; }
```

but we did not want to confuse the issue with another kind of const.)

Self-Test Exercises

4. Suppose you omit the `const` at the beginning of the declaration and definition of the overloaded plus operator for the class `Money`, so that the value is not returned by `const` value. Is the following legal?

```
Money m1(10.99), m2(23.57), m3(12.34);
(m1 + m2) = m3;
```

Is it legal if the definition of the class `Money` is as shown in Display 8.1, so that the plus operator returns its value by `const` value?

OVERLOADING UNARY OPERATORS

In addition to the binary operators, such as + in x + y, C++ has unary operators, such as the operator – when it is used to mean negation. A **unary operator** is an operator that takes only one operand (one argument). In the statement below, the unary operator – is used to set the value of a variable x equal to the negative of the value of the variable y:

unary
operator

```
x = -y;
```

The increment and decrement operators, ++ and --, are other examples of unary operators.

You can overload unary operators as well as binary operators. For example, we have overloaded the minus operator – for the type `Money` (Display 8.1) so that it has both a unary and a binary operator version of the subtraction/negation operator –. For example, suppose your program contains this class definition and the following code:

```
Money amount1(10), amount2(6), amount3;
```

Then the following sets the value of `amount3` to `amount1` minus `amount2`:

```
amount3 = amount1 - amount2;
```

The following will, then, output $4.00 to the screen:

```
amount3.output( );
```

On the other hand, the following will set `amount3` equal to the negative of `amount1`:

```
amount3 = -amount1;
```

The following will, then, output -$10.00 to the screen:

```
amount3.output( );
```

++ and --

You can overload the ++ and -- operators in ways similar to how we overloaded the negation operator in Display 8.1. If you overload the ++ and -- operators following the example of the minus sign – in Display 8.1, then the overloading definition will apply to the operator when it is used in prefix position, as in ++x and --x. Later in this chapter we will discuss overloading ++ and -- more fully and will then explain how to overload these operators for use in the postfix position.

■ OVERLOADING AS MEMBER FUNCTIONS

In Display 8.1 we overloaded operators as standalone functions defined outside the class. It is also possible to overload an operator as a member operator (member function). This is illustrated in Display 8.2.

Note that when a binary operator is overloaded as a member operator, there is only one parameter, not two. The calling object serves as the first parameter. For example, consider the following code:

```
Money cost(1, 50), tax(0, 15), total;
total = cost + tax;
```

When + is overloaded as a member operator, then in the expression cost + tax the variable cost is the calling object and tax is the single argument to +.

The definition of the member operator + is given in Display 8.2. Notice the following line from that definition:

```
int allCents1 = cents + dollars*100;
```

The expressions cents and dollars are member variables of the calling object, which in this case is the first operand. If this definition is applied to

```
cost + tax
```

then cents means cost.cents and dollars means cost.dollars.

Note that since the first operand is the calling object, you should, in most cases, add the const modifier to the end of the operator declaration and to the end of the operator definition. Whenever the operator invocation does not change the calling object (which is the first operand), good style dictates that you add the const to the end of the operator declaration and to the end of the operator definition, as illustrated in Display 8.2.

Overloading an operator as a member variable can seem strange at first, but it is easy to get used to the new details. Many experts advocate always overloading operators as member operators rather than as nonmembers (as in Display 8.1): It is more in the spirt of object-oriented programming and is a bit more efficient, since the definition can directly reference member variables and need not use accessor and mutator functions. However, as we will discover later in this chapter, overloading an operator as a member also has a significant disadvantage.

Display 8.2 Overloading Operators as Members *(part 1 of 2)*

```
1   #include <iostream>
2   #include <cstdlib>
3   #include <cmath>
4   using namespace std;

5   //Class for amounts of money in U.S. currency
6   class Money
7   {
8   public:
9       Money( );
10      Money(double amount);
11      Money(int dollars, int cents);
12      Money(int dollars);
13      double getAmount( ) const;
14      int getDollars( ) const;
15      int getCents( ) const;
16      void input( ); //Reads the dollar sign as well as the amount number.
17      void output( ) const;
18      const Money operator +(const Money& amount2) const;
19      const Money operator -(const Money& amount2) const;
20      bool operator ==(const Money& amount2) const;
21      const Money operator -( ) const;
22  private:
23      int dollars; //A negative amount is represented as negative dollars and
24      int cents; //negative cents. Negative $4.50 is represented as  4 and −50.

25      int dollarsPart(double amount) const;
26      int centsPart(double amount) const;
27      int round(double number) const;
28  };

29  int main( )
30  {
31          <If the main function is the same as in Display 8.1, then the screen dialogue
                will be the same as shown in Display 8.1.>
32  }

33
34  const Money Money::operator +(const Money& secondOperand) const
35  {
36      int allCents1 = cents + dollars*100;
37      int allCents2 = secondOperand.cents + secondOperand.dollars*100;
38      int sumAllCents = allCents1 + allCents2;
39      int absAllCents = abs(sumAllCents); //Money can be negative.
40      int finalDollars = absAllCents/100;
41      int finalCents = absAllCents%100;
```

This is Display 8.1 redone with the overloaded operators as member functions.

The calling object is the first operand.

Display 8.2   Overloading Operators as Members *(part 2 of 2)*

```
42        if (sumAllCents < 0)
43        {
44            finalDollars = -finalDollars;
45            finalCents = -finalCents;
46        }

47        return Money(finalDollars, finalCents);
48    }

49    const Money Money::operator -(const Money& secondOperand) const
50            <The rest of this definition is Self-Test Exercise 5.>

51    bool Money::operator ==(const Money& secondOperand) const
52    {
53        return ((dollars == secondOperand.dollars)
54                && (cents == secondOperand.cents));
55    }

56    const Money Money::operator -( ) const
57    {
58        return Money(-dollars, -cents);
59    }

60            <Definitions of all other member functions are the same as in Display 8.1.>
```

> ### Tip
>
> ### A CLASS HAS ACCESS TO ALL ITS OBJECTS
>
> When defining a member function or operator, you may access any private member variable (or function) of the calling object. However, you are allowed even more than that. You may access any private member variable (or private member function) of any object of the class being defined.
>
> For example, consider the following few lines that begin the definition of the plus operator for the class Money in Display 8.2:
>
> ```
> const Money Money::operator +(const Money& secondOperand) const
> {
>     int allCents1 = cents + dollars*100;
>     int allCents2 = secondOperand.cents + secondOperand.dollars*100;
> ```
>
> In this case, the plus operator is being defined as a member operator, so the variables cents and dollars, in the first line of the function body, are the member variables of the calling object

(which happens to be the first operand). However, it is also legal to access by name the member variables of the object secondOperand, as in the following line:

```
int allCents2 = secondOperand.cents + secondOperand.dollars*100;
```

This is legal because secondOperand is an object of the class Money and this line is in the definition of a member operator for the class Money. Many novice programmers mistakenly think they only have direct access to the private members of the calling object and do not realize that they have direct access to all objects of the class being defined.

Self-Test Exercises

5. Complete the definition of the member binary operator – in Display 8.2.

■ OVERLOADING FUNCTION APPLICATION ( )

The function call operator ( ) must be overloaded as a member function. It allows you to use an object of the class as if it were a function. If class AClass has overloaded the function application operator to have one argument of type int and anObject is an object of AClass, then anObject(42) invokes the overloaded function call operator ( ) with calling object anObject and argument 42. The type returned may be void or any other type.

The function call operator ( ) is unusual in that it allows any number of arguments. So, you can define several overloaded versions of the function call operator ( ).

Pitfall

OVERLOADING &&, ||, AND THE COMMA OPERATOR

The predefined versions of && and || that work for the type bool use short-circuit evaluation. However, when overloaded these operators perform complete evaluation. This is so contrary to what most programmers expect that it inevitably causes problems. It is best to just not overload these two operators.

The comma operator also presents problems. In its normal use the comma operator guarantees left-to-right evaluations. When overloaded no such guarantee is given. The comma operator is another operator it is safest to avoid overloading.

8.2 Friend Functions and Automatic Type Conversion

Trust your friends.

Common advice

Friend functions are nonmember functions that have all the privileges of member functions. Before we discuss friend functions in any detail, we discuss automatic type conversion via constructors, since that helps to explain one of the advantages of overloading operators (or any functions) as friend functions.

■ CONSTRUCTORS FOR AUTOMATIC TYPE CONVERSION

If your class definition contains the appropriate constructors, the system will perform certain type conversions automatically. For example, if your program contains the definition of the class Money either as given in Display 8.1 or as given in Display 8.2, you could use the following in your program:

```
Money baseAmount(100, 60), fullAmount;
fullAmount = baseAmount + 25;
fullAmount.output( );
```

The output would be

```
$125.60
```

The code above may look simple and natural enough, but there is one subtle point. The 25 (in the expression baseAmount + 25) is not of the appropriate type. In Display 8.1 we only overloaded the operator + so that it could be used with two values of type Money. We did not overload + so that it could be used with a value of type Money and an integer. The constant 25 can be considered to be of type int, but 25 cannot be used as a value of type Money unless the class definition somehow tells the system how to convert an integer to a value of type Money. The only way that the system knows that 25 means $25.00 is that we included a constructor that takes a single argument of type int. When the system sees the expression

```
baseAmount + 25
```

it first checks to see if the operator + has been overloaded for the combination of a value of type Money and an integer. Since there is no such overloading, the system next looks to see if there is a constructor that takes a single argument that is an integer. If it finds a constructor that takes a single integer argument, it uses that constructor to convert the integer 25 to a value of type Money. The one-argument constructor says that 25 should be converted to an object of type Money whose member variable dollars is equal to 25 and whose member variable cents is equal to 0. In other words, the constructor converts 25 to an object of type Money that represents $25.00. (The definition of the constructor is in Display 8.1.)

Note that this type conversion will not work unless there is a suitable constructor. If the class Money did not contain a constructor with one parameter of type int (or of some other number type, such as long or double), then the expression

```
baseAmount + 25
```

would produce an error message.

These automatic type conversions (produced by constructors) seem most common and compelling with overloaded numeric operators such as + and –. However, these automatic conversions apply in exactly the same way to arguments of ordinary functions, arguments of member functions, and arguments of other overloaded operators.

Pitfall **MEMBER OPERATORS AND AUTOMATIC TYPE CONVERSION**

When you overload a binary operator as a member operator, the two arguments are no longer symmetric. One is a calling object, and only the second "argument" is a true argument. This is not only unaesthetic but also has a very practical shortcoming. Any automatic type conversion will only apply to the second argument. So, for example, as we noted in the previous subsection, the following would be legal:

```
Money baseAmount(100, 60), fullAmount;
fullAmount = baseAmount + 25;
```

This is because Money has a constructor with one argument of type int, and so the value 25 will be considered an int value that is automatically converted to a value of type Money.

However, if you overload + as a member operator (as in Display 8.2), then you cannot reverse the two arguments to +. The following is illegal:

```
fullAmount = 25 + baseAmount;
```

because 25 cannot be a calling object. Conversion of int values to type Money works for arguments but not for calling objects.

On the other hand, if you overload + as a nonmember (as in Display 8.1), then the following is perfectly legal:

```
fullAmount = 25 + baseAmount;
```

This is the biggest advantage of overloading an operator as a nonmember.

Overloading an operator as a nonmember gives you automatic type conversion of all arguments. Overloading an operator as a member gives you the efficiency of bypassing accessor and mutator functions and directly accessing member variables. There is a way to overload an operator (and certain functions) that offers both of these advantages. It is called *overloading as a friend function* and is our next topic.

FRIEND FUNCTIONS

If your class has a full set of accessor and mutator functions, you can use the accessor and mutator functions to define nonmember overloaded operators (as in Display 8.1 as opposed to Display 8.2). However, although this may give you access to the private member variables, it may not give you efficient access to them. Look again at the definition of the overloaded addition operator + given in Display 8.1. Rather than just reading four member variables, it must incur the overhead of two invocations of get-Cents and two invocations of getDollars. This adds a bit of inefficiency and also can make the code harder to understand. The alternative of overloading + as a member gets around this problem at the price of losing automatic type conversion of the first operand. Overloading the + operator as a friend will allow us to both directly access member variables and have automatic type conversion for all operands.

friend
function

A **friend function** of a class is not a member function of the class, but it has access to the private members of that class (to both private member variables and private member functions) just as a member function does. To make a function a friend function, you must name it as a friend in the class definition. For example, in Display 8.3 we have rewritten the definition of the class Money yet another time. This time we have overloaded the operators as friends. You make an operator or function a friend of a class by listing the operator or function declaration in the definition of the class and placing the keyword friend in front of the operator or function declaration.

A friend operator or friend function has its declaration listed in the class definition, just as you would list the declaration of a member function, except that you precede the declaration by the keyword friend. However, a friend is *not* a member function; rather, it really is an ordinary function with extraordinary access to the data members of the class. The friend is defined exactly like the ordinary function it is. In particular, the operator definitions shown in Display 8.3 do not include the qualifier Money:: in the function heading. Also, you do not use the keyword friend in the function definition (only in the function declaration). The friend operators in Display 8.3 are invoked just like the nonfriend, nonmember operators in Display 8.1, and they have automatic type conversion of all arguments just like the nonfriend, nonmember operators in Display 8.1.

The most common kinds of friend functions are overloaded operators. However, any kind of function can be made a friend function.

A function (or overloaded operator) can be a friend of more than one class. To make it a friend of multiple classes, just give the declaration of the friend function in each class for which you want it to be a friend.

Many experts consider friend functions (and operators) to be in some sense not "pure." They feel that in the true spirit of object-oriented programming all operators and functions should be member functions. On the other hand, overloading operators as friends provides the pragmatic advantage of automatic type conversion in all arguments, and since the operator declaration is inside the class definitions, it provides at least a bit more encapsulation than nonmember, nonfriend operators. We have shown you three ways to overload operators: as nonmember nonfriends, as members, and as friends. You can decide for yourself which technique you prefer.

Display 8.3   Overloading Operators as Friends (part 1 of 2)

```
1   #include <iostream>
2   #include <cstdlib>
3   #include <cmath>
4   using namespace std;

5   //Class for amounts of money in U.S. currency
6   class Money
7   {
8   public:
9       Money( );
10      Money(double amount);
11      Money(int dollars, int cents);
12      Money(int dollars);
13      double getAmount( ) const;
14      int getDollars( ) const;
15      int getCents( ) const;
16      void input( ); //Reads the dollar sign as well as the amount number.
17      void output( ) const;
18      friend const Money operator +(const Money& amount1, const Money& amount2);
19      friend const Money operator -(const Money& amount1, const Money& amount2);
20      friend bool operator ==(const Money& amount1, const Money& amount2);
21      friend const Money operator -(const Money& amount);
22  private:
23      int dollars; //A negative amount is represented as negative dollars and
24      int cents; //negative cents. Negative $4.50 is represented as -4 and -50.

25      int dollarsPart(double amount) const;
26      int centsPart(double amount) const;
27      int round(double number) const;
28  },

29  int main( )
30  {
31          <If the main function is the same as in Display 8.1, then the screen dialogue
            will be the same as shown in Display 8.1.>
32  }

33
34  const Money operator +(const Money& amount1, const Money& amount2)
35  {
36      int allCents1 = amount1.cents + amount1.dollars*100;
37      int allCents2 = amount2.cents + amount2.dollars*100;
38      int sumAllCents = allCents1 + allCents2;
39      int absAllCents = abs(sumAllCents); //Money can be negative.
40      int finalDollars = absAllCents/100;
```

Display 8.3   Overloading Operators as Friends (part 2 of 2)

```
41        int finalCents = absAllCents%100;
```
Note that friends have direct access to member variables.

```
42        if (sumAllCents < 0)
43        {
44            finalDollars = -finalDollars;
45            finalCents = -finalCents;
46        }

47        return Money(finalDollars, finalCents);
48    }

49    const Money operator -(const Money& amount1, const Money& amount2)
50        <The complete definition is Self-Test Exercise 7.>

51    bool operator ==(const Money& amount1, const Money& amount2)
52    {
53        return ((amount1.dollars == amount2.dollars)
54                && (amount1.cents == amount2.cents));
55    }

56    const Money operator -(const Money& amount)
57    {
58        return Money(-amount.dollars, -amount.cents);
59    }
```

<Definitions of all other member functions are the same as in Display 8.1.>

```
60
```

FRIEND FUNCTIONS

A friend function of a class is an ordinary function except that it has access to the private members of objects of that class. To make a function a friend of a class, you must list the function declaration for the friend function in the class definition. The function declaration is preceded by the keyword friend. The function declaration may be placed in either the private section or the public section, but it will be a public function in either case, so it is clearer to list it in the public section.

SYNTAX OF A CLASS DEFINITION WITH FRIEND FUNCTIONS

```
class Class_Name
{
public:
    friend Declaration_for_Friend_Function_1
    friend Declaration_for_Friend_Function_2
         .
         .
         .
```
You need not list the friend functions first. You can intermix the order of these declarations.

```
        Member_Function_Declarations
private:
        Private_Member_Declarations
};
```

EXAMPLE

```
class FuelTank
{
public:
    friend void fillLowest(FuelTank& t1, FuelTank& t2);
    //Fills the tank with the lowest fuel level, or t1 if a tie.

    FuelTank(double theCapacity, double theLevel);
    FuelTank( );
    void input( );
    void output( ) const;
private:
    double capacity;//in liters
    double level;
};
```

A friend function is *not* a member function. A friend function is defined and called the same way as an ordinary function. You do not use the dot operator in a call to a friend function, and you do not use a type qualifier in the definition of a friend function.

Pitfall   **COMPILERS WITHOUT FRIENDS**

On some C++ compilers friend functions simply do not work as they are supposed to work. Worst of all, they may work sometimes and not work at other times. On these compilers friend functions do not always have access to private members of the class as they are supposed to. Presumably, this will be fixed in later releases of these compilers. In the meantime, you will have to work around this problem. If you have one of these compilers for which friend functions do not work, you must either use accessor functions to define nonmember functions and overloaded operators or you must overload operators as members.

FRIEND CLASSES

A class can be a **friend** of another class in the same way that a function can be a friend   friend class
of a class. If the class F is a friend of the class C, then every member function of the class
F is a friend of the class C. To make one class a friend of another, you must declare the
friend class as a friend within the other class.

forward declaration

When one class is a friend of another class, it is typical for the classes to reference each other in their class definitions. This requires that you include a **forward declaration** to the class defined second, as illustrated in the outline that follows this paragraph. Note that the forward declaration is just the heading of the class definition followed by a semicolon.

If you want the class F to be a friend of the class C, the general outline of how you set things up is as follows:

```
class F; //forward declaration

class C
{
public:
     ...
    friend class F;
     ...
};

class F
{
    ...
```

Complete examples using friend classes are given in Chapter 17. We will not be using friend classes until then.

Self-Test Exercises

6. What is the difference between a friend function for a class and a member function for the class?

7. Complete the definition of the friend subtraction operator – in Display 8.3.

8. Suppose you wish to overload the operator < so that it applies to the type Money defined in Display 8.3. What do you need to add to the definition of Money given in Display 8.3?

8.3 References and More Overloaded Operators

Do not mistake the pointing finger for the moon.

Zen Saying

This section covers some specialized, but important, overloading topics, including overloading the assignment operator and the <<, >>, [], ++, and −− operators. Because

RULES ON OVERLOADING OPERATORS

- When overloading an operator, at least one parameter (one operand) of the resulting overloaded operator must be of a class type.

- Most operators can be overloaded as a member of the class, a friend of the class, or a nonmember, nonfriend.

- The following operators can only be overloaded as (nonstatic) members of the class: =, [], ->, and ( ).

- You cannot create a new operator. All you can do is overload existing operators such as +, −, *, /, %, and so forth.

- You cannot change the number of arguments that an operator takes. For example, you cannot change % from a binary to a unary operator when you overload %; you cannot change ++ from a unary to a binary operator when you overload it.

- You cannot change the precedence of an operator. An overloaded operator has the same precedence as the ordinary version of the operator. For example, x*y + z always means (x*y) + z, even if x, y, and z are objects and the operators + and * have been overloaded for the appropriate classes.

- The following operators cannot be overloaded: the dot operator (.), the scope resolution operator (::), sizeof, ?:, and the operator .*, which is not discussed in this book.

- An overloaded operator cannot have default arguments.

you need to understand returning a reference to correctly overload some of these operators, we also discuss this topic.

REFERENCES

A **reference** is the name of a storage location.[2] You can have a standalone reference, as in the following:

```
int robert;
int& bob = robert;
```

This makes bob a reference to the storage location for the variable robert, which makes bob an alias for the variable robert. Any change made to bob will also be made to robert. Stated this way, it sounds like a standalone reference is just a way to make your code confusing and get you in trouble. In most instances, a standalone reference is just

reference

_____

[2] If you know about pointers, you will notice that a reference sounds like a pointer. A reference is essentially, but not exactly, a constant pointer. There are differences between pointers and references, and they are not completely interchangeable.

trouble, although there a few cases where it can be useful. We will not discuss standalone references any more, nor will we use them.

As you may suspect, references are used to implement the call-by-reference parameter mechanism. So, the concept is not completely new to this chapter, although the phrase *a reference* is new.

We are interested in references here because returning a reference will allow you to overload certain operators in a more natural way. Returning a reference can be viewed as something like returning a variable or, more precisely, an alias to a variable. The syntactic details are simple. You add an & to the return type. For example:

```
double& sampleFunction(double& variable);
```

Since a type like double& is a different type from double, you must use the & in both the function declaration and the function definition. The return expression must be something with a reference, such as a variable of the appropriate type. It cannot be an expression, such as X + 5. Although many compilers will let you do it (with unfortunate results), you also should not return a local variable because you would be generating an alias to a variable and immediately destroying the variable. A trivial example of the function definition is

```
double& sampleFunction(double& variable)
{
    return variable;
}
```

Of course, this is a pretty useless, even troublesome, function, but it illustrates the concept. For example, the following code will output 99 and then 42:

```
double m = 99;
cout << sampleFunction(m) << endl;
sampleFunction(m) = 42;
cout << m << endl;
```

We will only be returning a reference when defining certain kinds of overloaded operators.

L-VALUES AND R-VALUES

The term **l-value** is used for something that can appear on the left-hand side of an assignment operator. The term **r-value** is used for something that can appear on the right-hand side of an assignment operator.

If you want the object returned by a function to be an l-value, it must be returned by reference.

Pitfall

RETURNING A REFERENCE TO CERTAIN MEMBER VARIABLES

When a member function returns a member variable and that member variable is of some class type, then it should normally not be returned by reference. For example, consider

```
class A
{
public:
    const SomeClass getMember( ) { return member; }
        ...
private:
    SomeClass member;
        ...
};
```

where SomeClass is, of course, some class type. The function getMember should not return a reference, but should instead return by const value as we have done in the example.

The problem with returning a reference to a class type member variable is the same as what we described for returning the member variable by non-const value in the programming tip section of this chapter entitled **Returning Member Variables of a Class Type.** When returning a member variable which is itself of some class type it should normally be returned by const value. (Every such rule has rare exceptions.)

⬛ OVERLOADING >> AND <<

The operators >> and << can be overloaded so that you can use them to input and output objects of the classes you define. The details are not that different from what we have already seen for other operators, but there are some new subtleties.

The insertion operator << that we used with cout is a binary operator very much like + or –. For example, consider the following:

<< is an operator

```
cout << "Hello out there.\n";
```

The operator is <<, the first operand is the predefined object cout (from the library iostream), and the second operand is the string value "Hello out there.\n". The predefined object cout is of type ostream, and so when you overload <<, the parameter that receives cout will be of type ostream. You can change either of the two operands to <<. When we cover file I/O in Chapter 12 you will see how to create an object of type ostream that sends output to a file. (These file I/O objects as well as the objects cin and cout are called *streams*, which is why the library name is ostream.) The overloading that we create, with cout in mind, will turn out to also work for file output without any changes in the definition of the overloaded <<.

stream

In our previous definitions of the class Money (Display 8.1 through Display 8.3) we used the member function output to output values of type Money. This is adequate, but

overloading

it would be nicer if we could simply use the insertion operator `<<` to output values of type Money, as in the following:

```
Money amount(100);
cout << "I have " << amount << " in my purse.\n";
```

instead of having to use the member function output as shown below:

```
Money amount(100);
cout << "I have ";
amount.output( );
cout << " in my purse.\n";
```

One problem in overloading the operator `<<` is deciding what value, if any, should be returned when `<<` is used in an expression like the following:

```
cout << amount
```

The two operands in the above expression are cout and amount, and evaluating the expression should cause the value of amount to be written to the screen. But if `<<` is an operator like + or –, then the above expression should also return some value. After all, expressions with other operands, such as n1 + n2, return values. But what does cout `<<` amount return? To obtain the answer to that question, we need to look at a more complicated expression involving `<<`.

chains of `<<`   Let's consider the following expression, which involves evaluating a chain of expressions using `<<`:

```
cout << "I have " << amount << " in my purse.\n";
```

If you think of the operator `<<` as being analogous to other operators, such as +, then the above should be (and in fact is) equivalent to the following:

```
( (cout << "I have ") << amount ) << " in my purse.\n";
```

What value should `<<` return to make sense of the above expression? The first thing evaluated is the subexpression:

```
(cout << "I have ")
```

If things are to work out, then the above subexpression had better return cout so that the computation can continue as follows:

```
( cout << amount ) << " in my purse.\n";
```

And if things are to continue to work out, (cout `<<` amount) had better also return cout so that the computation can continue as follows:

```
cout << " in my purse.\n";
```

This is illustrated in Display 8.4. The operator << should return its first argument, which is of type ostream (the type of cout).

<< returns a stream

Thus, the declaration for the overloaded operator << (to use with the class Money) should be as follows:

```
class Money
{
public:
        . . .
    friend ostream& operator <<(ostream& outs, const Money& amount);
```

Display 8.4   << as an Operator

```
cout << "I have " << amount << " in my purse.\n";
```

means the same as

```
((cout << "I have ") << amount) << " in my purse.\n";
```

and is evaluated as follows:

First evaluate (cout << "I have "), which returns cout:
```
((cout << "I have ") << amount) << " in my purse.\n";
```
               The string "I have" is output.

```
(cout << amount) << " in my purse.\n";
```

Then evaluate (cout << amount), which returns cout:

```
(cout << amount) << " in my purse.\n";
```
               The value of amount is output.

```
cout << " in my purse.\n";
```

Then evaluate cout << " in my purse.\n", which returns cout:

```
cout << " in my purse.\n";
```
               The string "in my purse.\n" is output.

```
cout;
```
               Since there are no more << operators, the process ends.

Once we have overloaded the insertion (output) operator <<, we will no longer need the member function `output` and will delete `output` from our definition of the class `Money`. The definition of the overloaded operator << is very similar to the member function `output`. In outline form, the definition for the overloaded operator is as follows:

```
ostream& operator <<(ostream& outputStream, const Money& amount)
{
    <This part is the same as the body of
     Money::output which is given in Display 8.1 (except that
      dollars is replaced with amount.dollars
     and cents is replaced by amount.cents).>

    return outputStream;

}
```

**<< and >>
return
a reference**

Note that the operator returns a reference.

The extraction operator >> is overloaded in a way that is analogous to what we described for the insertion operator <<. However, with the extraction (input) operator >>, the second argument will be the object that receives the input value, so the second parameter must be an ordinary call-by-reference parameter. In outline form the definition for the overloaded extraction operator >> is as follows:

```
istream& operator >>(istream& inputStream, Money& amount)
{
    <This part is the same as the body of
     Money::input, which is given in Display 8.1 (except that
      dollars is replaced with amount.dollars
     and cents is replaced by amount.cents).>

    return inputStream;
}
```

The complete definitions of the overloaded operators << and >> are given in Display 8.5, where we have rewritten the class `Money` yet again. This time we have rewritten the class so that the operators << and >> are overloaded to allow us to use these operators with values of type `Money`.

Note that you cannot realistically overload >> or << as member operators. If << and >> are to work as we want, then the first operand (first argument) must be `cout` or `cin` (or some file I/O stream). But if we want to overload the operators as members of, say, the class `Money`, then the first operand would have to be the calling object and so would have to be of type `Money`, and that will not allow you to define the operators so they behave in the normal way for >> and <<.

Display 8.5   Overloading << and >> *(part 1 of 3)*

```
1    #include <iostream>
2    #include <cstdlib>
3    #include <cmath>
4    using namespace std;

5    //Class for amounts of money in U.S. currency
6    class Money
7    {
8    public:
9        Money( );
10       Money(double amount);
11       Money(int theDollars, int theCents);
12       Money(int theDollars);
13       double getAmount( ) const;
14       int getDollars( ) const;
15       int getCents( ) const;
16       friend const Money operator +(const Money& amount1, const Money& amount2);
17       friend const Money operator -(const Money& amount1, const Money& amount2);
18       friend bool operator ==(const Money& amount1, const Money& amount2);
19       friend const Money operator -(const Money& amount);
20       friend ostream& operator <<(ostream& outputStream, const Money& amount);
21       friend istream& operator >>(istream& inputStream, Money& amount);
22   private:
23       int dollars; //A negative amount is represented as negative dollars and
24       int cents; //negative cents. Negative $4.50 is represented as -4 and -50.

25       int dollarsPart(double amount) const;
26       int centsPart(double amount) const;
27       int round(double number) const;
28   };

29   int main( )
30   {
31       Money yourAmount, myAmount(10, 9);
32       cout << "Enter an amount of money: ";
33       cin >> yourAmount;
34       cout << "Your amount is " << yourAmount << endl;
35       cout << "My amount is " << myAmount << endl;

37       if (yourAmount == myAmount)
38           cout << "We have the same amounts.\n";
39       else
40           cout << "One of us is richer.\n";

41       Money ourAmount = yourAmount + myAmount;
```

Display 8.5   Overloading << and >> *(part 2 of 3)*

```
42        cout << yourAmount << " + " << myAmount
43             << " equals " << ourAmount << endl;
```
Since << returns a reference, you can chain << like this.
You can chain >> in a similar way.

```
44        Money diffAmount = yourAmount - myAmount;
45        cout << yourAmount << " - " << myAmount
46             << " equals " << diffAmount << endl;

47        return 0;
48    }
```

<Definitions of other member functions are as in Display 8.1.
Definitions of other overloaded operators are as in Display 8.3.>

```
49    ostream& operator <<(ostream& outputStream, const Money& amount)
50    {
51        int absDollars = abs(amount.dollars);
52        int absCents = abs(amount.cents);
53        if (amount.dollars < 0 || amount.cents < 0)
54            //accounts for dollars == 0 or cents == 0
55            outputStream << "$-";
56        else
57            outputStream << '$';
58        outputStream << absDollars;

59        if (absCents >= 10)
60            outputStream << '.' << absCents;
61        else
62            outputStream << '.' << '0' << absCents;

63        return outputStream;
64    }
65
66    //Uses iostream and cstdlib:
67    istream& operator >>(istream& inputStream, Money& amount)
68    {
69        char dollarSign;
70        inputStream >> dollarSign; //hopefully
71        if (dollarSign != '$')
72        {
73            cout << "No dollar sign in Money input.\n";
74            exit(1);
75        }

76        double amountAsDouble;
77        inputStream >> amountAsDouble;
78        amount.dollars = amount.dollarsPart(amountAsDouble);
```

In the main function, cout is plugged in for *outputStream.*

For an alternate input algorithm, see Self-Test Exercise 3 in Chapter 7.

Returns a reference

In the main function, cin is plugged in for *inputStream.*

Since this is not a member operator, you need to specify a calling object for member functions of Money.

Display 8.5   Overloading << and >> *(part 3 of 3)*

```
79        amount.cents = amount.centsPart(amountAsDouble);

80        return inputStream;
81    }
```

← Returns a reference

SAMPLE DIALOGUE

```
Enter an amount of money: $123.45
Your amount is $123.45
My amount is $10.09.
One of us is richer.
$123.45 + $10.09 equals $133.54
$123.45 - $10.09 equals $113.36
```

Self-Test Exercises

9. In Display 8.5, the definition of the overloaded operator << contains lines like the following:

   ```
   outputStream << "$-";
   ```

   Isn't this circular? Aren't we defining << in terms of <<?

10. Why can't we overload << or >> as member operators?

11. Below is the definition for a class called Percent. Objects of type Percent represent percentages such as 10% or 99%. Give the definitions of the overloaded operators >> and << so that they can be used for input and output with objects of the class Percent. Assume that input always consists of an integer followed by the character '%', such as 25%. All percentages are whole numbers and are stored in the int member variable named value. You do not need to define the other overloaded operators and do not need to define the constructor. You only have to define the overloaded operators >> and <<.

    ```cpp
    #include <iostream>
    using namespace std;
    class Percent
    {
    public:
        friend bool operator ==(const Percent& first,
                                const Percent& second);
        friend bool operator <(const Percent& first,
                               const Percent& second);
        Percent( );
    ```

```
        friend istream& operator >>(istream& inputStream,
                                    Percent& aPercent);
        friend ostream& operator <<(ostream& outputStream,
                                    const Percent& aPercent);
        //There would normally also be other members and friends.
private:
    int value;
};
```

OVERLOADING >> AND <<

The input and output operators >> and << can be overloaded just like any other operators. If you want the operators to behave as expected for cin, cout, and file I/O, then the value returned should be of type istream for input and ostream for output, and the value should be returned by reference.

DECLARATIONS

```
class Class_Name
{
        . . .
public:
        . . .
    friend istream& operator >>(istream& Parameter_1,
                                Class_Name& Parameter_2);

    friend ostream& operator <<(ostream& Parameter_3,
                                const Class_Name& Parameter_4);
        . . .
```

The operators do not need to be friends but cannot be members of the class being input or output.

DEFINITIONS

```
istream& operator >>(istream& Parameter_1,
                                Class_Name& Parameter_2)
{
        . . .
```

```
    }
ostream& operator <<(ostream& Parameter_3,
                        const Class_Name& Parameter_4)
{
        . . .

    }
```

If you have enough accessor and mutator functions, you can overload >> and << as nonfriend functions. However, it is natural and more efficient to define them as friends.

Tip

WHAT MODE OF RETURNED VALUE TO USE

A function can return a value of type T in four different ways:

By plain old value, as in the function declaration   T f( );

By constant value, as in the function declaration   const T f( );

By reference, as in the function declaration   T& f( );

By const reference, as in the function declaration   const T& f( );

There is not unanimous agreement on which to use when. So, do not expect too much consistency in usage. Even when an author or programmer has a clear policy, they seldom manage to follow it without exception. Still, some points are clear.

If you are returning a simple type, like int or char, there is no point in using a const when returning by value or by reference. So programmers typically do not use a const on the return type when it is a simple type. If you want the simple value returned to be allowed as an l-value, that is to be allowed on the left-hand side of an assignment statement, then return by reference; otherwise return the simple type by plain old value. Class types are not so simple. The rest of this discussion applies to returning an object of a class type.

The decision on whether or not to return by reference has to do with whether or not you want to be able to use the returned object as an as an l-value. If you want to return something that can be used as an l-value, that is, that can be used on the left-hand side of an assignment operator, you must return by reference and so must use an ampere sign & on the returned type.

Returning a local variable (or other short lived object) by reference, with or without a const, can produce problems and should be avoided.

For class types, the two returned type specifications const T and const T& are very similar. They both mean that you cannot change the returned object by invoking some mutator function directly on the returned object, as in

```
f( ).mutator( );
```

The returned value can still be copied to another variable with an assignment operator and that other variable can have the mutator function applied to it. If you cannot decide between the const T& and const T, use const T (without the ampersand). A const T& is perhaps a bit more efficient than a const T.[3] However, the difference is not typically that important and most programmers use const T rather than const T& as a retuned type specification. As noted earlier, const T& can sometimes cause problems.

The following summary may be of help. T is assumed to be a class type. Copy constructors are not covered until Chapter 10, but we include details about them here for reference value. If you have not yet read Chapter 10, simply ignore all references to copy constructors.

If a public member function returns a private class member variable, it should always have a const on the returned type, as we explained in the pitfall section of this chapter entitled **Returning Member Variables of a Class Type.** (One exception to this rule is that programmers normally always return a value of type string by ordinary value, not by const value. This is presumably because the type string is thought of as a simple type like int and char, even though string is a class type.)

The following summary may be of help. T is assumed to be a class type.

Simple retuning by value, as in the function declaration   T f( );
Cannot be used as an l-value, and the returned value can be changed directly as in f( ).mutator( ). Calls the copy constructor.

Returning by constant value, as in   const T f( );
This case is the same as the previous case, but the returned value cannot be changed directly as in f( ).mutator( ).

Returning by reference as in   T& f( );
Can be used as an l-value, and the returned value can be changed directly as in f( ).mutator( ). Does not call the copy constructor.

Returning by constant reference, as in   const T& f( );
Cannot be used as an l-value, and the returned value cannot be changed directly as in f( ).mutator( ). Does not call the copy constructor.

THE ASSIGNMENT OPERATOR

If you overload the assignment operator =, you must overload it as a member operator. If you do not overload the assignment operator =, then you automatically get an assignment operator for your class. This default assignment operator copies the values of member variables from one object of the class to the corresponding member variables of another object of the class. For simple classes, that is usually what you want. When we discuss pointers, this default assignment operator will not be what we want, and we will discuss overloading the assignment operator at that point.

---

[3] This is because const T& does not call the copy constructor while const T does call the copy constructor. Copy constructors are discussed in Chapter 10.

■ OVERLOADING THE INCREMENT AND DECREMENT OPERATORS

The increment and decrement operators ++ and -- each have two versions. They can do different things depending on whether they are used in prefix notation, ++x, or postfix (suffix) notation, x++. Thus, when overloading these operators, you need to somehow distinguish between the prefix and postfix versions so that you can have two versions of the overloaded operator. In C++ this distinction between prefix and postfix versions is handled in a way that at first reading (and maybe even on second reading) seems a bit contrived. If you overload the ++ operator in the regular way (as a nonmember operator with one parameter or as a member operator with no parameters), then you have overloaded the prefix form. To obtain the postfix version, x++ or x--, you add a second parameter of type int. This is just a marker for the compiler; you do not give a second int argument when you invoke x++ or x--.

prefix and postfix

For example, Display 8.6 contains the definition of a class whose data is pairs of integers. The increment operator ++ is defined so it works in both prefix and postfix notation. We have defined ++ so that it has the intuitive spirit of ++ on int variables. This is the best way to define ++, but you are free to define it to return any kind of type and perform any kind of action.

The definition of the postfix version ignores that int parameter, as shown in Display 8.6. When the compiler sees a++, it treats it as an invocation of IntPair::operator++(int), with a as the calling object.

The increment and decrement operator on simple types, such as int and char, return by reference in the prefix form and by value in the postfix form. If you want to emulate what happens with simple types when you overload these operators for your class types, then you would return by reference for the prefix form and by value for the postfix form. However, we find it opens the door to too many problems to return by reference with increment or decrement operators, and so we always simply return by value for all versions of the increment and decrement operators.

return by reference

Self-Test Exercises

12. Is the following legal? Explain your answer. (The definition of IntPair is given in Display 8.6.)

```
IntPair a(1,2);
(a++)++;
```

■ OVERLOADING THE ARRAY OPERATOR [ ]

You can overload the square brackets, [], for a class so that they can be used with objects of the class. If you want to use [] in an expression on the left-hand side of an assignment operator, then the operator must be defined to return a reference. When overloading [], the operator [] *must* be a member function.

Display 8.6   Overloading ++ *(part 1 of 2)*

```
1   #include <iostream>
2   #include <cstdlib>
3   using namespace std;
```

You need not give a parameter name in a function or operator declaration. For ++ it makes sense to give no parameter since the parameter is not used.

```
4   class IntPair
5   {
6   public:
7       IntPair(int firstValue, int secondValue);
8       IntPair operator++( ); //Prefix version
9       IntPair operator++(int); //Postfix version
10      void setFirst(int newValue);
11      void setSecond(int newValue);
12      int getFirst( ) const;
13      int getSecond( ) const;
14  private:
15      int first;
16      int second;
17  };

18  int main( )
19  {
20      IntPair a(1,2);
21      cout << "Postfix a++: Start value of object a: ";
22      cout << a.getFirst( ) << " " << a.getSecond( ) << endl;
23      IntPair b = a++;
24      cout << "Value returned: ";
25      cout << b.getFirst( ) << " " << b.getSecond( ) << endl;
26      cout << "Changed object: ";
27      cout << a.getFirst( ) << " " << a.getSecond( ) << endl;

28      a = IntPair(1, 2);
29      cout << "Prefix ++a: Start value of object a: ";
30      cout << a.getFirst( ) << " " << a.getSecond( ) << endl;
31      IntPair c = ++a;
32      cout << "Value returned: ";
33      cout << c.getFirst( ) << " " << c.getSecond( ) << endl;
34      cout << "Changed object: ";
35      cout << a.getFirst( ) << " " << a.getSecond( ) << endl;
36      return 0;
37  }

38
39  IntPair::IntPair(int firstValue, int secondValue)
40                      : first(firstValue), second(secondValue)
41  {/*Body intentionally empty*/}
```

Display 8.6 Overloading ++ (part 2 of 2)

```
42  IntPair IntPair::operator++(int ignoreMe) //Postfix version
43  {
44      int temp1 = first;
45      int temp2 = second;
46      first++;
47      second++;
48      return IntPair(temp1, temp2);
49  }

50  IntPair IntPair::operator++( ) //Prefix version
51  {
52      first++;
53      second++;
54      return IntPair(first, second);
55  }

56  void IntPair::setFirst(int newValue)
57  {
58      first = newValue;
59  }

60  void IntPair::setSecond(int newValue)
61  {
62      second = newValue;
63  }

64  int IntPair::getFirst( ) const
65  {
66      return first;
67  }

68  int IntPair::getSecond( ) const
69  {
70      return second;
71  }
```

SAMPLE DIALOGUE

```
Postfix a++: Start value of object a: 1 2
Value returned: 1 2
Changed object: 2 3
Prefix ++a: Start value of object a: 1 2
Value returned: 2 3
Changed object: 2 3
```

It may help to review the syntax for the operator [], since it is different from any other operator we have seen. Remember that [] is overloaded as a member operator; therefore one thing in an expression using [] must be the calling object. In the expression a[2], a is the calling object and 2 is the argument to the member operator []. When overloading [], this "index" parameter can be any type.

For example, in Display 8.7 we define a class called Pair whose objects behave like arrays of characters with the two indexes 1 and 2 (*not* 0 and 1). Note that the expressions a[1] and a[2] behave just like array indexed variables. If you look at the definition of the overloaded operator [], you will see that a reference is returned and that it is a reference to a member variable, not to the entire Pair object. This is because the member variable is analogous to an indexed variable of an array. When you change a[1] (in the sample code in Display 8.7), you want that to be a change to the member variable first. Note that this gives access to the private member variables to any program, for example, via a[1] and a[2] in the sample main function in Display 8.7. Although first and second are private members, the code is legal because it does not reference first and second by name but indirectly using the names a[1] and a[2].

Display 8.7   Overloading [] *(part 1 of 2)*

```
1   #include <iostream>
2   #include <cstdlib>
3   using namespace std;


4   class CharPair
5   {
6   public:
7       CharPair( ){/*Body intentionally empty*/}
8       CharPair(char firstValue, char secondValue)
9                    : first(firstValue), second(secondValue)
10      {/*Body intentionally empty*/}
11
12      char& operator[](int index);
13  private:
14      char first;
15      char second;
16  };


17  int main( )
18  {
19      CharPair a;
20      a[1] = 'A';
21      a[2] = 'B';
```

Display 8.7   Overloading [] *(part 2 of 2)*

```
22        cout << "a[1] and a[2] are:\n";
23        cout << a[1] << a[2] << endl;

24        cout << "Enter two letters (no spaces):\n";
25        cin >> a[1] >> a[2];
26        cout << "You entered:\n";
27        cout << a[1] << a[2] << endl;

28        return 0;
29    }
30
31    //Uses iostream and cstdlib:
32    char& CharPair::operator[](int index)
33    {
34        if (index == 1)
35            return first;
36        else if (index == 2)
37            return second;
38        else
39        {
40            cout << "Illegal index value.\n";
41            exit(1);
42        }
43    }
```

Note that you return the member variable, not the entire Pair object, because the member variable is analogous to an indexed variable of an array.

SAMPLE DIALOGUE

```
a[1] and a[2] are:
AB
Enter two letters (no spaces):
CD
You entered:
CD
```

OVERLOADING BASED ON L-VALUE VERSUS R-VALUE

Although we will not be doing it in this book, you can overload a function name (or operator) so that it behaves differently when used as an l-value and when it is used as an r-value. (Recall that an l-value means it can be used on the left-hand side of an assignment statement.) . For example, if you want a function f to behave differently depending on whether it is used as an l-value or an r-value, you can do so as follows:

```
class SomeClass
{
public:
    int& f( ); // will be used in any l-value invocation
    const int& f( ) const; // used in any r-value invocation
    ...
};
```

The two parameter lists need not be empty, but they should be the same (or else you just get simple overloading). Be sure to notice that the second declarations of f has two occurrences of const. You must include both occurrences of const. The ampersand signs & are of course also required.

Chapter Summary

- Operators, such as + and ==, can be overloaded so that they can be used with objects of a class type that you define.

- An operator is just a function that uses a different syntax for invocations.

- A friend function of a class is an ordinary function except that it has access to the private members of the class, just like member functions do.

- When an operator is overloaded as a member of a class, the first operand is the calling object.

- If your classes each have a full set of accessor functions, then the only reason to make a function a friend is to make the definition of the friend function simpler and more efficient, but that is often reason enough.

- A reference is a way of naming a variable. It is essentially an alias for the variable.

- When overloading the >> or << operators, the type returned should be a stream type and should be a reference, which is indicated by appending an & to the name of the returned type.

ANSWERS TO SELF-TEST EXERCISES

1. The difference between a (binary) operator (such as +, *, or /) and a function involves the syntax of how they are called. In a function call, the arguments are given in parentheses after the function name. With an operator the arguments are given before and after the operator. Also, you must use the reserved word operator in the operator declaration and in the definition of an overloaded operator.

2. Add the following declaration and function definition:

```
bool operator <(const Money& amount1, const Money& amount2);

bool operator <(const Money& amount1, const Money& amount2)
{
```

```
      int dollars1 = amount1.getDollars( );
      int dollars2 = amount2.getDollars( );
      int cents1 = amount1.getCents( );
      int cents2 = amount2.getCents( );
      return ((dollars1 < dollars2) ||
              ((dollars1 == dollars2) && (cents1 < cents2)));
}
```

3. When overloading an operator, at least one of the arguments to the operator must be of a class type. This prevents changing the behavior of + for integers.

4. If you omit the const at the beginning of the declaration and definition of the overloaded plus operator for the class Money, then the following is legal:

```
(m1 + m2) = m3;
```

If the definition of the class Money is as shown in Display 8.1, so that the plus operator returns by const value, then it is not legal.

5. const Money
```
         Money::operator -(const Money& secondOperand) const
{
      int allCents1 = cents + dollars*100;
      int allCents2 = secondOperand.cents
                    + secondOperand.dollars*100;
      int diffAllCents = allCents1 - allCents2;
      int absAllCents = abs(diffAllCents);
      int finalDollars = absAllCents/100;
      int finalCents = absAllCents%100;

      if (diffAllCents < 0)
      {
          finalDollars = -finalDollars;
          finalCents = -finalCents;
      }

      return Money(finalDollars, finalCents);
}
```

6. A friend function and a member function are alike in that they both can use any member of the class (either public or private) in their function definition. However, a friend function is defined and used just like an ordinary function; the dot operator is not used when you call a friend function and no type qualifier is used when you define a friend function. A member function, on the other hand, is called using an object name and the dot operator. Also, a member function definition includes a type qualifier consisting of the class name and the scope resolution operator, ::.

7. ```
//Uses cstdlib:
const Money operator -(const Money& amount1,
                                    const Money& amount2)
{
    int allCents1 = amount1.cents + amount1.dollars*100;
    int allCents2 = amount2.cents + amount2.dollars*100;
    int diffAllCents = allCents1 - allCents2;
    int absAllCents = abs(diffAllCents);

    int finalDollars = absAllCents/100;
    int finalCents = absAllCents%100;

    if (diffAllCents < 0)
    {
        finalDollars = -finalDollars;
        finalCents = -finalCents;
    }

    return Money(finalDollars, finalCents);
}
```

8. Add the following declaration and function definition:

```
friend bool operator <(const Money& amount1,
                            const Money& amount2);
```

```
bool operator <(const Money& amount1,
                    const Money& amount2)
{
    return ((amount1.dollars < amount2.dollars) ||
                ((amount1.dollars == amount2.dollars) &&
                (amount1.cents < amount2.cents)));
}
```

9. To understand why it is not circular, you need to think about the basic message of overloading: A single function or operator name can have two or more definitions. That means that two or more different operators (or functions) can share a single name. In the line

```
outputStream << "$-";
```

the operator << is the name of an operator defined in the library iostream to be used when the second argument is a quoted string. The operator named << that we define in Display 8.5 is a different operator that works when the second argument is of type Money.

10. If << and >> are to work as we want, then the first operand (first argument) must be cout or cin (or some file I/O stream). But if we want to overload the operators as members of, say, the class Money, then the first operand would have to be the calling object and so would have to be of type Money, and that is not what we want.
```

11.
```
//Uses iostream:
istream& operator >>(istream& inputStream,
                                Percent& aPercent)
{
    char percentSign;
    inputStream >> aPercent.value;
    inputStream >> percentSign;//Discards the % sign.
    return inputStream;
}

//Uses iostream:
ostream& operator <<(ostream& outputStream,
                                const Percent& aPercent)
{
    outputStream << aPercent.value << '%';
    return outputStream;
}
```

12. It is legal, but the meaning is not what you might want. (a++) increases the value of the member variables in a by one, but (a++)++ raises the value of the member variables in a++ by one, and a++ is a different object from a. (It is possible to define the increment operator so that (a++)++ will increase the value of the member variables by two but that requires use of the this pointer which is not discussed until Chapter 10.)

PROGRAMMING PROJECTS

1. Modify the definition of the class Money shown in Display 8.5 so that the following are added:

   a. The operators <, <=, >, and >= have each been overloaded to apply to the type Money. (*Hint:* See Self-Test Exercise 8.)

   b. The following member function has been added to the class definition. (We show the function declaration as it should appear in the class definition. The definition of the function itself will include the qualifier Money::.)

```
const Money percent(int percentFigure) const;
//Returns a percentage of the money amount in the calling object.
//For example, if percentFigure is 10, then the value returned is
//10% of the amount of money represented by the calling object.
```

   For example, if purse is an object of type Money whose value represents the amount $100.10, then the call

```
        purse.percent(10);
```

   returns 10% of $100.10; that is, it returns a value of type Money that represents the amount $10.01.

2. Define a class for rational numbers. A rational number is a number that can be represented as the quotient of two integers. For example, 1/2, 3/4, 64/2, and so forth are all rational numbers. (By 1/2 and so on we mean the everyday fraction, not the integer division this expression would produce in a C++ program.) Represent rational numbers as two values of type int, one for the numerator and one for the denominator. Call the class Rational. Include a constructor with two arguments that can be used to set the member variables of an object to any legitimate values. Also include a constructor that has only a single parameter of type int; call this single parameter wholeNumber and define the constructor so that the object will be initialized to the rational number wholeNumber/1. Include a default constructor that initializes an object to 0 (that is, to 0/1). Overload the input and output operators >> and <<. Numbers are to be input and output in the form 1/2, 15/32, 300/401, and so forth. Note that the numerator, the denominator, or both may contain a minus sign, so –1/2, 15/–32, and –300/–401 are also possible inputs. Overload all the following operators so that they correctly apply to the type Rational: ==, <, <=, >, >=, +, –, *, and /. Write a test program to test your class. *Hints:* Two rational numbers *a/b* and *c/d* are equal if *a*d* equals *c*b*. If *b* and *d* are *positive* rational numbers, *a/b* is less than *c/d* provided *a*d* is less than *c*b*. You should include a function to normalize the values stored so that, after normalization, the denominator is positive and the numerator and denominator are as small as possible. For example, after normalization 4/–8 would be represented the same as –1/2.

3. Define a class for complex numbers. A complex number is a number of the form

$$a + b*i$$

where for our purposes, *a* and *b* are numbers of type double, and *i* is a number that represents the quantity $\sqrt{-1}$. Represent a complex number as two values of type double. Name the member variables real and imaginary. (The variable for the number that is multiplied by *i* is the one called imaginary.) Call the class Complex. Include a constructor with two parameters of type double that can be used to set the member variables of an object to any values. Include a constructor that has only a single parameter of type double; call this parameter realPart and define the constructor so that the object will be initialized to realPart + 0*i. Include a default constructor that initializes an object to 0 (that is, to 0 + 0*i). Overload all the following operators so that they correctly apply to the type Complex: ==, +, –, *, >>, and <<. You should also write a test program to test your class. *Hints:* To add or subtract two complex numbers, add or subtract the two member variables of type double. The product of two complex numbers is given by the following formula:

$$(a + b*i)*(c + d*i) == (a*c - b*d) + (a*d + b*c)*i$$

In the interface file, you should define a constant i as follows:

```
const Complex i(0, 1);
```

This defined constant i will be the same as the *i* discussed above.

4. (Cumulatively modify the example from Display 8.7 as follows.

   a. In Display 8.7, replace the private char members first and second with an array of char of size 100 and a private data member named size.

      Provide a default constructor that initializes size to 10 and sets the first 10 of the char positions to '#'. (This only uses 10 of the possible 100 slots.)

      Provide an accessor function that returns the value of the private member size.

         Test.

   b. Add an operator[] member that returns a char& that allows the user to access or to set any member of the private data array using a non-negative index that is less than size.

      Test.

   c. Add a constructor that takes an int argument, sz, that sets the first sz members of the char array to '#'.

      Test.

   d. Add a constructor that takes an int argument, sz, and an array of char of size sz. The constructor should set the first sz members of the private data array to the sz members of the argument array of char.

      Test.

      NOTES: When you test, you should test with known good values, with data on boundaries and with deliberately bad values. You are not required to put checks for index out of bounds errors in your code, but that would be a nice touch. Error handling alternatives: Issue an error message then die (that is, call exit(1)) or give the user another chance to make a correct entry.

9 CHAPTER

Strings

9 Strings

Polonius: What do you read my lord?
Hamlet: Words, words, words

William Shakespeare, *Hamlet*

INTRODUCTION

This chapter discusses two types whose values represent strings of characters, such as "Hello". One type is just an array with base type char that stores strings of characters in the array and marks the end of the string with the null character, '\0'. This is the older way of representing strings, which C++ inherited from the C programming language. These sorts of strings are called *C-strings*. Although C-strings are an older way of representing strings, it is difficult to do any sort of string processing in C++ without at least passing contact with C-strings. For example, quoted strings, such as "Hello", are implemented as C-strings in C++.

The ANSI/ISO C++ standard includes a more modern string handling facility in the form of the class string. The class string is the second string type that we will discuss in this chapter. The full class string uses templates and so is similar to the template classes in the Standard Template Library (STL). Templates are covered in Chapter 16 and the STL is covered in Chapter 19. This chapter covers basic uses of the class string that do not require a knowledge of templates.

This material does not require extensive knowledge of arrays, but you should be familiar with basic array notation, such as a[i]. Section 5.1 of Chapter 5 covers more than enough material about arrays to allow you to read the material of this chapter. This material also does not require extensive knowledge of classes. Section 9.1 on C-strings and Section 9.2 on character manipulation can be covered before Chapters 6, 7, and 8, which cover classes. However, before reading Section 9.3 on the standard class string, you should read Chapter 6 and the following parts of Chapter 7: Section 7.1 and the subsection of Section 7.2 entitled "The const Parameter Modifier" along with its accompanying pitfall section.

9.1   An Array Type for Strings

In everything one must consider the end.

Jean de La Fontaine, *Fables, book III (1668)*

This section describes one way to represent strings of characters, which C++ inherited from the C language. Section 9.3 describes a string class that is a more modern way to represent strings. Although the string type described here may be a bit "old fashioned," it is still widely used and is an integral part of the C++ language.

◼ C-STRING VALUES AND C-STRING VARIABLES

One way to represent a string is as an array with base type char. However, if the string is "Hello", it is handy to represent it as an array of characters with six indexed variables: five for the five letters in "Hello" plus one for the character '\0', which serves as an end marker. The character '\0' is called the **null character** and is used as an end marker because it is distinct from all the "real" characters. The end marker allows your program to read the array one character at a time and know that it should stop reading when it reads the '\0'. A string stored in this way (as an array of characters terminated with '\0') is called a **C-string**.

We spell '\0' with two symbols when we write it in a program, but just like the newline character '\n', the character '\0' is really only a single character value. Like any other character value, '\0' can be stored in one variable of type char or one indexed variable of an array of characters.

null character, '\0'

C-string

THE NULL CHARACTER, '\0'

The null character, '\0', is used to mark the end of a C-string that is stored in an array of characters. When an array of characters is used in this way, the array is often called a C-string variable. Although the null character '\0' is written using two symbols, it is a single character that fits in one variable of type char or one indexed variable of an array of characters.

You have already been using C-strings. In C++, a literal string, such as "Hello" is stored as a C-string, although you seldom need to be aware of this detail.

C-string
variables

A **C-string variable** is just an array of characters. Thus, the following array declaration provides us with a C-string variable capable of storing a C-string value with nine or fewer characters:

```
char s[10];
```

The 10 is for the 9 letters in the string plus the null character '\0' to mark the end of the string.

A C-string variable is a partially filled array of characters. Like any other partially filled array, a C-string variable uses positions starting at indexed variable 0 through as many as are needed. However, a C-string variable does not use an int variable to keep track of how much of the array is currently being used. Instead, a string variable places the special symbol '\0' in the array immediately after the last character of the C-string. Thus, if s contains the string "Hi Mom!", the array elements are filled as shown below:

s[0]	s[1]	s[2]	s[3]	s[4]	s[5]	s[6]	s[7]	s[8]	s[9]
H	i		M	o	m	!	\0	?	?

The character '\0' is used as a sentinel value to mark the end of the C-string. If you read the characters in the C-string starting at indexed variable s[0], proceed to s[1], then to s[2], and so forth, you know that when you encounter the symbol '\0' you have reached the end of the C-string. Since the symbol '\0' always occupies one element of the array, the length of the longest string that the array can hold is one less than the size of the array.

C-string
variables vs.
arrays of
characters

The thing that distinguishes a C-string variable from an ordinary array of characters is that a C-string variable must contain the null character '\0' at the end of the C-string value. This is a distinction regarding how the array is used rather than a distinction regarding what the array is. *A C-string variable is an array of characters, but it is used in a different way.*

initializing
C-string
variables

You can initialize a C-string variable when you declare it, as illustrated by the following example:

```
char myMessage[20] = "Hi there.";
```

Notice that the C-string assigned to the C-string variable need not fill the entire array.

When you initialize a C-string variable, you can omit the array size and C++ will automatically make the size of the C-string variable one more than the length of the quoted string. (The one extra indexed variable is for '\0'.) For example:

```
char shortString[] = "abc";
```

is equivalent to

```
char shortString[4] = "abc";
```

C-String Variable Declaration

A C-string variable is the same thing as an array of characters, but it is used differently. A C-string variable is declared to be an array of characters in the usual way.

Syntax

```
char Array_Name[Maximum_C-string_Size + 1];
```

Example

```
char myCstring[11];
```

The + 1 allows for the null character '\0', which terminates any C-string stored in the array. For example, the C-string variable myCstring in the above example can hold a C-string that is ten or fewer characters long.

Be sure you do not confuse the following initializations:

```
char shortString[] = "abc";
```

and

```
char shortString[] = {'a', 'b', 'c'};
```

They are *not equivalent*. The first of these two possible initializations places the null character '\0' in the array after the characters 'a', 'b', and 'c'. The second one does not put a '\0' anyplace in the array.

Initializing a C-String Variable

A C-string variable can be initialized when it is declared, as illustrated by the following example:

```
char yourString[11] = "Do Be Do";
```

Initializing in this way automatically places the null character, '\0', in the array at the end of the C-string specified.

If you omit the number inside the square brackets, [], then the C-string variable will be given a size one character longer than the length of the C-string. For example, the following declares myString to have nine indexed variables (eight for the characters of the C-string "Do Be Do" and one for the null character '\0'):

```
char myString[] = "Do Be Do";
```

A C-string variable is an array, so it has indexed variables that can be used just like those of any other array. For example, suppose your program contains the following C-string variable declaration:

```
char ourString[5] = "Hi";
```

With ourString declared as above, your program has the following indexed variables: ourString[0], ourString[1], ourString[2], ourString[3], and ourString[4]. For example, the following will change the C-string value in ourString to a C-string of the same length consisting of all 'X' characters:

```
int index = 0;
while (ourString[index] != '\0')
{
    ourString[index] = 'X';
    index++;
}
```

When manipulating these indexed variables you should be very careful not to replace the null character '\0' with some other value. If the array loses the value '\0' it will no longer behave like a C-string variable. For example, the following will change the array happyString so that it no longer contains a C-string:

```
char happyString[7] = "DoBeDo";
happyString[6] = 'Z';
```

After the above code is executed, the array happyString will still contain the six letters in the C-string "DoBeDo", but happyString will no longer contain the null character '\0' to mark the end of the C-string. Many string-manipulating functions depend critically on the presence of '\0' to mark the end of the C-string value.

As another example, consider the above while loop that changes characters in the C-string variable ourString. That while loop changes characters until it encounters a '\0'. If the loop never encounters a '\0', then it could change a large chunk of memory to some unwanted values, which could make your program do strange things. As a safety feature, it would be wise to rewrite the above while loop as follows, so that if the null character '\0' is lost, the loop will not inadvertently change memory locations beyond the end of the array:

```
int index = 0;
while ( (ourString[index] != '\0') && (index < SIZE) )
{
    ourString[index] = 'X';
    index++;
}
```

SIZE is a defined constant equal to the declared size of the array ourString.

THE <cstring> LIBRARY

You do not need any include directive or using statement to declare and initialize C-strings. However, when processing C-strings you inevitably will use some of the predefined string functions in the library <cstring>. Thus, when using C-strings, you will normally give the following include directive near the beginning of the file containing your code:

```
#include <cstring>
```

The definitions in <cstring> are placed in the global namespace, not in the std namespace, and so no using statement is required.

Pitfall

USING = AND == WITH C-STRINGS

C-string values and C-string variables are not like values and variables of other data types, and many of the usual operations do not work for C-strings. You cannot use a C-string variable in an assignment statement using =. If you use == to test C-strings for equality, you will not get the result you expect. The reason for these problems is that C-strings and C-string variables are arrays.

Assigning a value to a C-string variable is not as simple as it is for other kinds of variables. The following is illegal:

```
char aString[10];
aString = "Hello";          ← Illegal!
```

assigning a
C-string
value

Although you can use the equal sign to assign a value to a C-string variable when the variable is declared, you cannot do it anywhere else in your program. Technically, the use of the equal sign in a declaration, as in

```
char happyString[7] = "DoBeDo";
```

is an initialization, not an assignment. If you want to assign a value to a C-string variable, you must do something else.

There are a number of different ways to assign a value to a C-string variable. The easiest way is to use the predefined function strcpy as shown below:

```
strcpy(aString, "Hello");
```

This will set the value of aString equal to "Hello". Unfortunately, this version of the function strcpy does not check to make sure the copying does not exceed the size of the string variable that is the first argument. Many, but not all, versions of C++ also have a version of strcpy that takes a third argument which gives the maximum number of characters to copy. If this third parameter is set to one less than the size of the array variable in the first argument position, then you obtain a safe version of strcpy (provided your version of C++ allows this third argument). For example:

```
char anotherString[10];
strcpy(anotherString, aStringVariable, 9);
```

With this version of strcpy, at most nine characters (leaving room for '\0') will be copied from the C-string variable aStringVariable no matter how long the string in aStringVariable may be.

testing
C-strings
for equality

You also cannot use the operator == in an expression to test whether two C-strings are the same. (Things are actually much worse than that. You can use == with C-strings, but it does not test for the C-strings being equal. So if you use == to test two C-strings for equality, you are likely to get incorrect results, but no error message!) To test whether two C-strings are the same, you can use the predefined function strcmp. For example:

```
if (strcmp(cString1, cString2))
    cout << "The strings are NOT the same.";
else
    cout << "The strings are the same.";
```

Note that the function strcmp works differently than you might guess. The comparison is true if the strings do not match. The function strcmp compares the characters in the C-string arguments a character at a time. If at any point the numeric encoding of the character from cString1 is less than the numeric encoding of the corresponding character from cString2, the testing stops at that point and a negative number is returned. If the character from cString1 is greater than the character from cString2, a positive number is returned. (Some implementations of strcmp return the difference of the character encoding, but you should not depend on that.) If the C-strings are the same, a 0 is returned. The ordering relationship used for comparing characters is called **lexicographic order**. The important point to note is that if both strings are in all uppercase or all lowercase, then lexicographic order is just alphabetic order.

lexicographic
order

We see that strcmp returns a negative value, a positive value, or zero depending on whether the C-strings compare lexicographically as lesser, greater, or equal. If you use strcmp as a Boolean expression in an if or a looping statement to test C-strings for equality, then the nonzero value will be converted to true if the strings are different, and the zero will be converted to false. Be sure that you remember this inverted logic in your testing for C-string equality.

C++ compilers that are compliant with the standard have a safer version of strcmp that has a third argument that gives the maximum number of characters to compare.

The functions strcpy and strcmp are in the library with the header file <cstring>, so to use them you must insert the following near the top of the file:

```
#include <cstring>
```

The definitions of strcpy and strcmp are placed in the global namespace, not in the std namespace, and so no using directive is required.

■ OTHER FUNCTIONS IN <cstring>

Display 9.1 contains a few of the most commonly used functions from the library with the header file <cstring>. To use them, insert the following near the top of the file:

```
#include <cstring>
```

Note that <cstring> places all these definitions in the global namespace, not in the std namespace, and so no using statement is required.

We have already discussed strcpy and strcmp. The function strlen is easy to understand and use. For example, strlen("dobedo") returns 6 because there are six characters in "dobedo".

The function strcat is used to concatenate two C-strings; that is, to form a longer string by placing the two shorter C-strings end-to-end. The first argument must be a C-string variable. The second argument can be anything that evaluates to a C-string value, such as a quoted string. The result is placed in the C-string variable that is the first argument. For example, consider the following:

```
char stringVar[20] = "The rain";
strcat(stringVar, "in Spain");
```

This code will change the value of stringVar to "The rainin Spain". As this example illustrates, you need to be careful to account for blanks when concatenating C-strings. If you look at the table in Display 9.1 you will see that there is a safer, three-argument version of the function strcat that is available in many, but not all, versions of C++.

Display 9.1 Some Predefined C-String Functions in <cstring> (part 1 of 2)

FUNCTION	DESCRIPTION	CAUTIONS
strcpy(*Target_String_Var, Src_String*)	Copies the C-string value *Src_String* into the C-string variable *Target_String_Var*.	Does not check to make sure *Target_String_Var* is large enough to hold the value *Src_String*.
strncpy(*Target_String_Var, Src_String, Limit*)	The same as the two-argument strcpy except that at most *Limit* characters are copied.	If *Limit* is chosen carefully, this is safer than the two-argument version of strcpy. Not implemented in all versions of C++.
strcat(*Target_String_Var, Src_String*)	Concatenates the C-string value *Src_String* onto the end of the C-string in the C-string variable *Target_String_Var*.	Does not check to see that *Target_String_Var* is large enough to hold the result of the concatenation.
strncat(*Target_String_Var, Src_String, Limit*)	The same as the two argument strcat except that at most *Limit* characters are appended.	If *Limit* is chosen carefully, this is safer than the two-argument version of strcat. Not implemented in all versions of C++.

Display 9.1 Some Predefined C-String Functions in `<cstring>` *(part 2 of 2)*

FUNCTION	DESCRIPTION	CAUTIONS
strlen(*Src_String*)	Returns an integer equal to the length of *Src_String*. (The null character, '\0', is not counted in the length.)	
strcmp(*String_1, String_2*)	Returns 0 if *String_1* and *String_2* are the same. Returns a value < 0 if *String_1* is less than *String_2*. Returns a value > 0 if *String_1* is greater than *String_2* (that is, returns a nonzero value if *String_1* and *String_2* are different). The order is lexicographic.	If *String_1* equals *String_2*, this function returns 0, which converts to false. Note that this is the reverse of what you might expect it to return when the strings are equal.
strncmp(*String_1, String_2, Limit*)	The same as the two-argument strcat except that at most *Limit* characters are compared.	If *Limit* is chosen carefully, this is safer than the two-argument version of strcmp. Not implemented in all versions of C++.

C-String Arguments and Parameters

A C-string variable is an array, so a C-string parameter to a function is simply an array parameter.

As with any array parameter, whenever a function changes the value of a C-string parameter, it is safest to include an additional int parameter giving the declared size of the C-string variable.

On the other hand, if a function only uses the value in a C-string argument but does not change that value, then there is no need to include another parameter to give either the declared size of the C-string variable or the amount of the C-string variable array that is filled. The null character, '\0', can be used to detect the end of the C-string value that is stored in the C-string variable.

Self-Test Exercises

1. Which of the following declarations are equivalent?

```
char stringVar[10] = "Hello";
char stringVar[10] = {'H', 'e', 'l', 'l', 'o', '\0'};
char stringVar[10] = {'H', 'e', 'l', 'l', 'o'};
char stringVar[6] = "Hello";
char stringVar[] = "Hello";
```

2. What C-string will be stored in `singingString` after the following code is run?

```
char singingString[20] = "DoBeDo";
strcat(singingString, " to you");
```

Assume that the code is embedded in a complete and correct program and that an `include` directive for `<cstring>` is in the program file.

3. What (if anything) is wrong with the following code?

```
char stringVar[] = "Hello";
strcat(stringVar, " and Good-bye.");
cout << stringVar;
```

Assume that the code is embedded in a complete program and that an `include` directive for `<cstring>` is in the program file.

4. Suppose the function `strlen` (which returns the length of its string argument) was not already defined for you. Give a function definition for `strlen`. Note that `strlen` has only one argument, which is a C-string. Do not add additional arguments; they are not needed.

5. What is the length (maximum) of a string that can be placed in the string variable declared by the following declaration? Explain.

```
char s[6];
```

6. How many characters are in each of the following character and string constants?
    a. `'\n'`
    b. `'n'`
    c. `"Mary"`
    d. `"M"`
    e. `"Mary\n"`

7. Since character strings are just arrays of `char`, why does the text caution you not to confuse the following declaration and initialization?

```
char shortString[] = "abc";
char shortString[] = { 'a', 'b', 'c'};
```

8. Given the following declaration and initialization of the string variable, write a loop to assign `'X'` to all positions of this string variable, keeping the length the same.

```
char ourString[15] = "Hi there!";
```

9. Given the declaration of a C-string variable, where `SIZE` is a defined constant:

```
char ourString[SIZE];
```

The C-string variable `ourString` has been assigned in code not shown here. For correct C-string variables, the following loop reassigns all positions of `ourString` the value `'X'`, leaving the length the same as before. Assume this code fragment is embedded in an otherwise complete and correct program. Answer the questions following this code fragment.

```
int index = 0;
while (ourString[index] != '\0')
{
    ourString[index] = 'X';
    index++;
}
```

a. Explain how this code can destroy the contents of memory beyond the end of the array.

b. Modify this loop to protect against inadvertently changing memory beyond the end of the array.

10. Write code using a library function to copy the string constant `"Hello"` into the string variable declared below. Be sure to `#include` the necessary header file to get the declaration of the function you use.

```
char aString[10];
```

11. What string will be output when this code is run? (Assume, as always, that this code is embedded in a complete, correct program.)
```
char song[10] = "I did it ";
char franksSong[20];
strcpy ( franksSong, song );
strcat ( franksSong, "my way!");
cout << franksSong << endl;
```

12. What is the problem (if any) with this code?

```
char aString[20] = "How are you? ";
strcat(aString, "Good, I hope.");
```

C-STRING INPUT AND OUTPUT

C-strings can be output using the insertion operator, <<. In fact, we have already been doing so with quoted strings. You can use a C-string variable in the same way. For example,

```
cout << news << " Wow.\n";
```

where news is a C-string variable.

It is possible to fill a C-string variable using the input operator >>, but there is one thing to keep in mind. As for all other types of data, all whitespace (blanks, tabs, and line breaks) are skipped when C-strings are read this way. Moreover, each reading of input stops at the next space or line break. For example, consider the following code:

```
char a[80], b[80];
cout << "Enter some input:\n";
cin >> a >> b;
cout << a << b << "END OF OUTPUT\n";
```

When embedded in a complete program, this code produces a dialogue like the following:

```
Enter some input:
Do be do to you!
DobeEND OF OUTPUT
```

The C-string variables a and b each receive only one word of the input: a receives the C-string value "Do" because the input character following **Do** is a blank; b receives "be" because the input character following **be** is a blank.

If you want your program to read an entire line of input, you can use the extraction operator, >>, to read the line one word at a time. This can be tedious and it still will not read the blanks in the line. There is an easier way to read an entire line of input and place the resulting C-string into a C-string variable: Just use the predefined member function getline, which is a member function of every input stream (such as cin or a   `getline` file input stream). The function getline has two arguments. The first argument is a C-string variable to receive the input and the second is an integer that typically is the declared size of the C-string variable. The second argument specifies the maximum number of array elements in the C-string variable that getline will be allowed to fill with characters. For example, consider the following code:

```
char a[80];
cout << "Enter some input:\n";
cin.getline(a, 80);
cout << a << "END OF OUTPUT\n";
```

When embedded in a complete program, this code produces a dialogue like the following:

```
Enter some input:
Do be do to you!
Do be do to you!END OF OUTPUT
```

With the function cin.getline, the entire line is read. The reading ends when the line ends, even though the resulting C-string may be shorter than the maximum number of characters specified by the second argument.

When `getline` is executed, the reading stops after the number of characters given by the second argument has been filled in the C-string array, even if the end of the line has not been reached. For example, consider the following code:

```
char shortString[5];
cout << "Enter some input:\n";
cin.getline(shortString, 5);
cout << shortString << "END OF OUTPUT\n";
```

When embedded in a complete program, this code produces a dialogue like the following:

```
Enter some input:
dobedowap
dobeEND OF OUTPUT
```

Notice that four, not five, characters are read into the C-string variable `shortString`, even though the second argument is 5. This is because the null character `'\0'` fills one array position. Every C-string is terminated with the null character when it is stored in a C-string variable, and this always consumes one array position.

input/output with files

The C-string input and output techniques we illustrated for `cout` and `cin` work the same way for input and output with files. The input stream `cin` can be replaced by an input stream that is connected to a file. The output stream `cout` can be replaced by an output stream that is connected to a file. (File I/O is discussed in Chapter 12.).

---

getline

The member function `getline` can be used to read a line of input and place the string of characters on that line into a C-string variable.

SYNTAX

```
cin.getline(String_Var, Max_Characters + 1);
```

One line of input is read from the stream *Input_Stream* and the resulting C-string is placed in *String_Var*. If the line is more than *Max_Characters* long, only the first *Max_Characters* on the line are read. (The +1 is needed because every C-string has the null character `'\0'` added to the end of the C-string and thus the string stored in *String_Var* is one longer than the number of characters read in.)

EXAMPLE

```
char oneLine[80];
cin.getline(oneLine, 80);
```

As you will see in Chapter 12, you can use an input stream connected to a text file in place of `cin`.

Self-Test Exercises

13. Consider the following code (and assume it is embedded in a complete and correct program and then run):

```
char a[80], b[80];
cout << "Enter some input:\n";
cin >> a >> b;
cout << a << '-' << b << "END OF OUTPUT\n";
```

If the dialogue begins as follows, what will be the next line of output?

```
Enter some input:
The
    time is now.
```

14. Consider the following code (and assume it is embedded in a complete and correct program and then run):

```
char myString[80];
cout << "Enter a line of input:\n";
cin.getline(myString, 6);
cout << myString << "<END OF OUTPUT";
```

If the dialogue begins as follows, what will be the next line of output?

```
Enter a line of input:
May the hair on your toes grow long and curly.
```

9.2   Character Manipulation Tools

> *They spell it Vinci and pronounce it Vinchy; foreigners always*
> *spell better than they pronounce.*

Mark Twain, *The Innocents Abroad*

Any form of string is ultimately composed of individual characters. Thus, when doing string processing it is often helpful to have tools at your disposal to test and manipulate individual values of type char. This section is about such tools.

CHARACTER I/O

All data is input and output as character data. When your program outputs the number 10, it is really the two characters '1' and '0' that are output. Similarly, when the user wants to type in the number 10, he or she types in the character '1' followed by the character '0'. Whether the computer interprets this "10" as two characters or as the number 10 depends on how your program is written. But, however your program is written, the computer hardware is always reading the characters '1' and '0', not the number 10. This conversion between characters and numbers is usually done automatically so that you need not think about such details; however, sometimes all this automatic help gets in the way. Therefore, C++ provides some low-level facilities for input and output of character data. These low-level facilities include no automatic conversions. This allows you to bypass the automatic facilities and do input/output in absolutely any way you want. You could even write input and output functions that can read and write int values in Roman numeral notation, if you wanted to be so perverse.

THE MEMBER FUNCTIONS get AND put

The function get allows your program to read in one character of input and store it in a variable of type char. Every input stream, whether it is an input-file stream or the stream cin, has get as a member function. We will describe get here as a member function of the object cin. (When we discuss file I/O in Chapter 12 we will see that it behaves exactly the same for input-file streams as it does for cin).

Before now, we have used cin with the extraction operator, >>, in order to read a character of input (or any other input, for that matter). When you use the extraction operator >>, some things are done for you automatically, such as skipping over whitespace. But sometimes you do not want to skip over whitespace. The member function cin.get reads the next input character no matter whether the character is whitespace or not.

cin.get

The member function get takes one argument, which should be a variable of type char. That argument receives the input character that is read from the input stream. For example, the following will read in the next input character from the keyboard and store it in the variable nextSymbol:

```
char nextSymbol;
cin.get(nextSymbol);
```

reading blanks and '\n'

It is important to note that your program can read any character in this way. If the next input character is a blank, this code will read the blank character. If the next character is the newline character '\n' (that is, if the program has just reached the end of an input line), then the above call to cin.get will set the value of nextSymbol equal to '\n'. For example, suppose your program contains the following code:

```
char c1, c2, c3;
cin.get(c1);
cin.get(c2);
cin.get(c3);
```

and suppose you type in the following two lines of input to be read by this code:

AB
CD

The value of c1 is set to 'A', the value of c2 is set to 'B', and the value of c3 is set to '\n'. The variable c3 is not set equal to 'C'.

One thing you can do with the member function get is to have your program detect the end of a line. The following loop will read a line of input and stop after passing the newline character '\n'. Any subsequent input will be read from the beginning of the next line. For this first example, we have simply echoed the input, but the same technique would allow you to do whatever you want with the input.

detecting the end of an input line

```
cout << "Enter a line of input and I will echo it:\n";
char symbol;
do
{
    cin.get(symbol);
    cout << symbol;
} while (symbol != '\n');
cout << "That's all for this demonstration.\n";
```

This loop will read any line of input and echo it exactly, including blanks. The following is a sample dialogue produced by this code:

```
Enter a line of input and I will echo it:
Do Be Do 1 2    34
Do Be Do 1 2    34
That's all for this demonstration.
```

Notice that the newline character '\n' is both read and output. Since '\n' is output, the string that begins with the word "That's" is on a new line.

'\n' AND "\n"

'\n' and "\n" sometimes seem like the same thing. In a cout statement, they produce the same effect, but they cannot be used interchangeably in all situations. '\n' is a value of type char and can be stored in a variable of type char. On the other hand, "\n" is a string that happens to be made up of exactly one character. Thus, "\n" is not of type char and cannot be stored in a variable of type char.

The member function put is analogous to the member function get except that it is used for output rather than input. The function put allows your program to output one character. The member function cout.put takes one argument, which should be an expression of type char, such as a constant or a variable of type char. The value of the argument is output to the screen when the function is called. For example, the following will output the letter 'a' to the screen:

put

```
cout.put('a');
```

THE MEMBER FUNCTION get

The function get can be used to read one character of input. Unlike the extraction operator, >>, get reads the next input character, no matter what that character is. In particular, get will read a blank or the newline character, '\n', if either of these are the next input character. The function get takes one argument, which should be a variable of type char. When get is called, the next input character is read and the argument variable has its value set equal to this input character.

EXAMPLE

```
char nextSymbol;
cin.get(nextSymbol);
```

As we will see in Chapter 12, if you wish to use get to read from a file, you use an input-file stream in place of the stream cin.

The function cout.put does not allow you to do anything you could not do with the insertion operator <<, but we include it for completeness. (When we discuss file I/O in Chapter 12, we will see that put can be used with an output stream connected to a text file and is not restricted to being used only with cout.)

If your program uses cin.get or cout.put, then just as with other uses of cin and cout, your program should include one of the following (or something similar):

```
#include <iostream>
using namespace std;
```

or

```
#include <iostream>
using std::cin;
using std::cout;
```

Example

CHECKING INPUT USING A NEWLINE FUNCTION

The function getInt in Display 9.2 asks the user if the input is correct and asks for a new value if the user says the input is incorrect. The program in Display 9.2 is just a driver program to test the function getInt, but the function, or one very similar to it, can be used in just about any kind of program that takes its input from the keyboard.

newLine( )

Notice the call to the function newLine( ). The function newLine reads all the characters on the remainder of the current line but does nothing with them. This amounts to discarding the remainder of the line. Thus, if the user types in No, then the program reads the first letter, which is N, and then calls the function newLine, which discards the rest of the input line. This means that if the user types 75 on the next input line, as shown in the sample dialogue, the program will read the number 75 and will not attempt to read the letter o in the word No. If the program did not include a call to the function newLine, then the next item read would be the o in the line containing No instead of the number 75 on the following line.

Display 9.2 Checking Input *(part 1 of 2)*

```
1    //Program to demonstrate the functions newLine and getInput
2    #include <iostream>
3    using namespace std;

4    void newLine( );
5    //Discards all the input remaining on the current input line.
6    //Also discards the '\n' at the end of the line.

7    void getInt(int& number);
8    //Sets the variable number to a
9    //value that the user approves of.


10   int main( )
11   {
12       int n;

13       getInt(n);
14       cout << "Final value read in = " << n << endl
15           << "End of demonstration.\n";

16       return 0;
17   }


18   //Uses iostream:
19   void newLine( )
20   {
21       char symbol;
22       do
23       {
24           cin.get(symbol);
25       } while (symbol != '\n');

26   }
27   //Uses iostream:
28   void getInt(int& number)
29   {
```

Display 9.2   Checking Input *(part 2 of 2)*

```
30        char ans;
31        do
32        {
33            cout << "Enter input number: ";
34            cin >> number;
35            cout << "You entered " << number
36                 << " Is that correct? (yes/no): ";
37            cin >> ans;
38            newLine( );
39        } while ((ans == 'N') || (ans == 'n'));
40    }
```

SAMPLE DIALOGUE

```
Enter input number: 57
You entered 57 Is that correct? (yes/no): No No No!
Enter input number: 75
You entered 75 Is that correct? (yes/no): yes
Final value read in = 75
End of demonstration.
```

Pitfall

UNEXPECTED '\n' IN INPUT

When using the member function get you must account for every character of input, even the characters you do not think of as being symbols, such as blanks and the newline character, '\n'. A common problem when using get is forgetting to dispose of the '\n' that ends every input line. If there is a newline character in the input stream that is not read (and usually discarded), then when your program next expects to read a "real" symbol using the member function get, it will instead read the character '\n'. To clear the input stream of any leftover '\n', you can use the function newLine, which we defined in Display 9.2 (or you can use the function ignore, which we discuss in the next subsection). Let's look at a concrete example.

It is legal to mix the different forms of cin. For example, the following is legal:

```
cout << "Enter a number:\n";
int number;
cin >> number;
cout << "Now enter a letter:\n";
char symbol;
cin.get(symbol);
```

However, this can produce problems, as illustrated by the following dialogue:

```
Enter a number:
21
Now enter a letter:
A
```

With this dialogue, the value of number will be 21 as you expect. However, if you expect the value of the variable symbol to be 'A', you will be disappointed. The value given to symbol is '\n'. After reading the number 21, the next character in the input stream is the newline character, '\n', and so that is read next. Remember, get does not skip over line breaks and spaces. (In fact, depending on what is in the rest of the program, you may not even get a chance to type in the **A**. Once the variable symbol is filled with the character '\n', the program proceeds to whatever statement is next in the program. If the next statement sends output to the screen, the screen will be filled with output before you get a chance to type in the **A**.)

The following rewriting of the above code will cause the above dialogue to fill the variable number with 21 and fill the variable symbol with 'A':

```cpp
cout << "Enter a number:\n";
int number;
cin >> number;
cout << "Now enter a letter:\n";
char symbol;
cin >> symbol;
```

Alternatively, you can use the function newLine, defined in Display 9.2, as follows:

```cpp
cout << "Enter a number:\n";
int number;
cin >> number;
newLine( );
cout << "Now enter a letter:\n";
char symbol;
cin.get(symbol);
```

As this second rewrite indicates, you can mix the two forms of cin and have your program work correctly, but it does require some extra care.

As a third alternative, you could use the function ignore, which we discuss in the next subsection.

THE putback, peek, AND ignore MEMBER FUNCTIONS

Sometimes your program needs to know the next character in the input stream. However, after reading the next character, it might turn out that you do not want to process that character and so would like to "put it back." For example, if you want your program to read up to but not include the first blank it encounters, then your program must read that first blank in order to know when to stop reading—but then that blank is no longer in the input stream. Some other part of your program might need to read

putback

and process this blank. One way to deal with this situation is to use the member function cin.putback. The function cin.putback takes one argument of type char and places the value of that argument back in the input stream so that it will be the next character to be read. The argument can be any expression that evaluates to a value of type char. The character that is put back into the input stream with the member function putback need not be the last character read; it can be any character you wish.

peek

The peek member function does what you might expect from its name. cin.peek( ) returns the next character to be read by cin, but it does not use up that character; the next read starts with that character. In other words, the peek function peeks ahead to tell your program what the next character to be read will be.

ignore

If you want to skip over input up to some designated character, such as the newline character '\n', you can use the ignore member function. For example, the following will skip over all input characters up to and including the newline character, '\n':

```
cin.ignore(1000, '\n');
```

The 1000 is the maximum number of characters to ignore. If the delimiter, in this case '\n', has not been found after 1000 characters, then no more characters are ignored. Of course, a different int argument can be used in place of 1000 and a different character argument can be used in place of '\n'.

As we will see in Chapter 12, the member functions putback, peek, and ignore can be used with cin replaced by a file input stream object for text file input.

Self-Test Exercises

15. Consider the following code (and assume that it is embedded in a complete and correct program and then run):

```
char c1, c2, c3, c4;
cout << "Enter a line of input:\n";
cin.get(c1);
cin.get(c2);
cin.get(c3);
cin.get(c4);
cout << c1 << c2 << c3 << c4 << "END OF OUTPUT";
```

If the dialogue begins as follows, what will be the next line of output?

```
Enter a line of input:
a b c d e f g
```

16. Consider the following code (and assume that it is embedded in a complete and correct program and then run):

```
char next;
int count = 0;
cout << "Enter a line of input:\n";
cin.get(next);
while (next != '\n')
{
    if ((count%2) == 0)          ← True if count is even
        cout << next;
    count++;
    cin.get(next);
}
```

If the dialogue begins as follows, what will be the next line of output?

```
Enter a line of input:
abcdef gh
```

17. Suppose that the program described in Self-Test Exercise 16 is run and the dialogue begins as follows (instead of beginning as shown in Self-Test Exercise 16). What will be the next line of output?

```
Enter a line of input:
0 1 2 3 4 5 6 7 8 9 10 11
```

18. Consider the following code (and assume that it is embedded in a complete and correct program and then run):

```
char next;
int count = 0;
cout << "Enter a line of input:\n";
cin >> next;
while (next != '\n')
{
    if ((count%2) == 0)
        cout << next;
    count++;
    cin >> next;
}
```

If the dialogue begins as follows, what will be the next line of output?

```
Enter a line of input:
0 1 2 3 4 5 6 7 8 9 10 11
```

■ CHARACTER-MANIPULATING FUNCTIONS

In text processing you often want to convert lowercase letters to uppercase or vice versa. The predefined function toupper can be used to convert a lowercase letter to an uppercase letter. For example, toupper('a') returns 'A'. If the argument to the function toupper is anything other than a lowercase letter, toupper simply returns the argument unchanged. So toupper('A') returns 'A', and toupper('?') returns '?'. The function tolower is similar except that it converts an uppercase letter to its lowercase version.

The functions toupper and tolower are in the library with the header file <cctype>, so any program that uses these functions, or any other functions in this library, must contain the following:

```
#include <cctype>
```

Note that <cctype> places all these definitions in the global namespace, and so no using directive is required. Display 9.3 contains descriptions of some of the most commonly used functions in the library <cctype>.

Display 9.3 **Some Functions in <cctype>** *(part 1 of 2)*

FUNCTION	DESCRIPTION	EXAMPLE
toupper(*Char_Exp*)	Returns the uppercase version of *Char_Exp* (as a value of type int).	char c = toupper('a'); cout << c; **Outputs:** A
tolower(*Char_Exp*)	Returns the lowercase version of *Char_Exp* (as a value of type int).	char c = tolower('A'); cout << c; **Outputs:** a

isupper(*Char_Exp*)	Returns true provided *Char_Exp* is an uppercase letter; otherwise, returns false.	if (isupper(c))
		    cout << "Is uppercase.";
		else
		    cout << "Is not uppercase.";

islower(*Char_Exp*)	Returns true provided *Char_Exp* is a lowercase letter; otherwise, returns false.	char c = 'a'; if (islower(c)) cout << c << " is lowercase."; **Outputs:** a is lowercase.

isalpha(*Char_Exp*)	Returns true provided *Char_Exp* is a letter of the alphabet; otherwise, returns false.	char c = '$';
		if (isalpha(c))
		    cout << "Is a letter.";
		else
		    cout << "Is not a letter.";
		Outputs: Is not a letter.

Display 9.3   Some Functions in <cctype> (part 2 of 2)

FUNCTION	DESCRIPTION	EXAMPLE

isdigit(*Char_Exp*)	Returns true provided *Char_Exp* is one of the digits '0' through '9'; otherwise, returns false.	`if (isdigit('3'))`
		`    cout << "It's a digit.";`
		`else`
		`    cout << "It's not a digit.";`
		Outputs: It's a digit.

isalnum(*Char_Exp*)	Returns true provided *Char_Exp* is either a letter or a digit; otherwise, returns false.	`if (isalnum('3') && isalnum('a'))`
		`    cout << "Both alphanumeric.";`
		`else`
		`    cout << "One or more are not.";`
		Outputs: Both alphanumeric.

isspace(*Char_Exp*)	Returns true provided *Char_Exp* is a whitespace character, such as the blank or newline character; otherwise, returns false.	`//Skips over one "word" and sets c`
		`//equal to the first whitespace`
		`//character after the "word":`
		`do`
		`{`
		`    cin.get(c);`
		`} while (! isspace(c));`

ispunct(*Char_Exp*)	Returns true provided *Char_Exp* is a printing character other than whitespace, a digit, or a letter; otherwise, returns false.	`if (ispunct('?'))`
		`    cout << "Is punctuation.";`
		`else`
		`    cout << "Not punctuation.";`

isprint(*Char_Fxp*)	Returns true provided *Char_Exp* is a printing character; otherwise, returns false.	
isgraph(*Char_Exp*)	Returns true provided *Char_Exp* is a printing character other than whitespace; otherwise, returns false.	
isctrl(*Char_Exp*)	Returns true provided *Char_Exp* is a control character; otherwise, returns false.	

The function isspace returns true if its argument is a whitespace character. **Whitespace** characters are all the characters that are displayed as blank space on the screen, including the blank character, the tab character, and the newline character, '\n'. If the argument to isspace is not a whitespace character, then isspace returns false. Thus, isspace(' ') returns true and isspace('a') returns false.

whitespace

For example, the following will read a sentence terminated with a period and echo the string with all whitespace characters replaced with the symbol '-':

```
char next;
do
{
    cin.get(next);
    if (isspace(next))
        cout << '-';
    else
        cout << next;
} while (next != '.');
```

For example, if the above code is given the following input:

Ahh   do be do.

it will produce the following output:

Ahh---do-be-do.

Pitfall

toupper AND tolower RETURN int VALUES

In many ways C++ considers characters to be whole numbers, similar to the numbers of type int. Each character is assigned a number. When the character is stored in a variable of type char, it is this number that is placed in the computer's memory. In C++ you can use a value of type char as a number, for example, by placing it in a variable of type int. You can also store a number of type int in a variable of type char (provided the number is not too large). Thus, the type char can be used as the type for characters or as a type for small whole numbers. Usually you need not be concerned with this detail and can simply think of values of type char as being characters without worrying about their use as numbers. However, when using some of the functions in <cctype>, this detail can be important. The functions toupper and tolower actually return values of type int rather than values of type char; that is, they return the number corresponding to the character we think of them as returning, rather than the character itself. Thus, the following will not output the letter 'A' but will instead output the number that is assigned to 'A':

```
cout << toupper('a');
```

To get the computer to treat the value returned by toupper or tolower as a value of type char (as opposed to a value of type int), you need to indicate that you want a value of type char. One way to do this is to place the value returned in a variable of type char. The following will output the character 'A', which is usually what we want:

```
char c = toupper('a');
cout << c;
```

Another way to get the computer to treat the value returned by toupper or tolower as a value of type char is to use a type cast, as follows:

```
cout << static_cast<char>(toupper('a'));
```

Self-Test Exercises

19. Consider the following code (and assume that it is embedded in a complete and correct program and then run):

```
cout << "Enter a line of input:\n";
char next;
do
{
    cin.get(next);
    cout << next;
} while ( (! isdigit(next)) && (next != '\n') );
cout << "<END OF OUTPUT";
```

If the dialogue begins as follows, what will be the next line of output?

```
Enter a line of input:
I'll see you at 10:30 AM.
```

20. Write some C++ code that will read a line of text and echo the line with all uppercase letters deleted.

21. Rewrite the definition of the newLine function in Display 9.2 but this time use the ignore member function.

9.3 The Standard Class string

*I try to catch every sentence, every word you and I say, and
quickly lock all these sentences and words away in my literary
storehouse because they might come in handy.*

Anton Chekhov, *The Seagull*

Section 9.1 introduced C-strings. These C-strings are simply arrays of characters terminated with the null character, '\0'. To manipulate these C-strings you need to worry about all the details of handling arrays. For example, when you want to add characters to a C-string and there is not enough room in the array, you must create another array to hold this longer string of characters. In short, C-strings require that you the programmer keep track of all the low-level details of how the C-strings are stored in memory. This is a lot of extra work and a source of programmer errors. The ANSI/ISO standard for C++ specified that C++ must now also have a class string that allows the programmer to treat strings as a basic data type without needing to worry about implementation details. This section introduces you to this string type.

■ INTRODUCTION TO THE STANDARD CLASS string

The class string is defined in the library whose name is also <string>, and the definitions are placed in the std namespace. To use the class string, therefore, your code must contain the following (or something more or less equivalent):

```
#include <string>
using namespace std;
```

The class string allows you to treat string values and string expressions very much like values of a simple type. You can use the = operator to assign a value to a string variable, and you can use the + sign to concatenate two strings. For example, suppose s1, s2, and s3 are objects of type string and both s1 and s2 have string values. Then s3 can be set equal to the concatenation of the string value in s1 followed by the string value in s2 as follows:

+ does concatenation

```
s3 = s1 + s2;
```

There is no danger of s3 being too small for its new string value. If the sum of the lengths of s1 and s2 exceeds the capacity of s3, then more space is automatically allocated for s3.

As we noted earlier in this chapter, quoted strings are really C-strings and so they are not literally of type string. However, C++ provides automatic type casting of quoted strings to values of type string. Thus, you can use quoted strings as if they were literal values of type string, and we (and most others) will often refer to quoted strings as if they were values of type string. For example,

```
s3 = "Hello Mom!";
```

sets the value of the string variable s3 to a string object with the same characters as in the C-string "Hello Mom!".

constructors

The class string has a default constructor that initializes a string object to the empty string. The class string also has a second constructor that takes one argument that is a standard C-string and so can be a quoted string. This second constructor initializes the string object to a value that represents the same string as its C-string argument. For example,

```
string phrase;
string noun("ants");
```

The first line declares the string variable phrase and initializes it to the empty string. The second line declares noun to be of type string and initializes it to a string value equivalent to the C-string "ants". Most programmers when talking loosely would say that "noun is initialized to "ants"," but there really is a type conversion here. The quoted string "ants" is a C-string, not a value of type string. The variable noun receives a string value that has the same characters as "ants" in the same order as "ants'", but the string value is not terminated with the null character '\0'. In theory, at least, you do not need to know or care whether the string value of noun is even stored in an array, as opposed to some other data structure.

There is an alternate notation for declaring a string variable and invoking the default constructor. The following two lines are exactly equivalent:

```
string noun("ants");
string noun = "ants";
```

These basic details about the class string are illustrated in Display 9.4. Note that, as illustrated there, you can output string values using the operator <<.

Consider the following line from Display 9.4:

```
phrase = "I love " + adjective + " " + noun + "!";
```

Display 9.4   Program Using the Class string

```
1    //Demonstrates the standard class string.
2    #include <iostream>
3    #include <string>
4    using namespace std;
                                    Initialized to the empty string.

5    int main( )
6    {
7        string phrase;                                      Two equivalent
8        string adjective("fried"), noun("ants");           ways of initializing
9        string wish = "Bon appetite!";                      a string variable

10       phrase = "I love " + adjective + " " + noun + "!";
11       cout << phrase << endl
12           << wish << endl;

13       return 0;
14   }
```

SAMPLE DIALOGUE

```
I love fried ants!
Bon appetite!
```

converting
C-string
constants to
the type
string

C++ must do a lot of work to allow you to concatenate strings in this simple and natural fashion. The string constant "I love " is not an object of type string. A string constant like "I love " is stored as a C-string (in other words, as a null-terminated array of characters). When C++ sees "I love " as an argument to +, it finds the definition (or overloading) of + that applies to a value such as "I love ". There are overloadings of the + operator that have a C-string on the left and a string on the right, as well as the reverse of this positioning. There is even a version that has a C-string on both sides of the + and produces a string object as the value returned. Of course, there is also the overloading you expect, with the type string for both operands.

C++ did not really need to provide all those overloading cases for +. If these overloadings were not provided, C++ would look for a constructor that can perform a type conversion to convert the C-string "I love " to a value for which + did apply. In this case, the constructor with the one C-string parameter would perform just such a conversion. However, the extra overloadings are presumably more efficient.

The class string is often thought of as a modern replacement for C-strings. However, in C++ you cannot easily avoid also using C-strings when you program with the class string.

THE CLASS string

The class string can be used to represent values that are strings of characters. The class string provides more versatile string representation than the C-strings discussed in Section 9.1.

The class string is defined in the library that is also named <string>, and its definition is placed in the std namespace. Programs that use the class string should therefore contain one of the following (or something more or less equivalent):

```
#include <string>
using namespace std;
```

or

```
#include <string>
using std::string;
```

The class string has a default constructor that initializes the string object to the empty string, and a constructor that takes a C-string as arguments and initializes the string object to a value that represents the string given as the argument. For example:

```
string s1, s2("Hello");
```

■ I/O WITH THE CLASS string

You can use the insertion operator >> and cout to output string objects just as you do for data of other types. This is illustrated in Display 9.4. Input with the class string is a bit more subtle.

The extraction operator, >>, and cin work the same for string objects as for other data, but remember that the extraction operator ignores initial whitespace and stops reading when it encounters more whitespace. This is as true for strings as it is for other data. For example, consider the following code:

```
string s1, s2;
cin >> s1;
cin >> s2;
```

If the user types in

May the hair on your toes grow long and curly!

then s1 will receive the value "May" with any leading (or trailing) whitespace deleted. The variable s2 receives the string "the". Using the extraction operator, >>, and cin, you can only read in words; you cannot read in a line or other string that contains a blank. Sometimes this is exactly what you want, but sometimes it is not at all what you want.

If you want your program to read an entire line of input into a variable of type string, you can use the function getline. The syntax for using getline with string objects is a bit different from what we described for C-strings in Section 9.1. You do not use cin.getline; instead, you make cin the first argument to getline.[1] (So, this version of getline is not a member function.)

getline

```
string line;
cout << "Enter a line of input:\n";
getline(cin, line);
cout << line << "END OF OUTPUT\n";
```

When embedded in a complete program, this code produces a dialogue like the following:

```
Enter some input:
Do be do to you!
Do be do to you!END OF OUTPUT
```

If there were leading or trailing blanks on the line, they too would be part of the string value read by getline. This version of getline is in the library <string>. (As we will

---

[1] This is a bit ironic, since the class string was designed using more modern object-oriented techniques, and the notation it uses for getline is the old fashioned, less object-oriented notation. This is an accident of history. This getline function was defined after the iostream library was already in use, so the designers had little choice but to make this getline a stand alone function.

see in Chapter 12, you can use a `stream` object connected to a text file in place of `cin` to do input from a file using `getline`.)

You cannot use `cin` and `>>` to read in a blank character. If you want to read one character at a time, you can use `cin.get`, which we discussed in Section 9.2. The function `cin.get` reads values of type `char`, not of type `string`, but it can be helpful when handling `string` input. Display 9.5 contains a program that illustrates both `getline` and `cin.get` used for `string` input. The significance of the function `newline` is explained in the pitfall entitled "Mixing `cin >> variable;` and `getline`."

Display 9.5   Program Using the Class `string` (part 1 of 2)

```
1   //Demonstrates getline and cin.get.
2   #include <iostream>
3   #include <string>
4   using namespace std;

5   void newLine( );
6   int main( )
7   {
8       string firstName, lastName, recordName;
9       string motto = "Your records are our records.";
10      cout << "Enter your first and last name:\n";
11      cin >> firstName >> lastName;
12      newLine( );

13      recordName = lastName + ", " + firstName;
14      cout << "Your name in our records is: ";
15      cout << recordName << endl;

16      cout << "Our motto is\n"
17           << motto << endl;
18      cout << "Please suggest a better (one line) motto:\n";
19      getline(cin, motto);
20      cout << "Our new motto will be:\n";
21      cout << motto << endl;

22      return 0;
23  }
24  //Uses iostream:
25  void newLine( )
26  {
```

Display 9.5   Program Using the Class string *(part 2 of 2)*

```
27      char nextChar;
28      do
29      {
30          cin.get(nextChar);
31      } while (nextChar != '\n');
32  }
```

SAMPLE DIALOGUE

```
Enter your first and last names:
  B'Elanna Torres
Your name in our records is: Torres, B'Elanna
Our motto is
Your records are our records.
Please suggest a better (one-line) motto:
Our records go where no records dared to go before.
Our new motto will be:
Our records go where no records dared to go before.
```

I/O WITH string OBJECTS

You can use the insertion operator << with cout to output string objects. You can input a string with the extraction operator >> and cin. When using >> for input, the code reads in a string delimited with whitespace. You can use the function getline to input an entire line of text into a string object.

EXAMPLES

```
string greeting("Hello"), response, nextLine;
cout << greeting;
cin >> response;
getline(cin, nextLine);
```

Self-Test Exercises

22. Consider the following code (and assume that it is embedded in a complete and correct program and then run):

```
string s1, s2;
cout << "Enter a line of input:\n";
```

```
cin >> s1 >> s2;
cout << s1 << "*" << s2 << "<END OF OUTPUT";
```

If the dialogue begins as follows, what will be the next line of output?

```
Enter a line of input:
A string is a joy forever!
```

23. Consider the following code (and assume that it is embedded in a complete and correct program and then run):

```
string s;
cout << "Enter a line of input:\n";
getline(cin, s);
cout << s << "<END OF OUTPUT";
```

If the dialogue begins as follows, what will be the next line of output?

```
Enter a line of input:
A string is a joy forever!
```

Tip

MORE VERSIONS OF getline

So far, we have described the following way of using getline:

```
string line;
cout << "Enter a line of input:\n";
getline(cin, line);
```

This version stops reading when it encounters the end-of-line marker, '\n'. There is a version that allows you to specify a different character to use as a stopping signal. For example, the following will stop when the first question mark is encountered:

```
string line;
cout << "Enter some input:\n";
getline(cin, line, '?');
```

It makes sense to use getline as if it were a void function, but it actually returns a reference to its first argument, which is cin in the above code. Thus, the following will read in a line of text into s1 and a string of nonwhitespace characters into s2:

```
string s1, s2;
getline(cin, s1) >> s2;
```

The invocation getline(cin, s1) returns a reference to cin, so that after the invocation of getline, the next thing to happen is equivalent to

```
cin >> s2;
```

This kind of use of getline seems to have been designed for use in a C++ quiz show rather than to meet any actual programming need, but it can come in handy sometimes.

Pitfall

MIXING cin >> variable; AND getline

Take care in mixing input using cin >> variable; with input using getline. For example, consider the following code:

```
int n;
string line;
cin >> n;
getline(cin, line);
```

When this code reads the following input, you might expect the value of n to be set to 42 and the value of line to be set to a string value representing "Hello hitchhiker.":

```
42
Hello hitchhiker.
```

However, while n is indeed set to the value of 42, line is set equal to the empty string. What happened?

Using cin >> n skips leading whitespace on the input but leaves the rest of the line, in this case just '\n', for the next input. A statement like

```
cin >> n;
```

always leaves something on the line for a following getline to read (even if it is just the '\n'). In this case, the getline sees the '\n' and stops reading, so getline reads an empty string. If you find your program appearing to mysteriously ignore input data, see if you have mixed these two kinds of input. You may need to use either the newLine function from Display 9.5 or the function ignore from the library iostream. For example,

```
cin.ignore(1000, '\n');
```

With these arguments, a call to the ignore member function will read and discard the entire rest of the line up to and including the '\n' (or until it discards 1000 characters if it does not find the end of the line after 1000 characters).

Other baffling problems can appear with programs that use `cin` with both `>>` and `getline`. Moreover, these problems can come and go as you move from one C++ compiler to another. When all else fails, or if you want to be certain of portability, you can resort to character-by-character input using `cin.get`.

These problems can occur with any of the versions of `getline` that we discuss in this chapter.

`getline` FOR OBJECTS OF THE CLASS `string`

The `getline` function for `string` objects has two versions:

```
istream& getline(istream& ins, string& strVar,
                           char delimiter);
```

and

```
istream& getline(istream& ins, string& strVar);
```

The first version of this function reads characters from the `istream` object given as the first argument (always `cin` in this chapter), inserting the characters into the `string` variable `strVar` until an instance of the `delimiter` character is encountered. The `delimiter` character is removed from the input and discarded. The second version uses '`\n`' for the default value of `delimiter`; otherwise, it works the same.

These `getline` functions return their first argument (always `cin` in this chapter), but they are usually used as if they were `void` functions.

STRING PROCESSING WITH THE CLASS `string`

The class `string` allows you to perform the same operations that you can perform with the C-strings we discussed in Section 9.1 and more. (A lot more! There are well over 100 members and other functions associated with the standard `string` class.)

You can access the characters in a `string` object in the same way that you access array elements, so `string` objects have the advantages of arrays of characters plus a number of advantages that arrays do not have, such as automatically increasing their capacity.

If `lastName` is the name of a `string` object, then `lastName[i]` gives access to the i th character in the string represented by `lastName`. This use of array square brackets is illustrated in Display 9.6.

length

Display 9.6 also illustrates the member function `length`. Every `string` object has a member function named `length` that takes no arguments and returns the length of the string represented by the `string` object. Thus, a `string` object not only can be used like

Display 9.6   A string Object Can Behave Like an Array

```
1    //Demonstrates using a string object as if it were an array.
2    #include <iostream>
3    #include <string>
4    using namespace std;

5    int main( )
6    {
7        string firstName, lastName;

8        cout << "Enter your first and last name:\n";
9        cin >> firstName >> lastName;

10       cout << "Your last name is spelled:\n";
11       int i;
12       for (i = 0; i < lastName.length( ); i++)
13       {
14           cout << lastName[i] << " ";
15           lastName[i] = '-';
16       }
17       cout << endl;
18       for (i = 0; i < lastName.length( ); i++)
19           cout << lastName[i] << " "; //Places a "-" under each letter.
20       cout << endl;

21       cout << "Good day " << firstName << endl;
22       return 0;
23   }
```

SAMPLE DIALOGUE

```
Enter your first and last names:
John Crichton
Your last name is spelled:
C r i c h t o n
- - - - - - - -
Good day John
```

an array, but the length member function makes it behave like a partially filled array that automatically keeps track of how many positions are occupied.

The array square brackets when used with an object of the class string do not check for illegal indexes. If you use an illegal index (that is, an index that is greater than or equal to the length of the string in the object), the results are unpredictable but are bound to be bad. You may just get strange behavior without any error message that tells you that the problem is an illegal index value. There is a member function named at that does check for an illegal index value. The member function named at behaves basically the same as the square brackets, except for two points: You use function notation with at, so instead of a[i], you use a.at(i), and the at member function checks to see if i evaluates to an illegal index. If the value of i in a.at(i) is an illegal index, you should get a runtime error message telling you what is wrong. In the following code fragment, the attempted access is out of range, yet, it probably will not produce an error message, although it will be accessing a nonexistent indexed variable:

```
string str("Mary");
cout << str[6] << endl;
```

The next example, however, will cause the program to terminate abnormally, so that you at least know something is wrong:

```
string str("Mary");
cout << str.at(6) << endl;
```

But, be warned that some systems give very poor error messages when a.at(i) has an illegal index i.

You can change a single character in the string by assigning a char value to the indexed variable, such as str[i]. Since the member function at returns a reference, this may also be done with the member function at. For example, to change the third character in the string object str to 'X', you can use either of the following code fragments:

```
str.at(2)='X';
```

or

```
str[2]='X';
```

As in an ordinary array of characters, character positions for objects of type string are indexed starting with 0, so that the third character in a string is in index position 2.

Display 9.7 gives a partial list of the member functions of the class string.

In many ways objects of the class string are better behaved than the C-strings we introduced in Section 9.1. In particular, the == operator on objects of the string class returns a result that corresponds to our intuitive notion of strings being equal; namely, it returns true if the two strings contain the same characters in the same order and returns false otherwise. Similarly, the comparison operators <, >, <=, and >= compare string objects using lexicographic ordering. (Lexicographic ordering is alphabetic ordering using the order of symbols given in the ASCII character set in Appendix 3. If the strings consist of all letters and are both either all uppercase or all lowercase letters, then for this case lexicographic ordering is the same as everyday alphabetical ordering.).

Display 9.7   Member Functions of the Standard Class string

EXAMPLE	REMARKS
Constructors	
`string str;`	Default constructor; creates empty `string` object `str`.
`string str("string");`	Creates a `string` object with data `"string"`.
`string str(aString);`	Creates a `string` object `str` that is a copy of `aString`. `aString` is an object of the class `string`.
Element access	
`str[i]`	Returns read/write reference to character in `str` at index `i`.
`str.at(i)`	Returns read/write reference to character in `str` at index `i`.
`str.substr(position, length)`	Returns the substring of the calling object starting at position and having `length` characters.
Assignment/Modifiers	
`str1 = str2;`	Allocates space and initializes it to `str2`'s data, releases memory allocated for `str1`, and sets `str1`'s size to that of `str2`.
`str1 += str2;`	Character data of `str2` is concatenated to the end of `str1`; the size is set appropriately.
`str.empty( )`	Returns `true` if `str` is an empty `string`; returns `false` otherwise.
`str1 + str2`	Returns a `string` that has `str2`'s data concatenated to the end of `str1`'s data. The size is set appropriately.
`str.insert(pos, str2)`	Inserts `str2` into `str` beginning at position `pos`.
`str.remove(pos, length)`	Removes substring of size `length`, starting at position `pos`.
Comparisons	
`str1 == str2   str1 != str2`	Compare for equality or inequality; returns a Boolean value.
`str1 < str2     str1 > str2`	Four comparisons. All are lexicographical comparisons.
`str1 <= str2   str1 >= str2`	
`str.find(str1)`	Returns index of the first occurrence of `str1` in `str`.
`str.find(str1, pos)`	Returns index of the first occurrence of string `str1` in `str`; the search starts at position `pos`.
`str.find_first_of(str1, pos)`	Returns the index of the first instance in `str` of any character in `str1`, starting the search at position `pos`.
`str.find_first_not_of (str1, pos)`	Returns the index of the first instance in `str` of any character *not* in `str1`, starting search at position `pos`.

= AND == ARE DIFFERENT FOR strings AND C-STRINGS

The operators =, ==, != , <, >, <=, and >=, when used with the standard C++ type string, produce results that correspond to our intuitive notion of how strings compare. They do not misbehave as they do with C-strings, as we discussed in Section 9.1.

Example

PALINDROME TESTING

A palindrome is a string that reads the same front to back as it does back to front. The program in Display 9.8 tests an input string to see if it is a palindrome. Our palindrome test will disregard all spaces and punctuation and will consider uppercase and lowercase versions of a letter to be the same when deciding if something is a palindrome. Some palindrome examples are as follows:

```
Able was I 'ere I saw Elba.
I Love Me, Vol. I.
Madam, I'm Adam.
A man, a plan, a canal, Panama.
Rats live on no evil star.
radar
deed
mom
racecar
```

The removePunct function is of interest in that it uses the string member functions substr and find. The member function substr extracts a substring of the calling object, given the position and length of the desired substring. The first three lines of removePunct declare variables for use in the function. The for loop runs through the characters of the parameter s one at a time and tries to find them in the punct string. To do this, a string that is the substring of s, of length 1 at each character position, is extracted. The position of this substring in punct is determined using the find member function. If this one-character string is not in the punct string, then the one-character string is concatenated to the noPunct string that is to be returned.

Display 9.8 Palindrome Testing Program (*part 1 of 4*)

```
1   //Test for palindrome property.
2   #include <iostream>
3   #include <string>
4   #include <cctype>
5   using namespace std;

6   void swap(char& v1, char& v2);
7   //Interchanges the values of v1 and v2.
```

```
 8   string reverse(const string& s);
 9   //Returns a copy of s but with characters in reverse order.

10   string removePunct(const string& s, const string& punct);
11   //Returns a copy of s with any occurrences of characters
12   //in the string punct removed.

13   string makeLower (const string& s);
14   //Returns a copy of s that has all uppercase
15   //characters changed to lowercase, with other characters unchanged.

16   bool isPal(const string& s);
17   //Returns true if s is a palindrome; false otherwise.

18   int main( )
19   {
20       string str;
21       cout << "Enter a candidate for palindrome test\n"
22            << "followed by pressing Return.\n";
23       getline(cin, str);

24       if (isPal(str))
25           cout << "\"" << str + "\" is a palindrome.";
26       else
27           cout << "\"" << str + "\" is not a palindrome.";
28       cout << endl;

29       return 0;
30   }


31
32   void swap(char& v1, char& v2)
33   {
34       char temp = v1;
35       v1 = v2;
36       v2 = temp;
37   }


38   string reverse(const string& s)
39   {
40       int start = 0;
41       int end = s.length( );
42       string temp(s);

43       while (start < end)
```

Display 9.8   Palindrome Testing Program (*part 3 of 4*)

```
44      {
45          end--;
46          swap(temp[start], temp[end]);
47          start++;
48      }

49      return temp;
50  }


51  //Uses <cctype> and <string>
52  string makeLower(const string& s)
53  {
54      string temp(s);
55      for (int i = 0; i < s.length( ); i++)
56          temp[i] = tolower(s[i]);

57
58      return temp;
59  }
60
61  string removePunct(const string& s, const string& punct)
62  {
63      string noPunct; //initialized to empty string
64      int sLength = s.length( );
65      int punctLength = punct.length( );
66      for (int i = 0; i < sLength; i++)
67      {
68          string aChar = s.substr(i,1); //A one-character string
69          int location = punct.find(aChar, 0);
70          //Find location of successive characters
71          //of src in punct.

72        if (location < 0 || location >= punctLength)
73            noPunct = noPunct + aChar; //aChar is not in punct, so keep it
74      }
75
76      return noPunct;
77  }


78  //uses functions makeLower, removePunct
79  bool isPal(const string& s)
80  {
81      string punct(",;:.?!'\" "); //includes a blank
82      string str(s);
83      str = makeLower(str);
```

Display 9.8 Palindrome Testing Program (*part 4 of 4*)

```
84        string lowerStr = removePunct(str, punct);

85        return (lowerStr == reverse(lowerStr));
86    }
```

SAMPLE DIALOGUES

```
Enter a candidate for palindrome test
followed by pressing Return.
Madam, I'm Adam.
"Madam, I'm Adam." is a palindrome.
```

```
Enter a candidate for palindrome test
followed by pressing Return.
Radar
"Radar" is a palindrome.
```

```
Enter a candidate for palindrome test
followed by pressing Return.
Am I a palindrome?
"Am I a palindrome?" is not a palindrome.
```

Self-Test Exercises

24. Consider the following code:

```
string s1, s2("Hello");
cout << "Enter a line of input:\n";
cin >> s1;
if (s1 == s2)
    cout << "Equal\n";
else
    cout << "Not equal\n";
```

If the dialogue begins as follows, what will be the next line of output?

```
Enter a line of input:
Hello friend!
```

25. What is the output produced by the following code?

```
string s1, s2("Hello");
s1 = s2;
s2[0] = 'J';
  cout << s1 << " " << s2;
```

■ CONVERTING BETWEEN string OBJECTS AND C-STRINGS

You have already seen that C++ will perform an automatic type conversion to allow you to store a C-string in a variable of type string. For example, the following will work fine:

```
char aCString[] = "This is my C-string.";
string stringVariable;
stringVariable = aCString;
```

However, the following will produce a compiler error message:

```
aCString = stringVariable; //ILLEGAL
```

The following is also illegal:

```
strcpy(aCString, stringVariable); //ILLEGAL
```

strcpy cannot take a string object as its second argument and there is no automatic conversion of string objects to C-strings, which is the problem we cannot seem to get away from.

c_str( )

To obtain the C-string corresponding to a string object you must perform an explicit conversion. This can be done with the string member function c_str( ). The correct version of the copying we have been trying to do is the following:

```
strcpy(aCString, stringVariable.c_str( )); //Legal;
```

Note that you need to use the strcpy function to do the copying. The member function c_str( ) returns the C-string corresponding to the string calling object. As we noted earlier in this chapter, the assignment operator does not work with C-strings. So, just in case you thought the following might work, we should point out that it too is illegal.

```
aCString = stringVariable.c_str( ); //ILLEGAL
```

Chapter Summary

- A C-string variable is the same thing as an array of characters, but it is used in a slightly different way. A string variable uses the null character, '\0', to mark the end of the string stored in the array.

- C-string variables usually must be treated like arrays rather than simple variables of the kind we used for numbers and single characters. In particular, you cannot assign a C-string value to a C-string variable using the equal sign, =, and you cannot compare the values in two C-string variables using the == operator. Instead, you must use special C-string functions to perform these tasks.

- The library <cctype> has a number of useful character-manipulating functions.

- You can use cin.get to read a single character of input without skipping over whitespace. The function cin.get reads the next character no matter what kind of character it is.

- Various versions of the getline function can be used to read an entire line of input from the keyboard.

- The ANSI/ISO standard <string> library provides a fully featured class called string that can be used to represent strings of characters.

- Objects of the class string are better behaved than C-strings. In particular, the assignment and equal operators, = and ==, have their intuitive meanings when used with objects of the class string.

ANSWERS TO SELF-TEST EXERCISES

1. The following two declarations are equivalent to each other (but not equivalent to any others):

   ```
   char stringVar[10] = "Hello";
   char stringVar[10] = {'H', 'e', 'l', 'l', 'o', '\0'};
   ```

   The following two declarations are equivalent to each other (but not equivalent to any others):

   ```
   char stringVar[6] = "Hello";
   char stringVar[] = "Hello";
   ```

   The following declaration is not equivalent to any of the others:

   ```
   char stringVar[10] = {'H', 'e', 'l', 'l', 'o'};
   ```

2. "DoBeDo to you"

3. The declaration means that `stringVar` has room for only six characters (including the null character, `'\0'`). The function `strcat` does not check that there is room to add more characters to `stringVar`, so `strcat` will write all the characters in the string `" and Good-bye."` into memory, even though that requires more memory than has been assigned to `stringVar`. This means memory that should not be changed will be changed. The net effect is unpredictable, but bad.

4. If `strlen` were not already defined for you, you could use the following definition:

```
int strlen(const char str[])
//Precondition: str contains a string value terminated
//with '\0'.
//Returns the number of characters in the string str (not
//counting '\0').
{
    int index = 0;
    while (str[index] != '\0')
        index++;
    return index;
}
```

5. The maximum number of characters is five because the sixth position is needed for the null terminator (`'\0'`).

6. a. 1

   b. 1

   c. 5 (including the `'\0'`)

   d. 2 (including the `'\0'`)

   e. 6 (including the `'\0'`)

7. These are *not equivalent.* The first of these places the null character `'\0'` in the array after the characters `'a'`, `'b'`, and `'c'`. The second only assigns the successive positions `'a'`, `'b'`, and `'c'` but does not put a `'\0'` anywhere.

8.
```
int index = 0;
while ( ourString[index] != '\0' )
{
    ourString[index] = 'X';
    index++;
}
```

9. a. If the C-string variable does not have a `null` terminator, `'\0'`, the loop can run beyond the memory allocated for the C-string, destroying the contents of memory there. To protect memory beyond the end of the array, change the `while` condition as shown in b.

   b. `while( ourString[index] != '\0' && index < SIZE )`

10. ```
    #include <cstring>
    //needed to get the declaration of strcpy
    ...
    strcpy(aString, "Hello");
    ```

11. I did it my way!

12. The string `"good, I hope."` is too long for `aString`. A chunk of memory that doesn't belong to the array `aString` will be overwritten.

13. The complete dialogue is as follows:
    ```
    Enter some input:
    The
        time is now.
    The-time<END OF OUTPUT
    ```

14. The complete dialogue is as follows:
    ```
    Enter a line of input:
    May the hair on your toes grow long and curly.
    May t<END OF OUTPUT
    ```

15. The complete dialogue is as follows:
    ```
    Enter a line of input:
    a b c d e f g
    a b END OF OUTPUT
    ```

16. The complete dialogue is as follows:
    ```
    Enter a line of input:
    abcdef gh
    ace h
    ```

    Note that the output is simply every other character of the input, and note that the blank is treated just like any other character.

17. The complete dialogue is as follows:
    ```
    Enter a line of input:
    0 1 2 3 4 5 6 7 8 9 10 11
    01234567891 1
    ```

    Be sure to note that only the `'1'` in the input string **10** is output. This is because `cin.get` is reading characters, not numbers, and so it reads the input **10** as the two characters `'1'` and `'0'`. Since this code is written to echo only every other character, the `'0'` is not output. Since the `'0'` is not output, the next character, which is a blank, is output, and so there is one blank in the output. Similarly, only one of the two `'1'` characters in **11** is output. If this is unclear, write the input on a sheet of paper and use a small square for the blank character. Then, cross out every other character; the output shown above is what is left.
    ```

18. This code contains an infinite loop and will continue as long as the user continues to give it input. The Boolean expression (next != '\n') is always true because next is filled via the statement

```
cin >> next;
```

and this statement always skips the newline character, '\n' (as well as any blanks). The code will run, and if the user gives no additional input, the dialogue will be as follows:

```
Enter a line of input:
0 1 2 3 4 5 6 7 8 9 10 11
0246811
```

This code outputs every other *nonblank* character. The two '1' characters in the output are the first character in the input **10** and the first character in the input **11**.

19. The complete dialogue is as follows:
```
Enter a line of input:
I'll see you at 10:30 AM.
I'll see you at 1<END OF OUTPUT
```

20. ```
cout << "Enter a line of input:\n";
char next;
do
{
    cin.get(next);
    if (!isupper(next))
        cout << next;
} while (next != '\n');
```

Note that you should use !isupper(next) and not use islower(next). This is because islower(next) returns false if next contains a character that is not a letter (such as the blank or comma symbol).

21. ```
//Uses iostream:
void newLine( )
{
    cin.ignore(10000, '\n');
}
```

Of course, this only works for lines less than about 10,000 characters, but any lines longer than that would likely indicate some other unrelated problem.

22. A*string<END OF OUTPUT

23. A string is a joy forever!<END OF OUTPUT

24. The complete dialogue is as follows:
    Enter a line of input:
    Hello friend!
    Equal

25. Hello Jello

PROGRAMMING PROJECTS

1. Write a program that will read in a sentence of up to 100 characters and output the sentence with spacing corrected and with letters corrected for capitalization. In other words, in the output sentence all strings of two or more blanks should be compressed to a single blank. The sentence should start with an uppercase letter but should contain no other uppercase letters. Do not worry about proper names; if their first letter is changed to lowercase, that is acceptable. Treat a line break as if it were a blank in the sense that a line break and any number of blanks are compressed to a single blank. Assume that the sentence ends with a period and contains no other periods. For example, the input

   **the   Answer to life, the Universe, and   everything
   IS 42.**

   should produce the following output:

   The answer to life, the universe, and everything is 42.

2. Write a program that will read in a line of text and output the number of words in the line and the number of occurrences of each letter. Define a word to be any string of letters that is delimited at each end by either whitespace, a period, a comma, or the beginning or end of the line. You can assume that the input consists entirely of letters, whitespace, commas, and periods. When outputting the number of letters that occur in a line, be sure to count uppercase and lowercase versions of a letter as the same letter. Output the letters in alphabetical order and list only those letters that occur in the input line. For example, the input line

   I say Hi.

   should produce output similar to the following:

   3 words
   1 a
   1 h
   2 i
   1 s
   1 y

3. Write a program that reads a person's name in the following format: first name, then middle name or initial, and then last name. The program then outputs the name in the following format:

`Last_Name, First_Name, Middle_Initial.`

For example, the input

Mary Average User

should produce the output

`User, Mary A.`

The input

Mary A. User

should also produce the output

`User, Mary A.`

Your program should place a period after the middle initial even if the input did not contain a period. Your program should allow for users who give no middle name or middle initial. In that case, the output, of course, contains no middle name or initial. For example, the input

Mary User

should produce the output

`User, Mary`

If you are using C-strings, assume that each name is at most 20 characters long. Alternatively, use the class `string`. (*Hint:* You may want to use three string variables rather than one large string variable for the input. You may find it easier to *not* use `getline`.)

4. Write a program that reads in a line of text and replaces all four-letter words with the word `"love"`. For example, the input string

I hate you, you dodo!

should produce the output:

`I love you, you love!`

Of course, the output will not always make sense. For example, the input string

John will run home.

should produce the output:

`Love love run love.`

If the four-letter word starts with a capital letter, it should be replaced by `"Love"`, not by `"love"`. You need not check capitalization, except for the first letter of a word. A word is any string consisting of the letters of the alphabet and delimited at each end by a blank, the end of the line, or any other character that is not a letter. Your program should repeat this action until the user says to quit.

5. Write a program that can be used to train the user to use less sexist language by suggesting alternative versions of sentences given by the user. The program will ask for a sentence, read the sentence into a `string` variable, and replace all occurrences of masculine pronouns with gender-neutral pronouns. For example, it will replace `"he"` by `"she or he"`. Thus, the input sentence

See an adviser, talk to him, and listen to him.

should produce the following suggested changed version of the sentence:

`See an adviser, talk to her or him, and listen to her or him.`

Be sure to preserve uppercase letters for the first word of the sentence. The pronoun `"his"` can be replaced by `"her(s)"`; your program need not decide between `"her"` and `"hers"`. Allow the user to repeat this for more sentences until the user says she or he is done. This will be a long program that requires a good deal of patience. Your program should not replace the string `"he"` when it occurs inside another word such as `"here"`. A word is any string consisting of the letters of the alphabet and delimited at each end by a blank, the end of the line, or any other character that is not a letter. Allow your sentences to be up to 100 characters long.

6. There is a CD available for purchase that contains `.jpeg` and `.gif` images of music that is in the public domain. The CD includes a file consisting of lines containing the names, then composers of that title, one per line. The name of the piece is first, then zero or more spaces then a dash (-) character, then one or more spaces, then the composer's name. The composer name may be only last name, or an initial and one name, or two names: first last, or three names: first middle last. There are a few tunes with "no author listed" as author. In the subsequent processing, "no author listed" should not be rearranged. Here is a very abbreviated list of the titles and authors.

   1. Adagio "MoonLight" Sonata - Ludwig Van Beethoven
   2. An Alexis - F.H. Hummel and J.N. Hummel
   3. A La Bien Aimee- Ben Schutt
   4. At Sunset- E. MacDowell
   5. Angelus- J. Massenet
   6. Anitra's Dance- Edward Grieg
   7. Ase's Death- Edward Grieg
   8. Au Matin- Benj. - Godard

   . . .

37. The Dying Poet - L. Gottschalk

38. Dead March - G.F. Handel

39. Do They Think of Me At Home - Chas. W. Glover

40. The Dearest Spot - W.T. Wrighton

1. Evening - L. Van Beethoven

2. Embarrassment - Franz Abt

3. Erin is my Home - no author listed

4. Ellen Bayne - Stephen C. Foster

. . .

9. Alla Mazurka- A. Nemerowsky

. . .

1. The Dying Volunteer - A.E. Muse

2. Dolly Day - Stephen C. Foster

3. Dolcy Jones - Stephen C. Foster

4. Dickory, Dickory, Dock - no author listed

5. The Dear Little Shamrock - no author listed

6. Dutch Warbler - no author listed

. . .

The ultimate task is to produce an alphabetized list of composers followed by a list of pieces by them alphabetized on the title within composer. This exercise is easier if it is broken into pieces:

Write code to:

a. Remove the lead numbers, any periods, and any spaces so that the first word of the title is the first word of the line.

b. Replace any multiple spaces with a single space.

c. A few titles may have several - characters, for example:

20. Ba- Be- Bi- Bo- Bu - no author listed

Replace all dash - characters on any line before the end of the line by a space except the last one.

d. The last word in the title may have the - character with no space between it and the = character. Put the space in.

e. When alphabetizing the title, you don't want to consider an initial "A", "An", or "The" in the title. Write code to move such initial words to just before the - character. A comma after the last word in the title is not required, but that would be a nice touch. This can be done after the composer's names are moved to the front, but obviously the code will be different.

f. Move the composer's names to the beginning of the line, followed by the - character, followed by the composition title.

g. Move any first initial, first and second names of the composer to after the composer's last name. If the composer is "no author listed" this should not be rearranged, so test for this combination.

h. Alphabetize by composer using any sort routine you know. You may ignore any duplicate composer's last name, such as CPE Bach and JS Bach, but sorting by composer's second name would be a nice touch. You may use the insertion sort, or selection sort, or bubble sort, or other sorting algorithm.

i. If you have not already done so, move "A", "An", or "The" that may begin a title to the end of the title. Then alphabetize within each composer by composition title.

j. Keep a copy of your design and your code. You will be asked to do this over using the STL vector container.

10

CHAPTER Pointers and Dynamic Arrays

10 Pointers and Dynamic Arrays

Memory is necessary for all the operations of reason.

Blaise Pascal, Pensées

INTRODUCTION

A *pointer* is a construct that gives you more control of the computer's memory. This chapter will show you how pointers are used with arrays and will introduce a new form of array called a *dynamically allocated array*. Dynamically allocated arrays (dynamic arrays for short) are arrays whose size is determined while the program is running, rather than being fixed when the program is written.

Before reading Sections 10.1 and 10.2 on pointers and dynamically allocated arrays you should first read Chapters 1 through 6 (omitting the coverage of vectors if you wish), but you need not read any of Chapters 7 through 9. You can even read Sections 10.1 and 10.2 after reading just Chapters 1 to 5, provided you ignore the few passages that mention classes.

Section 10.3 discusses some tools for classes that only become relevant once you begin to use pointers and dynamically allocated data (such as dynamically allocated arrays). Before covering Section 10.3, you should read Chapters 1 through 8, although you may omit the coverage of vectors if you wish.

You may cover this chapter, Chapter 11 on separate compilation and namespaces, Chapter 12 on file I/O, and Chapter 13 on recursion in any order. If you do not read the Chapter 11 section on namespaces before this chapter, you might find it profitable to review the section of Chapter 1 entitled "Namespaces."

10.1 Pointers

By indirections find directions out.

William Shakespeare, *Hamlet*

A **pointer** is the memory address of a variable. Recall from Chapter 5 that the computer's memory is divided into numbered memory locations (called *bytes*) and that variables are implemented as a sequence of adjacent memory locations. Recall also that sometimes the C++ system uses these memory addresses as names for the variables. If a variable is implemented as, say, three memory locations, then the address of the first of these memory locations is sometimes used as a name for that variable. For example, when the variable is used as a call-by-reference argument, it is this address, not the identifier name of the variable, that is passed to the calling function. An address that is used to name a variable in this way (by giving the address in memory where the variable starts) is called a *pointer* because the address can be thought of as "pointing" to the variable. The address "points" to the variable because it identifies the variable by telling *where* the variable is, rather than telling what the variable's name is.

You have already been using pointers in a number of situations. As noted in the previous paragraph, when a variable is a call-by-reference argument in a function call, the function is given this argument variable in the form of a pointer to the variable. As noted in Chapter 5, an array is given to a function (or to anything else, for that matter) by giving a pointer to the first array element. (At the time we called these pointers "memory addresses," but that is the same thing as a pointer.) These are two powerful uses for pointers, but they are handled automatically by the C++ system. This chapter shows you how to write programs that directly manipulate pointers rather than relying on the system to manipulate the pointers for you.

POINTER VARIABLES

A pointer can be stored in a variable. However, even though a pointer is a memory address and a memory address is a number, you cannot store a pointer in a variable of type int or double. A variable to hold a pointer must be declared to have a pointer type. For example, the following declares p to be a pointer variable that can hold one pointer that points to a variable of type double:

declaring pointer variables

```
double *p;
```

The variable p can hold pointers to variables of type double, but it cannot normally contain a pointer to a variable of some other type, such as int or char. Each variable type requires a different pointer type.[1]

In general, to declare a variable that can hold pointers to other variables of a specific type, you declare the pointer variable just as you would declare an ordinary variable of that type, but you place an asterisk in front of the variable name. For example, the following declares the variables p1 and p2 so they can hold pointers to variables of type int; it also declares two ordinary variables v1 and v2 of type int:

```
int *p1, *p2, v1, v2;
```

There must be an asterisk before *each* of the pointer variables. If you omit the second asterisk in the above declaration, then p2 will not be a pointer variable; it will instead be an ordinary variable of type int.

---

[1] There are ways to get a pointer of one type into a pointer variable for another type, but it does not happen automatically and is very poor style anyway.

POINTER VARIABLE DECLARATIONS

A variable that can hold pointers to other variables of type *Type_Name* is declared similar to the way you declare a variable of type *Type_Name*, except that you place an asterisk at the beginning of the variable name.

SYNTAX

Type_Name *Variable_Name1, *Variable_Name2,. . .;

EXAMPLE

```
double *pointer1, *pointer2;
```

ADDRESSES AND NUMBERS

A pointer is an address, and an address is an integer, but a pointer is not an integer. That is not crazy—that is abstraction! C++ insists that you use a pointer as an address and that you not use it as a number. A pointer is not a value of type int or of any other numeric type. You normally cannot store a pointer in a variable of type int. If you try, most C++ compilers will give you an error message or a warning message. Also, you cannot perform the normal arithmetic operations on pointers. (As you will see later in this chapter, you can perform a kind of addition and a kind of subtraction on pointers, but they are not the usual integer addition and subtraction.)

When discussing pointers and pointer variables, we usually speak of *pointing* rather than speaking of *addresses*. When a pointer variable, such as p1, contains the address of a variable, such as v1, the pointer variable is said to *point to the variable* v1 or to be *a pointer to the variable* v1.

the & operator

Pointer variables, like p1 and p2 declared above, can contain pointers to variables like v1 and v2. You can use the operator & to determine the address of a variable, and you can then assign that address to a pointer variable. For example, the following will set the variable p1 equal to a pointer that points to the variable v1:

```
p1 = &v1;
```

the * operator

dereferencing operator

You now have two ways to refer to v1: You can call it v1 or you can call it "the variable pointed to by p1." In C++, the way you say "the variable pointed to by p1" is *p1. This is the same asterisk that we used when we declared p1, but now it has yet another meaning. When the asterisk is used in this way it is called the **dereferencing operator**, and the pointer variable is said to be *dereferenced*.

POINTER TYPES

There is a bit of an inconsistency (or at least a potential for confusion) in how C++ names pointer types. If you want a parameter whose type is, for example, a pointer to variables of type `int`, then the type is written `int*`, as in the following example:

```
void manipulatePointer(int* p);
```

If you want to declare a variable of the same pointer type, the * goes with the variable, as in the following example:

```
int *p1, *p2;
```

In fact, the compiler does not care whether the * is attached to the `int` or the variable name, so the following are also accepted by the compiler and have the same meanings:

```
void manipulatePointer(int *p);//Accepted but not as nice.

int* p1, *p2;//Accepted but dangerous.
```

However, we find the first versions to be clearer. In particular, note that when declaring variables there must be one * for each pointer variable.

Putting these pieces together can produce some surprising results. Consider the following code:

```
v1 = 0;
p1 = &v1;
*p1 = 42;
cout << v1 << endl;
cout << *p1 << endl;
```

This code will output the following to the screen:

```
42
42
```

As long as `p1` contains a pointer that points to `v1`, then `v1` and `*p1` refer to the same variable. So when you set `*p1` equal to 42, you are also setting `v1` equal to 42.

The symbol & that is used to obtain the address of a variable is the same symbol that you use in function declarations to specify a call-by-reference parameter. This is not a coincidence. Recall that a call-by-reference argument is implemented by giving the address of the argument to the calling function. So, these two uses of the symbol & are very closely related, although they are not exactly the same.

The * and & Operators

The * operator in front of a pointer variable produces the variable to which it points. When used this way, the * operator is called the **dereferencing operator**.

The operator & in front of an ordinary variable produces the address of that variable; that is, it produces a pointer that points to the variable. The & operator is simply called the **address-of operator**.

For example, consider the declarations

```
double *p, v;
```

The following sets the value of p so that p points to the variable v:

```
p = &v;
```

*p produces the variable pointed to by p, so after the above assignment, *p and v refer to the same variable. For example, the following sets the value of v to 9.99, even though the name v is never explicitly used:

```
*p = 9.99;
```

pointers in assignment statements

You can assign the value of one pointer variable to another pointer variable. For example, if p1 is still pointing to v1, then the following will set p2 so that it also points to v1:

```
p2 = p1;
```

Provided we have not changed v1's value, the following will also output 42 to the screen:

```
cout << *p2;
```

Be sure you do not confuse

```
p1 = p2;
```

and

```
*p1 = *p2;
```

When you add the asterisk, you are not dealing with the pointers p1 and p2, but with the variables to which the pointers are pointing. This is illustrated in Display 10.1, in which variables are represented as boxes and the value of the variable is written inside the box. We have not shown the actual numeric addresses in the pointer variables because the numbers are not important. What is important is that the number is the address of some particular variable. So, rather than use the actual number of the

Display 10.1   Uses of the Assignment Operator with Pointer Variables

`p1 = p2;`

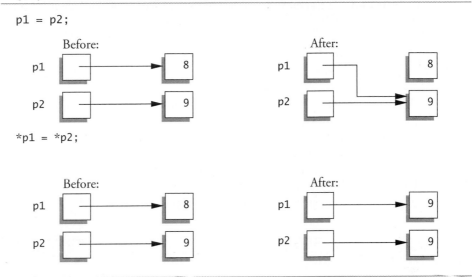

`*p1 = *p2;`

Pointer Variables Used with =

If p1 and p2 are pointer variables, then the statement

`p1 = p2;`

changes the value of p1 so that it is the memory address (pointer) in p2. A common way to think of this is that the assignment will change p1 so that it points to the same thing to which p2 is currently pointing.

address, we have merely indicated the address with an arrow that points to the variable with that address.

Since a pointer can be used to refer to a variable, your program can manipulate variables even if the variables have no identifiers to name them. The operator **new** can be used to create variables that have no identifiers to serve as their names. These nameless variables are referred to via pointers. For example, the following creates a new variable of type int and sets the pointer variable p1 equal to the address of this new variable (that is, p1 points to this new, nameless variable):

new

`p1 = new int;`

This new, nameless variable can be referred to as *p1 (that is, as the variable pointed to by p1). You can do anything with this nameless variable that you can do with any other variable of type int. For example, the following code reads a value of type int from the keyboard into this nameless variable, adds 7 to the value, and then outputs this new value:

```
cin >> *p1;
*p1 = *p1 + 7;
cout << *p1;
```

The new operator produces a new, nameless variable and returns a pointer that points to this new variable. You specify the type for this new variable by writing the type name after the new operator. Variables that are created using the new operator are **dynamic variable** called **dynamically allocated variables** or simply **dynamic variables**, because they are created and destroyed while the program is running. The program in Display 10.2 demonstrates some simple operations on pointers and dynamic variables. Display 10.3 graphically illustrates the working of the program in Display 10.2.

THE new OPERATOR

The new operator creates a new dynamic variable of a specified type and returns a pointer that points to this new variable. For example, the following creates a new dynamic variable of type MyType and leaves the pointer variable p pointing to this new variable:

```
MyType *p;
p = new MyType;
```

If the type is a class type, the default constructor is called for the newly created dynamic variable. You can specify a different constructor by including arguments as follows:

```
MyType *mtPtr;
mtPtr = new MyType(32.0, 17); // calls MyType(double, int);
```

A similar notation allows you to initialize dynamic variables of nonclass types, as illustrated below:

```
int *n;
n = new int(17); // initializes *n to 17
```

With earlier C++ compilers, if there was insufficient available memory to create the new variable, then new returned a special pointer named NULL. The C++ standard provides that if there is insufficient available memory to create the new variable, then the new operator, by default, terminates the program.

Display 10.2   Basic Pointer Manipulations

```
1    //Program to demonstrate pointers and dynamic variables.
2    #include <iostream>
3    using std::cout;
4    using std::endl;


5    int main( )
6    {
7        int *p1, *p2;


8        p1 = new int;
9        *p1 = 42;
10       p2 = p1;
11       cout << "*p1 == " << *p1 << endl;
12       cout << "*p2 == " << *p2 << endl;


13       *p2 = 53;
14       cout << "*p1 == " << *p1 << endl;
15       cout << "*p2 == " << *p2 << endl;


16       p1 = new int;
17       *p1 = 88;
18       cout << "*p1 == " << *p1 << endl;
19       cout << "*p2 == " << *p2 << endl;


20       cout << "Hope you got the point of this example!\n";
21       return 0;
22   }
```

SAMPLE DIALOGUE

```
*p1 == 42
*p2 == 42
*p1 == 53
*p2 == 53
*p1 == 88
*p2 == 53
Hope you got the point of this example!
```

Display 10.3   Explanation of Display 10.2

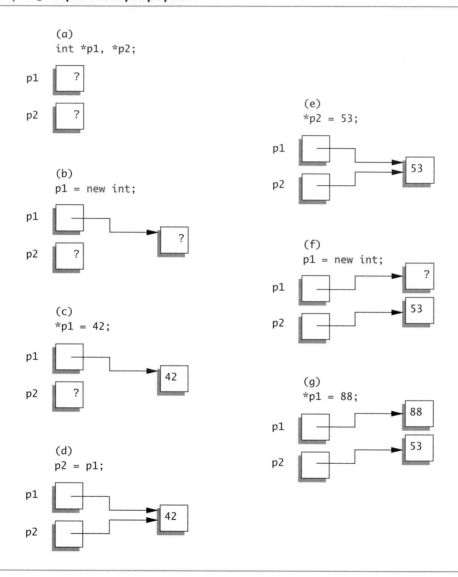

(a)
int *p1, *p2;

(b)
p1 = new int;

(c)
*p1 = 42;

(d)
p2 = p1;

(e)
*p2 = 53;

(f)
p1 = new int;

(g)
*p1 = 88;

When the new operator is used to create a dynamic variable of a class type, a constructor for the class is invoked. If you do not specify which constructor to use, the default constructor is invoked. For example, the following invokes the default constructor:

```
SomeClass *classPtr;
classPtr = new SomeClass; //Calls default constructor.
```

If you include constructor arguments, you can invoke a different constructor, as illustrated below:

```
classPtr = new SomeClass(32.0, 17);//Calls SomeClass(double, int).
```

A similar notation allows you to initialize dynamic variables of nonclass types, as illustrated below:

```
double *dPtr;
dPtr = new double(98.6); // Initializes *dPtr to 98.6.
```

A pointer type is a full-fledged type and can be used in the same ways as other types. In particular, you can have a function parameter of a pointer type and you can have a function that returns a pointer type. For example, the following function has a parameter that is a pointer to an int variable and returns a (possibly different) pointer to an int variable:

pointer parameters

```
int* findOtherPointer(int* p);
```

Self-Test Exercises

1. What is a pointer in C++?

2. Give at least three uses of the * operator. Name and describe each use.

3. What is the output produced by the following code?
   ```
   int *p1, *p2;
   p1 = new int;
   p2 = new int;
   *p1 = 10;
   *p2 = 20;
   cout << *p1 << " " << *p2 << endl;
   p1 = p2;
   cout << *p1 << " " << *p2 << endl;
   *p1 = 30;
   cout << *p1 << " " << *p2 << endl;
   ```

   How would the output change if you were to replace

   ```
   *p1 = 30;
   ```

   with the following?

   ```
   *p2 = 30;
   ```

4. What is the output produced by the following code?

   ```
   int *p1, *p2;
   p1 = new int;
   ```

```
p2 = new int;
*p1 = 10;
*p2 = 20;
cout << *p1 << " " << *p2 << endl;
*p1 = *p2; //This is different from Exercise 4
cout << *p1 << " " << *p2 << endl;
*p1 = 30;
cout << *p1 << " " << *p2 << endl;
```

■ BASIC MEMORY MANAGEMENT

freestore or
heap

A special area of memory, called the **freestore** or the **heap**, is reserved for dynamically allocated variables. Any new dynamic variable created by a program consumes some of the memory in the freestore. If your program creates too many dynamic variables, it will consume all the memory in the freestore. If this happens, any additional calls to new will fail. What happens when you use new after you have exhausted all the memory in the freestore (all the memory reserved for dynamically allocated variables) will depend on how up-to-date your compiler is. With earlier C++ compilers, if there was insufficient available memory to create the new variable, then new returned a special value named NULL. If you have a compiler that fully conforms to the newer C++ standard, then if there is insufficient available memory to create the new variable, the new operator terminates the program. Chapter 18 discusses ways to configure your program so that it can do things other than abort when new exhausts the freestore.[2]

If you have an older compiler, you can check to see if a call to new was successful by testing to see if NULL was returned by the call to new. For example, the following code tests to see if the attempt to create a new dynamic variable succeeded. The program will end with an error message if the call to new failed to create the desired dynamic variable:

```
int *p;
p = new int;
if (p == NULL)
{
    cout << "Error: Insufficient memory.\n";
    exit(1);
}
//If new succeeded, the program continues from here.
```

(Remember that since this code uses exit, you need an include directive for the library with header file <cstdlib> or, with some implementations, <stdlib.h>.)

---

[2] Technically, the new operator throws an exception, which, if not caught, terminates the program. It is possible to catch the exception and handle the exception. Exception handling is discussed in Chapter 18.

The constant NULL is actually the number 0, but we prefer to think of it and spell it as NULL make it clear that you mean this special-purpose value which you can assign to pointer variables. We will discuss other uses for NULL later in this book. The definition of the identifier NULL is in a number of the standard libraries, such as <iostream> and <cstddef>, so you should use an include directive for either <iostream>, <cstddef> (or another suitable library) when you use NULL.

NULL is 0

As we said, NUll is actually just the number 0. The definition of NULL is handled by the C++ preprocessor which replaces NULL with 0. Thus, the compiler never actually sees "NULL" and so there is no namespace issue and no using directive is needed for NULL.[3] While we prefer to use NULL rather than 0 in our code, we note that some authorities hold just the opposite view and advocate using 0 rather than NULL.

(Do not confuse the NULL pointer with the null character '\0' which is used to terminate C strings. They are not the same. One is the integer 0 while the other is the character '\0'.)

Newer compilers do not require the above explicit check to see if the new dynamic variable was created. On newer compilers, your program will automatically end with an error message if a call to new fails to create the desired dynamic variable. However, with any compiler, the above check will cause no harm and will make your program more portable.

NULL

NULL is a special constant pointer value that is used to give a value to a pointer variable that would not otherwise have a value. NULL can be assigned to a pointer variable of any type. The identifier NULL is defined in a number of libraries, including <iostream>. (The constant NULL is actually the integer 0.)

The size of the freestore varies from one implementation of C++ to another. It is typically large, and a modest program is not likely to use all the memory in the freestore. However, even in modest programs it is a good practice to recycle any freestore memory that is no longer needed. If your program no longer needs a dynamic variable, the memory used by that dynamic variable can be returned to the **freestore manager** which recycles the memory to create other dynamic variables. The **delete** operator eliminates a dynamic variable and returns the memory that the dynamic variable occupied to the freestore manager so that the memory can be reused. Suppose that p is a pointer variable that is pointing to a dynamic variable. The following will destroy the dynamic variable pointed to by p and return the memory used by the dynamic variable to the freestore manager for reuse:

delete

```
delete p;
```

---

[3] The details are as follows: The definition of NULL uses #define, a form of definition that was inherited from the C language and that is handled by the preprocessor.

THE delete OPERATOR

The delete operator eliminates a dynamic variable and returns the memory that the dynamic variable occupied to the freestore. The memory can then be reused to create new dynamic variables. For example, the following eliminates the dynamic variable pointed to by the pointer variable p:

```
delete p;
```

After a call to delete, the value of the pointer variable, like p above, is undefined. (A slightly different version of delete, discussed later in this chapter, is used when the dynamically allocated variable is an array.)

Pitfall   DANGLING POINTERS

When you apply delete to a pointer variable, the dynamic variable to which it is pointing is destroyed. At that point, the value of the pointer variable is undefined, which means that you do not know where it is pointing. Moreover, if some other pointer variable was pointing to the dynamic variable that was destroyed, then this other pointer variable is also undefined. These undefined pointer variables are called **dangling pointers**. If p is a dangling pointer and your program applies the dereferencing operator * to p (to produce the expression *p), the result is unpredictable and usually disastrous. Before you apply the dereferencing operator * to a pointer variable, you should be certain that the pointer variable points to some variable.

dangling
pointer

C++ has no built-in test to check whether a pointer variable is a dangling pointer. One way to avoid dangling pointers is to set any dangling pointer variable equal to NULL. Then your program can test the pointer variable to see if it is equal to NULL before applying the dereferencing operator * to the pointer variable. When you use this technique, you follow a call to delete by code that sets all dangling pointers equal to NULL. Remember, other pointer variables may become dangling pointers besides the one pointer variable used in the call to delete, so be sure to set *all* dangling pointers to NULL. It is up to the programmer to keep track of dangling pointers and set them to NULL or otherwise ensure that they are not dereferenced.

▪ DYNAMIC VARIABLES AND AUTOMATIC VARIABLES

Variables created with the new operator are called *dynamic variables* (or *dynamically allocated variables*) because they are created and destroyed while the program is running. Local variables—that is, variables declared within a function definition—also have a certain dynamic characteristic, but they are not called dynamic variables. If a variable is local to a function, then the variable is created by the C++ system when the function is called and is destroyed when the function call is completed. Since the main part of a program is really just a function called main, this is even true of the variables declared in the main part of your program. (Since the call to main does not end until the program ends, the variables declared in main are not destroyed until the program ends, but the mechanism for handling local variables is the same for main as for any other function.) These local variables are sometimes called **automatic variables** because their dynamic properties are controlled automatically for you. They are automatically created when the function in which they are declared is called and automatically destroyed when the function call ends.

automatic variable

Variables declared outside any function or class definition, including outside main, are called **global variables**. These global variables are sometimes called **statically allocated variables**, because they are truly static in contrast to dynamic and automatic variables. We discussed global variables briefly in Chapter 3. As it turns out, we have no need for global variables and have not used them.[4]

global variable

Tip

DEFINE POINTER TYPES

You can define a pointer type name so that pointer variables can be declared like other variables without the need to place an asterisk in front of each pointer variable. For example, the following defines a type called IntPtr, which is the type for pointer variables that contain pointers to int variables:

```
typedef int* IntPtr;
```

Thus, the following two pointer variable declarations are equivalent:

```
IntPtr p;
```

and

```
int *p;
```

You can use typedef to define an alias for any type name or definition. For example, the following defines the type name Kilometers to mean the same thing as the type name double:

typedef

```
typedef double Kilometers;
```

Once you have given this type definition, you can define a variable of type double as follows:

```
Kilometers distance;
```

Renaming existing types this way can occasionally be useful. However, our main use of typedef will be to define types for pointer variables.

Keep in mind that a typedef does not produce a new type but is simply an alias for the type definition. For example, given the previous definition of Kilometers, a variable of type

---

[4] Variables declared within a class using the modifier static are static in a different sense than the dynamic/static contrast we are discussing in this section.

Kilometers may be substituted for a parameter of type double. Kilometers and double are two names for the same type.

There are two advantages to using defined pointer type names, such as IntPtr defined previously. First, it avoids the mistake of omitting an asterisk. Remember, if you intend p1 and p2 to be pointers, then the following is a mistake:

```
int *p1, p2;
```

Since the * was omitted from the p2, the variable p2 is just an ordinary int variable, not a pointer variable. If you get confused and place the * on the int, the problem is the same but is more difficult to notice. C++ allows you to place the * on the type name, such as int, so that the following is legal:

```
int* p1, p2;
```

Although the above is legal, it is misleading. It looks like both p1 and p2 are pointer variables, but in fact only p1 is a pointer variable; p2 is an ordinary int variable. As far as the C++ compiler is concerned, the * that is attached to the identifier int may as well be attached to the identifier p1. One correct way to declare both p1 and p2 to be pointer variables is

```
int *p1, *p2;
```

An easier and less error-prone way to declare both p1 and p2 to be pointer variables is to use the defined type name IntPtr as follows:

```
IntPtr p1, p2;
```

The second advantage of using a defined pointer type, such as IntPtr, is seen when you define a function with a call-by-reference parameter for a pointer variable. Without the defined pointer type name, you would need to include both an * and an & in the declaration for the function, and the details can get confusing. If you use a type name for the pointer type, then a call-by-reference parameter for a pointer type involves no complications. You define a call-by-reference parameter for a defined pointer type just like you define any other call-by-reference parameter. Here's an example:

```
void sampleFunction(IntPtr& pointerVariable);
```

Self-Test Exercises

5. What unfortunate misinterpretation can occur with the following declaration?
   ```
   int* intPtr1, intPtr2;
   ```

6. Suppose a dynamic variable were created as follows:

   ```
   char *p;
   p = new char;
   ```

Assuming that the value of the pointer variable p has not changed (so it still points to the same dynamic variable), how can you destroy this new dynamic variable and return the memory it uses to the freestore manager so that the memory can be reused to create other new dynamic variables?

7. Write a definition for a type called NumberPtr that will be the type for pointer variables that hold pointers to dynamic variables of type double. Also, write a declaration for a pointer variable called myPoint, which is of type NumberPtr.

8. Describe the action of the new operator. What does the new operator return? What are the indications of errors?

TYPE DEFINITIONS

You can assign a name to a type definition and then use the type name to declare variables. This is done with the keyword typedef. These type definitions are normally placed outside the body of the main part of your program and outside the body of other functions, typically near the start of a file. That way the typedef is global and available to your entire program. We will use type definitions to define names for pointer types, as shown in the example below.

SYNTAX

```
typedef Known_Type_Definition New_Type_Name;
```

EXAMPLE

```
typedef int* IntPtr;
```

The type name IntPtr can then be used to declare pointers to dynamic variables of type int, as in the following example:

```
IntPtr pointer1, pointer2;
```

Pitfall   POINTERS AS CALL-BY-VALUE PARAMETERS

When a call-by-value parameter is of a pointer type, its behavior can occasionally be subtle and troublesome. Consider the function call shown in Display 10.4. The parameter temp in the function sneaky is a call-by-value parameter, and hence it is a local variable. When the function is called, the value of temp is set to the value of the argument p and the function body is executed. Since temp is a local variable, no changes to temp should go outside the function sneaky. In particular, the value of the pointer variable p should not be changed. Yet the sample dialogue makes it look like the value of the pointer variable p has changed. Before the call to the function sneaky, the value of *p was 77, and after the call to sneaky the value of *p is 99. What has happened?

The situation is diagrammed in Display 10.5. Although the sample dialogue may make it look as if p were changed, the value of p was not changed by the function call to sneaky. Pointer p has two things associated with it: p's pointer value and the value stored where p points. But the value of p is the pointer (that is, a memory address). After the call to sneaky, the variable p contains the same pointer value (that is, the same memory address). The call to sneaky has changed the value of the variable pointed to by p, but it has not changed the value of p itself.

If the parameter type is a class or structure type that has member variables of a pointer type, the same kind of surprising changes can occur with call-by-value arguments of the class type. However, for class types, you can avoid (and control) these surprise changes by defining a *copy constructor*, as described later in this chapter.

Display 10.4   A Call-by-Value Pointer Parameter *(part 1 of 2)*

```
1   //Program to demonstrate the way call-by-value parameters
2   //behave with pointer arguments.
3   #include <iostream>
4   using std::cout;
5   using std::cin;
6   using std::endl;

7   typedef int* IntPointer;

8   void sneaky(IntPointer temp);

9   int main( )
10  {
11      IntPointer p;

12      p = new int;
13      *p = 77;
14      cout << "Before call to function *p == "
15          << *p << endl;

16      sneaky(p);

17      cout << "After call to function *p == "
18          << *p << endl;

19      return 0;
20  }
```

Display 10.4   A Call-by-Value Pointer Parameter *(part 2 of 2)*

```
21   void sneaky(IntPointer temp)
22   {
23       *temp = 99;
24       cout << "Inside function call *temp == "
25            << *temp << endl;
26   }
```

SAMPLE DIALOGUE

```
Before call to function *p == 77
Inside function call *temp == 99
After call to function *p == 99
```

Display 10.5   The Function Call `sneaky(p);`

1. Before call to sneaky:

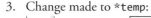

2. Value of p is plugged in for temp:

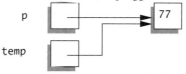

3. Change made to *temp:

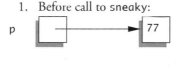

4. After call to sneaky:

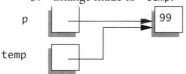

USES FOR POINTERS

Chapter 17 discusses ways to use pointers to create a number of useful data structures. This chapter only discusses one use of pointers, namely, to reference arrays, and in particular to create and reference a kind of array known as a *dynamically allocated array*. Dynamically allocated arrays are the topic of Section 10.2.

10.2 Dynamic Arrays

In this section you will see that array variables are actually pointer variables. You will also find out how to write programs with dynamically allocated arrays. A **dynamically allocated array** (also called simply a **dynamic array**) is an array whose size is not specified when you write the program, but is determined while the program is running.

dynamically allocated array

ARRAY VARIABLES AND POINTER VARIABLES

Chapter 5 described how arrays are kept in memory. At that point we discussed arrays in terms of memory addresses. But a memory address is a pointer. So, in C++ an array variable is actually a kind of pointer variable that points to the first indexed variable of the array. Given the following two variable declarations, p and a are both pointer variables:

```
int a[10];
typedef int* IntPtr;
IntPtr p;
```

The fact that a and p are both pointer variables is illustrated in Display 10.6. Since a is a pointer that points to a variable of type int (namely, the variable a[0]), the value of a can be assigned to the pointer variable p as follows:

```
p = a;
```

After this assignment, p points to the same memory location that a points to. Thus, p[0], p[1], . . . p[9] refer to the indexed variables a[0], a[1], . . . a[9]. The square bracket notation you have been using for arrays applies to pointer variables as long as the pointer variable points to an array in memory. After the above assignment, you can treat the identifier p as if it were an array identifier. You can also treat the identifier a as if it were a pointer variable, but there is one important reservation: *You cannot change the pointer value in an array variable.* If the pointer variable p2 has a value, you might be tempted to think the following is legal, but it is not:

```
a = p2;//ILLEGAL. You cannot assign a different address to a.
```

The underlying reason why this assignment does not work is that an array variable is not of type int*, but its type is a const version of int*. An array variable, like a, is a pointer variable with the modifier const, which means that its value cannot be changed.

(An array variable is actually more than an ordinary pointer variable since it carries some additional size information about the array, but an array variable does include a pointer to the array and the array variable can be assigned to a pointer variable. So, an array variable is a kind of pointer variable and can be treated like a pointer variable whose value cannot be changed.)

Display 10.6 Arrays and Pointer Variables

```
1    //Program to demonstrate that an array variable is a kind of pointer variable.
2    #include <iostream>
3    using std::cout;
4    using std::endl;

5    typedef int* IntPtr;

6    int main( )
7    {
8        IntPtr p;
9        int a[10];
10       int index;

11       for (index = 0; index < 10; index++)
12           a[index] = index;

13       p = a;

14       for (index = 0; index < 10; index++)
15           cout << p[index] << " ";
16       cout << endl;

17       for (index = 0; index < 10; index++)
18           p[index] = p[index] + 1;

19       for (index = 0; index < 10; index++)
20           cout << a[index] << " ";
21       cout << endl;

22       return 0;
23   }
```

Note that changes to the array p are also changes to the array a.

SAMPLE DIALOGUE

```
0 1 2 3 4 5 6 7 8 9
1 2 3 4 5 6 7 8 9 10
```

▨ CREATING AND USING DYNAMIC ARRAYS

One problem with the kinds of arrays we discussed in Chapter 5 is that you must specify the size of the array when you write the program—but you may not know what size array you need until the program is run. For example, an array might hold a list of student identification numbers, but the size of the class may be different each time the program is run. With the kinds of arrays you have used thus far, you must estimate the largest possible size you may need for the array and hope that size is large enough. There are two problems with this. First, you may estimate too low, and then your program will not work in all situations. Second, since the array might have many unused positions, this can waste computer memory. Dynamically allocated arrays avoid these problems. If your program uses a dynamically allocated array for student identification numbers, then the number of students can be entered as input to the program and the dynamically allocated array can be created to have a size exactly equal to the number of students.

creating a dynamic array

Dynamically allocated arrays are created using the new operator. The creation and use of dynamically allocated arrays is surprisingly simple. Since array variables are pointer variables, you can use the new operator to create dynamically allocated variables that are arrays and can treat these dynamically allocated arrays as if they were ordinary arrays. For example, the following creates a dynamically allocated array variable with ten array elements of type double:

```
typedef double* DoublePtr;
DoublePtr d;
d = new double[10];
```

To obtain a dynamically allocated array of elements of any other type, simply replace double with the desired type. In particular, you can replace the type double with a struct or class type. To obtain a dynamically allocated array variable of any other size, simply replace 10 with the desired size.

There are also a number of less-obvious things to notice about this example. First, the pointer type that you use for a pointer to a dynamically allocated array is the same as the pointer type you would use for a single element of the array. For instance, the pointer type for an array of elements of type double is the same as the pointer type you would use for a simple variable of type double. The pointer to the array is actually a pointer to the first indexed variable of the array. In the above example, an entire array with ten indexed variables is created, and the pointer p is left pointing to the first of these ten indexed variables.

Second, notice that when you call new, the size of the dynamically allocated array is given in square brackets after the type, which in this example is the type double. This tells the computer how much storage to reserve for the dynamic array. If you omitted the square brackets and the 10 in this example, the computer would allocate enough storage for only one variable of type double, rather than for an array of ten indexed variables of type double.

Display 10.7 contains a program that illustrates the use of a dynamically allocated array. The program searches a list of numbers stored in a dynamically allocated array. The size of the array is determined when the program is run. The user is asked how many numbers there will be, and then the new operator creates a dynamically allocated array of that size. The size of the dynamic array is given by the variable arraySize. The size of a dynamic array need not be given by a constant. It can, as in Display 10.7, be given by a variable whose value is determined when the program is run.

Display 10.7   A Dynamically Allocated Array *(part 1 of 2)*

```
 1   //Searches a list of numbers entered at the keyboard.
 2   #include <iostream>
 3   using std::cin;
 4   using std::cout;

 5   typedef int* IntPtr;

 6   void fillArray(int a[], int size);
 7   //Precondition: size is the size of the array a.
 8   //Postcondition: a[0] through a[size-1] have been
 9   //filled with values read from the keyboard.

10   int search(int a[], int size, int target);
11   //Precondition: size is the size of the array a.
12   //The array elements a[0] through a[size-1] have values.
13   //If target is in the array, returns the first index of target.
14   //If target is not in the array, returns -1.

15   int main( )
16   {
17       cout << "This program searches a list of numbers.\n";

18       int arraySize;
19       cout << "How many numbers will be on the list? ";
20       cin >> arraySize;
21       IntPtr a;
22       a = new int[arraySize];

23       fillArray(a, arraySize);

24       int target;
25       cout << "Enter a value to search for: ";
26       cin >> target;
27       int location = search(a, arraySize, target);
28       if (location == -1)
29           cout << target << " is not in the array.\n";
30       else
31           cout << target << " is element " << location << " in the array.\n";
32
33       delete [] a;
34
35       return 0;
36   }
```

Ordinary array parameters

The dynamic array a is used like an ordinary array.

Display 10.7   A Dynamically Allocated Array *(part 2 of 2)*

```
37   //Uses the library <iostream>:
38   void fillArray(int a[], int size)
39   {
40       cout << "Enter " << size << " integers.\n";
41       for (int index = 0; index < size; index++)
42           cin >> a[index];
43   }

44   int search(int a[], int size, int target)
45   {
46       int index = 0;
47       while ((a[index] != target) && (index < size))
48           index++;
49       if (index == size)//if target is not in a.
50           index = -1;
51       return index;
52   }
```

SAMPLE DIALOGUE

```
This program searches a list of numbers.
How many numbers will be on the list? 5
Enter 5 integers.
1 2 3 4 5
Enter a value to search for: 3
3 is element 2 in the array.
```

delete []

Notice the delete statement, which destroys the dynamically allocated array pointed to by a in Display 10.7. Since the program is about to end anyway, we did not really need this delete statement; if the program went on to do other things, however, you would want such a delete statement so that the memory used by this dynamically allocated array would be returned to the freestore manager. The delete statement for a dynamically allocated array is similar to the delete statement you saw earlier, except that with a dynamically allocated array you must include an empty pair of square brackets like so:

```
delete [] a;
```

The square brackets tell C++ that a dynamically allocated array variable is being eliminated, so the system checks the size of the array and removes that many indexed variables. If you omit the square brackets you will not be eliminating the entire array. For example:

```
delete a;
```

is not legal, but the error is not detected by most compilers. The C++ standard says that what happens when you do this is "undefined." That means the author of the compiler can have this do anything that is convenient (for the compiler writer, not for you). Always use the

```
delete [] arrayPtr;
```

syntax when you are deleting memory that was allocated with something like

```
arrayPtr = new MyType[37];
```

Also note the position of the square brackets in the `delete` statement

```
delete [] arrayPtr; //Correct
delete arrayPtr[]; //ILLEGAL!
```

You create a dynamically allocated array with a call to new using a pointer, such as the pointer *a* in Display 10.7. After the call to new, you should not assign any other pointer value to this pointer variable because that can confuse the system when the memory for the dynamic array is returned to the freestore manager with a call to `delete`.

Dynamically allocated arrays are created using new and a pointer variable. When your program is finished using a dynamically allocated array, you should return the array memory to the freestore manager with a call to `delete`. Other than that, a dynamically allocated array can be used just like any other array.

Example   **A FUNCTION THAT RETURNS AN ARRAY**

In C++ an array type is not allowed as the return type of a function. For example, the following is illegal:

```
int [] someFunction( );//ILLEGAL
```

If you want to create a function similar to this, you must return a pointer to the array base type and have the pointer point to the array. So, the function declaration would be as follows:

```
int* someFunction( );//Legal
```

An example of a function that returns a pointer to an array is given in Display 10.8.

Self-Test Exercises

9. Write a type definition for pointer variables that will be used to point to dynamically allocated arrays. The array elements are to be of type char. Call the type CharArray.

10. Suppose your program contains code to create a dynamically allocated array as follows:

```
int *entry;
entry = new int[10];
```

so that the pointer variable entry is pointing to this dynamically allocated array. Write code to fill this array with ten numbers typed in at the keyboard.

11. Suppose your program contains code to create a dynamically allocated array as in Self-Test Exercise 10, and suppose the pointer variable entry has not had its (pointer) value changed. Write code to destroy this dynamically allocated array and return the memory it uses to the freestore manager.

12. What is the output of the following code fragment?

```cpp
int a[10];
int arraySize = 10;
int *p = a;
int i;
for (i = 0; i < arraySize; i++)
    a[i] = i;
for (i = 0; i < arraySize; i++)
    cout << p[i] << " ";
cout << endl;
```

Display 10.8   Returning a Pointer to an Array (part 1 of 2)

```cpp
1   #include <iostream>
2   using std::cout;
3   using std::endl;

4   int* doubler(int a[], int size);
5   //Precondition; size is the size of the array a.
6   //All indexed variables of a have values.
7   //Returns: a pointer to an array of the same size as a in which
8   //each indexed variable is double the corresponding element in a.

9   int main( )
10  {
11      int a[] = {1, 2, 3, 4, 5};
12      int* b;

13      b = doubler(a, 5);

14      int i;
15      cout << "Array a:\n";
16      for (i = 0; i < 5; i++)
17          cout << a[i] << " ";
18      cout << endl;
```

Display 10.8   Returning a Pointer to an Array *(part 2 of 2)*

```
19        cout << "Array b:\n";
20        for (i = 0; i < 5; i++)
21            cout << b[i] << " ";
22        cout << endl;

23        delete[] b;
24        return 0;
25    }

26    int* doubler(int a[], int size)
27    {
28        int* temp = new int[size];

29        for (int i =0; i < size; i++)
30            temp[i] = 2*a[i];

31        return temp;
32    }
```

This call to delete is not really needed since the program is ending, but in another context it could be important to include this delete.

SAMPLE DIALOGUE

```
Array a:
1 2 3 4 5
Array b:
2 4 6 8 10
```

POINTER ARITHMETIC

You can perform a kind of arithmetic on pointers, but it is an arithmetic of addresses, not an arithmetic of numbers. For example, suppose your program contains the following code:

```
typedef double* DoublePtr;
DoublePtr d;
d = new double[10];
```

After these statements, d contains the address of the indexed variable d[0]. The expression d + 1 evaluates to the address of d[1], d + 2 is the address of d[2], and so forth. Notice that although the value of d is an address and an address is a number, d + 1 does not simply add 1 to the number in d. If a variable of type double requires eight bytes (eight memory locations) and d contains the address 2000, then d + 1 evaluates to the memory address 2008. Of course, the type double can be replaced by any other type, and then pointer addition moves in units of variables for that type.

addresses, not numbers

This pointer arithmetic gives you an alternative way to manipulate arrays. For example, if arraySize is the size of the dynamically allocated array pointed to by d, then the following will output the contents of the dynamic array:

```
for (int i = 0; i < arraySize; i++)
    cout << *(d + i)<< " ";
```

The above is equivalent to the following:

```
for (int i = 0; i < arraySize; i++)
    cout << d[i] << " ";
```

You may not perform multiplication or division of pointers. All you can do is add an integer to a pointer, subtract an integer from a pointer, or subtract two pointers of the same type. When you subtract two pointers, the result is the number of indexed variables between the two addresses. Remember, for subtraction of two pointer values, *these values must point into the same array!* It makes little sense to subtract a pointer that points into one array from another pointer that points into a different array.

++ and --

You can also use the increment and decrement operators, ++ and --, to perform pointer arithmetic. For example, d++ will advance the value of d so that it contains the address of the next indexed variable, and d-- will change d so that it contains the address of the previous indexed variable

■ MULTIDIMENSIONAL DYNAMIC ARRAYS

You can have multidimensional dynamic arrays. You just need to remember that multidimensional arrays are arrays of arrays or arrays of arrays of arrays and so forth. For example, to create a two-dimensional dynamic array you must remember that it is an array of arrays. To create a two-dimensional array of integers, you first create a one-dimensional dynamic array of pointers of type int*, which is the type for a one-dimensional array of ints. Then you create a dynamic array of ints for each element of the array.

A type definition may help to keep things straight. The following is the variable type for an ordinary one-dimensional dynamic array of ints:

```
typedef int* IntArrayPtr;
```

To obtain a three-by-four array of ints, you want an array whose base type is IntArrayPtr. For example:

```
IntArrayPtr *m = new IntArrayPtr[3];
```

This is an array of three pointers, each of which can name a dynamic array of ints, as follows:

```
for (int i = 0; i < 3; i++)
    m[i] = new int[4];
```

HOW TO USE A DYNAMIC ARRAY

- *Define a pointer type:* Define a type for pointers to variables of the same type as the elements of the array. For example, if the dynamic array is an array of `doubles`, you might use the following:

  ```
  typedef double* DoubleArrayPtr;
  ```

- *Declare a pointer variable:* Declare a pointer variable of this defined type. The pointer variable will point to the dynamically allocated array in memory and will serve as the name of the dynamic array.

  ```
  DoubleArrayPtr a;
  ```

  (Alternatively, without a defined pointer type, use `double *a;`).

- *Call new:* Create a dynamic array using the new operator:

  ```
  a = new double[arraySize];
  ```

  The size of the dynamic array is given in square brackets as in the above example. The size can be given using an `int` variable or other `int` expression. In the above example, `arraySize` can be a variable of type `int` whose value is determined while the program is running.

- *Use like an ordinary array:* The pointer variable, such as `a`, is used just like an ordinary array. For example, the indexed variables are written in the usual way: `a[0]`, `a[1]`, and so forth. The pointer variable should not have any other pointer value assigned to it, but should be used like an array variable.

- *Call delete [ ]:* When your program is finished with the dynamically allocated array variable, use `delete` and empty square brackets along with the pointer variable to eliminate the dynamic array and return the storage that it occupies to the freestore manager for reuse. For example:

  ```
  delete [] a;
  ```

The resulting array `m` is a three-by-four dynamic array. A simple program to illustrate this is given in Display 10.9.

Be sure to notice the use of `delete` in Display 10.9. Since the dynamic array `m` is an array of arrays, each of the arrays created with `new` in the `for` loop on lines 13 and 14 must be returned to the freestore manager with a call to `delete []`; then, the array `m` itself must be returned to the freestore manager with another call to `delete []`. There must be a call to `delete []` for each call to `new` that created an array. (Since the program ends right after the calls to `delete []`, we could safely omit the calls to `delete []`, but we wanted to illustrate their usage.)

`delete []`

Display 10.9   A Two-Dimensional Dynamic Array *(part 1 of 2)*

```
1    #include <iostream>
2    using std::cin;
3    using std::cout;
4    using std::endl;


5    typedef int* IntArrayPtr;


6    int main( )
7    {
8        int d1, d2;
9        cout << "Enter the row and column dimensions of the array:\n";
10       cin >> d1 >> d2;


11       IntArrayPtr *m = new IntArrayPtr[d1];
12       int i, j;
13       for (i = 0; i < d1; i++)
14           m[i] = new int[d2];
15       //m is now a d1–by–d2 array.


16       cout << "Enter " << d1 << " rows of "
17           << d2 << " integers each:\n";
18       for (i = 0; i < d1; i++)
19           for (j = 0; j < d2; j++)
20               cin >> m[i][j];


21       cout << "Echoing the two-dimensional array:\n";
22       for (i = 0; i < d1; i++)
23       {
24           for (j = 0; j < d2; j++)
25               cout << m[i][j] << " ";
26           cout << endl;
27       }
28
29       for (i = 0; i < d1; i++)
30           delete[] m[i];
31       delete[] m;


32       return 0;
33   }
```

Note that there must be one call to delete [] for each call to new that created an array.
(These calls to delete [] are not really needed since the program is ending, but in another context it could be important to include them.)

Display 10.9   **A Two-Dimensional Dynamic Array** *(part 2 of 2)*

SAMPLE DIALOGUE

```
Enter the row and column dimensions of the array:
3 4
Enter 3 rows of 4 integers each:
1 2 3 4
5 6 7 8
9 0 1 2
Echoing the two-dimensional array:
1 2 3 4
5 6 7 8
9 0 1 2
```

10.3 Classes, Pointers, and Dynamic Arrays

The combinations are endless.

Common advertisement copy

A dynamically allocated array can have a base type that is a class. A class can have a member variable that is a dynamically allocated array. You can combine classes and dynamically allocated arrays in just about any combination. There are a few more things to worry about when using classes and dynamically allocated arrays, but the basic techniques are the ones that you have already used. Many of the techniques presented in this section apply to all dynamically allocated structures, such as those we will discuss in Chapter 17, and not just to classes involving dynamically allocated arrays.

THE -> OPERATOR

C++ has an operator that can be used with a pointer to simplify the notation for specifying the members of a struct or a class. The **arrow operator**, ->, combines the actions of a dereferencing operator, *, and a dot operator to specify a member of a dynamic struct or class object that is pointed to by a given pointer. For example, suppose you have the following definition:

arrow operator

```
struct Record
{
    int number;
    char grade;
};
```

The following creates a dynamically allocated variable of type `Record` and sets the member variables of the dynamic `struct` variable to 2001 and `'A'`:

```
Record *p;
p = new Record;
p->number = 2001;
p->grade = 'A';
```

The notations

```
p->grade
```

and

```
(*p).grade
```

have the same meaning. However, the first is more convenient and is almost always the notation used.

THE this POINTER

When defining member functions for a class, you sometimes want to refer to the calling object. The `this` pointer is a predefined pointer that points to the calling object. For example, consider a class like the following:

```
class Sample
{
public:
    ...
    void showStuff( ) const;
    ...
private:
    int stuff;
    ...
};
```

The following two ways of defining the member function `showStuff` are equivalent:

```
void Sample::showStuff( ) const
{
    cout << stuff;
}

//Not good style, but this illustrates the this pointer:
void Sample::showStuff( )
{
    cout << this->stuff;
}
```

Notice that this is not the name of the calling object, but is the name of a pointer that points to the calling object. The this pointer cannot have its value changed; it always points to the calling object.

As our earlier comment indicated, you normally have no need for the pointer this. However, in a few situations it is handy. One place where the this pointer is commonly used is in overloading the assignment operator, =, which we discuss next.

Since the this pointer points to the calling object, you cannot use this in the definition of any static member functions. A static member function normally has no calling object to which the pointer this can point..

OVERLOADING THE ASSIGNMENT OPERATOR

In this book we usually use the assignment operator as if it were a void function. However, the predefined assignment operator returns a reference that allows for some specialized uses.

With the predefined assignment operator, you can chain assignment operators as follows: a = b = c;, which means a = (b = c);. The first operation, b = c, returns the new version of b. So, the action of

```
a = b = c;
```

is to set a as well as b equal to c. To ensure that your overloaded versions of the assignment operator can be used in this way, you need to define the assignment operator so it returns something of the same type as its left-hand side. As you will see shortly, the this pointer will allow you to do this. (No pun intended.) However, while this requires that the assignment operator return something of the type of its left-hand side, it does not require that it return a reference. Another use of the assignment operator explains why a reference is returned.

The reason that the predefined assignment operator returns a reference is so that you can invoke a member function with the value returned, as in

```
(a = b).f( );
```

where f is a member function. If you want your overloaded versions of the assignment operator to allow for invoking member functions in this way, then you should have them return a reference. This is not a very compelling reason for returning a reference, since this is a pretty minor property that is seldom used. However, it is traditional to return a reference, and it is not significantly more difficult to return a reference than to simply return a value.

For example, consider the following class (which might be used for some specialized string handling that is not easily handled by the predefined class string):

```
class StringClass
{
public:
    ...
    void someProcessing( );
    ...
    StringClass& operator=(const StringClass& rtSide);
    ...
private:
    char *a;//Dynamic array for characters in the string
    int capacity;//size of dynamic array a
    int length;//Number of characters in a
};
```

**= must be a
member**

As noted in Chapter 8, when you overload the assignment operator it must be a member of the class; it cannot be a friend of the class. That is why the above definition has only one parameter for operator. For example, consider the following:

```
s1 = s2;//s1 and s2 in the class StringClass
```

**calling object
for =**

In the above call, s1 is the calling object and s2 is the argument to the member operator =.

The following definition of the overloaded assignment operator can be used in chains of assignments like

```
s1 = s2 = s3;
```

and can be used to invoke member functions as follows:

```
(s1 = s2).someProcessing( );
```

The definition of the overloaded assignment operator uses the this pointer to return the object on the left side of the = sign (which is the calling object):

```
//This version does not work in all cases.
StringClass& StringClass::operator=(const StringClass& rtSide)
{
    capacity = rtSide.capacity;
    length = rtSide.length;
    delete [] a;
    a = new char[capacity];
    for (int i = 0; i < length; i++)
        a[i] = rtSide.a[i];

    return *this;
}
```

This version has a problem when used in an assignment with the same object on both sides of the assignment operator, like the following:

```
s = s;
```

When this assignment is executed, the following statement is executed:

```
delete [] a;
```

But the calling object is s, so this means

```
delete [] s.a;
```

The pointer s.a is then undefined. The assignment operator has corrupted the object s and this run of the program is probably ruined.

For many classes, the obvious definition for overloading the assignment operator does not work correctly when the same object is on both sides of the assignment operator. You should always check this case and be careful to write your definition of the overloaded assignment operator so that it also works in this case.

To avoid the problem we had with our first definition of the overloaded assignment operator, you can use the this pointer to test this special case as follows:

```
//Final version with bug fixed:
StringClass& StringClass::operator=(const StringClass& rtSide)
{
    if (this == &rtSide)
     //if the right side is the same as the left side
    {
        return *this;
    }
    else
    {
        capacity = rtSide.capacity;
        length = rtSide.length;
        delete [] a;
        a = new char[capacity];
        for (int i = 0; i < length; i++)
           a[i] = rtSide.a[i];

        return *this;
    }
}
```

A complete example with an overloaded assignment operator is given in the next programming example.

Example

A CLASS FOR PARTIALLY FILLED ARRAYS

The class PFArrayD in Displays 10.10 and 10.11 is a class for a partially filled array of doubles.[5] As shown in the demonstration program in Display 10.12, an object of the class PFArrayD can be accessed using the square brackets just like an ordinary array, but the object also automatically keeps track of how much of the array is in use. Thus, it functions like a partially filled array. The member function `getNumberUsed` returns the number of array positions used and can thus be used in a `for` loop as in the following sample code:

```
PFArrayD stuff(cap);//cap is an int variable.
  <some code to fill object stuff with elements.>
for (int index = 0; index < stuff.getNumberUsed( ); index++)
    cout << stuff[index] << " ";
```

An object of the class `PFArrayD` has a dynamic array as a member variable. This member variable array stores the elements. The dynamic array member variable is actually a pointer variable. In each constructor, this member variable is set to point at a dynamic array. There are also two member variables of type `int`: The member variable `capacity` records the size of the dynamic array, and the member variable `used` records the number of array positions that have been filled so far. As is customary with partially filled arrays, the elements must be filled in order, going first into position 0, then 1, then 2, and so forth.

An object of the class `PFArrayD` can be used as a partially filled array of `double`s. It has some advantages over an ordinary array of `double`s or a dynamic array of `double`s. Unlike the standard arrays, this array gives an error message if an illegal array index is used. Also, an object of the class `PFArrayD` does not require an extra `int` variable to keep track of how much of the array is used. (You may protest that "There is such an `int` variable. It's a member variable." However, that member variable is a private member variable in the implementation, and a programmer who uses the class `PFArrayD` need never be aware of that member variable.)

An object of the class `PFArrayD` only works for storing values of type `double`. When we discuss templates in Chapter 16, you will see that it would be easy to convert the definition to a template class that would work for any type, but for now we will settle for storing elements of type `double`.

Most of the details in the definition of the class `PFArrayD` use only items covered before now, but there are three new items: a copy constructor, a destructor, and an overloading of the assignment operator. We explain the overloaded assignment operator next and discuss the copy constructor and destructor in the next two subsections.

To see why you want to overload the assignment operator, suppose that the overloading of the assignment operator were omitted from Displays 10.10 and 10.11. Suppose `list1` and `list2` are then declared as follows:

```
PFArrayD list1(10), list2(20);
```

---

[5] If you have already read the section of Chapter 7 on vectors, you will notice that the class defined here is a weak version of a vector. Even though you can use a vector anyplace that you would use this class, this is still an instructive example using many of the techniques we discussed in this chapter. Moreover, this example will give you some insight into how a vector class might be implemented.

Display 10.10   Definition of a Class with a Dynamic Array Member

```
1
2    //Objects of this class are partially filled arrays of doubles.
3    class PFArrayD
4    {
5    public:
6        PFArrayD( );
7        //Initializes with a capacity of 50.

8        PFArrayD(int capacityValue);

                                                    ── Copy constructor
9        PFArrayD(const PFArrayD& pfaObject);

10       void addElement(double element);
11       //Precondition: The array is not full.
12       //Postcondition: The element has been added.

13       bool full( ) const { return (capacity == used); }
14       //Returns true if the array is full, false otherwise.

15       int getCapacity( ) const { return capacity; }

16       int getNumberUsed( ) const { return used; }

17       void emptyArray( ){ used = 0; }
18       //Empties the array.

19       double& operator[](int index);
20       //Read and change access to elements 0 through numberUsed - 1.

                                                    Overloaded
                                                    assignment
21       PFArrayD& operator =(const PFArrayD& rightSide);

22       ~PFArrayD( );
23   private:                                       Destructor
24       double *a; //For an array of doubles
25       int capacity; //For the size of the array
26       int used; //For the number of array positions currently in use

27   };
```

Display 10.11   Member Function Definitions for PFArrayD Class *(part 1 of 2)*

```
1
2   //These are the definitions for the member functions for the class PFArrayD.
3   //They require the following include and using directives:
4   //#include <iostream>
5   //using std::cout;

6   PFArrayD::PFArrayD( ) :capacity(50), used(0)
7   {
8       a = new double[capacity];
9   }

10  PFArrayD::PFArrayD(int size) :capacity(size), used(0)
11  {
12      a = new double[capacity];
13  }

14  PFArrayD::PFArrayD(const PFArrayD& pfaObject)
15    :capacity(pfaObject.getCapacity( )), used(pfaObject.getNumberUsed( ))
16  {
17      a = new double[capacity];
18      for (int i =0; i < used; i++)
19          a[i] = pfaObject.a[i];
20  }

21  void PFArrayD::addElement(double element)
22  {
23      if (used >= capacity)
24      {
25          cout << "Attempt to exceed capacity in PFArrayD.\n";
26          exit(0);
27      }
28      a[used] = element;
29      used++;
30  }
31
32  double& PFArrayD::operator[](int index)
33  {
34      if (index >= used)
35      {
36          cout << "Illegal index in PFArrayD.\n";
37          exit(0);
38      }

39      return a[index];
40  }
```

Display 10.11   **Member Function Definitions for PFArrayD Class** *(part 2 of 2)*

```
41   PFArrayD& PFArrayD::operator =(const PFArrayD& rightSide)
42   {
43       if (capacity != rightSide.capacity)
44       {
45           delete [] a;
46           a = new double[rightSide.capacity];
47       }

48       capacity = rightSide.capacity;
49       used = rightSide.used;
50       for (int i = 0; i < used; i++)
51           a[i] = rightSide.a[i];

52       return *this;
53   }

54   PFArrayD::~PFArrayD( )
55   {
56       delete [] a;
57   }
58
```

Note that this also checks for the case of having the same object on both sides of the assignment operator.

Display 10.12   **Demonstration Program for PFArrayD** *(part 1 of 3)*

```
1    //Program to demonstrate the class PFArrayD
2    #include <iostream>
3    using std::cin;
4    using std::cout;
5    using std::endl;

6    class PFArrayD
7    {
8        <The rest of the class definition is the same as in Display 10.10.>
9    };

10   void testPFArrayD( );
11   //Conducts one test of the class PFArrayD.

12   int main( )
13   {
14       cout << "This program tests the class PFArrayD.\n";
```

In Section 11.1 of Chapter 11 we show you how to divide this long file into three shorter files corresponding roughly to Displays 10.10, 10.11, and this display without the code from Displays 10.10 and 10.11.

Display 10.12   Demonstration Program for PFArrayD (part 2 of 3)

```
15        char ans;
16        do
17        {
18            testPFArrayD( );
19            cout << "Test again? (y/n) ";
20            cin >> ans;
21        }while ((ans == 'y') || (ans == 'Y'));


22        return 0;
23    }


24        <The definitions of the member functions for the class PFArrayD go here. >


25    void testPFArrayD( )
26    {
27        int cap;
28        cout << "Enter capacity of this super array: ";
29        cin >> cap;
30        PFArrayD temp(cap);


31
32        cout << "Enter up to " << cap << " nonnegative numbers.\n";
33        cout << "Place a negative number at the end.\n";


34        double next;
35        cin >> next;
36        while ((next >= 0) && (!temp.full( )))
37        {
38            temp.addElement(next);
39            cin >> next;
40        }


41        cout << "You entered the following "
42                << temp.getNumberUsed( ) << " numbers:\n";
43        int index;
44        int count = temp.getNumberUsed( );
45        for (index = 0; index < count; index++)
46            cout << temp[index] << " ";
47        cout << endl;
48        cout << "(plus a sentinel value.)\n";
49    }
```

Display 10.12   Demonstration Program for PFArrayD *(part 3 of 3)*

SAMPLE DIALOGUE

```
This program tests the class PFArrayD.
Enter capacity of this super array: 10
Enter up to 10 nonnegative numbers.
Place a negative number at the end.
1.1
2.2
3.3
4.4
-1
You entered the following 4 numbers:
1.1 2.2 3.3 4.4
(plus a sentinel value.)
Test again? (y/n) n
```

If list2 has been given a list of numbers with invocations of list2.addElement, then even though we are assuming that there is no overloading of the assignment operator, the following assignment statement is still defined, but its meaning may not be what you would like it to be:

```
list1 = list2;
```

With no overloading of the assignment operator, the default predefined assignment operator is used. As usual, this predefined version of the assignment operator copies the value of each of the member variables of list2 to the corresponding member variables of list1. Thus, the value of list1.a is changed to be the same as list2.a, the value of list1.capacity is changed to be the same as list2.capacity, and the value of list1.used is changed to be the same as list2.used. But this can cause problems.

The member variable list1.a contains a pointer, and the assignment statement sets this pointer equal to the same value as list2.a. Both list1.a and list2.a therefore point to the same place in memory. Thus, if you change the array list1.a, you will also change the array list2.a. Similarly, if you change the array list2.a, you will also change the array list1.a. This is not what we normally want. We usually want the assignment operator to produce a completely independent copy of the thing on the right-hand side. The way to fix this is to overload the assignment operator so that it does what we want it to do with objects of the class PFArrayD. This is what we have done in Displays 10.10 and 10.11.

The definition of the overloaded assignment operator in Display 10.11 is reproduced below:

```
PFArrayD& PFArrayD::operator =(const PFArrayD& rightSide)
{
```

```
        if (capacity != rightSide.capacity)
        {
            delete [] a;
            a = new double[rightSide.capacity];
        }

        capacity = rightSide.capacity;
        used = rightSide.used;
        for (int i = 0; i < used; i++)
            a[i] = rightSide.a[i];

        return *this;
}
```

= must be a member

When you overload the assignment operator it must be a member of the class; it cannot be a friend of the class. That is why the above definition has only one parameter. For example, consider the following:

```
list1 = list2;
```

calling object for =

In the above call, `list1` is the calling object and `list2` is the argument to the member operator =.

Notice that the capacities of the two objects are checked to see if they are equal. If they are not equal, then the array member variable a of the left side (that is, of the calling object) is destroyed using `delete` and a new array with the appropriate capacity is created using `new`. This ensures that the object on the left side of the assignment operator will have an array of the correct size, but also does something else that is very important: It ensures that if the same object occurs on both sides of the assignment operator, then the array named by the member variable a will not be deleted with a call to `delete`. To see why this is important, consider the following alternative and simpler definition of the overloaded assignment operator:

```
//This version has a bug:
PFArrayD& PFArrayD::operator =(const PFArrayD& rightSide)
{
    delete [] a;
    a = new double[rightSide.capacity];

    capacity = rightSide.capacity;
    used = rightSide.used;
    for (int i = 0; i < used; i++)
        a[i] = rightSide.a[i];

    return *this;
}
```

This version has a problem when used in an assignment with the same object on both sides of the assignment operator, like the following:

```
myList = myList;
```

When this assignment is executed, the first statement executed is

```
delete [] a;
```

But the calling object is myList, so this means

```
delete [] myList.a;
```

The pointer myList.a is then undefined. The assignment operator has corrupted the object myList. This problem cannot happen with the definition of the overloaded assignment operator we gave in Display 10.11.

SHALLOW COPY AND DEEP COPY

When defining an overloaded assignment operator or a copy constructor, if your code simply copies the contents of member variables from one object to the other that is known as a *shallow copy*. The default assignment operator and the default copy constructor perform shallow copies. If there are no pointers or dynamically allocated data involved, this works fine. If some member variable names a dynamic array or (points to some other dynamic structure), then you normally do not want a shallow copy. Instead, you want to create a copy of what each member variable is pointing to, so that you get a separate but identical copy, as illustrated in Display 10.11. This is called a *deep copy* and is what we normally do when overloading the assignment operator or defining a copy constructor.

▪ DESTRUCTORS

Dynamically allocated variables have one problem: They do not go away unless your program makes a suitable call to delete. Even if the dynamic variable was created using a local pointer variable and the local pointer variable goes away at the end of a function call, the dynamic variable will remain unless there is a call to delete. If you do not eliminate dynamic variables with calls to delete, the dynamic variables will continue to occupy memory space, which may cause your program to abort by using up all the memory in the freestore manager. Moreover, if the dynamic variable is embedded in the implementation details of a class, the programmer who uses the class may not know about the dynamic variable and cannot be expected to perform the calls to delete. In fact, since the data members are normally private members, the programmer normally *cannot* access the needed pointer variables and so *cannot* call delete with these pointer variables. To handle this problem, C++ has a special kind of member function called a *destructor.*

A **destructor** is a member function that is called automatically when an object of the class passes out of scope. If your program contains a local variable that names an

destructor

object from a class with a destructor, then when the function call ends, the destructor will be called automatically. If the destructor is defined correctly, the destructor will call `delete` to eliminate all the dynamically allocated variables created by the object. This may be done with a single call to `delete` or it may require several calls to `delete`. You may also want your destructor to perform some other clean-up details as well, but returning memory to the freestore manager for reuse is the main job of the destructor.

destructor
name

The member function `~PFArrayD` is the destructor for the class `PFArrayD` shown in Display 10.10. Like a constructor, a destructor always has the same name as the class of which it is a member, but the destructor has the tilde symbol, ~, at the beginning of its name (so you can tell that it is a destructor and not a constructor). Like a constructor, a destructor has no type for the value returned, not even the type `void`. A destructor has no parameters. Thus, a class can have only one destructor; you cannot overload the destructor for a class. Otherwise, a destructor is defined just like any other member function.

Notice the definition of the destructor `~PFArrayD` given in Display 10.11. `~PFArrayD` calls `delete` to eliminate the dynamically allocated array pointed to by the member pointer variable a. Look again at the function `testPFArrayD` in the sample program shown in Display 10.12. The local variable `temp` contains a dynamic array pointed to by the member variable `temp.a`. If this class did not have a destructor, then after the call to `testPFArrayD` ended, this dynamic array would still be occupying memory, even though the dynamic array is useless to the program. Moreover, every iteration of the do–while loop would produce another useless dynamic array to clutter up memory. If the loop is iterated enough times, the function calls could consume all the memory in the freestore manager and your program would then end abnormally.

DESTRUCTOR

The destructor of a class is a member function of a class that is called automatically when an object of the class goes out of scope. Among other things, this means that if an object of the class type is a local variable for a function, then the destructor is automatically called as the last action before the function call ends. Destructors are used to eliminate any dynamically allocated variables that have been created by the object so that the memory occupied by these dynamic variables is returned to the freestore manager for reuse. Destructors may perform other clean-up tasks as well. The name of a destructor must consist of the tilde symbol, ~, followed by the name of the class.

◼ COPY CONSTRUCTORS

copy
constructor

A **copy constructor** is a constructor that has one parameter that is of the same type as the class. The one parameter must be a call-by-reference parameter, and normally the parameter is preceded by the `const` parameter modifier, so it is a constant parameter. In all other respects a copy constructor is defined in the same way as any other constructor and can be used just like other constructors. For example, a program that uses the class PFArrayD defined in Display 10.10 might contain the following:

```
PFArrayD b(20);
for (int i = 0; i < 20; i++)
    b.addElement(i);
PFArrayD temp(b);//Initialized by the copy constructor
```

The object b is initialized with the constructor that has a parameter of type int. Similarly, the object temp is initialized by the constructor that has one argument of type const PFArrayD&. When used in this way a copy constructor is being used just like any other constructor.

A copy constructor should be defined so that the object being initialized becomes a complete, independent copy of its argument. So, in the declaration

```
PFArrayD temp(b);
```

the member variable temp.a should not be simply set to the same value as b.a; that would produce two pointers pointing to the same dynamic array. The definition of the copy constructor is shown in Display 10.11. Note that in the definition of the copy constructor, a new dynamic array is created and the contents of one dynamic array are copied to the other dynamic array. Thus, in the above declaration, temp is initialized so that its array member variable is different from the array member variable of b. The two array member variables, temp.a and b.a, contain the same values of type double, but if a change is made to one of these array member variables, it has no effect on the other array member variable. Thus, any change that is made to temp will have no effect on b.

As you have seen, a copy constructor can be used just like any other constructor. A copy constructor is also called automatically in certain other situations. Roughly speaking, whenever C++ needs to make a copy of an object, it automatically calls the copy constructor. In particular, the copy constructor is called automatically in three circumstances:

1. When a class object is being declared and is initialized by another object of the same type given in parentheses. (This is the case of using the copy constructor like any other constructor.)
2. When a function returns a value of the class type.
3. Whenever an argument of the class type is "plugged in" for a call-by-value parameter. In this case, the copy constructor defines what is meant by "plugging in."

If you do not define a copy constructor for a class, C++ will automatically generate a copy constructor for you. However, this default copy constructor simply copies the contents of member variables and does not work correctly for classes with pointers or dynamic data in their member variables. Thus, if your class member variables involve pointers, dynamic arrays, or other dynamic data, you should define a copy constructor for the class.

To see why you need a copy constructor, let's see what would happen if we did not define a copy constructor for the class PFArrayD. *Suppose we did not include the copy*

why a copy constructor is needed

constructor in the definition of the class PFArrayD and suppose we used a call-by-value parameter in a function definition, for example:

```
void showPFArrayD(PFArrayD parameter)
{
    cout << "The first value is: "
         << parameter[0] << endl;
}
```

Consider the following code, which includes a function call:

```
PFArrayD sample(2);
sample.addElement(5.5);
sample.addElement(6.6);
showPFArrayD(sample);
cout << "After call: " << sample[0] << endl;
```

Because no copy constructor is defined for the class PFArrayD, the class has a default copy constructor that simply copies the contents of member variables. Things then proceed as follows. When the function call is executed, the value of sample is copied to the local variable parameter, so parameter.a is set equal to sample.a. But these are pointer variables, so during the function call parameter.a and sample.a point to the same dynamic array, as follows:

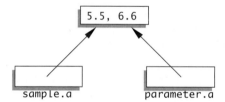

When the function call ends, the destructor for PFArrayD is called to return the memory used by parameter to the freestore manager so it can be reused. The definition of the destructor contains the following statement:

```
delete [] a;
```

Since the destructor is called with the object parameter, this statement is equivalent to

```
delete [] parameter.a;
```

which changes the picture to the following:

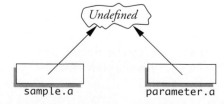

Since `sample.a` and `parameter.a` point to the same dynamic array, deleting `parameter.a` is the same as deleting `sample.a`. Thus, `sample.a` is undefined when the program reaches the statement

```
cout << "After call: " << sample[0] << endl;
```

so this `cout` statement is undefined. The `cout` statement may by chance give you the output you want, but sooner or later the fact that `sample.a` is undefined will produce problems. One major problem occurs when the object `sample` is a local variable in some function. In this case the destructor will be called with `sample` when the function call ends. That destructor call will be equivalent to

```
delete [] sample.a;
```

But, as we just saw, the dynamic array pointed to by `sample.a` has already been deleted once, and now the system is trying to delete it a second time. Calling `delete` twice to delete the same dynamic array (or any other variable created with `new`) can produce a serious system error that can cause your program to crash.

That was what would happen if there were no copy constructor. Fortunately, we included a copy constructor in our definition of the class `PFArrayD`, so the copy constructor is called automatically when the following function call is executed:

```
showPFArrayD(sample);
```

The copy constructor defines what it means to plug in the argument `sample` for the call-by-value parameter named `parameter`, so that now the picture is as follows:

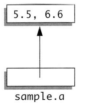
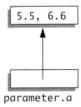

Thus, any change that is made to `parameter.a` has no effect on the argument `sample`, and there are no problems with the destructor. If the destructor is called for `parameter` and then called for `sample`, each call to the destructor deletes a different dynamic array.

When a function returns a value of a class type, the copy constructor is called automatically to copy the value specified by the `return` statement. If there is no copy constructor, problems similar to what we described for call-by-value parameters will occur. — **returned value**

If a class definition involves pointers and dynamically allocated memory using the `new` operator, you need to include a copy constructor. Classes that do not involve pointers or dynamically allocated memory do not need to define a copy constructor. — **when you need a copy constructor**

assignment
statements

Contrary to what you might expect, the copy constructor is *not* called when you set one object equal to another using the assignment operator.[6] However, if you do not like what the default assignment operator does, you can redefine the assignment operator as we have done in Displays 10.10 and 10.11.

COPY CONSTRUCTOR

A copy constructor is a constructor that has one call-by-reference parameter that is of the same type as the class. The one parameter must be a call-by-reference parameter; normally, the parameter is also a constant parameter—that is, it is preceded by the const parameter modifier. The copy constructor for a class is called automatically whenever a function returns a value of the class type. The copy constructor is also called automatically whenever an argument is plugged in for a call-by-value parameter of the class type. A copy constructor can also be used in the same ways as other constructors.

Any class that uses pointers and the new operator should have a copy constructor.

THE BIG THREE

The copy constructor, the = assignment operator, and the destructor are called the *big three* because experts say that if you need any of them, you need all three. If any of these is missing, the compiler will create it, but the created item might not behave as you want. Thus, it pays to define them yourself. The copy constructor and overloaded = assignment operator that the compiler generates for you will work fine if all member variables are of predefined types such as int and double. For any class that uses pointers and the new operator, it is safest to define your own copy constructor, overloaded =, and a destructor.

Self-Test Exercises

13. If a class is named MyClass and it has a constructor, what is the constructor named? If MyClass has a destructor what is the destructor named?

14. Suppose you change the definition of the destructor in Display 10.11 to the following. How would the sample dialogue in Display 10.12 change?

```
PFArrayD::~PFArrayD( )
{
```

---

[6] C++ makes a distinction between initialization (the three cases where the copy constructor is called) and assignment. Initialization uses the copy constructor to create a new object; the assignment operator takes an existing object and modifies it so that it is an identical copy (in all but location) of the right-hand side of the assignment.

```
        cout << "\nGood-bye cruel world! The short life of\n"
             << "this dynamic array is about to end.\n";
        delete [] a;
    }
```

15. The following is the first line of the copy constructor definition for the class `PFArrayD`. The identifier `PFArrayD` occurs three times and means something slightly different each time. What does it mean in each of the three cases?

    `PFArrayD::PFArrayD(const PFArrayD& pfaObject)`

16. Answer these questions about destructors.

    a. What is a destructor and what must the name of a destructor be?

    b. When is a destructor called?

    c. What does a destructor actually do?

    d. What *should* a destructor do?

17. a. Explain carefully why no overloaded assignment operator is needed when the only data consists of built-in types.

    b. Same as part a for a copy constructor.

    c. Same as part a for a destructor.

Chapter Summary

- A pointer is a memory address, so a pointer provides a way to indirectly name a variable by naming the address of the variable in the computer's memory.

- Dynamic variables (also called dynamically allocated variables) are variables that are created (and destroyed) while a program is running.

- Memory for dynamic variables is in a special portion of the computer's memory called the freestore managers. When a program is finished with a dynamic variable, the memory used by the dynamic variable can be returned to the freestore manager for reuse; this is done with a `delete` statement.

- A dynamically allocated array (also called simply a dynamic array) is an array whose size is determined when the program is running. A dynamic array is implemented as a dynamic variable of an array type.

- A destructor is a special kind of member function for a class. A destructor is called automatically when an object of the class passes out of scope. The main reason for destructors is to return memory to the freestore manager so the memory can be reused.

- A copy constructor is a constructor that has a single argument that is of the same type as the class. If you define a copy constructor, it will be called automatically whenever a function returns a value of the class type and whenever an argument is plugged in for a call-by-value parameter of the class type. Any class that uses pointers and the operator new should have a copy constructor.

- When overloading the assignment operator, it must be overloaded as a member operator. Be sure to check that your overloading works when the same variable is on both sides of the overloaded assignment operator.

ANSWERS TO SELF-TEST EXERCISES

1. A pointer is the memory address of a variable.

2. ```
   int *p;    // This declares a pointer to an int variable.
   *p = 17; //Here, * is the dereferencing operator. This assigns
               //17 to the memory location pointed to by p.
   void func(int* p); // Declares p to be a pointer value
                         // parameter.
   ```

3. ```
   10 20
   20 20
   30 30
   ```

   If you replace *p1 = 30; with *p2 = 30;, the output would be the same.

4. ```
   10 20
   20 20
   30 20
   ```

5. To the unwary or to the neophyte, this looks like two objects of type pointer to int, that is, int*. Unfortunately, the * binds to the *identifier*, not to the type (that is, not to the int). The result is that this declaration declares intPtr1 to be an int pointer, while intPtr2 is an ordinary int variable.

6. `delete p;`

7. ```
   typedef double* NumberPtr;
   NumberPtr myPoint;
   ```

8. The new operator takes a type for its argument. new allocates space on the freestore for a variable of the type of the argument. It returns a pointer to that memory, provided there is enough space. If there is not enough space, the new operator may return NULL, or may abort the program, depending on how your particular compiler works.

9. `typedef char* CharArray;`

10. ```
    cout << "Enter 10 integers:\n";
    for (int i = 0; i < 10; i++)
        cin >> entry[i];
    ```
    ```

11. `delete [] entry;`

12. `0 1 2 3 4 5 6 7 8 9`

13. The *constructor* is named `MyClass`, the same name as the name of the class. The *destructor* is named `~MyClass`.

14. The dialogue would change to the following:

```
This program tests the class PFArrayD.
Enter capacity of this super array: 10
Enter up to 10 nonnegative numbers.
Place a negative number at the end.
1.1
2.2
3.3
4.4
-1
You entered the following 4 numbers:
1.1 2.2 3.3 4.4
(plus a sentinel value.)

Good-bye cruel world! The short life of
this dynamic array is about to end.
Test again? (y/n) n
```

15. The `PFArrayD` before the `::` is the name of the class. The `PFArrayD` right after the `::` is the name of the member function. (Remember, a constructor is a member function that has the same name as the class.) The `PFArrayD` inside the parentheses is the type for the parameter `pfaObject`.

16. a. A destructor is a member function of a class. A destructor's name always begins with a tilde, , followed by the class name.

    b. A destructor is called when a class object goes out of scope.

    c. A destructor actually does whatever the class author programs it to do!

    d. A destructor is *supposed* to delete dynamic variables that have been allocated by constructors for the class. Destructors may also do other clean-up tasks.

17. In the case of the assignment operator = and the copy constructor, if there are only built-in types for data, the copy mechanism is exactly what you want, so the default works fine. In the case of the destructor, no dynamic memory allocation is done (no pointers), so the default do-nothing action is again what you want.

PROGRAMMING PROJECTS

1. Reread the code in Display 10.9. Then, write a class TwoD that implements the two-dimensional dynamic array of doubles using ideas from this display in its constructors. You should have a private member of type pointer to double to point to the dynamic array, and two int (or unsigned int) values that are MaxRows and MaxCols.

   You should supply a default constructor for which you are to choose a default maximum row and column sizes and a parameterized constructor that allows the programmer to set maximum row and column sizes.

   Further, you should provide a void member function that allows setting a particular row and column entry and a member function that returns a particular row and column entry as a value of type double.

   Remark: It's difficult or impossible (depending on the details) to overload [] so it works as you would like for two-dimensional arrays. So simply use accessor and mutator functions using ordinary function notation.

   Overload the + operator as a friend function to add two two-dimensional arrays. This function should return the TwoD object whose ith row, jth column element is the sum of the ith row, jth column element of the left-hand operand TwoD object and the ith row, jth column element of the right-hand operand TwoD object.

   Provide a copy constructor, an overloaded operator=, and a destructor.

   Declare class member functions that do not change the data as const members.

2. Using dynamic arrays, implement a polynomial class with polynomial addition, subtraction, and multiplication.

   Discussion: A variable in a polynomial does nothing but act as a placeholder for the coefficients. Hence, the only interesting thing about polynomials is the array of coefficients and the corresponding exponent. Think about the polynomial

   ```
   x*x*x + x + 1
   ```

   Where is the term in x*x? One simple way to implement the polynomial class is to use an array of doubles to store the coefficients. The index of the array is the exponent of the corresponding term. If a term is missing, then it simply has a zero coefficient.

   There are techniques for representing polynomials of high degree with many missing terms. These use so-called sparse matrix techniques. Unless you already know these techniques, or learn very quickly, don't use these techniques.

   Provide a default constructor, a copy constructor, and a parameterized constructor that enables an arbitrary polynomial to be constructed.

Supply an overloaded operator = and a destructor.

Provide these operations:

polynomial + polynomial, constant + polynomial, polynomial + constant,

polynomial – polynomial, constant – polynomial, polynomial – constant.

polynomial * polynomial, constant * polynomial, polynomial * constant,

Supply functions to assign and extract coefficients, indexed by exponent.

Supply a function to evaluate the polynomial at a value of type `double`.

You should decide whether to implement these functions as members, friends, or stand-alone functions.

11 CHAPTER

Separate Compilation and Namespaces

11 Separate Compilation and Namespaces

From mine own library with volumes that
I prize above my dukedom.

William Shakespeare, *The Tempest*

INTRODUCTION

This chapter covers two topics that have to do with how to organize a C++ program into separate parts. Section 11.1 on separate compilation discusses how a C++ program can be distributed across a number of files so that when some parts of the program change only those parts need to be recompiled and so that the separate parts can be more easily reused in other applications.

Section 11.2 discusses namespaces, which were introduced briefly in Chapter 1. Namespaces are a way of allowing you to reuse the names of classes, functions, and other items by qualifying the names to indicate different uses. Namespaces divide your code into sections so that the different sections may reuse the same names with differing meanings. They allow a kind of local meaning for names that is more general than local variables.

This chapter can be covered earlier than its location in the book. This chapter does not use any of the material from Chapters 5 (arrays), 9 (strings), 10 (pointers and dynamic arrays) or Section 7.3 (vectors) of Chapter 7.

11.1 Separate Compilation

Your "if" is the only peacemaker; much virtue in "if."

William Shakespeare, *As You Like It*

C++ has facilities for dividing a program into parts that are kept in separate files, compiled separately, and then linked together when (or just before) the program is run. You can place the definition for a class (and its associated function definitions) in files that are separate from the programs that use the class. In this way you can build up a library of classes so that many programs can use the same class. You can compile the class once and then use it in many different programs, just like you use the predefined libraries such as those with header files `iostream` and `cstdlib`. Moreover, you can define the class itself in two files so that the specification of what the class does is separate from how the class is implemented. If you only change the implementation of the class, then you need only recompile the file containing the class implementation. The other files, including the files containing the programs that use the class, need not be changed or even recompiled. This section tells you how to carry out this separate compilation of classes.

ENCAPSULATION REVIEWED

The principle of encapsulation says that you should separate the specification of how the class is used by a programmer from the details of how the class is implemented. The separation should be so complete that you can change the implementation without needing to change any program that uses the class. The way to ensure this separation can be summarized in three rules:

1. Make all the member variables private members of the class.

2. Make each of the basic operations for the class either a public member function of the class, a friend function, an ordinary function, or an overloaded operator. Group the class definition and the function and operator declarations (prototypes) together. This group, along with its accompanying comments, is called the **interface** for the class. Fully specify how to use each such function or operator in a comment given with the class or with the function or operator declaration.

interface

3. Make the implementation of the basic operations unavailable to the programmer who uses the class. The **implementation** consists of the function definitions and overloaded operator definitions (along with any helping functions or other additional items these definitions require).

Implementation

In C++, the best way to ensure that you follow these rules is to place the interface and the implementation of the class in separate files. As you might guess, the file that contains the interface is often called the **interface file**, and the file that contains the implementation is called the **implementation file**. The exact details of how to set up, compile, and use these files will vary slightly from one version of C++ to another, but the basic scheme is the same in all versions of C++. In particular, the details of what goes into the files is the same in all systems. The only things that vary are the commands used to compile and link these files. The details about what goes into these files are illustrated in the next subsection.

interface file and implementation file

A typical class has private member variables. Private member variables (and private member functions) present a problem to our basic philosophy of placing the interface and the implementation of a class in separate files. The public part of the definition for a class is part of the interface for the class, but the private part is part of the implementation. This is a problem because C++ will not allow you to split the class definition across two files. Thus, some sort of compromise is needed. The only sensible compromise is to place the entire class definition in the interface file. Since a programmer who is using the class cannot use any of the private members of the class, the private members will, in effect, still be hidden from the programmer.

Private members are part of the implementation.

■ HEADER FILES AND IMPLEMENTATION FILES

Display 11.1 contains the interface file for a class called DigitalTime. DigitalTime is a class whose values are times of day, such as 9:30. Only the public members of the class are part of the interface. The private members are part of the implementation, even though they are in the interface file. The label private: warns you that these private members are not part of the public interface. Everything that a programmer needs to know in order to use the class DigitalTime is explained in the comment at the start of the file and in the comments in the public section of the class definition. As noted in the comment at the top of the interface file, this class uses 24-hour notation, so, for instance, 1:30 P.M. is input and output as 13:30. This and the other details you must know in order to effectively use the class DigitalTime are included in the comments given with the member functions.

header files

We have placed the interface in a file named dtime.h. The suffix .h indicates that this is a **header file**. An interface file is always a header file and so always ends with the suffix .h. Any program that uses the class DigitalTime must contain an include directive like the following, which names this file:

```
#include "dtime.h"
```

include

When you write an include directive, you must indicate whether the header file is a predefined header file that is provided for you or is a header file that you wrote. If the header file is predefined, write the header file name in angular brackets, like <iostream>. If the header file is one that you wrote, write the header file name in quotes, like "dtime.h". This distinction tells the compiler where to look for the header file. If the header file name is in angular brackets, the compiler looks wherever the predefined header files are kept in your implementation of C++. If the header file name is in quotes, the compiler looks in the current directory or wherever programmer-defined header files are kept on your system.

file names

Any program that uses our DigitalTime class must contain the above include directive that names the header file dtime.h. That is enough to allow you to compile the program, but is not enough to allow you to run the program. In order to run the program you must write (and compile) the definitions of the member functions and the overloaded operators. We have placed these function and operator definitions in another file, which is called the *implementation file*. Although it is not required by most compilers, it is traditional to give the interface file and the implementation file the same name. The two files do, however, end in different suffixes. We have placed the interface for our class in the file named dtime.h and the implementation for our class in a file named dtime.cpp. The suffix you use for the implementation file depends on your version of C++. Use the same suffix for the implementation file as you normally use for files that contain C++ programs. (Other common suffixes are .cxx and .hxx.) The implementation file for our DigitalTime class is given in Display 11.2. After we explain how the various files for our class interact with each other, we will return to Display 11.2 and discuss the details of the definitions in this implementation file.

Display 11.1   Interface File for the DigitalTime Class

```
 1   //This is the header file dtime.h. This is the interface for the class DigitalTime.
 2   //Values of this type are times of day. The values are input and output in 24-hour
 3   //notation, as in 9:30 for 9:30 AM and 14:45 for 2:45 PM.
 4   #include <iostream>
 5   using namespace std;

 6   class DigitalTime
 7   {
 8   public:
 9       DigitalTime(int theHour, int theMinute);
10       DigitalTime( );
11       //Initializes the time value to 0:00 (which is midnight).

12       getHour( ) const;
13       getMinute( ) const;
14       void advance(int minutesAdded);
15       //Changes the time to minutesAdded minutes later.

16       void advance(int hoursAdded, int minutesAdded);
17       //Changes the time to hoursAdded hours plus minutesAdded minutes later.

18       friend bool operator ==(const DigitalTime& time1,
19                               const DigitalTime& time2);

20       friend istream& operator >>(istream& ins, DigitalTime& theObject);

21       friend ostream& operator <<(ostream& outs, const DigitalTime& theObject);
22       private:
```

These member variables and helping functions are part of the implementation. They are not part of the interface. The word private indicates that they are not part of the public interface.

```
23       int hour;
24       int minute;

25       static void readHour(int& theHour);
26       //Precondition: Next input to be read from the keyboard is
27       //a time in notation, like 9:45 or 14:45.
28       //Postcondition: theHour has been set to the hour part of the time.
29       //The colon has been discarded and the next input to be read is the minute.

30       static void readMinute(int& theMinute);
31       //Reads the minute from the keyboard after readHour has read the hour.

32       static int digitToInt(char c);
33       //Precondition: c is one of the digits '0' through '9'.
34       //Returns the integer for the digit; for example, digitToInt('3') returns 3.
35
36   };
```

Display 11.2 Implementation File *(part 1 of 3)*

```
1   //This is the implementation file dtime.cpp of the class DigitalTime.
2   //The interface for the class DigitalTime is in the header file dtime.h.
3   #include <iostream>
4   #include <cctype>
5   #include <cstdlib>
6   using namespace std;
7   #include "dtime.h"

8   //Uses iostream and cstdlib:
9   DigitalTime::DigitalTime(int theHour, int theMinute)
10  {
11      if (theHour < 0 || theHour > 24 || theMinute < 0 || theMinute > 59)
12      {
13          cout << "Illegal argument to DigitalTime constructor.";
14          exit(1);
15      }
16      else
17      {
18          hour = theHour;
19          minute = theMinute;
20      }

21      if (hour == 24)
22          hour = 0; //Standardize midnight as 0:00
23  }

24  DigitalTime::DigitalTime( )
25  {
26      hour = 0;
27      minute = 0;
28  }

29  int DigitalTime::getHour( ) const
30  {
31      return hour;
32  }

34  int DigitalTime::getMinute( ) const
35  {
36      return minute;
37  }

38  void DigitalTime::advance(int minutesAdded)
39  {
40      int grossMinutes = minute + minutesAdded;
41      minute = grossMinutes%60;
42      int hourAdjustment = grossMinutes/60;
```

Display 11.2   Implementation File *(part 2 of 3)*

```
43        hour = (hour + hourAdjustment)%24;
44    }

45    void DigitalTime::advance(int hoursAdded, int minutesAdded)
46    {
47        hour = (hour + hoursAdded)%24;
48        advance(minutesAdded);
49    }

50    bool operator ==(const DigitalTime& time1, const DigitalTime& time2)
51    {
52        return (time1.hour == time2.hour && time1.minute == time2.minute);
53    }

54    //Uses iostream:
55    ostream& operator <<(ostream& outs, const DigitalTime& theObject)
56    {
57        outs << theObject.hour << ':';
58        if (theObject.minute < 10)
59            outs << '0';
60        outs << theObject.minute;
61        return outs;
62    }
63
64    //Uses iostream:
65    istream& operator >>(istream& ins, DigitalTime& theObject)
66    {
67        DigitalTime::readHour(theObject.hour);
68        DigitalTime::readMinute(theObject.minute);
69        return ins;
70    }

71    int DigitalTime::digitToInt(char c)
72    {
73        return ( int(c) - int('0') );
74    }

75    //Uses iostream, cctype, and cstdlib:
76    void DigitalTime::readMinute(int& theMinute)
77    {
78        char c1, c2;
79        cin >> c1 >> c2;

80        if (!(isdigit(c1) && isdigit(c2)))
81        {
82            cout << "Error: illegal input to readMinute\n";
83            exit(1);
84    }
```

Display 11.2   Implementation File *(part 3 of 3)*

```
85        theMinute = digitToInt(c1)*10 + digitToInt(c2);

86        if (theMinute < 0 || theMinute > 59)
87        {
88            cout << "Error: illegal input to readMinute\n";
89            exit(1);
90        }
91   }
92
93   //Uses iostream, cctype, and cstdlib:
94   void DigitalTime::readHour(int& theHour)
95   {
96        char c1, c2;
97        cin >> c1 >> c2;
98        if ( !( isdigit(c1) && (isdigit(c2) || c2 == ':' ) ) )
99        {
100           cout << "Error: illegal input to readHour\n";
101           exit(1);
102       }

103       if (isdigit(c1) && c2 == ':')
104       {
105           theHour = DigitalTime::digitToInt(c1);
106       }
107       else //(isdigit(c1) && isdigit(c2))
108       {
109           theHour = DigitalTime::digitToInt(c1)*10
110                   + DigitalTime::digitToInt(c2);
111           cin >> c2; //discard ':'
112           if (c2 != ':')
113           {
114               cout << "Error: illegal input to readHour\n";
115               exit(1);
116           }
117       }

118       if (theHour == 24)
119           theHour = 0; //Standardize midnight as 0:00

120       if ( theHour < 0 || theHour > 23 )
121       {
122           cout << "Error: illegal input to readHour\n";
123           exit(1);
124       }
125   }
```

Any file that uses the class `DigitalTime` must contain the include directive

```
#include "dtime.h"
```

Thus, both the implementation file and the program file must contain the `include` directive that names the interface file. The file that contains the program (that is, the file that contains the `main` function) is often called the **application file** or **driver file.** Display 11.3 contains an application file with a very simple program that uses and demonstrates the `DigitalTime` class.

application file or driver file

The exact details of how to run this complete program, which is contained in three files, depend on what system you are using. However, the basic details are the same for all systems. You must compile the implementation file and you must compile the application file that contains the `main` function. You do not compile the interface file, which in this example is the file `dtime.h` given in Display 11.1. You do not need to compile the interface file because the compiler thinks the contents of this interface file are already contained in each of the other two files. Recall that both the implementation file and the application file contain the directive

compiling and running the program

```
#include "dtime.h"
```

Compiling your program automatically invokes a preprocessor that reads this `include` directive and replaces it with the text in the file `dtime.h`. Thus, the compiler sees the contents of `dtime.h`, and so the file `dtime.h` does not need to be compiled separately. (In fact, the compiler sees the contents of `dtime.h` twice: once when you compile the implementation file and once when you compile the application file.) This copying of the file `dtime.h` is only a conceptual copying. The compiler acts as if the contents of `dtime.h` were copied into each file that has the `include` directive. However, if you look in those files after they are compiled, you will only find the `include` directive; you will not find the contents of the file `dtime.h`.

Once the implementation file and the application file are compiled, you still need to connect these files so that they can work together. This is called **linking** the files and is done by a separate utility called a **linker**. The details of how to call the linker depends on what system you are using. Often, the command to run a program automatically invokes the linker, so you need not explicitly call the linker at all. After the files are linked, you can run your program.

linking

linker

This sounds like a complicated process, but many systems have facilities that manage much of this detail for you automatically or semiautomatically. On any system, the details quickly become routine. On UNIX systems, these details are handled by the **make** facility. In most **IDE**s (Integrated Development Environments) these various files are combined into something called a **project**.

make

project

Displays 11.1, 11.2, and 11.3 contain one complete program divided into pieces and placed in three different files. You could instead combine the contents of these three files into one file, and then compile and run this one file without all this fuss

Why separate files?

Display 11.3   Application File Using DigitalTime Class

```
1   //This is the application file timedemo.cpp, which demonstrates use of DigitalTime.
2   #include <iostream>
3   using namespace std;
4   #include "dtime.h"


5   int main( )
6   {
7       DigitalTime clock, oldClock;


8       cout << "You may write midnight as either 0:00 or 24:00,\n"
9            << "but I will always write it as 0:00.\n"
10           << "Enter the time in 24-hour notation: ";
11      cin >> clock;


12      oldClock = clock;
13      clock.advance(15);
14      if (clock == oldClock)
15          cout << "Something is wrong.";
16      cout << "You entered " << oldClock << endl;
17      cout << "15 minutes later the time will be "
18           << clock << endl;


19      clock.advance(2, 15);
20      cout << "2 hours and 15 minutes after that\n"
21           << "the time will be "
22           << clock << endl;


23      return 0;
24  }
```

SAMPLE DIALOGUE

```
You may write midnight as either 0:00 or 24:00,
but I will always write it as 0:00.
Enter the time in 24-hour notation: 11:15
You entered 11:15
15 minutes later the time will be 11:30
2 hours and 15 minutes after that
the time will be 13:45
```

about include directives and linking separate files. Why bother with three separate files? There are several advantages to dividing your program into separate files. Since you have the definition and the implementation of the class DigitalTime in files separate from the application file, you can use this class in many different programs without needing to rewrite the definition of the class in each of the programs. Moreover, you

DEFINING A CLASS IN SEPARATE FILES: A SUMMARY

You can define a class and place the definition of the class and the implementation of its member functions in separate files. You can then compile the class separately from any program that uses the class and you can use this same class in any number of different programs. The class is placed in files as follows:

1. Put the definition of the class in a header file called the *interface file*. The name of this header file ends in .h. The interface file also contains the declarations (prototypes) for any functions and overloaded operators that define basic class operations but that are not listed in the class definition. Include comments that explain how all these functions and operators are used.

2. The definitions of all the functions and overloaded operators mentioned above (whether they are members or friends or neither) are placed in another file called the *implementation file*. This file must contain an include directive that names the interface file described above. This include directive uses quotes around the file name, as in the following example:

   ```
   #include "dtime.h"
   ```

   The interface file and the implementation file traditionally have the same name, but end in different suffixes. The interface file ends in .h. The implementation file ends in the same suffix that you use for files that contain a complete C++ program. The implementation file is compiled separately before it is used in any program.

3. When you want to use the class in a program, you place the main part of the program (and any additional function definitions, constant declarations, and such) in another file called an *application file* or *driver file*. This file also must contain an include directive naming the interface file, as in the following example:

   ```
   #include "dtime.h"
   ```

   The application file is compiled separately from the implementation file. You can write any number of these application files to use with one pair of interface and implementation files. To run an entire program, you must first link the object code produced by compiling the application file and the object code produced by compiling the implementation file. (On some systems the linking may be done automatically or semiautomatically.)

If you use multiple classes in a program, then you simply have multiple interface files and multiple implementation files, each compiled separately.

need to compile the implementation file only once, no matter how many programs use the class DigitalTime. But there are more advantages than that. Since you have separated the interface from the implementation of your DigitalTime class, you can change the implementation file and will not need to change any program that uses the class. In fact, you will not even need to recompile the program. If you change the implementation file, you only need to recompile the implementation file and relink the files. Saving a bit of recompiling time is nice, but the big advantage is avoiding the need to rewrite code. You can use the class in many programs without writing the class code into each program. You can change the implementation of the class and you need not rewrite any part of any program that uses the class.

The details of the implementation of the class DigitalTime are discussed in the following example section.

Example

DigitalTime CLASS

Previously we described how the files in Displays 11.1, 11.2, and 11.3 divide a program into three files: the interface for the class DigitalTime, the implementation of the class DigitalTime, and an application that uses the class. Here we discuss the details of the class implementation. There is no new material in this example section, but if some of the details in the implementation (Display 11.2) are not completely clear to you, this section may shed some light on your confusion.

Most of the implementation details are straightforward, but there are two things that merit comment. Notice that the member function name advance is overloaded so that it has two function definitions. Also notice that the definition for the overloaded extraction (input) operator >> uses two helping functions called readHour and readMinute and that these two helping functions themselves use a third helping function called digitToInt. Let's discuss these points.

The class DigitalTime (Displays 11.1 and 11.2) has two member functions called advance. One version takes a single argument, that is, an integer giving the number of minutes to advance the time. The other version takes two arguments, one for a number of hours and one for a number of minutes, and advances the time by that number of hours plus that number of minutes. Notice that the definition of the two-argument version of advance includes a call to the one-argument version. Look at the definition of the two-argument version that is given in Display 11.2. First the time is advanced by hoursAdded hours and then the single-argument version of advance is used to advance the time by an additional minutesAdded minutes. At first this may seem strange, but it is perfectly legal. The two functions named advance are two different functions that, as far as the compiler is concerned, just coincidentally happen to have the same name.

Now let's discuss the helping functions. The helping functions readHour and readMinute read the input one character at a time and then convert the input to integer values that are placed in the member variables hour and minute. The functions readHour and readMinute read the hour and minute one digit at a time, so they are reading values of type char. This is more complicated than reading the input as int values, but it allows us to perform error checking to see whether the input is correctly formed and to issue an error message if the input is not well formed.

These helping functions readHour and readMinute use another helping function named dig-itToInt. The function digitToInt converts a digit, such as '3', to a number, such as 3. This function was given previously in this book as the answer to Self-Test Exercise 3 in Chapter 7.

Tip

REUSABLE COMPONENTS

A class developed and coded into separate files is a software component that can be used again and again in a number of different programs. A reusable component saves effort because it does not need to be redesigned, recoded, and retested for every application. A reusable component is also likely to be more reliable than a component that is used only once. It is likely to be more reliable for two reasons. First, you can afford to spend more time and effort on a component if it will be used many times. Second, if the component is used again and again, it is tested again and again. Every use of a software component is a test of that component. Using a software component many times in a variety of contexts is one of the best ways to discover any remaining bugs in the software.

USING #ifndef

We have given you a method for placing a program in three (or more) files: two for the interface and implementation of each class and one for the application part of the program. A program can be kept in more than three files. For example, a program might use several classes, and each class might be kept in a separate pair of files. Suppose you have a program spread across a number of files and that more than one file has an include directive for a class interface file such as the following:

```
#include "dtime.h"
```

Under these circumstances you can have files that include other files, and these other files may in turn include yet other files. This can easily lead to a situation in which a file, in effect, contains the definitions in dtime.h more than once. C++ does not allow you to define a class more than once, even if the repeated definitions are identical. Moreover, if you are using the same header file in many different projects, it becomes close to impossible to keep track of whether you included the class definition more than once. To avoid this problem, C++ provides a way of marking a section of code to say "if you have already included this stuff once before, do not include it again." The way this is done is quite intuitive, although the notation may look a bit weird until you get used to it. We will go through an example, explaining the details as we go.

The following directive **defines** DTIME_H: #define

```
#define DTIME_H
```

What this means is that the compiler's preprocessor puts DTIME_H on a list to indicate that DTIME_H has been seen. *Defined* is perhaps not the best word for this, since DTIME_H is not defined to mean anything but merely put on a list. The important point is that you can use another directive to test whether DTIME_H has been defined and so test whether a section of code has already been processed. You can use any (nonkeyword) identifier in place of DTIME_H, but you will see that there are standard conventions for which identifier you should use.

#ifndef

The following directive tests to see whether DTIME_H has been defined:

```
#ifndef DTIME_H
```

If DTIME_H has already been defined, then everything between this directive and the first occurrence of the following directive is skipped:

#endif

```
#endif
```

An equivalent way to state this, which may clarify the way the directives are spelled, is the following: If DTIME_H is *not* defined, then the compiler processes everything up to the next #endif. The *not* is why there is an n in #ifndef. (This may lead you to wonder whether there is a #ifdef directive as well as a #ifndef directive. There is, and it has the obvious meaning, but we will have no occasion to use #ifdef.)

Now consider the following code:

```
#ifndef DTIME_H
#define DTIME_H
 <a class definition>
#endif
```

If this code is in a file named dtime.h, then no matter how many times your program contains

```
#include "dtime.h"
```

the class will be defined only one time.

The first time

```
#include "dtime.h"
```

is processed, the flag DTIME_H is defined and the class is defined. Now, suppose the compiler again encounters

```
#include "dtime.h"
```

When the include directive is processed this second time, the directive

```
#ifndef DTIME_H
```

says to skip everything up to

```
#endif
```

and so the class is not defined again.

In Display 11.4 we have rewritten the header file dtime.h shown in Display 11.1, but this time we used these directives to prevent multiple definitions. With the version of dtime.h shown in Display 11.4, if a file contains the following include directive more than once, the class DigitalTime will still be defined only once:

```
#include "dtime.h"
```

You may use some other identifier in place of DTIME_H, but the normal convention is to use the name of the file written in all uppercase letters with the underscore used in place of the period. You should follow this convention so that others can more easily read your code and so that you do not have to remember the flag name. This way the flag name is determined automatically and there is nothing arbitrary to remember.

These same directives can be used to skip over code in files other than header files, but we will not have occasion to use these directives except in header files.

#ifndef

You can avoid multiple definitions of a class (or anything else) by using #ifndef in the header file (interface file), as illustrated in Display 11.4. If the file is included more than once, only one of the definitions included will be used.

Display 11.4   Avoiding Multiple Definitions of a Class

```
1   //This is the header file dtime.h. This is the interface for the class DigitalTime.
2   //Values of this type are times of day. The values are input and output in
3   //24-hour notation, as in 9:30 for 9:30 AM and 14:45 for 2:45 PM.

4   #ifndef DTIME_H
5   #define DTIME_H

6   #include <iostream>
7   using namespace std;

8   class DigitalTime
9   {

        <The definition of the class DigitalTime is the same as in Display 11.1.>

10  };

11  #endif //DTIME_H
```

Tip

DEFINING OTHER LIBRARIES

You need not define a class in order to use separate compilation. If you have a collection of related functions that you want; to make into a library of your own design, you can place the function declarations (prototypes) and accompanying comments in a header file and the function definitions in an implementation file, just as we outlined for classes. After that, you can use this library in your programs the same way you would use a class that you placed in separate files.

Self-Test Exercises

1. Suppose that you are defining a class and that you then want to use this class in a program. You want to separate the class and program parts into separate files as described in this chapter. State whether each of the following should be placed in the interface file, implementation file, or application file.

   a. The class definition

   b. The declaration for a function that is to serve as a class operation but that is neither a member nor a friend of the class

   c. The declaration for an overloaded operator that is to serve as a class operation but that is neither a member nor a friend of the class

   d. The definition for a function that is to serve as a class operation but that is neither a member nor a friend of the class

   e. The definition for a friend function that is to serve as a class operation

   f. The definition for a member function

   g. The definition for an overloaded operator that is to serve as a class operation but that is neither a member nor a friend of the class

   h. The definition for an overloaded operator that is to serve as a class operation and that is a friend of the class

   i. The `main` function of your program

2. Which of the following files has a name that ends in `.h`: the interface file for a class, the implementation file for the class, or the application file that uses the class?

3. When you define a class in separate files, there is an interface file and an implementation file. Which of these files needs to be compiled? (Both? Neither? Only one? If so, which one?)

4. Suppose you define a class in separate files and use the class in a program. Now suppose you change the class implementation file. Which of the following files, if any, needs to be recompiled: the interface file, the implementation file, and/or the application file?

5. Suppose you want to change the implementation of the class `DigitalTime` given in Displays 11.1 and 11.2. Specifically, you want to change the way the time is recorded. Instead of using the two private variables `hour` and `minute`, you want to use a single (private) `int` variable, which will be called `minutes`. In this new implementation the private variable `minutes` will record the time as the number of minutes since the time 0:00 (that is, since midnight). For example, 1:30 is recorded as `90` minutes, since it is 90 minutes past midnight. Describe how you need to change the interface and implementation files shown in Displays 11.1 and 11.2. You need not write out the files in their entirety; just indicate what items you need to change and how, in a very general way, you would change them.

11.2 Namespaces

What's in a name? That which we call a rose
By any other name would smell as sweet.

William Shakespeare, *Romeo and Juliet*

When a program uses different classes and functions written by different programmers there is a possibility that two programmers will use the same name for two different things. Namespaces are a way to deal with this problem. A **namespace** is a collection of name definitions, such as class definitions and variable declarations. A namespace can, in a sense, be turned on and off so that when some of its names would otherwise conflict with names in another namespace, it can be turned off.

namespace

NAMESPACES AND using DIRECTIVES

We have already been using the namespace that is named `std`. The `std` namespace contains all the names defined in many of the standard C++ library files (such as `iostream`). For example, when you place the following line at the start of a file,

```
#include <iostream>
```

it places all the name definitions (for names like `cin` and `cout`) into the `std` namespace. Your program does not know about names in the `std` namespace unless you specify that it is using the `std` namespace. To make all the definitions in the `std` namespace available to your code, insert the following `using` directive:

```
using namespace std;
```

A good way to see why you might want to include this `using` directive is to think about why you might want to *not* include it. If you do not include this `using` directive for the namespace `std`, then you can define `cin` and `cout` to have some meaning other than their standard meaning. (Perhaps you want to redefine `cin` and `cout` because you want them to behave a bit differently from the standard versions.) Their standard meaning is in the std namespace; without the using directive (or something like it), your code knows nothing about the std namespace, and so, as far as your code is concerned, the only definitions of cin and cout it knows are whatever definitions you give them.

global
namespace

Every bit of code you write is in some namespace. If you do not place the code in some specific namespace, then the code is in a namespace known as the **global namespace**. So far we have not placed any code we wrote in any namespace and so all our code has been in the global namespace. The global namespace does not have a using directive because you are always using the global namespace. You could say there is always an implicit automatic using directive that says you are using the global namespace.

Note that you can use more than one namespace in the same program. For example, we are always using the global namespace and we are usually using the std namespace. What happens if a name is defined in two namespaces and you are using both namespaces? This results in an error (either a compiler error or a run-time error, depending on the exact details). You can have the same name defined in two different namespaces, but if that is true, then you can only use one of those namespaces at a time. However, this does not mean you cannot use the two namespaces in the same program. You can use them each at different times in the same program.

For example, suppose NS1 and NS2 are two namespaces and suppose myFunction is a void function with no arguments that is defined in both namespaces but defined in different ways in the two namespaces. The following is then legal:

```
{
    using namespace NS1;
    myFunction( );
}
{
    using namespace NS2;
    myFunction( );
}
```

The first invocation would use the definition of myFunction given in the namespace NS1, and the second invocation would use the definition of myFunction given in the namespace NS2.

Recall that a *block* is a list of statements, declarations, and possibly other code enclosed in braces, {}. A using directive at the start of a block applies only to that block. Therefore the first using directive above applies only in the first block, and the second using directive applies only in the second block. The usual way of phrasing this is to say that the **scope** of the NS1 using directive is the first block, whereas the scope of the NS2 using directive is the second block. Note that because of this scope rule, we are able to use two conflicting namespaces in the same program (such as in a program that contains the two blocks we discussed in the previous paragraph).

scope

Normally, you place a using directive at the start of a block. If you place it further down in the block, however, you need to know its precise scope. The scope of a using directive runs from the place where it occurs to the end of the block. You may have a using directive for the same namespace in more than one block, so the entire scope of a namespace may cover multiple disconnected blocks. When you use a using directive in a block, it is typically the block consisting of the body of a function definition.

If you place a using directive at the start of a file (as we have usually done so far), then the using directive applies to the entire file. A using directive should normally be placed near the start of a file (or the start of a block), but the precise scope rule is that the scope of a using directive that is outside all blocks is from the occurrence of the using directive to the end of the file.

SCOPE RULE FOR USING DIRECTIVES

The scope of a using directive is the block in which it appears (more precisely, from the location of the using directive to the end of the block). If the using directive is outside all blocks, then it applies to all of the file that follows the using directive.

CREATING A NAMESPACE

To place some code in a namespace, you simply place it in a **namespace grouping** of the following form:

namespace grouping

```
namespace Name_Space_Name
{
    Some_Code
}
```

When you include one of these groupings in your code, you are said to place the names defined in *Some_Code* into the namespace *Name_Space_Name*. These names (really, the definitions of these names) can be made available with the using directive

```
using namespace Name_Space_Name;
```

For example, the following, taken from Display 11.5, places a function declaration in the namespace Space1:

```
namespace Space1
{
    void greeting( );
}
```

If you look again at Display 11.5, you see that the definition of the function greeting is also placed in namespace Space1. That is done with the following additional namespace grouping:

```
namespace Space1
{
    void greeting( )
    {
        cout << "Hello from namespace Space1.\n";
    }
}
```

Display 11.5   Namespace Demonstration (part 1 of 2)

```
1
2    #include <iostream>
3    using namespace std;

4    namespace Space1
5    {
6        void greeting( );
7    }

8    namespace Space2
9    {
10       void greeting( );
11   }

12   void bigGreeting( );

13   int main( )
14   {
15       {
16           using namespace Space2;
17           greeting( );
18       }

19       {
20           using namespace Space1;
21           greeting( );
22       }

23       bigGreeting( );

24       return 0;
25   }
```

Names in this block use definitions in namespaces Space2, std, and the global namespace. (pointing to lines 16–17)

Names in this block use definitions in namespaces Space1, std, and the global namespace. (pointing to line 20)

Names out here only use definitions in the namespace std and the global namespace. (pointing to line 23)

Display 11.5 **Namespace Demonstration** *(part 2 of 2)*

```
26
27  namespace Space1
28  {
29      void greeting( )
30      {
31          cout << "Hello from namespace Space1.\n";
32      }
33  }


34  namespace Space2
35  {
36      void greeting( )
37      {
38          cout << "Greetings from namespace Space2.\n";
39      }
40  }


41  void bigGreeting( )
42  {
43      cout << "A Big Global Hello!\n";
44  }
```

SAMPLE DIALOGUE

```
Greetings from namespace Space2.
Hello from namespace Space1.
A Big Global Hello!
```

Note that you can have any number of these namespace groupings for a single namespace. In Display 11.5, we used two namespace groupings for namespace Space1 and two other groupings for namespace Space2.

Every name defined in a namespace is available inside the namespace groupings, but the names can also be made available to code outside the namespace groupings. For example, the function declaration and function definition in the namespace Space1 can be made available with the using directive

```
using namespace Space1
```

as illustrated in Display 11.5.

PUTTING A DEFINITION IN A NAMESPACE

You place a name definition in a namespace by placing it in a *namespace grouping*, which has the following syntax:

```
namespace Namespace_Name
{
        Definition_1
        Definition_2
             .
             .
             .
        Definition_Last
}
```

You can have multiple namespace groupings (even in multiple files), and all the definitions in all the groupings will be in the same namespace.

Self-Test Exercises

6. Consider the program shown in Display 11.5. Could we use the name `greeting` in place of `bigGreeting`?

7. In Exercise 6, we saw that you could *not* add a definition for the following function to the global namespace:

```
void greeting( );
```

Can you add a definition for the following function declaration to the global namespace?

```
void greeting(int howMany );
```

USING DECLARATIONS

This subsection describes a way to qualify a single name so that you can make only one name from a namespace available to your program, rather than making all the names in a namespace available. We saw this technique in Chapter 1 and so this is a review and amplification of what we said in Chapter 1.

Suppose you are faced with the following situation. You have two namespaces, NS1 and NS2. You want to use the function `fun1` defined in NS1 and the function `fun2` defined in namespace NS2. The complication is that both NS1 and NS2 also define a function `myFunction`. (Assume all functions in this discussion take no arguments, so overloading does not apply.) There is a problem with

```
using namespace NS1;
using namespace NS2;
```

This would potentially provide conflicting definitions for myFunction. (If the name myFunction is never used, then most compilers will not detect the problem and will allow your program to compile and run.)

What you need is a way to say you are using fun1 in namespace NS1 and fun2 in namespace NS2 and nothing else in the namespaces NS1 and NS2. We have already been using a technique that can handle this situation. The following is your solution:

```
using NS1::fun1;
using NS2::fun2;
```

A qualification of the form

```
using Name_Space::One_Name;
```

makes the (definition of the) name One_Name from the namespace Name_Space available, but does not make any other names in Name_Space available. This is called a **using declaration**.

Note that the scope resolution operator :: that we use in these using declarations is the same as the scope resolution operator we use when defining member functions. These two uses of the scope resolution operator have a similarity. For example, Display 11.2 had the following function definition:

```
void DigitalTime::advance(int hoursAdded, int minutesAdded)
{
    hour = (hour + hoursAdded)%24;
    advance(minutesAdded);
}
```

In this case the :: means that we are defining the function advance for the class DigitalTime, as opposed to any other function named advance in any other class. Similarly,

```
using NS1::fun1;
```

means we are using the function named fun1 as defined in the namespace NS1, as opposed to any other definition of fun1 in any other namespace.

There are two differences between a *using declaration*, such as

```
using std::cout;
```

and a *using directive* such as

```
using namespace std;
```

The differences are:

1. A a using declaration makes only one name in the namespace available to your code, while a using directive makes all the names in a namespace available.

2. A using declaration introduces a name (like cout) into your code so no other use of the name can be made. However, a using directive only potentially introduces the names in the namespace.

using
NS1::fun1;

using
declaration

Point 1 is pretty obvious. Point 2 has some subtleties. For example, suppose the namespaces NS1 and NS2 both provide definitions for myFunction, but have no other name conflicts, then the following will produce no problems:

```
using namespace NS1;
using namespace NS2;
```

provided that (within the scope of these directives) the conflicting name myFunction is never used in your code.

On the other hand, the following is illegal, even if the function myFunction is never used:

```
using NS1::myFunction;
using NS2::myFunction;
```

using
directive

Sometimes this subtle point can be important, but it does not impinge on most routine code. So, we will often use the term **using directive** loosely to mean either a using directive or a using declaration.

◼ QUALIFYING NAMES

This section introduces a way to qualify names that we have not discussed before. Suppose that you intend to use the name fun1 as defined in the namespace NS1, but you only intend to use it one time (or a small number of times). You can name the function (or other item) using the name of the namespace and the scope resolution operator as follows:

```
NS1::fun1( );
```

This form is often used when specifying a parameter type. For example, consider

```
int getInput(std::istream inputStream)
. . .
```

In the function getInput, the parameter inputStream is of type istream, where istream is defined as in the std namespace. If this use of the type name istream is the only name you need from the std namespace (or if all the names you need are similarly qualified with std::), then you do *not* need

```
using namespace std;
```

or

```
using std::istream;
```

Note that you can use std::istream even within the scope of a using directive for another namespace which also defines the name istream. In this case std::istream and istream will have different definitions. For example, consider

```
using namespace MySpace;
void someFunction(istream p1, std::istream p2);
```

Assuming istream is a type defined in the namespace MySpace, then p1 will have the type istream as defined in MySpace and p2 will have the type istream as defined in the std namespace.

8. What is the output produced by the following program?

```cpp
#include <iostream>
using namespace std;

namespace Hello
{
    void message( );
}

namespace GoodBye
{
    void message( );
}

void message( );

int main( )
{
    using GoodBye::message;

    {
        using Hello::message;
        message( );
        GoodBye::message( );
    }

    message( );

    return 0;
}

void message( )
{
    cout << "Global message.\n";
}

namespace Hello
{
    void message( )
    {
```

```
            cout << "Hello.\n";
        }
    }

    namespace GoodBye
    {
        void message( )
        {
            cout << "Good-Bye.\n";
        }
    }
```

9. Write the declaration (prototype) for a void function named wow. The function wow has two parameters, the first of type speed as defined in the speedway namespace and the second of type speed as defined in the indy500 namespace.

Example

A CLASS DEFINITION IN A NAMESPACE

In Displays 11.6 and 11.7 we have again rewritten both the header file dtime.h for the class DigitalTime and the implementation file for the class DigitalTime. This time (no pun intended), we have placed the definition in a namespace called DTimeSavitch. Note that the namespace DTimeSavitch spans the two files dtime.h and dtime.cpp. A namespace can span multiple files.

If you rewrite the definition of the class DigitalTime as shown in Displays 11.6 and 11.7, then the application file in Display 11.3 needs to specify the namespace DTimeSavitch in some way, such as the following:

```
using namespace DTimeSavitch;
```

or

```
using DTimeSavitch::DigitalTime;
```

Tip

CHOOSING A NAME FOR A NAMESPACE

It is a good idea to include your last name or some other unique string in the names of your namespaces so as to reduce the chance that somebody else will use the same namespace name as you do. With multiple programmers writing code for the same project, it is important that namespaces that are meant to be distinct really do have distinct names. Otherwise, you can easily have multiple definitions of the same names in the same scope. That is why we included the name Savitch in the namespace DtimeSavitch in Display 11.9.

Display 11.6   Placing a Class in a Namespace (Header File)

```
1   //This is the header file dtime.h.
2   #ifndef DTIME_H
3   #define DTIME_H
```
A better version of this class definition will be given in Displays 11.8 and 11.9.

```
4   #include <iostream>
5   using std::istream;
6   using std::ostream;

7   namespace DTimeSavitch
8   {
9
10      class DigitalTime
11      {
12
13          <The definition of the class DigitalTime is the same as in Display 11.1.>
14      };
15
16  }// DTimeSavitch
```

Note that the namespace DTimeSavitch spans two files. The other is shown in Display 11.7.

```
17  #endif //DTIME_H
```

Display 11.7   Placing a Class in a Namespace (Implementation File)

```
1   //This is the implementation file dtime.cpp.
2   #include <iostream>
3   #include <cctype>
4   #include <cstdlib>
5   using std::istream;
6   using std::ostream;
7   using std::cout;
8   using std::cin;
9   #include "dtime.h"
```

You can use the single using directive
using namespace std;
in place of these four using declarations.
However, the four using declarations are a
preferable style.

```
10  namespace DTimeSavitch
11  {
12
13      <All the function definitions from Display 11.2 go here.>
14
15  }// DTimeSavitch
```

UNNAMED NAMESPACES

compilation
unit

A **compilation unit** is a file, such as a class implementation file, along with all the files that are #included in the file, such as the interface header file for the class. Every compilation unit has an unnamed namespace. A namespace grouping for the unnamed namespace is written in the same way as for any other namespace, but no name is given, as in the following example:

```
namespace
{
    void sampleFunction( )
         .
         .
         .
} //unnamed namespace
```

All the names defined in the unnamed namespace are local to the compilation unit, and so the names can be reused for something else outside the compilation unit. For example, Displays 11.8 and 11.9 show a rewritten (and final) version of the interface

Display 11.8   Hiding the Helping Functions in a Namespace (Interface File) *(part 1 of 2)*

```
1   //This is the header file dtime.h. This is the interface for the class DigitalTime.
2   //Values of this type are times of day. The values are input and output in 24-hour
3   //notation, as in 9:30 for 9:30 AM and 14:45 for 2:45 PM.
4   #ifndef DTIME_H
5   #define DTIME_H                      This is our final version of the class DigitalTime.
                                         This is the best version and the one you should use.
6   #include <iostream>                  The implementation to use with this interface is
7   using std::istream;                  given in Display 11.9.
8   using std::ostream;

9   namespace DTimeSavitch
10  {
11      class DigitalTime
12      {
13      public:
14          DigitalTime(int theHour, int theMinute);

15          DigitalTime( );
16          //Initializes the time value to 0:00 (which is midnight).

17          getHour( ) const;
18          getMinute( ) const;

19          void advance(int minutesAdded);
20          //Changes the time to minutesAdded minutes later.
```

Display 11.8   Hiding the Helping Functions in a Namespace (Interface File) *(part 2 of 2)*

```
21              void advance(int hoursAdded, int minutesAdded);
22              //Changes the time to hoursAdded hours plus minutesAdded minutes later.

23              friend bool operator ==(const DigitalTime& time1,
24                                      const DigitalTime& time2);
25              friend istream& operator >>(istream& ins, DigitalTime& theObject);
26              friend ostream& operator <<(ostream& outs,
27                                      const DigitalTime& theObject);
28      private:
29          int hour;                    Note that the helping functions are not
30          int minute;                  mentioned in the interface file.
31      };

32  } //DTimeSavitch
33  #endif //DTIME_H
```

Display 11.9   Hiding the Helping Functions in a Namespace (Implementation File) *(part 1 of 3)*

```
1   //This is the implementation file dtime.cpp of the class DigitalTime.
2   //The interface for the class DigitalTime is in the header file dtime.h.
3   #include <iostream>
4   #include <cctype>
5   #include <cstdlib>
6   using std::istream;
7   using std::ostream;
8   using std::cout;
9   using std::cin;
10  #include "dtime.h"

11  namespace         ←——— Specifies the unnamed namespace
12  {
13      int digitToInt(char c)
14      {                                Names defined in the unnamed namespace are
15          return ( int(c) - int('0') );   local to the compilation unit. So, these helping
16      }                                functions are local to the file dtime.cpp.

17      //Uses iostream, cctype, and cstdlib:
18      void readMinute(int& theMinute)
19      {
20          char c1, c2;
21          cin >> c1 >> c2;
22          if (!(isdigit(c1) && isdigit(c2)))
23          {
24              cout << "Error: illegal input to readMinute\n";
```

Display 11.9   Hiding the Helping Functions in a Namespace (Implementation File) *(part 2 of 3)*

```
25                exit(1);
26            }

27            theMinute = digitToInt(c1)*10 + digitToInt(c2);

28            if (theMinute < 0 || theMinute > 59)
29            {
30                cout << "Error: illegal input to readMinute\n";
31                exit(1);
32            }
33        }


34
35        //Uses iostream, cctype, and cstdlib:
36        void readHour(int& theHour)
37        {
38            char c1, c2;
39            cin >> c1 >> c2;
40            if ( !( isdigit(c1) && (isdigit(c2) || c2 == ':' ) ) )
41            {
42                cout << "Error: illegal input to readHour\n";
43                exit(1);
44            }

45            if (isdigit(c1) && c2 == ':')
46            {
47                theHour = digitToInt(c1);
48            }
49            else //(isdigit(c1) && isdigit(c2))
50            {
51                theHour = digitToInt(c1)*10 + digitToInt(c2);
52                cin >> c2; //discard ':'
53                if (c2 != ':')
54                {
55                    cout << "Error: illegal input to readHour\n";
56                    exit(1);
57                }
58            }

59            if (theHour == 24)
60                theHour = 0; //Standardize midnight as 0:00.

61            if ( theHour < 0 || theHour > 23 )
62            {
```

Display 11.9   Hiding the Helping Functions in a Namespace (Implementation File) *(part 3 of 3)*

```
63                  cout << "Error: illegal input to readHour\n";
64                  exit(1);
65            }
66        }
67  } //unnamed namespace
68
69  namespace DTimeSavitch
70  {
71      //Uses iostream:
72      istream& operator >>(istream& ins, DigitalTime& theObject)
73      {
74          readHour(theObject.hour);
75          readMinute(theObject.minute);
76          return ins;
77      }
```

Within the compilation unit (in this case dtime.cpp*), you can use names in the unnamed namespace without qualification.*

```
78      ostream& operator <<(ostream& outs, const DigitalTime& theObject)
```
<The body of the function definition is the same as in Display 11.2.>

```
79      bool operator ==(const DigitalTime& time1, const DigitalTime& time2)
```
<The body of the function definition is the same as in Display 11.2.>

```
80      DigitalTime::DigitalTime(int theHour, int theMinute)
```
<The body of the function definition is the same as in Display 11.2.>

```
81      DigitalTime::DigitalTime( )
```
<The body of the function definition is the same as in Display 11.2.>

```
82      int DigitalTime::getHour( ) const
```
<The body of the function definition is the same as in Display 11.2.>

```
83      int DigitalTime::getMinute( ) const
```
<The body of the function definition is the same as in Display 11.2.>

```
84      void DigitalTime::advance(int minutesAdded)
```
<The body of the function definition is the same as in Display 11.2.>

```
85      void DigitalTime::advance(int hoursAdded, int minutesAdded)
```
<The body of the function definition is the same as in Display 11.2.>

```
86  } //DTimeSavitch
```

and implementation file for the class `DigitalTime`. Note that the helping functions `readHour`, `readMinute`, and `digitToInt` are all in the unnamed namespace; thus they are local to the compilation unit. As illustrated in Display 11.10, the names in the unnamed namespace can be reused for something else outside the compilation unit. In Display 11.10, the function name `readHour` is reused for a different function in the application program.

Display 11.10   Hiding the Helping Functions in a Namespace (Application Program) *(part 1 of 2)*

```
1    //This is the application file timedemo.cpp. This program
2    //demonstrates hiding the helping functions in an unnamed namespace.

3    #include <iostream>
4    #include "dtime.h"

5    void readHour(int& theHour);

6    int main( )
7    {
8        using std::cout;
9        using std::cin;
10       using std::endl;

11       using DTimeSavitch::DigitalTime;

12       int theHour;
13       readHour(theHour);

14       DigitalTime clock(theHour, 0), oldClock;

15       oldClock = clock;
16       clock.advance(15);
17       if (clock == oldClock)
18           cout << "Something is wrong.";
19       cout << "You entered " << oldClock << endl;
20       cout << "15 minutes later the time will be "
21               << clock << endl;

22       clock.advance(2, 15);
23       cout << "2 hours and 15 minutes after that\n"
24               << "the time will be "
25               << clock << endl;

26       return 0;
27   }
```

If you place the using declarations here, then the program behavior will be the same. However, many authorities say that you should make the scope of each using declaration or using directive as small as is reasonable, and we wanted to give you an example of that technique.

This is a different function readHour than the one in the implementation file dtime.cpp (shown in Display 11.9).

Display 11.10   **Hiding the Helping Functions in a Namespace (Application Program)** *(part 2 of 2)*

```
28
29    void readHour(int& theHour)              When we gave these using declarations before,
30    {                                        they were in main, so their scope was main. Thus,
31        using std::cout;                     we need to repeat them here in order to use cin
32        using std::cin;                      and cout in readHour.
33
34        cout << "Let's play a time game.\n"
35             << "Let's pretend the hour has just changed.\n"
36             << "You may write midnight as either 0 or 24,\n"
37             << "but, I will always write it as 0.\n"
38             << "Enter the hour as a number (0 to 24): ";
39        cin >> theHour;
40    }
```

SAMPLE DIALOGUE

```
Let's play a time game.
Let's pretend the hour has just changed.
You may write midnight as either 0 or 24,
but, I will always write it as 0.
Enter the hour as a number (0 to 24): 11
You entered 11:00
15 minutes later the time will be 11:15
2 hours and 15 minutes after that
the time will be 13:30
```

If you look again at the implementation file Display 11.9, you will see that the helping functions digitToInt, readHour, and readMinute are used outside the unnamed namespace without any namespace qualifier. Any name defined in the unnamed namespace can be used without qualification anywhere in the compilation unit. (Of course, this needed to be so, since the unnamed namespace has no name to use for qualifying its names.)

It is interesting to note how unnamed namespaces interact with the C++ rule that you cannot have two definitions of a name in the same namespace. There is one unnamed namespace in each compilation unit. It is easily possible for compilation units to overlap. For example, both the implementation file for a class and an application program using the class would normally both include the header file (interface file) for the class. Thus, the header file is in two compilation units and hence participates in two unnamed namespaces. As dangerous as this sounds, it will normally produce no problems as long as each compilation unit's namespace makes sense when considered by itself. For example, if a name is defined in the unnamed namespace in the header file, it cannot be defined again in the unnamed namespace in either the implementation file or the application file. Thus, a name conflict is avoided.

UNNAMED NAMESPACE

You can use the *unnamed namespace* to make a definition local to a compilation unit. Each compilation unit has one unnamed namespace. All the identifiers defined in the unnamed namespace are local to the compilation unit. You place a definition in the unnamed namespace by placing the definition in a namespace grouping with no namespace name, as shown below:

```
namespace
{
    Definition_1
    Definition_2
        .
        .
        .
    Definition_Last
}
```

You can use any name in the unnamed namespace without qualifiers anyplace in the compilation unit. See Displays 11.8, 11.9, and 11.10 for a complete example.

Pitfall

CONFUSING THE GLOBAL NAMESPACE AND THE UNNAMED NAMESPACE

Do not confuse the global namespace with the unnamed namespace. If you do not put a name definition in a namespace grouping, then it is in the global namespace. To put a name definition in the unnamed namespace, you must put it in a namespace grouping that starts out as follows, without a name:

```
namespace
{
```

Names in the global namespace and names in the unnamed namespace may both be accessed without a qualifier. However, names in the global namespace have global scope (all the program files), whereas names in an unnamed namespace are local to a compilation unit.

This confusion between the global namespace and the unnamed namespace does not arise very much in writing code, since there is a tendency to think of names in the global namespace as being "in no namespace," even though that is not technically correct. However, the confusion can easily arise when discussing code.

Tip

UNNAMED NAMESPACES REPLACE THE static QUALIFIER

Earlier versions of C++ used the qualifier static to make a name local to a file. This use of static is being phased out, and you should instead use the unnamed namespace to make a name local to a compilation unit. Note that this use of static has nothing to do with the use of static to qualify class members (as discussed in the subsection "Static Members" of Chapter 7). So, since static used to mean more than one thing, it is probably good that one use of the word is being phased out.

Tip

HIDING HELPING FUNCTIONS

There are two good ways to hide a helping function for a class. You can make the function a private member function of the class or you can place the helping function in the unnamed namespace for the implementation file of the class. If the function naturally takes a calling object, then it should be made a private member function. If it does not naturally take a calling object, you can make it a static member function (for example, DigitalTime::readHour in Displays 11.1 and 11.2) or you can place it in the unnamed namespace of the implementation file (for example, readHour in Displays 11.8 and 11.9.)

If the helping function does not need a calling object, then placing the helping function in the unnamed namespace of the implementation file makes for cleaner code because it better separates interface and implementation into separate files and it avoids the need for so much function name qualification. For example, note that in Display 11.9 we can use the function name read-Hour unqualified since it is in the unnamed namespace, while in the version in Display 11.2 we need to use DigitalTime::readHour.

◼ NESTED NAMESPACES

It is legal to nest namespaces. When qualifying a name from a nested namespace, you simply qualify twice. For example, consider

```
namespace S1
{
    namespace S2
    {
        void sample( )
        {
            .
            .
            .
        }
```

```
        .
        .
        .
    } //S2
}//S1
```

To invoke `sample` outside the namespace S1, you use

```
S1::S2::sample( );
```

To invoke `sample` outside the namespace S2 but within namespace S1, you use

```
S2::sample( );
```

Alternatively, you could use a suitable `using` directive.

Tip

WHAT NAMESPACE SPECIFICATION SHOULD YOU USE?

You have three ways to specify that your code uses the definition of a function (or other item) named f that was defined in a namespace named theSpace. You can insert

```
using namespace theSpace;
```

Alternatively, you can insert

```
using theSpace::f;
```

Finally, you could omit the `using` directive altogether, but always qualify the function name by writing `theSpace::f` instead of just plain f.

Which form should you use? All three methods can be made to work, and authorities differ on what they recommend as the preferred style. However, to obtain the full value of namespaces, it is good to avoid the form

```
using namespace theSpace;
```

Placing such a `using` directive at the start of a file is little different than placing all definitions in the global namespace, which is what earlier versions of C++ actually did. So, this approach gets no value from the namespace mechanism. (If you place such a `using` directive inside a block, however, then it only applies to that block. This is another alternative, which is both sensible and advocated by many authorities.)

We prefer to use the second method most of the time, inserting statements like the following at the start of files:

```
using theSpace::f;
```

This allows you to omit names that are in the namespace but that are not used. That in turn avoids potential name conflicts. Moreover, it nicely documents which names you use, and it is not as messy as always qualifying a name with notation of the form theSpace::f.

If your files are structured so that different namespaces are used in different locations, it may sometimes be preferable to place your using directives and using declarations inside blocks, such as the bodies of function definitions, rather than at the start of the file.

Self-Test Exercises

10. Would the program in Display 11.10 behave any differently if you replaced the four using declarations

```
using std::cout;
using std::cin;
using std::endl;
using DTimeSavitch::DigitalTime;
```

with the following two using directives?

```
using namespace std;
using namespace DTimeSavitch;
```

11. What is the output produced by the following program?

```cpp
#include <iostream>
using namespace std;

namespace Sally
{
    void message( );
}

namespace
{
    void message( );
}

int main( )
{
    {
        message( );
        using Sally::message;
        message( );
    }
```

```
        message( );

        return 0;
}

namespace Sally
{
    void message( )
    {
        cout << "Hello from Sally.\n";
    }
}

namespace
{
    void message( )
    {
        cout << "Hello from unnamed.\n";
    }
}
```

12. What is the output produced by the following program?

```
#include <iostream>
using namespace std;

namespace Outer
{
    void message( );

    namespace Inner
    {
        void message( );
    }
}

int main( )
{
    Outer::message( );
    Outer::Inner::message( );

    using namespace Outer;
    Inner::message( );

    return 0;
}
```

```
namespace Outer
{
    void message( )
    {
        cout << "Outer.\n";
    }

    namespace Inner
    {
        void message( )
        {
            cout << "Inner.\n";
        }
    }
}
```

Chapter Summary

- You can define a class and place the definition of the class and the implementation of its member functions in separate files. You can then compile the class separately from any program that uses it, and you can use this same class in any number of different programs.

- A namespace is a collection of name definitions, such as class definitions and variable declarations.

- There are three ways to use a name from a namespace: by making all the names in the namespace available with a using directive, by making the single name available with a using declaration for the one name, or by qualifying the name with the name of the namespace and the scope resolution operator.

- You place a definition in a namespace by placing the definition in a namespace grouping for that namespace.

- The unnamed namespace can be used to make a name definition local to a compilation unit.

ANSWERS TO SELF-TEST EXERCISES

1. Parts a, b, and c go in the interface file; parts d through h go in the implementation file. (All the definitions of class operations of any sort go in the implementation file.) Part i (that is, the main part of your program) goes in the application file.

2. The name of the interface file ends in .h.

3. Only the implementation file needs to be compiled. The interface file does not need to be compiled.

4. Only the implementation file needs to be recompiled. You do, however, need to relink the files.

5. You need to delete the private member variables `hour` and `minute` from the interface file shown in Display 11.1 and replace them with the member variable `minutes` (with an `s`). You do not need to make any other changes in the interface file. In the implementation file, you need to change the definitions of all the constructors and other member functions, as well as the definitions of the overloaded operators, so that they work for this new way of recording time. (In this case, you do not need to change any of the helping functions `readHour`, `readMinute`, or `digitToInt`, but that might not be true for some other class or even some other reimplementation of this class.) For example, the definition of the overloaded operator, `>>`, could be changed to the following:

```
istream& operator >>(istream& ins,
                                DigitalTime& theObject)
{
    int inputHour, inputMinute;
    DigitalTime::readHour(inputHour);
    DigitalTime::readMinute(inputMinute);
    theObject.minutes = inputMinute + 60*inputHour;
    return ins;
}
```

You need not change any application files for programs that use the class. However, since the interface file is changed (as well as the implementation file), you will need to recompile any application files, and of course you will need to recompile the implementation file.

6. No. If you replace `bigGreeting` with `greeting`, you will have a definition for the name `greeting` in the global namespace. There are parts of the program where all the name definitions in the namespace `Space1` and all the name definitions in the global namespace are simultaneously available. In those parts of the program, there would be two distinct definitions for

```
void greeting( );
```

7. Yes. The additional definition would cause no problems because overloading is always allowed. When, for example, the namespace `Space1` and the global namespace are available, the function name `greeting` would be overloaded. The problem in Self-Test Exercise 6 was that there would sometimes be two definitions of the function name `greeting` with the same parameter lists.

8. `Hello`
   `Good-Bye`
   `Good-Bye`

9. `void wow(speedway::speed s1, indy500::speed s2);`

10. The program would behave exactly the same. However, most authorities favor using the using declaration, as we have done in Display 11.10. Note that with either, there are still two different functions named readHour. The one in Display 11.10 is different from the one defined in the unnamed namespace in Display 11.9.

11. Hello from unnamed.
    Hello from Sally.
    Hello from unnamed.

12. Outer.
    Inner.
    Inner.

PROGRAMMING PROJECTS

1. This exercise is intended to illustrate namespaces and separate compilation in your development environment. You should use the development environment you regularly use in this course for this exercise. In a file f.h, place a declaration of void f( ) in namespace A. In file g.h, place a declaration of void g( ) in namespace A. In files f.cpp and g.cpp, place the definitions of void f( ) and void g( ), respectively. Place the definitions of void f( ) and void g( ) in namespace A. The functions can do anything you want, but to keep track of execution include something like

   ```
   cout <<"Function_Name called" << endl;
   ```

   where *Function_Name* is the name of the particular function. In another file, main.cpp, put your main function, #include the minimum collection of files to provide access to the names from namespace A. In your main function call the functions f then g. Compile, link, and execute using your development environment. To provide access to names in namespaces, you may use local using declarations such as:

   ```
   using std::cout;
   ```

   or use local using directives such as:

   ```
   using namespace std;
   ```

   inside a block, or qualify names using the names of namespaces, such as std::cout. You may not use global namespace directives such as the following which are not in a block and apply to the entire file:

   ```
   using namespace std;
   ```

   Of course you must handle namespace A and function names f and g, in addition to possibly std and cout.

   After doing the above, write a one page description of how to create and use namespaces and separate compilation in your environment.

2. Obtain the source code for the `PFArrayD` class and the demonstration program from Displays 10.10, 10.11, and 10.10. Modify this program to use namespaces and separate compilation. Put the class definition and other function declarations in one file. Place the implementations in a separate file. Distribute the namespace definition across the two files. Place the demonstration program in a third file. To provide access to names in namespaces, you may use local `using` declarations such as:

```
using std::cout;
```

or use local `using` directives such as:

```
using namespace std;
```

inside a block, or qualify names using the names of namespaces, such as `std::cout`. You may not use global namespace directives such as the following which are not in a block and apply to the entire file:

```
using namespace std;
```

3. Extend the Programming Project 1 from Chapter 10 in which you implemented a two dimensional array class by placing the class definition and implementation in a namespace, then providing access to the names in the namespace. Test your code. To provide access to names in namespaces, you may use local `using` declarations such as

```
using std::cout;
```

or use local `using` directives such as:

```
using namespace std;
```

inside a block, or qualify names using the names of namespaces, such as `std::cout`. You may not use global namespace directives such as the following which are not in a block and apply to the entire file:

```
using namespace std;
```

12 CHAPTER

Streams and File I/O

Streams and File I/O

Fish say, they have their stream and pond;
But is there anything beyond?

Rupert Brooke, *Heaven* (1913)

As a leaf is carried by a stream, whether the stream ends in a
lake or in the sea, so too is the output of your program carried by
a stream not knowing if the stream goes to the screen or to a file.

Washroom Wall of a Computer Science Department (1995)

INTRODUCTION

Input is delivered to your program and output from your program is delivered to the output device via special objects known as *streams*. The term *stream* is supposed to convey the idea that the output is streamed to or from your program without your program being aware (or at least not very aware) of where the input data came from or where the output data goes. This should, and does, mean that file input is handled in essentially the same way as the keyboard input we have been using up to now and that file output is handled in essentially the same way as screen output.

File I/O makes a small but essential use of inheritance, which is not covered until Chapter 14. However, we have placed this chapter before the inheritance chapter because programmers often want to start using file I/O early. Therefore this chapter includes a brief introduction to what few inheritance details are needed for file I/O.

You may cover this chapter anytime after covering the material of Chapters 1 to 4 and 6 to 9; in other words, you may cover this chapter before Chapters 5, 10, and 11. Enough material to allow you to do simple file I/O can be covered even before reading all those chapters. The basic elements of file I/O, which are discussed in Section 12.1, may be covered anytime after reading Chapters 1 to 4, Chapter 6, and the subsection of Chapter 9 entitled "The Member Functions get and put." That subsection is self-contained and does not require reading any other parts of Chapter 9. All of Section 12.2, except for the subsection entitled "File Names as Input" may also be read after reading only Chapters 1 to 4, Chapter 6, and the subsection of Chapter 9 entitled "The Member Functions get and put."

If you have not read Chapter 11 on namespaces, you may want to review the subsection of Chapter 1 on namespaces.

12.1 I/O Streams

Good Heavens! For more than forty years I have been speaking prose without knowing it.

Molière, *Le Bourgeois Gentilhomme*

A **stream** is a flow of characters (or other kind of data). If the flow is into your program, the stream is called an **input stream**. If the flow is out of your program, the stream is called an **output stream**. If the input stream flows from the keyboard, then your program will take input from the keyboard. If the input stream flows from a file, then your program will take its input from that file. Similarly, an output stream can go to the screen or to a file.

stream
input stream
output stream

Although you may not realize it, you have already been using streams in your programs. The `cin` that you have already used is an input stream connected to the keyboard, and `cout` is an output stream connected to the screen. These two streams are automatically available to your program as long as it has both an `include` directive that names the header file `<iostream>` and a `using` directive for the `std` namespace. You can define other streams that come from or go to files; once you have defined them, you can use them in your program in the same way you use the streams `cin` and `cout`. For example, suppose your program defines a stream called `inStream` that comes from some file. (We'll tell you how to define it shortly.) You can then fill an `int` variable named `theNumber` with a number from this file by using the following in your program:

`cin` and `cout` are streams

```
int theNumber;
inStream >> theNumber;
```

Similarly, if your program defines an output stream named `outStream` that goes to another file, then you can output the value of the variable `theNumber` to this other file. The following will output the string `"theNumber is "` followed by the contents of the variable `theNumber` to the output file that is connected to the stream `outStream`:

```
outStream << "theNumber is " << theNumber << endl;
```

Once the streams are connected to the desired files, your program can do file I/O the same way it does I/O using the keyboard and screen.

FILE I/O

The files we will use for I/O in this chapter are text files; that is, they are the same kind of files as those that contain your C++ programs.

When your program takes input from a file, it is said to be **reading** from the file; when your program sends output to a file, it is said to be **writing** to the file. There are other ways of reading input from a file, but the method given in this subsection reads the file from the beginning to the end (or as far as the program gets before ending).

reading and writing

Using this method, your program is not allowed to back up and read anything in the file a second time. This is exactly what happens when your program takes input from the keyboard, so it should not seem new or strange. (As we will see, your program can reread a file starting from the beginning of the file, but this is starting over, not backing up.) Similarly, for the method presented here, your program writes output into a file starting at the beginning of the file and proceeding forward. Your program is not allowed to back up and change any output that it has previously written to the file. This is exactly what happens when your program sends output to the screen: You can send more output to the screen, but you cannot back up and change the screen output. The way that you get input from a file into your program or send output from your program into a file is to connect your program to the file by means of a stream.

To send output to a file, your program must first connect the file to a (stream) object of the class ofstream. To read input from a file, your program must first connect the file to a (stream) object of the class ifstream. The classes ifstream and ofstream are defined in the <fstream> library and placed in the std namespace. Thus, to do both file input and file output, your program would contain

<fstream>

```
#include <fstream>
using namespace std;
```

or

```
#include <fstream>
using std::ifstream;
using std::ofstream;
```

declaring streams

A stream must be declared just as you would declare any other class variable. Thus, you can declare inStream to be an input stream for a file and outStream to be an output stream for another file as follows:

```
ifstream inStream;
ofstream outStream;
```

connecting a stream to a file

open

Stream variables, such as inStream and outStream declared above, must each be connected to a file. This is called **opening the file** and is done with the member function named open. For example, suppose you want the input stream inStream connected to the file named infile.txt. Your program must then contain the following before it reads any input from this file:

```
inStream.open("infile.txt");
```

pathnames

You can specify a pathname (a directory or folder) when giving the file name. The details of how to specify a pathname vary a little from system to system, so consult with a local guru for the details (or do a little trial-and-error programming). In our examples we will use simple file names, which assumes that the file is in the same directory (folder) as the one in which your program is running.

Once you have declared an input stream variable and connected it to a file using the open function, your program can take input from the file using the extraction operator, >>, with the input stream variable used the same way as cin. For example, the following reads two input numbers from the file connected to inStream and places them in the variables oneNumber and anotherNumber:

```
int oneNumber, anotherNumber;
inStream >> oneNumber >> anotherNumber;
```

An output stream is opened (that is, connected to a file) in the same way as just described for input streams. For example, the following declares the output stream outStream and connects it to the file named outfile.txt:

```
ofstream outStream;
outStream.open("outfile.txt");
```

When used with a stream of type ofstream, the member function open will create the output file if it does not already exist. If the output file already exists, the member function open will discard the contents of the file so that the output file is empty after the call to open. (We will discuss other ways of opening a file a bit later in this chapter.)

After a file is connected to the stream outStream with a call to open, the program can send output to that file using the insertion operator <<. For example, the following writes two strings and the contents of the variables oneNumber and anotherNumber to the file that is connected to the stream outStream (which in this example is the file named outfile.txt):

```
outStream << "oneNumber = " << oneNumber
          << " anotherNumber = " << anotherNumber;
```

OVERLOADING OF >> AND << APPLIES TO FILES

As we pointed out in Chapter 8, if you overload >> and <<, then those overloadings apply to file input and output streams the same as they apply to cin and cout. (If you have not yet read Chapter 8, you can ignore this remark. It will be repeated for you in Chapter 8.)

Notice that when your program is dealing with a file, it is as if the file had two names. One is the usual name for the file that is used by the operating system, which is the **external file name**. In our sample code the external file names were infile.txt and outfile.txt. The external file name is in some sense the "real name" for the file. The conventions for spelling these external file names vary from one system to another. The names infile.txt and outfile.txt that we used in our examples may or may not look like file names on your system. You should name your files following whatever

external file name

conventions are used on your operating system. Although the external file name is the real name for the file, it is typically used only once in a program. The external file name is given as an argument to the function open, but after the file is opened, the file is always referred to by naming the stream that is connected to the file. Thus, within your program, the stream name serves as a second name for the file.

A FILE HAS TWO NAMES

Every input and every output file used by your program has two names. The external file name is the real name of the file, but it is used only in the call to the member function open, which connects the file to a stream. After the call to open, you always use the stream name as the name of the file.

The sample program in Display 12.1 reads three numbers from one file and writes their sum, as well as some text, to another file.

close

Every file should be **closed** when your program is finished getting input from the file or sending output to the file. Closing a file disconnects the stream from the file. A file is closed with a call to the function close. The following lines from the program in Display 12.1 illustrate how to use the function close:

```
inStream.close( );
outStream.close( );
```

Notice that the function close takes no arguments. If your program ends normally but without closing a file, the system will automatically close the file for you. However, it is good to get in the habit of closing files for at least two reasons. First, the system will only close files for you if your program ends normally. If your program ends abnormally due to an error, the file will not be closed and may be left in a corrupted state. If your program closes files as soon as it is finished with them, file corruption is less likely. Second, you may want your program to send output to a file and later read that output back into the program. To do this, your program should close the file after it is finished writing to the file, and then reopen the file with an input stream. (It is possible to open a file for both input and output, but this is done in a slightly different way.)

A less commonly used member function, but one you may eventually need, is flush, which is a member function of every output stream. For reasons of efficiency, output is often *buffered*—that is, temporarily stored someplace—before it is actually written to a file. The member function flush flushes the output stream so that all output that may have been buffered is physically written to the file. An invocation of close automatically invokes flush, so you very seldom need to use flush. The syntax for flush is indicated by the following example:

```
outStream.flush( );
```

Display 12.1   Simple File Input/Output

```
1   //Reads three numbers from the file infile.txt, sums the numbers,
2   //and writes the sum to the file outfile.txt.
3   #include <fstream>
4   using std::ifstream;
5   using std::ofstream;
6   using std::endl;
7
8   int main( )
9   {
10      ifstream inStream;
11      ofstream outStream;
12
13      inStream.open("infile.txt");
14      outStream.open("outfile.txt");
15
16      int first, second, third;
17      inStream >> first >> second >> third;
18      outStream << "The sum of the first 3\n"
19                << "numbers in infile.txt\n"
20                << "is " << (first + second + third)
21                << endl;
22
23      inStream.close( );
24      outStream.close( );
25
26      return 0;
27  }
```

A better version of this program is given in Display 12.3.

SAMPLE DIALOGUE

*There is no output to the screen
and no input from the keyboard.*

infile.txt
(Not changed by program)

```
1
2
3
4
```

outfile.txt
(After program is run)

```
The sum of the first 3
numbers in infile.txt
is 6
```

506 Streams and File I/O

RESTRICTIONS ON STREAM VARIABLES

You declare a stream variable (one of type `ifstream` or `ofstream`) in the usual way, but these variables cannot be used in some of the ways that other variables are used. You cannot use an assignment statement to assign a value to a stream variable. You can have a parameter of a stream type (`ifstream`, `ofstream`, or any other stream type), but it must be a call-by-reference parameter. It cannot be a call-by-value parameter.

■ APPENDING TO A FILE

When sending output to a file, your code must first use the member function `open` to open a file and connect it to a stream of type `ofstream`. The way we have done this thus far (with a single argument for the file name) always yields an empty file. If a file of the specified name already exists, its old contents are lost. There is an alternative way to open a file so that the output from your program will be appended to the file after any data already in the file.

To append your output to a file named `"important.txt"`, you would use a two-argument version of `open`, as illustrated by the following:

```
ofstream outStream;
outStream.open("important.txt", ios::app);
```

If the file `"important.txt"` does not exist, this will create an empty file with that name to receive your program's output; if the file already exists, then all the output from your program will be appended to the end of the file, so that old data in the file is not lost. This is illustrated in Display 12.2.

ios::app The second argument `ios::app` is a defined constant in the class `ios`. The class `ios` is defined in the `<iostream>` library (and also in some other stream libraries). The definition of the class `ios` is placed in the `std` namespace, so either of the following will make `ios` (and hence `ios::app`) available to your program:

```
#include <iostream>
using namespace std;
```

or

```
#include <iostream>
using std::ios;
```

Display 12.2 Appending to a File

```
1    //Appends data to the end of the file alldata.txt.
2    #include <fstream>
3    #include <iostream>
4    using std::ofstream;
5    using std::cout;
6    using std::ios;

7    int main( )
8    {
9        cout << "Opening data.txt for appending.\n";
10       ofstream fout;
11       fout.open("data.txt", ios::app);

12       fout << "5 6 pick up sticks.\n"
13            << "7 8 ain't C++ great!\n";

14       fout.close( );
15       cout << "End of appending to file.\n";

16       return 0;
17   }
```

SAMPLE DIALOGUE

data.txt
(Before program is run)

```
1 2 bucket my shoe.
3 4 shut the door.
```

data.txt
(After program is run)

```
1 2 bucket my shoe.
3 4 shut the door.
5 6 pick up sticks
7 8 ain't C++ great!
```

SCREEN OUTPUT

```
Opening data.txt for appending.
End of appending to file.
```

APPENDING TO A FILE

If you want to append data to a file so that it goes after any existing contents of the file, open the file as follows.

SYNTAX

```
Output_Stream.open(File_Name, ios::app);
```

EXAMPLE

```
ofstream outStream;
outStream.open("important.txt", ios::app);
```

Tip

ANOTHER SYNTAX FOR OPENING A FILE

Each of the classes ifstream and ofstream has constructors that allow you to specify a file name and sometimes other parameters for opening a file. A few examples will make the syntax clear.

The two statements

```
ifstream inStream;
inStream.open("infile.txt");
```

can be replaced by the following equivalent line:

```
ifstream inStream("infile.txt");
```

The two statements

```
ofstream outStream;
outStream.open("outfile.txt");
```

can be replaced by the following equivalent line:

```
ofstream outStream("outfile.txt");
```

As our final example, the two lines

```
ofstream outStream;
outStream.open("important.txt", ios::app);
```

are equivalent to the following:

```
ofstream outStream("important.txt", ios::app);
```

Tip

CHECK THAT A FILE WAS OPENED SUCCESSFULLY

A call to open can be unsuccessful for a number of reasons. For example, if you try to open an input file and there is no file with the external name that you specified, then the call to open will fail. As another example, an attempt to open an output file could fail because the file exists and your program (that is, your account) does not have write permission for the file. When such things happen, you may not receive an error message and your program may simply proceed to do something unexpected. Thus, you should always follow a call to open with a test to see whether the call to open was successful, and end the program (or take some other appropriate action) if the call to open was unsuccessful.

You can use the member function named `fail` to test whether or not a stream operation has failed. There is a member function named `fail` for each of the classes `ifstream` and `ofstream`. The `fail` function takes no arguments and returns a `bool` value.

the member function `fail`

You should place a call to `fail` immediately after each call to open; if the call to open fails, the function `fail` will return `true`. For example, if the following call to open fails, then the program will output an error message and end; if the call succeeds, the `fail` function returns `false` and the program will continue.

```
inStream.open("stuff.txt");
if (inStream.fail( ))
{
    cout << "Input file opening failed.\n";
    exit(1);
}
```

Display 12.3 contains the program from Display 12.1 rewritten to include tests to see if the input and output files were opened successfully. It processes files in exactly the same way as the program in Display 12.1. In particular, assuming that the file `infile.txt` exists and has the contents shown in Display 12.1, the program in Display 12.3 will create the file `outfile.txt` that is shown in Display 12.1. However, if there were something wrong and one of the calls to open failed, then the program in Display 12.3 would end and send an appropriate error message to the screen. For example, if there were no file named `infile.txt`, then the call to `inStream.open` would fail, the program would end, and an error message would be written to the screen. Notice that we used `cout` to output the error message; this is because we want the error message to go to the screen, as opposed to going to a file. Since this program uses `cout` to output to the screen (as well as doing file I/O), we have added an `include` directive for the header file `<iostream>`. (Actually, your program does not need to have #include <iostream> when your program has #include <fstream>, but it causes no problems to include it, and it reminds you that the program is using screen output in addition to file I/O.)

Display 12.3   File I/O with Checks on open

```
1    //Reads three numbers from the file infile.txt and writes the sum to the
2    //file outfile.txt.
3    #include <fstream>
4    #include <iostream>
5    #include <cstdlib> //for exit
6    using std::ifstream;
7    using std::ofstream;
8    using std::cout;
9    using std::endl;

10   int main( )
11   {
12       ifstream inStream;
13       ofstream outStream;

14       inStream.open("infile.txt");
15       if (inStream.fail( ))
16       {
17           cout << "Input file opening failed.\n";
18           exit(1);
19       }

20       outStream.open("outfile.txt");
21       if (outStream.fail( ))
22       {
23           cout << "Output file opening failed.\n";
24           exit(1);
25       }

26       int first, second, third;
27       inStream >> first >> second >> third;
28       outStream << "The sum of the first 3\n"
29                 << "numbers in infile.txt\n"
30                 << "is " << (first + second + third) << endl;

31       inStream.close( );
32       outStream.close( );
33       return 0;
34   }
```

SAMPLE DIALOGUE (if the file infile.txt does not exist)

```
Input file opening failed.
```

SUMMARY OF FILE I/O STATEMENTS

In this example the input comes from a file with the name infile.txt, and the output goes to a file with the name outfile.txt.

- Place the following include directives in your program file:

```
#include <fstream>          For file I/O
#include <iostream>         For cout
#include <cstdlib>          For exit
```

Add the following using directives (or something similar):

```
using std::ifstream;
using std::ofstream;
using std::cout;
using std::endl;   //if endl is used.
```

- Choose a stream name for the input stream and declare it to be a variable of type ifstream. Choose a stream name for the output file and declare it to be of type ofstream. For example:

```
ifstream inStream;
ofstream outStream;
```

- Connect each stream to a file using the member function open with the external file name as an argument. Remember to use the member function fail to test that the call to open was successful:

```
inStream.open("infile.txt");
if (inStream.fail( ))
{
    cout << "Input file opening failed.\n";
    exit(1);
}

outStream.open("outfile.txt");
if (outStream.fail( ))
{
    cout << "Output file opening failed.\n";
    exit(1);
}
```

- Use the stream inStream to get input from the file infile.txt just like you use cin to get input from the keyboard. For example:

```
inStream >> someVariable >> someOtherVariable;
```

■ Use the stream outStream to send output to the file outfile.txt just like you use cout to send output to the screen. For example:

```
outStream << "someVariable = "
          << someVariable << endl;
```

■ Close the streams using the function close:

```
inStream.close( );
outStream.close( );
```

Self-Test Exercises

1. Suppose you are writing a program that uses a stream called fin, which will be connected to an input file, and a stream called fout, which will be connected to an output file. How do you declare fin and fout? What include directive, if any, do you need to place in your program file?

2. Suppose you are continuing to write the program discussed in the previous exercise and you want your program to take its input from the file stuff1.txt and send its output to the file stuff2.txt. What statements do you need to place in your program in order to connect the stream fin to the file stuff1.txt and to connect the stream fout to the file stuff2.txt? Be sure to include checks to make sure that the openings were successful.

3. Suppose that you are still writing the same program that we discussed in the previous two exercises and you reach the point at which you no longer need to get input from the file stuff1.txt and no longer need to send output to the file stuff2.txt. How do you close these files?

4. Suppose you want to change the program in Display 12.1 so that it sends its output to the screen instead of the file outfile.txt. (The input should still come from the file infile.txt.) What changes do you need to make to the program?

5. A programmer has read half of the lines in a file. What must the programmer do to the file to enable reading the first line a second time?

▪ CHARACTER I/O

Chapter 9 described character I/O from the keyboard with cin and to the screen with cout. All those details apply equally well to file I/O. Just use an input stream connected to a file in place of cin or an output stream connected to a file in place of cout. In particular, get, getline, putback, peek, and ignore work the same for file input as they do for keyboard input;[1] put works the same for file output as it does for screen output.

CHECKING FOR THE END OF A FILE

A common way of processing an input file is to use a loop that processes data from the file until the end of the file is reached. There are two standard ways to test for the end of a file. The most straightforward way is to use the eof member function.

Every input-file stream has a member function called eof that can be used to test for reaching the end of the input file. The function eof takes no arguments, so if the input stream is called fin, then a call to the function eof is written

eof
member
function

```
fin.eof( )
```

This is a Boolean expression that can be used to control a while loop, do-while loop, or an if-else statement. This expression returns true if the program has read past the end of the input file; otherwise, it returns false.

Since we usually want to test that we are *not* at the end of a file, a call to the member function eof is typically used with a *not* in front of it. Recall that in C++ the symbol ! is used to express *not*. For example, the entire contents of the file connected to the input stream inStream can be written to the screen with the following while loop:

ending
an input
loop with
the eof
function

```
inStream.get(next);
while (! inStream.eof( ))
{
    cout << next;
    inStream.get(next);
}
```

If you prefer, you can use cout.put(next) here.

The above while loop reads each character from the input file into the char variable next using the member function get, and then it writes the character to the screen. After the program has passed the end of the file, the value of inStream.eof( ) changes from false to true. Thus,

```
(! inStream.eof( ))
```

changes from true to false and the loop ends.

Notice that inStream.eof( ) does not become true until the program attempts to read one character beyond the end of the file. For example, suppose the file contains the following (without any newline character after the c):

```
ab
c
```

---

[1] If you have not yet read about getline, putback, peek, or ignore, do not be concerned. They are not used in this chapter, except for one brief reference to ignore at the very end of this chapter. You can ignore that one reference to ignore.

This is actually the following list of four characters:

ab<the newline character '\n'>c

The above loop will read an 'a' and write it to the screen, then read a 'b' and write it to the screen, then read the newline character '\n' and write it to the screen, and then read a 'c' and write it to the screen. At that point the loop will have read all the characters in the file. However, inStream.eof( ) will still be false. The value of inStream.eof( ) will not change from false to true until the program tries to read one more character. That is why the above while loop ends with inStream.get(next). The loop needs to read one extra character in order to end the loop.

There is a special end-of-file marker at the end of a file. The member function eof does not change from false to true until this end-of-file marker is read. That's why the previous while loop could read one character beyond what you think of as the last character in the file. However, this end-of-file marker is not an ordinary character and should not be manipulated like an ordinary character. You can read this end-of-file marker, but you should not write it out again. If you write out the end-of-file marker, the result is unpredictable. The system automatically places this end-of-file marker at the end of each file for you.

the macho
way to
test for end
of file

The second way to check for the end of the file is to note (and use) the fact that a read with an extraction operator actually returns a Boolean value. The expression

```
(inStream >> next)
```

returns true if the read was successful and returns false when your code attempts to read beyond the end of the file. For example, the following will read all the numbers in a file of integers connected to the input stream inStream and compute their sum in the variable sum:

```
double next, sum = 0;
while (inStream >> next)
    sum = sum + next;
cout << "the sum is " << sum << endl;
```

The above loop may look a bit peculiar, because inStream >> next reads a number from the stream inStream and returns a Boolean value. An expression involving the extraction operator >> is simultaneously both an action and a Boolean condition.[2] If there is another number to be input, then the number is read and the Boolean value true is returned, so the body of the loop is executed one more time. If there are no more numbers to be read in, then nothing is input and the Boolean value false is returned, so the loop ends. In this example the type of the input variable next was

---

[2] Technically, the Boolean condition works this way: The returned value of the operator >> is an input stream reference (istream& or ifstream&), as explained in Chapter 8. This stream reference is automatically converted to a bool value. The resulting value is true if the stream was able to extract data, and false otherwise.

double, but this method of checking for the end of the file works the same way for other data types, such as int and char.

This second method of testing for the end of a file is preferred by many C++ programmers for what appears to be a cultural reason. It was commonly used in C programming. It is also possible that, depending on implementation details, this second method might be a bit more efficient. In any event, whether you use this second method or not, you need to know it so you can understand other programmer's code.

An illustration of using the eof member function is given in Display 12.4.

Display 12.4   Checking for the End of a File *(part 1 of 2)*

```
1
2    //Copies story.txt to numstory.txt,
3    //but adds a number to the beginning of each line.
4    //Assumes story.txt is not empty.
5    #include <fstream>
6    #include <iostream>
7    #include <cstdlib>

8    using std::ifstream;
9    using std::ofstream;
10   using std::cout;


11   int main( )
12   {
13       ifstream fin;
14       ofstream fout;


15       fin.open("story.txt");
16       if (fin.fail( ))
17       {
18           cout << "Input file opening failed.\n";
19           exit(1);
20       }


21       fout.open("numstory.txt");
22       if (fout.fail( ))
23       {
24           cout << "Output file opening failed.\n";
25           exit(1);
26       }
```

Display 12.4   Checking for the End of a File *(part 2 of 2)*

```
27
28      char next;
29      int n = 1;
30      fin.get(next);
31      fout << n << " ";
32      while (! fin.eof( ))
33      {
34          fout << next;
35          if (next == '\n')
36          {
37              n++;
38              fout << n << ' ';
39          }
40          fin.get(next);
41      }

42      fin.close( );
43      fout.close( );

44      return 0;
45  }
```

Notice that the loop ends with a read (fin.get). The member function fin.eof does not return true until your program tries to read one more character after reading the last character in the file.

SAMPLE DIALOGUE

*There is no output to the screen
and no input from the keyboard.*

story.txt
(Not changed by program)

```
The little green men had
pointed heads and orange
toes with one long curly
hair on each toe.
```

numstory.txt
(After program is run)

```
1 The little green men had
2 pointed heads and orange
3 toes with one long curly
4 hair on each toe.
```

Self-Test Exercises

6. What output will be produced when the following lines are executed, assuming the file list.txt contains the data shown (and assuming the lines are embedded in a complete and correct program with the proper include and using directives)?

```
ifstream ins;
ins.open("list.txt");
```

```
    int count = 0, next;
    while (ins >> next)
    {
        count++;
        cout << next << endl;
    }
    ins.close( );
    cout << count;
```

The file `list.txt` contains the following three numbers (and nothing more):

```
1 2
   3
```

7. Write the definition for a **void** function called **toScreen**. The function **toScreen** has one formal parameter called **fileStream**, which is of type **ifstream**. The precondition and postcondition for the function are given below.

```
//Precondition: The stream fileStream has been connected
//to a file with a call to the member function open. The
//file contains a list of integers (and nothing else).
//Postcondition: The numbers in the file connected to
//fileStream have been written to the screen one per line.
//(This function does not close the file.)
```

12.2   Tools for Stream I/O

> *You shall see them on a beautiful quarto page, where a neat*
> *rivulet of text shall meander through a meadow of margin.*
>
> Richard Brinsley Sheridan, *The School for Scandal*

FILE NAMES AS INPUT

Thus far, we have written the literal file names for our input and output files into the code of our programs. We did this by giving the file name as the argument to a call to the function open, as in the following example:

```
inStream.open("infile.txt");
```

You can instead read the file name in from the keyboard, as illustrated by the following: **as a C-string**

```
char fileName[16];
ifstream inStream;
```

```
cout << "Enter file name (maximum of 15 characters):\n";
cin >> fileName;
inStream.open(fileName);
```

Note that our code reads the file name as a C-string. The member function open takes an argument that is a C-string. You cannot use a string variable as an argument to open, and there is no predefined type cast operator to convert from a string object to a C-string. However, as an alternative, you can read the file name into a string variable and use the string member function c_str( ) to produce the corresponding C-string value for open. The code would be as follows:

```
string fileName;
ifstream inStream;

cout << "Enter file name:\n";
cin >> fileName;
inStream.open(fileName.c_str( ));
```

Note that when you use a string variable for the file name, there is essentially no limit to the size of the file name.[3]

FORMATTING OUTPUT WITH STREAM FUNCTIONS

You can control the format of your output to a file or to the screen with commands that determine such details as the number of spaces between items and the number of digits after the decimal point. For example, in Chapter 1 we gave the following "magic formula" to use for outputting amounts of money:

```
cout.setf(ios::fixed);
cout.setf(ios::showpoint);
cout.precision(2);
```

We are now in a position to explain these and other formulas for formatting output.

The first thing to note is that you can use these formatting commands on any output stream. Output streams connected to a file have these same member functions as the object cout. If outStream is a file output stream (of type ofstream), you can format output in the same way:

```
outStream.setf(ios::fixed);
outStream.setf(ios::showpoint);
outStream.precision(2);
```

To explain this magic formula, we will consider the member functions in reverse order.

---

[3] The lack of accommodation for the type string within the iostream library is because iostream was written before the string type was added to the C++ libraries.

Every output stream has a member function named precision. When your program executes a call to precision such as the one above for the stream outStream, then
from that point on in your program, any number with a decimal point that is output to
that stream will be written with a total of two significant figures or with two digits after
the decimal point, depending on when your compiler was written. The following is
some possible output from a compiler that sets two significant digits:

precision

```
23.     2.2e7    2.2    6.9e-1    0.00069
```

The following is some possible output from a compiler that sets two digits after the
decimal point:

```
23.56   2.26e7   2.21   0.69      0.69e-4
```

In this book, we assume the compiler sets two digits after the decimal point. Of course,
you can use a different argument than 2 to obtain more or less precision.

Every output stream has a member function named setf that can be used to set certain flags. These **flags** are constants in the class ios, which is in the std namespace.
When set with a call to setf, the flags determine certain behaviors of the output
stream. Below are the two calls to the member function setf with the stream out-
Stream as the calling object:

setf
flag

```
outStream.setf(ios::fixed);
outStream.setf(ios::showpoint);
```

Each of these flags is an instruction to format output in one of two possible ways. What
it causes the stream to do depends on the flag.

The flag ios::fixed causes the stream to output floating-point numbers in what is
called **fixed-point notation**, which is a fancy phrase for the way we normally write
numbers. If the flag ios::fixed is set (by a call to setf), then all floating-point numbers (such as numbers of type double) that are output to that stream will be written in
ordinary everyday notation, rather than e-notation.

ios::fixed
fixed-point
notation

The flag ios::showpoint tells the stream to always include a decimal point in floating-
point numbers. If the number to be output has a value of 2.0, then it will be output as
2.0 and not simply as 2; that is, the output will include the decimal point even if all the
digits after the decimal point are 0. Some common flags and the actions they cause are
described in Display 12.5.

ios::show-
point

You can set multiple flags with a single call to setf. Simply connect the various flags
with '|' symbols, as illustrated below:[4]

```
outStream.setf(ios::fixed | ios::showpoint | ios::right);
```

---

[4] The | operator is bitwise-or. You are literally or-ing a bitwise mask that indicates the flag set-
tings, although you need not be aware of this low level detail.

Display 12.5 Formatting Flags for `setf`

FLAG	MEANING OF SETTING THE FLAG	DEFAULT
`ios::fixed`	Floating-point numbers are not written in e-notation. (Setting this flag automatically unsets the flag `ios::scientific`.)	Not set
`ios::scientific`	Floating-point numbers are written in e-notation. (Setting this flag automatically unsets the flag `ios::fixed`.) If neither `ios::fixed` nor `ios::scientific` is set, then the system decides how to output each number.	Not set
`ios::showpoint`	A decimal point and trailing zeros are always shown for floating-point numbers. If it is not set, a number with all zeros after the decimal point might be output without the decimal point and following zeros.	Not set
`ios::showpos`	A plus sign is output before positive integer values.	Not set
`ios::right`	If this flag is set and some field-width value is given with a call to the member function `width`, then the next item output will be at the right end of the space specified by `width`. In other words, any extra blanks are placed before the item output. (Setting this flag automatically unsets the flag `ios::left`.)	Set
`ios::left`	If this flag is set and some field-width value is given with a call to the member function `width`, then the next item output will be at the left end of the space specified by `width`. In other words, any extra blanks are placed after the item output. (Setting this flag automatically unsets the flag `ios::right`.)	Not set
`ios::dec`	Integers are output in decimal (base 10) notation.	Set
`ios::oct`	Integers are output in octal (base 8) notation.	Not set
`ios::hex`	Integers are output in hexadecimal (base 16) notation.	Not set
`ios::uppercase`	An uppercase E is used instead of a lowercase e in scientific notation for floating-point numbers. Hexadecimal numbers are output using uppercase letters.	Not set
`ios::showbase`	Shows the base of an output number (leading 0 for octal, leading 0x for hexadecimal).	Not set

width

Output streams have other member functions besides `precision` and `setf`. One very commonly used formatting function is `width`. For example, consider the following call to `width` made by the stream `cout`:

```
cout << "Start Now";
cout.width(4);
cout << 7 << endl;
```

This code will cause the following line to appear on the screen:

```
Start Now    7
```

This output has exactly three spaces between the letter 'w' and the number 7. The width function tells the stream how many spaces to use when giving an item as output. In this case the number 7 occupies only one space and width is set to use four spaces, so three of the spaces are blank. If the output requires more space than you specified in the argument to width, then as much additional space as is needed will be used. The entire item is always output, no matter what argument you give to width.

THE CLASS ios

The class ios has a number of important defined constants, such as ios::app (used to indicate that you are appending to a file) and the flags listed in Display 12.5. The class ios is defined in libraries for output streams, such as <iostream> and <fstream>. One way to make the class ios and hence all these constants (all these flags) available to your code is the following:

```
#include <iostream> //or #include <fstream> or both
using std::ios;
```

Any flag that is set may be unset. To unset a flag, use the function unsetf. For exam- **unsetf** ple, the following will cause your program to stop including plus signs on positive integers that are output to the stream cout:

```
cout.unsetf(ios::showpos);
```

When a flag is set, it remains set until it is unset. The effect of a call to precision stays in effect until the precision is reset. However, the member function width behaves differently. A call to width applies only to the next item that is output. If you want to output 12 numbers, using four spaces to output each number, then you must call width 12 times. If this becomes a nuisance, you may prefer to use the manipulator setw that is described in the next subsection.

MANIPULATORS

A **manipulator** is a function that is called in a nontraditional way. Manipulators are **manipulator** placed after the insertion operator <<, just as if the manipulator function call were an item to be output. Like traditional functions, manipulators may or may not have arguments. We have already seen one manipulator, endl. This subsection discusses two manipulators called setw and setprecision.

The manipulator setw and the member function width (which you have already **setw** seen) do exactly the same thing. You call the setw manipulator by writing it after the insertion operator, <<, as if it were to be sent to the output stream, and this in turn calls the member function width. For example, the following will output the numbers 10, 20, and 30, using the field widths specified:

```
cout << "Start" << setw(4) << 10
     << setw(4) << 20 << setw(6) << 30;
```

The preceding statement will produce the following output:

```
Start  10  20    30
```

(There are two spaces before the 10, two spaces before the 20, and four spaces before the 30.)

Like the member function width, a call to setw applies only to the next item output, but it is easier to include multiple calls to setw than it is to make multiple calls to width.

setprecision

The manipulator setprecision does the same thing as the member function precision (which you have already seen). However, a call to setprecision is written after the insertion operator, <<, in a manner similar to how you call the setw manipulator. For example, the following will output the numbers listed using the number of digits after the decimal point that are indicated by the call to setprecision:

```
cout.setf(ios::fixed);
cout.setf(ios::showpoint);
cout << "$" << setprecision(2) << 10.3 << endl
     << "$" << 20.5 << endl;
```

The above statement will produce the following output:

```
$10.30
$20.50
```

When you set the number of digits after the decimal point using the manipulator setprecision, then just as was the case with the member function precision, the setting stays in effect until you reset it to some other number by another call to either setprecision or precision.

<iomanip>

To use either of the manipulators setw or setprecision, you must include the following directive in your program:

```
#include <iomanip>
using namespace std;
```

or must use one of the other ways of specifying the names and namespace, such as the following:

```
#include <iomanip>
using std::setw;
using std::setprecision;
```

■ SAVING FLAG SETTINGS

A function should not have unwanted or unexpected side effects. For example, a function to output amounts of money might contain

```
cout.setf(ios::fixed);
cout.setf(ios::showpoint);
cout.precision(2);
```

After the function invocation ends, these settings will still be in effect. If you do not want such side effects, you can save and restore the original settings.

The function `precision` has been overloaded so that with no arguments it returns the current precision setting so the setting can later be restored.

The flags set with `setf` are easy to save and restore. The member function `flags` is overloaded to provide a way to save and then restore the flag settings. The member function `cout.flags( )` returns a value of type `long` that codes all the flag settings. The flags can be reset by using this `long` value as an argument to `cout.flags`. These techniques work the same for file output streams as they do for `cout`.

For example, a function to save and restore these settings could be structured as follows:

```
void outputStuff(ofstream& outStream)
{
    int precisionSetting = outStream.precision( );
    long flagSettings = outStream.flags( );
    outStream.setf(ios::fixed);
    outStream.setf(ios::showpoint);
    outStream.precision(2);
        Do whatever you want here.
    outStream.precision(precisionSetting);
    outStream.flags(flagSettings);
}
```

Another way to restore settings is

```
cout.setf(0, ios::floatfield);
```

An invocation of the member function `setf` with these arguments will restore the default `setf` settings. Note that these are the default values, not necessarily the settings before the last time they were changed. Also note that the default setting values are implementation-dependent. Finally, note that this does not reset `precision` settings or any settings that are not set with `setf`.

■ MORE OUTPUT STREAM MEMBER FUNCTIONS

Display 12.6 summarizes some of the formatting member functions for the class ostream and some of the manipulators. Remember that to use the manipulators you need the following (or something similar):

```
#include <iomanip>
using namespace std;
```

Display 12.6   Formatting Tools for the Class ostream

FUNCTION	DESCRIPTION	CORRESPONDING MANIPULATOR
setf(*ios_Flag*)	Sets flags as described in Display 12.5	setiosflags(*ios_Flag*)
unsetf(*ios_Flag*)	Unsets flag	resetiosflags(*ios_Flag*)
setf(0, ios::floatfield)	Restores default flag settings	None
precision(int)	Sets precision for floating-point number output	setprecision(int)
precision( )	Returns the current precision setting	None
width(int)	Sets the output field width; applies only to the next item output	setw(int)
fill(char)	Specifies the fill character when the output field is larger than the value output; the default is a blank	setfill(char)

Self-Test Exercises

8. What output will be produced when the following lines are executed?

```
cout << "*";
cout.width(5);
cout << 123
     << "*" << 123 << "*" << endl;
cout << "*" << setw(5) << 123
     << "*" << 123 << "*" << endl;
```

9. What output will be produced when the following lines are executed?

```
cout << "*" << setw(5) << 123;
cout.setf(ios::left);
cout << "*" << setw(5) << 123;
```

```
cout.setf(ios::right);
cout << "*" << setw(5) << 123 << "*" << endl;
```

10. What output will be produced when the following lines are executed?

```
cout << "*" << setw(5) << 123 << "*"
    << 123 << "*" << endl;
cout.setf(ios::showpos);
cout << "*" << setw(5) << 123 << "*"
    << 123 << "*" << endl;
cout.unsetf(ios::showpos);
cout.setf(ios::left);
cout << "*" << setw(5) << 123 << "*"
    << setw(5) << 123 << "*" << endl;
```

11. What output will be sent to the file `stuff.txt` when the following lines are executed?

```
ofstream fout;
fout.open("stuff.txt");
fout << "*" << setw(5) << 123 << "*"
    << 123 << "*" << endl;
fout.setf(ios::showpos);
fout << "*" << setw(5) << 123 << "*"
    << 123 << "*" << endl;
fout.unsetf(ios::showpos);
fout.setf(ios::left);
fout << "*" << setw(5) << 123 << "*"
    << setw(5) << 123 << "*" << endl;
```

12. What output will be produced when the following line is executed (assuming the line is embedded in a complete and correct program with the proper `include` and `using` directives)?

```
cout << "*" << setw(3) << 12345 << "*" << endl;
```

Example

CLEANING UP A FILE FORMAT

The program in Display 12.7 takes its input from the file `rawdata.txt` and writes its output, in a neat format, both to the screen and to the file `neat.txt`. The program copies numbers from the file `rawdata.txt` to the file `neat.txt`, but it uses formatting instructions to write them in a neat way. The numbers are written one per line in a field of width 12, which means that each number is preceded by enough blanks so that the blanks plus the number occupy 12 spaces. The numbers are written in ordinary notation; that is, they are not written in e-notation. Each number is written with five digits after the decimal point and with a plus or minus sign. The program uses a function, named `makeNeat`, that has formal parameters for the input-file stream and the output-file stream.

Display 12.7   Formatting Output *(part 1 of 2)*

```
1   //Reads all the numbers in the file rawdata.dat and writes the numbers
2   //to the screen and to the file neat.dat in a neatly formatted way.
3   #include <iostream>
4   #include <fstream>
5   #include<cstdlib>
6   #include <iomanip>  ←——————————— Needed for setw
7   using std::ifstream;
8   using std::ofstream;
9   using std::cout;
10  using std::endl;                        Stream parameters must
11  using std::ios;                         be call-by-reference parameters.
12  using std::setw;

13  void makeNeat(ifstream& messyFile, ofstream& neatFile,
14              int numberAfterDecimalpoint, int fieldWidth);
15  //Precondition: The streams messyFile and neatFile have been connected to
16  //two different files. The file named messyFile contains only floating-point
17  //numbers. Postcondition: The numbers in the file connected to messyFile
18  //have been written to the screen and to the file connected to the stream
19  //neatFile. The numbers are written one per line, in fixed-point notation
20  //(that is, not in e-notation), with numberAfterDecimalpoint digits after
21  //the decimal point; each number is preceded by a plus or minus sign and each
22  //number is in a field of width fieldWidth. (This function does not close
23  //the file.)

24  int main( )
25  {
26      ifstream fin;
27      ofstream fout;

28      fin.open("rawdata.txt");
29      if (fin.fail( ))
30      {
31          cout << "Input file opening failed.\n";
32          exit(1);
33      }

34
35      fout.open("neat.txt");
36      if (fout.fail( ))
37      {
38          cout << "Output file opening failed.\n";
39          exit(1);
40      }
41    makeNeat(fin, fout, 5, 12);

42      fin.close( );
43      fout.close( );
```

Display 12.7   Formatting Output *(part 2 of 2)*

```
44        cout << "End of program.\n";
45        return 0;
46   }

47   //Uses <iostream>, <fstream>, and <iomanip>:
48   void makeNeat(ifstream& messyFile, ofstream& neatFile,
49               int numberAfterDecimalpoint, int fieldWidth)
50   {
51       neatFile.setf(ios::fixed);
52       neatFile.setf(ios::showpoint);
53       neatFile.setf(ios::showpos);
54       neatFile.precision(numberAfterDecimalpoint);

55       cout.setf(ios::fixed);
56       cout.setf(ios::showpoint);
57       cout.setf(ios::showpos);
58       cout.precision(numberAfterDecimalpoint);

59       double next;
60       while (messyFile >> next)
61       {
62           cout << setw(fieldWidth) << next << endl;
63           neatFile << setw(fieldWidth) << next << endl;
64       }
65   }
```

setf and precision behave the same for a file output stream as they do for cout.

Satisfied if there is a next number to read

Works the same for file output streams as it does for cout

rawdata.txt
(Not changed by program)

```
10.37      -9.89897
2.313    -8.950   15.0

    7.33333   92.8765
-1.237568432e2
```

neat.txt
(After program is run)

```
+10.37000
 -9.89897
 +2.31300
 -8.95000
+15.00000
 +7.33333
+92.87650
-123.75684
```

SCREEN OUTPUT

```
+10.37000
 -9.89897
 +2.31300
 -8.95000
+15.00000
 +7.33333
+92.87650
-123.75684
End of program.
```

Example

EDITING A TEXT FILE

The program discussed here is a very simple example of text editing applied to files. This program can be used to automatically generate C++ advertising material from existing C advertising material (in a rather simplistic way). The program takes its input from a file that contains advertising copy that says good things about C and writes similar advertising copy about C++ in another file. The file that contains the C advertising copy is called cad.txt, and the new file that receives the C++ advertising copy is called cppad.txt. The program is shown in Display 12.8. The program simply reads every character in the file cad.txt and copies the characters to the file cppad.txt. Every character is copied unchanged, except that when the uppercase letter 'C' is read from the input file, the program writes the string "C++" to the output file. This program assumes that whenever the letter 'C' occurs in the input file, it names the C programming language; so this change is exactly what is needed to produce the updated advertising copy.

Notice that the line breaks are preserved when the program reads characters from the input file and writes the characters to the output file. The newline character '\n' is treated just like any other character. It is read from the input file with the member function get, and it is written to the output file using the insertion operator, <<. We must use the member function get to read the input (rather than the extraction operator, >>) because we want to read whitespace.

12.3 Stream Hierarchies: A Preview of Inheritance

One very useful way to organize classes is by means of the "derived from" relationship. When we say that one class is *derived from* another class we mean that the derived class was obtained from the other class by adding features. For example, the class of input-*file* streams is derived from the class of *all* input streams by adding additional member functions such as open and close. The stream cin belongs to the class of all input streams, but does *not* belong to the class of input-file streams because cin has no member functions named open and close. This section introduces the notion of a derived class as a way to think about and organize the predefined stream classes. (Chapter 14 shows how to use the idea of a derived class to define classes of your own.)

INHERITANCE AMONG STREAM CLASSES

Both the predefined stream cin and an input-file stream are input streams. So in some sense they are similar. For example, you can use the extraction operator, >>, with either kind of stream. On the other hand, an input-file stream can be connected to a file using the member function open, but the stream cin has no member function named open. An input-file stream is a similar but different kind of stream than cin. An input-file stream is of type ifstream. The object cin is an object of the class istream (spelled without the 'f'). The classes ifstream and istream are different but closely related types. The class ifstream is a *derived class* of the class istream. Let's see what that means.

Display 12.8   Editing a File of Text *(part 1 of 2)*

```
1    //Program to create a file called cplusad.txt that is identical to the file
2    //cad.txt except that all occurrences of 'C' are replaced by "C++". Assumes
3    //that the uppercase letter 'C' does not occur in cad.txt except as the
4    //name of the C programming language.
5    #include <fstream>
6    #include <iostream>
7    #include <cstdlib>
8    using std::ifstream;
9    using std::ofstream;
10   using std::cout;


11   void addPlusPlus(ifstream& inStream, ofstream& outStream);
12   //Precondition: inStream has been connected to an input file with open.
13   //outStream has been connected to an output file with open.
14   //Postcondition: The contents of the file connected to inStream have been
15   //copied into the file connected to outStream, but with each 'C' replaced
16   //by "C++". (The files are not closed by this function.)


17   int main( )
18   {
19       ifstream fin;
20       ofstream fout;


21       cout << "Begin editing files.\n";


22       fin.open("cad.txt");
23       if (fin.fail( ))
24       {
25           cout << "Input file opening failed.\n";
26           exit(1);
27       }


28       fout.open("cppad.txt");
29       if (fout.fail( ))
30       {
31           cout << "Output file opening failed.\n";
32           exit(1);
33       }


34       addPlusPlus(fin, fout);
```

Display 12.8   Editing a File of Text *(part 2 of 2)*

```
35        fin.close( );
36        fout.close( );

37        cout << "End of editing files.\n";
38        return 0;
39   }

40   void addPlusPlus(ifstream& inStream, ofstream& outStream)
41   {
42        char next;

43        inStream.get(next);
44        while (! inStream.eof( ))
45        {
46            if (next == 'C')
47                outStream << "C++";
48            else
49                outStream << next;

50            inStream.get(next);
51        }
52   }
```

cad.txt
(Not changed by program)

```
C is one of the world's most modern
programming languages. There is no
language as versatile as C, and C
is fun to use.
```

cppad.txt
(After program is run)

```
C++ is one of the world's most modern
programming languages. There is no
language as versatile as C++, and C++
is fun to use.
```

SCREEN OUTPUT

```
Begin editing files.
End of editing files.
```

When we say that some class D is a **derived class** of some other class B, it means that class D has all the features of class B but it also has added features. For example, any stream of type istream (without the 'f') can be used with the extraction operator, >>. The class ifstream (with the 'f') is a derived class of the class istream, so an object of type ifstream can be used with the extraction operator, >>. An object of the class ifstream has all the properties of an object of type istream. In particular, an object of the class ifstream *is also an object of type* istream.

However, ifstream has added features so that you can do more with an object of type ifstream than you can with an object that is only of type istream. For example, one added feature is that a stream of type ifstream can be used with the function open. The stream cin is only of type istream and not of type ifstream. You cannot use cin with the function open. Notice that the relationship between the classes ifstream and istream is not symmetric. Every object of type ifstream is of type istream (a file input stream is an input stream), but an object of type istream need not be of type ifstream (the object cin is of type istream but not of type ifstream).

The idea of a derived class is really quite common. An example from everyday life may help to make the idea clearer. The class of all convertibles, for instance, is a derived class of the class of all automobiles. Every convertible is an automobile, but a convertible is not just an automobile. A convertible is a special kind of automobile with special properties that other kinds of automobiles do not have. If you have a convertible, you can lower the top so that the car is open. (You might say that a convertible has an "open" function as an added feature.)

If D is a derived class of the class B, then every object of type D is also of type B. A convertible is also an automobile. A file input stream (object of the class ifstream) is also an input stream (also an object of the class istream). So, if we use istream as the type for a function parameter, rather than using ifstream, then more objects can be plugged in for the parameter. Consider the following two function definitions, which differ only in the type of the parameter (and the function name):

```
void twoSumVersion1(ifstream& sourceFile)//ifstream with an 'f'
{
    int n1, n2;
    sourceFile >> n1 >> n2;
    cout << n1 << " + " << n2 << " = " << (n1 + n2) << endl;
}
```

and

```
void twoSumVersion2(istream& sourceFile)//istream without an 'f'
{
    int n1, n2;
    sourceFile >> n1 >> n2;
    cout << n1 << " + " << n2 << " = " << (n1 + n2) << endl;
}
```

derived class

With twoSumVersion1, the argument must be of type ifstream. So if fileIn is a file input stream connected to a file, then

```
twoSumVersion1(fileIn);
```

is legal, but

```
twoSumVersion1(cin); //ILLEGAL
```

is not legal, because cin is not of type ifstream. The object cin is only a stream and only of type istream; cin is not a file input stream.

The function twoSumVersion2 is more versatile. Both of the following are legal:

```
twoSumVersion2(fileIn);
twoSumVersion2(cin);
```

The moral is clear: Use istream, not ifstream, as a parameter type whenever you can. When choosing a parameter type, use the most general type you can. (To draw a real-life analogy: You might prefer to own a convertible, but you would not want a garage that could only hold a convertible. What if you borrowed a sedan from a friend? You'd still want to be able to park the sedan in your garage.)

You cannot always use the parameter type istream instead of the parameter type ifstream. If you define a function with a parameter of type istream, then that parameter can only use istream member functions. In particular, it cannot use the functions open and close. If you cannot keep all calls to the member functions open and close outside the function definition, then you must use a parameter of type ifstream.

ostream **and** ofstream

So far we have discussed two classes for input streams: istream and its derived class ifstream. The situation with output streams is similar. Chapter 1 introduced the output streams cout and cerr, which are in the class ostream. This chapter introduced the file output streams, which are in the class ofstream (with an 'f'). The class ostream is the class of all output streams. The streams cout and cerr are of type ostream, but not of type ofstream. In contrast to cout or cerr, an output-file stream is declared to be of type ofstream. The class ofstream of output-file streams is a derived class of the class ostream. For example, the following function writes the word "Hello" to the output stream given as its argument.

```
void sayHello(ostream& anyOutStream)
{
    anyOutStream << "Hello";
}
```

The first of the following calls writes "Hello" to the screen; the second writes "Hello" to the file with the external file name afile.txt.

```
ofstream fout;
fout.open("afile.txt");
sayHello(cout);
sayHello(fout);
```

Note that an output-file stream is of type ofstream *and* of type ostream.

Derived classes are often discussed using the metaphor of inheritance and family relationships. If class D is a derived class of class B, then class D is called a **child** of class B and class B is called a **parent** of class D. The derived class is said to **inherit** the member functions of its parent class. For example, every convertible inherits the fact that it has four wheels from the class of all automobiles, and every input-file stream inherits the extraction operator, >>, from the class of all input streams. This is why the topic of derived classes is often called *inheritance*.

inheritance

child

parent

MAKING STREAM PARAMETERS VERSATILE

If you want to define a function that takes an input stream as an argument and you want that argument to be cin in some cases and an input-file stream in other cases, then use a formal parameter of type istream (without an 'f'). However, an input-file stream, even if used as an argument of type istream, must still be declared to be of type ifstream (with an 'f').

Similarly, if you want to define a function that takes an output stream as an argument and you want that argument to be cout in some cases and an output-file stream in other cases, then use a formal parameter of type ostream. However, an output-file stream, even if used as an argument of type ostream, must still be declared to be of type ofstream (with an 'f'). You cannot open or close a stream parameter of type istream or ostream. Open these objects before passing them to your function and close them after the function call.

The stream classes istream and ostream are defined in the iostream library and placed in the std namespace. One way to make them available to your code is the following:

```
#include <iostream>
using std::istream;
using std::ostream;
```

Example

ANOTHER newLine FUNCTION

As an example of how you can make a stream function more versatile, consider the function new-Line that we defined in Display 9.2. That function works only for input from the keyboard, which is input from the predefined stream cin. The function newLine in Display 9.2 has no arguments. Below we have rewritten the function newLine so that it has a formal parameter of type istream for the input stream:

```
//Uses <iostream>:
void newLine(istream& inStream)
{
    char symbol;
    do
    {
```

```
        inStream.get(symbol);
    } while (symbol != '\n');
}
```

Now, suppose your program contains this new version of the function newLine. If your program is taking input from an input stream called fin (which is connected to an input file), the following will discard all the input left on the line currently being read from the input file:

```
newLine(fin);
```

If your program is also reading some input from the keyboard, the following will discard the remainder of the input line that was typed in at the keyboard:

```
newLine(cin);
```

If your program has only the above rewritten version of newLine, which takes a stream argument such as fin or cin, you must always give the stream name, even if the stream name is cin. But thanks to overloading, you can have both versions of the function newLine in the same program: the version with no arguments that is given in Display 9.2 and the version with one argument of type istream that we just defined. In a program with both definitions of newLine, the following two calls are equivalent:

```
newLine(cin);
```

and

```
newLine( );
```

You do not really need two versions of the function newLine. The version with one argument of type istream can serve all your needs. However, many programmers find it convenient to have a version with no arguments for keyboard input, since keyboard input is used so frequently.

An alternative to having two overloaded versions of the newLine function is to use a default argument (as discussed in Chapter 4). In the following code, we have rewritten the newLine function a third time:

```
//Uses <iostream>:
void newLine(istream& inStream = cin)
{
    char symbol;
    do
    {
        inStream.get(symbol);
    } while (symbol != '\n');
}
```
If we call this function as

```
newLine( );
```

the formal parameter takes the default argument `cin`. If we call this as

```
newLine(fin);
```

the formal parameter takes the argument `fin`.

An alternative to using this `newLine` function is to use the function `ignore`, which we discussed in Chapter 9. The function `ignore` is a member of every input-file stream as well as a member of `cin`.

ignore

Self-Test Exercises

13. What is the type of the stream `cin`? What is the type of the stream `cout`?

14. Define a function called `copyChar` that takes one argument that is an input stream. When called, `copyChar` will read one character of input from the input stream given as its argument and will write that character to the screen. You should be able to call your function using either `cin` or an input-file stream as the argument to your function `copyChar`. (If the argument is an input-file stream, then the stream is connected to a file before the function is called, so `copyChar` will not open or close any files.) For example, the first of the following two calls to `copyChar` will copy a character from the file `stuff.txt` to the screen, and the second will copy a character from the keyboard to the screen:

```
ifstream fin;
fin.open("stuff.txt");
copyChar(fin);
copyChar(cin);
```

15. Define a function called `copyLine` that takes one argument that is an input stream. When called, `copyLine` reads one line of input from the input stream given as its argument and writes that line to the screen. You should be able to call your function using either `cin` or an input-file stream as the argument to your function `copyLine`. (If the argument is an input-file stream, then the stream is connected to a file before the function is called, so `copyLine` will not open or close any files.) For example, the first of the following two calls to `copyLine` will copy a line from the file `stuff.txt` to the screen, and the second will copy a line from the keyboard to the screen:

```
ifstream fin;
fin.open("stuff.txt");
copyLine(fin);
copyLine(cin);
```

16. Define a function called `sendLine` that takes one argument that is an output stream. When called, `sendLine` reads one line of input from the keyboard and outputs the line to the output stream given as its argument. You should be able to call your function using either `cout` or an output-file stream as the argument to your function `sendLine`. (If the

argument is an output-file stream, then the stream is connected to a file before the function is called, so sendLine will not open or close any files.) For example, the first of the following calls to sendLine will copy a line from the keyboard to the file morestuf.txt, and the second will copy a line from the keyboard to the screen:

```
ofstream fout;
fout.open("morestuf.txt");
cout << "Enter 2 lines of input:\n";
sendLine(fout);
sendLine(cout);
```

17. Is the following statement true or false? If it is false, correct it. In either event, explain it carefully.

A function written using a parameter of class ifstream or ofstream can be called with istream or ostream arguments, respectively.

12.4   Random Access to Files

Any time, any where.

Common response to a challenge for a confrontation

The streams for sequential access to files, which we discussed in the previous sections of this chapter, are the ones most often used for file access in C++. However, some applications that require very rapid access to records in very large databases require some sort of random access to particular parts of a file. Such applications might best be done with specialized database software. But perhaps you are given the job of writing such a package in C++, or perhaps you are just curious about how such things are done in C++. C++ does provide for random access to files so that your program can both read from and write to random locations in a file. This section gives a brief glimpse of this random access to files. This is not a complete tutorial on random access to files, but will let you know the name of the main stream class used and the important issues you will encounter.

If you want to be able to both read and write to a file in C++, you use the stream class fstream that is defined in the <fstream> library. The definition of fstream is placed in the std namespace.

Details about opening a file and connecting it to a stream in the class fstream are basically the same as discussed for the classes ifstream and ofstream, except that fstream has a second argument to open. This second argument specifies whether the stream is used for input, output, or both input and output. For example, a program that does both input and output to a file named "stuff" might start as follows:

```
#include <fstream>
using namespace std;

int main( )
{
    fstream rwStream;
    rwStream.open("stuff", ios::in | ios::out);
```

If you prefer, you may use the following in place of the last two of the previous lines:

```
fstream rwStream("stuff", ios::in | ios::out);
```

After this, your program can read from the file "stuff" using the stream fstream and can also write to the file "stuff" using the same stream. There is no need to close and reopen the file when you change from reading to writing or from writing to reading. Moreover, you have random access for reading and writing to any location in the file. However, there are other complications.

At least two complications arise when reading and writing with random access via an fstream: (1) You normally work in bytes using the type char or arrays of char and need to handle type conversions on your own, and (2) you typically need to position a pointer (indicating where the read or write begins) before each read or write.

The constraints of finding a position and replacing one portion of a file with new data mean that most such random-access I/O is done by reading or writing records (in the form of structs or classes). One record (or an integral number of records) is read or written after each positioning of the pointer.

Each fstream object has a member function named seekp that is used to position the put-pointer at the location where you wish to write ("put") data. The function seekp takes a single argument, which is the address of the first byte to be written next. The first byte in the file is numbered zero. For example, to position the pointer in the file connected to the fstream rwStream at the 1000th byte, the invocation would be as follows:

```
rwStream.seekp(1000);
```

Of course, you need to know how many bytes a record requires. The sizeof operator can be used to determine the number of bytes needed for an object of a class or struct. Actually, sizeof can be applied to any type, object, or value. It returns the size of its argument in bytes. The operator sizeof is part of the core C++ language and requires no include directive or using directive. Some sample invocations are as follows:

`sizeof(s)` (where s is `string s = "Hello";`)
`sizeof(10)`
`sizeof(double)`
`sizeof(MyStruct)` (where MyStruct is a defined type)

Each of these returns an integer giving the size of its argument in bytes.

To position the put-pointer at the 100th record of type MyStruct in a file containing nothing but records of type MyStruct, the invocation of seekp would be

```
rwStream.seekp(100*sizeof(MyStruct) - 1);
```

The member function seekg is used to position the get-pointer to indicate where reading ("getting") of the next byte will take place. It is completely analogous to seekp.

With the setup we have shown, you can write to the file "stuff" and read from the file "stuff" using the fstream rwStream with the member functions put and get. There is also a member function write that can write multiple bytes and a member function read that can read multiple bytes.

Theoretically, you now know enough to do random-access file I/O. In reality, this is just a taste of what is involved. This section was designed to let you know what it is all about in a general sort of way. If you intend to do any real programming of random-access file I/O, you should consult a more advanced and more specialized book.

Chapter Summary

- A stream of type ifstream can be connected to a file with a call to the member function open. Your program can then take input from that file.

- A stream of type ofstream can be connected to a file with a call to the member function open. Your program can then send output to that file.

- You should use the member function fail to check whether a call to open was successful.

- Stream member functions, such as width, setf, and precision, can be used to format output. These output functions work the same for the stream cout, which is connected to the screen, and for output streams connected to files.

- A function may have formal parameters of a stream type, but they must be call-by-reference parameters. They cannot be call-by-value parameters. The type ifstream can be used for an input-file stream, and the type ofstream can be used for an output-file stream. (See the next summary point for other type possibilities.)

- If you use istream (spelled without the 'f') as the type for an input stream parameter, then the argument corresponding to that formal parameter can be either the stream cin or an input-file stream of type ifstream (spelled with the 'f'). If you use ostream (spelled without the 'f') as the type for an output stream parameter, then the argument corresponding to that formal parameter can be either the stream cout, the stream cerr, or an output-file stream of type ofstream (spelled with the 'f').

- The member function eof can be used to test when a program has reached the end of an input file.

ANSWERS TO SELF-TEST EXERCISES

1. The streams `fin` and `fout` are declared as follows:

```
ifstream fin;
ofstream fout;
```

The `include` directive that goes at the top of your file is

```
#include <fstream>
```

Since the definitions are placed in the `std` namespace you should also have one of the following (or something similar):

```
using std::ifstream;
using std::ofstream;
```

or

```
using namespace std;
```

2.
```
fin.open("stuff1.txt");
if (fin.fail( ))
{
    cout << "Input file opening failed.\n";
    exit(1);
}

fout.open("stuff2.txt");
if (fout.fail( ))
{
    cout << "Output file opening failed.\n";
    exit(1);
}
```

3.
```
fin.close( );
fout.close( );
```

4. You need to replace the stream `outStream` with the stream `cout`. Note that you do not need to declare `cout`, you do not need to call `open` with `cout`, and you do not need to close `cout`.

5. This is "starting over." The file must be closed and opened again. This action puts the read position at the start of the file, ready to be read again.

6. 1
   2
   3
   3

7. ```
void toScreen(ifstream& fileStream)
{
    int next;
    while (fileStream >> next)
        cout << next << endl;
}
```

8. ```
*   123*123*
*   123*123*
```

Each of the spaces contains exactly two blank characters. Notice that a call to width or to setw only lasts for one output item.

9. ```
*   123*123   *   123*
```

Each of the spaces consists of exactly two blank characters.

10. ```
*   123*123*
* +123*+123*
*123  *123   *
```

There is just one space between the '*' and the '+' on the second line. Each of the other spaces contains exactly two blank characters.

11. The output to the file stuff.txt will be exactly the same as the output given in the answer to Self-Test Exercise 10.

12. ```
12345
```

Notice that the entire integer is output even though this requires more space than was specified by setw.

13. cin is of type istream; cout is of type ostream.

14. ```
void copyChar(istream& sourceFile)
{
    char next;
    sourceFile.get(next);
    cout << next;
}
```

15. ```
void copyLine(istream& sourceFile)
{
    char next;
    do
    {
        sourceFile.get(next);
        cout << next;
    }while (next != '\n');
}
```
```

16.
```
void sendLine(ostream& targetStream)
{
    char next;
    do
    {
        cin.get(next);
        targetStream << next;
    }while (next != '\n');
}
```

17. False. The situation stated here is the reverse of the correct situation. Any stream that is of type `ifstream` is also of type `istream`, so a formal parameter of type `istream` can be replaced by an argument of type `ifstream` in a function call, and similarly for the streams `ostream` and `ofstream`.

PROGRAMMING PROJECTS

1. Write a program that will search a file of numbers of type `int` and write the largest and the smallest numbers to the screen. The file contains nothing but numbers of type `int` separated by blanks or line breaks.

2. Write a program that takes its input from a file of numbers of type `double` and outputs the average of the numbers in the file to the screen. The file contains nothing but numbers of type `double` separated by blanks and/or line breaks.

3. a. Compute the median of a data file. The *median* is the number that has the same number of data elements greater than the number as there are less than the number. For purposes of this problem, you are to assume that the data is sorted (that is, is in increasing order). The median is the middle element of the file if there are an odd number of elements, or is the average of the two middle elements if the file has an even number of elements. You will need to open the file, count the members, close the file and calculate the location of the middle of the file, open the file again (recall the 'start over' discussion at the beginning of this chapter), count up to the file entries you need, and calculate the middle.

   b. For a sorted file, a quartile is one of three numbers: The first has one-fourth the data values less than or equal to it, one-fourth the data values between the first and second numbers (up to and including the second number), one-fourth the data points between the second and the third (up to and including the third number), and one-fourth above the third quartile. Find the three quartiles for the data file you used for part a. Note that "one-fourth" means as close to one-fourth as possible.

   Hint: You should recognize that having done part a you have one-third of your job done. (You have the second quartile already.) You also should recognize that you have done almost all the work toward finding the other two quartiles as well.

4. Write a program that takes its input from a file of numbers of type `double`. The program outputs to the screen the average and standard deviation of the numbers in the file. The file contains nothing but numbers of type `double` separated by blanks and/or line breaks. The

standard deviation of a list of numbers n_1, n_2, n_3, and so forth, is defined as the square root of the average of the following numbers:

$$(n_1 - a)^2, \ (n_2 - a)^2, \ (n_3 - a)^2, \text{ and so forth}$$

The number a is the average of the numbers n_1, n_2, n_3, and so forth.

Hint: Write your program so that it first reads the entire file and computes the average of all the numbers, then closes the file, then reopens the file and computes the standard deviation. You will find it helpful to first do Programming Project 2 and then modify that program to obtain the program for this project.

5. Write a program that gives and takes advice on program writing. The program starts by writing a piece of advice to the screen and asking the user to type in a different piece of advice. The program then ends. The next person to run the program receives the advice given by the person who last ran the program. The advice is kept in a file, and the contents of the file change after each run of the program. You can use your editor to enter the initial piece of advice in the file so that the first person who runs the program receives some advice. Allow the user to type in advice of any length (any number of lines long). The user is told to end his or her advice by pressing the Return key two times. Your program can then test to see that it has reached the end of the input by checking to see when it reads two consecutive occurrences of the character '\n'.

6. Write a program that merges the numbers in two files and writes all the numbers into a third file. Your program takes input from two different files and writes its output to a third file. Each input file contains a list of numbers of type int in sorted order from the smallest to the largest. After the program is run, the output file will contain all the numbers in the two input files in one longer list in sorted order from smallest to largest. Your program should define a function that is called with the two input-file streams and the output-file stream as three arguments.

7. Write a program to generate personalized junk mail. The program takes input both from an input file and from the keyboard. The input file contains the text of a letter, except that the name of the recipient is indicated by the three characters #N#. The program asks the user for a name and then writes the letter to a second file but with the three letters #N# replaced by the name. The three-letter string #N# will occur exactly once in the letter.

Hint: Have your program read from the input file until it encounters the three characters #N#, and have it copy what it reads to the output file as it goes. When it encounters the three letters #N#, it then sends output to the screen asking for the name from the keyboard. You should be able to figure out the rest of the details. Your program should define a function that is called with the input- and output-file streams as arguments. If this is being done as a class assignment, obtain the file names from your instructor.

Harder version: Allow the string #N# to occur any number of times in the file. In this case the name is stored in two string variables. For this version assume that there is a first name and last name but no middle names or initials.

8. Write a program to compute numeric grades for a course. The course records are in a file that will serve as the input file. The input file is in the following format: Each line contains a student's last name, then one space, then the student's first name, then one space, then ten quiz scores all on one line. The quiz scores are whole numbers and are separated by one space. Your program will take its input from this file and send its output to a second file. The data in the output file will be the same as the data in the input file except that there will be one additional number (of type `double`) at the end of each line. This number will be the average of the student's ten quiz scores. Use at least one function that has file streams as all or some of its arguments.

9. Enhance the program you wrote for Programming Project 8 in all the following ways.

   - The list of quiz scores on each line will contain ten or fewer quiz scores. (If there are fewer than ten quiz scores that means that the student missed one or more quizzes.) The average score is still the sum of the quiz scores divided by 10. This amounts to giving the student a `0` for any missed quiz.
   - The output file will contain a line (or lines) at the beginning of the file explaining the output. Use formatting instructions to make the layout neat and easy to read.
   - After placing the desired output in an output file, your program will close all files and then copy the contents of the "output" file to the "input" file so that the net effect is to change the contents of the input file.

   Use at least two functions that have file streams as all or some of their arguments.

10. Write a program that will compute the average word length (average number of characters per word) for a file that contains some text. A word is defined to be any string of symbols that is preceded and followed by one of the following at each end: a blank, a comma, a period, the beginning of a line, or the end of a line. Your program should define a function that is called with the input-file stream as an argument. This function should also work with the stream `cin` as the input stream, although the function will not be called with `cin` as an argument in this program. If this is being done as a class assignment, obtain the file names from your instructor.

11. Write a program that will correct a C++ program that has errors in which operator, `<<` or `>>`, it uses with `cin` and `cout`. The program replaces each (incorrect) occurrence of

    `cin <<`

    with the corrected version

    `cin >>`

    and each (incorrect) occurrence of

    `cout >>`

    with the corrected version

    `cout <<`

For an easier version, assume that there is always exactly one blank symbol between any occurrence of `cin` and a following `<<`, and similarly assume that there is always exactly one blank space between each occurrence of `cout` and a following `>>`. For a harder version, allow for the possibility that there may be any number of blanks, even zero blanks, between `cin` and `<<` and between `cout` and `>>`; in this harder case, the replacement corrected version has only one blank between the `cin` or `cout` and the following operator. The program to be corrected is in one file and the corrected version is output to a second file. Your program should define a function that is called with the input- and output-file streams as arguments. (*Hint:* Even if you are doing the harder version, you will probably find it easier and quicker to first do the easier version and then modify your program so that it performs the harder task.)

12. Write a program that allows the user to type in any one-line question and then answers that question. The program will not really pay any attention to the question, but will simply read the question line and discard all that it reads. It always gives one of the following answers:

```
I'm not sure but I think you will find the answer in Chapter #N.
That's a good question.
If I were you, I would not worry about such things.
That question has puzzled philosophers for centuries.
I don't know. I'm just a machine.
Think about it and the answer will come to you.
I used to know the answer to that question, but I've forgotten it.
The answer can be found in a secret place in the woods.
```

These answers are stored in a file (one answer per line), and your program simply reads the next answer from the file and writes it out as the answer to the question. After your program has read the entire file, it simply closes the file, reopens the file, and starts down the list of answers again.

Whenever your program outputs the first answer, it should replace the two symbols `#N` with a number between 1 and 20 (including the possibility of 1 and 20). In order to choose a number between 1 and 20, your program should initialize a variable to `20` and decrease the variable's value by 1 each time it outputs a number so that the chapter numbers count backward from 20 to 1. When the variable reaches the value `0`, your program should change its value back to `20`. Give the number 20 the name `NUMBER_OF_CHAPTERS` with a global named constant declaration using the `const` modifier. (*Hint:* Use the function `new-Line` defined in this chapter.)

13. This project is the same as Programming Project 12 except that in this project your program will use a more sophisticated method for choosing the answer to a question. When your program reads a question, it counts the number of characters in the question and stores the number in a variable named `count`. It then responds with answer number `count%ANSWERS`. The first answer in the file is answer number 0, the next is answer number 1, then 2, and so forth. `ANSWERS` is defined in a constant declaration, as shown below, so that it is equal to the number of answers in the answer file:

```
const int ANSWERS = 8;
```

This way you can change the answer file so that it contains more or fewer answers and you need change only the constant declaration to make your program work correctly for a different number of possible answers. Assume that the answer listed first in the file will always be the following, even if the answer file is changed:

```
I'm not sure but I think you will find the answer in Chapter #N.
```

When replacing the two characters #N with a number, use the number (count%NUMBER_OF_CHAPTERS + 1), where count is the variable discussed above, and NUMBER_OF_CHAPTERS is a global named constant defined to be equal to the number of chapters in this book.

14. This program numbers the lines found in a text file.

    Write a program that reads text from a file and outputs each line preceded by a line number. Print the line number right-adjusted in a field of three spaces. Follow the line number with a colon, then one space, then the text of the line. You should get a character at a time, and write code to ignore leading blanks on each line. You may assume that the lines are short enough to fit within a line on the screen. Otherwise, allow default printer or screen output behavior if the line is too long (that is, wrap or truncate).

    A somewhat harder version determines the number of spaces needed in the field for the line numbers by counting lines before processing the lines of the file. This version of the program should insert a new line after the last complete word that will fit within a 72-character line.

15. In this program you are to process text to create a KWIX table (Key Word In conteXt table). The idea is to produce a list of keywords (not programming language keywords, rather words that have important technical meaning in a discussion), then for each instance of each keyword, place the keyword, the line number of the context, and the keyword in its context in the table. There may be more than one context for a given keyword. The sequence of entries within a keyword is to be the order of occurrence in the text. For this problem, "context" is a user-selected number of words before the keyword, the keyword itself, and a user-selected number of words after the keyword.

    The table has an alphabetized column of keywords followed by a line number(s) where the keyword occurs, followed by a column of all contexts within which the keyword occurs. See the example below. For a choice of text consult your instructor.

    Hints: To get your list of keywords, you should choose and type in several paragraphs from the text, then omit from your paragraph "boring" words such as forms of the verb "to be"; pronouns such as I, me, he, she, her, you, us, them, who, which, etc.; Finally, sort the keyword list and remove duplicates. The better job you do at this, the more useful output you will get.

    Example: A paragraph and its KWIX Listing:

    There are at least two complications when reading and writing with random access via an fstream: (1) You normally work in bytes using the type `char` or arrays of `char` and need to handle type conversions on your own, and (2) You typically need to position a pointer (indicating where the read or write begins) before each read or write.

KWIX Listing:

Keyword	Line Number	Keyword in Context
access	2	with random *access* via
arrays	3	*char* or *arrays* of
bytes	2	work in *bytes* using
char	3	the type *char* or
char	3	array of *char* and
conversions	3	handle type *conversions* on

The table is longer than these sample entries.

13 CHAPTER

Recursion

13 Recursion

After a lecture on cosmology and the structure of the solar system, William James was accosted by a little old lady.

"Your theory that the sun is the center of the solar system, and the earth is a ball which rotates around it has a very convincing ring to it, Mr. James, but it's wrong. I've got a better theory," said the little old lady.

"And what is that, madam?" inquired James politely.

"That we live on a crust of earth which is on the back of a giant turtle."

Not wishing to demolish this absurd little theory by bringing to bear the masses of scientific evidence he had at his command, James decided to gently dissuade his opponent by making her see some of the inadequacies of her position.

"If your theory is correct, madam," he asked, "what does this turtle stand on?"

"You're a very clever man, Mr. James, and that's a very good question" replied the little old lady, "but I have an answer to it. And it is this: the first turtle stands on the back of a second, far larger, turtle, who stands directly under him."

"But what does this second turtle stand on?" persisted James patiently.

To this the little old lady crowed triumphantly. "It's no use, Mr. James— it's turtles all the way down."

J. R. Ross, *Constraints on Variables in Syntax*

INTRODUCTION

A function definition that includes a call to itself is said to be *recursive*. Like most modern programming languages, C++ allows functions to be recursive. If used with a little care, recursion can be a useful programming technique. This chapter introduces the basic techniques needed for defining successful recursive functions. There is nothing in this chapter that is truly unique to C++. If you are already familiar with recursion you can safely skip this chapter.

This chapter only uses material from Chapters 1 to 5. Sections 13.1 and 13.2 do not use any material from Chapter 5, so you can cover recursion any time after Chapter 4. If you have not read Chapter 11, you may find it helpful to review the section of Chapter 1 on namespaces.

Recursive void functions

I remembered too that night which is at the middle of the Thousand and One Nights when Scheherazade (through a magical oversight of the copyist) begins to relate word for word the story of the Thousand and One Nights, establishing the risk of coming once again to the night when she must repeat it, and thus to infinity.

Jorge Luis Borges, *The Garden of Forking Paths*

When you are writing a function to solve a task, one basic design technique is to break the task into subtasks. Sometimes it turns out that at least one of the subtasks is a smaller example of the same task. For example, if the task is to search a list for a particular value, you might divide this into the subtask of searching the first half of the list and the subtask of searching the second half of the list. The subtasks of searching the halves of the list are "smaller" versions of the original task. Whenever one subtask is a smaller version of the original task to be accomplished, you can solve the original task using a recursive function. We begin with a simple example to illustrate this technique.

RECURSION

In C++ a function definition may contain a call to the function being defined. In such cases the function is said to be **recursive**.

Example

VERTICAL NUMBERS

Display 13.1 contains a demonstration program for a recursive function named writeVertical that takes one (nonnegative) int argument and writes that int to the screen, with the digits going down the screen one per line. For example, the invocation

    writeVertical(1234);

would produce the output

    1
    2
    3
    4

The task to be performed by writeVertical may be broken down into the following two cases:

- *Simple case:* If n < 10, then write the number n to the screen.

After all, if the number is only one digit long, the task is trivial.

- *Recursive case:* If n $>=$ 10, then do two subtasks:
  1. Output all the digits except the last digit.
  2. Output the last digit.

For example, if the argument were 1234, the first subtask would output

```
1
2
3
```

and the second subtask would output 4. This decomposition into subtasks can be used to derive the function definition.

Subtask 1 is a smaller version of the original task, so we can implement this subtask with a recursive call. Subtask 2 is just the simple case we listed above. Thus, an outline of our algorithm for the function writeVertical with parameter n is given by the following pseudocode:

```
if (n < 10)
{
    cout << n << endl;
}
else //n is two or more digits long:
{
    writeVertical(the number n with the last digit removed);
    cout << the last digit of n << endl;
}
```

Recursive subtask

If you observe the following identities, it is easy to convert this pseudocode to a complete C++ function definition:

```
n/10  is the number n with the last digit removed.
n%10  is the last digit of n.
```

For example, 1234/10 evaluates to 123, and 1234%10 evaluates to 4.

The complete code for the function is as follows:

```
void writeVertical(int n)
{
    if (n < 10)
    {
        cout << n << endl;
    }
    else //n is two or more digits long:
    {
        writeVertical(n/10);
        cout << (n%10) << endl;
    }
}
```

Display 13.1 A Recursive void Function

```
1   //Program to demonstrate the recursive function writeVertical.
2   #include <iostream>
3   using std::cout;
4   using std::endl;

5   void writeVertical(int n);
6   //Precondition: n >= 0.
7   //Postcondition: The number n is written to the screen vertically,
8   //with each digit on a separate line.

9   int main( )
10  {
11      cout << "writeVertical(3):" << endl;
12      writeVertical(3);

13      cout << "writeVertical(12):" << endl;
14      writeVertical(12);

15      cout << "writeVertical(123):" << endl;
16      writeVertical(123);

17      return 0;
18  }

19  //uses iostream:
20  void writeVertical(int n)
21  {
22      if (n < 10)
23      {
24          cout << n << endl;
25      }
26      else //n is two or more digits long:
27      {
28          writeVertical(n/10);
29          cout << (n%10) << endl;
30      }
31  }
```

SAMPLE DIALOGUE

```
writeVertical(3):
3
writeVertical(12):
1
2
writeVertical(123):
1
2
3
```

■ TRACING A RECURSIVE CALL

Let's see exactly what happens when the following function call is made (as in Display 13.1):

```
writeVertical(123);
```

When this function call is executed, the computer proceeds just as it would with any function call. The argument 123 is substituted for the parameter n, and the body of the function is executed. After the substitution of 123 for n, the code to be executed is equivalent to the following:

```
if (123 < 10)
{
    cout << 123 << endl;
}
else //n is two or more digits long:
{
    writeVertical(123/10);          Computation will
    cout << (123%10) << endl;       stop here until the recursive
}                                   call returns.
```

Since 123 is not less than 10, the else part is executed. However, the else part begins with the following function call:

```
writeVertical(n/10);
```

which (since n is equal to 123) is the call

```
writeVertical(123/10);
```

which is equivalent to

```
writeVertical(12);
```

When execution reaches this recursive call, the current function computation is placed in suspended animation and the recursive call is executed. When this recursive call is finished, the execution of the suspended computation will return to this point and the suspended computation will continue from there.

The recursive call

```
writeVertical(12);
```

is handled just like any other function call. The argument 12 is substituted for the parameter n, and the body of the function is executed. After substituting 12 for n, there are two computations, one suspended and one active, as follows:

```
if (123 < 10)
{
     cout <    if (12 < 10)
}            {
else //n i        cout << 12 << endl;
{            }
     writeV   else //n is two or more digits long:
     cout <   {
}                writeVertical(12/10);      Computation will
                 cout << (12%10) << endl;    stop here until
             }                               the recursive call
                                             returns.
```

Since 12 is not less than 10, the else part is executed. However, as you already saw, the else part begins with a recursive call. The argument for the recursive call is n/10, which in this case is equivalent to 12/10. So this second computation of the function writeVertical is suspended and the following recursive call is executed:

```
writeVertical(12/10);
```

which is equivalent to

```
writeVertical(1);
```

At this point there are two suspended computations waiting to resume, and the computer begins to execute this new recursive call, which is handled just like all the previous recursive calls. The argument 1 is substituted for the parameter n, and the body of the function is executed. At this point, the computation looks like the following:

```
if (123 < 10)
{
   c  if (12 < 10)
}     {
else      if (1 < 10)
{         {
              cout << 1 << endl;     No recursive
    }         }                      call this time
    w  else   else //n is two or more digits long:
    c  {      {
}     }           writeVertical(1/10);
                  cout << (1%10) << endl;
              }
```

When the body of the function is executed this time, something different happens. Since 1 is less than 10, the Boolean expression in the if-else statement is true, so the statement before the else is executed. That statement is simply a cout statement that writes the argument 1 to the screen, and so the call writeVertical(1) writes 1 to the screen and ends without any recursive call.

When the call writeVertical(1) ends, the suspended computation that is waiting for it to end resumes where that suspended computation left off, as shown by the following:

```
if (123 < 10)
{
    c            if (12 < 10)
}                {
else                 cout << 12 << endl;
{                }
    w            else //n is two or more digits long:
    c            {
}                    writeVertical(12/10);◄─────── Computation resumes here.
                     cout << (12%10) << endl;
                 }
```

When this suspended computation resumes, it executes a cout statement that outputs the value 12%10, which is 2. That ends that computation, but there is yet another suspended computation waiting to resume.

When this last suspended computation resumes, the situation is as follows:

```
if (123 < 10)
{
    cout << 123 << endl;
}
else //n is two or more digits long:
{
    writeVertical(123/10);◄─────── Computation resumes here.
    cout << (123%10) << endl;
}
```

This last suspended computation outputs the value 123%10, which is 3. The execution of the original function call then ends. And, sure enough, the digits 1, 2, and 3 have been written to the screen one per line, in that order.

A CLOSER LOOK AT RECURSION

The definition of the function writeVertical uses recursion. Yet we did nothing new or different in evaluating the function call writeVertical(123). We treated it just like any of the function calls we saw in previous chapters. We simply substituted the argument 123 for the parameter n and then executed the code in the body of the function definition. When we reached the recursive call

```
writeVertical(123/10);
```

we simply repeated this process one more time.

The computer keeps track of recursive calls in the following way. When a function is called, the computer plugs in the arguments for the parameter(s) and begins to execute the code. If it should encounter a recursive call, it temporarily stops its computation because it must know the result of the recursive call before it can proceed. It saves all the information it needs to continue the computation later on, and proceeds to evaluate the recursive call. When the recursive call is completed, the computer returns to finish the outer computation.

how recursion works

The C++ language places no restrictions on how recursive calls are used in function definitions. However, in order for a recursive function definition to be useful, it must be designed so that any call of the function must ultimately terminate with some piece of code that does not depend on recursion. The function may call itself, and that recursive call may call the function again. The process may be repeated any number of times. However, the process will not terminate unless eventually one of the recursive calls does not depend on recursion in order to return a value. The general outline of a successful recursive function definition is as follows:

how recursion ends

- One or more cases in which the function accomplishes its task by using one or more recursive calls to accomplish one or more smaller versions of the task.
- One or more cases in which the function accomplishes its task without the use of any recursive calls. These cases without any recursive calls are called **base cases** or **stopping cases**.

base case or stopping case

Often an if-else statement determines which of the cases will be executed. A typical scenario is for the original function call to execute a case that includes a recursive call. That recursive call may in turn execute a case that requires another recursive call. For some number of times each recursive call produces another recursive call, but eventually one of the stopping cases should apply. Every call of the function must eventually lead to a stopping case or else the function call will never end because of an infinite chain of recursive calls. (In practice, a call that includes an infinite chain of recursive calls will usually terminate abnormally rather than actually running forever.)

The most common way to ensure that a stopping case is eventually reached is to write the function so that some (positive) numeric quantity is decreased on each recursive call and to provide a stopping case for some "small" value. This is how we designed the function writeVertical in Display 13.1. When the function writeVertical is called, that call produces a recursive call with a smaller argument. This continues with each recursive call producing another recursive call until the argument is less than 10. When the argument is less than 10, the function call ends without producing any more recursive calls and the process works its way back to the original call and then ends.

GENERAL FORM OF A RECURSIVE FUNCTION DEFINITION

The general outline of a successful recursive function definition is as follows:

- One or more cases that include one or more recursive calls to the function being defined. These recursive calls should solve "smaller" versions of the task performed by the function being defined.

- One or more cases that include no recursive calls. These cases without any recursive calls are called *base cases* or *stopping cases*.

Pitfall   **INFINITE RECURSION**

infinite recursion

In the example of the function writeVertical discussed in the previous subsections, the series of recursive calls eventually reached a call of the function that did not involve recursion (that is, a stopping case was reached). If, on the other hand, every recursive call produces another recursive call, then a call to the function will, in theory, run forever. This is called **infinite recursion**. In practice, such a function will typically run until the computer runs out of resources and the program terminates abnormally.

Examples of infinite recursion are not hard to come by. The following is a syntactically correct C++ function definition that might result from an attempt to define an alternative version of the function writeVertical:

```
void newWriteVertical(int n)
{
    newWriteVertical(n/10);
    cout << (n%10) << endl;
}
```

If you embed this definition in a program that calls this function, the compiler will translate the function definition to machine code and you can execute the machine code. Moreover, the definition even has a certain reasonableness to it. It says that to output the argument to new-WriteVertical, first output all but the last digit and then output the last digit. However, when called, this function will produce an infinite sequence of recursive calls. If you call new-WriteVertical(12), that execution will stop to execute the recursive call newWriteVertical (12/10), which is equivalent to newWriteVertical(1). The execution of that recursive call will, in turn, stop to execute the recursive call

```
newWriteVertical(1/10);
```

which is equivalent to

```
newWriteVertical(0);
```

That, in turn, will stop to execute the recursive call newWriteVertical(0/10); which is also equivalent to

```
newWriteVertical(0);
```

and that will produce another recursive call to again execute the same recursive function call newWriteVertical(0);, and so on, forever. Since the definition of newWriteVertical has no stopping case, the process will proceed forever (or until the computer runs out of resources).

Self-Test Exercises

1. What is the output of the following program?

```
#include <iostream>
using std::cout;
void cheers(int n);

int main( )
{
    cheers(3);
    return 0;
}

void cheers(int n)
{
    if (n == 1)
    {
        cout << "Hurray\n";
    }
    else
    {
        cout << "Hip ";
        cheers(n - 1);
    }
}
```

2. Write a recursive void function that has one parameter that is a positive integer and that writes out that number of asterisks (*) to the screen, all on one line.

3. Write a recursive void function that has one parameter that is a positive integer. When called, the function writes its argument to the screen backward. That is, if the argument is 1234, it outputs the following to the screen:

4321

4. Write a recursive void function that takes a single int argument n and writes the integers 1, 2, . . . , n.

5. Write a recursive **void** function that takes a single **int** argument n and writes integers n, n–1, . . . , 3, 2, 1. (*Hint:* Notice that you can get from the code for Exercise 4 to that for this exercise, or vice versa, by an exchange of as little as two lines.)

STACKS FOR RECURSION

stack

To keep track of recursion (and a number of other things), most computer systems make use of a structure called a *stack*. A **stack** is a very specialized kind of memory structure that is analogous to a stack of paper. In this analogy there is an inexhaustible supply of extra blank sheets of paper. To place some information in the stack, it is written on one of these sheets of paper and placed on top of the stack of papers. To place more information in the stack, a clean sheet of paper is taken, the information is written on it, and this new sheet of paper is placed on top of the stack. In this straightforward way more and more information may be placed on the stack.

Getting information out of the stack is also accomplished by a very simple procedure. The top sheet of paper can be read, and when it is no longer needed, it is thrown away.

last-in/
first-out

There is one complication: Only the top sheet of paper is accessible. In order to read, say, the third sheet from the top, the top two sheets must be thrown away. Since the last sheet that is put on the stack is the first sheet taken off the stack, a stack is often called a **last-in/first-out** memory structure.

Using a stack, the computer can easily keep track of recursion. Whenever a function is called, a new sheet of paper is taken. The function definition is copied onto this sheet of paper, and the arguments are plugged in for the function parameters. Then the computer starts to execute the body of the function definition. When it encounters a recursive call, it stops the computation it is doing on that sheet in order to compute the value returned by the recursive call. But before computing the recursive call, it saves enough information so that when it does finally determine the value returned by the recursive call, it can continue the stopped computation. This saved information is written on a sheet of paper and placed on the stack. A new sheet of paper is used for the recursive call. The computer writes a second copy of the function definition on this new sheet of paper, plugs in the arguments for the function parameters, and starts to execute the recursive call. When it gets to a recursive call within the recursively called copy, it repeats the process of saving information on the stack and using a new sheet of paper for the new recursive call. This process is illustrated in the subsection entitled "Tracing a Recursive Call." Even though we did not call it a stack at the time, the figures of computations placed one on top of the other illustrate the actions of the stack.

This process continues until some recursive call to the function completes its computation without producing any more recursive calls. When that happens, the computer turns its attention to the top sheet of paper on the stack. This sheet contains the partially completed computation that is waiting for the recursive computation that just ended. Thus, it is possible to proceed with that suspended computation. When that suspended computation ends, the computer discards that sheet of paper and the suspended computation that is below it on the stack becomes the computation on top of the stack. The computer turns its attention to the suspended computation that is now on the top of the stack, and so forth. The process continues until the computation on the bottom sheet is completed. Depending on how many recursive calls are made and how the function definition is written, the stack may grow and shrink in any fashion. Notice that the sheets in the stack can only be accessed in a last-in/first-out fashion, but that is exactly what is needed to keep track of recursive calls. Each suspended version is waiting for the completion of the version directly above it on the stack.

Needless to say, computers do not have stacks of paper. This is just an analogy. The computer uses portions of memory rather than pieces of paper. The content of one of these portions of memory ("sheets of paper") is called an **activation frame**. These activation frames are handled in the last-in/first-out manner we just discussed. (These activation frames do not contain a complete copy of the function definition, but merely reference a single copy of the function definition. However, an activation frame contains enough information to allow the computer to act as if the activation frame contained a complete copy of the function definition.)

activation frame

STACK

A stack is a last-in/first-out memory structure. The first item referenced or removed from a stack is always the last item entered into the stack. Stacks are used by computers to keep track of recursion (and for other purposes).

Pitfall   STACK OVERFLOW

There is always some limit to the size of the stack. If there is a long chain in which a function makes a recursive call to itself, and that call results in another recursive call, and that call produces yet another recursive call, and so forth, then each recursive call in this chain will cause another activation frame to be placed on the stack. If this chain is too long, the stack will attempt to grow beyond its limit. This is an error condition known as a **stack overflow**. If you receive an error message that says "stack overflow," it is likely that some function call has produced an excessively long chain of recursive calls. One common cause of stack overflow is infinite recursion. If a function is recursing infinitely, then it will eventually try to make the stack exceed any stack size limit.

stack overflow

■ RECURSION VERSUS ITERATION

Recursion is not absolutely necessary. In fact, some programming languages do not allow it. Any task that can be accomplished using recursion can also be done in some other way without using recursion. For example, Display 13.2 contains a nonrecursive

Display 13.2   Iterative Version of the Function in Display 13.1

```
1   //Uses iostream:
2   void writeVertical(int n)
3   {
4       int nsTens = 1;
5       int leftEndPiece = n;
6       while (leftEndPiece > 9)
7       {
8           leftEndPiece = leftEndPiece/10;
9           nsTens = nsTens*10;
10      }
11      //nsTens is a power of ten that has the same number
12      //of digits as n. For example, if n is 2345, then
13      //nsTens is 1000.
14
15      for (int powerOf10 = nsTens;
16              powerOf10 > 0; powerOf10 = powerOf10/10)
17      {
18          cout << (n/powerOf10) << endl;
19          n = n%powerOf10;
20      }
    }
```

version of the function given in Display 13.1. The nonrecursive version of a function typically uses a loop (or loops) of some sort in place of recursion. For that reason, the nonrecursive version is usually referred to as an **iterative version**. If the definition of the function writeVertical given in Display 13.1 is replaced by the version given in Display 13.2, the output will be the same. As is true in this case, a recursive version of a function can sometimes be much simpler than an iterative version.

iterative
version

A recursively written function will usually run slower and use more storage than an equivalent iterative version. The computer must do a good deal of work manipulating the stack in order to keep track of the recursion. However, since the system does all this for you automatically, using recursion can sometimes make your job as a programmer easier and can sometimes produce code that is easier to understand.

efficiency

Self-Test Exercises

6. If your program produces an error message that says "stack overflow," what is a likely source of the error?

7. Write an iterative version of the function cheers defined in Self-Test Exercise 1.

8. Write an iterative version of the function defined in Self-Test Exercise 2.

9. Write an iterative version of the function defined in Self-Test Exercise 3.

10. Trace the recursive solution you made to Self-Test Exercise 4.

11. Trace the recursive solution you made to Self-Test Exercise 5.

13.2 Recursive Functions That Return a Value

To iterate is human, to recurse divine.

Anonymous

GENERAL FORM FOR A RECURSIVE FUNCTION THAT RETURNS A VALUE

The recursive functions you have seen thus far are all void functions, but recursion is not limited to void functions. A recursive function can return a value of any type. The technique for designing recursive functions that return a value is basically the same as that for void functions. An outline for a successful recursive function definition that returns a value is as follows:

- One or more cases in which the value returned is computed in terms of calls to the same function (that is, using recursive calls). As was the case with void functions, the arguments for the recursive calls should intuitively be "smaller."

- One or more cases in which the value returned is computed without the use of any recursive calls. These cases without any recursive calls are called *base cases* or *stopping cases* (just as they were with void functions).

This technique is illustrated in the next programming example.

Example   **ANOTHER POWERS FUNCTION**

Chapter 3 introduced the predefined function pow that computes powers. For example, pow(2.0, 3.0) returns $2.0^{3.0}$, so the following sets the variable result equal to 8.0:

```
double result = pow(2.0, 3.0);
```

The function pow takes two arguments of type double and returns a value of type double. Display 13.3 contains a recursive definition for a function that is similar but that works with the type int rather than double. This new function is called power. For example, the following will set the value of result2 equal to 8, since 2^3 is 8:

```
int result2 = power(2, 3);
```

Our main reason for defining the function power is to have a simple example of a recursive function, but there are situations in which the function power would be preferable to the function

Display 13.3   The Recursive Function power

```
1    //Program to demonstrate the recursive function power.
2    #include <iostream>
3    #include <cstdlib>
4    using std::cout;
5    using std::endl;


6    int power(int x, int n);
7    //Precondition: n >= 0.
8    //Returns x to the power n.


9    int main( )
10   {
11       for (int n = 0; n < 4; n++)
12           cout << "3 to the power " << n
13                 << " is " << power(3, n) << endl;


14       return 0;
15   }


16   //uses iostream and cstdlib:
17   int power(int x, int n)
18   {
19       if (n < 0)
20       {
21           cout << "Illegal argument to power.\n";
22           exit(1);
23       }


24       if (n > 0)
25           return ( power(x, n - 1)*x );
26       else // n == 0
27           return (1);
28   }
```

SAMPLE DIALOGUE

```
3 to the power 0 is 1
3 to the power 1 is 3
3 to the power 2 is 9
3 to the power 3 is 27
```

pow. The function pow returns a value of type double, which is only an approximate quantity. The function power returns a value of type int, which is an exact quantity. In some situations, you might need the additional accuracy provided by the function power.

The definition of the function power is based on the following formula:

x^n is equal to $x^{n-1} * x$

Translating this formula into C++ says that the value returned by power(x, n) should be the same as the value of the expression

```
power(x, n - 1)*x
```

The definition of the function power given in Display 13.3 does return this value for power (x, n), provided n > 0.

The case where n is equal to 0 is the stopping case. If n is 0, then power(x, n) simply returns 1 (since x^0 is 1).

Let's see what happens when the function power is called with some sample values. First consider the following simple expression:

```
power(2, 0)
```

When the function is called, the value of x is set equal to 2, the value of n is set equal to 0, and the code in the body of the function definition is executed. Since the value of n is a legal value, the if-else statement is executed. Since this value of n is not greater than 0, the return statement after the else is used, so the function call returns 1. Thus, the following would set the value of result3 equal to 1:

```
int result3 - power(2, 0);
```

Now let's look at an example that involves a recursive call. Consider the expression

```
power(2, 1)
```

When the function is called, the value of x is set equal to 2, the value of n is set equal to 1, and the code in the body of the function definition is executed. Since this value of n is greater than 0, the following return statement is used to determine the value returned:

```
return ( power(x, n - 1)*x );
```

which in this case is equivalent to

```
return ( power(2, 0)*2 );
```

At this point the computation of power(2, 1) is suspended, a copy of this suspended computation is placed on the stack, and the computer then starts a new function call to compute the value of power(2, 0). As you have already seen, the value of power(2, 0) is 1. After determining the value of power(2, 0), the computer replaces the expression power(2, 0) with its value of 1 and resumes the suspended computation. The resumed computation determines the final value for power(2, 1) from the above return statement as follows:

power(2, 0)*2 is 1*2, which is 2.

Thus, the final value returned for power(2, 1) is 2. So, the following would set the value of result4 equal to 2:

```
int result4 = power(2, 1);
```

Larger numbers for the second argument will produce longer chains of recursive calls. For example, consider the statement

```
cout << power(2, 3);
```

The value of power(2, 3) is calculated as follows:

```
power(2, 3) is power(2, 2)*2
  power(2, 2) is power(2, 1)*2
    power(2, 1) is power(2, 0)*2
      power(2, 0) is 1 (stopping case)
```

When the computer reaches the stopping case power(2, 0), there are three suspended computations. After calculating the value returned for the stopping case, it resumes the most recently suspended computations to determine the value of power(2, 1). After that, the computer completes each of the other suspended computations, using each value computed as a value to plug into another suspended computation, until it reaches and completes the computation for the original call, power(2, 3). The details of the entire computation are illustrated in Display 13.4.

Self-Test Exercises

12. What is the output of the following program?

```
#include <iostream>
using std::cout;
using std::endl;

int mystery(int n);
//Precondition n >= 1.

int main( )
{
    cout << mystery(3) << endl;
    return 0;
}

int mystery(int n)
{
```

Display 13.4   Evaluating the Recursive Function Call power(2,3)

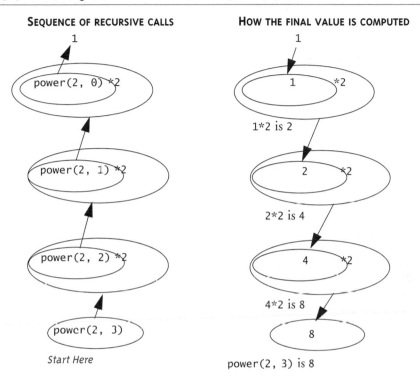

SEQUENCE OF RECURSIVE CALLS

HOW THE FINAL VALUE IS COMPUTED

power(2, 0) *2

power(2, 1) *2

power(2, 2) *2

power(2, 3)

Start Here

1*2 is 2

2*2 is 4

4*2 is 8

power(2, 3) is 8

```
        if (n <= 1)
            return 1;
        else
            return ( mystery(n - 1) + n );
    }
```

13. What is the output of the following program? What well-known mathematical function is rose?

```
#include <iostream>
using std::cout;
using std::endl;

int rose(int n);
//Precondition: n >= 0.

int main( )
{
    cout << rose(4) << endl;
```

```
        return 0;
    }

    int rose(int n)
    {
        if (n <= 0)
            return 1;
        else
            return ( rose(n - 1) * n );
    }
```

14. Redefine the function **power** so that it also works for negative exponents. In order to do this you will also have to change the type of the value returned to **double**. The function declaration and header comment for the redefined version of **power** are as follows:

```
double power(int x, int n);
//Precondition: If n < 0, then x is not 0.
//Returns x to the power n.
```

Hint: x^{-n} is equal to $1/(x^{n})$.

13.3 Thinking Recursively

There are two kinds of people in the world, those who divide the world into two kinds of people and those who do not.

Anonymous

RECURSIVE DESIGN TECHNIQUES

When defining and using recursive functions, you do not want to be continually aware of the stack and the suspended computations. The power of recursion comes from the fact that you can ignore that detail and let the computer do the bookkeeping for you. Consider the example of the function power in Display 13.3. The way to think of the definition of power is as follows:

```
power(x, n)
```

returns

```
power(x, n - 1)*x
```

Since x^n is equal to $x^{n-1} * x$, this is the correct value to return, provided that the computation will always reach a stopping case and will correctly compute the stopping case. So, after checking that the recursive part of the definition is correct, all you need check is that the chain of recursive calls will always reach a stopping case and that the stopping case always returns the correct value.

When designing a recursive function, you need not trace out the entire sequence of recursive calls for the instances of that function in your program. If the function returns a value, all you need do is check that the following three properties are satisfied:

1. There is no infinite recursion. (A recursive call may lead to another recursive call and that may lead to another, and so forth, but every such chain of recursive calls eventually reaches a stopping case.)

2. Each stopping case returns the correct value for that case.

3. For the cases that involve recursion: *If* all recursive calls return the correct value, *then* the final value returned by the function is the correct value.

criteria for functions that return a value

For example, consider the function power in Display 13.3.

1. *There is no infinite recursion:* The second argument to power(x, n) is decreased by 1 in each recursive call, so any chain of recursive calls must eventually reach the case power(x, 0), which is the stopping case. Thus, there is no infinite recursion.

2. *Each stopping case returns the correct value for that case:* The only stopping case is power(x, 0). A call of the form power(x, 0) always returns 1, and the correct value for x^0 is 1. So the stopping case returns the correct value.

3. *For the cases that involve recursion: If all recursive calls return the correct value, then the final value returned by the function is the correct value:* The only case that involves recursion is when n > 1. When n > 1, power(x, n) returns

    power(x, n − 1)*x

    To see that this is the correct value to return, note that *if* power(x, n − 1) returns the correct value, *then* power(x, n − 1) returns x^{n-1} and so power(x, n) returns

    $x^{n-1} * x$

    which is x^n, and that is the correct value for power(x, n).

That's all you need to check to be sure that the definition of power is correct. (The above technique is known as *mathematical induction,* a concept that you may have heard about in a mathematics class. However, you do not need to be familiar with the term *mathematical induction* in order to use this technique.)

We gave you three criteria to use in checking the correctness of a recursive function that returns a value. Basically the same rules can be applied to a recursive void function. If you show that your recursive void function definition satisfies the following three criteria, then you will know that your void function performs correctly:

1. There is no infinite recursion.

2. Each stopping case performs the correct action for that case.

3. For each of the cases that involve recursion: *If* all recursive calls perform their actions correctly, *then* the entire case performs correctly.

criteria for void functions

■ BINARY SEARCH

This subsection develops a recursive function that searches an array to determine whether it contains a specified value. For example, the array may contain a list of numbers for credit cards that are no longer valid. A store clerk needs to search the list to see if a customer's card is valid or invalid.

The indexes of the array a are the integers 0 through finalIndex. To make the task of searching the array easier, we will assume that the array is sorted. Hence, we know the following:

a[0] ≤ a[1] ≤ a[2] ≤... ≤ a[finalIndex]

When searching an array, you are likely to want to know both whether the value is in the list and, if it is, where it is in the list. For example, if we are searching for a credit card number, then the array index may serve as a record number. Another array indexed by these same indexes may hold a phone number or other information to use for reporting the suspicious card. Hence, if the sought-after value is in the array, we will want our function to tell where that value is in the array.

Now let us proceed to produce an algorithm to solve this task. It will help to visualize the problem in very concrete terms. Suppose the list of numbers is so long that it takes a book to list them all. This is in fact how invalid credit card numbers are distributed to stores that do not have access to computers. If you are a clerk and are handed a credit card, you must check to see if it is on the list and hence invalid. How would you proceed? Open the book to the middle and see if the number is there. If it is not and it is smaller than the middle number, then work backward toward the beginning of the book. If the number is larger than the middle number, work your way toward the end of the book. This idea produces our first draft of an algorithm:

algorithm— first version

```
found = false;//so far.
mid = approximate midpoint between 0 and finalIndex;
if (key == a[mid])
{
    found = true;
    location = mid;
}
else if (key < a[mid])
    search a[0] through a[mid - 1];
else if (key > a[mid])
    search a[mid + 1] through a[finalIndex];
```

Since the searchings of the shorter lists are smaller versions of the very task we are designing the algorithm to perform, this algorithm naturally lends itself to the use of recursion. The smaller lists can be searched with recursive calls to the algorithm itself.

Our pseudocode is a bit too imprecise to be easily translated into C++ code. The problem has to do with the recursive calls. There are two recursive calls shown:

```
search a[0] through a[mid - 1];
```

and

```
search a[mid + 1] through a[finalIndex];
```

To implement these recursive calls we need two more parameters. A recursive call specifies that a subrange of the array is to be searched. In one case it is the elements indexed by 0 through mid - 1. In the other case it is the elements indexed by mid + 1 through finalIndex. The two extra parameters will specify the first and last indexes of the search, so we will call them first and last. Using these parameters for the lowest and highest indexes, instead of 0 and finalIndex, we can express the pseudocode more precisely, as follows:

algorithm—
first
refinement

```
To search a[first] through a[last] do the following:
found = false;//so far.
mid = approximate midpoint between first and last;
if (key == a[mid])
{
    found = true;
    location = mid;
}
else if (key < a[mid])
    search a[first] through a[mid - 1];
else if (key > a[mid])
    search a[mid + 1] through a[last];
```

To search the entire array, the algorithm would be executed with first set equal to 0 and last set equal to finalIndex. The recursive calls will use other values for first and last. For example, the first recursive call would set first equal to 0 and last equal to the calculated value mid - 1.

As with any recursive algorithm, we must ensure that our algorithm ends rather than producing infinite recursion. If the sought-after number is found on the list, then there is no recursive call and the process terminates, but we need some way to detect when the number is not on the list. On each recursive call the value of first is increased or the value of last is decreased. If they ever pass each other and first actually becomes larger than last, we will know that there are no more indexes left to check and that the number key is not in the array. If we add this test to our pseudocode, we obtain a complete solution, as shown in Display 13.5.

stopping
case

algorithm—
final version

Display 13.5   Pseudocode for Binary Search

```
    int a[Some_Size_Value];
```

ALGORITHM TO SEARCH a[first] THROUGH a[last]

```
        //Precondition:
        //a[first]<= a[first + 1] <= a[first + 2] <=... <= a[last]
```

TO LOCATE THE VALUE KEY:

```
        if (first > last) //A stopping case
            found = false;
        else
        {
            mid = approximate midpoint between first and last;
            if (key == a[mid]) //A stopping case
            {
                found = false;
                location = mid;
            }
            else if key < a[mid] //A case with recursion
                search a[first] through a[mid – 1];
            else if key > a[mid] //A case with recursion
                search a[mid + 1] through a[last];
        }
```

CODING

Now we can routinely translate the pseudocode into C++ code. The result is shown in Display 13.6. The function search is an implementation of the recursive algorithm given in Display 13.5. A diagram of how the function performs on a sample array is given in Display 13.7.

Notice that the function search solves a more general problem than the original task. Our goal was to design a function to search an entire array, yet the search function will let us search any interval of the array by specifying the index bounds first and last. This is common when designing recursive functions. Frequently, it is necessary to solve a more general problem in order to be able to express the recursive algorithm. In this case, we only wanted the answer in the case where first and last are set equal to 0 and finalIndex. However, the recursive calls will set them to values other than 0 and finalIndex.

Display 13.6 Recursive Function for Binary Search *(part 1 of 2)*

```
1    //Program to demonstrate the recursive function for binary search.
2    #include <iostream>
3    using std::cin;
4    using std::cout;
5    using std::endl;
6    const int ARRAY_SIZE = 10;


7    void search(const int a[], int first, int last,
8                         int key, bool& found, int& location);
9    //Precondition: a[first] through a[last] are sorted in increasing order.
10   //Postcondition: if key is not one of the values a[first] through a[last],
11   //then found == false; otherwise, a[location] == key and found == true.


12   int main( )
13   {
14       int a[ARRAY_SIZE];
15       const int finalIndex = ARRAY_SIZE - 1;
```

<This portion of the program contains some code to fill and sort
the array a. The exact details are irrelevant to this example.>

```
16       int key, location;
17       bool found;
18       cout << "Enter number to be located: ";
19       cin >> key;
20       search(a, 0, finalIndex, key, found, location);

21       if (found)
22           cout << key << " is in index location "
23                << location << endl;
24       else
25           cout << key << " is not in the array." << endl;

26       return 0;
27   }
28   void search(const int a[], int first, int last,
29                         int key, bool& found, int& location)
30   {
31       int mid;
32       if (first > last)
33       {
34           found = false;
35       }
```

Display 13.6   Recursive Function for Binary Search *(part 2 of 2)*

```
36        else
37        {
38            mid = (first + last)/2;

39            if (key == a[mid])
40            {
41                found = true;
42                location = mid;
43            }
44            else if (key < a[mid])
45            {
46                search(a, first, mid – 1, key, found, location);
47            }
48            else if (key > a[mid])
49            {
50                search(a, mid + 1, last, key, found, location);
51            }
52        }
53    }
```

CHECKING THE RECURSION

The subsection entitled "Recursive Design Techniques" gave three criteria that you should check to ensure that a recursive void function definition is correct. Let's check these three things for the function search given in Display 13.6.

1. *There is no infinite recursion:* On each recursive call the value of first is increased or the value of last is decreased. If the chain of recursive calls does not end in some other way, then eventually the function will be called with first larger than last, which is a stopping case.

2. *Each stopping case performs the correct action for that case:* There are two stopping cases, when first > last and when key == a[mid]. Let's consider each case.

   If first > last, there are no array elements between a[first] and a[last] and so key is not in this segment of the array. (Nothing is in this segment of the array!) So, if first > last, the function search correctly sets found equal to false.

   If key == a[mid], the algorithm correctly sets found equal to true and location equal to mid. Thus, both stopping cases are correct.

3. *For each of the cases that involve recursion, if all recursive calls perform their actions correctly, then the entire case performs correctly:* There are two cases in which there are recursive calls, when key < a[mid] and when key > a[mid]. We need to check each of these two cases.

   First suppose key < a[mid]. In this case, since the array is sorted, we know that if key is anywhere in the array, then key is one of the elements a[first] through a[mid – 1].

Display 13.7   Execution of the Function search

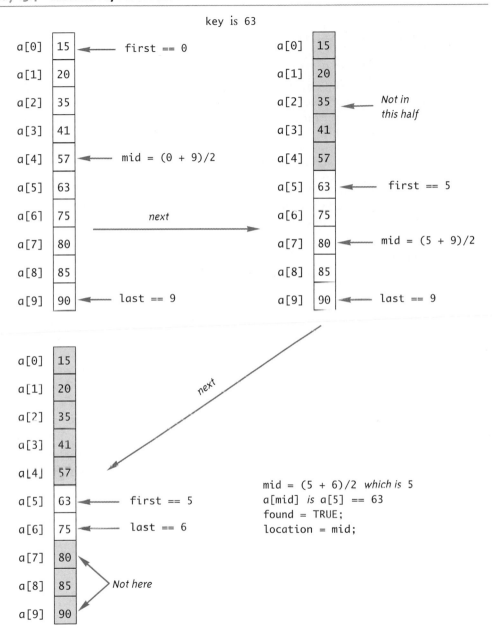

key is 63

a[0] 15 ⟵ first == 0   a[0] 15
a[1] 20   a[1] 20
a[2] 35   a[2] 35 ⟵ Not in
a[3] 41   a[3] 41   this half
a[4] 57 ⟵ mid = (0 + 9)/2   a[4] 57
a[5] 63   a[5] 63 ⟵ first == 5
a[6] 75   next   a[6] 75
a[7] 80   ⟶   a[7] 80 ⟵ mid = (5 + 9)/2
a[8] 85   a[8] 85
a[9] 90 ⟵ last == 9   a[9] 90 ⟵ last == 9

a[0] 15
a[1] 20   next
a[2] 35
a[3] 41
a[4] 57
a[5] 63 ⟵ first == 5   mid = (5 + 6)/2 *which is* 5
a[6] 75 ⟵ last == 6   a[mid] *is* a[5] == 63
a[7] 80   found = TRUE;
a[8] 85 ⟩ Not here   location = mid;
a[9] 90

Thus, the function need only search these elements, which is exactly what the recursive call

```
search(a, first, mid - 1, key, found, location);
```

does. So if the recursive call is correct, then the entire action is correct.

Next, suppose key > a[mid]. In this case, since the array is sorted, we know that if key is anywhere in the array, then key is one of the elements a[mid + 1] through a[last]. Thus, the function need only search these elements, which is exactly what the recursive call

```
search(a, mid + 1, last, key, found, location);
```

does. So if the recursive call is correct, then the entire action is correct. Thus, in both cases the function performs the correct action (assuming that the recursive calls perform the correct action).

The function search passes all three of our tests, so it is a good recursive function definition.

EFFICIENCY

The binary search algorithm is extremely fast compared with an algorithm that simply tries all array elements in order. In the binary search, you eliminate about half the array from consideration right at the start. You then eliminate a quarter, then an eighth of the array, and so forth. These savings add up to a dramatically fast algorithm. For an array of 100 elements, the binary search will never need to compare more than 7 array elements to the key. A simple serial search could compare as many as 100 array elements to the key and on the average will compare about 50 array elements to the key. Moreover, the larger the array is, the more dramatic the savings will be. On an array with 1000 elements, the binary search will only need to compare about 10 array elements to the key value, as compared to an average of 500 for the simple serial search algorithm.

An iterative version of the function search is given in Display 13.8. On some systems the iterative version will run more efficiently than the recursive version. The algorithm for the iterative version was derived by mirroring the recursive version. In the iterative version, the local variables first and last mirror the roles of the parameters in the recursive version, which are also named first and last. As this example illustrates, it often makes sense to derive a recursive algorithm even if you expect to later convert it to an iterative algorithm.

Display 13.8   Iterative Version of Binary Search

FUNCTION DECLARATION

```
void search(const int a[], int lowEnd, int highEnd,
                            int key, bool& found, int& location);
//Precondition: a[lowEnd] through a[highEnd] are sorted in increasing
//order.
//Postcondition: If key is not one of the values a[lowEnd] through
//a[highEnd], then found == false; otherwise, a[location] == key and
//found == true.
```

FUNCTION DEFINITION

```
void search(const int a[], int lowEnd, int highEnd,
                            int key, bool& found, int& location)
{
    int first = lowEnd;
    int last = highEnd;
    int mid;

    found = false;//so far
    while ( (first <= last) && !(found) )
    {
        mid = (first + last)/2;
        if (key == a[mid])
        {
            found = true;
            location = mid;
        }
        else if (key < a[mid])
        {
            last = mid - 1;
        }
        else if (key > a[mid])
        {
            first = mid + 1;
        }
    }
}
```

Self-Test Exercises

15. Write a recursive function definition for the following function:

```
int squares(int n);
//Precondition: n >= 1
//Returns the sum of the squares of the numbers 1 through n.
```

For example, `squares(3)` returns 14 because $1^2 + 2^2 + 3^2$ is 14.

Chapter Summary

- If a problem can be reduced to smaller instances of the same problem, then a recursive solution is likely to be easy to find and implement.

- A recursive algorithm for a function definition normally contains two kinds of cases: one or more cases that include at least one recursive call and one or more stopping cases in which the problem is solved without any recursive calls.

- When writing a recursive function definition, always check to see that the function will not produce infinite recursion.

- When you define a recursive function, use the three criteria given in the subsection "Recursive Design Techniques" to check that the function is correct.

- When designing a recursive function to solve a task, it is often necessary to solve a more general problem than the given task. This may be required to allow for the proper recursive calls, since the smaller problems may not be exactly the same problem as the given task. For example, in the binary search problem, the task was to search an entire array, but the recursive solution is an algorithm to search any portion of the array (either all of it or a part of it).

ANSWERS TO SELF-TEST EXERCISES

1. `Hip Hip Hurray`

2.
```
using std::cout;
void stars(int n)
{
    cout << '*';
    if (n > 1)
        stars(n - 1);
}
```

The following is also correct, but is more complicated:

```
void stars(int n)
{
    if (n <= 1)
```

```
    {
        cout << '*';
    }
    else
    {
        stars(n - 1);
        cout << '*';
    }
}
```

3. ```
   using std::cout;
   void backward(int n)
   {
       if (n < 10)
       {
           cout << n;
       }
       else
       {
           cout << (n%10);//write last digit
           backward(n/10);//write the other digits backward
       }
   }
   ```

4–5. The answer to 4 is writeUp;. The answer to 5 is writeDown;.

```
#include <iostream>
using std::cout;
using std::endl;

void writeDown(int n)
{
    if (n >= 1)
    {
        cout << n << " "; //write while the
                          //recursion winds
        writeDown(n - 1);
    }
}


// 5
void writeUp(int n)
{
    if (n >= 1)
    {
        writeUp(n - 1);
        cout << n << " "; //write while the
                          //recursion unwinds
```
```

```
        }
    }

    //testing code for both Exercises 4 and 5
    int main( )
     {
        cout << "calling writeUp(" << 10 << ")\n";
        writeUp(10);
        cout << endl;
        cout << "calling writeDown(" << 10 << ")\n";
        writeDown(10);
        cout << endl;
        return 0;
     }

    /* Test results
    calling writeUp(10)
    1 2 3 4 5 6 7 8 9 10
    calling writeDown(10)
    10 9 8 7 6 5 4 3 2 1*/
```

6. An error message that says "stack overflow" is telling you that the computer has attempted to place more activation frames on the stack than are allowed on your system. A likely cause of this error message is infinite recursion.

7. ```
   using std::cout;
   void cheers(int n)
   {
       while (n > 1)
       {
           cout << "Hip ";
           n--;
       }
       cout << "Hurray\n";
   }
   ```

8. ```
   using std::cout;
   void stars(int n)
   {
       for (int count = 1; count <= n; count++)
           cout << '*';
   }
   ```

9. ```
   using std::cout;
   void backward(int n)
   {
       while (n >= 10)
   ```
   ```

```
    {
        cout << (n%10);//write last digit
        n = n/10;//discard the last digit
    }
    cout << n;
}
```

10. Trace for Self-Test Exercise 4. If n = 3, the code to be executed is

```
if (3 >= 1)
    {
        writeDown(3 - 1);
    }
```

On the next recursion, n = 2 and the code to be executed is

```
if (2 >= 1)
    {
        writeDown(2 - 1)
    }
```

On the next recursion, n = 1 and the code to be executed is

```
if (1 >= 1)
    {
        writeDown(1 - 1)
    }
```

On the final recursion, n = 0 and the true clause is not executed:

```
if (0 >= 1) // condition false
    {
                    // this clause is skipped
    ┝
```

The recursion unwinds, the cout << n << " "; line of code is executed for each recursive call that was on the stack, with n = 3, then n = 2, and finally n = 1. The output is 3 2 1.

11. Trace for Self-Test Exercise 5. If n = 3, the code to be executed is

```
if (3 >= 1)
{
    cout << 3 << " ";
    writeUp(3 - 1);
}
```

On the next recursion, n = 2 and the code to be executed is

```
if (2 >= 1)
{
    cout << 2 << " ";
    writeUp(2 - 1);
```

```
}
```

On the next recursion, n = 1 and the code to be executed is

```
if (1 >= 1)
{
    cout << 1 << " ";
    writeUp(1 - 1);
}
```

On the final recursion, n = 0 and the code to be executed is

```
if (0 >= 1) // condition false, body skipped
{
    // skipped
}
```

The recursions unwind; the output (obtained by working through the stack) is 1 2 3.

12. 6

13. The output is 24. The function is the factorial function, usually written $n!$ and defined as follows:

$n!$ is equal to $n*(n-1)*(n-2)*...*1$

14.
```
//Uses iostream and cstdlib:
double power(int x, int n)
{
    if (n < 0 && x == 0)
    {
        cout << "Illegal argument to power.\n";
        exit(1);
    }

    if (n < 0)
        return ( 1/power(x, -n));
    else if (n > 0)
        return ( power(x, n - 1)*x );
    else // n == 0
        return (1.0);
}
```

15.
```
int squares(int n)
{
    if (n <= 1)
        return 1;
    else
        return ( squares(n - 1) + n*n );
}
```

PROGRAMMING PROJECTS

1. Write a recursive function definition for a function that has one parameter n of type int and that returns the nth Fibonacci number. The Fibonacci numbers are F_0 is 1, F_1 is 1, F_2 is 2, F_3 is 3, F_4 is 5, and in general

   $$F_{i+2} = F_i + F_{i+1} \text{ for } i = 0, 1, 2, \ldots$$

2. The formula for computing the number of ways of choosing r different things from a set of n things is the following:

   ```
   C(n, r) = n!/(r!*(n - r)!)
   ```

   The factorial function $n!$ is defined by

   ```
   n! = n*(n-1)*(n-2)*. . .*1
   ```

   Discover a recursive version of the formula for $C(n, r)$ and write a recursive function that computes the value of the formula. Embed the function in a program and test it.

3. Write a recursive function that has an argument that is an array of characters and two arguments that are array indexes. The function should reverse the order of those entries in the array whose indexes are between the two bounds. For example, if the array is

   ```
   a[1] == 'A' a[2] == 'B' a[3] == 'C' a[4] == 'D' a[5] == 'E'
   ```

   and the bounds are 2 and 5, then after the function is run the array elements should be

   ```
   a[1] == 'A' a[2] == 'E' a[3] == 'D' a[4] == 'C' a[5] == 'B'
   ```

   Embed the function in a program and test it. After you have fully debugged this function, define another function that takes a single argument that is an array that contains a string value; the function should reverse the spelling of the string value in the array argument. This function will include a call to the recursive definition you did for the first part of this project. Embed this second function in a program and test it.

4. Write an iterative version of the recursive function in the previous project. Embed it in a program and test it.

5. Towers of Hanoi. There is a story about Buddhist monks who are playing this puzzle with 64 stone disks. The story claims that when the monks finish moving the disks from one post to a second via the third post, time will end. Eschatology (concerns about the end of time) and theology will be left to those better qualified; our interest is limited to the recursive solution to the problem.

   A stack of n disks of decreasing size is placed on one of three posts. The task is to move the disks one at a time from the first post to the second. To do this, any disk can be moved from any post to any other post, subject to the rule that you can never place a larger disk over a smaller disk. The (spare) third post is provided to make the solution possible. Your task is to write a recursive function that describes instructions for a solution to this problem. We don't have graphics available, so you should output a sequence of instructions that will solve the problem.

Hint: If you could move n–1 of the disks from the first post to the third post using the second post as a spare, the last disk could be moved from the first post to the second post. Then by using the same technique (whatever that may be) you can move the n–1 disks from the third post to the second post, using the first disk as a spare. There! You have the puzzle solved. You only have to decide what the nonrecursive case is, what the recursive case is, and when to output instructions to move the disks.

6. (You need to have first done Programming Project 1.) In this exercise you will compare the efficiency of a recursive and an iterative function to compute the Fibonacci number.

   a. Examine the recursive function computation of Fibonacci numbers. Note that each Fibonacci number is recomputed many times. To avoid this recomputation, do programming problem 1 iteratively, rather than recursively; that is, do the problem with a loop. You should compute each Fibonacci number once on the way to the number requested and discard the numbers when they are no longer needed.

   b. Time the solution for project 1 and part a of this project in finding the 1st, 3rd, 5th, 7th, 9th, 11th, 13th, and 15th Fibonacci numbers. Determine how long each function takes. Compare and comment on your results.

   Hints: If you are running Linux, you can use the Bash 'time' utility. It gives real time (as in wall clock time), user time (time measured by cpu cycles devoted to your program), and sys time (cpu cycles devoted to tasks other than your program). If you are running in some other environment, you will have to read your manual, or ask your instructor, to find out how to measure the time a program takes to run.

7. (You need to have first done Programming Project 6.) When computing a Fibonacci number using the most straight forward recursive function definition, the recursive solution recomputes each Fibonacci number too many times. To compute $F_{i+2} = F_i + F_{i+1}$, it computes all the numbers computed in F_i a second time in computing F_{i+1}. You can avoid this by saving the numbers in an array while computing F_i. Write another version of your recursive Fibonacci function based on this idea. In the recursive solution for calculating the Nth Fibonacci number, declare an array of size N. Array entry with index i stores the ith ($i \leq N$) Fibonacci number as it is computed the first time. Then use the array to avoid the second (redundant) recalculation of the Fibonacci numbers. Time this solution as in Programming Project 6, and compare it to your results for the iterative solution.

14 CHAPTER

Inheritance

14 Inheritance

Like mother, like daughter

Common saying

INTRODUCTION

Object-oriented programming is a popular and powerful programming technique. Among other things, it provides for a dimension of abstraction known as *inheritance*. This means that a very general form of a class can be defined and compiled. Later, more specialized versions of that class may be defined and can inherit the properties of the general class. This chapter covers inheritance in general and, more specifically, how it is realized in C++.

This chapter does not use any of the material presented in Chapter 12 (file I/O) or Chapter 13 (recursion). It also does not use the material in Section 7.3 of Chapter 7, which covers vectors. Section 14.1 also does not use any material from Chapter 10 (pointers and dynamic arrays).

14.1 Inheritance Basics

If there is anything that we wish to change in the child, we should first examine it and see whether it is not something that could better be changed in ourselves.

Carl Gustav Jung, *The Integration of the Personality*

derived class
base class

Inheritance is the process by which a new class—known as a **derived class**—is created from another class, called the **base class**. A derived class automatically has all the member variables and all the ordinary member functions that the base class has, and can have additional member functions and additional member variables.

DERIVED CLASSES

Suppose we are designing a record-keeping program that has records for salaried employees and hourly employees. There is a natural hierarchy for grouping these classes. These are all classes of people who share the property of being employees.

Employees who are paid an hourly wage are one subset of employees. Another subset consists of employees who are paid a fixed wage each month or week. Although the program may not need any type corresponding to the set of all employees, thinking in terms of the more general concept of employees can be useful. For example, all employees have names and Social Security numbers, and the member functions for setting and changing names and Social Security numbers will be the same for salaried and hourly employees.

Within C++ you can define a class called Employee that includes all employees, whether salaried or hourly, and then use this class to define classes for hourly employees and salaried employees.

The class Employee will also contain member functions that manipulate the data fields of the class Employee. Displays 14.1 and 14.2 show one possible definition for the class Employee.

Display 14.1   Interface for the Base Class Employee

```
 1
 2   //This is the header file employee.h.
 3   //This is the interface for the class Employee.
 4   //This is primarily intended to be used as a base class to derive
 5   //classes for different kinds of employees.
 6   #ifndef EMPLOYEE_H
 7   #define EMPLOYEE_H

 8   #include <string>
 9   using std::string;

10   namespace SavitchEmployees
11   {

12       class Employee
13       {
14       public:
15           Employee( );
16           Employee(string theName, string theSsn);
17           string getName( ) const;
18           string getSsn( ) const;
19           double getNetPay( ) const;
20           void setName(string newName);
21           void setSsn(string newSsn);
22           void setNetPay(double newNetPay);
23           void printCheck( ) const;
24       private:
25           string name;
26           string ssn;
27           double netPay;
28       };

29   }//SavitchEmployees

30   #endif //EMPLOYEE_H
```

Display 14.2   Implementation for the Base Class Employee *(part 1 of 2)*

```
1
2    //This is the file employee.cpp.
3    //This is the implementation for the class Employee.
4    //The interface for the class Employee is in the header file employee.h.
5    #include <string>
6    #include <cstdlib>
7    #include <iostream>
8    #include "employee.h"
9    using std::string;
10   using std::cout;

11   namespace SavitchEmployees
12   {
13       Employee::Employee( ) : name("No name yet"), ssn("No number yet"), netPay(0)
14       {
15           //deliberately empty
16       }

17       Employee::Employee(string theName, string theNumber)
18           : name(theName), ssn(theNumber), netPay(0)
19       {
20           //deliberately empty
21       }

22       string Employee::getName( ) const
23       {
24           return name;
25       }

26       string Employee::getSsn( ) const
27       {
28           return ssn;
29       }
30
31       double Employee::getNetPay( ) const
32       {
33           return netPay;
34       }

35       void Employee::setName(string newName)
36       {
37           name = newName;
38       }

39       void Employee::setSsn(string newSsn)
```

Display 14.2   Implementation for Class Employee *(part 2 of 2)*

```
40        {
41            ssn = newSsn;
42        }

43        void Employee::setNetPay (double newNetPay)
44        {
45            netPay = newNetPay;
46        }

47        void Employee::printCheck( ) const
48        {
49            cout << "\nERROR: printCheck FUNCTION CALLED FOR AN \n"
50                 << "UNDIFFERENTIATED EMPLOYEE. Aborting the program.\n"
51                 << "Check with the author of the program about this bug.\n";
52            exit(1);
53        }

54    }//SavitchEmployees
```

You can have an (undifferentiated) Employee object, but our reason for defining the class Employee is so that we can define derived classes for different kinds of employees. In particular, the function printCheck will always have its definition changed in derived classes so that different kinds of employees can have different kinds of checks. This is reflected in the definition of the function printCheck for the class Employee (Display 14.2). It makes little sense to print a check for such an (undifferentiated) Employee. We know nothing about this employee. Consequently, we implemented the function printCheck of the class Employee so that the program stops with an error message if printCheck is called for a base class Employee object. As you will see, derived classes will have enough information to redefine the function printCheck to produce meaningful employee checks.

A class that is derived from the class Employee will automatically have all the member variables of the class Employee (name, ssn, and netPay). A class that is derived from the class Employee will also have all the member functions of the class Employee, such as printCheck, getName, setName, and the other member functions listed in Display 14.1. This is usually expressed by saying that the derived class **inherits** the member variables and member functions.

inherits

The interface files with the class definitions of two derived classes of the class Employee are given in Displays 14.3 (HourlyEmployee) and 14.4 (SalariedEmployee). We have placed the class Employee and the two derived classes in the same namespace. C++ does not require that they be in the same namespace, but since they are related classes, it makes sense to put them in the same namespace. We will first discuss the derived class HourlyEmployee, given in Display 14.3.

Display 14.3   Interface for the Derived Class HourlyEmployee

```
 1
 2   //This is the header file hourlyemployee.h.
 3   //This is the interface for the class HourlyEmployee.
 4   #ifndef HOURLYEMPLOYEE_H
 5   #define HOURLYEMPLOYEE_H

 6   #include <string>
 7   #include "employee.h"

 8   using std::string;

 9   namespace SavitchEmployees
10   {

11       class HourlyEmployee : public Employee
12       {
13       public:
14           HourlyEmployee( );
15           HourlyEmployee(string theName, string theSsn,
16                               double theWageRate, double theHours);
17           void setRate(double newWageRate);
18           double getRate( ) const;
19           void setHours(double hoursWorked);
20           double getHours( ) const;
21           void printCheck( ) ;            You only list the declaration of an
22       private:                           inherited member function if you want
23           double wageRate;               to change the definition of the
24           double hours;                  function.
25       };

26   }//SavitchEmployees

27   #endif //HOURLYEMPLOYEE_H
```

Note that the definition of a derived class begins like any other class definition but adds a colon, the reserved word public, and the name of the base class to the first line of the class definition, as in the following (from Display 14.3):

```
class HourlyEmployee : public Employee
{
```

The derived class (such as HourlyEmployee) automatically receives all the member variables and member functions of the base class (such as Employee) and can add additional member variables and member functions.

Display 14.4   **Interface for the Derived Class** SalariedEmployee

```
1
2   //This is the header file salariedemployee.h.
3   //This is the interface for the class SalariedEmployee.
4   #ifndef SALARIEDEMPLOYEE_H
5   #define SALARIEDEMPLOYEE_H

6   #include <string>
7   #include "employee.h"

8   using std::string;

9   namespace SavitchEmployees
10  {

11      class SalariedEmployee : public Employee
12      {
13      public:
14          SalariedEmployee( );
15          SalariedEmployee (string theName, string theSsn,
16                                       double theWeeklySalary);
17          double getSalary( ) const;
18          void setSalary(double newSalary);
19          void printCheck( );
20      private:
21          double salary;//weekly
22      };

23  }//SavitchEmployees

24  #endif //SALARIEDEMPLOYEE_H
```

The definition of the class HourlyEmployee does not mention the member variables name, ssn, and netPay, but every object of the class HourlyEmployee has member variables named name, ssn, and netPay. The member variables name, ssn, and netPay are inherited from the class Employee. The class HourlyEmployee declares two additional member variables named wageRate, and hours. Thus, every object of the class Hourly-Employee has five member variables named name, ssn, netPay, wageRate, and hours. Note that the definition of a derived class (such as HourlyEmployee) only lists the added member variables. The member variables defined in the base class are not mentioned. They are provided automatically to the derived class.

Just as it inherits the member variables of the class Employee, so too the class Hour-lyEmployee inherits all the member functions from the class Employee. Thus, the class HourlyEmployee inherits the member functions getName, getSsn, getNetPay, setName, setSsn, setNetPay, and printCheck from the class Employee.

INHERITED MEMBERS

A derived class automatically has all the member variables and all the ordinary member functions of the base class. (As discussed later in this chapter, there are some specialized member functions, such as constructors, that are not automatically inherited.) These members from the base class are said to be *inherited*. These inherited member functions and inherited member variables are, with one exception, not mentioned in the definition of the derived class, but they are automatically members of the derived class. As explained in the text, you do mention an inherited member function in the definition of the derived class if you want to change the definition of the inherited member function.

In addition to the inherited member variables and member functions, a derived class can add new member variables and new member functions. The new member variables and the declarations for the new member functions are listed in the class definition. For example, the derived class HourlyEmployee adds the two member variables wageRate and hours and adds the new member functions setRate, getRate, setHours, and getHours. This is shown in Display 14.3. Note that you do not give the declarations of the inherited member functions unless you want to change the definitions of the inherited member functions, which is a point that we will discuss shortly. For now, do not worry about the details of the constructor definition for the derived class. We will discuss constructors in the next subsection.

In the implementation file for the derived class, such as the implementation of HourlyEmployee in Display 14.5, you give the definitions of all the added member functions. Note that you do not give definitions for the inherited member functions unless the definition of the member function is changed in the derived class, a point we discuss next.

PARENT AND CHILD CLASSES

When discussing derived classes, it is common to use terminology derived from family relationships. A base class is often called a **parent class**. A derived class is then called a **child class**. This makes the language of inheritance very smooth. For example, we can say that a child class inherits member variables and member functions from its parent class. This analogy is often carried one step further. A class that is a parent of a parent of a parent of another class (or some other number of "parent of" iterations) is often called an **ancestor class**. If class A is an ancestor of class B, then class B is often called a **descendant** of class A.

---

redefining

The definition of an inherited member function can be changed in the definition of a derived class so that it has a meaning in the derived class that is different from what it is in the base class. This is called **redefining** the inherited member function. For example, the member function printCheck( ) is redefined in the definition of the derived class HourlyEmployee. To redefine a member function definition, simply list it in the class definition and give it a new definition, just as you would do with a member function that is added in the derived class. This is illustrated by the redefined function print-Check( ) of the class HourlyEmployee (Displays 14.3 and 14.5).

Display 14.5   **Implementation for the Derived Class HourlyEmployee** *(part 1 of 2)*

```cpp
1    //This is the file hourlyemployee.cpp.
2    //This is the implementation for the class HourlyEmployee.
3    //The interface for the class HourlyEmployee is in
4    //the header file hourlyemployee.h.
5    #include <string>
6    #include <iostream>
7    #include "hourlyemployee.h"
8    using std::string;
9    using std::cout;
10   using std::endl;

11   namespace SavitchEmployees
12   {

13       HourlyEmployee::HourlyEmployee( ) : Employee( ), wageRate(0), hours(0)
14       {
15           //deliberately empty
16       }

17       HourlyEmployee::HourlyEmployee(string theName, string theNumber,
18                                       double theWageRate, double theHours)
19           : Employee(theName, theNumber), wageRate(theWageRate), hours(theHours)
20       {
21           //deliberately empty
22       }

23       void HourlyEmployee::setRate(double newWageRate)
24       {
25           wageRate = newWageRate;
26       }

27       double HourlyEmployee::getRate( ) const
28       {
29           return wageRate;
30       }
31
32       void HourlyEmployee::setHours(double hoursWorked)
33       {
34           hours = hoursWorked;
35       }
```

Display 14.5   Implementation for the Derived Class HourlyEmployee (part 2 of 2)

```
36     double HourlyEmployee::getHours( ) const
37     {
38         return hours;
39     }

40     void HourlyEmployee::printCheck( )
41     {
42         setNetPay(hours * wageRate);

43         cout << "\n_____\n";
44         cout << "Pay to the order of " << getName( ) << endl;
45         cout << "The sum of " << getNetPay( ) << " Dollars\n";
46         cout << "_____\n";
47         cout << "Check Stub: NOT NEGOTIABLE\n";
48         cout << "Employee Number: " << getSsn( ) << endl;
49         cout << "Hourly Employee. \nHours worked: " << hours
50             << " Rate: " << wageRate << " Pay: " << getNetPay( ) << endl;
51         cout << "_____\n";
52     }

53 }//SavitchEmployees
```

We have chosen to set netPay as part of the printCheck function because that is when it is used. In any event, this is an accounting question, not a programming question. But, note that C++ allows us to drop the const on the function printCheck when we redefine it in a derived class.

SalariedEmployee is another example of a derived class of the class Employee. The interface for the class SalariedEmployee is given in Display 14.4, and its implementation is given in Display 14.6. An object declared to be of type SalariedEmployee has all the member functions and member variables of Employee plus the new members given in the definition of the class SalariedEmployee. This is true even though the class SalariedEmployee lists none of the inherited variables and only lists one function from the class Employee, namely, the function printCheck, which will have its definition changed in SalariedEmployee. The class SalariedEmployee, nonetheless, has the three member variables name, ssn, and netPay, as well as the member variable salary. Notice that you do not have to declare the member variables and member functions of the class Employee, such as name and setName, in order for SalariedEmployee to have these members. The class SalariedEmployee gets these inherited members automatically without the programmer doing anything.

Note that the class Employee has all the code that is common to the two classes HourlyEmployee and SalariedEmployee. This saves you the trouble of writing identical code two times: once for the class HourlyEmployee and once for the class SalariedEmployee. Inheritance allows you to reuse the code in the class Employee.

Display 14.6   Implementation for the Derived Class SalariedEmployee *(part 1 of 2)*

```
1
2    //This is the file salariedemployee.cpp
3    //This is the implementation for the class SalariedEmployee.
4    //The interface for the class SalariedEmployee is in
5    //the header file salariedemployee.h.
6    #include <iostream>
7    #include <string>
8    #include "salariedemployee.h"
9    using std::string;
10   using std::cout;
11   using std::endl;

12   namespace SavitchEmployees
13   {
14       SalariedEmployee::SalariedEmployee( ) : Employee( ), salary(0)
15       {
16           //deliberately empty
17       }

18       SalariedEmployee::SalariedEmployee(string theName, string theNumber,
19                                   double theWeeklyPay)
20                       : Employee(theName, theNumber), salary(theWeeklyPay)
21       {
22           //deliberately empty
23       }

24       double SalariedEmployee::getSalary( ) const
25       {
26           return salary;
27       }

28       void SalariedEmployee::setSalary(double newSalary)
29       {
30           salary = newSalary;
31       }
32
33       void SalariedEmployee::printCheck( )
34       {
35           setNetPay(salary);
36           cout << "\n_____\n";
37           cout << "Pay to the order of " << getName( ) << endl;
38           cout << "The sum of " << getNetPay( ) << " Dollars\n";
39           cout << "_____\n";
40           cout << "Check Stub NOT NEGOTIABLE \n";
41           cout << "Employee Number: " << getSsn( ) << endl;
```

Display 14.6   Implementation for the Derived Class SalariedEmployee *(part 2 of 2)*

```
42            cout << "Salaried Employee. Regular Pay: "
43                  << salary << endl;
44            cout << "_____\n";
45        }
46   }//SavitchEmployees
```

■ CONSTRUCTORS IN DERIVED CLASSES

A constructor in a base class is not inherited in the derived class, but you can invoke a constructor of the base class within the definition of a derived class constructor, which is all you need or normally want. A constructor for a derived class uses a constructor from the base class in a special way. A constructor for the base class initializes all the data inherited from the base class. Thus, a constructor for a derived class begins with an invocation of a constructor for the base class. The special syntax for invoking the base class constructor is illustrated by the constructor definitions for the class HourlyEm-ployee given in Display 14.5. In what follows we have reproduced (with minor changes in the line breaks to make it fit the text column) one of the constructor defini-tions for the class HourlyEmployee taken from that display:

```
HourlyEmployee::HourlyEmployee(string theName,
        string theNumber, double theWageRate, double theHours)
    : Employee(theName, theNumber),
                wageRate(theWageRate), hours(theHours)
{
    //deliberately empty
}
```

The portion after the colon is the initialization section of the constructor definition for the constructor HourlyEmployee::HourlyEmployee. The part Employee(theName, theNumber) is an invocation of the two-argument constructor for the base class Employee. Note that the syntax for invoking the base class constructor is analogous to the syntax used to set member variables: The entry wageRate(theWageRate) sets the value of the member variable wageRate to theWageRate; the entry Employee(theName, theNumber) invokes the base class constructor Employee with the arguments theName and theNumber. Since all the work is done in the initialization section, the body of the constructor definition is empty.

Below we reproduce the other constructor for the class HourlyEmployee from Dis-play 14.5:

```
HourlyEmployee::HourlyEmployee( ) : Employee( ), wageRate(0),
                                                hours(0)
{
    //deliberately empty
}
```

AN OBJECT OF A DERIVED CLASS HAS MORE THAN ONE TYPE

In everyday experience an hourly employee is an employee. In C++ the same sort of thing holds. Since HourlyEmployee is a derived class of the class Employee, every object of the class HourlyEmployee can be used anyplace an object of the class Employee can be used. In particular, you can use an argument of type HourlyEmployee when a function requires an argument of type Employee. You can assign an object of the class HourlyEmployee to a variable of type Employee. (But be warned: You cannot assign a plain old Employee object to a variable of type HourlyEmployee. After all, an Employee is not necessarily an HourlyEmployee.) Of course, the same remarks apply to any base class and its derived class. You can use an object of a derived class anyplace that an object of its base class is allowed.

More generally, an object of a class type can be used anyplace that an object of any of its ancestor classes can be used. If class Child is derived from class Ancestor and class Grandchild is derived from class Child, then an object of class Grandchild can be used anyplace an object of class Child can be used, and the object of class Grandchild can also be used anyplace that an object of class Ancestor can be used.

In this constructor definition the default (zero-argument) version of the base class constructor is called to initialize the inherited member variables. You should always include an invocation of one of the base class constructors in the initialization section of a derived class constructor.

If a constructor definition for a derived class does not include an invocation of a constructor for the base class, then the default (zero-argument) version of the base class constructor will be invoked automatically. So, the following definition of the default constructor for the class HourlyEmployee (with Employee( ) omitted) is equivalent to the version we just discussed:

```
HourlyEmployee::HourlyEmployee( ) : wageRate(0), hours(0)
{
    //deliberately empty
}
```

However, we prefer to always explicitly include a call to a base class constructor, even if it would be invoked automatically.

A derived class object has all the member variables of the base class. When a derived class constructor is called, these member variables need to be allocated memory and should be initialized. This allocation of memory for the inherited member variables must be done by a constructor for the base class, and the base class constructor is the most convenient place to initialize these inherited member variables. That is why you should always include a call to one of the base class constructors when you define a constructor for a derived class. If you do not include a call to a base class constructor (in the initialization section of the definition of a derived class constructor), then the default (zero-argument) constructor of the base class is called automatically. (If there is no default constructor for the base class, an error occurs.)

order of
constructor
calls

The call to the base class constructor is the first action taken by a derived class constructor. Thus, if class B is derived from class A and class C is derived from class B, then when an object of class C is created, first a constructor for class A is called, then a constructor for B is called, and finally the remaining actions of the class C constructor are taken.

CONSTRUCTORS IN DERIVED CLASSES

A derived class does not inherit the constructors of its base class. However, when defining a constructor for the derived class, you can and should include a call to a constructor of the base class (within the initialization section of the constructor definition).

If you do not include a call to a constructor of the base class, then the default (zero-argument) constructor of the base class will automatically be called when the derived class constructor is called.

Pitfall

USE OF PRIVATE MEMBER VARIABLES FROM THE BASE CLASS

An object of the class HourlyEmployee (Displays 14.3 and 14.5) inherits a member variable called name from the class Employee (Displays 14.1 and 14.2). For example, the following would set the value of the member variable name of the object joe to "Josephine" (it also sets the member variable ssn to "123–45–6789" and both wageRate and hours to 0):

```
HourlyEmployee joe("Josephine", "123–45–6789", 0, 0);
```

If you want to change joe.name to "Mighty-Joe", you can do so as follows:

```
joe.setName("Mighty-Joe");
```

You must be a bit careful about how you manipulate inherited member variables such as name. The member variable name of the class HourlyEmployee was inherited from the class Employee, but the member variable name is a private member variable in the definition of the class Employee. That means that name can only be directly accessed within the definition of a member function in the class Employee. A member variable (or member function) that is private in a base class is not accessible *by name* in the definition of a member function for *any other class, not even in a member function definition of a derived class.* Thus, although the class HourlyEmployee does have a member variable named name (inherited from the base class Employee), it is illegal to directly access the member variable name in the definition of any member function in the class definition of HourlyEmployee.

For example, the following are the first few lines from the body of the member function Hourly-Employee::printCheck (taken from Display 14.5):

```
void HourlyEmployee::printCheck( )
{
    setNetPay(hours * wageRate);

    cout << "\n_____\n";
    cout << "Pay to the order of " << getName( ) << endl;
    cout << "The sum of " << getNetPay( ) << " Dollars\n";
```

You might have wondered why we needed to use the member function setNetPay to set the value of the netPay member variable. You might be tempted to rewrite the start of the member function definition as follows:

```
void HourlyEmployee::printCheck( )
{
    netPay = hours * wageRate;            Illegal use of netPay
```

As the comment indicates, this will not work. The member variable netPay is a private member variable in the class Employee, and although a derived class like HourlyEmployee inherits the variable netPay, it cannot access it directly. It must use some public member function to access the member variable netPay. The correct way to accomplish the definition of printCheck in the class HourlyEmployee is the way we did it in Display 14.5 (part of which was displayed earlier).

The fact that name and netPay are inherited variables that are private in the base class also explains why we needed to use the accessor functions getName and getNetPay in the definition of HourlyEmployee::printCheck instead of simply using the variable names name and net-Pay. You cannot mention a private inherited member variable by name. You must instead use public accessor and mutator member functions (such as getName and setName) that were defined in the base class. (Recall that an accessor function is a function that allows you to access member variables of a class and a mutator function is one that allows you to change member variables of a class. Accessor and mutator functions were covered in Chapter 6.)

The fact that a private member variable of a base class cannot be accessed in the definition of a member function of a derived class often seems wrong to people. After all, if you are an hourly employee and you want to change your name, nobody says, "Sorry, name is a private member variable of the class Employee." After all, if you are an hourly employee, you are also an employee. In Java, this is also true; an object of the class HourlyEmployee is also an object of the class Employee. However, the laws regarding the use of private member variables and private member functions in C++ must be as we described, or else they would be compromised. If private member variables of a class were accessible in member function definitions of a derived class, then anytime you wanted to access a private member variable, you could simply create a derived class and access it in a member function of that class, which would mean that all private member variables would be accessible to anybody who wanted to put in a little extra effort. This scenario illustrates the problem, but the big problem is unintentional errors rather than intentional subversion. If private member variables of a class were accessible in member function definitions of a derived class, then the member variables might be changed by mistake or in inappropriate ways. (Remember, accessor and mutator functions can guard against inappropriate changes to member variables.)

We will discuss one possible way to get around this restriction on private member variables of the base class in the subsection entitled "The protected Qualifier" a bit later in this chapter.

Pitfall   PRIVATE MEMBER FUNCTIONS ARE EFFECTIVELY NOT INHERITED

As noted in the previous Pitfall section, a member variable (or member function) that is private in a base class is not directly accessible outside the interface and implementation of the base class, *not even in a member function definition for a derived class.* Note that private member functions are just like private variables in terms of not being directly available. In the case of member functions, however, the restriction is more dramatic. A private variable can be accessed indirectly via an accessor or mutator member function. A private member function is simply not available. It is just as if the private member function were not inherited.

This should not be a problem. Private member functions should be used just as helping functions, and so their use should be limited to the class in which they are defined. If you want a member function to be used as a helping member function in a number of inherited classes, then it is not *just* a helping function, and you should make the member function public.

THE protected QUALIFIER

As you have seen, you cannot access a private member variable or private member function in the definition or implementation of a derived class. There is a classification of member variables and functions that allows them to be accessed by name in a derived class, but not anyplace else, such as in some class that is not a derived class. If you use the qualifier protected, rather than private or public, before a member variable or member function of a class, then for any class or function other than a derived class the effect is the same as if the member variable were labeled private; however, in a derived class the variable can be accessed by name.

For example, consider the class HourlyEmployee, which was derived from the base class Employee. We were required to use accessor and mutator member functions to manipulate the inherited member variables in the definition of HourlyEmployee::print-Check. If all the private member variables in the class Employee were labeled with the keyword protected instead of private, the definition of HourlyEmployee::print-Check in the derived class Employee could be simplified to the following:

protected

```
void HourlyEmployee::printCheck( )
//Only works if the member variables of Employee are marked
//protected instead of private.
```

```
{
    netPay = hours * wageRate;

    cout << "\n_____\n";
    cout << "Pay to the order of " << name << endl;
    cout << "The sum of " << netPay << " Dollars\n";
    cout << "_____\n";
    cout << "Check Stub: NOT NEGOTIABLE\n";
    cout << "Employee Number: " << ssn << endl;
    cout << "Hourly Employee. \nHours worked: " << hours
         << " Rate: " << wageRate << " Pay: " << netPay << endl;
    cout << "_____\n";
}
```

In the derived class HourlyEmployee, the inherited member variables name, netPay, and ssn can be accessed by name provided they are marked as protected (as opposed to private) in the base class Employee. However, in any class that is not derived from the class Employee, these member variables are treated as if they were marked private.

Member variables that are marked protected in the base class act as though they were also marked protected in any derived class. For example, suppose you define a derived class PartTimeHourlyEmployee of the class HourlyEmployee. The class Part-TimeHourlyEmployee inherits all the member variables of the class HourlyEmployee, including the member variables that HourlyEmployee inherits from the class Employee. The class PartTimeHourlyEmployee will thus have the member variables netPay, name, and ssn. If these member variables were marked protected in the class Employee, then they can be used by name in the definitions of functions of the class PartTimeHourly-Employee.

Except for derived classes (and derived classes of derived classes, etc.), a member variable that is marked protected is treated the same as if it were marked private.

We include this discussion of protected member variables primarily because you will see them used and should be familiar with them. Many, but not all, programming authorities say it is bad style to use protected member variables because doing so compromises the principle of hiding the class implementation. They say that all member variables should be marked private. If all member variables are marked private, the inherited member variables cannot be accessed by name in derived class function definitions. However, this is not as bad as it sounds. The inherited private member variables can be accessed indirectly by invoking inherited functions that either read or change the private inherited variables. Since authorities differ on whether you should use protected members, you will have to make your own decision on whether to use them.

PROTECTED MEMBERS

If you use the qualifier protected, rather than private or public, before a member variable of a class, then for any class or function other than a derived class the effect is the same as if the member variable were labeled private. However, in the definition of a member function of a derived class the variable can be accessed by name. Similarly, if you use the qualifier protected before a member function of a class, then for any class or function other than a derived class the effect is the same as if the member variable were labeled private. However, in the definition of a member function of a derived class the protected function can be used.

Protected members are inherited in the derived class as if they were marked protected in the derived class. In other words, if a member is marked as protected in a base class, then it can be accessed by name in the definitions of all descendant classes, not just in those classes directly derived from the base class.

Self-Test Exercises

1. Is the following program legal (assuming appropriate #include and using directives are added)?

```
void showEmployeeData(const Employee object);

int main( )
{
    HourlyEmployee joe("Mighty Joe",
                        "123-45-6789", 20.50, 40);
    SalariedEmployee boss("Mr. Big Shot",
                        "987-65-4321", 10500.50);
    showEmployeeData(joe);
    showEmployeeData(boss);

    return 0;
}

void showEmployeeData(const Employee object)
{
    cout << "Name: " << object.getName( ) << endl;
    cout << "Social Security Number: "
        << object.getSsn( ) << endl;
}
```

2. Give a definition for a class SmartBut that is a derived class of the base class Smart given below. Do not bother with #include directives or namespace details.

```
class Smart
{
```

```
public:
    Smart( );
    void printAnswer( ) const;
protected:
    int a;
    int b;
};
```

This class should have an additional data field, `crazy`, of type `bool`; one additional member function that takes no arguments and returns a value of type `bool`; and suitable constructors. The new function is named `isCrazy`. You do not need to give any implementations, just the class definition.

3. Is the following a legal definition of the member function `isCrazy` in the derived class `SmartBut` discussed in Self-Test Exercise 2? Explain your answer. (Remember, the question asks if it is legal, not if it is a sensible definition.)

```
bool SmartBut::isCrazy( ) const
{
    if (a > b)
        return crazy;
    else
        return true;
}
```

REDEFINITION OF MEMBER FUNCTIONS

In the definition of the derived class `HourlyEmployee` (Display 14.3), we gave the declaration for the new member functions `setRate`, `getRate`, `setHours`, and `getHours`. We also gave the function declaration for only one of the member functions inherited from the class `Employee`. The inherited member functions whose function declarations were not given (such as `setName` and `setSsn`) are inherited unchanged. They have the same definition in the class `HourlyEmployee` as they do in the base class `Employee`. When you define a derived class like `HourlyEmployee`, you only list the function declarations for the inherited member functions whose definitions you want to change to have different definitions in the derived class. If you look at the implementation of the class `Hourly-Employee` (Display 14.5), you will see that we have redefined the inherited member function `printCheck`. The class `SalariedEmployee` also gives a new definition to the member function `printCheck`, as shown in Display 14.6. Moreover, the two classes give different definitions from each other. The function `printCheck` is *redefined* in the derived classes.

Display 14.7 gives a demonstration program that illustrates the use of the derived classes `HourlyEmployee` and `SalariedEmployee`.

REDEFINING AN INHERITED FUNCTION

A derived class inherits all the member functions (and member variables) that belong to the base class. However, if a derived class requires a different implementation for an inherited member function, the function may be redefined in the derived class. When a member function is redefined, you must list its declaration in the definition of the derived class, even though the declaration is the same as in the base class. If you do not wish to redefine a member function that is inherited from the base class, do not list it in the definition of the derived class.

Display 14.7   Using Derived Classes (*part 1 of 2*)

```
1   #include <iostream>
2   #include "hourlyemployee.h"
3   #include "salariedemployee.h"
4   using std::cout;
5   using std::endl;
6   using SavitchEmployees::HourlyEmployee;
7   using SavitchEmployees::SalariedEmployee;

8   int main( )
9   {
10      HourlyEmployee joe;
11      joe.setName("Mighty Joe");
12      joe.setSsn("123-45-6789");
13      joe.setRate(20.50);
14      joe.setHours(40);
15      cout << "Check for " << joe.getName( )
16           << " for " << joe.getHours( ) << " hours.\n";
17      joe.printCheck( );
18      cout << endl;

19      SalariedEmployee boss("Mr. Big Shot", "987-65-4321", 10500.50);
20      cout << "Check for " << boss.getName( ) << endl;
21      boss.printCheck( );

22      return 0;
23   }
```

The functions setName, setSsn, setRate, setHours, and getName are inherited unchanged from the class Employee. The function printCheck is redefined. The function getHours was added to the derived class HourlyEmployee.

Display 14.7   Using Derived Classes *(part 2 of 2)*

SAMPLE DIALOGUE

```
Check for Mighty Joe for 40 hours.
_____
Pay to the order of Mighty Joe
The sum of 820 Dollars
_____
Check Stub: NOT NEGOTIABLE
Employee Number: 123-45-6789
Hourly Employee.
Hours worked: 40 Rate: 20.5 Pay: 820

_____


Check for Mr. Big Shot
_____
Pay to the order of Mr. Big Shot
The sum of 10500.5 Dollars

_____
Check Stub NOT NEGOTIABLE
Employee Number: 987-65-4321
Salaried Employee. Regular Pay: 10500.5
_____
```

▨ REDEFINING VERSUS OVERLOADING

Do not confuse *redefining* a function definition in a derived class with *overloading* a function name. When you redefine a function definition, the new function definition given in the derived class has the same number and types of parameters. When you overload a function, the function in the derived class has a different number of parameters or a parameter of a different type from the function in the base class, and the derived class has both functions. For example, suppose we added a function with the following function declaration to the definition of the class HourlyEmployee:

```
void setName(string firstName, string lastName);
```

The class HourlyEmployee would have this two-argument function setName and would also inherit the following one argument function setName:

```
void setName(string newName);
```

The class HourlyEmployee would have two functions named setName. This would be *overloading* the function name setName.

On the other hand, both the class `Employee` and the class `HourlyEmployee` define a function with the following function declaration:

```
void printCheck( );
```

In this case, the class `HourlyEmployee` has only one function named `printCheck`, but the definition of the function `printCheck` for the class `HourlyEmployee` is different from its definition for the class `Employee`. In this case, the function `printCheck` has been *redefined*.

If you get redefining and overloading confused, you do have one consolation: They are both legal. So, it is more important to learn how to use them than it is to learn to distinguish between them. Nonetheless, you should learn the difference between them.

SIGNATURE

A function's **signature** is the function's name with the sequence of types in the parameter list, not including the `const` keyword and the ampersand, `&`. When you overload a function name, the two definitions of the function name must have different signatures using this definition of signature. (Some authorities include the `const` and/or ampersand as part of the signature, but we wanted a definition that works for explaining overloading.) A function that has the same name in a derived class as in the base class but has a different signature is overloaded, not redefined.

(As we noted in Chapter 4, some compilers will, in fact, allow you to overload on the basis of `const` versus no `const`, but you should not count on this. The C++ standard says it is not allowed.)

ACCESS TO A REDEFINED BASE FUNCTION

Suppose you redefine a function so that it has a different definition in the derived class from what it had in the base class. The definition that was given in the base class is not completely lost to the derived class objects. However, if you want to invoke the version of the function given in the base class with an object in the derived class, you need some way to say "use the definition of this function as given in the base class (even though I am an object of the derived class)." The way you say this is to use the scope resolution operator with the name of the base class. An example should clarify the details.

Consider the base class `Employee` (Display 14.1) and the derived class `HourlyEmployee` (Display 14.3). The function `printCheck( )` is defined in both classes. Now suppose you have an object of each class, as in the following:

```
Employee JaneE;
HourlyEmployee SallyH;
```

Then

```
JaneE.printCheck( );
```

uses the definition of printCheck given in the class Employee, and

```
SallyH.printCheck( );
```

uses the definition of printCheck given in the class HourlyEmployee.

But suppose you want to invoke the version of printCheck given in the definition of the base class Employee with the derived class object SallyH as the calling object for printCheck. You do that as follows:

```
SallyH.Employee::printCheck( );
```

Of course, you are unlikely to want to use the version of printCheck given in the particular class Employee, but with other classes and other functions, you may occasionally want to use a function definition from a base class with a derived class object. An example is given in Self-Test Exercise 6.

FUNCTIONS THAT ARE NOT INHERITED

As a general rule, if Derived is a derived class with base class Base, then all "normal" functions in the class Base are usable inherited members of the class Derived. However, there are some special functions that are, for all practical purposes, not inherited. We have already seen that, as a practical matter, constructors are not inherited and that private member functions are not inherited. Destructors (discussed in Section 14.2) are also effectively not inherited.

The copy constructor is not inherited, but if you do not define a copy constructor in a derived class (or any class, for that matter), C++ will automatically generate a copy constructor for you. However, this default copy constructor simply copies the contents of member variables and does not work correctly for classes with pointers or dynamic data in their member variables. Thus, if your class member variables involve pointers, dynamic arrays, or other dynamic data, you should define a copy constructor for the class. This applies whether or not the class is a derived class.

The assignment operator = is also not inherited. If the base class Base defines the assignment operator, but the derived class Derived does not define the assignment operator, then the class Derived will have an assignment operator, but it will be the default assignment operator that C++ creates (when you do not define =); it will not have anything to do with the base class assignment operator defined in Base. Techniques for defining the assignment operator are discussed in the subsection "Assignment Operators and Copy Constructors in Derived Classes" of Section 14.2.

It is natural that constructors, destructors, and the assignment operator are not inherited. To correctly perform their tasks they need information that the base class does not possess; namely, they need to know about the new member variables introduced in the derived class.

4. The class `SalariedEmployee` inherits both of the functions `getName` and `printCheck` (among other things) from the base class `Employee`, yet only the function declaration for the function `printCheck` is given in the definition of the class `SalariedEmployee`. Why isn't the function declaration for the function `getName` given in the definition of `SalariedEmployee`?

5. Give a definition for a class `TitledEmployee` that is a derived class of the base class `SalariedEmployee` given in Display 14.4. The class `TitledEmployee` has one additional member variable of type `string` called `title`. It also has two additional member functions: `getTitle`, which takes no arguments and returns a `string`, and `setTitle`, which is a `void` function that takes one argument of type `string`. It also redefines the member function `setName`. You do not need to give any implementations, just the class definition. However, do give all needed `#include` directives and all `using namespace` directives. Place the class `TitledEmployee` in the namespace `SavitchEmployees`.

6. Give the definitions of the constructors for the class `TitledEmployee` that you gave as the answer to Self-Test Exercise 5. Also, give the redefinition of the member function `setName`. The function `setName` should insert the title into the name. Do not bother with `#include` directives or namespace details.

7. You know that an overloaded assignment operator and a copy constructor are not inherited. Does this mean that if you do not define an overloaded assignment operator or a copy constructor for a derived class, then that derived class will have no assignment operator and no copy constructor?

14.2   Programming with Inheritance

The devil is in the details.

Common saying

This section presents some of the more subtle details regarding inheritance and presents another complete example, plus some discussion on inheritance and related programming techniques. The material in this section uses dynamic arrays (Chapter 10), and most of the topics are only relevant to classes that use dynamic arrays or pointers and other dynamic data.

ASSIGNMENT OPERATORS AND COPY CONSTRUCTORS IN DERIVED CLASSES

Overloaded assignment operators and constructors are not inherited. However, they can be used—and in almost all cases must be used—in the definitions of overloaded assignment operators and copy constructors in derived classes.

When overloading the assignment operator in a derived class, you normally use the overloaded assignment operator from the base class. To help understand the code outline we will give, remember that an overloaded assignment operator must be defined as a member function of the class.

If `Derived` is a class derived from `Base`, then the definition of the overloaded assignment operator for the class `Derived` would typically begin with something like the following:

```
Derived& Derived::operator =(const Derived& rightSide)
{
    Base::operator =(rightSide);
```

The first line of code in the body of the definition is a call to the assignment operator of the `Base` class. This takes care of the inherited member variables and their data. The definition of the overloaded assignment operator would then go on to set the new member variables that were introduced in the definition of the class `Derived`. A complete example that includes this technique is given in the programming example "Partially Filled Array with Backup" later in this chapter.

A similar situation holds for defining the copy constructor in a derived class. If `Derived` is a class derived from `Base`, then the definition of the copy constructor for the class `Derived` would typically use the copy constructor for the class `Base` to set the inherited member variables and their data. The code would typically begin with something like the following:

```
Derived::Derived(const Derived& Object)
                    : Base(Object), <probably more initializations>
{
```

The invocation of the base class copy constructor `Base(Object)` sets the inherited member variables of the `Derived` class object being created. Note that since `Object` is of type `Derived`, it is also of type `Base`; therefore, `Object` is a legal argument to the copy constructor for the class `Base`. A complete example that includes a copy constructor in a base class is given in the programming example "Partially Filled Array with Backup" later in this chapter.

Of course, these techniques do not work unless you have a correctly functioning assignment operator and a correctly functioning copy constructor for the base class. This means that the base class definition must include a copy constructor and that either the default automatically created assignment operator works correctly for the base class or the base class has an overloaded definition of the assignment operator.

DESTRUCTORS IN DERIVED CLASSES

If a base class has a correctly functioning destructor, it is relatively easy to define a correctly functioning destructor in a class derived from the base class. When the destructor for the derived class is invoked, it automatically invokes the destructor of the base class, so there is no need for the explicit writing of a call to the base class destructor; it always happens automatically. The derived class destructor thus need only worry about using delete on the member variables (and any data they point to) that are added in the derived class. It is the job of the base class destructor to invoke delete on the inherited member variables.

If class B is derived from class A and class C is derived from class B, then when an object of class C goes out of scope, first the destructor for the class C is called, then the destructor for class B is called, and finally the destructor for class A is called. Note that the order of destructor calls is the reverse of the order in which constructors are called. We give an example of writing a destructor in a derived class in the programming example "Partially Filled Array with Backup."

Example

PARTIALLY FILLED ARRAY WITH BACKUP

This example presents a derived class of the partially filled array class PFArrayD that we presented in Chapter 10 (Display 10.10). For reference we repeat the header file for the base class PFArrayD in Display 14.8. We repeat as much as we will discuss of the implementation for the base class PFArrayD in Display 14.9. Note that we have made one important change to the definition presented in Chapter 10. We have changed the member variables from private to protected. This will allow member functions in the derived class to access the member variables by name.

We will define a derived class called PFArrayDBak using PFArrayD as a base class. An object of the derived class PFArrayDBak will have all the member functions of the base class PFArrayD and can be used just like an object of the class PFArrayD, but an object of the class PFArrayD–Bak will have the following added feature: There is a member function called backup that can make a backup copy of all the data in the partially filled array, and at any later time the programmer can use the member function restore to restore the partially filled array to the state it was in just before the last invocation of backup. If the meaning of these added member functions is not clear, you should peek ahead to the sample demonstration program shown in Display 14.12.

The interface for the derived class PFArrayDBak is shown in Display 14.10. The class PFArrayD–Bak adds two member variables to hold a backed-up copy of the partially filled array: a member variable b of type double* that will point to a dynamic array with the backup version of the (inherited) working array, and an int member variable named usedB to indicate how much of the backed-up array b is filled with data. Since there is no way to change the capacity of a PFArrayD (or a PFArrayDBak), there is no need to back up the capacity value. All the basic functions for handling a partially filled array are inherited unchanged from the base class PFArrayD. These inherited functions manipulate the inherited array a and the inherited int variable used just as they did in the base class PFArrayD.

The implementation of the new member functions for the class PFArrayDBak is shown in Display 14.11. The constructors of the derived class PFArrayDBak rely on the constructors of the base class to set up the regular partially filled array (inherited member variables a, used, and capacity). Each constructor also creates a new dynamic array of the same size as the array a. This second array is the array b used for backing up the data in a.

Display 14.8   Interface for the Base Class PFArrayD

```
1   //This is the header file pfarrayd.h. This is the interface for the class
2   //PFArrayD. Objects of this type are partially filled arrays of doubles.
3   #ifndef PFARRAYD_H
4   #define PFARRAYD_H
```
This class is the same as the one in Display 10.10, except that we have made the member variables protected instead of private.
```
5   class PFArrayD
6   {
7   public:
8       PFArrayD( );
9       //Initializes with a capacity of 50.
```
It would be good to place this class in a namespace, but we have not done so in order to keep the example simple.
```
10      PFArrayD(int capacityValue);

11      PFArrayD(const PFArrayD& pfaObject);

12      void addElement(double element);
13      //Precondition: The array is not full.
14      //Postcondition: The element has been added.

15      bool full( ) const;
16      //Returns true if the array is full, false otherwise.

17      int getCapacity( ) const;

18      int getNumberUsed( ) const;

19      void emptyArray( );
20      //Resets the number used to zero, effectively emptying the array.

21      double& operator[](int index);
22      //Read and change access to elements 0 through numberUsed - 1.

23      PFArrayD& operator =(const PFArrayD& rightSide);

24      ~PFArrayD( );
25  protected:
26      double *a; //for an array of doubles.
27      int capacity; //for the size of the array.
28      int used; //for the number of array positions currently in use.
29  };

30  #endif //PFARRAYD_H
```

Display 14.9 Implementation for the Base Class PFArrayD *(part 1 of 2)*

```
1   #include <iostream>
2   using std::cout;
3   #include "pfarrayd.h"

4   PFArrayD::PFArrayD( ) : capacity(50), used(0)
5   {
6       a = new double[capacity];
7   }

8   PFArrayD::PFArrayD(int size) : capacity(size), used(0)
9   {
10      a = new double[capacity];
11  }

12  PFArrayD::PFArrayD(const PFArrayD& pfaObject)
13    :capacity(pfaObject.getCapacity( )), used(pfaObject.getNumberUsed( ))
14  {
15      a = new double[capacity];
16      for (int i =0; i < used; i++)
17          a[i] = pfaObject.a[i];
18  }

19  double& PFArrayD::operator[](int index)
20  {
21      if (index >= used)
22      {
23          cout << "Illegal index in PFArrayD.\n";
24          exit(0);
25      }

26      return a[index];
27  }
28
29  PFArrayD& PFArrayD::operator =(const PFArrayD& rightSide)
30  {
31      if (capacity != rightSide.capacity)
32      {
33          delete [] a;
34          a = new double[rightSide.capacity];
35      }

36      capacity = rightSide.capacity;
37      used = rightSide.used;
38      for (int i = 0; i < used; i++)
39          a[i] = rightSide.a[i];
```

This is part of the implementation file pfarrayd.cpp. The complete implementation is given in Display 10.11, but what is shown here is all you should need for this chapter.

Display 14.9   Implementation for the Base Class PFArrayD *(part 2 of 2)*

```
40        return *this;
41    }

42    PFArrayD::~PFArrayD( )
43    {
44        delete [] a;
45    }
```

Display 14.10   Interface for the Derived Class PFArrayDBak

```
 1    //This is the header file pfarraydbak.h. This is the interface for the class
 2    //PFArrayDBak. Objects of this type are partially filled arrays of doubles.
 3    //This version allows the programmer to make a backup copy and restore
 4    //to the last saved copy of the partially filled array.
 5    #ifndef PFARRAYDBAK_H
 6    #define PFARRAYDBAK_H
 7    #include "pfarrayd.h"

 8    class PFArrayDBak : public PFArrayD
 9    {
10    public:
11        PFArrayDBak( );
12        //Initializes with a capacity of 50.

13        PFArrayDBak(int capacityValue);

14        PFArrayDBak(const PFArrayDBak& Object);

15        void backup( );
16        //Makes a backup copy of the partially filled array.

17        void restore( );
18        //Restores the partially filled array to the last saved version.
19        //If backup has never been invoked, this empties the partially filled
20        //array.

21        PFArrayDBak& operator =(const PFArrayDBak& rightSide);

22        ~PFArrayDBak( );
23    private:
24        double *b; //for a backup of main array.
25        int usedB; //backup for inherited member variable used.
26    };

27    #endif //PFARRAYD_H
```

Display 14.11   Implementation for the Derived Class PFArrayDBak *(part 1 of 2)*

```
1   //This is the file pfarraydbak.cpp.
2   //This is the implementation of the class PFArrayDBak.
3   //The interface for the class PFArrayDBak is in the file pfarraydbak.h.
4   #include "pfarraydbak.h"
5   #include <iostream>
6   using std::cout;

7   PFArrayDBak::PFArrayDBak( ) : PFArrayD( ), usedB(0)
8   {
9       b = new double[capacity];
10  }

11  PFArrayDBak::PFArrayDBak(int capacityValue) : PFArrayD(capacityValue), usedB(0)
12  {
13      b = new double[capacity];
14  }

15  PFArrayDBak::PFArrayDBak(const PFArrayDBak& oldObject)
16                  : PFArrayD(oldObject), usedB(0)
17  {
18      b = new double[capacity];
19      usedB = oldObject.usedB;
20      for (int i = 0; i < usedB; i++)
21          b[i] = oldObject.b[i];
22  }

23  void PFArrayDBak::backup( )
24  {
25      usedB = used;
26      for (int i = 0; i < usedB; i++)
27          b[i] = a[i];
28  }
29
30  void PFArrayDBak::restore( )
31  {
32      used = usedB;
33      for (int i = 0; i < used; i++)
34          a[i] = b[i];
35  }

36  PFArrayDBak& PFArrayDBak::operator =(const PFArrayDBak& rightSide)
37  {
38      PFArrayD::operator =(rightSide);
39      if (capacity != rightSide.capacity)
40      {
41          delete [] b;
```

Note that b is a copy of the array a. We do not want to use b = a;.

You use a call to the base class assignment operator in order to assign to the base class member variables.

Display 14.11   Implementation for PFArrayDBak Class *(part 2 of 2)*

```
42              b = new double[rightSide.capacity];
43         }

44         usedB = rightSide.usedB;
45         for (int i = 0; i < usedB; i++)
46             b[i] = rightSide.b[i];

47         return *this;
48     }

49     PFArrayDBak::~PFArrayDBak( )
50     {
51         delete [] b;
52     }
```

The destructor for the base class PFArrayD is called automatically, and it performs `delete [] a;`.

The member function backup copies data from the partially filled array (a and used) to the backup locations b and usedB with the following code:

```
usedB = used;
for (int i = 0; i < usedB; i++)
    b[i] = a[i];
```

You should note that the member variables a and used in the base class are protected and not private. Otherwise, the above code would be illegal because it accesses the inherited member variables a and used by name.

The member function restore simply reverses things and copies from b and usedB to a and used.

The definition of the overloaded assignment operator for the derived class PFArrayDBak begins with an invocation of the assignment operator for the base class PFArrayD. This copies all the data from the member variables a, used, and capacity from the object on the right-hand side of the assigment operator (from the parameter rightSide) to the object on the left-hand side of the assignment operator (the calling object). We are relying on the fact that this was done properly in the definition of the overloaded assignment operator in the base class. That is, we rely on the base class assignment operator to behave correctly when the same object (for the inherited part) occurs on both sides of the assignment operator, and we assume that the copying actions make an independent copy of the array a. The code in the body of the overloaded assignment operator for the derived class PFArrayDBak needs to create a similarly independent copy of the array b.

Since the objects on the right and left sides of the assignment operators may have different capacities, we must create a new array b (in most cases). This is done as follows:

```
if (capacity != rightSide.capacity)
{
```

```
        delete [] b;
        b = new double[rightSide.capacity];
    }
```

Note that the Boolean expression in the if statement ensures that b will not be deleted when the objects on either side of the assignment operator have the same capacity. In particular, this ensures that when the same object appears on both sides of the assignment operator, the array b is not deleted. After this, the copying of data is routine.

Note that the destructor for the class PFArrayDBak has no explicit mention of the inherited member variable a. It simply sends the b array memory back to the freestore for recycling with the following:

```
    delete [] b;
```

The memory for the inherited array a is also sent back to the freestore, even though you do not see any mention of a in the destructor for the derived class PFArrayDBak. When the destructor for the derived class PFArrayDBak is invoked, it ends its action by automatically invoking the destructor for the base class PFArrayD, and that destructor includes the following code to dispose of a:

```
    delete [] a;
```

A demonstration program for our class PFArrayDBak is given in Display 14.12.

Display 14.12   Demonstration Program for the Class PFArrayDBak (part 1 of 3)

```
1   //Program to demonstrate the class PFArrayDBak.
2   #include <iostream>
3   #include "pfarraydbak.h"
4   using std::cin;
5   using std::cout;
6   using std::endl;

7   void testPFArrayDBak( );
8   //Conducts one test of the class PFArrayDBak.

9   int main( )
10  {
11      cout << "This program tests the class PFArrayDBak.\n";

12      char ans;
13      do
14      {
15          testPFArrayDBak( );
16          cout << "Test again? (y/n) ";
```

Display 14.12   Demonstration Program for the Class PFArrayDBak *(part 2 of 3)*

```
17              cin >> ans;
18          }while ((ans == 'y') || (ans == 'Y'));

19          return 0;
20  }

21  void testPFArrayDBak( )
22  {
23      int cap;
24      cout << "Enter capacity of this super array: ";
25      cin >> cap;
26      PFArrayDBak a(cap);

27      cout << "Enter up to " << cap << " nonnegative numbers.\n";
28      cout << "Place a negative number at the end.\n";

29      double next;

30      cin >> next;
31      while ((next >= 0) && (!a.full( )))
32      {
33          a.addElement(next);
34          cin >> next;
35      }

36      if (next >= 0)
37      {
38          cout << "Could not read all numbers.\n";
39          //Clear the unread input:
40          while (next >= 0)
41              cin >> next;
42      }

43      int count = a.getNumberUsed( );
44      cout << "The following " << count
45          << " numbers read and stored:\n";
46      int index;
47      for (index = 0; index < count; index++)
48          cout << a[index] << " ";
49      cout << endl;

50      cout << "Backing up array.\n";
51      a.backup( );

52      cout << "Emptying array.\n";
```

Display 14.12   Demonstration Program for the Class PFArrayDBak *(part 3 of 3)*

```
53        a.emptyArray( );
54        cout << a.getNumberUsed( )
55              << " numbers are now stored in the array.\n";

56        cout << "Restoring array.\n";
57        a.restore( );
58        count = a.getNumberUsed( );
59        cout << "The following " << count
60              << " numbers are now stored:\n";
61        for (index = 0; index < count; index++)
62            cout << a[index] << " ";
63        cout << endl;
64    }
```

SAMPLE DIALOGUE

```
This program tests the class PFArrayDBak.
Enter capacity of this super array: 10
Enter up to 10 nonnegative numbers.
Place a negative number at the end.
1 2 3 4 5 –1
The following 5 numbers read and stored:
1 2 3 4 5
Backing up array.
Emptying array.
0 numbers are now stored in the array.
Restoring array.
The following 5 numbers are now stored:
1 2 3 4 5
Test again? (y/n) y
Enter capacity of this super array: 5
Enter up to 5 nonnegative numbers.
Place a negative number at the end.
1 2 3 4 5 6 7 –1
Could not read all numbers.
The following 5 numbers read and stored:
1 2 3 4 5
Backing up array.
Emptying array.
0 numbers are now stored in the array.
Restoring array.
The following 5 numbers are now stored:
1 2 3 4 5
Test again? (y/n) n
```

SAME OBJECT ON BOTH SIDES OF THE ASSIGNMENT OPERATOR

Whenever you overload an assignment operator, always make sure your definition works when the same object occurs on both sides of the assignment operator. In most cases, you will need to make this a special case with some code of its own. An example of this is given in the programming example "Partially Filled Array with Backup."

---

8. Suppose Child is a class derived from the class Parent and that the class Grandchild is a class derived from the class Child. This question is concerned with the constructors and destructors for the three classes Parent, Child, and Grandchild. When a constructor for the class Grandchild is invoked, what constructors are invoked and in what order? When the destructor for the class Grandchild is invoked, what destructors are invoked and in what order?

9. Is the following alternative definition of the default constructor for the class PFArrayDBak (Displays 14.10 and 14.11) legal? (The invocation of the constructor from the base class has been omitted.) Explain your answer.

```
PFArrayDBak::PFArrayDBak( ) : usedB(0)
{
    b = new double[capacity];
}
```

ALTERNATE IMPLEMENTATION OF PFArrayDBak

At first glance it may seem that we needed to make the member variables of the base class PFArrayD protected in order to give the definitions of the member functions for the derived class PFArrayDBak. After all, many of the member functions manipulate the inherited member variables a, used, and capacity. The implementation we gave in Display 14.11 does indeed refer to a, used, and capacity by name, and so those particular definitions do depend on these member variables being protected in the base class (as opposed to private). However, we have enough accessor and mutator functions in the base class that with just a bit more thinking, we can rewrite the implementation of the derived class PFArrayDBak so that it works even if all the member variables in the base class PFArrayD are private (rather than protected).

Display 14.13 shows an alternate implementation for the class PFArrayDBak that works fine even if all the member variables in the base class are private instead of protected. The parts that differ from our previous implementation are shaded. Most changes are obvious, but there are a few points that merit notice.

Consider the member function backup. In our previous implementation (Display 14.11), we copied the array entries from a to b. Since a is now private, we cannot access it by name, but we have overloaded the array square brackets operator (operator[]) so that it applies to objects of type PFArrayD, and this operator is inherited in PFArrayDBak. We simply use operator[] with the calling object. The net effect is to copy from the array a to the array b, but we never mention the private array a by name. The code is as follows:

```
usedB = getNumberUsed( );
for (int i = 0; i < usedB; i++)
    b[i] = operator[](i);
```

Be sure to note the syntax for calling an operator of the class being defined. If superArray is an object of the class PFArrayDBak, then in the invocation superArray.backup( ), the notation operator[](i) means superArray[i].

We could have used the notation operator[](i) in our definition of the member function restore, but it is just as easy to empty the array a with the inherited member function empty-Array and then add the backed-up elements using addElement. This way, we also set the private member variable used in the process.

With this alternate implementation, the class PFArrayDBak is used just as it was with the previous implementation. In particular, the demonstration program in Display 14.12 works exactly the same for either implementation.

Tip

A CLASS HAS ACCESS TO PRIVATE MEMBERS OF ALL OBJECTS OF THE CLASS

Consider the following lines from the implementation of the overloaded assignment operator given in Display 14.13:

```
usedB = rightSide.usedB;
for (int i = 0; i < usedB; i++)
    b[i] = rightSide.b[i];
```

You might object that rightSide.usedB and rightSide.b[i] are illegal since usedB and b are private member variables of some object other than the calling object. Normally that objection would be correct. However, the object rightSide is of the same type as the class being defined, and so this is legal.

In the definition of a class, you can access private members of any object of the class, not just private members of the calling object.

Display 14.13   Alternate Implementation of PFArrayDBak *(part 1 of 2)*

```
1   //This is the file pfarraydbak.cpp.
2   //This is the implementation of the class PFArrayDBak.
3   //The interface for the class PFArrayDBak is in the file pfarraydbak.h.
4   #include "pfarraydbak.h"
5   #include <iostream>
6   using std::cout;

7   PFArrayDBak::PFArrayDBak( ) : PFArrayD( ), usedB(0)
8   {
9       b = new double[getCapacity( )];
10  }

11  PFArrayDBak::PFArrayDBak(int capacityValue) : PFArrayD(capacityValue), usedB(0)
12  {
13      b = new double[getCapacity( )];
14  }

15  PFArrayDBak::PFArrayDBak(const PFArrayDBak& oldObject)
16                  : PFArrayD(oldObject), usedB(0)
17  {
18      b = new double[getCapacity( )];
19      usedB = oldObject.usedB;
20      for (int i = 0; i < usedB; i++)
21          b[i] = oldObject.b[i];
22  }
```

This implementation works even if all the member variables in the base class are private (rather than protected).

```
23  void PFArrayDBak::backup( )
24  {
25      usedB = getNumberUsed( );
26      for (int i = 0; i < usedB; i++)
27          b[i] = operator[](i);
28  }
29
30  void PFArrayDBak::restore( )
31  {
32      emptyArray( );

33      for (int i = 0; i < usedB; i++)
34          addElement(b[i]);
35  }
```

Invocation of the square brackets operator with the calling object

```
36  PFArrayDBak& PFArrayDBak::operator =(const PFArrayDBak& rightSide)
37  {
38      PFArrayD::operator =(rightSide);
```

Display 14.13   **Alternate Implementation of PFArrayDBak** *(part 2 of 2)*

```
39          if (getCapacity( ) != rightSide.getCapacity( ))
40          {
41              delete [] b;
42              b = new double[rightSide.getCapacity( )];
43          }

44          usedB = rightSide.usedB;
45          for (int i = 0; i < usedB; i++)
46              b[i] = rightSide.b[i];

47          return *this;
48      }


49      PFArrayDBak::~PFArrayDBak( )
50      {
51          delete [] b;
52      }
```

Tip

"Is a" versus "Has a"

"is a"
relation-
ship

"has a"
relation-
ship

Early in this chapter we defined a derived class called HourlyEmployee using the class Employee as the base class. In such a case an object of the derived class HourlyEmployee is also of type Employee. Stated more simply, an HourlyEmployee *is an* Employee. This is an example of the "is a" relationship between classes. It is one way to make a more complex class from a simpler class.

Another way to make a more complex class from a simpler class is known as the "has a" relationship. For example, if you have a class Date that records a date, then you might add a date of employment to the Employee class by adding a member variable of type Date to the Employee class. In this case we say an Employee "has a" Date. As another example, if we have an appopriately named class to simulate a jet engine and we are defining a class to simulate a passenger airplane, then we can give the PassengerAirPlane class one or more member variables of type JetEngine. In this case we say that a PassengerAirPlane "has a" JetEngine.

In most situations you can make your code work with either an "is a" relationship or a "has a" relationship. It seems silly (and it is silly) to make the PassengerAirPlane class a derived class of the JetEngine class, but it can be done and can be made to work (perhaps with difficulty). Fortunately, the best programming technique is to simply follow what sounds most natural in English. It makes more sense to say "A passenger airplane has a jet engine" than it does to say "A passenger airplane is a jet engine." So, it makes better programming sense to have JetEngine as a member variable of a PassengerAirPlane class. It makes little sense to make the Passen-gerAirPlane class a derived class of the JetEngine class.

Self-Test Exercises

10. Suppose you define a function with a parameter of type PFArrayD. Can you plug in an object of the class PFArrayDBak as an argument for this function?

11. Would the following be legal for the definition of a member function to add to the class Employee (Display 14.1)? (Remember, the question is whether it is legal, not whether it is sensible.)

```
void Employee::doStuff( )
{
    Employee object("Joe", "123-45-6789");
    cout << "Hello " << object.name << endl;
}
```

PROTECTED AND PRIVATE INHERITANCE

So far, all our definitions of derived classes included the keyword public in the class heading, as in the following:

```
class SalariedEmployee : public Employee
{
```

This may lead you to suspect that the word public can be replaced with either protected or private to obtain a different kind of inheritance. In this case, your suspicion would be correct. However, protected and private inheritance are seldom used. We include a brief description of them for the sake of completeness.

The syntax for protected and private inheritance is illustrated by the following:

```
class SalariedEmployee : protected Employee
{
```

If you use the keyword protected for inheritance, then members that are public in the base class are protected in the derived class when they are inherited. If you use the keyword private for inheritance, then all members of the base class (public, protected, and private) are inaccessible in the derived class; in other words, all members are inherited as if they were marked private in the base class.

Moreover, with protected and private inheritance, an object of the derived class cannot be used as an argument that has the type of the base class. If Derived is derived from Base using protected or private (instead of public), then an object of type Derived is not an object of type Base; the "is a" relationship does not hold with protected and private inheritance. The idea is that with protected and private inheritance the base class is simply a tool to use in defining the derived class. Although protected and private inheritance can be made to work for some purposes, they are, as you might suspect, seldom used, and any use they do have can be achieved in other ways.

The details about protected and private inheritance are summarized in Display 14.14.

Display 14.14 Public, Protected, and Private Inheritance

ACCESS SPECIFIER IN BASE CLASS	TYPE OF INHERITANCE (SPECIFIER AFTER CLASS NAME IN DERIVED CLASS DEFINITION)		
	public	protected	private
public	Public	Protected	Private (Can only be used by name in definitions of member functions and friends)
protected	Protected	Protected	Private (Can only be used by name in definitions of member functions and friends)
private	Cannot be accessed by name in the derived class	Cannot be accessed by name in the derived class	Cannot be accessed by name in the derived class

Entries show how inherited members are treated in the derived class.

Note that protected and private inheritance are not inheritance in the sense we described for public inheritance. With protected or private inheritance the base class is only a tool to be used in the derived class.

MULTIPLE INHERITANCE

It is possible for a derived class to have more than one base class. The syntax is very simple: All the base classes are listed, separated by commas. However, the possibilities for ambiguity are numerous. What if two base classes have a function with the same name and parameter types? Which is inherited? What if two base classes have a member variable with the same name? All these questions can be answered, but these and other problems make multiple inheritance a very dangerous business. Some authorities consider multiple inheritance so dangerous that it should not be used at all. That may or may not be too extreme a position, but it is true that you should not seriously attempt multiple inheritance until you are a very experienced C++ programmer. At that point, you will realize that you can almost always avoid multiple inheritance by using some less dangerous technique. We will not discuss multiple inheritance in this book, but leave it for more advanced references.

Chapter Summary

■ Inheritance provides a tool for code reuse by deriving one class from another, adding features to the derived class.

■ Derived class objects inherit the members of the base class, and may add members.

■ If a member variable is private in a base class, then it cannot be accessed by name in a derived class.

■ Private member functions are not inherited.

■ A member function may be redefined in a derived class so that it performs differently from how it performs in the base class. The declaration for a redefined member function must be given in the class definition of the derived class, even though it is the same as in the base class.

■ A protected member in the base class can be accessed by name in the definition of a member function of a publicly derived class.

■ An overloaded assignment operator is not inherited. However, the assignment operator of a base class can be used in the definition of an overloaded assignment operator of a derived class.

■ Constructors are not inherited. However, a constructor of a base class can be used in the definition of a constructor for a derived class.

ANSWERS TO SELF-TEST EXERCISES

1. Yes. You can plug in an object of a derived class for a parameter of the base class type. An `HourlyEmployee` is an `Employee`. A `SalariedEmployee` is an `Employee`.

2.
```
class SmartBut : public Smart
{
public:
    SmartBut( );
    SmartBut(int newA, int newB, bool newCrazy);
    bool isCrazy( ) const;
private:
    bool crazy;
};
```

3. It is legal because `a` and `b` are marked `protected` in the base class `Smart` and so they can be accessed by name in a derived class. If `a` and `b` had instead been marked `private`, then this would be illegal.

4. The declaration for the function `getName` is not given in the definition of `Salaried-Employee` because it is not redefined in the class `SalariedEmployee`. It is inherited unchanged from the base class `Employee`.

5.
```cpp
#include <iostream>
#include "salariedemployee.h"
using namespace std;
namespace SavitchEmployees
{
    class TitledEmployee : public SalariedEmployee
    {
    public:
        TitledEmployee( );
        TitledEmployee(string theName, string theTitle,
                       string theSsn, double theSalary);
        string getTitle( ) const;
        void setTitle(string theTitle);
        void setName(string theName);
    private:
        string title;
    };
}//SavitchEmployees
```

6.
```cpp
namespace SavitchEmployees
{
    TitledEmployee::TitledEmployee( )
          : SalariedEmployee( ), title("No title yet")
    {
        //deliberately empty
    }

    TitledEmployee::TitledEmployee(string theName,
                       string theTitle,
                       string theSsn, double theSalary)
        : SalariedEmployee(theName, theSsn, theSalary),
                       title(theTitle)
    {
        //deliberately empty
    }

    void TitledEmployee::setName(string theName)
    {
        Employee::setName(title + theName);
    }
}//SavitchEmployees
```

7. No. If you do not define an overloaded assignment operator or a copy constructor for a derived class, then a default assignment operator and a default copy constructor will be defined for the derived class. However, if the class involves pointers, dynamic arrays, or other dynamic data, then it is almost certain that neither the default assignment operator nor the default copy constructor will behave as you want them to.

8. The constructors are called in the following order: first `Parent`, then `Child`, and finally `Grandchild`. The destructors are called in the reverse order: first `Grandchild`, then `Child`, and finally `Parent`.

9. Yes, it is legal and has the same meaning as the definition given in Display 14.11. If no base class constructor is called, then the default constructor for the base class is called automatically.

10. Yes. An object of a derived class is also an object of its base class. A `PFArrayDBak` is a `PFArrayD`.

11. Yes, it is legal. One reason you might think it illegal is that `name` is a private member variable. However, `object` is in the class `Employee`, which is the class that is being defined, so we have access to all member variables of all objects of the class `Employee`.

PROGRAMMING PROJECTS

1. Write a program that uses the class `SalariedEmployee` given in Display 14.4. Your program is to define a derived class called `Administrator`, which is to be derived from the class `SalariedEmployee`. You are allowed to change `private` in the base class to `protected`. You are to supply the following additional data and function members:
   - A member variable of type `string` that contains the administrator's title, (such as Director or Vice President).
   - A member variable of type `string` that contains the company area of responsibility (such as Production, Accounting, or Personnel).
   - A member variable of type `string` that contains the name of this administrator's immediate supervisor.
   - A `protected` member variable of type `double` that holds the administrator's annual salary. It is possible for you to use the existing salary member if you did the change recommended above.
   - A member function called `setSupervisor`, which changes the supervisor name.
   - A member function for reading in an administrator's data from the keyboard.
   - A member function called `print`, which outputs the object's data to the screen.
   - Finally, an overloading of the member function `printCheck( )` with appropriate notations on the check.

2. Add temporary, administrative, permanent, and other classifications of employee to the hierarchy from Displays 14.1, 14.3, and 14.4. Implement and test this hierarchy. Test all member functions. A user interface with a menu would be a nice touch for your test program.

3. Give the definition of a class named `Doctor` whose objects are records for a clinic's doctors. This class will be a derived class of the class `SalariedEmployee` given in Display 14.4. A `Doctor` record has the doctor's specialty (such as "Pediatrician," "Obstetrician," "General Practitioner," etc., so use type `string`), and office visit fee (use type `double`). Be sure your class has a reasonable complement of constructors and accessor methods, an overloaded assignment operator, and a copy constructor. Write a driver program to test all your methods.

4. Create a base class called Vehicle that has the manufacturer's name (type string), number of cylinder's in the engine (type int), and owner (type Person given below). Then create a class called Truck that is derived from Vehicle and has additional properties, the load capacity in tons (type double since it may contain a fractional part) and towing capacity in pounds (type int). Be sure your classes have a reasonable complement of constructors and accessor methods, an overloaded assignment operator, and a copy constructor. Write a driver program that tests all your methods.

The definition of the class Person is below. The implementation of the class is part of this programming project.

```
class Person
{
public:
    Person();
    Person(string theName);
    Person(const Person& theObject);
    string getName() const;
    Person& operator=(const Person& rtSide);
    friend istream& operator >>(istream& inStream,
                                    Person& personObject);
    friend ostream& operator <<(ostream& outStream,
                                const Person& personObject);
private:
    string name;
};
```

5. Give the definition of two classes, Patient and Billing, whose objects are records for a clinic. Patient will be derived from the class Person given in Programming Project 4. A Patient record has the patient's name (inherited from the class Person) and primary physician, of type Doctor defined in Programming Project 3. A Billing object will contain a Patient object and a Doctor object, and an amount due of type double. Be sure your classes have a reasonable complement of constructors and accessor methods, an overloaded assignment operator, and a copy constructor. First write a driver program to test all your methods, then write a test program that creates at least two patients, at least two doctors, at least two Billing records, then prints out the total income from the Billing records.

15 CHAPTER

Polymorphism and Virtual Functions

15

Polymorphism and Virtual Functions

I did it my way.

Frank Sinatra

INTRODUCTION

Polymorphism refers to the ability to associate many meanings to one function name by means of a special mechanism known as *virtual functions* or *late binding*. Polymorphism is one of the fundamental mechanisms of a popular and powerful programming philosophy known as *object-oriented programming*. Wow, lots of fancy words! This chapter will explain them.

Section 15.1 does not require the material from Chapters 10 (pointers and dynamic arrays), 12 (file I/O), or 13 (recursion). Section 15.2 does not require the material from Chapters 12 (file I/O) or 13 (recursion), but does require the material from Chapter 10 (pointers and dynamic arrays).

15.1 Virtual Function Basics

virtual adj. 1. Existing or resulting in essence or effect though not in actual fact, form, or name.

The American Heritage Dictionary of the English Language, Third Edition

A *virtual* function is so named because it may, in a sense to be made clear, be used before it is defined. Virtual functions will prove to be another tool for software reuse.

LATE BINDING

Virtual functions are best explained by an example. Suppose you are designing software for a graphics package that has classes for several kinds of figures, such as rectangles, circles, ovals, and so forth. Each figure might be an object of a different class. For example, the `Rectangle` class might have member variables for a height, width, and center point, while the `Circle` class might have member variables for a center point and a radius. In a well-designed programming project, all of these classes would probably be descendants of a single parent class called, for example, `Figure`. Now, suppose you want a function to draw a figure on the screen. To draw a circle, you need different instructions from those you need to draw a rectangle. So, each class needs to have a different function to draw its kind of figure. However, because the functions belong to the classes, they can all be called draw. If r is a Rectangle object and c is a Circle object, then r.draw( ) and c.draw( ) can be functions implemented with different code. All this is not news, but now we move on to something new: virtual functions defined in the parent class Figure.

The parent class Figure may have functions that apply to all figures. For example, it might have a function called center that moves a figure to the center of the screen by erasing it and then redrawing it in the center of the screen. The function Figure::center might use the function draw to redraw the figure in the center of the screen. When you think of using the inherited function center with figures of the classes Rectangle and Circle, you begin to see that there are complications here.

To make the point clear and more dramatic, let's suppose that the class Figure is already written and in use and that at some later time you add a class for a brand-new kind of figure, say, the class Triangle. Now, Triangle can be a derived class of the class Figure, and so the function center will be inherited from the class Figure. The function center should therefore apply to (and perform correctly for) all Triangles. But there is a complication. The function center uses draw, and the function draw is different for each type of figure. The inherited function center (if nothing special is done) will use the definition of the function draw given in the class Figure, and that function draw does not work correctly for Triangles. We want the inherited member function center to use the function Triangle::draw rather than the function Figure::draw. But the class Triangle—and therefore the function Triangle::draw—was not even written when the function center (defined in the class Figure) was written and compiled! How can the function center possibly work correctly for Triangles? The compiler did not know anything about Triangle::draw at the time that center was compiled! The answer is that it can apply provided draw is a *virtual function*.

When you make a function **virtual**, you are telling the compiler "I do not know how this function is implemented. Wait until it is used in a program, and then get the implementation from the object instance." The technique of waiting until runtime to determine the implementation of a function is often called **late binding** or **dynamic binding**. Virtual functions are the way C++ provides late binding. But enough introduction. We need an example to make this come alive (and to teach you how to use virtual functions in your programs). To explain the details of virtual functions in C++, we will use a simplified example from an application area other than drawing figures.

virtual function

late binding or dynamic binding

■ VIRTUAL FUNCTIONS IN C++

Suppose you are designing a record-keeping program for an automobile parts store. You want to make the program versatile, but you are not sure you can account for all possible situations. For example, you want to keep track of sales, but you cannot anticipate all types of sales. At first, there will only be regular sales to retail customers who go to the store to buy one particular part. However, later you may want to add sales with discounts or mail order sales with a shipping charge. All these sales will be for an item with a basic price and ultimately will produce some bill. For a simple sale, the bill is just the basic price, but if you later add discounts, then some kinds of bills will also depend on the size of the discount. Your program will need to compute daily gross sales, which intuitively should just be the sum of all the individual sales bills. You may also want to calculate the largest and smallest sales of the day or the average sale for the day. All these can be calculated from the individual bills, but many of the functions for computing the bills will not be added until later, when you decide what types of sales you will be dealing with. To accommodate this, we make the function for computing the bill a virtual function. (For simplicity in this first example, we assume that each sale is for just one item, although with derived classes and virtual functions we could, but will not here, account for sales of multiple items.)

Displays 15.1 and 15.2 contain the interface and implementation for the class Sale. All types of sales will be derived classes of the class Sale. The class Sale corresponds to

Display 15.1   Interface for the Base Class Sale

```
 1
 2    //This is the header file sale.h.
 3    //This is the interface for the class Sale.
 4    //Sale is a class for simple sales.

 5    #ifndef SALE_H
 6    #define SALE_H


 7    namespace SavitchSale
 8    {

 9        class Sale
10        {
11        public:
12            Sale( );
13            Sale(double thePrice);
14            double getPrice( ) const;
15            void setPrice(double newPrice);
16            virtual double bill( ) const;
17            double savings(const Sale& other) const;
18            //Returns the savings if you buy other instead of the calling object.
19        private:
20            double price;
21        };

22        bool operator < (const Sale& first, const Sale& second);
23        //Compares two sales to see which is larger.

24    }//SavitchSale

25    #endif // SALE_H
```

Display 15.2   Implementation of the Base Class Sale *(part 1 of 2)*

```
1
2   //This is the file sale.cpp.
3   //This is the implementation for the class Sale.
4   //The interface for the class Sale is in the file sale.h.

5   #include <iostream>
6   #include "sale.h"
7   using std::cout;

8   namespace SavitchSale
9   {

10      Sale::Sale( ) : price(0)
11      {
12          //Intentionally empty
13      }

14      Sale::Sale(double thePrice)
15      {
16          if (thePrice >= 0)
17              price = thePrice;
18          else
19          {
20              cout << "Error: Cannot have a negative price!\n";
21              exit(1);
22          }
23      }

24      double Sale::bill( ) const
25      {
26          return price;
27      }

28      double Sale::getPrice( ) const
29      {
30          return price;
31      }
32
33      void Sale::setPrice(double newPrice)
34      {
35          if (newPrice >= 0)
36              price = newPrice;
37          else
38          {
39              cout << "Error: Cannot have a negative price!\n";
40              exit(1);
```

Display 15.2   Implementation of the Base Class Sale *(part 2 of 2)*

```
41              }
42          }

43          double Sale::savings(const Sale& other) const
44          {
45              return (bill( ) - other.bill( ));
46          }

47          bool operator < (const Sale& first, const Sale& second)
48          {
49              return (first.bill( ) < second.bill( ));
50          }

51    }//SavitchSale
```

simple sales of a single item with no added discounts or charges. Notice the reserved word `virtual` in the declaration for the member function `bill` (Display 15.1). Notice (Display 15.2) that the member function `savings` and the overloaded operator, `<`, each use the function `bill`. Since `bill` is declared to be a virtual function, we can later define derived classes of the class `Sale` and define their versions of the member function `bill`, and the definitions of the member function `savings` and the overloaded operator, `<`, which we gave with the class `Sale`, will use the version of the member function `bill` that corresponds to the object of the derived class.

For example, Displays 15.3 and 15.4 show the derived class `DiscountSale`. Notice that the class `DiscountSale` requires a different definition for its version of the member function `bill`. Nonetheless, when the member function `savings` and the overloaded operator, `<`, are used with an object of the class `DiscountSale`, they will use the version of the function definition for `bill` that was given with the class `DiscountSale`. This is indeed a pretty fancy trick for C++ to pull off. Consider the function call `d1.savings(d2)` for objects `d1` and `d2` of the class `DiscountSale`. The definition of the function `savings` (even for an object of the class `DiscountSale`) is given in the implementation file for the base class `Sale`, which was compiled before we even thought of the class `DiscountSale`. Yet, in the function call `d1.savings(d2)`, the line that calls the function `bill` knows enough to use the definition of the function `bill` given for the class `DiscountSale`.

How does this work? In order to write C++ programs you can just assume it happens by magic, but the real explanation was given in the introduction to this section. When you label a function `virtual`, you are telling the C++ environment "Wait until this function is used in a program, and then get the implementation corresponding to the calling object."

Display 15.5 gives a sample program that illustrates how the virtual function `bill` and the functions that use `bill` work in a complete program.

Display 15.3   Interface for the Derived Class DiscountSale

```
1
2   //This is the file discountsale.h.
3   //This is the interface for the class DiscountSale.

4   #ifndef DISCOUNTSALE_H
5   #define DISCOUNTSALE_H
6   #include "sale.h"

7   namespace SavitchSale
8   {

9       class DiscountSale : public Sale
10      {

11      public:
12          DiscountSale( );
13          DiscountSale(double thePrice, double theDiscount);
14          //Discount is expressed as a percentage of the price.
15          //A negative discount is a price increase.
16          double getDiscount( ) const;
17          void setDiscount(double newDiscount);
18          double bill( ) const;
19      private:
20          double discount;

21      };

22  }//SavitchSale

23  #endif //DISCOUNTSALE_H
```

Since bill was declared virtual in the base class, it is automatically virtual in the derived class DiscountSale. You can add the modifier virtual to the declaration of bill or omit it as here; in either case bill is virtual in the class DiscountSale. (We prefer to include the word virtual in all virtual function declarations, even if it is not required. We omitted it here to illustrate that it is not required.)

Display 15.4   Implementation for the Derived Class DiscountSale *(part 1 of 2)*

```
1
2   //This is the implementation for the class DiscountSale.
3   //This is the file discountsale.cpp.
4   //The interface for the class DiscountSale is in the header file
5   //discountsale.h.
6   #include "discountsale.h"

7   namespace SavitchSale
8   {
9       DiscountSale::DiscountSale( ) : Sale( ), discount(0)
10      {
```

Display 15.4   Implementation for the Derived Class DiscountSale *(part 2 of 2)*

```
11            //Intentionally empty
12        }

13        DiscountSale::DiscountSale(double thePrice, double theDiscount)
14                : Sale(thePrice), discount(theDiscount)
15        {
16            //Intentionally empty
17        }

18        double DiscountSale::getDiscount( ) const
19        {
20            return discount;
21        }

22        void DiscountSale::setDiscount(double newDiscount)
23        {
24            discount = newDiscount;
25        }

26        double DiscountSale::bill( ) const
27        {
28            double fraction = discount/100;
29            return (1 - fraction)*getPrice( );
30        }

31    }//SavitchSale
```

You do not repeat the qualifier virtual in the function definition.

Display 15.5   Use of a Virtual Function *(part 1 of 2)*

```
1
2    //Demonstrates the performance of the virtual function bill.
3    #include <iostream>
4    #include "sale.h" //Not really needed, but safe due to ifndef.
5    #include "discountsale.h"
6    using std::cout;
7    using std::endl;
8    using std::ios;
9    using namespace SavitchSale;

10   int main( )
11   {
```

Display 15.5   Use of a Virtual Function *(part 2 of 2)*

```
12      Sale simple(10.00);//One item at $10.00.
13      DiscountSale discount(11.00, 10);//One item at $11.00 with a 10% discount.

14      cout.setf(ios::fixed);
15      cout.setf(ios::showpoint);
16      cout.precision(2);

17      if (discount < simple)
18      {
19          cout << "Discounted item is cheaper.\n";
20          cout << "Savings is $" << simple.savings(discount) << endl;
21      }
22      else
23          cout << "Discounted item is not cheaper.\n";

24      return 0;
25  }
```

The objects discount and simple use different code for the member function bill when the less-than comparison is made. Similar remarks apply to savings.

SAMPLE DIALOGUE

```
Discounted item is cheaper.
Savings is $0.10
```

VIRTUAL FUNCTION

A virtual function is indicated by including the modifier virtual in the member function declaration (which is given in the definition of the class).

If a function is virtual and a new definition of the function is given in a derived class, then for any object of the derived class, that object will always use the definition of the virtual function that was given in the derived class, even if the virtual function is used indirectly by being invoked in the definition of an inherited function. This method of deciding which definition of a virtual function to use is known as *late binding*.

POLYMORPHISM

Polymorphism refers to the ability to associate many meanings to one function name by means of the late-binding mechanism. Thus, polymorphism, late binding, and virtual functions are really all the same topic.

OVERRIDING

When a virtual function definition is changed in a derived class, programmers often say the function definition is **overridden**. In the C++ literature a distinction is usually made between the terms *redefined* and *overridden*. Both terms refer to changing the definition of the function in a derived class. If the function is a virtual function, this act is called *overriding*. If the function is not a virtual function, it's called *redefining*. This may seem like a silly distinction to you the programmer, since you do the same thing in both cases, but the two cases are treated differently by the compiler.

Tip

THE VIRTUAL PROPERTY IS INHERITED

The property of being a virtual function is inherited. For example, since bill was declared to be virtual in the base class Sale (Display 15.1), the function bill is automatically virtual in the derived class DiscountSale (Display 15.3). So, the following two declarations of the member function bill would be equivalent in the definition of the derived class DiscountSale:

```
double bill( ) const;
virtual double bill( ) const;
```

Thus, if SuperDiscountSale is a derived class of the class DiscountSale that inherits the function savings, and if the function bill is given a new definition for the class SuperDiscountSale, then all objects of the class SuperDiscountSale will use the definition of the function bill given in the definition of the class SuperDiscountSale. Even the inherited function savings (which includes a call to the function bill) will use the definition of bill given in SuperDiscountSale whenever the calling object is in the class SuperDiscountSale.

Tip

WHEN TO USE A VIRTUAL FUNCTION

There are clear advantages to using virtual functions and no clear disadvantages that we have seen so far. So, why not make all member functions virtual? In fact, why not define the C++ compiler so that (like some other languages, such as Java) all member functions are automatically virtual? The answer is that there is a large overhead to making a function virtual. Doing so uses more storage and makes your program run slower than if the function were not virtual. That is why the designers of C++ gave the programmer control over which member functions are virtual and which are not. If you expect to need the advantages of a virtual member function, then make that member function virtual. If you do not expect to need the advantages of a virtual function, then your program will run more efficiently if you do not make the member function virtual.

Self-Test Exercises

1. Explain the difference among the terms *virtual function*, *late binding*, and *polymorphism*.

2. Suppose you modify the definitions of the class Sale (Display 15.1) by deleting the reserved word virtual. How would that change the output of the program in Display 15.5?

Pitfall   **OMITTING THE DEFINITION OF A VIRTUAL MEMBER FUNCTION**

It is wise to develop incrementally. This means code a little, then test a little, then code a little more and test a little more, and so forth. However, if you try to compile classes with virtual member functions but do not implement each member, you may run into some very-hard-to-understand error messages, even if you do not call the undefined member functions!

If any virtual member functions are not implemented before compiling, the compilation fails with error messages similar to this:

Undefined reference to *Class_Name* virtual table.

Even if there is *no derived class* and there is *only one* virtual member function, but that function does not have a definition, this kind of message still occurs.

What makes the error messages very hard to decipher is that without definitions for the functions declared virtual, there will be further error messages complaining about an undefined reference to default constructors, even if these constructors really are already defined.

Of course, you may use some trivial definition for a virtual function until you are ready to define the "real" version of the function.

This caution does not apply to *pure virtual functions*, which we discuss in the next section. As you will see, pure virtual functions are not supposed to have a definition.

ABSTRACT CLASSES AND PURE VIRTUAL FUNCTIONS

You can encounter situations in which you want to have a class to use as a base class for a number of other classes, but you do not have any meaningful definition to give to one or more of its member functions. When we introduced virtual functions we discussed one such scenario. Let's review it now.

Suppose you are designing software for a graphics package that has classes for several kinds of figures, such as rectangles, circles, ovals, and so forth. Each figure might be an object of a different class, such as the Rectangle class or the Circle class. In a well-designed programming project, all of these classes would probably be descendants of a single parent class called, for example, Figure. Now, suppose you want a function to draw a figure on the screen. To draw a circle, you need different instructions from those you need to draw a rectangle. So, each class needs to have a different function to draw its kind of figure. If r is a Rectangle object and c is a Circle object, then r.draw( ) and c.draw( ) can be functions implemented with different code.

The parent class Figure may have a function called center that moves a figure to the center of the screen by erasing it and then redrawing it in the center of the screen. The function Figure::center might use the function draw to redraw the figure in the center of the screen. By making the member function draw a virtual function, you can write the code for the member function Figure::center in the class Figure and know that when it is used for a derived class, say Circle, the definition of draw in the class Circle will be the definition used. You never plan to create an object of type Figure. You only intend to create objects of the derived classes, such as Circle and Rectangle. So, the definition that you give to Figure::draw will never be used. However, based only on what we covered so far, you would still need to give a definition for Figure::draw, even though it could be trivial.

pure virtual function

If you make the member function Figure::draw a **pure virtual function**, then you do not need to give any definition to that member function. The way to make a member function into a pure virtual function is to mark it as virtual and to add the annotation = 0 to the member function declaration, as in the following example:

```
virtual void draw( ) = 0;
```

Any kind of member can be made a pure virtual function. It need not be a void function with no parameters as in our example.

abstract class

A class with one or more pure virtual functions is called an **abstract class**. An abstract class can only be used as a base class to derive other classes. You cannot create objects of an abstract class, since it is not a complete class definition. An abstract class is a partial class definition because it can contain other member functions that are not pure virtual functions. An abstract class is also a type, so you can write code with parameters of the abstract class type and it will apply to all objects of classes that are descendants of the abstract class.

If you derive a class from an abstract class, the derived class will itself be an abstract class unless you provide definitions for all the inherited pure virtual functions (and also do not introduce any new pure virtual functions). If you do provide definitions for all the inherited pure virtual functions (and also do not introduce any new pure virtual functions), the resulting class is not an abstract class, which means you can create objects of the class.

Example   **AN ABSTRACT CLASS**

In Display 15.6 we have slightly rewritten the class Employee from Display 14.1. This time we have made Employee an abstract class. The following line (highlighted in Display 15.6) is the only thing that is different from our previous definition of Employee (Display 14.1):

```
virtual void printCheck( ) const = 0;
```

The word virtual and the = 0 in the member function heading tell the compiler that this is a pure virtual function and that therefore the class Employee is now an abstract class. The implementation for the class Employee includes no definition for the class Employee::printCheck, but otherwise the implementation of the class Employee is the same as before (that is, the same as in Display 14.2).

It makes sense that there is no definition for the member function Employee::printCheck, since you do not know what kind of check to write until you know with what kind of employee you are dealing. In our first definition of the class Employee (Displays 14.1 and 14.2) we were forced to give a definition to Employee::printCheck and so gave one that output an error message saying that the function should not be invoked. We now have a more elegant solution. By making Employee::printCheck a pure virtual function, we have set things up so that the compiler will enforce the ban against invoking Employee::printCheck.

Display 15.6 **Interface for the Abstract Class Employee** *(part 1 of 2)*

```
1
2    //This is the header file employee.h.
3    //This is the interface for the abstract class Employee.

4    #ifndef EMPLOYEE_H              This is an improved version of the class
5    #define EMPLOYEE_H              Employee given in Display 14.1.

6    #include <string>
7    using std::string;

8    namespace SavitchEmployees    The implementation for this class is the same as in
9    {                              Display 14.2, except that no definition is given for
                                    the member function printCheck( ).
10       class Employee
11       {

12       public:
13           Employee( );
14           Employee(string theName, string theSsn);
15           string getName( ) const;
16           string getSsn( ) const;
17           double getNetPay( ) const;
18           void setName(string newName);
19           void setSsn(string newSsn);
20           void setNetPay(double newNetPay);
21           virtual void printCheck( ) const = 0;      A pure virtual function
22       private:
23           string name;
24           string ssn;
```

Display 15.6   Interface for the Abstract Class Employee *(part 2 of 2)*

```
25          double netPay;

26      };

27  }//SavitchEmployees

28  #endif //EMPLOYEE_H
```

Self-Test Exercises

3. Is it legal to have an abstract class in which all member functions are pure virtual functions?

4. Given the definition of the class Employee in Display 15.6, which of the following are legal?

a.

```
Employee joe;
joe = Employee( );
```

b.

```
class HourlyEmployee : public Employee
{
public:
    HourlyEmployee( );
    <Some more legal member function definitions, none of which are pure virtual functions. >
private:
    double wageRate;
    double hours;
};

int main( )
{
    Employee joe;
    joe = HourlyEmployee( );
```

c.

```
bool isBossOf(const Employee& e1, const Employee& e2);
```

15.2   Pointers and Virtual Functions

Beware lest you lose the substance by grasping at the shadow.

Aesop, *The Dog and the Shadow*

This section explores some of the more subtle points about virtual functions. To understand this material, you need to have covered the material on pointers given in Chapter 10.

■ VIRTUAL FUNCTIONS AND EXTENDED TYPE COMPATIBILITY

If Derived is a derived class of the base class Base, then you can assign an object of type Derived to a variable (or parameter) of type Base, but not the other way around. If you consider a concrete example, this becomes sensible. For example, DiscountSale is a derived class of Sale (Displays 15.1 and 15.3). You can assign an object of the class DiscountSale to a variable of type Sale, since a DiscountSale is a Sale. However, you cannot do the reverse assignment, since a Sale is not necessarily a DiscountSale. The fact that you can assign an object of a derived class to a variable (or parameter) of its base class is critically important for reuse of code via inheritance. However, it does have its problems.

For example, suppose a program or unit contains the following class definitions:

```
class Pet
{
public:
    string name;
    virtual void print( ) const;
};

class Dog : public Pet
{
public:
    string breed;
    virtual void print( ) const; //keyword virtual not needed,
                                 //but put here for clarity.
};

Dog vdog;
Pet vpet;
```

Now concentrate on the data members, name and breed. (To keep this example simple, we have made the member variables public. In a real application, they should be private and have functions to manipulate them.)

Anything that is a `Dog` is also a `Pet`. It would seem to make sense to allow programs to consider values of type `Dog` to also be values of type `Pet`, and hence the following should be allowed:

```
vdog.name = "Tiny";
vdog.breed = "Great Dane";
vpet = vdog;
```

C++ does allow this sort of assignment. You may assign a value, such as the value of `vdog`, to a variable of a parent type, such as `vpet`, but you are not allowed to perform the reverse assignment. Although the above assignment is allowed, the value that is assigned to the variable `vpet` loses its `breed` field. This is called the **slicing problem**. The following attempted access will produce an error message:

```
cout << vpet.breed;
        // Illegal: class Pet has no member named breed
```

You can argue that this makes sense, since once a `Dog` is moved to a variable of type `Pet` it should be treated like any other `Pet` and not have properties peculiar to `Dogs`. This makes for a lively philosophical debate, but it usually just makes for a nuisance when programming. The dog named Tiny is still a Great Dane and we would like to refer to its breed, even if we treated it as a `Pet` someplace along the way.

Fortunately, C++ does offer us a way to treat a `Dog` as a `Pet` without throwing away the name of the breed. To do this, we use pointers to dynamic variables.

Suppose we add the following declarations:

```
Pet *ppet;
Dog *pdog;
```

If we use pointers and dynamic variables, we can treat Tiny as a `Pet` without losing his breed. The following is allowed.[1]

```
pdog = new Dog;
pdog->name = "Tiny";
pdog->breed = "Great Dane";
ppet = pdog;
```

Moreover, we can still access the `breed` field of the node pointed to by `ppet`. Suppose that

```
Dog::print( ) const;
```

has been defined as follows:

```
void Dog::print( ) const
{
```

slicing
problem

----

[1] If you are not familiar with the `->` operator, see the subsection of Chapter 10 entitled "The `->` Operator."

```
        cout << "name: " << name << endl;
        cout << "breed: " << breed << endl;
    }
```

The statement

```
    ppet->print( );
```

will cause the following to be printed on the screen:

```
name: Tiny
breed: Great Dane
```

This nice ouput happens by virtue of the fact that print( ) is a virtual member function. (No pun intended.) We have included test code in Display 15.7.

Display 15.7   Defeating the Slicing Problem (*part 1 of 2*)

```
 1    //Program to illustrate use of a virtual function to defeat the slicing
 2    //problem.
 3    #include <string>
 4    #include <iostream>
 5    using std::string;
 6    using std::cout;
 7    using std::endl;

 8    class Pet
 9    {
10    public:
11        string name;
12        virtual void print( ) const;
13    };

14    class Dog : public Pet
15    {
16    public:
17        string breed;
18        virtual void print( ) const;
19    };

20    int main( )
21    {
22        Dog vdog;
23        Pet vpet;
24        vdog.name = "Tiny";
25        vdog.breed = "Great Dane";
26        vpet = vdog;
27        cout << "The slicing problem:\n";
```

We have made the member variables public to keep the example simple. In a real application they should be private and accessed via member functions.

Keyword virtual is not needed here, but we put it here for clarity.

Display 15.7   Defeating the Slicing Problem (*part 2 of 2*)

```
28        //vpet.breed; is illegal since class Pet has no member named breed.
29        vpet.print( );
30        cout << "Note that it was print from Pet that was invoked.\n";

31        cout << "The slicing problem defeated:\n";
32        Pet *ppet;
33        ppet = new Pet;
34        Dog *pdog;
35        pdog = new Dog;
36        pdog->name = "Tiny";
37        pdog->breed = "Great Dane";
38        ppet = pdog;
39        ppet->print( );
40        pdog->print( );

41        //The following, which accesses member variables directly
42        //rather than via virtual functions, would produce an error:
43        //cout << "name: " << ppet->name << "  breed: "
44        //     << ppet->breed << endl;
45        //It generates an error message saying
46        //class Pet has no member named breed.

47        return 0;
48    }

49  void Dog::print( ) const
50  {
51      cout << "name: " << name << endl;
52      cout << "breed: " << breed << endl;
53  }

54  void Pet::print( ) const
55  {
56      cout << "name: " << name << endl;
57  }
```

These two print the same output:
name: Tiny
breed: Great Dane

Note that no breed is mentioned

SAMPLE DIALOGUE

```
The slicing problem:
name: Tiny
Note that it was print from Pet that was invoked.
The slicing problem defeated:
name: Tiny
breed: Great Dane
name: Tiny
breed: Great Dane
```

Object-oriented programming with dynamic variables is a very different way of viewing programming. This can all be bewildering at first. It will help if you keep two simple rules in mind:

1. If the domain type of the pointer pAncestor is an ancestor class for the domain type of the pointer pDescendant, then the following assignment of pointers is allowed:

```
pAncestor = pDescendant;
```

Moreover, none of the data members or member functions of the dynamic variable being pointed to by pDescendant will be lost.

2. Although all the extra fields of the dynamic variable are there, you will need virtual member functions to access them.

Pitfall

THE SLICING PROBLEM

Although it is legal to assign a derived class object to a base class variable, assigning a derived class object to a base class object slices off data. Any data members in the derived class object that are not also in the base class will be lost in the assignment, and any member functions that are not defined in the base class are similarly unavailable to the resulting base class object.

For example, if Dog is a derived class of Pet, then the following is legal:

```
Dog vdog;
Pet vpet;
vpet = vdog;
```

However, vpet cannot be a calling object for a member function from Dog unless the function is also a member function of Pet, and all the member variables of vdog that are not inherited from the class Pet are lost. This is the slicing problem.

Note that simply making a member function virtual does not defeat the slicing problem. Note the following code from Display 15.7:

```
Dog vdog;
Pet vpet;

vdog.name = "Tiny";
vdog.breed = "Great Dane";
vpet = vdog;
. . .
vpet.print( );
```

Although the object in vdog is of type Dog, when vdog is assigned to the variable vpet (of type Pet) it becomes an object of type Pet. So, vpet.print( ) invokes the version of print( ) defined in Pet, not the version defined in Dog. This happens despite the fact that print( ) is virtual. In order to defeat the slicing problem, the function must be virtual *and* you must use pointers and dynamic variables.

Self-Test Exercises

5. Why can't you assign a base class object to a derived class variable?

6. What is the problem with the (legal) assignment of a derived class object to a base class variable?

7. Suppose the base class and the derived class each has a member function with the same signature. When you have a base class pointer to a derived class object and call a function member through the pointer, discuss what determines which function is actually called, the base class member function or the derived class member function.

Tip

MAKE DESTRUCTORS VIRTUAL

It is a good policy to always make destructors virtual, but before we explain why this is a good policy we need to say a word or two about how destructors and pointers interact and about what it means for a destructor to be virtual.

Consider the following code, where SomeClass is a class with a destructor that is not virtual:

```
SomeClass *p = new SomeClass;
    . . .
delete p;
```

When delete is invoked with p, the destructor of the class SomeClass is automatically invoked. Now, let's see what happens when a destructor is marked virtual.

The easiest way to describe how destructors interact with the virtual function mechanism is that destructors are treated as if all destructors had the same name (even though they do not really have the same name). For example, suppose Derived is a derived class of the class Base and suppose the destructor in the class Base is marked virtual. Now consider the following code:

```
Base *pBase = new Derived;
    . . .
delete pBase;
```

When delete is invoked with pBase, a destructor is called. Since the destructor in the class Base was marked virtual and the object pointed to is of type Derived, the destructor for the class Derived is called (and it in turn calls the destructor for the class Base). If the destructor in the class Base had not been declared as virtual, then only the destructor in the class Base would be called.

Another point to keep in mind is that when a destructor is marked virtual, then all destructors of derived classes are automatically virtual (whether or not they are marked virtual). Again, this behavior is as if all destructors had the same name (even though they do not).

Now we are ready to explain why all destructors should be virtual. Consider what happens when destructors are not declared as virtual in a base class. In particular consider the base class PFArrayD (partially filled array of doubles) and its derived class PFArrayDBak (partially filled array of doubles with backup). We discussed these classes in Chapter 14. That was before we knew about virtual functions, and so the destructor in the base class PFArrayD was not marked virtual. In Display 15.8 we have summarized all the facts we need about the classes PFArrayD and PFArrayDBak so that you need not look back to Chapter 14.

Consider the following code:

```
PFArrayD *p = new PFArrayDBak;
    . . .
delete p;
```

Since the destructor in the base class is not marked virtual, only the destructor for the base class (PFArrayD) will be invoked. This will return the memory for the member array a (declared in PFArrayD) to the freestore, but the memory for the member array b (declared in PFArrayD–Bak) will never be returned to the freestore (until the program ends).

On the other hand, if (unlike Display 15.8) the destructor for the base class PFArrayD were marked virtual, then when delete is applied to p, the constructor for the class PFArrayDBak would be invoked (since the object pointed to is of type PFArrayDBak). The destructor for the class PFArrayDBak would delete the array b and then automatically invoke the constructor for the base class PFArrayD, and that would delete the member array a. So, with the base class destructor marked as virtual, all the memory is returned to the freestore. To prepare for eventualities such as these, it is best to always mark destructors as virtual.

DOWNCASTING AND UPCASTING

You might think some sort of type casting would allow you to easily get around the slicing problem. However, things are not that simple. The following is illegal:

```
Pet vpet;
Dog vdog; //Dog is a derived class with base class Pet.
. . .
vdog = static_cast<Dog>(vpet); //ILLEGAL!
```

However, casting in the other direction is perfectly legal and does not even need a casting operator:

```
vpet = vdog; //Legal (but does produce the slicing problem.)
```

Casting from a descendant type to an ancestor type is known as **upcasting**, since you are moving up the class hierarchy. Upcasting is safe because you are simply disregarding some information (disregarding member variables and functions). So, the following is perfectly safe:

```
vpet = vdog;
```

upcasting

Display 15.8   Review of the Classes PFArrayD and PFArrayDBak

```
class PFArrayD
{
public:
    PFArrayD( );
        . . .
    ~PFArrayD( );
protected:
    double *a; //for an array of doubles.
    int capacity; //for the size of the array.
    int used; //for the number of array positions currently in use.
};

PFArrayD::PFArrayD( ) : capacity(50), used(0)
{
    a = new double[capacity];          Some details about the base class PFArrayD.
}                                      A more complete definition of PFArrayD is
                                       given in Displays 14.8 and 14.9, but this display
                                       has all the details you need for this chapter.
PFArrayD::~PFArrayD( )
{
    delete [] a;
}
```

```
class PFArrayDBak : public PFArrayD        The destructors should be virtual, but
{                                          we had not yet covered virtual
public:                                    functions when we wrote these classes.
    PFArrayDBak( );
        . . .
    ~PFArrayDBak( );
private:
    double *b; //for a backup of main array.
    int usedB; //backup for inherited member variable used.
};

PFArrayDBak::PFArrayDBak( ) : PFArrayD( ), usedB(0)
{
    b = new double[capacity];
}                                   Some details about the derived class PFArrayDBak.
                                    A complete definition of PFArrayDBak is given in
PFArrayDBak::~PFArrayDBak( )         Displays 14.10 and 14.11, but this display has all the details
{                                    you need for this chapter.
    delete [] b;
}
```

Casting from an ancestor type to a descended type is called **downcasting** and is very downcasting dangerous, since you are assuming that information is being added (added member variables and functions). The `dynamic_cast` that we discussed briefly in Chapter 1 is used for downcasting. It is of some possible use in defeating the slicing problem but is dangerously unreliable and fraught with pitfalls. A `dynamic_cast` may allow you to downcast, but it only works for pointer types, as in the following:

```
Pet *ppet;
ppet = new Dog;
Dog *pdog = dynamic_cast<Dog*>(ppet); //Dangerous!
```

We have had downcasting fail even in situations as simple as this, and so we do not recommend it.

The `dynamic_cast` is supposed to inform you if it fails. If the cast fails, the `dynamic_cast` should return `NULL` (which is really the integer 0).[2]

If you want to try downcasting keep the following points in mind:

1. You need to keep track of things so that you know the information to be added is indeed present.

2. Your member functions must be virtual, since `dynamic_cast` uses the virtual function information to perform the cast.

HOW C++ IMPLEMENTS VIRTUAL FUNCTIONS

You need not know how a compiler works in order to use it. That is the principle of information hiding, which is basic to all good program design philosophies. In particular, you need not know how virtual functions are implemented in order to use virtual functions. However, many people find that a concrete model of the implementation helps their understanding, and when reading about virtual functions in other books you are likely to encounter references to the implementation of virtual functions. So, we will give a brief outline of how they are implemented. All compilers for all languages (including C++) that have virtual functions typically implement them in basically the same way.

If a class has one or more member functions that are virtual, the compiler creates what is called a **virtual function table** for that class. This table has a pointer (memory virtual address) for each virtual member function. The pointer points to the location of the function correct code for that member function. If one virtual function was inherited and not table changed, then its table entry points to the definition for that function that was given in the parent class (or other ancestor class if need be). If another virtual function had a new definition in the class, then the pointer in the table for that member function points to that definition. (Remember that the property of being a virtual function is

---

[2] The standard says "The value of a failed cast to pointer type is the null pointer of the required result type. A failed cast to a reference type throws a `bad_cast`."

inherited, so once a class has a virtual function table, then all its descendant classes have a virtual function table.)

Whenever an object of a class with one or more virtual functions is created, another pointer is added to the description of the object that is stored in memory. This pointer points to the class's virtual function table. When you make a call to a member function using a pointer (yep, another one) to the object, the runtime system uses the virtual function table to decide which definition of a member function to use; it does not use the type of the pointer.

Of course, this all happens automatically, so you need not worry about it. A compiler writer is even free to implement virtual functions in some other way as long as it works correctly (although it never actually is implemented in a different way).

Self-Test Exercises

8. Why is the following illegal?

```
Pet vpet;
Dog vdog; //Dog is a derived class with base class Pet.
. . .
vdog = static_cast<Dog>(vpet); //ILLEGAL!
```

Chapter Summary

■ Late binding means that the decision of which version of a member function is appropriate is decided at runtime. In C++, member functions that use late binding are called virtual functions. *Polymorphism* is another word for late binding.

■ A pure virtual function is a member function that has no definition. A pure virtual function is indicated by the word virtual and the notation = 0 in the member function declaration. A class with one or more pure virtual functions is called an *abstract class*.

■ An abstract class is a type and can be used as a base class to derive other classes. However, you cannot create an object of an abstract class type (unless it is an object of some derived class).

■ You can assign an object of a derived class to a variable of its base class (or any ancestor class), but the member variables that are not in the base class are lost. This is known as *the slicing problem*.

■ If the domain type of the pointer pAncestor is a base class for the domain type of the pointer pDescendant, then the following assignment of pointers is allowed:

```
pAncestor = pDescendant;
```

Moreover, none of the data members or member functions of the dynamic variable being pointed to by pDescendant will be lost. Although all the extra fields of the dynamic variable are there, you will need virtual member functions to access them.

■ It is a good programming practice to make destructors virtual.

ANSWERS TO SELF-TEST EXERCISES

1. In essence there is no difference among the three terms. They all refer to the same topic. There is only a slight difference in their usage. (*Virtual function* is a kind of member function, *late binding* refers to the mechanism used to decide which function definition to use when a function is virtual, and *polymorphism* is another name for late binding.)

2. The output would change to the following:

```
Discounted item is not cheaper.
```

3. Yes, it is legal to have an abstract class in which all member functions are pure virtual functions.

4. a. Illegal, because Employee is an abstract class.

   b. Legal.

   c. Legal, because an abstract class is a type.

5. There would be no members to assign to the derived class's added members.

6. Although it is legal to assign a derived class object to a base class variable, this discards the parts of the derived class object that are not members of the base class. This situation is known as *the slicing problem.*

7. If the base class function carries the virtual modifier, then the derived class member function is called. If the base class member function does not have the virtual modifier, then the base class member function is called.

8. Since Dog can have more member variables than Pet, the object vpet may not have enough data for all the member variables of type Dog.

PROGRAMMING PROJECTS

1. Consider a graphics system that has classes for various figures, say rectangles, squares, triangles, circles, and so on. For example, a rectangle might have data members height, width, and center point, while a square and circle might have only a center point and an edge length or radius, respectively. In a well-designed system these would be derived from a common class, Figure. You are to implement such a system.

   The class Figure is the base class. You should add only Rectangle and Triangle classes derived from Figure. Each class has stubs for member functions erase and draw. Each of these member functions outputs a message telling what function has been called and what the class of the calling object is. Since these are just stubs, they do nothing more than output this message. The member function center calls erase and draw to erase and redraw the figure at the center. Because you have only stubs for erase and draw, center will not do any "centering" but will call the member functions erase and draw. Also, add an output message in the member function center that announces that center is being called. The member functions should take no arguments. There are three parts to this project:

a. Do the class definitions using no virtual functions. Compile and test.

b. Make the base class member functions virtual. Compile and test.

c. Explain the difference in results.

For a real example, you would have to replace the definition of each of these member functions with code to do the actual drawing. You will be asked to do this in Programming Project 2.

Use the following main function for all testing:

```
//This program tests Programming Problem 1.

#include <iostream>
#include "figure.h"
#include "rectangle.h"
#include "triangle.h"
using std::cout;
int main( )
{
    Triangle tri;
    tri.draw( );
    cout <<
      "\nDerived class Triangle object calling center( ).\n";
    tri.center( ); //Calls draw and center

    Rectangle rect;
    rect.draw( );
    cout <<
      "\nDerived class Rectangle object calling center().\n";
    rect.center( ); //Calls draw and center
    return 0;
}
```

2. Flesh out Programming Problem 1. Give new definitions for the various constructors and member functions Figure::center, Figure::draw, Figure::erase, Triangle::draw, Triangle::erase, Rectangle::draw and Rectangle::erase so that the draw functions actually draw figures on the screen by placing the character '*' at suitable locations on the screen. For the erase functions, you can simply clear the screen (by outputting blank lines or by doing something more sophisticated). There are a lot of details in this and you will have to decide on some of them on your own.

16 CHAPTER

Templates

16 Templates

All men are mortal.
Aristotle is a man.
Therefore, Aristotle is mortal.

All X's are Y.
Z is an X.
Therefore, Z is Y.

All cats are mischievous.
Garfield is a cat.
Therefore, Garfield is mischievous.

A Short Lesson on Syllogisms

INTRODUCTION

This chapter discusses C++ templates, which allow you to define functions and classes that have parameters for type names. This enables you to design functions that can be used with arguments of different types and to define classes that are much more general than those you have seen before this chapter.

Section 16.1 requires only material from Chapters 1 through 5. Section 16.2 uses material from Section 16.1 as well as Chapters 1 through 11 but does not require the material from Chapter 12 through 15. Section 16.3 requires the previous sections as well as Chapter 14 on inheritance and all the chapters needed for Section 16.2. Section 16.3 does mark some member functions as virtual. Virtual functions are covered in Chapter 15. However, this use of virtual functions is not essential to the material presented. It is possible to read Section 16.3 ignoring (or even omitting) all occurrences of the keyword virtual.

16.1 Function Templates

Many of our previously discussed C++ function definitions have an underlying algorithm that is much more general than the algorithm we gave in the function definition. For example, consider the function swapValues, which we first discussed in Chapter 4. For reference, we now repeat the function definition:

```
void swapValues(int& variable1, int& variable2)
{
    int temp;
```

```
    temp = variable1;
    variable1 = variable2;
    variable2 = temp;
}
```

Notice that the function swapValues applies only to variables of type int. Yet the algorithm given in the function body could just as well be used to swap the values in two variables of type char. If we want to also use the function swapValues with variables of type char, we can overload the function name swapValues by adding the following definition:

```
void swapValues(char& variable1, char& variable2)
{
    char temp;

    temp = variable1;
    variable1 = variable2;
    variable2 = temp;
}
```

But there is something inefficient and unsatisfying about these two definitions of the swapValues function: They are almost identical. The only difference is that one definition uses the type int in three places and the other uses the type char in the same three places. Proceeding in this way, if we wanted to have the function swapValues apply to pairs of variables of type double, we would have to write a third almost identical function definition. If we wanted to apply swapValues to still more types, the number of almost identical function definitions would be even larger. This would require a good deal of typing and would clutter up our code with lots of definitions that look identical. We should be able to say that the following function definition applies to variables of any type:

```
void swapValues(Type_Of_The_Variables& variable1,
                        Type_Of_The_Variables& variable2)
{
    Type_Of_The_Variables temp;

    temp = variable1;
    variable1 = variable2;
    variable2 = temp;
}
```

As we will see, something like this is possible. We can define one function that applies to all types of variables, although the syntax is a bit more complicated than what we have shown above. The proper syntax is described in the next subsection.

■ SYNTAX FOR FUNCTION TEMPLATES

Display 16.1 shows a C++ template for the function swapValues. This function template allows you to swap the values of any two variables, of any type, as long as the two variables have the same type. The definition and the function declaration begin with the line

```
template<class T>
```

template prefix

type parameter

A template overloads the function name

This is often called the **template prefix**, and it tells the compiler that the definition or function declaration that follows is a **template** and that T is a **type parameter**. In this context the word class actually means *type*.[1] As we will see, the type parameter T can be replaced by any type, whether the type is a class or not. Within the body of the function definition the type parameter T is used just like any other type.

The function template definition is, in effect, a large collection of function definitions. For the function template for swapValues shown in Display 16.1, there is, in effect, one function definition for each possible type name. Each of these definitions is obtained by replacing the type parameter T with a type name. For example, the function definition shown below is obtained by replacing T with the type name double:

```
void swapValues(double& variable1, double& variable2)
{
    double temp;

    temp = variable1;
    variable1 = variable2;
    variable2 = temp;
}
```

Another definition for swapValues is obtained by replacing the type parameter T in the function template with the type name int. Yet another definition is obtained by replacing the type parameter T with char. The one function template shown in Display 16.1 overloads the function name swapValues so that there is a slightly different function definition for every possible type.

The compiler will not literally produce definitions for every possible type for the function name swapValues, but it will behave exactly as if it had produced all those function definitions. A separate definition will be produced for each different type for which you use the template, but not for any types you do not use. Only one definition is generated for a single type regardless of the number of times you use the template for that type. Notice that the function swapValues is called twice in Display 16.1: One

---

[1] In fact, the ANSI/ISO standard provides that the keyword typename may be used instead of class in the template prefix. It would make more sense to use the keyword typename rather than class, but everybody uses class, so we will do the same. (It is often true that consistency in coding is more important than optimality.)

Display 16.1   A Function Template

```
1    //Program to demonstrate a function template.
2    #include <iostream>
3    using std::cout;
4    using std::endl;

5    //Interchanges the values of variable1 and variable2.
6    //The assignment operator must work for the type T.
7    template<class T>
8    void swapValues(T& variable1, T& variable2)
9    {
10        T temp;

11        temp = variable1;
12        variable1 = variable2;
13        variable2 = temp;
14   }

15   int main( )
16   {
17        int integer1 = 1, integer2 - 2;
18        cout << "Original integer values are "
19             << integer1 << " " << integer2 << endl;
20        swapValues(integer1, integer2);
21        cout << "Swapped integer values are "
22             << integer1 << " " << integer2 << endl;

23        char symbol1 = 'A', symbol2 = 'B';
24        cout << "Original character values are: "
25             << symbol1 << " " << symbol2 << endl;
26        swapValues(symbol1, symbol2);
27        cout << "Swapped character values are: "
28             << symbol1 << " " << symbol2 << endl;
29        return 0;
30   }
```

Compilers still have problems with templates. To be certain that your templates work on the widest selection of compilers, place the template definition in the same file in which it is used and have the template definition precede all uses of the template.

SAMPLE DIALOGUE

```
Original integer values are: 1 2
Swapped integer values are: 2 1
Original character values are: A B
Swapped character values are: B A
```

time the arguments are of type int, and the other time the arguments are of type char. Consider the following function call from Display 16.1:

```
swapValues(integer1, integer2);
```

When the C++ compiler gets to this function call, it notices the types of the arguments—in this case, int—and then it uses the template to produce a function definition with the type parameter T replaced with the type name int. Similarly, when the compiler sees the function call

```
swapValues(symbol1, symbol2);
```

it notices the types of the arguments—in this case, char—and then it uses the template to produce a function definition with the type parameter T replaced with the type name char.

calling a function template

Notice that you need not do anything special when you call a function that is defined with a function template; you call it just as you would any other function. The compiler does all the work of producing the function definition from the function template.

A function template may have a function declaration and a definition, just like an ordinary function. You may be able to place the function declaration and definition for a function template in the same locations that you place function declarations and definitions for ordinary functions. However, separate compilation of template definitions and template function declarations is not yet implemented on most compilers, so it is safest to place your template function definition in the file where you invoke the template function, as we did in Display 16.1. In fact, most compilers require that the template function definition appear before the first invocation of the template. You may simply #include the file containing your template function definitions prior to calling the template function. Your particular compiler may behave differently; you should ask a local expert about the details.

In the function template in Display 16.1 we used the letter T as the parameter for the type. This is traditional but is not required by the C++ language. The type parameter can be any identifier (other than a keyword). T is a good name for the type parameter, but other names can be used.

more than one type parameter

It is possible to have function templates that have more than one type parameter. For example, a function template with two type parameters named T1 and T2 would begin as follows:

```
template<class T1, class T2>
```

However, most function templates require only one type parameter. You cannot have unused template parameters; that is, each template parameter must be used in your template function.

Pitfall

COMPILER COMPLICATIONS

Many compilers do not allow separate compilation of templates, so you may need to include your template definition with your code that uses it. As usual, at least the function declaration must precede any use of the function template.

Some C++ compilers have additional special requirements for using templates. If you have trouble compiling your templates, check your manuals or check with a local expert. You may need to set special options or rearrange the way you order the template definitions and the other items in your files.

The template program layout that seems to work with the widest selection of compilers is the following: Place the template definition in the same file in which it is used and have the template definition precede all uses (all invocations) of the template. If you want to place your function template definition in a file separate from your application program, you can #include the file with the function template definition in the application file.

Self-Test Exercises

1. Write a function template named maximum. The function takes two values of the same type as its arguments and returns the larger of the two arguments (or either value if they are equal). Give both the function declaration and the function definition for the template. You will use the operator < in your definition. Therefore, this function template will apply only to types for which < is defined. Write a comment for the function declaration that explains this restriction.

2. We have used three kinds of absolute value function: abs, labs, and fabs. These functions differ only in the type of their argument. It might be better to have a function template for the absolute value function. Give a function template for an absolute value function called absolute. The template will apply only to types for which < is defined, for which the unary negation operator is defined, and for which the constant 0 can be used in a comparison with a value of that type. Thus, the function absolute can be called with any of the number types, such as int, long, and double. Give both the function declaration and the function definition for the template.

3. Define or characterize the template facility for C++.

4. In the template prefix

   ```
   template <class T>
   ```

   what kind of variable is the parameter T? Choose from the answers listed below.

   a. T must be a class.

   b. T must *not* be a class.

   c. T can be only a type built into the C++ language.

   d. T can be any type, whether built into C++ or defined by the programmer.

   e. T can be any kind of type, whether built into C++ or defined by the programmer, but T does have some requirements that must be met. (What are they?)

FUNCTION TEMPLATE

The function definition and the function declaration for a function template are each prefaced with the following:

```
template<class Type_Parameter>
```

The function declaration (if used) and definition are then the same as any ordinary function declaration and definition, except that the *Type_Parameter* can be used in place of a type.

For example, the following is a function declaration for a function template:

```
template<class T>
void showStuff(int stuff1, T stuff2, T stuff3);
```

The definition for this function template might be as follows:

```
template<class T>
void showStuff(int stuff1, T stuff2, T stuff3)
{
    cout << stuff1 << endl
         << stuff2 << endl
         << stuff3 << endl;
}
```

The function template given in this example is equivalent to having one function declaration and one function definition for each possible type name. The type name is substituted for the type parameter (which is T in the example above). For instance, consider the following function call:

```
showStuff(2, 3.3, 4.4);
```

When this function call is executed, the compiler uses the function definition obtained by replacing T with the type name double. A separate definition will be produced for each different type for which you use the template, but not for any types you do not use. Only one definition is generated for a specific type regardless of the number of times you use the template.

ALGORITHM ABSTRACTION

As we saw in our discussion of the swapValues function, there is a very general algorithm for interchanging the value of two variables that applies to variables of any type. Using a function template, we were able to express this more general algorithm in C++. This is a very simple example of algorithm abstraction. When we say we are using **algorithm abstraction**, we mean that we are expressing our algorithms in a very general way so that we can ignore incidental detail and concentrate on the substantive part of the algorithm. Function templates are one feature of C++ that supports algorithm abstraction.

A GENERIC SORTING FUNCTION

Chapter 5 gave the selection sorting algorithm for sorting an array of values of type int. The algorithm was realized in C++ code as the function sort, given in Display 5.8. Below we repeat the definitions of this function sort:

```
void sort(int a[], int numberUsed)
{
    int indexOfNextSmallest;
    for (int index = 0; index < numberUsed - 1; index++)
    {//Place the correct value in a[index]:
        indexOfNextSmallest =
                    indexOfSmallest(a, index, numberUsed);
        swapValues(a[index], a[indexOfNextSmallest]);
        //a[0] <= a[1] <=...<= a[index] are the smallest of the
        // original array elements. The rest of the elements
        //are in the remaining positions.
    }
}
```

If you study the above definition of the function sort you will see that the base type of the array is never used in any significant way. If we replaced the base type of the array in the function header with the type double, we would obtain a sorting function that applies to arrays of values of type double. Of course, we also must adjust the helping functions so that they apply to arrays of elements of type double. Let's consider the helping functions that are called inside the body of the function sort. The two helping functions are swapValues and indexOfSmallest.

We already saw that swapValues can apply to variables of any type for which the assignment operator works, provided we define it as a function template (as in Display 16.1). Let's see if indexOfSmallest depends in any significant way on the base type of the array being sorted. The definition of indexOfSmallest is repeated below so you can study its details.

```
int indexOfSmallest(const int a[], int startIndex, int numberUsed)
{
    int min = a[startIndex],
        indexOfMin = startIndex;
    for (int index = startIndex + 1; index < numberUsed; index++)
        if (a[index] < min)
        {
            min = a[index];
            indexOfMin = index;
            //min is the smallest of a[startIndex] through a[index]
        }

    return indexOfMin;
}
```

The function `indexOfSmallest` also does not depend in any significant way on the base type of the array. If we replace the two highlighted instances of the type `int` with the type `double`, then we will have changed the function `indexOfSmallest` so that it applies to arrays whose base type is `double`.

To change the function `sort` so that it can be used to sort arrays with the base type `double`, we only need to replace a few instances of the type name `int` with the type name `double`. Moreover, there is nothing special about the type `double`. We can do a similar replacement for many other types. The only thing we need to know about the type is that the assignment operator and the operator, <, are defined for that type. This is the perfect situation for function templates. If we replace a few instances of the type name `int` (in the functions `sort` and `indexOfSmallest`) with a type parameter, then the function `sort` can sort an array of values of any type, provided that the values of that type can be assigned with the assignment operator and compared using the < operator. In Display 16.2 we have written just such a function template.

Notice that the function template `sort` shown in Display 16.2 can be used with arrays of values that are not numbers. In the demonstration program, the function template `sort` is called to sort an array of characters. Characters can be compared using the < operator, which compares characters according to the order of their ASCII numbers (see Appendix 3). Thus, when applied to two upper-case letters, the operato, <, tests to see if the first character comes before the second in alphabetic order. Also, when applied to two lowercase letters, the operator, <, tests to see if the first character comes before the second in alphabetic order. When you mix uppercase and lowercase letters, the situation is not so well behaved, but the program shown in Display 16.2 deals only with uppercase letters. In that program an array of uppercase letters is sorted into alphabetical order with a call to the function template `sort`. (The function template `sort` will even sort an array of objects of a class that you define, provided you overload the < operator to apply to objects of the class.)

Our generic sorting function has separated the implementation from the declaration of the sorting function by placing the definition of the sorting function in the file `sort.cpp` (Display 16.3). However, most compilers do not allow for separate compilation of templates in the usual sense. So, we have separated the implementation from the programmer's point of view, but from the compiler's point of view it looks like everything is in one file. The file `sort.cpp` is `#included` in our main file, so it is as if everything were in one file. Note that the include directive for `sort.cpp` is placed before any invocation of the functions defined by templates. For most compilers this is the only way you can get templates to work.

Display 16.2   A Generic Sorting Function *(part 1 of 3)*

```
1   //Demonstrates a template function that implements
2   //a generic version of the selection sort algorithm.
3   #include <iostream>
4   using std::cout;
5   using std::endl;

6   template<class T>
7   void sort(T a[], int numberUsed);
```

Display 16.2   A Generic Sorting Function *(part 2 of 3)*

```
8    //Precondition: numberUsed <= declared size of the array a.
9    //The array elements a[0] through a[numberUsed - 1] have values.
10   //The assignment and < operator work for values of type T.
11   //Postcondition: The values of a[0] through a[numberUsed - 1] have
12   //been rearranged so that a[0] <= a[1] <=... <= a[numberUsed - 1].

13   template<class T>
14   void swapValues(T& variable1, T& variable2);
15   //Interchanges the values of variable1 and variable2.
16   //The assignment operator must work correctly for the type T.

17   template<class T>
18   int indexOfSmallest(const T a[], int startIndex, int numberUsed);
19   //Precondition: 0 <= startIndex < numberUsed. Array elements have values.
20   //The assignment and < operator work for values of type T.
21   //Returns the index i such that a[i] is the smallest of the values
22   //a[startIndex], a[startIndex + 1],..., a[numberUsed - 1].

23   #include "sort.cpp"   ←───────────────      This is equivalent to placing the function
                                                 template definitions in this file at this location.
24   int main( )
25   {
26       int i;
27       int a[10] = {9, 8, 7, 6, 5, 1, 2, 3, 0, 4};
28       cout << "Unsorted integers:\n";
29       for (i = 0; i < 10; i++)
30           cout << a[i] << " ";
31       cout << endl;
32       sort(a, 10);
33       cout << "In sorted order the integers are:\n";
34       for (i = 0; i < 10; i++)
35           cout << a[i] << " ";
36       cout << endl;
37       double b[5] = {5.5, 4.4, 1.1, 3.3, 2.2};
38       cout << "Unsorted doubles:\n";
39       for (i = 0; i < 5; i++)
40           cout << b[i] << " ";
41       cout << endl;
42       sort(b, 5);
43       cout << "In sorted order the doubles are:\n";
44       for (i = 0; i < 5; i++)
45           cout << b[i] << " ";
46       cout << endl;

47       char c[7] = {'G', 'E', 'N', 'E', 'R', 'I', 'C'};
48       cout << "Unsorted characters:\n";
```

Display 16.2   A Generic Sorting Function (*part 3 of 3*)

```
49        for (i = 0; i < 7; i++)
50            cout << c[i] << " ";
51        cout << endl;
52        sort(c, 7);
53        cout << "In sorted order the characters are:\n";
54        for (i = 0; i < 7; i++)
55            cout << c[i] << " ";
56        cout << endl;

57        return 0;
58    }
```

SAMPLE DIALOGUE

```
Unsorted integers:
9 8 7 6 5 1 2 3 0 4
In sorted order the integers are:
0 1 2 3 4 5 6 7 8 9
Unsorted doubles:
5.5 4.4 1.1 3.3 2.2
In sorted order the doubles are:
1.1 2.2 3.3 4.4 5.5
Unsorted characters:
G E N E R I C
In sorted order the characters are:
C E E G I N R
```

Display 16.3   Implementation of the Generic Sorting Function (*part 1 of 2*)

```
1   // This is the file sort.cpp.

2   template<class T>
3   void sort(T a[], int numberUsed)
4   {
5       int indexOfNextSmallest;
6       for (int index = 0; index < numberUsed - 1; index++)
7       {//Place the correct value in a[index]:
8           indexOfNextSmallest =
9               indexOfSmallest(a, index, numberUsed);
10          swapValues(a[index], a[indexOfNextSmallest]);
11        //a[0] <= a[1] <=...<= a[index] are the smallest of the original array
12        //elements. The rest of the elements are in the remaining positions.
13       }
     }
```

Display 16.3   Implementation of the Generic Sorting Function *(part 2 of 2)*

```
14    template<class T>
15    void swapValues(T& variable1, T& variable2)
              <The rest of the definition of swapValues is given in Display 16.1.>

16    template<class T>
17    int indexOfSmallest(const T a[], int startIndex, int numberUsed)
18    {
19        T min = a[startIndex]; ←────────────    Note that the type parameter may be
20        int indexOfMin = startIndex;            used in the body of the function
                                                  definition
21        for (int index = startIndex + 1; index < numberUsed; index++)
22            if (a[index] < min)
23            {
24                min = a[index];
25                indexOfMin = index;
26                //min is the smallest of a[startIndex] through a[index].
27            }

28        return indexOfMin;
29    }
```

Tip

HOW TO DEFINE TEMPLATES

When we defined the function templates in Display 16.3, we started with a function that sorts an array of elements of type int. We then created a template by replacing the base type of the array with the type parameter T. This is a good general strategy for writing templates. If you want to write a function template, first write a version that is not a template at all but is just an ordinary function. Then completely debug the ordinary function, and finally convert the ordinary function to a template by replacing some type names with a type parameter. There are two advantages to this method. First, when you are defining the ordinary function, you are dealing with a much more concrete case, which makes the problem easier to visualize. Second, you have fewer details to check at each stage; when worrying about the algorithm itself, you need not concern yourself with template syntax rules.

Pitfall

USING A TEMPLATE WITH AN INAPPROPRIATE TYPE

You can use a template function with any type for which the code in the function definition makes sense. However, all the code in the template function must makes sense and must behave in an appropriate way. For example, you cannot use the swapValues template (Display 16.1) with the type parameter replaced by a type for which the assignment operator does not work at all, or does not work "correctly."

As a more concrete example, suppose that your program defines the template function swapValues as in Display 16.1. You cannot add the following to your program.

```
int a[10], b[10];
  <some code to fill arrays>
swapValues(a, b);
```

This code will not work, because assignment does not work with array types:

Self-Test Exercises

5. Display 5.6 shows a function called search, which searches an array for a specified integer. Give a function template version of search that can be used to search an array of elements of any type. Give both the function declaration and the function definition for the template. (*Hint:* It is almost identical to the function given in Display 5.6.)

6. Compare and contrast overloading of a function name with the definition of a function template for the function name.

7. (This exercise is only for those who have already read at least Chapter 6 on structures and classes and preferably also read Chapter 8 on overloading operators.) Can you use the sort template function (Display 16.3) to sort an array with base type DayOfYear defined in Display 6.4?

8. (This exercise is only for those who have already read Chapter 10 on pointers and dynamic arrays.)

Although the assignment operator does not work with ordinary array variables, it does work with pointer variables that are used to name dynamic arrays. Suppose that your program defines the template function swapValues as in Display 16.1 and contains the following code. What is the output produced by this code?

```
typedef int* ArrayPointer;
ArrayPointer a, b, c;
a = new int[3];
b = new int[3];

int i;
for (i = 0; i < 3; i++)
{
    a[i] = i;
    b[i] = i*100;
}
c = a;

cout << "a contains: ";
for (i = 0; i < 3; i++)
    cout << a[i] << " ";
cout << endl;
```

```
cout << "b contains: ";
for (i = 0; i < 3; i++)
    cout << b[i] << " ";
cout << endl;
cout << "c contains: ";
for (i = 0; i < 3; i++)
    cout << c[i] << " ";
cout << endl;

swapValues(a, b);
b[0] = 42;

cout << "After swapping a and b,\n"
     << "and changing b:\n";
cout << "a contains: ";
for (i = 0; i < 3; i++)
    cout << a[i] << " ";
cout << endl;
cout << "b contains: ";
for (i = 0; i < 3; i++)
    cout << b[i] << " ";
cout << endl;
cout << "c contains: ";
for (i = 0; i < 3; i++)
    cout << c[i] << " ";
cout << endl;
```

16.2 Class Templates

*Equal wealth and equal opportunities of culture ... have simply
made us all members of one class.*

Edward Bellamy, *Looking Backward 2000–1887*

As you saw in the previous section, function definitions can be made more general by using templates. In this section you will see that templates can also make class definitions more general.

SYNTAX FOR CLASS TEMPLATES

The syntax details for class templates are basically the same as those for function templates. The following is placed before the template definition:

```
template<class T>
```

type parameter

The type parameter T is used in the class definition just like any other type. As with function templates, the type parameter T represents a type that can be any type at all; the type parameter does not have to be replaced with a class type. As with function templates, you may use any (nonkeyword) identifier instead of T, although it is traditional to use T.

Display 16.4 (part 1) shows an example of a class template. An object of this class contains a pair of values of type T: If T is int, the object values are pairs of integers; if T is char, the object values are pairs of characters, and so on.[2]

declaring objects

Once the class template is defined, you can declare objects of this class. The declaration must specify what type is to be filled in for T. For example, the following declares the object score so it can record a pair of integers and declares the object seats so it can record a pair of characters:

```
Pair<int> score;
Pair<char> seats;
```

The objects are then used just like any other objects. For example, the following sets score to be 3 for the first team and 0 for the second team:

```
score.setFirst(3);
score.setSecond(0);
```

Display 16.4 (Part 1) Class Template Definition

```
1    //Class for a pair of values of type T:
2    template<class T>
3    class Pair
4    {
5    public:
6        Pair( );
7        Pair(T firstValue, T secondValue);
8        void setFirst(T newValue);
9        void setSecond(T newValue);
10       T getFirst( ) const;
11       T getSecond( ) const;
12   private:
13       T first;
14       T second;
15   };
```

---

[2] Pair is a template version of the class intPair given in Display 8.6. However, since they would not be appropriate for all types T, we have omitted the increment and decrement operators.

Display 16.4   (Part 2) Some Sample Member Function Definitions

```
16   template<class T>
17   Pair<T>::Pair(T firstValue, T secondValue)
18   {
19       first = firstValue;
20       second = secondValue;
21   }

22   template<class T>                          Not all the member functions
23   void Pair<T>::setFirst(T newValue)         are shown here.
24   {
25       first = newValue;
26   }

27   template<class T>
28   T Pair<T>::getFirst( ) const
29   {
30       return first;
31   }
```

The member functions for a class template are defined the same way as member functions for ordinary classes. The only difference is that the member function definitions are themselves templates. For example, Display 16.4 (part 2) shows appropriate definitions for the member functions setFirst and getFirst, and for the constructor with two arguments for the template class Pair. Notice that the class name before the scope resolution operator is Pair<T>, not simply Pair, but that the constructor name after the scope resolution operator is the simple name Pair without any <T>.

defining member functions

The name of a class template may be used as the type for a function parameter. For example, the following is a possible function declaration for a function with a parameter for a pair of integers:

class templates as parameters

```
int addUp(const Pair<int>& thePair);
//Returns the sum of the two integers in thePair.
```

Note that we specified the type—in this case, int—that is to be filled in for the type parameter T.

You can even use a class template within a function template. For example, rather than defining the specialized function addUp given above, you could instead define a function template as follows so that the function applies to all kinds of numbers:

```
template<class T>
T addUp(const Pair<T>& thePair);
//Precondition: The operator + is defined for values of type T.
//Returns the sum of the two values in thePair.
```

restrictions
on the
type
parameter

Almost all template class definitions have some restrictions on what types can reasonable be substituted for the type parameter (or parameters). Even a straightforward template class like Pair does not work well with absolutely all types T. The type Pair<T> will not be well behaved unless the assignment operator and copy constructor are well behaved for the type T, since the assignment operator is used in member function definitions and since there are member functions with call-by-value parameters of type T. If T involves pointers and dynamic variables, then T should also have a suitable destructor. However, these are requirements you might expect a well-behaved class type T to have. So, these requirements are minimal. With other template classes the requirements on the types that can be substituted for a type parameter may be more restrictive.

CLASS TEMPLATE SYNTAX

A class template definition and the definitions of its member functions are prefaced with the following:

```
template<class Type_Parameter>
```

The class and member function definitions are then the same as for any ordinary class, except that the *Type_Parameter* can be used in place of a type.

For example, the following is the beginning of a class template definition:

```
template<class T>
class Pair
{
public:
    Pair( );
    Pair(T firstValue, T secondValue);
        . . .
```

Member functions and overloaded operators are then defined as function templates. For example, the definition of the two-argument constructor for the above sample class template would begin as follows:

```
template<class T>
Pair<T>::Pair(T firstValue, T secondValue)
{
    . . .
```

You can specialize a class template by giving a type argument to the class name, as in the following example:

```
Pair<int>
```

The specialized class name, like Pair<int>, can then be used just like any class name. It can be used to declare objects or to specify the type of a formal parameter.

TYPE DEFINITIONS

You can define a new class type name that has the same meaning as a specialized class template name, such as Pair<int>. The syntax for such a defined class type name is as follows:

```
typedef Class_Name<Type_Argument> New_Type_Name;
```

For example:

```
typedef Pair<int> PairOfInt;
```

The type name PairOfInt can then be used to declare objects of type Pair<int>, as in the following example:

```
PairOfInt pair1, pair2;
```

The type name PairOfInt can also be used to specify the type of a formal parameter or used anyplace else a type name is allowed.

Self-Test Exercises

9. Give the definition for the default (zero-argument) constructor for the class template Pair in Display 16.4.

10. Give the complete definition for the following function, which was discussed in the previous subsection:

```
int addUp(const Pair<int>& thePair);
//Returns the sum of the two integers in thePair.
```

11. Give the complete definition for the following template function, which was discussed in the previous subsection:

```
template<class T>
T addUp(const Pair<T>& thePair);
//Precondition: The operator + is defined for values of type T.
//Returns the sum of the two values in thePair
```

Example

AN ARRAY TEMPLATE CLASS

In Chapter 10 we defined a class for a partially filled array of doubles (Displays 10.10 and 10.11). In this example, we convert that definition to a template class for a partially filled array of values of any type. The template class PFArray has a type parameter T for the base type of the array.

The conversion is routine. We just replace double (when it occurs as the base type of the array) with the type parameter T and convert both the class definition and the member function definitions to template form. The template class definition is given in Display 16.5. The member function template definitions are given in Display 16.6.

namespace

Note that we have placed the template definitions in a namespace. Namespaces are used with templates in the same way as they are used with simple, nontemplate definitions.

separate compilation

A sample application program is given in Display 16.7. Note that we have separated the class template interface, implementation, and application program into three files. Unfortunately, these files cannot be used for the traditional method of separate compilation. Most compilers do not yet accommodate such separate compilation. So, we do the best we can by #include−ing the interface and implementation files in the application file. To the compiler, that makes it look like everything is in one file.

Display 16.5   Interface for the PFArray Template Class (part 1 of 2)

```
1   //This is the header file pfarray.h. This is the interface for the class
2   //PFArray. Objects of this type are partially filled arrays with base type T.
3   #ifndef PFARRAY_H
4   #define PFARRAY_H

5   namespace PFArraySavitch
6   {
7       template<class T>
8       class PFArray
9       {
10      public:
11          PFArray( ); //Initializes with a capacity of 50.

12          PFArray(int capacityValue);

13          PFArray(const PFArray<T>& pfaObject);

14          void addElement(T element);
15          //Precondition: The array is not full.
16          //Postcondition: The element has been added.

17          bool full( ) const; //Returns true if the array is full; false, otherwise.

18          int getCapacity( ) const;

19          int getNumberUsed( ) const;

20          void emptyArray( );
21          //Resets the number used to zero, effectively emptying the array.
```

Display 16.5   Interface for the PFArray Template Class _(part 2 of 2)_

```
22          T& operator[](int index);
23          //Read and change access to elements 0 through numberUsed - 1.

24          PFArray<T>& operator =(const PFArray<T>& rightSide);

25          virtual ~PFArray( );
26      private:
27          T *a; //for an array of T.
28          int capacity; //for the size of the array.
29          int used; //for the number of array positions currently in use.
30      };
31  }// PFArraySavitch
32  #endif //PFARRAY_H
```

Display 16.6   Implementation for PFArray Template Class _(part 1 of 3)_

```
1   //This is the implementation file pfarray.cpp.
2   //This is the implementation of the template class PFArray.
3   //The interface for the template class PFArray is in the file pfarray.h.

4   #include "pfarray.h"
5   #include <iostream>
6   using std::cout;

7   namespace PFArraySavitch
8   {
9       template<class T>
10      PFArray<T>::PFArray( ) :capacity(50), used(0)
11      {
12          a = new T[capacity];
13      }

14      template<class T>
15      PFArray<T>::PFArray(int size) :capacity(size), used(0)
16      {
17          a = new T[capacity];
18      }

19      template<class T>
20      PFArray<T>::PFArray(const PFArray<T>& pfaObject)
21        :capacity(pfaObject.getCapacity( )), used(pfaObject.getNumberUsed( ))
22      {
23          a = new T[capacity];
24          for (int i = 0; i < used; i++)
25              a[i] = pfaObject.a[i];
```

Note that the T is used before the scope resolution operator, but no T is used for the constructor name

Display 16.6   Implementation for PFArray Template Class *(part 2 of 3)*

```
26          }
27
28          template<class T>
29          void PFArray<T>::addElement(T element)
30          {
31              if (used >= capacity)
32              {
33                  cout << "Attempt to exceed capacity in PFArray.\n";
34                  exit(0);
35              }
36              a[used] = element;
37              used++;
38          }

39          template<class T>
40          bool PFArray<T>::full( ) const
41          {
42              return (capacity == used);
43          }

44          template<class T>
45          int PFArray<T>::getCapacity( ) const
46          {
47              return capacity;
48          }

49          template<class T>
50          int PFArray<T>::getNumberUsed( ) const
51          {
52              return used;
53          }

54          template<class T>
55          void PFArray<T>::emptyArray( )
56          {
57              used = 0;
58          }
59
60          template<class T>
61          T& PFArray<T>::operator[](int index)
62          {
63              if (index >= used)
64              {
65                  cout << "Illegal index in PFArray.\n";
66                  exit(0);
```

Display 16.6   Implementation for PFArray Template Class *(part 3 of 3)*

```
67              }

68          return a[index];
69      }

70      template<class T>
71      PFArray<T>& PFArray<T>::operator =(const PFArray<T>& rightSide)
72      {
73          if (capacity != rightSide.capacity)
74          {
75              delete [] a;
76              a = new T[rightSide.capacity];
77          }

78          capacity = rightSide.capacity;
79          used = rightSide.used;
80          for (int i = 0; i < used; i++)
81              a[i] = rightSide.a[i];

82          return *this;
83      }

84      template<class T>
85      PFArray<T>::~PFArray( )
86      {
87          delete [] a;
88      }
89  }// PFArraySavitch
```

Display 16.7   Demonstration Program for Template Class PFArray *(part 1 of 3)*

```
1   //Program to demonstrate the template class PFArray.
2   #include <iostream>
3   #include <string>
4   using std::cin;
5   using std::cout;
6   using std::endl;
7   using std::string;

8   #include "pfarray.h"
9   #include "pfarray.cpp"
10  using PFArraySavitch::PFArray;

11  int main( )
12  {
```

Display 16.7   Demonstration Program for Template Class PFArray *(part 2 of 3)*

```
13        PFArray<int> a(10);

14        cout << "Enter up to 10 nonnegative integers.\n";
15        cout << "Place a negative number at the end.\n";
16        int next;
17        cin >> next;
18        while ((next >= 0) && (!a.full( )))
19        {
20            a.addElement(next);
21            cin >> next;
22        }
23        if (next >= 0)
24        {
25            cout << "Could not read all numbers.\n";
26            //Clear the unread input:
27            while (next >= 0)
28                cin >> next;
29        }

30        cout << "You entered the following:\n ";
31        int index;
32        int count = a.getNumberUsed( );
33        for (index = 0; index < count; index++)
34            cout << a[index] << " ";
35        cout << endl;
36
37        PFArray<string> b(3);

38        cout << "Enter three words:\n";
39        string nextWord;
40        for (index = 0; index < 3; index++)
41        {
42            cin >> nextWord;
43            b.addElement(nextWord);
44        }

45        cout << "You wrote the following:\n";
46        count = b.getNumberUsed( );
47        for (index = 0; index < count; index++)
48            cout << b[index] << " ";
49        cout << endl;
50        cout << "I hope you really mean it.\n";

51        return 0;
52    }
```

Display 16.7   Demonstration Program for Template Class PFArray (part 3 of 3)

SAMPLE DIALOGUE

```
Enter up to 10 nonnegative integers.
Place a negative number at the end.
1 2 3 4 5 –1
You entered the following:
1 2 3 4 5
Enter three words:
I love you
You wrote the following:
I love you
I hope you really mean it.
```

FRIEND FUNCTIONS

Friend functions are used with template classes in the same way that they are used with ordinary classes. The only difference is that you must include a type parameter where appropriate.

Self-Test Exercises

12. What do you have to do to make the following function a friend of the template class PFArray in Display 16.5?

```
void showData(PFArray<T> theObject);
//Displays the data in theObject to the screen.
//Assumes that << is defined for values of type T.
```

THE vector AND basic_string TEMPLATES

If you have not yet done so, this would be a good time to read Section 7.3 of Chapter 7, which covers the template class vector.

vector

Another predefined template class is the basic_string template class. The class basic_string is a template class that can deal with strings of elements of any type. The class basic_string<char> is the class for strings of characters. The class basic_string<double> is the class for strings of numbers of type double. The class basic_string<YourClass> is the class for strings of objects of the class YourClass (whatever that may be).

basic_string

string

You have already been using a special case of the basic_string template class. The unadorned name string, which we have been using, is an alternate name for the class basic_string<char>. All the member functions you learned for the class string apply and behave similarly for the template class basic_string<T>.

The template class basic_string is defined in the library with header file <string>, and the definition is placed in the std namespace. When using the class basic_string you therefore need the following or something similar near the beginning of your file:

```
#include <string>
using namespace std;
```

or

```
#include <string>
using std::basic_string;
using std::string; //Only if you use the name string by itself
```

16.3 Templates and Inheritance

The ruling ideas of each age have ever been the ideas of its ruling class.

Karl Marx and Friedrich Engels, *The Communist Manifesto*

There is very little new to learn about templates and inheritance. To define a derived template class, you start with a template class (or sometimes a nontemplate class) and derive another template class from it. You do this in the same way that you derive an ordinary class from an ordinary base class. An example should clarify any questions you might have about syntax details.

Example

TEMPLATE CLASS FOR A PARTIALLY FILLED ARRAY WITH BACKUP

Chapter 14 (Displays 14.10 and 14.11) defined the class PFArrayDBak for partially filled arrays of double with backup. We defined it as a derived class of PFArrayD (Displays 14.8 and 14.9). The class PFArrayD was a class for a partially filled array, but it only worked for the base type double. Displays 16.5 and 16.6 converted the class PFArrayD to the template class PFArray so that it would work for any type as the array base type. In this program we will define a template class PFArrayBak for a partially filled array with backup that will work for any type as the array base type. We will define the template class PFArrayBak as a derived class of the template PFArray. We can do this almost automatically by starting with the regular derived class PFArarryDBak and replacing all occurrences of the array base type double with a type parameter T, replacing the class PFArrayD with the template class PFArray, and cleaning up the syntax so it fully conforms to template syntax.

The interface to the template class PFArrayBak is given in Display 16.8. Note that the base class is PFArray<T> with the array parameter, not simply PFArray. If you think about it, you will realize that you need the <T>. A partially filled array of T with backup is a derived class of a partially filled array of T. The T is important, and how it is used is important.

The implementation for the template class PFArrayBak is given in Display 16.9. In what follows we reproduce the first constructor definition in the implementation:

```
template<class T>
PFArrayBak<T>::PFArrayBak( ) : PFArray<T>( ), usedB(0)
{
    b = new T[getCapacity( )];
}
```

Note that, as with any definition of a template class function, it starts with

```
template<class T>
```

Also notice that the base type of the array (given after the new) is the type parameter T. Other details may not be quite as obvious, but do make sense.

Next consider the following line:

```
PFArrayBak<T>::PFArrayBak( ) : PFArray<T>( ), usedB(0)
```

As with any definition of a template class function, the definition has PFArray<T> with the type parameter before the scope resolution operator, but the constructor name is just plain-old PFArrayBak without any type parameter. Also notice that the base class constructor includes the type parameter T in the initialization PFArray<T>( ). This is so that the constructor will match the base type PFArray<T> as given in the following line of the interface:

```
class PFArrayBak : public PFArray<T>
```

A sample program using the template class PFArrayBak is given in Display 16.10.

Display 16.8 Interface for the Template Class PFArrayBak (part 1 of 2)

```
1   //This is the header file pfarraybak.h. This is the interface for the
2   //template class PFArrayBak. Objects of this type are partially filled
3   //arrays of any type T. This version allows the programmer to make a backup
4   //copy and restore to the last saved copy of the partially filled array.
5   #ifndef PFARRAYBAK_H
6   #define PFARRAYBAK_H
7   #include "pfarray.h"

8   namespace PFArraySavitch
9   {
```

Display 16.8   Interface for the Template Class PFArrayBak *(part 2 of 2)*

```
10      template<class T>
11      class PFArrayBak : public PFArray<T>
12      {
13      public:
14          PFArrayBak( );
15          //Initializes with a capacity of 50.

16          PFArrayBak(int capacityValue);

17          PFArrayBak(const PFArrayBak<T>& Object);

18          void backup( );
19          //Makes a backup copy of the partially filled array.

20          void restore( );
21          //Restores the partially filled array to the last saved version.
22          //If backup has never been invoked, this empties the partially
23          //filled array.

24          PFArrayBak<T>& operator =(const PFArrayBak<T>& rightSide);

25          virtual ~PFArrayBak( );
26      private:
27          T *b; //for a backup of main array.
28          int usedB; //backup for inherited member variable used.
29      };

30  }// PFArraySavitch
31  #endif //PFARRAY_H
```

Display 16.9   Implementation for the Template Class PFArrayBak *(part 1 of 3)*

```
1   //This is the file pfarraybak.cpp.
2   //This is the implementation for the template class PFArrayBak. The
3   //interface for the template class PFArrayBak is in the file pfarraybak.h.
4   #include "pfarraybak.h"
5   #include <iostream>
6   using std::cout;

7   namespace PFArraySavitch
8   {

9       template<class T>
10      PFArrayBak<T>::PFArrayBak( ) : PFArray<T>( ), usedB(0)
```

Display 16.9 Implementation for the Template Class PFArrayBak (part 2 of 3)

```
11      {
12          b = new T[getCapacity( )];
13      }

14      template<class T>
15      PFArrayBak<T>::PFArrayBak(int capacityValue)
16                      : PFArray<T>(capacityValue), usedB(0)
17      {
18          b = new T[getCapacity( )];
19      }

20      template<class T>
21      PFArrayBak<T>::PFArrayBak(const PFArrayBak<T>& oldObject)
22                      : PFArray<T>(oldObject), usedB(0)
23      {
24          b = new T[getCapacity( )];
25          usedB = oldObject.getNumberUsed();
26          for (int i = 0; i < usedB; i++)
27              b[i] = oldObject.b[i];
28      }
29      template<class T>
30      void PFArrayBak<T>::backup( )
31      {
32          usedB = getNumberUsed( );
33          for (int i = 0; i < usedB; i++)
34              b[i] = operator[](i);
35      }

36      template<class T>
37      void PFArrayBak<T>::restore( )
38      {
39          emptyArray( );

40          for (int i = 0; i < usedB; i++)
41              addElement(b[i]);
42      }

43      template<class T>
44      PFArrayBak<T>& PFArrayBak<T>::operator =(const PFArrayBak<T>& rightSide)
45      {
46          PFArray<T>::operator =(rightSide);

47          if (getCapacity( ) != rightSide.getCapacity( ))
48          {
49              delete [] b;
50              b = new T[rightSide.getCapacity( )];
51          }
```

Display 16.9   Implementation for the Template Class PFArrayBak (*part 3 of 3*)

```
52              usedB = rightSide.usedB;
53              for (int i = 0; i < usedB; i++)
54                  b[i] = rightSide.b[i];

55              return *this;
56          }

57          template<class T>
58          PFArrayBak<T>::~PFArrayBak( )
59          {
60              delete [] b;
61          }
62      }// PFArraySavitch
```

Display 16.10   Demonstration Program for Template Class PFArrayBak (*part 1 of 2*)

```
1    //Program to demonstrate the template class PFArrayBak.
2    #include <iostream>
3    #include <string>
4    using std::cin;
5    using std::cout;
6    using std::endl;
7    using std::string;

8    #include "pfarraybak.h"
9    #include "pfarray.cpp"
10   #include "pfarraybak.cpp"
11   using PFArraySavitch::PFArrayBak;

12   int main( )
13   {
14       int cap;
15       cout << "Enter capacity of this super array: ";
16       cin >> cap;
17       PFArrayBak<string> a(cap);

18       cout << "Enter " << cap << " strings\n";
19       cout << "separated by blanks.\n";

20       string next;
21       for (int i = 0; i < cap; i++)
22       {
23           cin >> next;
24           a.addElement(next);
25       }
```

Do not forget to include the implementation of the base class template

Display 16.10 **Demonstration Program for Template Class PFArrayBak** *(part 2 of 2)*

```
26        int count = a.getNumberUsed( );
27        cout << "The following " << count
28            << " strings read and stored:\n";
29        int index;
30        for (index = 0; index < count; index++)
31            cout << a[index] << " ";
32        cout << endl;

33        cout << "Backing up array.\n";
34        a.backup( );

35        cout << "Emptying array.\n";
36        a.emptyArray( );
37        cout << a.getNumberUsed( )
38            << " strings are now stored in the array.\n";

39        cout << "Restoring array.\n";
40        a.restore( );
41        count - a.getNumberUsed( );
42        cout << "The following " << count
43            << " strinss are now stored:\n";
44        for (index = 0; index < count; index++)
45            cout << a[index] << " ";
46        cout << endl;

47        cout << "End of demonstration.\n";
48        return 0;
49    }
```

SAMPLE DIALOGUE

```
Enter capacity of this super array: 3
Enter 3 strings
separated by blanks.
I love you
The following 3 strings read and stored:
I love you
Backing up array.
Emptying array.
0 strings are now stored in the array.
Restoring array.
The following 3 strings are now stored:
I love you
End of demonstration.
```

Self-Test Exercises

13. Is it legal for a derived template class to start as shown below? The template class TwoDimPFArrayBak is designed to be a two-dimensional partially filled array with backup.

```
template<class T>
class TwoDimPFArrayBak : public PFArray< PFArray<T> >
{
public:
    TwoDimPFArrayBak( );
```

Note that the space in < PFArray<T> > is important, or at least the last space is. If the space between the next-to-last > and the last > is omitted, then the compiler may interpret >> to be the extraction operator used for input in expressions like cin >> n; rather than interpreting it as a nested < >.

14. Give the heading for the default (zero-argument) constructor for the class TwoDimPFArrayBak given in Self-Test Exercise 13. (Assume all instance variables are initialized in the body of the constructor definition, so you are not being ask to do that.)

Chapter Summary

- Using function templates, you can define functions that have a parameter for a type.
- Using class templates, you can define a class with a type parameter for subparts of the class.
- The predefined vector and basic_string classes are actually template classes.
- You can define a template class that is a derived class of a template base class.

ANSWERS TO SELF-TEST EXERCISES

1. Function declaration:

```
template<class T>
T maximum(T first, T second);
//Precondition: The operator < is defined for the type T.
//Returns the maximum of first and second.
```

Definition:
```
template<class T>
T maximum(T first, T second)
{
    if (first < second)
        return second;
    else
        return first;
}
```

2. Function declaration:

```
template<class T>
T absolute(T value);
//Precondition: The expressions x < 0 and -x are defined
//whenever x is of type T.
//Returns the absolute value of its argument.
```

Definition:

```
template<class T>
T absolute(T value)
{
    if (value < 0)
        return -value;
    else
        return value;
}
```

3. Templates provide a facility to allow the definition of functions and classes that have parameters for type names.

4. e. Any type, whether a primitive type (provided by C++) or a type defined by the user (a class or struct type, an enum type, or a type defined array, or int, float, double, etc.), but T must be a type for which the code in the template makes sense. For example, for the swapValues template function (Display 16.1), the type T must have a correctly working assignment operator.

5. The function declaration and function definition are given below. They are basically identical to those for the versions given in Display 5.6 except that two instances of int are changed to T in the parameter list.

Function declaration:

```
template<class T>
int search(const T a[], int numberUsed, T target);
//Precondition: numberUsed is <= the declared size of a.
//Also, a[0] through a[numberUsed -1] have values.
//Returns the first index such that a[index] == target,
//provided there is such an index, otherwise returns -1.
```

Definition:

```
template<class T>
int search(const T a[], int numberUsed, T target)
{
    int index = 0;
    bool found = false;
    while ((!found) && (index < numberUsed))
        if (target == a[index])
            found = true;
        else
```

```
        index++;

    if (found)
        return index;
    else
        return -1;
}
```

6. Function overloading only works for types for which an overloading is provided. (Overloading may work for types that automatically convert to some type for which an overloading is provided, but it may not do what you expect.) The template solution will work for any type that is defined at the time of invocation, provided that the template function body makes sense for that type.

7. No, you cannot use an array with base type DayOfYear with the template function sort because the < operator is not defined on values of type DayOfYear. (If you overload < , as we discussed in Chapter 8, to give a suitable ordering on values of type DayOfYear, then you can use an array with base type DayOfYear with the template function sort. For example, you might overload < so it means one date comes before the other on the calendar and then sort an array of dates by calendar ordering.)

8.
```
a contains: 0 1 2
b contains: 0 100 200
c contains: 0 1 2
After swapping a and b,
and changing b:
a contains: 0 100 200
b contains: 42 1 2
c contains: 42 1 2
```

Note that before swapValues(a, b); c is an alias (another name for) the array a. After swapValues(a, b); c is an alias for b. Although the values of a and b are in some sense swapped, things are not as simple as you might have hoped. With pointer variables, there can be side effects of using swapValues.

The point illustrated here is that the assignment operator is not as well behaved as you might want on array pointers and so the template swapValues does not work as you might want with variables that are pointers to arrays. The assignment operator does not do element by element swapping but merely swaps two pointers. So, the swapValues function used with pointers to arrays simply swaps two pointers. It might be best to not use swapValues with pointers to arrays (or any other pointers), unless you are very aware of how it behaves on the pointers. The swapValues template function used with a type T is only as good, or as bad, as the assignment operator is on type T.

9. Since the type can be any type at all, there are no natural candidates for the default initialization values. So this constructor does nothing, but it does allow you to declare (uninitialized) objects without giving any constructor arguments.

```
template<class T>
Pair<T>::Pair( )
{
//Do nothing.
}
```

10.
```
int addUp(const Pair<int>& thePair)
{
    return (thePair.getFirst( ) + thePair.getSecond( ));
}
```

11.
```
template<class T>
T addUp(const Pair<T>& thePair)
{
    return (thePair.getFirst( ) + thePair.getSecond( ));
}
```

12. You add the following to the public section of the template class definition of PFArray:

```
friend void showData(PFArray<T> theObject);
//Displays the data in theObject to the screen.
//Assumes that << is defined for values of type T.
```

You also need to add a function template definition of showData. One possible definition is as follows:

```
namespace PFArraySavitch
{
    template<class T>
    void showData(PFArray< T > theObject)
    {
        for (int i = 0; i < theObject.used; i++)
            cout << theObject[i] << endl;
    }
}//PFArraySavitch
```

13. Yes, it is perfectly legal. There are other, possibly preferable, ways to accomplish the same thing, but this is legal and not even crazy.

14.
```
template<class T>
TwoDimPFArrayBak<T>::TwoDimPFArrayBak( )
                    : PFArray< PFArray<T> >( )
```

PROGRAMMING PROJECTS

1. Write a template version of the iterative binary search from Display 13.8. Specify requirements on the template parameter type. Discuss the requirements on the template parameter type.

2. Write a template version of the recursive binary search from Display 13.6. Specify requirements on the template parameter type. Discuss the requirements on the template parameter type.

3. The template sort routine Display 16.3 is based on an algorithm called the *selection sort* Another related sorting algorithm is called **insertion sort**. The insertion sort algorithm is the sort method used to sort a Bridge hand. Consider each element in turn, inserting it into its proper place among the elements at the start of the array that are already sorted. The element being considered is inserted by moving the larger elements "to the right" to make space and inserting the vacated place. For example, the following shows the steps in a selection sort of an array of ints a. The values of a[0] through a[4] are given on each line. The asterisk marks the boundary between the sorted and unsorted portions of the array.

```
2 * 5 3 4
2 5 * 3 4
2 3 5 * 4
2 3 4 5 *
```

First, write an insertion sort function that works for ints. Next, write the template version of this sort function. Finally, test thoroughly using several primitive types, and test using a type you create with the minimal machinery necessary to use the sort routine.

CHAPTER 17

Linked Data Structures

17 Linked Data Structures

If somebody there chanced to be
Who loved me in a manner true
My heart would point him out to me
And I would point him out to you.

Gilbert and Sullivan, *Ruddigore*

INTRODUCTION

A *linked list* is a list constructed using pointers. A linked list is not fixed in size but can grow and shrink while your program is running. A *tree* is another kind of data structure constructed using pointers. This chapter introduces the use of pointers for building such data structures. The Standard Template Library (STL) has predefined versions of these and other similar data structures. The STL is covered in Chapter 19. It often makes more sense to use the predefined data structures in the STL rather than defining your own data structures. However, there are cases where you need to define your own data structures using pointers. (Somebody had to define the STL.) Also, this material will give you some insight into how the STL might have been defined and will introduce you to some basic widely used material.

Linked data structures create their structures using dynamic variables, created with the new operator, and pointers to connect these variables. This gives you complete control over how you build and manage your data structures, including how you manage memory. This allows you to sometimes do things more efficiently. For example, it is easier and faster to insert a value into a sorted linked list than into a sorted array.

There are basically three ways to handle data structures of the kind discussed in this chapter:

1. The C-style approach of using global functions and structs with everything public

2. Using classes with all member variables private and using accessor and mutator functions

3. Using friend classes (or something similar, such as private or protected inheritance or locally defined classes)

We give examples of all three methods. We introduce linked lists using method 1. We then present more details about basic linked lists and introduce both the stack and queue data structures using method 2. We give an alternate definition of our queue template class using friend classes (method 3) and use friend classes (method 3) to present a tree template class. This way you can see the virtues and shortcomings of each approach. Our personal preference is to use friend classes, but each method has its own advocates.

Sections 17.1 through 17.3 do not use the material in Chapters 13 through 15 (recursion, inheritance, and polymorphism), with one small exception: We have marked our class destructors with the modifier `virtual` following the advice given in Chapter 15. If you have not yet read about virtual functions (Chapter 15), you can pretend that "`virtual`" does not appear in the code. For what is done in this chapter it makes no difference whether "`virtual`" is present or not. Section 17.4 uses recursion (Chapter 13) but does not use Chapters 14 and 15.

17.1 | Nodes and Linked Lists

A linked list, such as the one diagrammed in Display 17.1, is a simple example of a dynamic data structure. It's called a **dynamic data structure** because each of the boxes in Display 17.1 is a variable of a `struct` or class type that has been dynamically created with the new operator. In a dynamic data structure, these boxes, known as **nodes**, contain pointers, diagrammed as arrows, that point to other nodes. This section introduces the basic techniques for building and maintaining linked lists.

dynamic data structure

NODES

A structure like the one shown in Display 17.1 consists of items that we have drawn as boxes connected by arrows. The boxes are called *nodes*, and the arrows represent pointers. Each of the nodes in Display 17.1 contains a string value, an integer, and a pointer

node structures

Display 17.1 Nodes and Pointers

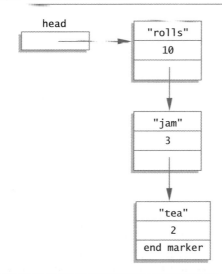

that can point to other nodes of the same type. Note that pointers point to the entire node, not to the individual items (such as 10 or "rolls") that are inside the node.

Nodes are implemented in C++ as structs or classes. For example, the struct type definitions for a node of the type shown in Display 17.1, along with the type definition for a pointer to such nodes, can be as follows:

```
struct ListNode
{
    string item;
    int count;
    ListNode *link;
};

typedef ListNode* ListNodePtr;
```

The order of the type definitions is important. The definition of ListNode must come first, since it is used in the definition of ListNodePtr.

The box labeled head in Display 17.1 is not a node but a pointer variable that can point to a node. The pointer variable head is declared as follows:

```
ListNodePtr head;
```

Even though we have ordered the type definitions to avoid some illegal forms of circularity, the above definition of the struct type ListNode is still circular. The definition of the type ListNode uses the type name ListNode to define the member variable link. There is nothing wrong with this particular circularity, which is allowed in C++. One indication that this definition is not logically inconsistent is the fact that you can draw pictures, such as Display 17.1, that represent such structures.

We now have pointers inside structs and have these pointers pointing to structs that contain pointers, and so forth. In such situations the syntax can sometimes get involved, but in all cases the syntax follows those few rules we have described for pointers and structs. As an illustration, suppose the declarations are as above, the situation is as diagrammed in Display 17.1, and you want to change the number in the first node from 10 to 12. One way to accomplish this is with the following statement:

```
(*head).count = 12;
```

The expression on the left side of the assignment operator may require a bit of explanation. The variable head is a pointer variable. The expression *head is thus the thing it points to, namely the node (dynamic variable) containing "rolls" and the integer 10. This node, referred to by *head, is a struct, and the member variable of this struct, which contains a value of type int, is called count; therefore, (*head).count is the name of the int variable in the first node. The parentheses around *head are not optional. You want the dereferencing operation, *, to be performed before the dot operation. However, the dot operator has higher precedence than the dereferencing operator, *, and so without the parentheses, the dot operation would be performed first (and that would produce an error). The next paragraph describes a shortcut notation that can avoid this worry about parentheses.

the –>
operator

C++ has an operator that can be used with a pointer to simplify the notation for specifying the members of a struct or a class. Chapter 10 introduced the arrow operator, –>, but we have not used it extensively before now. So, a review is in order. The arrow operator combines the actions of a dereferencing operator, *, and a dot operator to specify a member of a dynamic struct or class object that is pointed to by a given pointer. For example, the previous assignment statement for changing the number in the first node can be written more simply as

```
head->count = 12;
```

This assignment statement and the previous one mean the same thing, but this one is the form normally used.

The string in the first node can be changed from "rolls" to "bagels" with the following statement:

```
head->item = "bagels";
```

The result of these changes to the first node in the list is diagrammed in Display 17.2.

THE ARROW OPERATOR, –>

The arrow operator, –>, specifies a member of a struct or a member of a class object that is pointed to by a pointer variable. The syntax is

Pointer_Variable–>Member_Name

The above refers to a member of the struct or class object pointed to by the *Pointer_Variable*. Which member it refers to is given by the *Member_Name*. For example, suppose you have the following definition:

```
struct Record
{
    int number;
    char grade;
};
```

The following creates a dynamic variable of type Record and sets the member variables of the dynamic struct variable to 2001 and 'A':

```
Record *p;
p = new Record;
p->number = 2001;
p->grade = 'A';
```

Display 17.2   Accessing Node Data

```
head->count = 12;
head->item = "bagels";
```

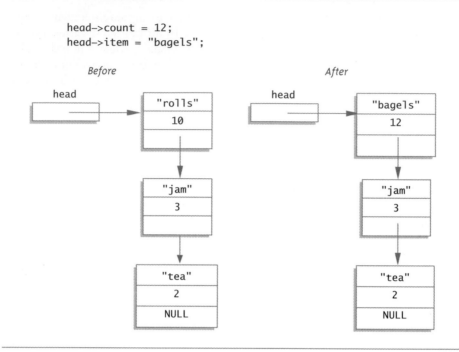

NULL

Look at the pointer member in the last node in the list shown in Display 17.2. This last node has the word NULL written where there should be a pointer. In Display 17.1 we filled this position with the phrase "end marker," but "end marker" is not a C++ expression. In C++ programs we use the constant NULL as a marker to signal the end of a linked list (or the end of any other kind of linked data structure).

NULL is typically used for two different (but often coinciding) purposes. First, NULL is used to give a value to a pointer variable that otherwise would not have any value. This prevents an inadvertent reference to memory, since NULL is not the address of any memory location. The second category of use is that of an end marker. A program can step through the list of nodes as shown in Display 17.2 and know that it has come to the end of the list when the program reaches the node that contains NULL.

NULL is 0

As noted in Chapter 10, the constant NULL is actually the number 0, but we prefer to think of it and spell it as NULL to make it clear that it means this special-purpose value that you can assign to pointer variables. The definition of the identifier NULL is in a number of the standard libraries, such as <iostream> and <cstddef>, so you should use an include directive with either <iostream>, <cstddef>, or some other suitable library when you use NULL. The definition of NULL is handled by the C++ preprocessor, which replaces NULL with 0. Thus, the compiler never actually sees "NULL" and so there are no namespace issues; therefore, no using directive is needed for NULL.

A pointer can be set to NULL using the assignment operator, as in the following, which declares a pointer variable called there and initializes it to NULL:

```
double *there = NULL;
```

The constant NULL can be assigned to a pointer variable of any pointer type.

NULL

NULL is a special constant value that is used to give a value to a pointer variable that would not otherwise have a value. NULL can be assigned to a pointer variable of any type. The identifier NULL is defined in a number of libraries including the library with header file <cstddef> and the library with header file <iostream>. The constant NULL is actually the number 0, but we prefer to think of it and spell it as NULL.

Self-Test Exercises

1. Suppose your program contains the following type definitions:

```
struct Box
{
    string name;
    int number;
    Box *next;
};

typedef Box* BoxPtr;
```

What is the output produced by the following code?

```
BoxPtr head;
head = new Box;
head->name = "Sally";
head->number = 18;
cout << (*head).name << endl;
cout << head->name << endl;
cout << (*head).number << endl;
cout << head->number << endl;
```

2. Suppose that your program contains the type definitions and code given in Self-Test Exercise 1. That code creates a node that contains the string "Sally" and the number 18. What code would you add to set the value of the member variable next of this node equal to NULL?

3. Given the following structure definition:

```
struct ListNode
{
    string item;
    int count;
    ListNode *link;
};
ListNode *head = new ListNode;
```

Give code to assign the string "Wilbur's brother Orville" to the member variable item of the variable to which head points.

LINKED LISTS AS ARGUMENTS

You should always keep one pointer variable pointing to the head of a linked list. This pointer variable is a way to name the linked list. When you write a function that takes a linked list as an argument, this pointer (which points to the head of the linked list) can be used as the linked list argument.

■ LINKED LISTS

linked list

head

Lists such as those shown in Display 17.1 are called *linked lists*. A **linked list** is a list of nodes in which each node has a member variable that is a pointer that points to the next node in the list. The first node in a linked list is called the **head**, which is why the pointer variable that points to the first node is named head. Note that the pointer named head is not itself the head of the list but only points to the head of the list. The last node has no special name, but it does have a special property: It has NULL as the value of its member pointer variable. To test whether a node is the last node, you need only test whether the pointer variable in the node is equal to NULL.

node type definition

Our goal in this section is to write some basic functions for manipulating linked lists. For variety, and to simplify the notation, we will use a simpler type of data for the nodes than that used in Display 17.2. These nodes will contain only an integer and a pointer. However, we will make our nodes more complicated in one sense. We will make our nodes objects of a class, rather than just a simple struct. The node and pointer type definitions that we will use are as follows:

```
class IntNode
{
public:
    IntNode( ){}
    IntNode(int theData, IntNode* theLink)
            : data(theData), link(theLink){}
```

```
      IntNode* getLink( ) const { return link; }
      int getData( ) const { return data; }
      void setData(int theData) { data = theData; }
      void setLink(IntNode* pointer) { link = pointer; }
  private:
      int data;
      IntNode *link;
  };
  typedef IntNode* IntNodePtr;
```

Note that all the member functions in the class IntNode are simple enough to have inline definitions.

Notice the two-parameter constructor for the class IntNode. It will allow us to create nodes with a specified integer as data and with a specified link member. For example, if p1 points to a node n1, then the following creates a new node pointed to by p2 such that this new node has data 42 and has its link member pointing to n1:

```
IntNodePtr p2 = new IntNode(42, p1);
```

After we derive some basic functions for creating and manipulating linked lists with this node type, we will convert the node type and the functions to template versions so they will work to store any type of data in the nodes.

As a warm-up exercise, let's see how we might construct the start of a linked list with nodes of this type. We first declare a pointer variable, called head, that will point to the head of our linked list:

a one-node linked list

```
IntNodePtr head;
```

To create our first node, we use the operator new to create a new dynamic variable that will become the first node in our linked list:

```
head = new IntNode;
```

We then give values to the member variables of this new node:

```
head->setData(3);
head->setLink(NULL);
```

Notice that the pointer member of this node is set equal to NULL because this node is the last node in the list (as well as the first node in the list). At this stage our linked list looks like this:

That was more work than we needed to do. By using the `IntNode` constructor with two parameters, we can create our one-node linked list much easier. The following is an easier way to obtain the one-node linked list just pictured:

```
head = new IntNode(3, NULL);
```

As it turns out, we will always create new nodes using this two-argument constructor for `IntNode`. Many programs would even omit the zero-argument constructor from the definition of `IntNode` so that it would be impossible to create a node without specifying values for each member variable.

Our one-node list was built in an ad hoc way. To have a larger linked list, your program must be able to add nodes in a systematic way. We next describe one simple way to insert nodes in a linked list.

■ INSERTING A NODE AT THE HEAD OF A LIST

In this subsection we assume that our linked list already contains one or more nodes, and we develop a function to add another node. The first parameter for the insertion function will be a call-by-reference parameter for a pointer variable that points to the head of the linked list, that is, a pointer variable that points to the first node in the linked list. The other parameter will give the number to be stored in the new node. The function declaration for our insertion function is as follows:

```
void headInsert(IntNodePtr& head, int theData);
```

To insert a new node into the linked list, our function will use the `new` operator and our two-argument constructor for `IntNode`. The new node will have `theData` as its data and will have its link member pointing to the first node in the linked list (before insertion). The dynamic variable is created as follows:

```
new IntNode(theData, head)
```

We want the pointer `head` to point to this new node, so the function body can simply be

```
{
    head = new IntNode(theData, head);
}
```

Display 17.3 contains a diagram of the action

```
head = new IntNode(theData, head);
```

when `theData` is 12. The complete function definition is given in Display 17.4.

You will want to allow for the possibility that a list contains nothing. For example, a shopping list might have nothing in it because there is nothing to buy this week. A list with nothing in it is called an **empty list**. A linked list is named by naming a pointer that points to the head of the list, but an empty list has no head node. To specify an

empty list

Display 17.3   Adding a Node to the Head of a Linked List

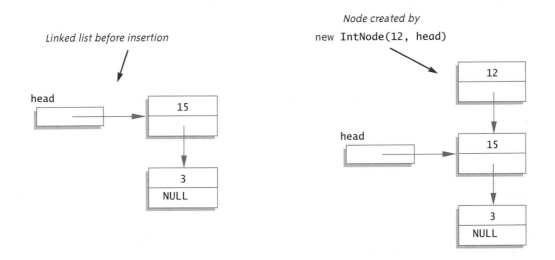

Linked list before insertion

Node created by
new IntNode(12, head)

Linked list after execution of
head = new IntNode(12, head);

empty list, you use the value NULL. If the pointer variable head is supposed to point to the head node of a linked list and you want to indicate that the list is empty, then set the value of head as follows:

```
head = NULL;
```

Whenever you design a function for manipulating a linked list, you should always check to see if it works on the empty list. If it does not, you may be able to add a special case for the empty list. If you cannot design the function to apply to the empty list, then your program must be designed to handle empty lists some other way or to avoid them completely. Fortunately, the empty list can often be treated just like any other list. For example, the function headInsert in Display 17.4 was designed with nonempty lists as the model, but a check will show that it works for the empty list as well.

Pitfall

LOSING NODES

You might be tempted to write the function definition for headInsert (Display 17.4) using the zero-argument constructor to set the member variables of the new node. If you were to try, you might start the function as follows:

```
head = new IntNode;
head->setData(theData);
```

At this point the new node is constructed, contains the correct data, and is pointed to by the pointer head—all as it is supposed to be. All that is left to do is attach the rest of the list to this node by setting the pointer member in this new node so that it points to what was formerly the first node of the list. You could do it with the following, if only you could figure out what pointer to put in place of the question mark:

```
head->setLink(?);
```

Display 17.5 shows the situation when the new data value is 12 and illustrates the problem. If you were to proceed in this way, there would be nothing pointing to the node containing 15. Since there is no named pointer pointing to it (or to a chain of pointers extending to that node), there is no way the program can reference this node. The node and all nodes below this node are lost. A program cannot make a pointer point to any of these nodes, nor can it access the data in these nodes or do anything else to the nodes. It simply has no way to refer to the nodes. Such a situation ties up memory for the duration of the program. A program that loses nodes is sometimes said to have a **memory leak**. A significant memory leak can result in the program running out of memory and terminating abnormally. Worse, a memory leak (lost nodes) in an ordinary user's program can, in rare situations, cause the operating system to crash. To avoid such lost nodes, the program must always keep some pointer pointing to the head of the list, usually the pointer in a pointer variable like head.

memory leak

Display 17.4   Functions for Adding a Node to a Linked List

NODE AND POINTER TYPE DEFINITIONS

```
class IntNode
{
public:
    IntNode( ){}
    IntNode(int theData, IntNode* theLink)
            : data(theData), link(theLink){}
    IntNode* getLink( ) const { return link; }
    int getData( ) const { return data; }
    void setData(int theData) { data = theData; }
    void setLink(IntNode* pointer) { link = pointer; }
private:
    int data;
    IntNode *link;
};

typedef IntNode* IntNodePtr;
```

FUNCTION TO ADD A NODE AT THE HEAD OF A LINKED LIST

FUNCTION DECLARATION

```
void headInsert(IntNodePtr& head, int theData);
//Precondition: The pointer variable head points to
//the head of a linked list.
//Postcondition: A new node containing theData
//has been added at the head of the linked list.
```

FUNCTION DEFINITION

```
void headInsert(IntNodePtr& head, int theData)
{
    head = new IntNode(theData, head);
}
```

FUNCTION TO ADD A NODE IN THE MIDDLE OF A LINKED LIST

FUNCTION DECLARATION

```
void insert(IntNodePtr afterMe, int theData);
//Precondition: afterMe points to a node in a linked list.
//Postcondition: A new node containing theData
//has been added after the node pointed to by afterMe.
```

FUNCTION DEFINITION

```
void insert(IntNodePtr afterMe, int theData)
{
    afterMe->setLink(new IntNode(theData, afterMe->getLink( )));
}
```

Display 17.5   Lost Nodes

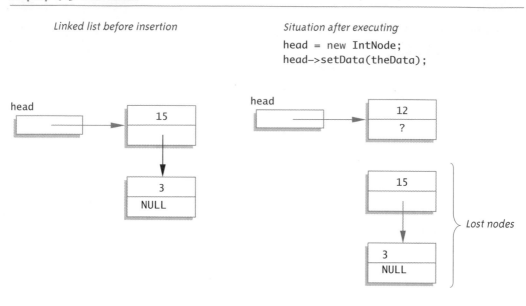

Linked list before insertion

Situation after executing
```
head = new IntNode;
head->setData(theData);
```

INSERTING AND REMOVING NODES INSIDE A LIST

inserting in the middle of a list

We next design a function to insert a node at a specified place in a linked list. If you want the nodes in some particular order, such as numerical or alphabetical, you cannot simply insert the node at the beginning or end of the list. We will therefore design a function to insert a node after a specified node in the linked list.

We assume that some other function or program part has correctly placed a pointer called afterMe pointing to some node in the linked list. We want the new node to be placed after the node pointed to by afterMe, as illustrated in Display 17.6. The same technique works for nodes with any kind of data, but to be concrete, we are using the same type of nodes as in previous subsections. The type definitions are given in Display 17.4. The function declaration for the function we want to define is given below:

```
void insert(IntNodePtr afterMe, int theData);
//Precondition: afterMe points to a node in a linked list.
//Postcondition: A new node containing theData
//has been added after the node pointed to by afterMe.
```

The new node is inserted inside the list in basically the same way a node is added to the head (start) of a list, which we have already discussed. The only difference is that we use the pointer afterMe->link instead of the pointer head. The insertion is done as follows:

```
afterMe->setLink(new IntNode(theData, afterMe->getLink( )));
```

Display 17.6   Inserting in the Middle of a Linked List

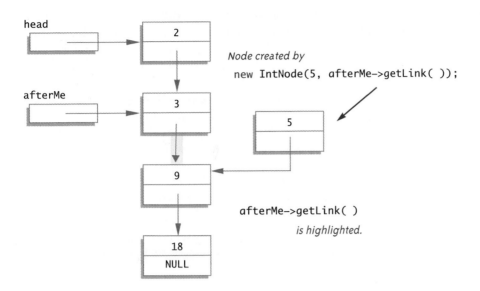

head

2

Node created by
   new IntNode(5, afterMe->getLink( ));

afterMe

3

5

9

afterMe->getLink( )

is highlighted.

18

NULL

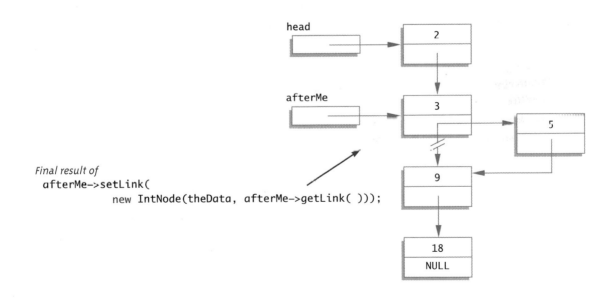

head

2

afterMe

3

5

Final result of
   afterMe->setLink(
         new IntNode(theData, afterMe->getLink( )));

9

18

NULL

The details with `theData` equal to 5 are pictured in Display 17.6, and the final function definition is given in Display 17.4.

insertion at the ends

If you go through the code for the function `insert`, you will see that it works correctly even if the node pointed to by `afterMe` is the last node in the list. However, `insert` will not work for inserting a node at the beginning of a linked list. The function `headInsert` given in Display 17.4 can be used to insert a node at the beginning of a list.

comparison to arrays

By using the function `insert` you can maintain a linked list in numerical or alphabetical order or in some other ordering. You can squeeze a new node into the correct position by simply adjusting two pointers. This is true no matter how long the linked list is or where in the list you want the new data to go. If you instead used an array, much, and in extreme cases all, of the array would have to be copied in order to make room for a new value in the correct spot. Despite the overhead involved in positioning the pointer `afterMe`, inserting into a linked list is frequently more efficient than inserting into an array.

removing a node

Removing a node from a linked list is also quite easy. Display 17.7 illustrates the method. Once the pointers `before` and `discard` have been positioned, all that is required to remove the node is the following statement:

```
before->setLink(discard->getLink( ));
```

This is sufficient to remove the node from the linked list. However, if you are not using this node for something else, you should destroy the node and return the memory it uses for recycling; you can do this with a call to `delete` as follows:

```
delete discard;
```

As we noted in Chapter 10, the memory for dynamic variables is kept in an area of memory known as the *freestore*. Because the freestore is not unlimited, when a dynamic variable (node) is no longer needed by your program, you should return this memory for recycling using the `delete` operator. We include a review of the `delete` operator in the accompanying box.

THE delete OPERATOR

The `delete` operator eliminates a dynamic variable and returns the memory that the dynamic variable occupied to the freestore. The memory can then be reused to create new dynamic variables. For example, the following eliminates the dynamic variable pointed to by the pointer variable p:

```
delete p;
```

After a call to `delete`, the value of the pointer variable, like p above, is undefined.

Display 17.7   Removing a Node

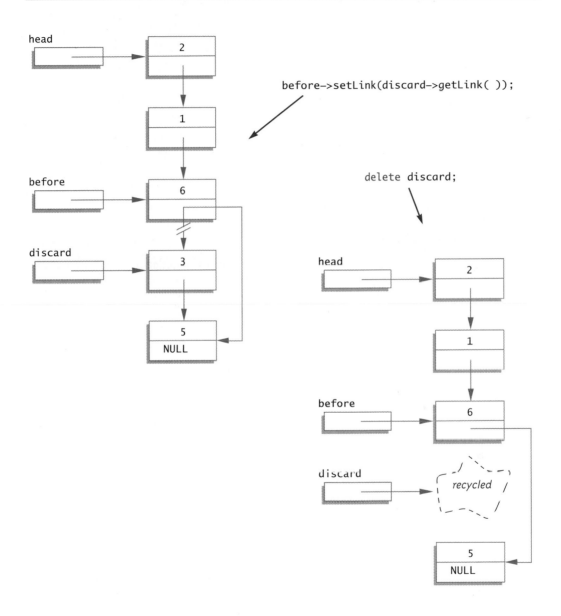

Pitfall

Pitfall   USING THE ASSIGNMENT OPERATOR WITH DYNAMIC DATA STRUCTURES

If head1 and head2 are pointer variables and head1 points to the head node of a linked list, the following will make head2 point to the same head node and hence the same linked list:

```
head2 = head1;
```

However, you must remember that there is only one linked list, not two. If you change the linked list pointed to by head1, then you will also change the linked list pointed to by head2, because they are the same linked lists.

If head1 points to a linked list and you want head2 to point to a second, identical *copy* of this linked list, the above assignment statement will not work. Instead, you must copy the entire linked list node by node.

▧ SEARCHING A LINKED LIST

Next we will design a function to search a linked list in order to locate a particular node. We will use the same node type, called IntNode, that we used in the previous subsections. (The definitions of the node and pointer types are given in Display 17.4.) The function we design will have two arguments: the linked list and the integer we want to locate. The function will return a pointer that points to the first node that contains that integer. If no node contains the integer, the function will return NULL. This way our program can test whether the int is in the list by checking to see if the function returns a pointer value that is not equal to NULL. The function declaration and header comment for our function are as follows:

search
```
IntNodePtr search(IntNodePtr head, int target);
//Precondition: The pointer head points to the head of a
//linked list. The pointer variable in the last node is NULL.
//If the list is empty, then head is NULL.
//Returns a pointer that points to the first node that contains the
//target. If no node contains the target, the function returns NULL.
```

We will use a local pointer variable, called here, to move through the list looking for the target. The only way to move around a linked list, or any other data structure made up of nodes and pointers, is to follow the pointers. Thus, we will start with here pointing to the first node and move the pointer from node to node, following the pointer out of each node. This technique is diagrammed in Display 17.8.

Display 17.8   Searching a Linked List

target is 6

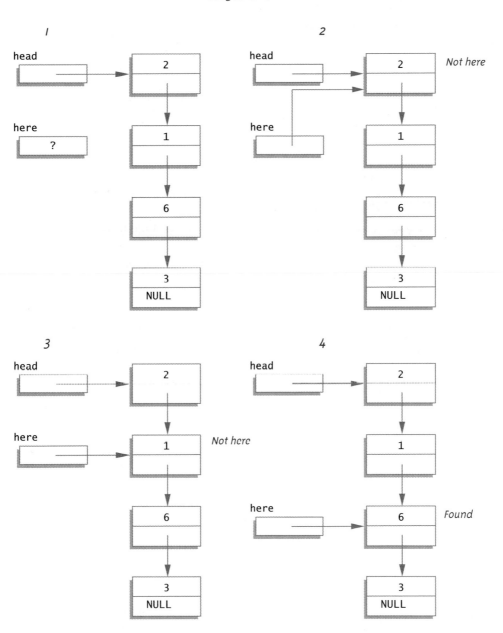

Since empty lists present some minor problems that would clutter our discussion, we will at first assume that the linked list contains at least one node. Later we will come back and make sure the algorithm works for the empty list as well. This search technique yields the following algorithm:

algorithm

Pseudocode for search Function

Make the pointer variable here *point to the head node (that is, first node) of the linked list.*

```
while (here is not pointing to a node containing target
                     and here is not pointing to the last node)
{
    Make here point to the next node in the list.
}

if (the node pointed to by here contains target)
    return here;
else
    return NULL;
```

To move the pointer here to the next node, we must think in terms of the named pointers we have available. The next node is the one pointed to by the pointer member of the node currently pointed to by here. The pointer member of the node currently pointed to by here is given by the expression

```
here->getLink( )
```

To move here to the next node, we want to change here so that it points to the node that is pointed to by the above-named pointer. Hence, the following will move the pointer here to the next node in the list:

```
here = here->getLink( );
```

Putting these pieces together yields the following refinement of the algorithm pseudo-code for the search function:

algorithm
refinement

```
here = head;

while (here->getData( ) != target && here->getLink( ) != NULL)
    here = here->getLink( );

if (here->getData( ) == target)
    return here;
else
    return NULL;
```

Notice the Boolean expression in the while statement. We test to see if here is pointing to the last node by testing to see if the member variable here->getLink( ) is equal to NULL.

We still must go back and take care of the empty list. If we check the previous code, we find that there is a problem with the empty list. If the list is empty, then here is equal to NULL and hence the following expressions are undefined:

```
here->getData( )
here->getLink( )
```

When here is NULL, it is not pointing to any node, so there is no data member or link member. Hence, we make a special case of the empty list.   The complete function definition is given in Display 17.9.

Display 17.9   Function to Locate a Node in a Linked List

FUNCTION DECLARATION

```
IntNodePtr search(IntNodePtr head, int target);
//Precondition: The pointer head points to the head of a
//linked list. The pointer variable in the last node is NULL.
//If the list is empty, then head is NULL.
//Returns a pointer that points to the first node that contains the
//target. If no node contains the target, the function returns NULL.
```

FUNCTION DEFINITION

The definitions of IntNode and IntNodePtr are given in Display 17.4.

```
//Uses cstddef:
IntNodePtr search(IntNodePtr head, int target)
{
        IntNodePtr here = head;

        if (here == NULL) //if empty list
        {
            return NULL;
        }
        else
        {
            while (here->getData( ) != target && here->getLink( ) != NULL)
                here = here->getLink( );

            if (here->getData( ) == target)
                return here;
            else
                return NULL;
        }
}
```

4. Write type definitions for the nodes and pointers in a linked list. Call the node type Node-Type and call the pointer type PointerType. The linked lists will be lists of letters.

5. A linked list is normally referred to via a pointer that points to the first node in the list, but an empty list has no first node. What pointer value is normally used to represent an empty list?

6. Suppose your program contains the following type definitions and pointer variable declarations:

```
struct Node
{
    double data;
    Node *next;
};

typedef Node* Pointer;
Pointer p1, p2;
```

Suppose p1 points to a node of the above type that is in a linked list. Write code that will make p1 point to the next node in this linked list. (The pointer p2 is for the next exercise and has nothing to do with this exercise.)

7. Suppose your program contains type definitions and pointer variable declarations as in Self-Test Exercise 6. Suppose further that p2 points to a node of the above type that is in a linked list and which is not the last node on the list. Write code that will delete the node *after* the node pointed to by p2. After this code is executed, the linked list should be the same, except that there will be one less node in the linked list. (*Hint:* You may want to declare another pointer variable to use.)

8. Suppose your program contains the following type definitions and pointer variable declarations:

```
class Node
{
public:
    Node(double theData, Node* theLink)
            : data(theData), next(theLink){}
    Node* getLink( ) const { return next; }
    double getData( ) const { return data; }
    void setData(double theData) { data = theData; }
    void setLink(Node* pointer) { next = pointer; }
private:
    double data;
    Node *next;
};
```

```
typedef Node* Pointer;
Pointer p1, p2;
```

Suppose p1 points to a node of the above type that is in a linked list. Write code that will make p1 point to the next node in this linked list. (The pointer p2 is for the next exercise and has nothing to do with this exercise.)

9. Suppose your program contains type definitions and pointer variable declarations as in Self-Test Exercise 8. Suppose further that p2 points to a node of the above type that is in a linked list and which is not the last node on the list. Write code that will delete the node *after* the node pointed to by p2. After this code is executed, the linked list should be the same, except that there will be one less node in the linked list. (*Hint:* You may want to declare another pointer variable to use.)

10. Choose an ending to the following statement, and explain:

For a large array and a large list holding the same type objects, inserting a new object at a known location into the middle of a linked list compared to insertion in an array is

a.   more efficient.

b.   less efficient.

c.   about the same.

Example

TEMPLATE VERSION OF LINKED LIST TOOLS

It is a routine matter to convert our type definitions and function definitions to templates so that they will work for linked lists with data of any type T in the nodes. However, there are some details to worry about. The heart of what you need to do is replace the data type of the data in a node (the type int in Display 17.4) by a type parameter T and insert the following at the appropriate locations:

```
template<class T>
```

However, you should also do a few more things to account for the fact that the type T might be a class type. Since the type T might be a class type, a value parameter of type T should be changed to a constant reference parameter and a returned type of type T should have a const added so that it is returned by constant value. (The reason for returning by const value is explained in Chapter 8.)

The final templates with the changes we described are shown in Displays 17.10 and 17.11. It was necessary to do one more change from the simple case of a linked list of integers. Since template typedefs are not implemented in most compilers, we have not been able to use them. This means that on occasion we needed to use the following hard-to-read parameter type specification:

```
Node<T>*&
```

> This is a call-by-reference parameter for a pointer to a node of type Node<T>. Below, we have reproduced a function declaration from Display 17.11 so you can see this parameter type specification in context:
>
> ```
> template<class T>
> void headInsert(Node<T>*& head, const T& theData);
> ```

Display 17.10   Interface File for a Linked List Library (part 1 of 2)

```
1    //This is the header file listtools.h. This contains type definitions and
2    //function declarations for manipulating a linked list to store data of any
3    //type T. The linked list is given as a pointer of type Node<T>* that points
4    //to the head (first) node of the list. The implementation of the functions
5    //is given in the file listtools.cpp.
6    #ifndef LISTTOOLS_H
7    #define LISTTOOLS_H
8    namespace LinkedListSavitch
9    {
10       template<class T>
11       class Node
12       {
13       public:
14           Node(const T& theData, Node<T>* theLink) : data(theData), link(theLink){}
15           Node<T>* getLink( ) const { return link; }
16           const T getData( ) const { return data; }
17           void setData(const T& theData) { data = theData; }
18           void setLink(Node<T>* pointer) { link = pointer; }
19       private:
20           T data;
21           Node<T> *link;
22       };

23       template<class T>
24       void headInsert(Node<T>*& head, const T& theData);
25       //Precondition: The pointer variable head points to
26       //the head of a linked list.
27       //Postcondition: A new node containing theData
28       //has been added at the head of the linked list.

29       template<class T>
30       void insert(Node<T>* afterMe, const T& theData);
31       //Precondition: afterMe points to a node in a linked list.
32       //Postcondition: A new node containing theData
33       //has been added after the node pointed to by afterMe.
```

It would be acceptable to use T as a parameter type where we have used const T&. We used a constant reference parameter because we anticipate that T will frequently be a class type.

Display 17.10   Interface File for Linked List Library *(part 2 of 2)*

```
34
35        template<class T>
36        void deleteNode(Node<T>* before);
37        //Precondition: The pointer before points to a node that has
38        //at least one node after it in the linked list.
39        //Postcondition: The node after the node pointed to by before
40        //has been removed from the linked list and its storage
41        //returned to the freestore.

42        template<class T>
43        void deleteFirstNode(Node<T>*& head);
44        //Precondition: The pointer head points to the first
45        //node in a linked list with at least one node.
46        //Postcondition: The node pointed to by head has been removed
47        //from the linked list and its storage returned to the freestore.

48        template<class T>
49        Node<T>* search(Node<T>* head, const T& target);
50        //Precondition: The pointer head points to the head of a linked list.
51        //The pointer variable in the last node is NULL.
52        //== is defined for type T.
53        //(== is used as the criterion for being equal.)
54        //If the list is empty, then head is NULL.
55        //Returns a pointer that points to the first node that
56        //is equal to the target. If no node equals the target,
57        //then the function returns NULL.
58    }//LinkedListSavitch

59    #endif //LISTTOOLS_H
```

Display 17.11   Implementation File for a Linked List Library *(part 1 of 2)*

```
1     //This is the implementation file listtools.cpp. This file contains
2     //function definitions for the functions declared in listtools.h.
3     #include <cstddef>
4     #include "listtools.h"

5     namespace LinkedListSavitch
6     {
7         template<class T>
8         void headInsert(Node<T>*& head, const T& theData)
9         {
10            head = new Node<T>(theData, head);
11        }
```

Display 17.11   Implementation File for a Linked List Library *(part 2 of 2)*

```
12      template<class T>
13      void insert(Node<T>* afterMe, const T& theData)
14      {
15          afterMe->setLink(new Node<T>(theData, afterMe->getLink( )));
16      }

17      template<class T>
18      void deleteNode(Node<T>* before)
19      {
20          Node<T> *discard;
21          discard = before->getLink( );
22          before->setLink(discard->getLink( ));
23          delete discard;
24      }

25      template<class T>
26      void deleteFirstNode(Node<T>*& head)
27      {
28          Node<T> *discard;
29          discard = head;
30          head = head->getLink( );
31          delete discard;
32      }

33
34      //Uses cstddef:
35      template<class T>
36      Node<T>* search(Node<T>* head, const T& target)
37      {
38          Node<T>* here = head;

39          if (here == NULL) //if empty list
40          {
41              return NULL;
42          }
43          else
44          {
45              while (here->getData( ) != target && here->getLink( ) != NULL)
46                  here = here->getLink( );

47              if (here->getData( ) == target)
48                  return here;
49              else
50                  return NULL;
51          }
52      }
53  }//LinkedListSavitch
```

17.2 **Linked List Applications**

*But many who are first now will be last, and many who are last
now will be first.*

Matthew 19:30

First come first served

A common (and more secular) saying

Linked lists have many applications. This section presents only two small examples of
their use, namely, two class template definitions that each use a linked list as the heart
of their implementation.

Example

A STACK TEMPLATE CLASS

A **stack** is a data structure that retrieves data in the reverse of the order in which the data is stored.   **stack**
Suppose you place the letters 'A', 'B', and then 'C' in a stack. When you take these letters out
of the stack, they will be removed in the order 'C', then 'B', and then 'A'. This use of a stack is
diagrammed in Display 17.12. As shown there, you can think of a stack as a hole in the ground. In
order to get something out of the stack, you must first remove the items on top of the one you
want. For this reason a stack is often called a *last-in/first-out* data structure.   **last-in/
first-out**

STACKS

A stack is a last-in/first-out data structure; that is, data items are retrieved in the opposite order
to which they were placed in the stack.

Stacks are used for many language processing tasks. Chapter 13 discussed how the computer system uses a stack to keep track of C++ function calls. However, here we will only be concerned with
one very simple application. Our goal in this example is to show how you can use the linked list
techniques to implement specific data structures, such as a stack.

The interface for our stack class is given in Display 17.13. This is a template class with a type
parameter T for the type of data stored in the stack. One item stored in the stack is a value of type
T. In the example we present, T is replaced by the type char. However, in most applications an
item stored in the stack is likely to be a struct or class object. Each record (item of type T) that is
stored in the stack is called a **stack frame**, which will explain why we occasionally use stack–   **stack frame**
Frame as an identifier name in the definition of the stack template class. There are two basic

Display 17.12   A Stack

pushing

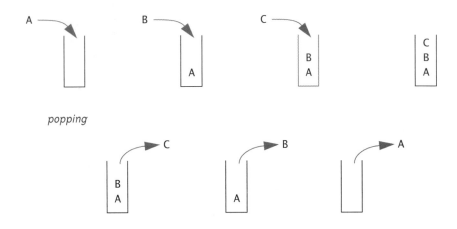

popping

Display 17.13   Interface File for a Stack Template Class *(part 1 of 2)*

```
1   //This is the header file stack.h. This is the interface for the class
2   //Stack, which is a template class for a stack of items of type T.
3   #ifndef STACK_H
4   #define STACK_H
5   namespace StackSavitch
6   {
7       template<class T>
8       class Node
9       {
10      public:
11          Node(T theData, Node<T>* theLink) : data(theData), link(theLink){}
12          Node<T>* getLink( ) const { return link; }
13          const T getData( ) const { return data; }
14          void setData(const T& theData) { data = theData; }
15          void setLink(Node<T>* pointer) { link = pointer; }
16      private:
17          T data;
18          Node<T> *link;
19      };
20      template<class T>
21      class Stack
22      {
```

You might prefer to replace the parameter type T with const T&.

Display 17.13   Interface File for a Stack Template Class *(part 2 of 2)*

```
23        public:
24            Stack( );
25            //Initializes the object to an empty stack.

                                                  ─── Copy constructor
26            Stack(const Stack<T>& aStack); ◄─────

27            Stack<T>& operator =(const Stack<T>& rightSide);

28            virtual ~Stack( );◄───────────── The destructor destroys the stack and
                                              returns all the memory to the freestore.
29            void push(T stackFrame);
30            //Postcondition: stackFrame has been added to the stack.

31            T pop( );
32            //Precondition: The stack is not empty.
33            //Returns the top stack frame and removes that top
34            //stack frame from the stack.

35            bool isEmpty( ) const;
36            //Returns true if the stack is empty. Returns false otherwise.
37        private:
38            Node<T> *top;
39        };

40    }//StackSavitch
41    #endif //STACK_H
```

operations you can perform on a stack: adding an item to the stack and removing an item from the stack. Adding an item is called **pushing** the item onto the stack, and so we called the member function that does this push. Removing an item from a stack is called **popping** the item off the stack, and so we called the member function that does this pop.

pushing

popping

The names push and pop derive from a particular way of visualizing a stack. A stack is analogous to a mechanism that is sometimes used to hold plates in a cafeteria. The mechanism stores plates in a hole in the countertop. There is a spring underneath the plates with its tension adjusted so that only the top plate protrudes above the countertop. If this sort of mechanism were used as a stack data structure, the data would be written on plates (which might violate some health laws, but still makes a good analogy). To add a plate to the stack, you put it on top of the other plates, and the weight of this new plate pushes down the spring. When you remove a plate, the plate below it pops into view.

Display 17.14 shows a simple program that illustrates how the Stack class is used. This program reads a line of text one character at a time and places the characters in a stack. The program then removes the characters one by one and writes them to the screen. Because data is removed from a

Display 17.14 Program Using the Stack Template Class

```
1   //Program to demonstrate use of the Stack template class.
2   #include <iostream>
3   #include "stack.h"
4   #include "stack.cpp"
5   using std::cin;
6   using std::cout;
7   using std::endl;
8   using StackSavitch::Stack;

9   int main( )
10  {
11      char next, ans;

12      do
13      {
14          Stack<char> s;
15          cout << "Enter a line of text:\n";
16          cin.get(next);
17          while (next != '\n')
18          {
19              s.push(next);
20              cin.get(next);
21          }

22          cout << "Written backward that is:\n";
23          while ( ! s.isEmpty( ) )
24              cout << s.pop( );
25          cout << endl;

26          cout << "Again?(y/n): ";          The ignore member of cin is
27          cin >> ans;                       discussed in Chapter 9. It discards
28          cin.ignore(10000, '\n');          input remaining on the line.
29      }while (ans != 'n' && ans != 'N');

30      return 0;
31  }
```

SAMPLE DIALOGUE

```
Enter a line of text:
straw
Written backward that is:
warts
Again?(y/n): y
Enter a line of text:
I love C++
Written backward that is:
++C evol I
Again?(y/n): n
```

stack in the reverse of the order in which it enters the stack, the output shows the line written backward. We have #included the implementation of the Stack class in our application program, as we normally do with template classes. That means we cannot run or even compile our application program until we do the implementation of our Stack class template.

The definitions of the member functions for the template class Stack are given in the implementation file shown in Display 17.15. Our stack class is implemented as a linked list in which the head of the list serves as the top of the stack. The member variable top is a pointer that points to the head of the linked list. The pointer top serves the same purpose as the pointer head did in our previous discussions of linked lists.

PUSH AND POP

Adding a data item to a stack data structure is referred to as *pushing* the data item onto the stack. Removing a data item from a stack is referred to as *popping* the item off the stack.

Display 17.15   Implementation of the Stack Template Class *(part 1 of 2)*

```
1   //This is the implementation file stack.cpp.
2   //This is the implementation of the template class Stack.
3   //The interface for the template class Stack is in the header file stack.h.

4   #include <iostream>
5   #include <cstdlib>
6   #include <cstddef>
7   #include "stack.h"
8   using std::cout;


9   namespace StackSavitch
10  {

11      //Uses cstddef:
12      template<class T>
13      Stack<T>::Stack( ) : top(NULL)
14      {
15          //Intentionally empty
16      }


17      template<class T>
18      Stack<T>::Stack(const Stack<T>& aStack)
19          <The definition of the copy constructor is Self-Test Exercise 12. >
```

Display 17.15   Implementation of the Stack Template Class *(part 2 of 2)*

```
20    template<class T>
21    Stack<T>& Stack<T>::operator =(const Stack<T>& rightSide)
22          <The definition of the overloaded assignment operator is Self-Test Exercise 13.>

23    template<class T>
24    Stack<T>::~Stack( )
25    {
26        T next;
27        while (! isEmpty( ))
28            next = pop( );//pop calls delete.
29    }


31    //Uses cstddef:
32    template<class T>
33    bool Stack<T>::isEmpty( ) const
34    {
35        return (top == NULL);
36    }

37    template<class T>
38    void Stack<T>::push(T stackFrame)
39        <The rest of the definition is Self-Test Exercise 11.>

40    //Uses cstdlib and iostream:
41    template<class T>
42    T Stack<T>::pop( )
43    {
44        if (isEmpty( ))
45        {
46            cout << "Error: popping an empty stack.\n";
47            exit(1);
48        }

49        T result = top->getData( );

50        Node<T> *discard;
51        discard = top;
52        top = top->getLink( );

53        delete discard;

54        return result;
55    }

56  }//StackSavitch
```

Writing the definition of the member function push is Self-Test Exercise 11. However, we have already given the algorithm for this task. The code for the push member function is essentially the same as the function headInsert shown in Display 17.11, except that in the member function push we use a pointer named top in place of a pointer named head.

An empty stack is just an empty linked list, so an empty stack is implemented by setting the pointer top equal to NULL. Once you realize that NULL represents the empty stack, the implementations of the default constructor and of the member function empty are obvious.

empty stack

The definition of the copy constructor is a bit more complicated but does not use any techniques we have not already discussed. The details are left to Self-Test Exercise 12.

The pop member function first checks to see if the stack is empty. If the stack is not empty, it proceeds to remove the top character in the stack. It sets the local variable result equal to the top symbol on the stack as follows:

```
T result = top->getData( );
```

After the data in the top node is saved in the variable result, the pointer top is moved to the next node in the linked list, effectively removing the top node from the list. The pointer top is moved with the statement

```
top = top->getLink( );
```

However, before the pointer top is moved, a temporary pointer, called discard, is positioned so that it points to the node that is about to be removed from the list. The storage for the removed node can then be recycled with the following call to delete:

```
delete discard;
```

Each node that is removed from the linked list by the member function pop has its memory recycled with a call to delete, so all that the destructor needs to do is remove each item from the stack with a call to pop. Each node will then have its memory returned to the freestore for recycling.

destructor

Self-Test Exercises

11. Give the definition of the member function push of the template class Stack described in Displays 17.13 and 17.15.

12. Give the definition of the copy constructor for the template class Stack described in Displays 17.13 and 17.15.

13. Give the definition of the overloaded assignment operator for the template class Stack described in Displays 17.13 and 17.15.

| Example | **A QUEUE TEMPLATE CLASS** |

queue

A stack is a last-in/first-out data structure. Another common data structure is a **queue**, which handles data in a *first-in/first-out* fashion. A queue can be implemented with a linked list in a manner similar to our implementation of the Stack template class. However, a queue needs a pointer at both the head of the list and at the end of the linked list, since action takes place in both locations. It is easier to remove a node from the head of a linked list than from the other end of the linked list. Therefore, our implementation will remove nodes from the head of the list

front

back

(which we will now call the **front** of the list) and will add nodes to the other end of the list, which we will now call the **back** of the list (or the back of the queue).

The definition of the Queue template class is given in Display 17.16. A sample application that uses the class Queue is shown in Display 17.17. The definitions of the member functions are left as Self-Test Exercises (but remember that the answers are given at the end of the chapter should you have any problems filling in the details).

QUEUE

A queue is a first-in/first-out data structure; that is, the data items are removed from the queue in the same order that they were added to the queue.

Display 17.16   Interface File for a Queue Template Class *(part 1 of 2)*

```
 1
 2   //This is the header file queue.h. This is the interface for the class
 3   //Queue, which is a template class for a queue of items of type T.
 4   #ifndef QUEUE_H
 5   #define QUEUE_H
 6   namespace QueueSavitch
 7   {
 8       template<class T>
 9       class Node
10       {
11       public:
12           Node(T theData, Node<T>* theLink) : data(theData), link(theLink){}
13           Node<T>* getLink( ) const { return link; }
14           const T getData( ) const { return data; }
15           void setData(const T& theData) { data = theData; }
16           void setLink(Node<T>* pointer) { link = pointer; }
17       private:
18           T data;
```

This is the same definition of the template class Node that we gave for the stack interface in Display 17.13. See the tip "A Comment on Namespaces" for a discussion of this duplication.

Display 17.16   Interface File for a Queue Template Class (part 2 of 2)

```
19          Node<T> *link;
20       };
```

You might prefer to replace the
parameter type T with const T&.

```
21       template<class T>
22       class Queue
23       {
24       public:
25           Queue( );
26           //Initializes the object to an empty queue.


27           Queue(const Queue<T>& aQueue);
```
—— *Copy constructor*

```
28           Queue<T>& operator =(const Queue<T>& rightSide);

29           virtual ~Queue( );
```
The destructor destroys the
queue and returns all the
memory to the freestore.

```
30
31           void add(T item);
32           //Postcondition: item has been added to the back of the queue.


33           T remove( );
34           //Precondition: The queue is not empty.
35           //Returns the item at the front of the queue
36           //and removes that item from the queue.


37           bool isEmpty( ) const;
38           //Returns true if the queue is empty. Returns false otherwise.
39       private:
40           Node<T> *front;//Points to the head of a linked list.
41                       //Items are removed at the head
42           Node<T> *back;//Points to the node at the other end of the linked list.
43                       //Items are added at this end.
44       };


45   }//QueueSavitch


46   #endif //QUEUE_H
```

Display 17.17   Program Using the Queue Template Class *(part 1 of 2)*

```
1    //Program to demonstrate use of the Queue template class.
2    #include <iostream>
3    #include "queue.h"
4    #include "queue.cpp"
5    using std::cin;
6    using std::cout;
7    using std::endl;
8    using QueueSavitch::Queue;


9    int main( )
10   {
11       char next, ans;                  Contrast this with the similar program using a stack
                                          instead of a queue that we gave in Display 17.14.

12       do
13       {
14           Queue<char> q;
15           cout << "Enter a line of text:\n";
16           cin.get(next);
17           while (next != '\n')
18           {
19               q.add(next);
20               cin.get(next);
21           }


22           cout << "You entered:\n";
23           while ( ! q.isEmpty( ) )
24               cout << q.remove( );
25           cout << endl;

26           cout << "Again?(y/n): ";
27           cin >> ans;
28           cin.ignore(10000, '\n');
29       }while (ans != 'n' && ans != 'N');


30       return 0;
31   }
```

Display 17.17 **Program Using the** Queue **Template Class** *(part 2 of 2)*

SAMPLE DIALOGUE

```
Enter a line of text:
straw
You entered:
straw
Again?(y/n): y
Enter a line of text:
I love C++
You entered:
I love C++
Again?(y/n): n
```

Tip

A COMMENT ON NAMESPACES

Notice that both of the namespaces StackSavitch (Display 17.13) and QueueSavitch (Display 17.16) define a template class called Node. As it turns out, the two definitions of Node are the same, but the point discussed here is the same whether the two definitions are the same or different. C++ does not allow you to define the same identifier twice, even if the two definitions are the same, unless the two names are somehow distinguished. In this case, the two definitions are allowed because they are in two different namespaces. It is even legal to use both the Stack template class and the Queue template class in the same program. However, you should use

```
using StackSavitch::Stack;
using QueueSavitch::Queue;
```

rather than

```
using namespace StackSavitch;
using namespace QueueSavitch;
```

Most compilers will allow either set of using directives if you do not use the identifier Node, but the second set of using directives provides two definitions of the identifier Node and therefore should be avoided.

It would be fine to also use either, but not both, of the following:

```
using StackSavitch::Node;
```

or

```
using QueueSavitch::Node;
```

14. Give the definitions for the default (zero-argument) constructor and the member functions Queue<T>::isEmpty for the template class Queue (Display 17.16).

15. Give the definitions for the member functions Queue<T>::add and Queue<T>::remove for the template class Queue (Display 17.16).

16. Give the definition for the destructor for the template class Queue (Display 17.16).

17. Give the definition for the copy constructor for the template class Queue (Display 17.16).

18. Give the definition for the overloaded assignment operator for the template class Queue (Display 17.16).

FRIEND CLASSES AND SIMILAR ALTERNATIVES

You may have found it a nuisance to use the accessor and mutator functions getLink and setLink in the template class Node (see Display 17.13 or Display 17.16). You might be tempted to avoid the invocations of getLink and setLink by simply making the member variable link of the class Node public instead of private. Before you abandon the principle of making all member variables private, note two things. First, using getLink and setLink is not really any harder for you the programmer than directly accessing the links in the nodes. (However, getLink and setLink do introduce some overhead and so may slightly reduce efficiency.) Second, there is a way to avoid using getLink and setLink and instead directly access the links of nodes without making the link member variable public. Let's explore this second possibility.

friend class

Chapter 8 discussed friend functions. As you will recall, if f is a friend function of a class C, then f is not a member function of C; however, when you write the definition of the function f, you can access private members of C just as you can in the definitions of member functions of C. A class can be a **friend** of another class in the same way that a function can be a friend of a class. If the class F is a friend of the class C, then every member function of the class F is a friend of the class C. Thus, if, for example, the Queue template class were a friend of the Node template class, then the private link member variables would be directly available in the definitions of the member functions of Queue. The details are outlined in Display 17.18.

forward declaration

When one class is a friend of another class, it is typical for the classes to reference each other in their class definitions. This requires that you include a **forward declaration** to the class or class template defined second, as illustrated in Display 17.18. Note that the forward declaration is just the heading of the class or class template definition followed by a semicolon. A complete example using a friend class is given in Section 17.4 (see "A Tree Template Class").

Display 17.18   A Queue Template Class as a Friend of the Node Class *(part 1 of 2)*

```
 1
 2   //This is the header file queue.h. This is the interface for the class
 3   //Queue, which is a template class for a queue of items of type T.
 4   #ifndef QUEUE_H
 5   #define QUEUE_H
 6   namespace QueueSavitch
 7   {
 8       template<class T>
 9       class Queue;
10
11       template<class T>
12       class Node
13       {
14       public:
15           Node(T theData, Node<T>* theLink) : data(theData), link(theLink){}
16           friend class Queue<T>;
17       private:
18           T data;
19           Node<T> *link;
20       };
21       template<class T>
22       class Queue
23       {
24   <The definition of the template class Queue is identical to the one given in Display 17.16. However, the
25   definitions of the member functions will be different from the ones we gave (in the Self-Test Exercises)
26   for the nonfriend version of Queue.>
27   }//QueueSavitch
28   #endif //QUEUE_H
```

A forward declaration. Do not forget the semicolon.

This is an alternate approach to that given in Display 17.16. In this version the Queue template class is a friend of the Node template class.

If Node<T> is only used in the definition of the friend class Queue<T>, there is no need for mutator or accessor functions.

```
29   #include <iostream>
30   #include <cstdlib>
31   #include <cstddef>
32   #include "queue.h"
33   using std::cout;
34   namespace QueueSavitch
35   {
36       template<class T> //Uses cstddef:
37       void Queue<T>::add(T item)
38       {
39           if (isEmpty( ))
```

The implementation file would contain these definitions and the definitions of the other member functions similarly modified to allow access by name to the link and data member variables of the nodes.

Display 17.18   A Queue Template Class as a Friend of the Node Class *(part 2 of 2)*

```
40                  front = back = new Node<T>(item, NULL);
41             else
42             {
43                 back->link = new Node<T>(item, NULL);
44                 back = back->link;
45             }
46         }
```
If efficiency is a major issue, you might want to use
(front == NULL) instead of (isEmpty( ).

```
47         template<class T> //Uses cstdlib and iostream:
48         T Queue<T>::remove( )
49         {
50             if (isEmpty( ))
51             {
52                 cout << "Error: Removing an item from an empty queue.\n";
53                 exit(1);
54             }

55             T result = front->data;
```
Contrast these implementations with the ones given as the
answer to Self-Test Exercise 15.

```
56             Node<T> *discard;
57             discard = front;
58             front = front->link;
59             if (front == NULL) //if you removed the last node
60                 back = NULL;

61             delete discard;
62             return result;
63         }
64     }//QueueSavitch
```

Two approaches that serve pretty much the same purpose as friend classes and which can be used in pretty much the same way with classes and template classes such as Node and Queue are (1) using protected or private inheritance to derive Queue from Node, and (2) giving the definition of Node within the definition of Queue, so that Node is a local class (template) definition. (Protected inheritance is discussed in Chapter 14, and classes defined locally within a class are discussed in Chapter 7.)

17.3 Iterators

*The white rabbit put on his spectacles. "Where shall I begin,
please your Majesty?" he asked.
"Begin at the beginning," the King said, very gravely, "And go
on till you come to the end: then stop."*

Lewis Carroll, *Alice in Wonderland*

An important notion in data structures is that of an iterator. An **iterator** is a construct (typically an object of some iterator class) that allows you to cycle through the data items stored in a data structure so that you can perform whatever action you want on each data item.

iterator

ITERATOR

An iterator is a construct (typically an object of some iterator class) that allows you to cycle through the data items stored in a data structure so that you can perform whatever action you want on each data item in the data structure.

POINTERS AS ITERATORS

The basic ideas, and in fact the prototypical model, for iterators can easily be seen in the context of linked lists. A linked list is one of the prototypical data structures, and a pointer is a prototypical example of an iterator. You can use a pointer as an iterator by moving through the linked list one node at a time starting at the head of the list and cycling through all the nodes in the list. The general outline is as follows:

```
Node_Type *iterator;
for (iterator = Head; iterator != NULL; iterator = iterator->Link)
    Do whatever you want with the node pointed to by iterator;
```

where *Head* is a pointer to the head node of the linked list and *Link* is the name of the member variable of a node that points to the next node in the list.

For example, to output the data in all the nodes in a linked list of the kind we discussed in Section 17.1, you could use the following:

```
IntNode *iterator;
for(iterator = head; iterator != NULL; iterator = iterator->getLink( ))
    cout << (iterator->getData( ));
```

The definition of `IntNode` is given in Display 17.4.

Note that you test to see if two pointers are pointing to the same node by comparing them with the equal operator, `==`. A pointer is a memory address. If two pointer variables contain the same memory address, then they compare as equal and they point to the same node. Similarly, you can use `!=` to compare two pointers to see if they do not point to the same node.

■ ITERATOR CLASSES

iterator class

An **iterator class** is a more versatile and more general notion than a pointer. It very often does have a pointer member variable as the heart of its data, as in the next programming example, but that is not required. For example, the heart of the iterator might be an array index. An iterator class has functions and overloaded operators that allow you to use pointer syntax with objects of the iterator class no matter what you use for the underlying data structure, node type, or basic location marker (pointer or array index or whatever). Moreover, it provides a general framework that can be used across a wide range of data structures.

An iterator class typically has the following overloaded operators:

++ Overloaded increment operator, which advances the iterator to the next item.

−− Overloaded decrement operator, which moves the iterator to the previous item.

== Overloaded equality operator to compare two iterators and return `true` if they both point to the same item.

!= Overloaded not-equal operator to compare two iterators and return `true` if they do not point to the same item.

*   Overloaded dereferencing operator that gives access to one item. (Often it returns a reference to allow both read and write access.)

When thinking of this list of operators you can use a linked list as a concrete example. In that case, remember that the items in the list are the data in the list, not the entire nodes and not the pointer members of the nodes. Everything but the data items is implementation detail that is meant to be hidden from the programmer who uses the iterator and data structure classes.

An iterator is used in conjunction with some particular structure class that stores data items of some type. The data structure class normally has the following member functions that provide iterators for objects of that class:

begin( ): A member function that takes no argument and returns an iterator that is located at ("points to") the first item in the data structure.

end( ): A member function that takes no argument and returns an iterator that can be used to test for having cycled through all items in the data structure. If `i` is an iterator and `i` has been advanced *beyond* the last item in the data structure, then `i` should equal `end( )`.

Using an iterator, you can cycle through the items in a data structure ds as follows:

```
for (i = ds.begin( ); i != ds.end( ); i++)
    process *i //*i is the current data item.
```

where i is an iterator. Chapter 19 discusses iterators with a few more items and refinements than these, but these will do for an introduction.

This abstract discussion will not come alive until we give an example. So, let's walk through an example.

ITERATOR CLASS

An iterator class typically has the following overloaded operators: ++, move to next item; −−, move to previous item; ==, overloaded equality; !=, overloaded not-equal operator; and *, overloaded dereferencing operator that gives access to one data item.

The data structure corresponding to an iterator class typically has the following two member functions: begin( ), which returns an iterator that is located at ("points to") the first item in the data structure; and end( ), which returns an iterator that can be used to test for having cycled through all items in the data structure. If i is an iterator and i has been advanced *beyond* the last item in the data structure, then i should equal end( ).

Using an iterator, you can cycle through the items in a data structure ds as follows:

```
for (i = ds.begin( ); i != ds.end( ); i++)
    process *i //*i is the current data item.
```

Example

AN ITERATOR CLASS

Display 17.19 contains the definition of an iterator class that can be used for data structures, such as a stack or queue, that are based on a linked list. We have placed the node class and the iterator class into a namespace of their own. This makes sense, since the iterator is intimately related to the node class and since any class that uses this node class can also use the iterator class. This iterator class does not have a decrement operator, because a definition of a decrement operator depends on the details of the linked list and does not depend solely on the type Node<T>. (There is nothing wrong with having the definition of the iterator depend on the underlying linked list. We have just decided to avoid this complication.)

As you can see, the template class ListIterator is essentially a pointer wrapped in a class so that it can have the needed member operators. The definitions of the overload operators are straightforward and in fact so short that we have defined all of them as inline functions. Note that

Display 17.19   An Iterator Class for Linked Lists *(part 1 of 2)*

```
1    //This is the header file iterator.h. This is the interface for the class
2    //ListIterator, which is a template class for an iterator to use with linked
3    //lists of items of type T. This file also contains the node type for a
4    //linked list.
5    #ifndef ITERATOR_H
6    #define ITERATOR_H

7    namespace ListNodeSavitch
8    {
9        template<class T>
10       class Node
11       {
12       public:
13           Node(T theData, Node<T>* theLink) : data(theData), link(theLink){}
14           Node<T>* getLink( ) const { return link; }
15           const T getData( ) const { return data; }
16           void setData(const T& theData) { data = theData; }
17           void setLink(Node<T>* pointer) { link = pointer; }
18       private:
19           T data;
20           Node<T> *link;
21       };
22
23       template<class T>
24       class ListIterator
25       {
26       public:
27           ListIterator( ) : current(NULL) {}

28           ListIterator(Node<T>* initial) : current(initial) {}

29           const T operator *( ) const { return current->getData( ); }
30           //Precondition: Not equal to the default constructor object;
31           //that is, current != NULL.

32           ListIterator operator ++( ) //Prefix form
33           {
34               current = current->getLink( );
35               return *this;
36           }
37           ListIterator operator ++(int) //Postfix form
38           {
39               ListIterator startVersion(current);
40               current = current->getLink( );
```

Note that the dereferencing operator * produces the data member of the node, not the entire node. This version does not allow you to change the data in the node.

Display 17.19   An Iterator Class for Linked Lists *(part 2 of 2)*

```
41                    return startVersion;
42              }
43              bool operator ==(const ListIterator& rightSide) const
44              { return (current == rightSide.current); }

45              bool operator !=(const ListIterator& rightSide) const
46              { return (current != rightSide.current); }

47              //The default assignment operator and copy constructor
48              //should work correctly for ListIterator.
49          private:
50              Node<T> *current;
51          };

52  }//ListNodeSavitch

53  #endif //ITERATOR_H
```

the dereferencing operator, *, produces the data member variable of the node pointed to. Only the data member variable is data. The pointer member variable in a node is part of the implementation detail that the user programmer should not need to be concerned with.

You can use the ListIterator class as an iterator for any class based on a linked list that uses the template class Node. As an example, we have rewritten the template class Queue so that it has iterator facilities. The interface for the template class Queue is given in Display 17.20. This definition of the Queue template is the same as our previous version (Display 17.16) except that we have added a type definition as well as the following two member functions:

```
Iterator begin( ) const { return Iterator(front); }
Iterator end( ) const { return Iterator( ); }
//The end iterator has end( ).current == NULL.
```

Let's discuss the member functions first.

The member function begin( ) returns an iterator located at ("pointing to") the front node of the queue, which is the head node of the underlying linked list. Each application of the increment operator, ++, moves the iterator to the next node. Thus, you can move through the nodes, and hence the data, in a queue named q as follows:

```
for (i = q.begin( ); Stopping_Condition; i++)
    process *i //*i is the current data item.
```

Display 17.20   Interface File for a Queue with Iterators Template Class

```
1  //This is the header file queue.h. This is the interface for the class
2  //Queue, which is a template class for a queue of items of type T, including
3  //iterators.
4  #ifndef QUEUE_H
5  #define QUEUE_H
6  #include "iterator.h"
7  using namespace ListNodeSavitch;
```

The definitions of Node<T> and
ListIterator<T> are in the namespace
ListNodeSavitch in the file iterator.h.

```
8  namespace QueueSavitch
9  {
10     template<class T>
11     class Queue
12     {
13     public:
14         typedef ListIterator<T> Iterator;

15         Queue( );
16         Queue(const Queue<T>& aQueue);
17         Queue<T>& operator =(const Queue<T>& rightSide);
18         virtual ~Queue( );
19         void add(T item);
20         T remove( );
21         bool isEmpty( ) const;

22         Iterator begin( ) const { return Iterator(front); }
23         Iterator end( ) const { return Iterator( ); }
24         //The end iterator has end( ).current == NULL.
25         //Note that you cannot dereference the end iterator.
26     private:
27         Node<T> *front;//Points to the head of a linked list.
28                       //Items are removed at the head
29         Node<T> *back;//Points to the node at the other end of the linked
30                       //list.
31                       //Items are added at this end.
32     };

33  }//QueueSavitch

34  #endif //QUEUE_H
```

where i is a variable of the iterator type.

The member function end( ) returns an iterator whose current member variable is NULL. Thus, when the iterator i has passed the last node, the Boolean expression

```
i != q.end( )
```

changes from true to false. This is the desired *Stopping_Condition*. This queue class and iterator class allow you to cycle through the data in the queue in the way we outlined for an iterator:

```
for (i = q.begin( ); i != q.end( ); i++)
    process *i //*i is the current data item.
```

Note that i is not equal to q.end( ) when i is at the last node. The iterator i is not equal to q.end( ) until i has been advanced one position past the last node. To remember this detail, think of q.end( ) as being an end marker like NULL; in this case it is essentially a version of NULL. A sample program that uses such a for loop is shown in Display 17.21.

Notice the type definition in our new queue template class:

typedef

```
typedef ListIterator<T> Iterator;
```

This typedef is not absolutely necessary. You can always use ListIterator<T> instead of the type name Iterator. However, this type definition does make for cleaner code. With this type definition, an iterator for the class Queue<char> is written

```
Queue<char>::Iterator i;
```

This makes it clear with which class the iterator is meant to be used.

The implementation of our new template class Queue is given in Display 17.22. Since the only member functions we added to this new Queue class are defined inline, the implementation file contains nothing really new, but we include the implementation file to show how it is laid out and to show which directives it would include.

Display 17.21   Program Using the Queue Template Class with Iterators *(part 1 of 2)*

```
1   //Program to demonstrate use of the Queue template class with iterators.
2   #include <iostream>
3   #include "queue.h"//not needed
4   #include "queue.cpp"
5   #include "iterator.h"//not needed
6   using std::cin;
7   using std::cout;
8   using std::endl;
9   using namespace QueueSavitch;

10  int main( )
11  {
12      char next, ans;
13      do
14      {
15          Queue<char> q;
16          cout << "Enter a line of text:\n";
17          cin.get(next);
18          while (next != '\n')
19          {
20              q.add(next);
21              cin.get(next);
22          }
23          cout << "You entered:\n";
24          Queue<char>::Iterator i;

25          for (i = q.begin( ); i != q.end( ); i++)
26              cout << *i;
27          cout << endl;

28          cout << "Again?(y/n): ";
29          cin >> ans;
30          cin.ignore(10000, '\n');
31      }while (ans != 'n' && ans != 'N');

32      return 0;
33  }
34
```

Even though they are not needed, many programmers prefer to include these include directives for the sake of documentation.

If your compiler is unhappy with Queue<char>::Iterator i; try
using namespace ListNodeSavitch; ListIterator<char> i;

Display 17.21   Program Using the Queue Template Class with Iterators *(part 2 of 2)*

SAMPLE DIALOGUE

```
Enter a line of text:
Where shall I begin?
You entered:
Where shall I begin?
Again?(y/n): y
Enter a line of text:
Begin at the beginning
You entered:
Begin at the beginning
Again?(y/n): n
```

Display 17.22   Implementation File for a Queue with Iterators Template Class *(part 1 of 2)*

```
1    //This is the file queue.cpp. This is the implementation of the template
2    //class Queue. The interface for the template class Queue is in the header
3    //file queue.h.
4    #include <iostream>
5    #include <cstdlib>
6    #include <cstddef>
7    #include "queue.h"
8    using std::cout;

9    using namespace ListNodeSavitch;
10   namespace QueueSavitch
11   {
12       template<class T>
13       Queue<T>::Queue( ) : front(NULL), back(NULL)
14           <The rest of the definition is given in the answer to Self-Test Exercise 14.>

15       template<class T>
16       Queue<T>::Queue(const Queue<T>& aQueue)
17           <The rest of the definition is given in the answer to Self-Test Exercise 17.>

18       template<class T>
19       Queue<T>& Queue<T>::operator =(const Queue<T>& rightSide)
20           <The rest of the definition is given in the answer to Self-Test Exercise 18.>
```

The member function definitions are the same as in the previous version of the Queue template. This is given to show the file layout and use of namespaces.

Display 17.22   Implementation File for a Queue with Iterators Template Class *(part 2 of 2)*

```
21        template<class T>
22        Queue<T>::~Queue( )
23            <The rest of the definition is given in the answer to Self-Test Exercise 16.>

24        template<class T>
25        bool Queue<T>::isEmpty( ) const
26            <The rest of the definition is given in the answer to Self-Test Exercise 14.>

27        template<class T>
28        void Queue<T>::add(T item)
29            <The rest of the definition is given in the answer to Self-Test Exercise 15.>

30        template<class T>
31        T Queue<T>::remove( )
32            <The rest of the definition is given in the answer to Self-Test Exercise 15.>
33    }//QueueSavitch
34    #endif //QUEUE_H
```

Self-Test Exercises

19. Write the definition of the template function inQ shown below. Use iterators. Use the definition of Queue given in Display 17.20.

```
template<class T>
bool inQ(Queue<T> q, T target);
//Returns true if target is in the queue q;
//otherwise, returns false.
```

17.4   Trees

I think that I shall never see a data structure as useful as a tree.

Anonymous

A detailed treatment of trees is beyond the scope of this chapter. The goal of this chapter is to teach you the basic techniques for constructing and manipulating data structures based on nodes and pointers. The linked list served as a good example for our discussion. However, there is one detail about the nodes in a linked list that is quite restricted: They have only one pointer member variable to point to another node. A tree node has two (and in some applications more than two) member variables for pointers to other nodes. Moreover, trees are a very important and widely used data structure. So, we will briefly outline the general techniques used to construct and manipulate trees.

This section uses recursion, which is covered in Chapter 13.

■ TREE PROPERTIES

A tree is a data structure that is structured as shown in Display 17.23. Note that a tree must have the sort of structure illustrated in Display 17.23. In particular, in a tree you can reach any node from the top (root) node by some path that follows the links (pointers). Note that there are no cycles in a tree. If you follow the pointers, you eventually get to an "end." A definition for a node class for this sort of tree of ints is also shown in Display 17.23. Note that each node has two links (two pointers) coming from it. This sort of tree is called a **binary tree** because it has exactly two link member variables. There are other kinds of trees with different numbers of link member variables, but the binary tree is the most common case.

binary tree

The pointer named root serves a purpose similar to that of the pointer head in a linked list (Display 17.1). The node pointed to by the root pointer is called the **root node**. Note that the pointer root is not itself the root node, but rather points to the root node. Any node in the tree can be reached from the root node by following the links.

root node

The term *tree* may seem like a misnomer. The root is at the top of the tree and the branching structure looks more like a root branching structure than a true tree branching structure. The secret to the terminology is to turn the picture (Display 17.23) upside down. The picture then does resemble the branching structure of a tree and the root node is where the tree's root would begin. The nodes at the ends of the branches with both link member variables set to NULL are known as **leaf nodes**, a terminology that may now make some sense.

leaf node

By analogy to an empty linked list, an empty tree is denoted by setting the pointer variable root equal to NULL.

empty tree

Note that a tree has a recursive structure. Each tree has two subtrees whose root nodes are the nodes pointed to by the leftLink and rightLink of the root node. These two subtrees are circled in Display 17.23. This natural recursive structure make trees particularly amenable to recursive algorithms. For example, consider the task of searching the tree in such a way that you visit each node and do something with the data in the node (such as writing it to the screen). The general plan of attack is as follows:

Preorder Processing

preorder

1. Process the data in the root node.

2. Process the left subtree.

3. Process the right subtree.

Display 17.23   A Binary Tree

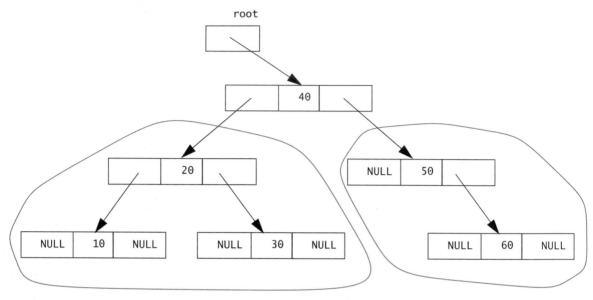

Left subtree

Right subtree

```
class IntTreeNode
{
public:
    IntTreeNode(int theData, IntTreeNode* left, IntTreeNode* right)
        : data(theData), leftLink(left), rightLink(right){}
private:
    int data;
    IntTreeNode *leftLink;
    IntTreeNode *rightLink;
};


IntTreeNode *root;
```

You can obtain a number of variants on this search process by varying the order of these three steps. Two more versions are given below.

In-order Processing

1. Process the left subtree.
2. Process the data in the root node.
3. Process the right subtree.

Postorder Processing

1. Process the left subtree.
2. Process the right subtree.
3. Process the data in the root node.

The tree in Display 17.23 has stored each number in the tree in a special way known as the **Binary Search Tree Storage Rule**. The rule is given in the accompanying box. A tree that satisfies the Binary Search Tree Storage Rule is referred to as a **binary search tree**.

BINARY SEARCH TREE STORAGE RULE

1. All the values in the left subtree are less than the value in the root node.

2. All the values in the right subtree are greater than or equal to the value in the root node.

3. This rule applies recursively to each of the two subtrees.

(The base case for the recursion is an empty tree, which is always considered to satisfy the rule.)

Note that if a tree satisfies the Binary Search Tree Storage Rule and you output the values using the in-order processing method, the numbers will be output in order from smallest to largest.

For trees that follow the Binary Search Tree Storage Rule and which are short and fat rather than long and thin, values can be very quickly retrieved from the tree using a binary search algorithm that is similar in spirit to the binary search algorithm presented in Display 13.5. The topic of searching and maintaining a binary storage tree to realize this efficiency is a large topic that goes beyond what we have room for here.

Example

A TREE TEMPLATE CLASS

Display 17.24 contains the definition of a template class for a binary search tree. In this example, we have made the SearchTree class a friend class of the TreeNode class. This allows us to access the node member variables by name in the definitions of the tree class member variables. The implementation of this SearchTree class is given in Display 17.25, and a demonstration program is given in Display 17.26.

This template class is designed to give you the flavor of tree processing, but it is not really a complete example. A real class would have more member functions. In particular, a real tree class would have a copy constructor and an overloaded assignment operator. We have omitted these to conserve space.

There are some things to observe about the function definitions in the class SearchTree. The functions insert and inTree are overloaded. The single-argument versions are the ones we need. However, the clearest algorithms are recursive, and the recursive algorithms require one additional parameter for the root of a subtree. Therefore, we defined private helping functions with two arguments for each of these functions and implemented the recursive algorithms in the two-parameter function. The single-parameter function then simply makes a call to the two-parameter version with the subtree root parameter set equal to the root of the entire tree. A similar situation holds for the overloaded member function name inorderShow. The function delete-Subtree serves a similar purpose for the destructor function.

Finally, it is important to note that the insert function builds a tree that satisfies the Binary Search Tree Storage Rule. Since insert is the only function available to build trees for this template class, objects of this tree template class will always satisfy the Binary Search Tree Storage Rule. The function inTree uses the fact that the tree satisfies the Binary Search Tree Storage Rule in its algorithms. This makes searching the tree very efficient. Of course this means that the < operator must be defined for the type T of data stored in the tree. To make things work correctly, the operation < should satisfy the following rules when applied to values of type T:

- *Transitivity:* $a < b$ and $b < c$ implies $a < c$.
- *Antisymmetry:* If a and b are not equal, then either $a < b$ or $b < a$, but not both.
- *Irreflexive:* You never have $a < a$.

Most natural orders satisfy these rules.[1]

---

[1] Note that you normally have both a "less-than-or-equal" relation and a "less-than" relation. These rules apply to only the "less-than" relation. You can actually make do with an even weaker notion of ordering known as a *strict weak ordering* which is defined in Chapter 19, but that is more detail than you need for normally encountered orderings.

Display 17.24   Interface File for a Tree Template Class

```
1   //Header file tree.h. The only way to insert data in a tree is with the
2   //insert function. So, the tree satisfies the Binary Search Tree Storage
3   //Rule. The function inTree depends on this. < must be defined and give a
4   //well-behaved ordering to the type T.
5   #ifndef TREE_H
6   #define TREE_H
7   namespace TreeSavitch
8   {
9       template<class T>
10      class SearchTree; //forward declaration

11      template<class T>
12      class TreeNode
13      {
14      public:
15          TreeNode( ) : root(NULL){}
16          TreeNode(T theData, TreeNode<T>* left, TreeNode<T>* right)
17              : data(theData), leftLink(left), rightLink(right){}
18          friend class SearchTree<T>;
19      private:
20          T data;
21          TreeNode<T> *leftLink;
22          TreeNode<T> *rightLink;
23      };

24
25      template<class T>
26      class SearchTree
27      {
28      public:
29          SearchTree( ) . root(NULL)[]
30          virtual ~SearchTree( );
31          void insert(T item); //Adds item to the tree.
32          bool inTree(T item) const;
33          void inorderShow( ) const;
34      private:
35          void insert(T item, TreeNode<T>*& subTreeRoot);
36          bool inTree(T item, TreeNode<T>* subTreeRoot) const;
37          void deleteSubtree(TreeNode<T>*& subTreeRoot);
38          void inorderShow(TreeNode<T>* subTreeRoot) const;
39          TreeNode<T> *root;
40      };
41  } //TreeSavitch

42  #endif
```

The SearchTree template class should have a copy constructor, an overloading of the assignment operator, and other member functions. However, we have omitted these functions to keep this example short. A real template class would contain more member functions and overloaded operators.

Display 17.25   Implementation File for a Tree Template Class *(part 1 of 2)*

```
1    //This is the implementation file tree.cpp. This is the implementation for
2    //the template class SearchTree. The interface is in the file tree.h.
3    namespace TreeSavitch
4    {
5        template<class T>
6        void SearchTree<T>::insert(T item, TreeNode<T>*& subTreeRoot)
7        {
8            if (subTreeRoot == NULL)
9                subTreeRoot = new TreeNode<T>(item, NULL, NULL);
10           else if (item < subTreeRoot->data)
11               insert(item, subTreeRoot->leftLink);
12           else //item >= subTreeRoot->data
13               insert(item, subTreeRoot->rightLink);
14       }
15       template<class T>
16       void SearchTree<T>::insert(T item)
17       {
18           insert(item, root);
19       }

20       template<class T>
21       bool SearchTree<T>::inTree(T item, TreeNode<T>* subTreeRoot) const
22       {
23           if (subTreeRoot == NULL)
24               return false;
25           else if (subTreeRoot->data == item)
26               return true;
27           else if (item < subTreeRoot->data)
28               return inTree(item, subTreeRoot->leftLink);
29           else //item >= link->data
30               return inTree(item, subTreeRoot->rightLink);
31       }

32       template<class T>
33       bool SearchTree<T>::inTree(T item) const
34       {
35           return inTree(item, root);
36       }
37       template<class T> //uses iostream:
38       void SearchTree<T>::inorderShow(TreeNode<T>* subTreeRoot) const
39       {
40           if (subTreeRoot != NULL)
41           {
42               inorderShow(subTreeRoot->leftLink);
43               cout << subTreeRoot->data << " ";
```

If all data is entered using the function insert, the tree will satisfy the Binary Search Tree Storage Rule. (note beside lines 12–14)

The function inTree uses a binary search algorithm that is a variant of the one given in Display 13.5. (note beside lines 23–26)

Uses in-order traversal of the tree. (note beside line 43)

Display 17.25   **Implementation File for a Tree Template Class** *(part 2 of 2)*

```
44                inorderShow(subTreeRoot->rightLink);
45            }
46        }

47        template<class T> //uses iostream:
48        void SearchTree<T>::inorderShow( ) const
49        {
50            inorderShow(root);
51        }

52        template<class T>
53        void SearchTree<T>::deleteSubtree(TreeNode<T>*& subTreeRoot)
54        {
55            if (subTreeRoot != NULL)
56            {
57                deleteSubtree(subTreeRoot->leftLink);

58                deleteSubtree(subTreeRoot->rightlink);

59                //subTreeRoot now points to a one node tree.
60                delete subTreeRoot;
61                subTreeRoot = NULL;
62            }
63        }

64        template<class T>
65        SearchTree<T>::~SearchTree( )
66        {
67            deleteSubtree(root);
68        }
69    }//TreeSavitch
```

Uses postorder traversal of the tree.

Self-Test Exercises

20. Define the following member functions, which could be added to the class SearchTree in Display 17.24. These functions display the data encountered in a preorder and postorder traversal of the tree, respectively. Define a private helping function for each function, as we did for SearchTree<T>::inorderShow.

```
void SearchTree<T>::preorderShow( ) const
void SearchTree<T>::postorderShow( ) const
```

Display 17.26   Demonstration Program for the Tree Template Class

```
1   //Demonstration program for the Tree template class.
2   #include <iostream>
3   #include "tree.h"
4   #include "tree.cpp"
5   using std::cout;
6   using std::cin;
7   using std::endl;
8   using TreeSavitch::SearchTree;


9   int main( )
10  {
11      SearchTree<int> t;


12      cout << "Enter a list of nonnegative integers.\n"
13          << "Place a negative integer at the end.\n";
14      int next;
15      cin >> next;
16      while (next >= 0)
17      {
18          t.insert(next);
19          cin >> next;
20      }


21      cout << "In sorted order: \n";
22      t.inorderShow( );
23      cout << endl;


24      return 0;
25  }
```

SAMPLE DIALOGUE

```
Enter a list of nonnegative integers.
Place a negative integer at the end.
40 30 20 10 11 22 33 44 −1
In sorted order:
10 11 20 22 30 33 40 44
```

Chapter Summary

- A node is a struct or class object that has one or more member variables that are pointer variables. These nodes can be connected by their member pointer variables to produce data structures that can grow and shrink in size while your program is running.

- A linked list is a list of nodes in which each node contains a pointer to the next node in the list.

- The end of a linked list (or other linked data structure) is indicated by setting the pointer member variable equal to NULL.

- A stack is a first-in/last-out data structure. A queue is a first-in/first-out data structure. Both can be implemented using a linked list.

- An iterator is a construct (typically an object of some iterator class) that allows you to cycle through data items stored in a data structure.

- A tree is a data structure whose nodes have two (or more) member variables for pointers to other nodes. If a tree satisfies the Binary Search Tree Storage Rule, then a function can be designed to rapidly find data in the tree.

ANSWERS TO SELF-TEST EXERCISES

1. Sally
   Sally
   18
   18

   Note that (*head).name and head->name mean the same thing. Similarly, (*head).number and head->number mean the same thing.

2. The best answer is

   ```
   head->next = NULL;
   ```

   However, the following is also correct:

   ```
   (*head).next = NULL;
   ```

3. head->item = "Wilbur's brother Orville";

4. ```
   class NodeType
   {
   public:
       NodeType( ){}
       NodeType(char theData, NodeType* theLink)
               : data(theData), link(theLink){}
       NodeType* getLink( ) const { return link; }
       char getData( ) const { return data; }
       void setData(char theData) { data = theData; }
   ```
   ```

```
      void setLink(NodeType* pointer) { link = pointer; }
  private:
      char data;
      NodeType *link;
  };

  typedef NodeType* PointerType;
```

5. The value NULL is used to indicate an empty list.

6. `p1 = p1-> next;`

7.
```
Pointer discard;
discard = p2->next;//discard points to the node to be deleted.
p2->next = discard->next;
```

This is sufficient to delete the node from the linked list. However, if you are not using this node for something else, you should destroy the node with a call to `delete` as follows:

```
delete discard;
```

8. `p1 = p1->getLink( );`

9.
```
Pointer discard;
discard = p2->getLink( );//points to node to be deleted.
p2->setLink(discard->getLink( ));
```

This is sufficient to delete the node from the linked list. However, if you are not using this node for something else, you should destroy the node with a call to `delete` as follows:

```
delete discard;
```

10. a. Inserting a new item at a known location into a large linked list is more efficient than inserting into a large array. If you are inserting into a list, you have about five operations, most of which are pointer assignments, regardless of the list size. If you insert into an array, on the average you have to move about half the array entries to insert a data item.

    For small lists, the answer is c, about the same.

11. Note that this function is essentially the same as `headInsert` in Display 17.11.

```
template<class T>
void Stack<T>::push(T stackFrame)
{
    top = new Node<T>(stackFrame, top);
}
```

12.
```
//Uses cstddef:
template<class T>
Stack<T>::Stack(const Stack<T>& aStack)
{
    if (aStack.isEmpty( ))
```

```cpp
            top = NULL;
    else
    {
        Node<T> *temp = aStack.top;//temp moves
                //through the nodes from top to bottom of aStack.
        Node<T> *end;//Points to end of the new stack.

        end = new Node<T>(temp->getData( ), NULL);
        top = end;
        //First node created and filled with data.
        //New nodes are now added AFTER this first node.

        temp = temp->getLink( );//move temp to second node
                    //or NULL if there is no second node.
        while (temp != NULL)
        {
            end->setLink(
                    new Node<T>(temp->getData( ), NULL));
            temp = temp->getLink( );
            end = end->getLink( );
        }
        //end->link == NULL;
    }
}

13. template<class T>
    Stack<T>& Stack<T>::operator =(const Stack<T>& rightSide)
    {
        if (top == rightSide.top) //if two stacks are the same
            return *this;
        else //send left side back to freestore
        {
            T next;
            while (! isEmpty( ))
                next = pop( );//remove calls delete.
        }

        if (rightSide.isEmpty())
        {
            top = NULL;
            return *this;
        }
        else
        {
            Node<T> *temp = rightSide.top;//temp moves through
                    //the nodes from front top to bottom of rightSide.

            Node<T> *end;//Points to end of the left-side stack.
            end = new Node<T>(temp->getData( ), NULL);
```

```
            top = end;;
            //First node created and filled with data.
            //New nodes are now added AFTER this first node.

            temp = temp->getLink();//Move temp to second node
                    //or set to NULL if there is no second node.

            while (temp != NULL)
            {
                end->setLink(
                        new Node<T>(temp->getData(), NULL));
                temp = temp->getLink();
                end = end->getLink();
            }
            //end->link == NULL;

            return *this;
        }
    }
```

14. The following should be placed in the namespace QueueSavitch:

```
    //Uses cstddef:
    template<class T>
    Queue<T>::Queue( ) : front(NULL), back(NULL)
    {
        //Intentionally empty.
    }

    //Uses cstddef:
    template<class T>
    bool Queue<T>::isEmpty( ) const
    {
        return (back == NULL);//front == NULL would also work
    }
```

15. The following should be placed in the namespace QueueSavitch:

```
    //Uses cstddef:
    template<class T>
    void Queue<T>::add(T item)
    {
        if (isEmpty( ))
            front = back = new Node<T>(item, NULL);//Sets both
                        //front and back to point to the only node
        else
        {
            back->setLink(new Node<T>(item, NULL));
            back = back->getLink( );
```

```
        }
    }

    //Uses cstdlib and iostream:
    template<class T>
    T Queue<T>::remove( )
    {
        if (isEmpty( ))
        {
            cout << "Error: Removing an item from an empty queue.\n";
            exit(1);
        }

        T result = front->getData( );

        Node<T> *discard;
        discard = front;
        front = front->getLink( );
        if (front == NULL) //if you removed the last node
            back - NULL;

        delete discard;

        return result;
    }
```

16. The following should be placed in the namespace QueueSavitch:

```
    template<class T>
    Queue<T>::~Queue( )
    {
        T next;
        while (! isEmpty( ))
            next = remove( );//remove calls delete.
    }
```

17. The following should be placed in the namespace QueueSavitch:

```
    //Uses cstddef:
    template<class T>
    Queue<T>::Queue(const Queue<T>& aQueue)
    {
        if (aQueue.isEmpty( ))
            front = back = NULL;
        else
        {
            Node<T> *temp = aQueue.front;//temp moves
            //through the nodes from front to back of aQueue.

            back = new Node<T>(temp->getData( ), NULL);
```

```
        front = back;
        //First node created and filled with data.
        //New nodes are now added AFTER this first node.

        temp = temp->getLink( );//temp now points to second
                //node or NULL if there is no second node.

        while (temp != NULL)
        {
            back->setLink(new Node<T>(temp->getData( ), NULL));
            back = back->getLink( );
            temp = temp->getLink( );

        }
        //back->link == NULL
    }
}
```

18. The following should be placed in the namespace QueueSavitch:

```
//Uses cstddef:
template<class T>
Queue<T>& Queue<T>::operator =(const Queue<T>& rightSide)
{
    if (front == rightSide.front)//if the queues are the same
        return *this;
    else //send left side back to freestore
    {
        T next;
        while (! isEmpty( ))
            next = remove( );//remove calls delete.
    }

    if (rightSide.isEmpty( ))
    {
        front = back = NULL;
        return *this;
    }
    else
    {
        Node<T> *temp = rightSide.front;//temp moves
            //through the nodes from front to back of rightSide.

        back = new Node<T>(temp->getData( ), NULL);
        front = back;
        //First node created and filled with data.
        //New nodes are now added AFTER this first node.

        temp = temp->getLink( );//temp now points to second
```

```
                    //node or NULL if there is no second node.

        while (temp != NULL)
        {
            back->setLink(
                    new Node<T>(temp->getData( ), NULL));
            back = back->getLink( );
            temp = temp->getLink( );
        }
        //back->link == NULL;

        return *this;
    }
}
```

19.
```
using namespace ListNodeSavitch;
using namespace QueueSavitch;
template<class T>
bool inQ(Queue<T> q, T target)
{
    Queue<T>::Iterator i;
    i = q.begin( );
    while ((i != q.end( )) && (*i != target))
            i++;
    return (i != q.end());
}
```

Note that the following **return** statement does not work, since it can cause a dereferencing of NULL, which is illegal. The error would be a runtime error, not a compiler error.

```
return (*i == target);
```

20. The template class **SearchTree** needs function declarations added. These are just the definitions.

```
template<class T> //uses iostream:
void SearchTree<T>::preorderShow( ) const
{
    preorderShow(root);
}

template<class T> //uses iostream:
void SearchTree<T>::preorderShow(
                    TreeNode<T>* subTreeRoot) const
{
    if (subTreeRoot != NULL)
    {
        cout << subTreeRoot->data << " ";
        preorderShow(subTreeRoot->leftLink);
```

```
            preorderShow(subTreeRoot->rightLink);
    }
}


template<class T> //uses iostream:
void SearchTree<T>::postorderShow( ) const
{
    postorderShow(root);
}

template<class T> //uses iostream:
void SearchTree<T>::postorderShow(
                        TreeNode<T>* subTreeRoot) const
{
    if (subTreeRoot != NULL)
    {
        postorderShow(subTreeRoot->leftLink);
        postorderShow(subTreeRoot->rightLink);
        cout << subTreeRoot->data << " ";
    }
}
```

PROGRAMMING PROJECTS

1. Write a `void` function that takes a linked list of integers and reverses the order of its nodes. The function will have one call-by-reference parameter that is a pointer to the head of the list. After the function is called, this pointer will point to the head of a linked list that has the same nodes as the original list but in the reverse of the order they had in the original list. Note that your function will neither create nor destroy any nodes. It will simply rearrange nodes. Place your function in a suitable test program.

2. Write a function called `mergeLists` that takes two call-by-reference arguments that are pointer variables that point to the heads of linked lists of values of type `int`. The two linked lists are assumed to be sorted so that the number at the head is the smallest number, the number in the next node is the next smallest, and so forth. The function returns a pointer to the head of a new linked list that contains all the nodes in the original two lists. The nodes in this longer list are also sorted from smallest to largest values. Note that your function will neither create nor destroy any nodes. When the function call ends, the two pointer variable arguments should have the value `NULL`.

3. Design and implement a class that is a class for polynomials. The polynomial

$$a_n x^n + a_{n-1} x^{n-1} + \ldots + a_0$$

will be implemented as a linked list. Each node will contain an `int` value for the power of x and an `int` value for the corresponding coefficient. The class operations should include addition, subtraction, multiplication, and evaluation of a polynomial. Overload the operators $+$, $-$, and $*$ for addition, subtraction, and multiplication. Evaluation of a polynomial is implemented as a member function with one argument of type `int`. The evaluation member function returns the value obtained by plugging in its argument for x and performing the indicated operations.

Include four constructors: a default constructor, a copy constructor, a constructor with a single argument of type `int` that produces the polynomial that has only one constant term that is equal to the constructor argument, and a constructor with two arguments of type `int` that produces the one-term polynomial whose coefficient and exponent are given by the two arguments. (In the previous notation the polynomial produced by the one-argument constructor is of the simple form consisting of only a_0. The polynomial produced by the two-argument constructor is of the slightly more complicated form $a_n x^n$.) Include a suitable destructor. Include member functions to input and output polynomials.

When the user inputs a polynomial, the user types in the following:

$$a_n x^\wedge n + a_{n-1} x^\wedge n-1 + \ldots + a_0$$

However, if a coefficient a_i is 0, the user may omit the term $a_i x^\wedge$ i. For example, the polynomial

$$3x^4 + 7x^2 + 5$$

can be input as

```
3x^4 + 7x^2 + 5
```

It could also be input as

```
3x^4 + 0x^3 + 7x^2 + 0x^1 + 5
```

If a coefficient is negative, a minus sign is used in place of a plus sign, as in the following examples:

```
3x^5 - 7x^3 + 2x^1 - 8
-7x^4 + 5x^2 + 9
```

A minus sign at the front of the polynomial, as in the second of the above two examples, applies only to the first coefficient; it does not negate the entire polynomial. Polynomials are output in the same format. In the case of output, the terms with 0 coefficients are not output. To simplify input, you can assume that polynomials are always entered one per line and that there will always be a constant term a_0. If there is no constant term, the user enters 0 for the constant term, as in the following:

```
12x^8 + 3x^2 + 0
```

4. Part A. The annotation in Display 17.24 says that a real `SearchTree` template class should have a copy constructor, an overloaded assignment operator, other overloaded operators, and other member functions. Obtain the code for Display 17.24 and add declarations for

the following functions and overloaded operators: the default constructor, copy constructor, `delete`, overloaded `operator, =, makeEmpty`, `height, size, preOrderTraversal`, `inOrderTraversal`, and `postOrderTraversal`. The functions `preOrderTraversal`, `inOrderTraversal`, and `postOrderTraversal` each call a global function `process` to process the nodes as they are encountered. The function `process` is a friend of the `SearchTree` class and for this exercise it is only a stub.

Supply preconditions and postconditions for these functions describing what each function should do.

The function `height` has no parameters and returns the height of the tree. The height of the tree is the maximum of the heights of all the nodes. The height of a node is the number of links between it and the root node.

The function `size` has no parameters and returns the number of nodes in the tree.

The function `makeEmpty` removes all the nodes from the tree and returns the memory used by the nodes for reuse. The `makeEmpty` function leaves the root pointer with the value `NULL`.

Part B. Implement the member and friend functions and overloaded operators. Note that some of the functions listed here are already implemented in the text. You should make full use of the text's code. You should test your package thoroughly.

Part C: Design and implement an iterator class for the tree class. You will need to decide what a `begin`, and `end`, element means for your `searchTree`, and what will be the next element the `++` operator will point to.

Hint 1: You might maintain a private size variable that is increased by insertion and decreased by deletion, and whose value is returned by the `size` function. An alternative (use this if you know calls to size will be quite infrequent) is to calculate the size when you need it by traversing the tree. Similar techniques, though with more sophisticated details, can be used to implement the `height` function.

Hint 2: Do these a few members at a time. Compile and test after doing each group of a few members. You will be glad you did it this way.

Hint 3: Before you write the operator, =, and copy constructor, note that their jobs have a common task—duplicating another tree. Write a `copyTree` function that abstracts out the common task of the copy constructor and operator, =. Then write these two important functions using the common code.

Hint 4: The function `makeEmpty` and the destructor have a common tree destruction task.

18 CHAPTER

Exception Handling

18 Exception Handling

It's the exception that proves the rule.

Common maxim

INTRODUCTION

One way to write a program is to first assume that nothing unusual or incorrect will happen. For example, if the program takes an entry off a list, you might assume that the list is not empty. Once you have the program working for the core situation where things always go as planned, you can then add code to take care of the exceptional cases. C++ has a way to reflect this approach in your code. Basically, you write your code as if nothing very unusual happens. After that, you use the C++ exception handling facilities to add code for those unusual cases.

Exception handling is commonly used to handle error situations, but perhaps a better way to view exceptions is as a way to handle exceptional situations. After all, if your code correctly handles an "error," then it no longer is an error.

Perhaps the most important use of exceptions is to deal with functions that have some special case that is handled differently depending on how the function is used. Perhaps the function will be used in many programs, some of which will handle the special case in one way, while others will handle it in some other way. For example, if there is a division by zero in the function, then it may turn out that for some invocations of the function the program should end, but for other invocations of the function something else should happen. You will see that such a function can be defined to throw an exception if the special case occurs; that exception will allow the special case to be handled outside the function. Thus, the special case can be handled differently for different invocations of the function.

In C++, exception handling proceeds as follows: Either some library software, or your code, provides a mechanism that signals when something unusual happens. This is called *throwing an exception*. At another place in your program you place the code that deals with the exceptional case. This is called *handling the exception*. This method of programming makes for cleaner code. Of course, we still need to explain the details of how you do this in C++.

Most of this chapter only uses material from Chapters 1 through 9. However, the sections "Exception Specification in Derived Classes" and "Exception Class Hierarchies" use material from Chapter 14. The section "Testing for Available Memory" uses material from Chapter 17. Any or all of these listed sections may be omitted without hurting the continuity of the chapter. The section "Exception Specification" has one paragraph that refers to derived classes (Chapter 14), but that paragraph may be omitted.

18.1 Exception Handling Basics

> *Well, the program works for most cases. I didn't know it had to work for that case.*
>
> Computer Science Student, *Appealing a grade*

Exception handling is meant to be used sparingly and in situations that are more involved than what is reasonable to include in a simple introductory example. So, we will teach you the exception handling details of C++ by means of simple examples that would not normally use exception handling. This makes a lot of sense for learning about the exception handling details of C++, but do not forget that these first examples are toy examples; in practice, you would not use exception handling for anything that simple.

■ A TOY EXAMPLE OF EXCEPTION HANDLING

For this example, suppose that milk is such an important food in our culture that people almost never run out of it, but still we would like our programs to accommodate the very unlikely situation of running out of milk. The basic code, which assumes we do not run out of milk, might be as follows:

```
cout << "Enter number of donuts:\n";
cin >> donuts;
cout << "Enter number of glasses of milk:\n";
cin >> milk;
dpg = donuts/static_cast<double>(milk);
cout << donuts << " donuts.\n"
     << milk << " glasses of milk.\n"
     << "You have " << dpg
     << " donuts for each glass of milk.\n";
```

If there is no milk, then this code will include a division by zero, which is an error. To take care of this special situation where we run out of milk, we can add a test. The complete program with this added test for the special situation is shown in Display 18.1. The program in Display 18.1 does not use exception handling. Now, let's see how this program can be rewritten using the C++ exception handling facilities.

In Display 18.2, we have rewritten the program from Display 18.1 using an exception. This is only a toy example, and you would probably not use an exception in this case. However, it does give us a simple example to work with. Although the program as

Display 18.1   Handling a Special Case without Exception Handling

```cpp
1    #include <iostream>
2    using std::cin;
3    using std::cout;


4    int main( )
5    {
6        int donuts, milk;
7        double dpg;
8        cout << "Enter number of donuts:\n";
9        cin >> donuts;
10       cout << "Enter number of glasses of milk:\n";
11       cin >> milk;


12       if (milk <= 0)
13       {
14           cout << donuts << " donuts, and No Milk!\n"
15                << "Go buy some milk.\n";
16       }
17       else
18       {
19           dpg = donuts/static_cast<double>(milk);
20           cout << donuts << " donuts.\n"
21                << milk << " glasses of milk.\n"
22                << "You have " << dpg
23                << " donuts for each glass of milk.\n";
24       }


25       cout << "End of program.\n";
26       return 0;
27   }
```

SAMPLE DIALOGUE

```
Enter number of donuts:
12
Enter number of glasses of milk:
0
12 donuts, and No Milk!
Go buy some milk.
End of program.
```

Display 18.2   Same Thing Using Exception Handling *(part 1 of 2)*

```
1
2    #include <iostream>
3    using std::cin;
4    using std::cout;

5    int main( )
6    {
7        int donuts, milk;
8        double dpg;

9        try
10       {
11           cout << "Enter number of donuts:\n";
12           cin >> donuts;
13           cout << "Enter number of glasses of milk:\n";
14           cin >> milk;

16           if (milk <= 0)
17                   throw donuts;

18           dpg = donuts/static_cast<double>(milk);
19           cout << donuts << " donuts.\n"
20                << milk << " glasses of milk.\n"
21                << "You have " << dpg
22                << " donuts for each glass of milk.\n";
23       }
24       catch(int e)
25       {
26           cout << e << " donuts, and No Milk!\n"
27                << "Go buy some milk.\n";
28       }

29       cout << "End of program.\n";
30       return 0;
31   }
```

This is just a toy example to learn C++ syntax. Do not take it as an example of good typical use of exception handling.

SAMPLE DIALOGUE 1

```
Enter number of donuts:
12
Enter number of glasses of milk:
6
12 donuts.
6 glasses of milk.
You have 2 donuts for each glass of milk.
End of program.
```

Display 18.2   Same Thing Using Exception Handling *(part 2 of 2)*

SAMPLE DIALOGUE 2

```
Enter number of donuts:
12
Enter number of glasses of milk:
0
12 donuts, and No Milk!
Go buy some milk.
End of program.
```

a whole is not simpler, at least the part between the words try and catch is cleaner, which hints at the advantage of using exceptions. Look at the code between the words try and catch. It is basically the same as the code in Display 18.1, except that rather than the big if-else statement (highlighted in Display 18.1), this new program has the following smaller if statement (plus some simple nonbranching statements):

```
if (milk <= 0)
    throw donuts;
```

This if statement says that if there is no milk, then do something exceptional. That something exceptional is given after the word catch. The idea is that the normal situation is handled by the code following the word try, and that exceptional situations are handled by the code following the word catch. Thus, we have separated the normal case from the exceptional case. In this toy example that does not really buy us too much, but in other situations it will prove to be very helpful. Let's look at the details.

try block

The basic way of handling exceptions in C++ consists of the try-throw-catch threesome. A **try block** has the following syntax:

```
try
{
    Some_Code
}
```

This try block contains the code for the basic algorithm that tells what to do when everything goes smoothly. It is called a try block because you are not 100% sure that all will go smoothly, but you want to "give it a try."

If something unusual does happen, you want to throw an exception, which is a way of indicating that something unusual happened. So the basic outline, when we add a throw, is as follows:

```
try
{
```

```
        Code_To_Try
        Possibly_Throw_An_Exception
        More_Code
    }
```

The following is an example of a try block with a throw statement included (copied from Display 18.2):

```
try
{
    cout << "Enter number of donuts:\n";
    cin >> donuts;
    cout << "Enter number of glasses of milk:\n";
    cin >> milk;

    if (milk <= 0)
            throw donuts;

    dpg = donuts/static_cast<double>(milk);
    cout << donuts << " donuts.\n"
        << milk << " glasses of milk.\n"
        << "You have " << dpg
        << " donuts for each glass of milk.\n";
}
```

The following statement **throws** the int value donuts:

```
throw donuts;
```

throw statement

The value thrown (in this case, donuts) is sometimes called an **exception**; the execution of a throw statement is called **throwing an exception**. You can throw a value of any type. In this case, an int value is thrown.

exception throwing an exception

When something is "thrown," something goes from one place to another place. In C++ what goes from one place to another is the flow of control (as well as the value thrown). When an exception is thrown, the code in the surrounding try block stops executing and another portion of code, known as a **catch block**, begins execution. Executing the catch block is called **catching the exception** or **handling the exception**. When an exception is thrown, it should ultimately be handled by (caught by) some catch block. In Display 18.2, the appropriate catch block immediately follows the try block. We repeat the catch block in what follows:

catch block

handling the exception

```
catch(int e)
{
    cout << e << " donuts, and No Milk!\n"
        << "Go buy some milk.\n";
}
```

---

throw STATEMENT

SYNTAX

throw *Expression_for_Value_to_Be_Thrown*;

When the throw statement is executed, the execution of the enclosing try block is stopped. If the try block is followed by a suitable catch block, then flow of control is transferred to the catch block. A throw statement is almost always embedded in a branching statement, such as an if statement. The value thrown can be of any type.

EXAMPLE

```
if (milk <= 0)
    throw donuts;
```

This catch block looks very much like a function definition that has a parameter of type int. It is not a function definition, but in some ways a catch block is like a function. It is a separate piece of code that is executed when your program encounters (and executes) the following (within the preceding try block):

```
throw Some_int;
```

So, this throw statement is similar to a function call, but instead of calling a function, it calls the catch block and says to execute the code in the catch block. A catch block is often referred to as an **exception handler**, which is a term that suggests that a catch block has a function-like nature.

exception handler

What is that identifier e in the following line from a catch block?

```
catch(int e)
```

catch-block parameter

That identifier e looks like a parameter and acts very much like a parameter. In fact, the identifier, such as e, in the catch–block heading is called the **catch-block parameter**. Each catch block can have at most one catch-block parameter. The catch–block parameter does two things:

1. The catch–block parameter is preceded by a type name that specifies what kind of thrown value the catch block can catch.
2. The catch–block parameter gives you a name for the thrown value that is caught, so you can write code in the catch block that does things with that value.

We will discuss these two functions of the catch–block parameter in reverse order. This subsection discusses using the catch–block parameter as a name for the value that was thrown and is caught. The subsection entitled "Multiple Throws and Catches," later in this chapter, discusses which catch block (which exception handler) will process a value that is thrown. Our current example has only one catch block. A common name for a catch-block parameter is e, but you can use any legal identifier in place of e.

Let's see how the catch block in Display 18.2 works. When a value is thrown, execution of the code in the try block ends and control passes to the catch block (or blocks) that is placed right after the try block. The catch block from Display 18.2 is reproduced here:

```
catch(int e)
{
    cout << e << " donuts, and No Milk!\n"
        << "Go buy some milk.\n";
}
```

When a value is thrown, the thrown value must be of type int in order for this particular catch block to apply. In Display 18.2, the value thrown is given by the variable donuts; because donuts is of type int, this catch block can catch the value thrown.

Suppose the value of donuts is 12 and the value of milk is 0, as in the second sample dialogue in Display 18.2. Since the value of milk is not positive, the throw statement within the if statement is executed. In that case the value of the variable donuts is thrown. When the catch block in Display 18.2 catches the value of donuts, the value of donuts is plugged in for the catch-block parameter e and the code in the catch block is executed, producing the following output:

```
12 donuts, and No Milk!
Go buy some milk.
```

If the value of donuts is positive, the throw statement is not executed. In this case the entire try block is executed. After the last statement in the try block is executed, the statement after the catch block is executed. Note that if no exception is thrown, the catch block is ignored.

This discussion makes it sound like a try-throw-catch setup is equivalent to an if-else statement. It almost is equivalent, except for the value thrown. A try-throw-catch setup is like an if-else statement *with the added ability to send a message to one of the branches*. This does not sound much different from an if-else statement, but it turns out to be a big difference in practice.

To summarize in a more formal tone, a try block contains some code that we are assuming includes a throw statement. The throw statement is normally executed only in exceptional circumstances, but when it is executed, it throws a value of some type. When an exception (a value such as donuts in Display 18.2) is thrown, the try block ends. All the rest of the code in the try block is ignored and control passes to a suitable catch block. A catch block applies only to an immediately preceding try block. If the exception is thrown, then that exception object is plugged in for the catch-block parameter, and the statements in the catch block are executed. For example, if you look at the dialogues in Display 18.2, you will see that as soon as the user enters a nonpositive number, the try block stops and the catch block is executed. For now, we will

---

catch–BLOCK PARAMETER

The catch–block parameter is an identifier in the heading of a catch block that serves as a placeholder for an exception (a value) that might be thrown. When a suitable value is thrown in the preceding try block, that value is plugged in for the catch–block parameter. (In order for the catch block to be executed the value throw must be of the type given for its catch–block parameter.) You can use any legal (nonreserved-word) identifier for a catch–block parameter.

EXAMPLE

```
catch(int e)
{
    cout << e << " donuts, and No Milk!\n"
        << "Go buy some milk.\n";
}
```

e is the catch–block parameter.

---

assume that every try block is followed by an appropriate catch block. We will later discuss what happens when there is no appropriate catch block.

If no exception (no value) is thrown in the try block, then after the try block is completed, program execution continues with the code after the catch block. In other words, if no exception is thrown, the catch block is ignored. Most of the time when the program is executed, the throw statement will not be executed, and so in most cases the code in the try block will run to completion and the code in the catch block will be ignored completely.

---

try–throw–catch

The basic mechanism for throwing and catching exceptions is a try-throw-catch sequence. The throw statement throws the exception (a value). The catch block catches the exception (the value). When an exception is thrown, the try block ends and then the code in the catch block is executed. After the catch block is completed, the code after the catch block or blocks is executed (provided the catch block has not ended the program or performed some other special action).

(The type of the thrown exception must match the type listed for the catch–block parameter or else the exception will not be caught by that catch block. This point is discussed further in the subsection "Multiple Throws and Catches.")

If no exception is thrown in the try block, then after the try block is completed, program execution continues with the code after the catch block or blocks. (In other words, if no exception is thrown, the catch block or blocks are ignored.)

Self-Test Exercises

1. What output is produced by the following code?

```
int waitTime = 46;

try
{
    cout << "Try block entered.\n";
    if (waitTime > 30)
        throw waitTime;
    cout << "Leaving try block.\n";
}

catch(int thrownValue)
{
    cout << "Exception thrown with\n"
        << "waitTime equal to " << thrownValue << endl;
}
cout << "After catch block" << endl;
```

2. What would be the output produced by the code in Self-Test Exercise 1 if we made the following change? Change the line

```
int waitTime = 46;
```

to

```
int waitTime = 12;
```

3. In the code given in Self-Test Exercise 1, what is the `throw` statement?

4. What happens when a `throw` statement is executed? (Tell what happens in general, not simply what happens in the code in Self-Test Exercise 1 or some other sample code.)

5. In the code given in Self-Test Exercise 1, what is the `try` block?

6. In the code given in Self-Test Exercise 1, what is the `catch` block?

7. In the code given in Self-Test Exercise 1, what is the `catch–block` parameter?

DEFINING YOUR OWN EXCEPTION CLASSES

A `throw` statement can throw a value of any type. A common thing to do is to define a class whose objects can carry the precise kinds of information you want thrown to the `catch` block. An even more important reason for defining a specialized exception class is so that you can have a different type to identify each possible kind of exceptional situation.

An exception class is just a class. What makes it an exception class is how it is used. Still, it pays to take some care in choosing an exception class's name and other details.

Display 18.3 contains an example of a program with a programmer-defined exception class. This is just a toy program to illustrate some C++ details about exception handling. It uses much too much machinery for such a simple task, but it is an otherwise uncluttered example of some C++ details.

Notice the `throw` statement, reproduced in what follows:

```
throw NoMilk(donuts);
```

The part `NoMilk(donuts)` is an invocation of a constructor for the class `NoMilk`. The constructor takes one `int` argument (in this case, `donuts`) and creates an object of the class `NoMilk`. That object is then thrown.

MULTIPLE THROWS AND CATCHES

A `try` block can potentially throw any number of exception values, which can be of differing types. In any one execution of the `try` block, at most one exception will be thrown (since a `throw` statement ends the execution of the `try` block), but different types of exception values can be thrown on different occasions when the `try` block is executed. Each `catch` block can only catch values of one type, but you can catch exception values of differing types by placing more than one `catch` block after a `try` block. For example, the program in Display 18.4 has two `catch` blocks after its `try` block.

Note that there is no parameter in the `catch` block for `DivideByZero`. If you do not need a parameter, you can simply list the type with no parameter. This is discussed a bit more in the programming tip section entitled "Exception Classes Can Be Trivial."

Display 18.3 Defining Your Own Exception Class

```
1   #include <iostream>
2   using std::cin;
3   using std::cout;


4   class NoMilk
5   {
6   public:
7       NoMilk( ) {}
8       NoMilk(int howMany) : count(howMany) {}
9       int getCount( ) const { return count; }
10  private:
11      int count;
12  };


13  int main( )
14  {
15      int donuts, milk;
16      double dpg;
17      try
18      {
19          cout << "Enter number of donuts:\n";
20          cin >> donuts;
21          cout << "Enter number of glasses of milk:\n";
22          cin >> milk;


23          if (milk <= 0)
24                  throw NoMilk(donuts);


25          dpg = donuts/static_cast<double>(milk);
26          cout << donuts << " donuts.\n"
27              << milk << " glasses of milk.\n"
28              << "You have " << dpg
29              << " donuts for each glass of milk.\n";
30      }
31      catch(NoMilk e)
32      {
33          cout << e.getCount( ) << " donuts, and No Milk!\n"
34              << "Go buy some milk.\n";
35      }
36      cout << "End of program.\n";
37      return 0;
38  }
```

This is just a toy example to learn C++ syntax. Do not take it as an example of good typical use of exception handling.

The sample dialogues are the same as in Display 18.2.

Display 18.4   Catching Multiple Exceptions *(part 1 of 2)*

```
1   #include <iostream>
2   #include <string>                    Exception classes can have their own interface and
3   using std::cin;                      implementation files and can be put in a namespace.
4   using std::cout;                     This is another toy example.
5   using std::endl;
6   using std::string;

7   class NegativeNumber
8   {
9   public:
10      NegativeNumber( ){}
11      NegativeNumber(string theMessage): message(theMessage) {}
12      string getMessage( ) const { return message; }
13  private:
14      string message;
15  };

16  class DivideByZero
17  {};

18  int main( )
19  {
20      int pencils, erasers;
21      double ppe; //pencils per eraser

22      try
23      {
24          cout << "How many pencils do you have?\n";
25          cin >> pencils;
26          if (pencils < 0)
27              throw NegativeNumber("pencils");

28          cout << "How many erasers do you have?\n";
29          cin >> erasers;
30          if (erasers < 0)
31              throw NegativeNumber("erasers");

32          if (erasers != 0)
33              ppe = pencils/static_cast<double>(erasers);
34          else
35              throw DivideByZero( );

36          cout << "Each eraser must last through "
37              << ppe << " pencils.\n";
38      }
```

Display 18.4   Catching Multiple Exceptions *(part 2 of 2)*

```
39      catch(NegativeNumber e)
40      {
41          cout << "Cannot have a negative number of "
42              << e.getMessage( ) << endl;
43      }
44      catch(DivideByZero)
45      {
46          cout << "Do not make any mistakes.\n";
47      }

48      cout << "End of program.\n";
49      return 0;
50  }
```

If the catch–block parameter is not used, you need not give it in the heading.

SAMPLE DIALOGUE 1

```
How many pencils do you have?
5
How many erasers do you have?
2
Each eraser must last through 2.5 pencils
End of program.
```

SAMPLE DIALOGUE 2

```
How many pencils do you have?
−2
Cannot have a negative number of pencils
End of program.
```

SAMPLE DIALOGUE 3

```
How many pencils do you have?
5
How many erasers do you have?
0
Do not make any mistakes.
End of program.
```

Pitfall

CATCH THE MORE SPECIFIC EXCEPTION FIRST

When catching multiple exceptions, the order of the `catch` blocks can be important. When an exception value is thrown in a `try` block, the `catch` blocks that follow it are tried in order, and the first one that matches the type of the exception thrown is the one that is executed.

catch (...)

For example, the following is a special kind of `catch` block that will catch a thrown value of any type:

```
catch (...)
{
    <Place whatever you want in here.>
}
```

The three dots do not stand for something omitted. You actually type in those three dots in your program. This makes a good default `catch` block to place after all other `catch` blocks. For example, we could add it to the `catch` blocks in Display 18.4 as follows:

```
catch(NegativeNumber e)
{
    cout << "Cannot have a negative number of "
        << e.getMessage( ) << endl;
}
catch(DivideByZero)
{
    cout << "Do not make any mistakes.\n";
}
catch (...)
{
    cout << "Unexplained exception.\n";
}
```

However, it only makes sense to place this default `catch` block at the end of a list of `catch` blocks. For example, suppose we instead used:

```
catch(NegativeNumber e)
{
    cout << "Cannot have a negative number of "
        << e.getMessage( ) << endl;
}
catch (...)
{
    cout << "Unexplained exception.\n";
}
catch(DivideByZero)
{
    cout << "Do not make any mistakes.\n";
}
```

With this second ordering, an exception (a thrown value) of type NegativeNumber will be caught by the NegativeNumber catch block as it should be. However, if a value of type DivideByZero were thrown, it would be caught by the block that starts catch(...). So, the DivideByZero catch block could never be reached. Fortunately, most compilers will tell you if you make this sort of mistake.

Tip

EXCEPTION CLASSES CAN BE TRIVIAL

Below we have reproduced the definition of the exception class DivideByZero from Display 18.4:

```
class DivideByZero
{};
```

This exception class has no member variables and no member functions (other than the default constructor). It has nothing but its name, but that is useful enough. Throwing an object of the class DivideByZero can activate the appropriate catch block, as it does in Display 18.4.

When using a trivial exception class, you normally do not have anything you can do with the exception (the thrown value) once control gets to the catch block. The exception is just being used to get you to the catch block. Thus, you can omit the catch-block parameter. In fact, you can omit the catch-block parameter any time you do not need it, whether the exception type is trivial or not.

THROWING AN EXCEPTION IN A FUNCTION

Sometimes it makes sense to delay handling an exception. For example, you might have a function with code that throws an exception if there is an attempt to divide by zero, but you may not want to catch the exception in that function. Perhaps some programs that use that function should simply end if the exception is thrown, and other programs that use the function should do something else. Thus, you would not know what to do with the exception if you caught it inside the function. In these cases, it makes sense to not catch the exception in the function definition, but instead to have any program (or other code) that uses the function place the function invocation in a try block and catch the exception in a catch block that follows that try block.

Look at the program in Display 18.5. It has a try block, but there is no throw statement visible in the try block. The statement that does the throwing in that program is

```
if (bottom == 0)
    throw DivideByZero( );
```

This statement is not visible in the try block. However, it is in the try block in terms of program execution, because it is in the definition of the function safeDivide and there is an invocation of safeDivide in the try block.

Display 18.5   Throwing an Exception Inside a Function *(part 1 of 2)*

```
1   #include <iostream>
2   #include <cstdlib>
3   using std::cin;
4   using std::cout;
5   using std::endl;

6   class DivideByZero
7   {};

8   double safeDivide(int top, int bottom) throw (DivideByZero);

9   int main( )
10  {
11      int numerator;
12      int denominator;
13      double quotient;
14      cout << "Enter numerator:\n";
15      cin >> numerator;
16      cout << "Enter denominator:\n";
17      cin >> denominator;

18      try
19      {
20          quotient = safeDivide(numerator, denominator);
21      }
22      catch(DivideByZero)
23      {
24          cout << "Error: Division by zero!\n"
25              << "Program aborting.\n";
26          exit(0);
27      }

28      cout << numerator << "/" << denominator
29          << " = " << quotient << endl;

30      cout << "End of program.\n";
31      return 0;
32  }
33
34  double safeDivide(int top, int bottom) throw (DivideByZero)
35  {
36      if (bottom == 0)
37          throw DivideByZero( );

38      return top/static_cast<double>(bottom);
39  }
```

Display 18.5   **Throwing an Exception Inside a Function** *(part 2 of 2)*

SAMPLE DIALOGUE 1

```
Enter numerator:
5
Enter denominator:
10
5/10 = 0.5
End of Program.
```

SAMPLE DIALOGUE 2

```
Enter numerator:
5
Enter denominator:
0
Error: Division by zero!
Program aborting.
```

The meaning of throw (DivideByZero) in the declaration of safeDivide is discussed in the next subsection.

EXCEPTION SPECIFICATION

If a function does not catch an exception, it should at least warn programmers that any invocation of the function might possibly throw an exception. If there are exceptions that might be thrown but not caught in the function definition, those exception types should be listed in an **exception specification**, which is illustrated by the following function declaration from Display 18.5:

exception specification

```
double safeDivide(int top, int bottom) throw (DivideByZero);
```

As illustrated in Display 18.5, the exception specification should appear in both the function declaration and the function definition. If a function has more than one function declaration, then all the function declarations must have identical exception specifications. The exception specification for a function is also sometimes called the **throw list**.

throw list

If more than one possible exception can be thrown in the function definition, the exception types are listed separated by commas, as illustrated in what follows:

```
void someFunction( ) throw (DivideByZero, SomeOtherException);
```

All exception types listed in the exception specification are treated normally. When we say the exception is treated normally we mean it is treated as we have described before this subsection. In particular, you can place the function invocation in a `try` block followed by a `catch` block to catch that type of exception and if the function throws the exception (and does not catch it inside the function), then the `catch` block following the `try` block will catch the exception.

If there is no exception specification (no throw list) at all (not even an empty one), then the code behaves the same as if all possible exception types were listed in the exception specification; that is, any exception that is thrown is treated normally.

What happens when an exception is thrown in a function but is not listed in the exception specification (and not caught inside the function)? This is neither a compile time error nor a runtime error. In such cases the function `unexpected( )` is called. You can change the behavior of the function `unexpected`, but the default behavior is to call the function `terminate( )`, which ends the program. In particular, notice that if an exception is thrown in a function but is not listed in the exception specification (and not caught inside the function), then it will not be caught by any `catch` block in your program but will instead result in an invocation of `unexpected( )` whose default behavior is to end your program.

Keep in mind that the exception specification is for exceptions that "get outside" the function. If they do not get outside the function, they do not belong in the exception specification. If they get outside the function, they belong in the exception specification no matter where they originate. If an exception is thrown in a `try` block that is inside a function definition and is caught in a `catch` block inside the function definition, then its type need not be listed in the exception specification. If a function definition includes an invocation of another function and that other function can throw an exception that is not caught, then the type of the exception should be placed in the exception specification.

You might think that the possibility of throwing an exception that is not caught and is not on the throw list should be checked by the compiler and produce a compiler error. However, because of the details of exceptions in C++, it is not possible for the compiler to perform the check. The check must be done at runtime.[1]

To say that a function should not throw any exceptions that are not caught inside the function, use an empty exception specification like so:

```
void someFunction( ) throw ( );
```

By way of summary:

```
void someFunction( ) throw (DivideByZero, SomeOtherException);
//Exceptions of type DivideByZero or SomeOtherException are
//treated normally. All other exceptions invoke unexpected( ).
```

---

[1] This is not true in all programming languages. It depends on the details of how the exception specification details are defined for the language.

```
void someFunction( ) throw ( );
//Empty exception list, so all exceptions invoke unexpected( ).

void someFunction( );
//All exceptions of all types are treated normally.
```

The default action of unexpected( ) is to end the program. You need not use any special include or using directives to gain the default behavior of unexpected( ). You normally have no need to redefine the behavior of unexpected( ); however, the behavior of unexpected( ) can be changed with the function set_unexpected. If you need to use set_unexpected, you should consult a more advanced book for the details.

Keep in mind that an object of a derived class is also an object of its base class. So, if D is a derived class of class B and B is in the exception specification, then a thrown object of class D will be treated normally, since it is an object of class B. However, no automatic type conversions are done. If double is in the exception specification, that does not account for throwing an int value. You would need to include both int and double in the exception specification.

One final warning: Not all compilers treat the exception specification as they are supposed to. Some compilers essentially treat the exception specification as a comment; with those compilers, the exception specification has no effect on your code. This is another reason to place all exceptions which might be thrown by your functions in the throw specification. This way all compilers will treat your exceptions the same way. Of course, you could get the same compiler consistency by not having any throw specification at all, but then your program would not be as well documented and you would not get the extra error checking provided by compilers that do use the throw specification. With a compiler that does process the throw specification, your program will terminate as soon as it throws an exception that you did not anticipate. (Note that this is a runtime behavior, but which runtime behavior you get depends on your compiler.)

Warning!

Pitfall

EXCEPTION SPECIFICATION IN DERIVED CLASSES

When you redefine or override a function definition in a derived class, it should have the same exception specification as it had in the base class, or it should have an exception specification whose exceptions are a subset of those in the base class exception specification. Put another way, when you redefine or override a function definition, you cannot add any exceptions to the exception specification (but you can delete some exceptions if you want). This makes sense, since an object of the derived class can be used anyplace an object of the base class can be used, and so a redefined or overwritten function must fit any code written for an object of the base class.

Self-Test Exercises

8. What is the output produced by the following program?

```cpp
#include <iostream>
using std::cout;

void sampleFunction(double test) throw (int);

int main( )
{
    try
    {
        cout << "Trying.\n";
        sampleFunction(98.6);
        cout << "Trying after call.\n";
    }
    catch(int)
    {
        cout << "Catching.\n";
    }

    cout << "End program.\n";
    return 0;
}
void sampleFunction(double test) throw (int)
{
    cout << "Starting sampleFunction.\n";
    if (test < 100)
        throw 42;
}
```

9. What is the output produced by the program in Self-Test Exercise 8 when the following change is made to the program? Change

```cpp
sampleFunction(98.6);
```

in the try block to

```cpp
sampleFunction(212);
```

18.2 Programming Techniques for Exception Handling

Only use this in exceptional circumstances.

Warren Peace, *The Lieutenant's Tool*

So far we have shown lots of code that explains how exception handling works in C++, but we have not shown an example of a program that makes good and realistic use of exception handling. However, now that you know the mechanics of exception handling, this section can go on to explain exception handling techniques.

WHEN TO THROW AN EXCEPTION

We have given some very simple code to illustrate the basic concepts of exception handling. However, our examples were unrealistically simple. A more complicated but better guideline is to separate throwing an exception and catching the exception into separate functions. In most cases, you should include any throw statement within a function definition, list the exception in an exception specification for that function, and place the catch clause in a different function. Thus, the preferred use of the try–throw–catch triad is as illustrated here:

```
void functionA( ) throw (MyException)
{
        .
        .
        .
    throw MyException(<Maybe an argument>);
        .
        .
        .
}
```

Then, in some other function (perhaps even some other function in some other file), you have the following:

```
void functionB( )
{
        .
        .
        .
```

```
try
{
        .
        .
        .
    functionA( );
        .
        .
        .
}
catch(MyException e)
{
            <Handle exception>
}
        .
        .
        .
}
```

Even this kind of use of a throw statement should be reserved for cases where it is unavoidable. If you can easily handle a problem in some other way, do not throw an exception. Reserve throw statements for situations in which the way the exceptional condition is handled depends on how and where the function is used. If the way that the exceptional condition is handled depends on how and where the function is invoked, then the best thing to do is let the programmer who invokes the function handle the exception. In all other situations, it is preferable to avoid throwing exceptions. Let's outline a sample scenario of this kind of situation.

Suppose you are writing a library of functions to deal with patient monitoring systems for hospitals. One function might compute the patient's average daily temperature by accessing the patients record in some file and dividing the sum of the temperatures by the number of times the temperature was taken. Now suppose these functions are used for creating different systems to be used in different situations. What should happen if the patient's temperature was never taken and so the averaging would involve a divides by zero? In an intensive care unit, this would indicate something is very wrong, such as the patient is lost. (It has been known to happen.) So for that system, when this potential division by zero would occur, an emergency message should be sent out. However, for a system to be used in a less urgent setting, such as outpatient care or even in some noncritical wards, it might have no significance and so a simple note in the patient's records would suffice. In this scenario the function for doing the averaging of the temperatures should throw an exception when this division by zero occurs, list the exception in the exception specifications, and let each system handle the exception case in the way that is appropriate to that system.

WHEN TO THROW AN EXCEPTION

For the most part, throw statements should be used within functions and listed in an exception specification for the function. Moreover, they should be reserved for situations in which the way the exceptional condition is handled depends on how and where the function is used. If the way that the exceptional condition is handled depends on how and where the function is invoked, then the best thing to do is let the programmer who invokes the function handle the exception. In other situations, it is almost always preferable to avoid throwing an exception.

Pitfall   UNCAUGHT EXCEPTIONS

Every exception that is thrown by your code should be caught someplace in your code. If an exception is thrown but not caught anywhere, the program will end.

Technically speaking, if an exception is thrown but not caught, then the function terminate( ) is called. The default meaning for terminate( ) is to end your program. You can change the meaning from the default, but that is seldom needed and we will not go into the details here.

An exception that is thrown in a function but is not caught either inside or outside the function has two possible cases. If the exception is not listed in the exception specification, then the function unexpected( ) is called. If the exception is not listed in the exception specification, the function terminate( ) is called. But unless you change the default behavior of unexpected( ), unexpected( ) calls terminate( ). So, the result is the same in both cases. If an exception is thrown in a function but not caught either inside or outside the function, then your program ends.

terminate()

unexpected()

Pitfall   NESTED try-catch BLOCKS

You can place a try block and following catch blocks inside a larger try block or inside a larger catch block. In rare cases this may be useful, but if you are tempted to do this, you should suspect that there is a nicer way to organize your program. It is almost always better to place the inner try-catch blocks inside a function definition and place an invocation of the function in the outer try or catch block (or maybe just eliminate one or more try blocks completely).

If you place a try block and following catch blocks inside a larger try block, and an exception is thrown in the inner try block but not caught in any of the inner catch blocks, then the exception is thrown to the outer try block for processing and might be caught by a catch block following the outer try block.

OVERUSE OF EXCEPTIONS

Exceptions allow you to write programs whose flow of control is so involved that it is almost impossible to understand the program. Moreover, this is not hard to do. Throwing an exception allows you to transfer flow of control from anyplace in your program to almost anyplace else in your program. In the early days of programming, this sort of unrestricted flow of control was allowed via a construct known as a goto. Programming experts now agree that such unrestricted flow of control is very poor programming style. Exceptions allow you to revert to these bad old days of unrestricted flow of control. Exceptions should be used sparingly and only in certain ways. A good rule is the following: If you are tempted to include a throw statement, then think about how you might write your program or class definition without this throw statement. If you can think of an alternative that produces reasonable code, then you probably do not want to include the throw statement.

EXCEPTION CLASS HIERARCHIES

It can be very useful to define a hierarchy of exception classes. For example, you might have an ArithmeticError exception class and then define an exception class Divide-ByZeroError that is a derived class of ArithmeticError. Since a DivideByZeroError is an ArithmeticError, every catch block for an ArithmeticError will catch a Divide-ByZeroError. If you list ArithmeticError in the exception specification, then you have, in effect, also added DivideByZeroError to the exception specification, whether or not you list DivideByZeroError by name in the exception specification.

TESTING FOR AVAILABLE MEMORY

In Chapter 17 we created new dynamic variables with code similar to the following:

```
struct Node
{
    int data;
    Node *link;
};
typedef Node* NodePtr;
    ...
NodePtr pointer = new Node;
```

This works fine as long as there is sufficient memory available to create the new node. But what happens if there is not sufficient memory? If there is insufficient memory to create the node, then a bad_alloc exception is thrown.

bad_alloc

Since new will throw a bad_alloc exception when there is not enough memory to create the node, you can check for running out of memory as follows:

```
try
{
```

```
        NodePtr pointer = new Node;
}
catch (bad_alloc)
{
        cout << "Ran out of memory!";
}
```

Of course, you can do other things besides simply giving a warning message, but the details of what you do will depend on your particular programming task.

The definition of bad_alloc is in the library with header file <new> and is placed in the std namespace. So, when using bad_alloc, your program should contain the following (or something similar):

```
#include <new>
using std::bad_alloc;
```

RETHROWING AN EXCEPTION

It is legal to throw an exception within a catch block. In rare cases you may want to catch an exception and then, depending on the details, decide to throw the same or a different exception for handling farther up the chain of exception handling blocks.

Self-Test Exercises

10. What happens when an exception is never caught?

11. Can you nest a try block inside another try block?

Chapter Summary

- Exception handling allows you to design and code the normal case for your program separately from the code that handles exceptional situations.
- An exception can be thrown in a try block. Alternatively, an exception can be thrown in a function definition that does not include a try block (or does not include a catch block to catch that type of exception). In this case, an invocation of the function can be placed in a try block.
- An exception is caught in a catch block.
- A try block may be followed by more than one catch block. In this case, always list the catch block for a more specific exception class before the catch block for a more general exception class.
- The best use of exceptions is to throw an exception in a function (but not catch it in the function) whenever the way the exception is handled will vary from one invocation of

the function to another. There is seldom any other situation that can profitably benefit from throwing an exception.

- If an exception is thrown in a function but not caught in that function, then the exception type should be listed in an exception specification for that function.
- If an exception is thrown but never caught, then the default behavior is to end your program.
- Do not overuse exceptions.

ANSWERS TO SELF-TEST EXERCISES

1. ```
Try block entered.
Exception thrown with
waitTime equal to 46
After catch block.
```

2. ```
Try block entered.
Leaving try block.
After catch block.
```

3. `throw waitTime;`

   Note that the following is an if statement, not a throw statement, even though it contains a throw statement:

   ```
   if (waitTime > 30)
       throw waitTime;
   ```

4. When a throw statement is executed, that is the end of the enclosing try block. No other statements in the try block are executed, and control passes to the following catch block or blocks. When we say control passes to the following catch block, we mean that the value thrown is plugged in for the catch-block parameter (if any) and the code in the catch block is executed.

5. ```
try
{
    cout << "Try block entered.";
    if (waitTime > 30)
        throw waitTime);
    cout << "Leaving try block.";
}
```

6. ```
catch(int thrownValue)
{
    cout << "Exception thrown with\n"
         << "waitTime equal to" << thrownValue << endl;
}
```

7. thrownValue is the catch–block parameter.

8. Trying.
   Starting sampleFunction.
   Catching.
   End of program.

9. Trying.
   Starting sampleFunction.
   Trying after call.
   End of program.

10. If an exception is not caught anywhere, then your program ends. Technically speaking, if an exception is thrown but not caught, then the function terminate( ) is called. The default meaning for terminate( ) is to end your program.

11. Yes, you can have a try block and corresponding catch blocks inside another larger try block. However, it would probably be better to place the inner try and catch blocks in a function definition and place an invocation of the function in the larger try block.

PROGRAMMING PROJECTS

1. Obtain the source code for the PFArray class from Chapter 10. Modify the definition of the overloaded operator, [], so it throws an OutOfRange exception if an index that is out of range is used or if an attempt is made to add an element beyond the capacity of the implementation. OutOfRange is an exception class that you define. The exception class should have a private int member and a private string member, and a public constructor that has int and string arguments. The offending index value along with a message should be stored in the exception object. You choose the message to describe the situation. Write a suitable test program to test the modified class PFArray.

2. (Based on a problem in Stroustrup, *The C++ Programming Language*, 3rd edition) Write a program consisting of functions calling one another to a calling depth of 10. Give each function an argument that specifies the level at which it is to throw an exception. The main function prompts for and receives input that specifies the calling depth (level) at which an exception will be thrown. The main function then calls the first function. The main function catches the exception and displays the level at which the exception was thrown. Don't forget the case where the depth is 0, where main must both throw and catch the exception.

   Hints: You could use 10 different functions or 10 copies of the same function that call one another, but don't. Rather, for compact code, use a main function that calls another function that calls itself recursively. Suppose you do this; is the restriction on the calling depth necessary? This can be done without giving the function any additional arguments, but if you cannot do it that way, try adding an additional argument to the function.

19 CHAPTER

Standard Template Library

19 Standard Template Library

Libraries are not made; they grow.

Augustine Birrell

INTRODUCTION

STL

In Chapter 17 we constructed our own versions of the stack and queue data structures. A large collection of standard structures for holding data exists. Because they are so standard it makes sense to have standard portable implementations of these data structures. The **Standard Template Library (STL)** includes libraries for such data structures. Included in the STL are implementations of the stack, queue, and many other standard data structures. When discussed in the context of the STL, these data structures are usually called *container classes* because they are used to hold collections of data. Chapter 7 presented a preview of the STL by describing the vector template class, which is one of the container classes in the STL. This chapter presents an overview of some of the basic classes included in the STL. Because the STL is very large, we will not be able to give a comprehensive treatment of it here, but we will present enough to get you started using some basic STL container classes as well as some of the other items in the STL.

The STL was developed by Alexander Stepanov and Meng Lee at Hewlett-Packard and was based on research by Stepanov, Lee, and David Musser. It is a collection of libraries written in the C++ language. Although the STL is not part of the core C++ language, it is part of the C++ standard, and so any implementation of C++ that conforms to the standard includes the STL. As a practical matter, you can consider the STL to be part of the C++ language.

As its name suggests, the classes in the STL are template classes. A typical container class in the STL has a type parameter for the type of data to be stored in the container class.

The STL container classes make extensive use of iterators, which are objects that facilitate cycling through the data in a container. An introduction to the general concept of an iterator was given in Section 17.3 of Chapter 17. Although this chapter does not presuppose that you have read that section, most readers will find it helpful to read that section before reading this chapter. As defined in the STL, iterators are very general and can be used for more than just cycling through the few container classes we will discuss. Our discussion of iterators will be specialized to simple uses with the container classes discussed in this chapter. This should make the concept come alive in a concrete setting and should give you enough understanding to feel comfortable reading more advanced texts on the STL. There are numerous books dedicated to the STL.

The STL also includes implementations of many important generic algorithms, such as searching and sorting. The algorithms are implemented as template functions. After discussing the container classes, we will describe some of these algorithm implementations.

The STL differs from other C++ libraries, such as <iostream> for example, in that the classes and algorithms are *generic*, which is another way of saying that they are template classes and template functions.

If you have not already done so, you should read Section 7.3 of Chapter 7, which covers the vector template class of the STL. Although the current chapter does not use any of the material in Chapter 17, most readers will find that reading Chapter 17 before this chapter will aid their comprehension of this chapter by giving sample concrete implementations of some of the abstract ideas intrinsic to the STL. This chapter does not use any of the material in Chapters 12 to 15.

19.1 Iterators

To iterate is human, and programmers are human.

Anonymous

If you have not yet done so, you should read Chapter 10 on pointers and arrays and also read Section 7.3 of Chapter 7, which covers vectors. Vectors are one of the container template classes in the STL. Iterators are a generalization of pointers. This section shows how to use iterators with vectors. Other container template classes that we introduce in Section 19.2 use iterators in the same way. So, all that you learn about iterators in this section will apply across a wide range of containers rather than applying solely to vectors. This reflects one of the basic tenets of the STL philosophy: The semantics, naming, and syntax for iterator usage should be (and is) uniform across different container types.

ITERATOR BASICS

An **iterator** is a generalization of a pointer, and in fact is typically even implemented using a pointer, but the abstraction of an iterator is designed to spare you the details of the implementation and give you a uniform interface to iterators that is the same across different container classes. Each container class has its own iterator types, just like each data type has its own pointer type. But just as all pointer types behave essentially the same for dynamic variables of their particular data type, so too does each iterator type behave the same, but each iterator is used only with its own container type.

An iterator is not a pointer, but you will not go far wrong if you think of it and use it as if it were a pointer. Like a pointer variable, an iterator variable is located at (points

iterator

to) one data entry in the container. You manipulate iterators using the following over-loaded operators that apply to iterator objects:

- Prefix and postfix increment operators (++) for advancing the iterator to the next data item.

- Prefix and postfix decrement operators (−−) for moving the iterator to the previous data item.

- Equal and unequal operators (== and !=) to test whether two iterators point to the same data location.

- A dereferencing operator (*) so that if p is an iterator variable, then *p gives access to the data located at (pointed to by) p. This access may be read only, write only, or allow both reading and changing of the data, depending on the particular container class.

Not all iterators have all of these operators. However, the vector template class is an example of a container whose iterators have all these operators and more.

A container class has member functions that get the iterator process started. After all, a new iterator variable is not located at (pointing to) any data in the container. Many container classes, including the vector template class, have the following member functions that return iterator objects (iterator values) that point to special data elements in the data structure:

- c.begin( ) returns an iterator for the container c that points to the "first" data item in the container c.

- c.end( ) returns something that can be used to test when an iterator has passed beyond the last data item in a container c. The iterator c.end( ) is completely anal-ogous to NULL when used to test whether a pointer has passed the last node in a linked list of the kind discussed in Chapter 17. The iterator c.end( ) is thus an iter-ator that is not located at a data item but that is a kind of end marker or sentinel.

For many container classes, these tools allow you to write for loops that cycle through all the elements in a container object c, as follows:

```
//p is an iterator variable of the type for the container object c.

for (p = c.begin( ); p != c.end( ); p++)
    process *p //*p is the current data item.
```

That's the big picture. Now lets look at the details in the concrete setting of the vector template container class.

Display 19.1 illustrates the use of iterators with the vector template class. Keep in mind that each container type in the STL has its own iterator types, although they are all used in the same basic ways. The iterators we want for a vector of ints are of type

```
std::vector<int>::iterator
```

Display 19.1 Iterators Used with a Vector

```
1   //Program to demonstrate STL iterators.
2   #include <iostream>
3   #include <vector>
4   using std::cout;
5   using std::endl;
6   using std::vector;
7   using std::vector<int>::iterator;

8   int main( )
9   {
10      vector<int> container;

11      for (int i = 1; i <= 4; i++)
12          container.push_back(i);

13      cout << "Here is what is in the container:\n";
14      iterator p;
15      for (p = container.begin( ); p != container.end( ); p++)
16          cout << *p << " ";
17      cout << endl;

18      cout << "Setting entries to 0:\n";
19      for (p = container.begin( ); p != container.end( ); p++)
20          *p = 0;

21      cout << "Container now contains:\n";
22      for (p = container.begin( ); p != container.end( ); p++)
23          cout << *p << " ";
24      cout << endl;

25      return 0;
26  }
```

SAMPLE DIALOGUE

```
Here is what is in the container:
1 2 3 4
Setting entries to 0:
Container now contains:
0 0 0 0
```

Another container class is the `list` template class. Iterators for `list`s of `int`s are of type

```
std::list<int>::iterator
```

In the program in Display 19.1 we specialize the type name `iterator` so it applies to iterators for vectors of `int`s. The type name `iterator` that we want in Display 19.1 is defined in the template class `vector`. Thus, if we specialize the template class `vector` to `int`s and want the iterator type for `vector<int>`, we want the type

```
vector<int>::iterator;
```

Because the `vector` definition places the name `vector` in the `std` namespace, the entire `using` declaration is as follows:

```
using std::vector<int>::iterator;
```

The basic use of iterators with `vector` (or any container class) is illustrated by the following lines from Display 19.1:

```
iterator p;
for (p = container.begin( ); p != container.end( ); p++)
    cout << *p << " ";
```

Recall that `container` is of type `vector<int>`, and that the type `iterator` really means `vector<int>::iterator`.

A vector `v` can be thought of as a linear arrangement of its data elements. There is a first data element `v[0]`, a second data element `v[1]`, and so forth. An iterator `p` is an object that can be *located at* one of these elements (think "points to" one of these elements). An iterator can move its location from one element to another element. If `p` is located at, say, `v[7]`, then `p++` moves `p` so it is located at `v[8]`. This allows an iterator to move through the vector from the first element to the last element, but it needs to find the first element and needs to know when it has seen the last element.

You can tell if an iterator is at the same location as another iterator by using the operator, `==`. Thus, if you have an iterator pointing to the first, last, or other element, you could test another iterator to see if it is located at the first, last, or other element.

If `p1` and `p2` are two iterators, then the comparison

```
p1 == p2
```

is `true` when and only when `p1` and `p2` are located at the same element. (This is analogous to pointers. If `p1` and `p2` were pointers, this comparison would be `true` if they pointed to the same thing.) As usual, `!=` is just the negation of `==`, and so

```
p1!= p2
```

is `true` when `p1` and `p2` are not located at the same element.

The member function begin( ) is used to position an iterator at the first element in a container. For vectors, and many other container classes, the member function begin( ) returns an iterator located at the first element. (For a vector v the first element is v[0].) Thus,

```
iterator p = v.begin( );
```

initializes the iterator variable p to an iterator located at the first element. The basic for loop for visiting all elements of the vector v is therefore

```
iterator p;
for (p = v.begin( ); Boolean_Expression; p++)
    Action_At_Location p;
```

The desired stopping condition is

```
p = v.end( )
```

The member function end( ) returns a sentinel value that can be checked to see if an iterator has passed the last element. If p is located at the last element, then after p++, the test p = v.end( )changes from false to true. So the correct *Boolean_Expression* is the negation of this stopping condition:

```
iterator p;
for (p = v.begin( ); p != v.end( ); p++)
    Action_At_Location p;
```

Note that p != v.end( ) does not change from true to false until after p's location has advanced past the last element. So, v.end( ) is not located at any element. The value v.end( ) is a special value that serves as a sentinel. It is not an iterator, but you can compare v.end( ) to an iterator using == and !=. The value v.end( ) is analogous to the value NULL that is used to mark the end of a linked list of the kind discussed in Chapter 17.

The following for loop from Display 19.1 uses this same technique with the vector named container:

```
iterator p;
for (p = container.begin( ); p != container.end( ); p++)
    cout << *p << " ";
```

The action taken at the location of the iterator p is

```
cout << *p << " ";
```

The dereferencing operator, *, is overloaded for STL container iterators so that *p produces the element at location p. In particular, for a vector container, *p produces the element located at the iterator p. The above cout statement thus outputs the element located at the iterator p, and so the entire for loop outputs all the elements in the vector container.

The dereferencing operator *p always produces the element located at the iterator p. In some situations *p produces read-only access, which does not allow you to change the element. In other situations it gives you access to the element and will let you change the element. For vectors, *p will allow you to change the element located at p, as illustrated by the following for loop from Display 19.1:

```
for (p = container.begin( ); p != container.end( ); p++)
    *p = 0;
```

This for loop cycles through all the elements in the vector container and changes all the elements to 0.

ITERATOR

An iterator is an object that can be used with a container to gain access to elements in the container. An iterator is a generalization of the notion of a pointer. The operators ==, !=, ++, and -- behave the same for iterators as they do for pointers. The basic outline of how an iterator can cycle through all the elements in a container is as follows:

```
iterator p;
for (p = container.begin( ); p != container.end( ); p++)
    Process_Element_At_Location p;
```

The member function begin( ) returns an iterator located at the first element. The member function end( ) returns a value that serves as a sentinel value one location past the last element in the container.

DEREFERENCING

The dereferencing operator, *p, when applied to an iterator p, produces the element located at the iterator p. In some situations *p produces read-only access, which does not allow you to change the element. In other situations it gives you access to the element and will let you change the element.

Self-Test Exercises

1. If v is a vector, what does v.begin( ) return? What does v.end( ) return?

2. If p is an iterator for a vector object v, what is *p?

3. Suppose v is a vector of ints. Write a for loop that will output all the elements of p except for the first element.

KINDS OF ITERATORS

Different containers have different kinds of iterators. Iterators are classified according to the kinds of operations that work on them. Vector iterators are of the most general form; that is, all the operations work with vector iterators. Thus, we will again use the vector container to illustrate iterators. In this case we use a vector to illustrate the iterator operations of *decrement* and *random access*. Display 19.2 shows another program using a vector object named container and an iterator p.

The decrement operator is used on line 30 of Display 19.2. As you would expect, p-- moves the iterator p to the previous location. The decrement operator, --, is similar to the increment operator, ++, but it moves the iterator in the opposite direction.

Display 19.2   Bidirectional and Random-Access Iterator Use *(part 1 of 2)*

```
1   //Program to demonstrate bidirectional and random-access iterators.
2   #include <iostream>
3   #include <vector>
4   using std::cout;
5   using std::endl;
6   using std::vector;
7   using std::vector<char>::iterator;

8   int main( )
9   {
10      vector<char> container;

11      container.push_back('A');
12      container.push_back('B');
13      container.push_back('C');
14      container.push_back('D');

15      for (int i = 0; i < 4; i++)
16          cout << "container[" << i << "] == "
17              << container[i] << endl;

18      iterator p = container.begin( );
19      cout << "The third entry is " << container[2] << endl;
20      cout << "The third entry is " << p[2] << endl;
21      cout << "The third entry is " << *(p + 2) << endl;

22      cout << "Back to container[0].\n";
23      p = container.begin( );
24      cout << "which has value " << *p << endl;

25      cout << "Two steps forward and one step back:\n";
26      p++;
27      cout << *p << endl;
```

Three different notations for the same thing

This notation is specialized to vectors and arrays.

These two work for any random-access iterator.

Display 19.2   Bidirectional and Random Access Iterator Use *(part 2 of 2)*

```
28        p++;
29        cout << *p << endl;
30        p--;          ←————————————    This works for any
31        cout << *p << endl;             bidirectional iterator.

32        return 0;
33    }
```

SAMPLE DIALOGUE

```
container[0] == A
container[1] == B
container[2] == C
container[3] == D
The third entry is C
The third entry is C
The third entry is C
Back to container[0].
which has value A
Two steps forward and one step back:
B
C
B
```

The increment and decrement operators can be used in either prefix (++p) or postfix (p++) notation. In addition to changing p, they also return a value. The details of the value returned are completely analogous to what happens with the increment and decrement operators on int variables. In prefix notation, first the variable is changed and then the changed value is returned. In postfix notation, the value is returned before the variable is changed. We prefer not to use the increment and decrement operators as expressions that return a value; we use them only to change the variable value.

The following lines from Display 19.2 illustrate the fact that with vector iterators you have random access to the elements of a vector, such as container:

```
iterator p = container.begin( );
cout << "The third entry is " << container[2] << endl;
cout << "The third entry is " << p[2] << endl;
cout << "The third entry is " << *(p + 2) << endl;
```

random access

Random access means that you can go directly to any particular element in one step. We have already used container[2] as a form of random access to a vector. This is simply the square bracket operator that is standard with arrays and vectors. What is new is that you can use this same square bracket notation with an iterator. The expression p[2] is a way to obtain access to the element indexed by 2.

The expressions p[2] and *(p + 2) are completely equivalent. By analogy to pointer arithmetic (see Chapter 10), (p + 2) names the location two places beyond p. Since p is at the first (index 0) location in the previous code, (p + 2) is at the third (index 2) location. The expression (p + 2) returns an iterator. The expression *(p + 2) dereferences that iterator. Of course, you can replace 2 with a different nonnegative integer to obtain a pointer to a different element.

Be sure to note that neither p[2] nor (p + 2) changes the value of the iterator in the iterator variable p. The expression (p + 2) returns another iterator at another location, but it leaves p where it was. Something similar happens with p[2] behind the scenes. Also note that the meaning of p[2] and (p + 2) depends on the location of the iterator in p. For example, (p + 2) means two locations beyond the location of p, wherever that may be.

For example, suppose the previously discussed code from Display 19.2 were replaced with the following (note the added p++):

```
iterator p = container.begin( );
p++;
cout << "The third entry is " << container[2] << endl;
cout << "The third entry is " << p[2] << endl;
cout << "The third entry is " << *(p + 2) << endl;
```

The output of these three couts would no longer be

```
The third entry is C
The third entry is C
The third entry is C
```

but would instead be

```
The third entry is C
The third entry is D
The third entry is D
```

The p++ moves p from location 0 to location 1, and so (p + 2) is now an iterator at location 3, not location 2. So, *(p + 2) and p[2] are equivalent to container[3], not container[2].

We now know enough about how to operate on iterators to make sense of how iterators are classified. The main kinds of iterators are as follows.

Forward iterators: ++ works on the iterator.

Bidirectional iterators: Both ++ and -- work on the iterator.

Random-access iterators: ++, --, and random access all work with the iterator.

Note that these are increasingly strong categories: Every random-access iterator is also a bidirectional iterator, and every bidirectional iterator is also a forward iterator.

As we will see, different template container classes have different kinds of iterators. The iterators for the vector template class are random-access iterators.

Note that the names *forward iterator*, *bidirectional iterator*, and *random-access iterator* refer to kinds of iterators, not type names. An actual type name would be something like `std::vector<int>::iterator`, which in this case happens to be a random-access iterator.

KINDS OF ITERATOR

Different containers have different kinds of iterators. The following are the main kinds of iterators.

Forward iterators: ++ works on the iterator.

Bidirectional iterators: Both ++ and -- work on the iterator.

Random-access iterators: ++, --, and random access all work with the iterator.

Self-Test Exercises

4. Suppose the vector v contains the letters 'A', 'B', 'C', and 'D' in that order. What is the output of the following code?

```
using std::vector<char>::iterator;
   . . .
iterator i = v.begin( );
i++;
cout << *(i + 2) << " ";
i--;
cout << i[2] << " ";
cout << *(i + 2) << " ";
```

■ CONSTANT AND MUTABLE ITERATORS

constant iterator

mutable iterator

The categories of forward iterator, bidirectional iterator, and random-access iterator each subdivide into two categories—*constant* and *mutable*—depending on how the dereferencing operator behaves with the iterator. With a **constant iterator** the dereferencing operator produces a read-only version of the element. With a constant iterator p, you can use *p to assign it to a variable or output it to the screen, for example, but you cannot change the element in the container by, for example, assigning to *p. With a **mutable iterator** p, *p can be assigned a value, and that will change the corresponding element in the container. Phrased another way, with a mutable iterator p, *p returns an lvalue. The vector iterators are mutable, as shown by the following lines from Display 19.1:

```
cout << "Setting entries to 0:\n";
for (p = container.begin( ); p != container.end( ); p++)
    *p = 0;
```

If a container has only constant iterators, you cannot obtain a mutable iterator for the container. However, if a container has mutable iterators and you want a constant iterator for the container, you can have it. You might want a constant iterator as a kind of error checking device if you intend that your code should not change the elements in the container. For example, the following will produce a constant iterator for a vector container named container:

```
std::vector<char>::const_iterator p = container.begin( );
```

or equivalently

```
using std::vector<char>::const_iterator;
const_iterator p = container.begin( );
```

With p declared in this way, the following would produce an error message:

```
*p = 'Z';
```

For example, Display 19.2 would behave exactly the same if you changed

```
using std::vector<int>::iterator;
```

to

```
using std::vector<int>::const_iterator;
```

and replaced

```
iterator p;
```

with

```
const_iterator p;
```

However, a similar change would not work in Display 19.1 because of the following line from the program in Display 19.1:

```
*p = 0;
```

Note that const_iterator is a type name, whereas *constant iterator* is the name of a kind of iterator. However, every iterator of a type named const_iterator will be a constant iterator.

CONSTANT ITERATOR

A *constant iterator* is an iterator that does not allow you to change the element at its location.

■ REVERSE ITERATORS

Sometimes you want to cycle through the elements in a container in reverse order. If you have a container with bidirectional iterators, you might be tempted to try the following:

```
iterator p;
for (p = container.end( ); p != container.begin( ); p--)
    cout << *p << " ";
```

This code will compile, and you may be able to get something like this to work on some systems, but there is something fundamentally wrong with it: `container.end( )` is not a regular iterator but only a sentinel, and `container.begin( )` is not a sentinel.

Fortunately, there is an easy way to do what you want. For a container with bidirectional iterators, there is a way to reverse everything using a kind of iterator known as a **reverse iterator**. The following will work fine:

reverse
iterator

```
reverse_iterator rp;
for (rp = container.rbegin( ); rp != container.rend( ); rp++)
    cout << *rp << " ";
```

rbegin( )

rend( )

The member function `rbegin( )` returns an iterator located at the last element. The member function `rend( )` returns a sentinel the marks the "end" of the elements in the reverse order. Note that for an iterator of type `reverse_iterator`, the increment operator, ++, moves backward through the elements. In other words, the meanings of -- and ++ are interchanged. The program in Display 19.3 demonstrates a reverse iterator.

`reverse_iterator` type also has a constant version, which is named `const_reverse_iterator`.

REVERSE ITERATORS

A reverse iterator can be used to cycle through all elements of a container with bidirectional iterators. The elements are visited in reverse order. The general scheme is as follows:

```
reverse_iterator rp;
for (rp = c.rbegin( ); rp != c.rend( ); rp++)
    Process_At_Location p;
```

The object c is a container class with bidirectional iterators.

When using `reverse_iterator` you need to have some sort of using declaration or something equivalent. For example, if c is a `vector<int>`, the following will suffice:

```
using std::vector<int>::reverse_iterator;
```

Display 19.3   Reverse Iterator

```
1   //Program to demonstrate a reverse iterator.
2   #include <iostream>
3   #include <vector>
4   using std::cout;
5   using std::endl;
6   using std::vector;
7   using std::vector<char>::iterator;
8   using std::vector<char>::reverse_iterator;

9   int main( )
10  {
11      vector<char> container;

12      container.push_back('A');
13      container.push_back('B');
14      container.push_back('C');

15      cout << "Forward:\n";
16      iterator p;
17      for (p = container.begin( ); p != container.end( ); p++)
18          cout << *p << " ";
19      cout << endl;

20      cout << "Reverse:\n";
21      reverse_iterator rp;
22      for (rp = container.rbegin( ); rp != container.rend( ); rp++)
23          cout << *rp << " ";
24      cout << endl;

25      return 0;
26  }
```

SAMPLE DIALOGUE

```
Forward:
A B C
Reverse:
C B A
```

Pitfall

COMPILER PROBLEMS

Some compilers have problems with iterator declarations. You can declare an iterator in different ways. For example, we have been using the following:

```
using std::vector<char>::iterator;
. . .
iterator p;
```

Alternatively, you could use the following:

```
std::vector<char>::iterator p;
```

You could also use the following, which is not quite as nice:

```
using namespace std;
. . .
vector<char>::iterator p;
```

There are other similar variations.

Your compiler should accept any of these alternatives. However, we have found that some compilers will accept only certain of these alternatives. If one form does not work with your compiler, try another.

■ OTHER KINDS OF ITERATORS

input iterator

output iterator

There are other kinds of iterators, which we will not cover in this book. We will briefly mention two kinds of iterators whose names you may encounter. An **input iterator** is essentially a forward iterator that can be used with input streams. An **output iterator** is essentially a forward iterator that can be used with output streams. For more details you will need to consult a more advanced reference.

Self-Test Exercises

5. Suppose the vector v contains the letters 'A', 'B', 'C', and 'D' in that order. What is the output of the following code?

```
using std::vector<char>::reverse_iterator;
 . . .
reverse_iterator i = v.rbegin( );
i++; i++;
cout << *i << " ";
i--;
cout << *i << " ";
```

6. Suppose you want to run the following code, where v is a vector of ints:

```
for (p = v.begin( ); p != v.end( ); p++)
    cout << *p << " ";
```

Which of the following are possible ways to declare p?

```
std::vector<int>::iterator p;
std::vector<int>::const_iterator p;
```

19.2 Containers

You can put all your eggs in one basket,
but be sure it's a good basket.

Walter Savitch, *Absolute C++*

container class

The **container classes** of the STL are different kinds of structures for holding data, such as lists, queues, and stacks. Each is a template class with a parameter for the particular type of data to be stored. So, for example, you can specify a list to be a list of ints or doubles or strings, or any class or struct type you wish. Each container template class may have its own specialized accessor and mutator functions for adding data and removing data from the container. Different container classes may have different kinds of iterators. For example, one container class may have bidirectional iterators whereas another container class may have only forward iterators. However, whenever they are defined, the iterator operators and the member functions begin( ) and end( ) have the same meaning for all STL container classes.

SEQUENTIAL CONTAINERS

A sequential container arranges its data items into a list such that there is a first element, a next element, and so forth, up to a last element. The linked lists we discussed in Chapter 17 are examples of a kind of sequential container. The lists we discussed in Chapter 17 are sometimes called **singly linked lists** because there is only one link from one location to another. The STL has no container corresponding to such a singly linked list, although some implementations do offer an implementation of a singly linked list, typically under the name slist. The simplest list that is part of the STL is the **doubly linked list**, which is the template class named list. The difference between these two kinds of lists is illustrated in Display 19.4.[1]

singly linked list

doubly linked list

---

[1] The Silicon Graphics version of the STL includes slist and is distributed with the g++ compiler. SGI provides a very useful reference document for its STL version that is applicable to almost everyone's STL. At the time this book went to print, it was available on the web at http://www.sgi.com/.

Display 19.4   Two Kinds of Lists

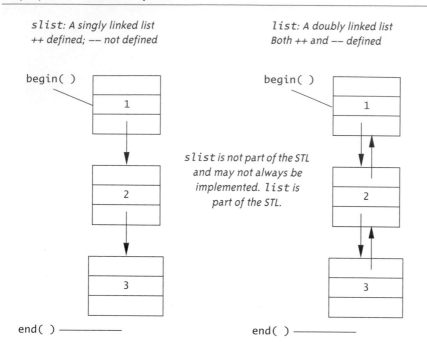

slist: A singly linked list
++ defined; −− not defined

list: A doubly linked list
Both ++ and −− defined

begin( )

1

2

3

end( )

begin( )

1

2

3

end( )

*slist is not part of the STL
and may not always be
implemented. list is
part of the STL.*

**slist and
list**

The lists in Display 19.4 contain the three integer values 1, 2, and 3 in that order. The types for the two lists are slist<int> and list<int>. The display also indicates the location of the iterators begin( ) and end( ). We have not yet told you how you can enter the integers into the lists.

In Display 19.4 we have drawn our singly and doubly linked lists as nodes and pointers of the form discussed in Chapter 17. The STL class list and the nonstandard class slist might (or might not) be implemented in this way. However, when using the STL template classes, you are shielded from these implementation details. So, you simply think in terms of locations for the data (which may or may not be nodes) and of iterators (not pointers). You can think of the arrows in Display 19.4 as indicating the directions for ++ (which is down) and −− (which is up in Display 19.4).

We presented the template class slist to help give a context for the sequential containers. It corresponds to what we discussed in Chapter 17 and is the first thing that comes to the mind of most programmers when you mention *linked lists*. However, since the template class slist is not standard we will not discuss it further. If your implementation offers the template class slist and you want to use it, the details are similar to those we will describe for list, except that the decrement operators −− (prefix and postfix) are not defined for slist.

A simple program using the STL template class `list` is given in Display 19.5. The function `push_back` adds an element to the end of the list. Notice that for the `list` template class, the dereferencing operator gives you access for reading and for changing the data. Also notice that with the `list` template class and all the template classes and iterators of the STL, all definitions are placed in the `std` namespace.

push_back

Display 19.5   Using the `list` Template Class

```
1    //Program to demonstrate the STL template class list.
2    #include <iostream>
3    #include <list>
4    using std::cout;
5    using std::endl;
6    using std::list;
7    using std::list<int>::iterator;

8    int main( )
9    {
10       list<int> listObject;

11       for (int i = 1; i <= 3; i++)
12           listObject.push_back(i);
13       cout << "List contains:\n";
14       iterator iter;
15       for (iter = listObject.begin( ); iter != listObject.end( ); iter++)
16           cout << *iter << " ";
17       cout << endl;

18       cout << "Setting all entries to 0:\n";
19       for (iter = listObject.begin( ); iter != listObject.end( ); iter++)
20           *iter = 0;

21       cout << "List now contains:\n";
22       for (iter = listObject.begin( ); iter != listObject.end( ); iter++)
23           cout << *iter << " ";
24       cout << endl;

25       return 0;
26   }
```

SAMPLE DIALOGUE

```
List contains:
1 2 3
Setting all entries to 0:
List now contains:
0 0 0
```

Note that Display 19.5 would compile and run exactly the same if we replaced list and list<int> with vector and vector<int>, respectively. This uniformity of usage is a key part of the STL syntax.

There are, however, differences between a vector and a list container. One of the main differences is that a vector container has random-access iterators whereas a list has only bidirectional iterators. For example, if you start with Display 19.2, which uses random access, and replace all occurrences of vector and vector<char> with list and list<char>, respectively, and then compile the program, you will get a compiler error. (You will get an error message even if you delete the statements containing container[i] or container[2].)

The basic sequential container template classes of the STL are listed in Display 19.6. Other containers, such as stacks and queues, can be obtained from these using techniques discussed in the subsection entitled "The Container Adapters stack and queue." A sample of some member functions of the sequential container classes is given in Display 19.7. All these sequence template classes have a destructor that returns storage for recycling.

memory management

Display 19.6   STL Basic Sequential Containers

TEMPLATE CLASS NAME	ITERATOR TYPE NAMES	KIND OF ITERATORS	LIBRARY HEADER FILE
slist (Warning: slist is not part of the STL.)	slist<T>::iterator slist<T>::const_iterator	Mutable forward Constant forward	<slist> (Depends on implementation and may not be available.)
list	list<T>::iterator list<T>::const_iterator list<T>::reverse_iterator list<T>::const_reverse_iterator	Mutable bidirectional Constant bidirectional Mutable bidirectional Constant bidirectional	<list>
vector	vector<T>::iterator vector<T>::const_iterator vector<T>::reverse_iterator vector<T>::const_reverse_iterator	Mutable random access Constant random access Mutable random access Constant random access	<vector>
deque	deque<T>::iterator deque<T>::const_iterator deque<T>::reverse_iterator deque<T>::const_reverse_iterator	Mutable random access Constant random access Mutable random access Constant random access	<deque>

Display 19.7   Some Sequential Container Member Functions

MEMBER FUNCTION (c IS A CONTAINER OBJECT)	MEANING
c.size( )	Returns the number of elements in the container.
c.begin( )	Returns an iterator located at the first element in the container.
c.end( )	Returns an iterator located one beyond the last element in the container.
c.rbegin( )	Returns an iterator located at the last element in the container. Used with reverse_iterator. Not a member of slist.
c.rend( )	Returns an iterator located one beyond the first element in the container. Used with reverse_iterator. Not a member of slist.
c.push_back(Element)	Inserts the Element at the end of the sequence. Not a member of slist.
c.push_front(Element)	Inserts the Element at the front of the sequence. Not a member of vector.
c.insert(Iterator, Element)	Inserts a copy of Element before the location of Iterator.
c.erase(Iterator)	Removes the element at location Iterator. Returns an iterator at the location immediately following. Returns c.end( ) if the last element is removed.
c.clear( )	A void function that removes all the elements in the container.
c.front( )	Returns a reference to the element in the front of the sequence. Equivalent to *(c.begin( )).
c1 == c2	True if c1.size( ) == c2.size( ) and each element of c1 is equal to the corresponding element of c2.
c1 != c2	!(c1 == c2)

All the sequence containers discussed in this section also have a default constructor, a copy constructor, and various other constructors for initializing the container to default or specified elements. Each also has a destructor that returns all storage for recycling, and a well-behaved assignment operator.

Deque is pronounced "d-queue" or "deck" and stands for "doubly ended queue." A deque is a kind of super queue. With a queue you add data at one end of the data sequence and remove data from the other end. With a deque you can add data at either end and remove data from either end. The template class deque is a template class for a deque with a parameter for the type of data stored.

deque

SEQUENTIAL CONTAINERS

A sequential container arranges its data items into a list so that there is a first element, a next element, and so forth, up to a last element. The sequential container template classes that we have discussed are slist, list, vector, and deque.

Pitfall   **ITERATORS AND REMOVING ELEMENTS**

Adding or removing an element to or from a container can affect other iterators. In general, there is no guarantee that the iterators will be located at the same element after an addition or deletion. Some containers do, however, guarantee that the iterators will not be moved by additions or deletions, except of course if the iterator is located at an element that is removed.

Of the template classes we have seen so far, list and slist guarantee that their iterators will not be moved by additions or deletions, except of course if the iterator is located at an element that is removed. The template classes vector and deque make no such guarantee.

Tip   **TYPE DEFINITIONS IN CONTAINERS**

The STL container classes contain type definitions that can be handy when programming with these classes. We have already seen that STL container classes may contain the type names iterator, const_iterator, reverse_iterator, and const_reverse_iterator (and hence must contain their type definitions behind the scene). There are typically other type definitions as well.

The type value_type is the type of the elements stored in the container, and size_type is an unsigned integer type that is the return type for the member function size. For example, list<int>::value_type is another name for int. All the template classes we have discussed so far have the defined types value_type and size_type.

Self-Test Exercises

7. What is a major difference between vector and list?

8. Which of the template classes slist, list, vector, and deque have the member function push_back?

9. Which of the template classes slist, list, vector, and deque have random-access iterators?

10. Which of the template classes slist, list, vector, and deque can have mutable iterators?

■ THE CONTAINER ADAPTERS stack AND queue

Container adapters are template classes that are implemented on top of other classes. For example, the stack template class is by default implemented on top of the deque template class, which means that buried in the implementation of the stack is a deque where all the data resides. However, you are shielded from this implementation detail and see a stack as a simple last-in/first-out data structure.

Other container adapter classes are the queue and priority_queue template classes. Stacks and queues were discussed in Chapter 17. A **priority queue** is a queue with the additional property that each entry is given a priority when it is added to the queue. If all entries have the same priority, then entries are removed from a priority queue in the same manner as they are removed from a queue. If items have different priorities, the higher-priority items are removed before lower-priority items. We will not discuss priority queues in any detail, but mention it for those who may be familiar with the concept.

priority queue

Although an adapter template class has a default container class on top of which it is built, you may choose to specify a different underlying container, for efficiency or other reasons, depending on your application. For example, any sequence container may serve as the underlying container for the stack template class, and any sequence container other than vector may serve as the underlying container for the queue template class. The default underlying data structure is the deque for both the stack and the queue. For a priority_queue the default underlying container is a vector. If you are happy with the default underlying container type, then a container adapter looks like any other template container class to you. For example, the type name for the stack template class using the default underlying container is stack<int> for a stack of ints. If you wish to specify that the underlying container is instead the vector template class, you would use stack<int, vector<int> > as the type name. We will always use the default underlying container.

If you do specify an underlying container, be warned that you should not place two > symbols in the type expression without a space in between them, or the compiler can be confused. Use stack<int, vector<int> >, with a space between the last two >'s. Do not use stack<int, vector<int>>.

Warning!

The member functions and other details about the stack template class are given in Display 19.8. For the queue template class these details are given in Display 19.9. A simple example of using the stack template class is given in Display 19.10.

Self-Test Exercises

11. What kind of iterators (forward, bidirectional, or random-access) does the stack template adapter class have?

12. What kind of iterators (forward, bidirectional, or random-access) does the queue template adapter class have?

13. If s is a stack<char>, what is the type of the returned value of s.pop( )?

Display 19.8   The stack Template Class

stack ADAPTER TEMPLATE CLASS DETAILS

Type name: stack<T> or stack<T, *Sequence_Type*> for a stack of elements of type T.

Library header: <stack>, which places the definition in the std namespace.

Defined types: value_type, size_type.

There are no iterators.

SAMPLE MEMBER FUNCTIONS

MEMBER FUNCTION (s IS A STACK OBJECT)	MEANING
s.size( )	Returns the number of elements in the stack.
s.empty( )	Returns true if the stack is empty; otherwise, returns false.
s.top( )	Returns a mutable reference to the top member of the stack.
s.push(*Element*)	Inserts a copy of *Element* at the top of the stack.
s.pop( )	Removes the top element of the stack. Note that pop is a void function. It does not return the element removed.
s1 == s2	True if s1.size( ) == s2.size( ) and each element of s1 is equal to the corresponding element of s2; otherwise, returns false.

The stack template class also has a default constructor, a copy constructor, and a constructor that takes an object of any sequence class and initializes the stack to the elements in the sequence. It also has a destructor that returns all storage for recycling, and a well-behaved assignment operator.

■ THE ASSOCIATIVE CONTAINERS set AND map

key

Associative containers are basically very simple databases. They store data, such as structs or any other type of data. Each data item has an associated value known as its **key**. For example, if the data is a struct with an employee's record, the key might be the employee's Social Security number. Items are retrieved on the basis of the key. The key type and the type for data to be stored need not have any relationship to one another, although they often are related. A very simple case is when each data item is its own key. For example, in a set every element is its own key.

set

The set template class is, in some sense, the simplest container you can imagine. It stores elements without repetition. The first insertion places an element in the set. Additional insertions after the first have no effect, so that no element appears more than once. Each element is its own key. Basically, you just add or delete elements and ask if an element is in the set or not. Like all STL classes, the set template class was

Display 19.9   The queue Template Class

queue **ADAPTER TEMPLATE CLASS DETAILS**

Type name: queue<T> or queue<*Sequence_Type*, T> for a queue of elements of type T. For efficiency reasons, the *Sequence_Type* cannot be a vector type.

Library header: <queue>, which places the definition in the std namespace.

Defined types: value_type, size_type.

There are no iterators.

SAMPLE MEMBER FUNCTIONS

MEMBER FUNCTION (q IS A QUEUE OBJECT)	MEANING
q.size( )	Returns the number of elements in the queue.
q.empty( )	Returns true if the queue is empty; otherwise, returns false.
q.front( )	Returns a mutable reference to the front member of the queue.
q.back( )	Returns a mutable reference to the last member of the queue.
q.push(*Element*)	Adds *Element* to the back of the queue.
q.pop( )	Removes the front element of the queue. Note that pop is a void function. It does not return the element removed.
q1 == q2	True if q1.size( ) == q2.size( ) and each element of q1 is equal to the corresponding element of q2; otherwise, returns false.

The queue template class also has a default constructor, a copy constructor, and a constructor that takes an object of any sequence class and initializes the stack to the elements in the sequence. It also has a destructor that returns all storage for recycling, and a well-behaved assignment operator.

Display 19.10   Program Using the stack Template Class *(part 1 of 2)*

```
1   //Program to demonstrate use of the stack template class from the STL.
2   #include <iostream>
3   #include <stack>
4   using std::cin;
5   using std::cout;
6   using std::endl;
7   using std::stack;

8   int main( )
9   {
```

Display 19.10   Program Using the stack Template Class (part 2 of 2)

```
10      stack<char> s;

11      cout << "Enter a line of text:\n";
12      char next;
13      cin.get(next);
14      while (next != '\n')
15      {
16          s.push(next);
17          cin.get(next);
18      }

19      cout << "Written backward that is:\n";
20      while ( ! s.empty( ) )
21      {
22          cout << s.top( );
23          s.pop( );
24      }
25      cout << endl;

26      return 0;
27  }
```

The member function pop removes one element, but does not return that element. pop is a void function. Therefore, we needed to use top to read the element we removed.

SAMPLE DIALOGUE

```
Enter a line of text:
straw
Written backward that is:
warts
```

written with efficiency as a goal. To work efficiently, a set object stores its values in sorted order. You can specify the order used for storing elements as follows:

```
set<T, Ordering> s;
```

Ordering should be a well-behaved ordering relation that takes two arguments of type T and returns a bool value.[2] T is the type of elements stored. If no ordering is specified,

---

[2] The ordering must be a *strict weak ordering*. Most typical ordering used to implement the < operator is strict weak ordering. For those who want the details: A strict weak ordering must be: (irreflexive) Ordering(x, x) is always false; (antisymmetric) Ordering(x, y) implies !Ordering(y, x); (transitive) Ordering(x, y) and Ordering(y, z) implies Ordering(x, z); and (transitivity of equivalence) if x is equivalent to y and y is equivalent to z, then x is equivalent to z. Two elements x and y are equivalent if Ordering(x, y) and Ordering(y, x) are both false.

then the ordering is assumed to use the < relational operator. Some basic details about the set template class are given in Display 19.11. A simple example that shows how to use some of the member functions of the template class set is given in Display 19.12 .

A **map** is essentially a function given as a set of ordered pairs. For each value first that appears in a pair, there is at most one value second such that the pair (first, second) is in the map. The template class map implements map objects in the STL. For example, if

map

Display 19.11   The set Template Class

---

set TEMPLATE CLASS DETAILS

Type name: set<T> or set<T, *Ordering*> for a set of elements of type T. The *Ordering* is used to sort elements for storage. If no *Ordering* is given, the ordering used is the binary operator, <.

Library header: <set> which places the definition in the std namespace.

Defined types include value_type, size_type.

Iterators: iterator, const_iterator, reverse_iterator, and const_reverse_iterator. All iterators are bidirectional and those not including const_ are mutable. begin( ), end( ), rbegin( ), and rend( ) have the expected behavior. Adding or deleting elements does not affect iterators, except for an iterator located at the element removed.

SAMPLE MEMBER FUNCTIONS

MEMBER FUNCTION (s IS A SET OBJECT)	MEANING
s.insert(*Element*)	Inserts a copy of *Element* in the set. If *Element* is already in the set, this has no effect.
s.erase(*Element*)	Removes *Element* from the set. If *Element* is not in the set, this has no effect.
s.find(*Element*)	Returns a mutable iterator located at the copy of *Element* in the set. If *Element* is not in the set, s.end( ) is returned.
s.erase(*Iterator*)	Erases the element at the location of the *Iterator*.
s.size( )	Returns the number of elements in the set.
s.empty( )	Returns true if the set is empty; otherwise, returns false.
s1 == s2	Returns true if the sets contain the same elements; otherwise, returns false.

The set template class also has a default constructor, a copy constructor, and other specialized constructors not mentioned here. It also has a destructor that returns all storage for recycling, and a well-behaved assignment operator.

Display 19.12   Program Using the set Template Class

```
1   //Program to demonstrate use of the set template class.
2   #include <iostream>
3   #include <set>
4   using std::cout;
5   using std::endl;
6   using std::set;
7   using std::set<char>::const_iterator;

8   int main( )
9   {
10      set<char> s;

11      s.insert('A');
12      s.insert('D');
13      s.insert('D');
14      s.insert('C');
15      s.insert('C');
16      s.insert('B');

17      cout << "The set contains:\n";
18      const_iterator p;
19      for (p = s.begin( ); p != s.end( ); p++)
20      cout << *p << " ";
21      cout << endl;

22      cout << "Removing C.\n";
23      s.erase('C');
24      for (p = s.begin( ); p != s.end( ); p++)
25      cout << *p << " ";
26      cout << endl;

27      return 0;
28  }
```

No matter how many times you add an element to a set, the set contains only one copy of that element.

SAMPLE DIALOGUE

```
The set contains:
A B C D
Removing C.
A B D
```

you want to assign a unique number to each string name, you could declare a map object as follows:

```
map<string, int> numberMap;
```

For string values known as *keys*, the numberMap object can associate a unique int value.

Like a set object, a map object stores its elements in sorted order by its key values. You can specify the ordering on keys as a third entry in the angular brackets, < >. If you do not specify an ordering, a default ordering is used. The restrictions on orderings you can use are the same as those on the orderings allowed for the set template class. Note that the ordering is on key values only. The second type can be any type and need not have anything to do with any ordering. As with the set object, the sorting of the stored entries in a map object is done for reasons of efficiency.

Some basic details about the map template class are given in Display 19.13. In order to understand these details, you need to first know something about the pair template class.

The STL template class pair<T1, T2> has objects that are pairs of values such that the   pair
first element is of type T1 and the second is of type T2. If aPair is an object of type pair<T1, T2>, then aPair.first is the first element, which is of type T1, and aPair.second is the second element, which is of type T2. The member variables first and second are public member variables, so no accessor or mutator functions are needed.

The header file for the pair template is <utility>. So, to use the pair template class, you need the following, or something like it, in your file:

```
#include<utility>
using std::pair;
```

We will mention two other associative containers, although we will not give any details about them. The template classes multiset and multimap are essentially the same as set and map, respectively, except that multiset allows repetition of elements and multimap allows multiple values to be associated with each key value.

■ EFFICIENCY

The STL was designed with efficiency as an important consideration. In fact, the STL implementations strive to be optimally efficient. For example, the set and map elements are stored in sorted order so that algorithms that search for the elements can be more efficient.

Each of the member functions for each of the template classes has a guaranteed maximum running time. These maximum running times are expressed using what is called big-*O* notation, which we discuss in Section 19.3. (Section 19.3 also gives some guaranteed running times for some of the container member functions we have already discussed. These are given in the subsection entitled "Container Access Running Times.") When using more advanced references or even later in this chapter, you will be told the guaranteed maximum running times for certain functions.

map TEMPLATE CLASS DETAILS

Type name: map<*KeyType*, T> or map<*KeyType*, T, *Ordering*> for a map that associates ("maps") elements of type *KeyType* to elements of type T. The *Ordering* is used to sort elements by key value for efficient storage. If no *Ordering* is given, the ordering used is the binary operator, <.

Library header: <map>, which places the definition in the std namespace.

Defined types include key_type for the type of the key values, mapped_type for the type of the values mapped to, and size_type. (So, the defined type key_type is simply what we called *KeyType* above.)

Iterators: iterator, const_iterator, reverse_iterator, and const_reverse_iterator. All iterators are bidirectional. Those iterators not including const_ are neither constant nor mutable but something in between. For example, if p is of type iterator, then you can change the key value but not the value of type T. Perhaps it is best, at least at first, to treat all iterators as if they were constant. begin( ), end( ), rbegin( ), and rend( ) have the expected behavior. Adding or deleting elements does not affect iterators, except for an iterator located at the element removed.

SAMPLE MEMBER FUNCTIONS

MEMBER FUNCTION (m IS A MAP OBJECT)	MEANING
m.insert(*Element*)	Inserts *Element* in the map. *Element* is of type pair<*KeyType*, T>. Returns a value of type pair<iterator, bool>. If the insertion is successful, the second part of the returned pair is true and the iterator is located at the inserted element.
m.erase(*Target_Key*)	Removes the element with the key *Target_Key*.
m.find(*Target_Key*)	Returns an iterator located at the element with key value *Target_Key*. Returns m.end( ) if there is no such element.
m.size( )	Returns the number of pairs in the map.
m.empty( )	Returns true if the map is empty; otherwise, returns false.
m1 == m2	Returns true if the maps contain the same pairs; otherwise, returns false.

The map template class also has a default constructor, a copy constructor, and other specialized constructors not mentioned here. It also has a destructor that returns all storage for recycling, and a well-behaved assignment operator.

14. Why are the elements in the `set` template class stored in sorted order?

15. Can a `set` have elements of a class type?

16. Suppose `s` is of the type `set<char>`. What value is returned by `s.find('A')` if `'A'` is in s? What value is returned if `'A'` is not in s?

19.3 Generic Algorithms

"And if you take one from three hundred and sixty-five, what remains?"
"Three hundred and sixty-four, of course."
Humpty Dumpty looked doubtful. "I'd rather see that done on paper,"
he said.

Lewis Carroll, *Through the Looking-Glass*

This section covers some basic function templates in the STL. We cannot give you a comprehensive description of them all here, but we will present a large enough sample to give you a good feel for what is contained in the STL and to give you sufficient detail to start using these template functions.

These template functions are sometimes called **generic algorithms**. The term *algorithm* is used for a reason. Recall that an algorithm is just a set of instructions for performing a task. An algorithm can be presented in any language, including a programming language like C++. But, when using the word *algorithm*, programmers typically have in mind a less formal presentation given in English or pseudocode. As such, it is often thought of as an abstraction of the code defining a function. It gives the important details but not the fine details of the coding. The STL specifies certain details about the algorithms underlying the STL template functions, which is why they are sometimes called *generic algorithms*. These STL function templates do more than just deliver a value in any way that the implementers wish. The function templates in the STL come with minimum requirements that must be satisfied by their implementations if they are to satisfy the standard. In most cases they must be implemented with a guaranteed running time. This adds an entirely new dimension to the idea of a function interface. In the STL the interface not only tells a programmer what the function does and how to use the functions, but also how rapidly the task will be done. In some cases the standard even specifies the particular algorithm that is used, although not the exact details of the coding. Moreover, when it does specify the particular algorithm, it does so because of the known efficiency of the algorithm. The key new point is the specification of an efficiency guarantee for the code. In this chapter we will use the terms *generic algorithm*, *generic function*, and *STL function template* to all mean the same thing.

generic
algorithm

In order to have some terminology to discuss the efficiency of these template functions or generic algorithms, we first present some background on how the efficiency of algorithms is usually measured.

■ RUNNING TIMES AND BIG-O NOTATION

If you ask a programmer how fast his or her program is, you might expect an answer like "two seconds." However, the speed of a program cannot be given by a single number. A program will typically take a longer amount of time on larger inputs than it will on smaller inputs. You would expect that a program for sorting numbers would take less time to sort ten numbers than it would to sort one thousand numbers. Perhaps it takes two seconds to sort ten numbers, but ten seconds to sort one thousand numbers. How then should the programmer answer the question "How fast is your program?" The programmer would have to give a table of values showing how long the program took for different sizes of input. For example, the table might be as shown in Display 19.14. This table does not give a single time, but instead gives different times for a variety of different input sizes.

mathematical function

The table is a description of what is called a **function** in mathematics. Just as a (non-void) C++ function takes an argument and returns a value, so too does this function take an argument, which is an input size, and returns a number, which is the time the program takes on an input of that size. If we call this function T, then $T(10)$ is 2 seconds, $T(100)$ is 2.1 seconds, $T(1,000)$ is 10 seconds, and $T(10,000)$ is 2.5 minutes. The table is just a sample of some of the values of this function T. The program will take some amount of time on inputs of every size. So although they are not shown in the table, there are also values for $T(1)$, $T(2)$, . . ., $T(101)$, $T(102)$, and so forth. For any positive integer N, $T(N)$ is the amount of time it takes for the program to sort N numbers. The function T is called the **running time** of the program.

running time

So far we have been assuming that this sorting program will take the same amount of time on any list of N numbers. That need not be true. Perhaps it takes much less time if the list is already sorted or almost sorted. In that case, $T(N)$ is defined to be the time taken by the "hardest" list, that is, the time taken on that list of N numbers that makes the program run the longest. This is called the **worst-case running time**. In this

worst case running time

Display 19.14   **Some Values of a Running Time Function**

INPUT SIZE	RUNNING TIME
10 numbers	2 seconds
100 numbers	2.1 seconds
1,000 numbers	10 seconds
10,000 numbers	2.5 minutes

chapter we will always mean worst-case running time when we give a running time for an algorithm or for some code.

The time taken by a program or algorithm is often given by a formula, such as $4N + 3$, $5N + 4$, or N^2. If the running time $T(N)$ is $5N + 5$, then on inputs of size N the program will run for $5N + 5$ time units.

Below is some code to search an array a with N elements to determine whether a particular value target is in the array:

```
int i = 0;
bool found = false;
while (( i < N) && !(found))
    if (a[i] == target)
        found = true;
    else
        i++;
```

We want to compute some estimate of how long it will take a computer to execute this code. We would like an estimate that does not depend on which computer we use, either because we do not know which computer we will use or because we might use several different computers to run the program at different times.

One possibility is to count the number of "steps," but it is not easy to decide what a step is. In this situation the normal thing to do is count the number of **operations**. The term *operations* is almost as vague as the term *step*, but there is at least some agreement in practice about what qualifies as an operation. Let us say that, for this C++ code, each application of any of the following will count as an operation: =, <, &&, !, [], ==, and ++. The computer must do other things besides carry out these operations, but these seem to be the main things that it is doing, and we will assume that they account for the bulk of the time needed to run this code. In fact, our analysis of time will assume that everything else takes no time at all and that the total time for our program to run is equal to the time needed to perform these operations. Although this is an idealization that clearly is not completely true, it turns out that this simplifying assumption works well in practice, and so it is often made when analyzing a program or algorithm.

operations

Even with our simplifying assumption, we still must consider two cases: Either the value target is in the array or it is not. Let us first consider the case when target is not in the array. The number of operations performed will depend on the number of array elements searched. The operation = is performed two times before the loop is executed. Since we are assuming that target is not in the array, the loop will be executed N times, one for each element of the array. Each time the loop is executed, the following operations are performed: <, &&, !, [], ==, and ++. This adds five operations for each of N loop iterations. Finally, after N iterations, the Boolean expression is again checked and found to be false. This adds a final three operations (<, &&, !).[3] If we tally all these

---

[3] Because of short-circuit evaluation, !(found) is not evaluated, so we actually get two, not three, operations. However, the important thing is to obtain a good upper bound. If we add in one extra operation that is not significant.

operations, we get a total of $6N + 5$ operations when the target is not in the array. We will leave it as an exercise for the reader to confirm that if the target is in the array, then the number of operations will be $6N + 5$ *or less*. Thus, the worst-case running time is $T(N) = 6N + 5$ operations for any array of N elements and any value of target.

We just determined that the worst-case running time for our search code is $6N + 5$ operations. But an operation is not a traditional unit of time, like a nanosecond, second, or minute. If we want to know how long the algorithm will take on some particular computer, we must know how long it takes that computer to perform one operation. If an operation can be performed in one nanosecond, then the time will be $6N + 5$ nanoseconds. If an operation can be performed in one second, the time will be $6N + 5$ seconds. If we use a slow computer that takes ten seconds to perform an operation, the time will be $60N + 50$ seconds. In general, if it takes the computer c nanoseconds to perform one operation, then the actual running time will be approximately $c(6N + 5)$ nanoseconds. (We said *approximately* because we are making some simplifying assumptions and therefore the result may not be the absolutely exact running time.) This means that our running time of $6N + 5$ is a very crude estimate. To get the running time expressed in nanoseconds, you must multiply by some constant that depends on the particular computer you are using. Our estimate of $6N + 5$ is only accurate to within a constant multiple.

big-*O* notation

Estimates on running time, such as the one we just went through, are normally expressed in something called **big-*O* notation**. (The *O* is the letter "Oh," not the digit zero.) Suppose we estimate the running time to be, say, $6N + 5$ operations, and suppose we know that no matter what the exact running time of each different operation may turn out to be, there will always be some constant factor c such that the real running time is less than or equal to

$$c(6N + 5)$$

Under these circumstances, we say that the code (or program or algorithm) runs in time $O(6N + 5)$. This is usually read as "big-*O* of $6N + 5$." We need not know what the constant c will be. In fact, it will undoubtedly be different for different computers, but we must know that there is one such c for any reasonable computer system. If the computer is very fast, the c might be less than 1—say, 0.001. If the computer is very slow, the c might be very large—say, 1,000. Moreover, since changing the units (say from nanosecond to second) only involves a constant multiple, there is no need to give any units of time.

Be sure to notice that a big-*O* estimate is an upper-bound estimate. We always approximate by taking numbers on the high side rather than the low side of the true count. Also notice that when performing a big-*O* estimate, we need not determine an exact count of the number of operations performed. We only need an estimate that is correct up to a constant multiple. If our estimate is twice as large as the true number, that is good enough.

size of task

An order-of-magnitude estimate, such as the previous $6N + 5$, contains a parameter for the size of the task solved by the algorithm (or program or piece of code). In our sample case, this parameter N was the number of array elements to be searched. Not surprisingly, it takes longer to search a larger number of array elements than it does to search a smaller number of array elements. Big-O running-time estimates are always expressed as a function of the size of the problem. In this chapter, all our algorithms will involve a range of values in some container. In all cases N will be the number of elements in that range.

The following is an alternative, pragmatic way to think about big-O estimates:

Only look at the term with the highest exponent and do not pay attention to constant multiples.

For example, all of the following are $O(N^2)$:

$$N^2 + 2N + 1, \quad 3N^2 + 7, \quad 100N^2 + N$$

All of the following are $O(N^3)$:

$$N^3 + 5N^2 + N + 1, \quad 8N^3 + 7, \quad 100N^3 + 4N + 1$$

These big-O running-time estimates are admittedly crude, but they do contain some information. They will not distinguish between a running time of $5N + 5$ and a running time of $100N$, but they do let us distinguish between some running times and so determine that some algorithms are faster than others. Look at the graphs in Display 19.15 and notice that all the graphs for functions that are $O(N)$ eventually fall below the graph for the function $0.5N^2$. The result is inevitable: An $O(N)$ algorithm will always run faster than any $O(N^2)$ algorithm, provided we use large enough values of N. Although an $O(N^2)$ algorithm could be faster than an $O(N)$ algorithm for the problem size you are handling, programmers have found that, in practice, $O(N)$ algorithms perform better than $O(N)$ algorithms for most practical applications that are intuitively "large." Similar remarks apply to any other two different big-O running times.

Some terminology will help with our descriptions of generic algorithm running times. **Linear running time** means a running time of $T(N) = aN + b$. A linear running time is always an $O(N)$ running time. **Quadratic running time** means a running time with a highest term of N^2. A quadratic running time is always an $O(N^2)$ running time. We will also occasionally have logarithms in running-time formulas. Those normally are given without any base, since changing the base is just a constant multiple. If you see log N, think log base 2 of N, but it would not be wrong to think log base 10 of N. Logarithms are very slow growing functions. So, a $O(\log N)$ running time is very fast.

In many cases, our running-time estimates will be better than big-O estimates. In particular, when we specify a linear running time, that is a tight upper bound and you can think of the running time as being exactly $T(N) = cN$, although the c is still not specified.

linear running time

quadratic running time

Display 19.15 Comparison of Running Times

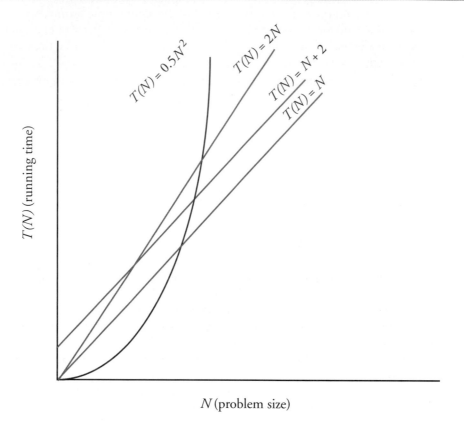

■ CONTAINER ACCESS RUNNING TIMES

Now that we know about big-O notation, we can express the efficiency of some of the accessing functions for container classes which we discussed in Section 19.2. Insertions at the back of a vector (push_back), the front or back of a deque (push_back and push_front), and anywhere in a list (insert) are all $O(1)$ (that is, a constant upper bound on the running time that is independent of the size of the container). Insertion or deletion of an arbitrary element for a vector or deque is $O(N)$ where N is the number of elements in the container. For a set or map finding (find) is $O(\log N)$ where N is the number of elements in the container.

17. Show that a running time $T(N) = aN + b$ is an $O(N)$ running time. (*Hint:* The only issue is the plus b. Assume N is always at least 1.)

18. Show that for any two bases a and b for logarithms, if a and b are both greater than 1, then there is a constant c such that $\log_a N \le c(\log_b N)$. Thus, there is no need to specify a base in $O(\log N)$. That is, $O(\log_a N)$ and $O(\log_b N)$ mean the same thing.

NONMODIFYING SEQUENCE ALGORITHMS

This section describes template functions that operate on containers but do not modify the contents of the container in any way. A good simple and typical example is the generic find function.

The generic find function is similar to the find member function of the set template class but is a different find function. The generic find function can be used with any of the STL sequence container classes. Display 19.16 shows a sample use of the generic find function used with the class vector<char>. The function in Display 19.16 would behave exactly the same if we replaced vector<char> by list<char> throughout, or if we replaced vector<char> by any other sequence container class. That is one of the reasons why the functions are called *generic*. One definition of the find function works for a wide selection of containers.

If the find function does not find the element it is looking for, it returns its second iterator argument, which need not be equal to some end( ) as it is in Display 19.16. Sample Dialogue 2 in that display shows the situation when find does not find what it is looking for.

Does find work with absolutely any container? No, not quite. To start with, it takes iterators as arguments, and some containers, such as stack, do not have iterators. To use the find function, the container must have iterators, the elements must be stored in a linear sequence so that the ++ operator moves iterators through the container, and the elements must be comparable using ==. In other words, the container must have forward iterators (or some stronger kind of iterators, such as bidirectional iterators).

When presenting generic function templates, we will describe the iterator type parameter by using the name of the required kind of iterator as the type parameter name. So, ForwardIterator should be replaced by a type that is a type for some kind of forward iterator, such as the iterator type in a list, vector, or other container template class. Remember, a bidirectional iterator is also a forward iterator, and a random-access iterator is also a bidirectional iterator. Thus, the type name ForwardIterator can be used with any iterator type that is a bidirectional or random-access iterator type as well as a plain-old forward iterator type. In some cases when we specify ForwardIterator, you

Display 19.16   The Generic find Function *(part 1 of 2)*

```
1    //Program to demonstrate use of the generic find function.
2    #include <iostream>
3    #include <vector>
4    #include <algorithm>
5    using std::cin;
6    using std::cout;
7    using std::endl;
8    using std::vector;
9    using std::vector<char>::const_iterator;
10   using std::find;

11   int main( )
12   {
13       vector<char> line;

14       cout << "Enter a line of text:\n";
15       char next;
16       cin.get(next);
17       while (next != '\n')
18       {
19           line.push_back(next);
20           cin.get(next);
21       }

22       const_iterator where;
23       where = find(line.begin( ), line.end( ), 'e');
24       //where is located at the first occurrence of 'e' in v.

25       const_iterator p;
26       cout << "You entered the following before you entered your first e:\n";
27       for (p = line.begin( ); p != where; p++)
28           cout << *p;
29       cout << endl;

30       cout << "You entered the following after that:\n";
31       for (p = where; p != line.end( ); p++)
32           cout << *p;
33       cout << endl;

34       cout << "End of demonstration.\n";
35       return 0;
36   }
```

If find does not find what it is looking for, it returns its second argument.

Display 19.16   The Generic find Function (part 2 of 2)

SAMPLE DIALOGUE 1

```
Enter a line of text
A line of text.
You entered the following before you entered your first e:
A lin
You entered the following after that:
e of text.
End of demonstration.
```

SAMPLE DIALOGUE 2

```
Enter a line of text
I will not!
You entered the following before you entered your first e:
I will not!  ◄──────────────────────────        If find does not find what it
You entered the following after that:               is looking for, it returns
                                                    line.end( ).
End of demonstration.
```

can use an even simpler iterator kind, namely, an input iterator or output iterator. Because we have not discussed input and output iterators, however, we do not mention them in our function template declarations.

Remember that the names *forward iterator*, *bidirectional iterator*, and *random-access iterator* refer to kinds of iterators, not type names. The actual type names will be something like std::vector<int>::iterator, which in this case happens to be a random-access iterator.

Display 19.17 gives a sample of some nonmodifying generic functions in the STL. Display 19.17 uses a notation that is common when discussing container iterators. The iterator locations encountered in moving from an iterator first to, but not including, an iterator last are called the **range [first, last)**. For example, the following for loop outputs all the elements in the range [first, last):

**range
[first,
last)**

```
for (iterator p = first; p != last; p++)
    cout << *p << endl;
```

Note that when two ranges are given, they need not be in the same container or even the same type of container. For example, for the search function, the ranges [first1, last1) and [first2, last2) may be in the same or different containers.

Display 19.17   Some Nonmodifying Generic Functions

These functions all work for forward iterators, which means they also work for bidirectional and random-access iterators. (In some cases they even work for other kinds of iterators that we have not covered in any detail.)

```
template <class ForwardIterator, class T>
ForwardIterator find(ForwardIterator first,
                                    ForwardIterator last, const T& target);
//Traverses the range [first, last) and returns an iterator located at
//the first occurrence of target. Returns second if target is not found.
//Time complexity: linear in the size of the range [first, last).


template <class ForwardIterator, class T>
int⁴ count(ForwardIterator first, ForwardIterator last, const T& target);
//Traverse the range [first, last) and returns the number
//of elements equal to target.
//Time complexity: linear in the size of the range [first, last).


template <class ForwardIterator1, class ForwardIterator2>
bool equal(ForwardIterator1 first1, ForwardIterator1 last1,
                               ForwardIterator2 first2);
//Returns true if [first1, last1) contains the same elements in the same order as
//the first last1-first1 elements starting at first2. Otherwise, returns false.
//Time complexity: linear in the size of the range [first, last).


template <class ForwardIterator1, class ForwardIterator2>
ForwardIterator1 search(ForwardIterator1 first1, ForwardIterator1 last1,
                     ForwardIterator2 first2, ForwardIterator2 last2);
//Checks to see if [first2, last2) is a subrange of [first1, last1).
//If so, it returns an iterator located in [first1, last1) at the start of
//the first match. Returns last1 if a match is not found.
//Time complexity: quadratic in the size of the range [first1, last1).


template <class ForwardIterator, class T>
bool binary_search(ForwardIterator first, ForwardIterator last, const T& target);
//Precondition: The range [first, last) is sorted into ascending order using <.
//Uses the binary search algorithm to determine if target is in the range [first,
//last). Time complexity: For random access iterators O(log N). For non-random-
//access iterators linear in N, where N is the size of the range [first, last).
```

---

⁴ The actual return type is an integer type that we have not discussed, but the returned value should be assignable to a variable of type int.

RANGE [FIRST, LAST)

The movement from some iterator first, often container.begin( ), up to but not including some location last, often container.end( ), is so common it has come to have a special name, range [first, last). For example, the following code outputs all elements in the range [c.begin( ), c.end( )), where c is some container object, such as a vector:

```
for (iterator p = c.begin( ); p != c.end( ); p++)
    cout << *p << endl;
```

Notice that there are three search functions in Display 19.17: find, search, and binary_search. The function search searches for a subsequence, while the find and binary_search functions search for a single value. How do you decide whether to use find or binary_search when searching for a single element? One function returns an iterator whereas the other returns just a Boolean value, but that is not the biggest difference. The binary_search function requires that the range being searched be sorted (into ascending order using <) and run in time $O(\log N)$, whereas the find function does not require that the range be sorted, but only guarantees linear time. If you have or can have the elements in sorted order, you can search for them much more quickly by using binary_search.

Note that with the binary_search function you are guaranteed that the implementation will use the binary search algorithm, which was discussed in Chapter 13. The importance of using the binary search algorithm is that it guarantees a very fast running time, $O(\log N)$. If you have not read Chapter 13 and have not otherwise heard of a binary search, just think of it as a very efficient search algorithm that requires that the elements be sorted. Those are the only two points about binary searches that are relevant to the material in this chapter.

Self-Test Exercises

19. Replace all occurrences of the identifier vector with the identifier list in Display 19.16. Compile and run the program.

20. Suppose v is an object of the class vector<int>. Use the search generic function (Display 19.17) to write some code to determine whether or not v contains the number 42 immediately followed by 43. You need not give a complete program, but do give all necessary include and using directives. (*Hint:* It may help to use a second vector.)

◼ MODIFYING SEQUENCE ALGORITHMS

Display 19.18 contains descriptions of some of the generic functions in the STL that change the contents of a container in some way.

Remember that adding or removing an element to or from a container can affect any of the other iterators. There is no guarantee that the iterators will be located at the same element after an addition or deletion unless the container template class makes such a guarantee. Of the template classes we have seen, `list` and `slist` guarantee that their iterators will not be moved by additions or deletions, except of course if the iterator is located at an element that is removed. The template classes `vector` and `deque` make no such guarantee. Some of the function templates in Display 19.18 guarantee the values of some specific iterators; you can, of course, count on those guarantees no matter what the container is.

Self-Test Exercises

21. Can you use the `random_shuffle` template function with a `list` container?

22. Can you use the `copy` template function with `vector` containers, even though `copy` requires forward iterators and `vector` has random-access iterators?

◼ SET ALGORITHMS

Display 19.19 shows a sample of the generic set operation functions defined in the STL. Note that generic algorithms assume that the containers store their elements in sorted order. The containers `set`, `map`, `multiset`, and `multimap` do store their elements in sorted order; therefore, all the functions in Display 19.19 apply to these four template class containers. Other containers, such as `vector`, do not store their elements in sorted order; these functions should not be used with such containers. The reason for requiring that the elements be sorted is so that the algorithms can be more efficient.

Self-Test Exercises

23. The mathematics course version of a set does not keep its elements in sorted order, and it has a `union` operator. Why does the `set_union` template function require that the containers keep their elements in sorted order?

Display 19.18 **Some Modifying Generic Functions**

```
template <class T>
void swap(T& variable1, T& variable2);
//Interchanges the values of variable1 and variable2.
```

The name of the iterator type parameter tells the kind of iterator for which the function works. Remember that these are minimum iterator requirements. For example, ForwardIterator works for forward iterators, bidirectional iterators, and random-access iterators.

```
template <class ForwardIterator1, class ForwardIterator2>
ForwardIterator2 copy(ForwardIterator1 first1, ForwardIterator1 last1,
                      ForwardIterator2 first2);
//last2 is such that the ranges [first1, last1) and [first2, last2) are the
//same size. Action: Copies the elements at locations [first1, last1) to
//locations [first2, last2). Returns last2.
//Time complexity: linear in the size of the range [first1, last1).


template <class ForwardIterator, class T>
ForwardIterator remove(ForwardIterator first, ForwardIterator last,
                                              const T& target);
//Removes those elements equal to target from the range [first, last). The size of
//the container is not changed. The removed values equal to target are moved to
//the end of the range [first, last). There is then an iterator i in this range
//such that all the values not equal to target are in [first, i). This i is
//returned. Time complexity: linear in the size of the range [first, last).


template <class BidirectionalIterator>
void reverse(BidirectionalIterator first, BidirectionalIterator last);
//Reverses the order of the elements in the range [first, last).
//Time complexity: linear in the size of the range [first, last).


template <class RandomAccessIterator>
void random_shuttle(RandomAccessIterator first, RandomAccessIterator last);
//Uses a pseudorandom number generator to randomly reorder the elements
//in the range [first, last).
//Time complexity: linear in the size of the range [first, last).
```

SORTING ALGORITHMS

Display 19.20 gives the declarations and documentation for two template functions: one to sort a range of elements and one to merge two sorted ranges of elements. Note that the sorting function sort guarantees a running time of $O(N \log N)$. Although it is beyond the scope of this book, it can be shown that you cannot write a sorting algorithm that is faster than $O(N \log N)$. So, this function guarantees that the sorting algorithm is as fast as possible, up to a constant multiple.

Display 19.19   **Set Operations**

These functions work for sets, maps, multisets, and multimaps (and other containers) but do not work for all containers. For example, they do not work for vectors, lists, or deques unless their contents are sorted. For these to work, the elements in the container must be stored in sorted order. These all work for forward iterators, which means they also work for bidirectional and random-access iterators. (In some cases they even work for other kinds of iterators that we have not covered in any detail.)

```
template <class ForwardIterator1, class ForwardIterator2>
bool includes(ForwardIterator1 first1, ForwardIterator1 last1,
              ForwardIterator2 first2, ForwardIterator2 last2);
//Returns true if every element in the range [first2, last2) also occurs in the
//range [first1, last1). Otherwise, returns false.
//Time complexity: linear in the size of [first1, last1) plus [first2, last2).
```

```
template <class ForwardIterator1, class ForwardIterator2, class ForwardIterator3>
void² set_union(ForwardIterator1 first1, ForwardIterator1 last1,
              ForwardIterator2 first2, ForwardIterator2 last2,
                                    ForwardIterator3 result);
//Creates a sorted union of the two ranges [first1, last1) and [first2, last2).
//The union is stored starting at result.
//Time complexity: linear in the size of [first1, last1) plus [first2, last2).
```

```
template <class ForwardIterator1, class ForwardIterator2, class ForwardIterator3>
void² set_intersection(ForwardIterator1 first1, ForwardIterator1 last1,
                     ForwardIterator2 first2, ForwardIterator2 last2,
                                    ForwardIterator3 result);
//Creates a sorted intersection of the two ranges [first1, last1) and
//[first2, last2). The intersection is stored starting at result.
//Time complexity: linear in the size of [first1, last1) plus [first2, last2).
```

```
template <class ForwardIterator1, class ForwardIterator2, class ForwardIterator3>
void² set_difference(ForwardIterator1 first1, ForwardIterator1 last1,
              ForwardIterator2 first2, ForwardIterator2 last2,
                                    ForwardIterator3 result);
//Creates a sorted set difference of the two ranges [first1, last1) and
//[first2, last2). The difference consists of the elements in the first range
//that are not in the second. The result is stored starting at result.
//Time complexity: linear in the size of [first1, last1) plus [first2, last2).
```

---

[2] Returns an iterator of type ForwardIterator3 but can be used as a void function.

Display 19.20   Some Generic Sorting Algorithms

```
template <class RandomAccessIterator>
void sort(RandomAccessIterator first, RandomAccessIterator last);
//Sorts the elements in the range [first, last) into ascending order.
//Time complexity: O(N log N), where N is the size of the range [first, last).

template <class ForwardIterator1, class ForwardIterator2, class ForwardIterator3>
void merge(ForwardIterator1 first1, ForwardIterator1 last1,
                   ForwardIterator2 first2, ForwardIterator2 last2,
                   ForwardIterator3 result);
//Precondition: The ranges [first1, last1) and [first2, last2) are sorted.
//Action: Merges the two ranges into a sorted range [result, last3) where
//last3 = result + (last1 - first1) + (last2 - first2).
//Time complexity: linear in the size of the range [first1, last1)
//plus the size of [first2, last2).
```

> *Sorting uses the < operator, and so the < operator must be defined. There are other versions, not given here, that allow you to provide the ordering relation. "Sorted" means sorted into ascending order.*

Chapter Summary

- An iterator is a generalization of a pointer. Iterators are used to move through the elements in some range of a container. The operations ++, --, and dereferencing * are usually defined for an iterator.

- Container classes with iterators have member functions end( ) and begin( ) that return iterator values such that you can process all the data in the container as follows:

  ```
  for (p = c.begin( ); p != c.end( ); p++)
      process *p //*p is the current data item.
  ```

- The main kinds of iterators are as follows.

  Forward iterators: ++ works on the iterator.

  Bidirectional iterators: Both ++ and -- work on the iterator.

  Random-access iterators: ++, --, and random access all work with the iterator.

- With a constant iterator p, the dereferencing operator *p produces a read-only version of the element. With a mutable iterator p, *p can be assigned a value.

- A bidirectional container has reverse iterators that allow your code to cycle through the elements in the container in reverse order.

- The main container template classes in the STL are list, which has mutable bidirectional iterators; and the template classes vector and deque, both of which have mutable random-access iterators.

- stack and queue are container adapter classes, which means they are built on top of other container classes. A stack is a last-in/first-out container. A queue is a first-in/first-out container.

- The set, map, multiset, and multimap container template classes store their elements in sorted order for efficiency of search algorithms. A set is a simple collection of elements. A map allows storing and retrieving by key values. The multiset class allows repetitions of entries. The multimap class allows a single key to be associated with multiple data items.

- The STL includes template functions to implement generic algorithms with guarantees on their maximum running time.

ANSWERS TO SELF-TEST EXERCISES

1. v.begin( ) returns an iterator located at the first element of v. v.end( ) returns a value that serves as a sentinel value at the end of all the elements of v.

2. *p is the dereferencing operator applied to p. *p is a reference to the element at location p.

3.
```
using std::vector<int>::iterator;
    . . .
iterator p;
for (p = v.begin( ), p++; p != v.end( ); p++)
    cout << *p << " ";
```

4. D C C

5. B C

6. Either would work.

7. A major difference is that a vector container has random-access iterators, whereas list has only bidirectional iterators.

8. All except slist.

9. vector and deque.

10. They all can have mutable iterators.

11. The stack template adapter class has no iterators.

12. The queue template adapter class has no iterators.

13. No value is returned; pop is a void function.

14. To facilitate an efficient search for elements.

15. Yes, they can be of any type, although there is only one type for each object. The type parameter in the template class is the type of element stored.

16. If 'A' is in s, then s.find('A') returns an iterator located at the element 'A'. If 'A' is not in s, then s.find('A') returns s.end( ).

17. Just note that $aN + b \leq (a + b)N$, as long as $1 \leq N$.

18. This is mathematics, not C++. So, = will mean *equals*, not assignment.

    First note that $\log a\ N = (\log a\ b)(\log b\ N)$.

    To see this first identity just note that if you raise a to the power $\log a\ N$ you get N and if you raise a to the power $(\log a\ b)(\log b\ N)$ you also get N.

    If you set $c = (\log a\ b)$ you get $\log a\ N = c(\log b\ N)$.

19. The programs should run exactly the same.

20.
```
#include <iostream>
#include <vector>
#include <algorithm>
using std::cout;
using std::vector;
using std::vector<int>::const_iterator;
using std::search;

  ...
vector<int> target;
target.push_back(42);
target.push_back(43);
const_iterator result = search(v.begin( ), v.end( ),
                        target.begin( ), target.end( ));
if (result != v.end( ))
    cout << "Found 42, 43.\n";
else
    cout << "42, 43 not there.\n";
```

21. No, you must have random-access iterators, and the list template class only has bidirectional iterators.

22. Yes, a random-access iterator is also a forward iterator.

23. The set_union template function requires that the containers keep their elements in sorted order to allow the function template to be implemented in a more efficient way.

PROGRAMMING PROJECTS

1. The point of this exercise is to demonstrate that: An object that *behaves* like an iterator *is* an iterator. More precisely, if an object accesses some container and behaves like an iterator of a particular strength, then that object can be used as an iterator to manipulate the container with any of the generic functions that require an iterator having that strength. However, while the generic algorithms can be used with this container, the *member* functions, such as begin and end, will (of course) not be present (for example, in an array) unless they have

been explicitly coded for that container. We will restrict this exercises to arrays of `double`, but the same message would hold true for any base type.

a. Argue from the properties of random access iterators that a pointer that points to an element of an array behaves exactly as a random access iterator.

b. Argue further that

i) the name of the array is a pointer to `double` that points to the first element and so the array name can serve as a "begin" iterator and

ii) that (the array's name) + (the size of the array) can serve as an "end" pointer. (Of course, this points *one past* the end, as it should.)

c. Write a short program in which you declare an array of `double` of size 10, populate this array with 10 `double`s. Then call the `sort` generic algorithm with these pointer values as arguments and display the results.

2. This problem intends to illustrate removal of several instances of a particular item from a container with the `remove` generic function. A side effect is to examine the behavior of the generic function `remove` that comes with your compiler. (We have observed some variation in the behavior of `remove` from one compiler to another.) Before you start, look up the behavior of the `remove` generic algorithm as described by your favorite STL document or web site. (For example, point your browser at `www.sgi.com`, click the "fast find" down arrow, click STL, click index, scroll down to and click `remove`. This worked as of the publication date.)

a. Modify the array declaration in Programming Project 1 to include several elements with the same value (say, 4.0, but you can use any value for this exercise). Make sure that some of these are not all together. Use the modifying generic function `remove` (see Display 19.18) to remove all elements 4.0 (that is, the value you duplicated in building the array.) Test.

b. Use the array of `double` from part a) to build a `list` and a `vector` that have the same contents as the array. Do this using the container constructor that takes two iterators as arguments. The `vector` and `list` classes each have a constructor that takes two iterators as arguments and initializes the `vector` or `list` to the items in the iterator interval. The iterators can be located in any container, including in an array. Build the `vector` and `list` using the array name for the begin iterator and the name + array length as the end iterator for the two constructor arguments. Use the modifying algorithm `remove` (Display 19.18) to remove from the `list` and from the `vector` all elements equal to 4.0 (or the value you duplicated in building the array.) Display the contents of the `vector` and `list` and explain the results.

c. Modify the code from part b) to assign to an iterator variable of appropriate type the iterator value returned by the call to the `remove` generic function. Review the documentation for `remove` to be certain you know what these iterator values mean. Output the contents of the array, the `vector` and the `list`, `begin()` to `end()`, using the "begin" and "end" we described above for the array. Output the contents of the two containers starting at the iterator retuned from `remove` to the `end()` of each container. Explain your results.

3. A **prime** number is an integer greater than 1 and divisible only by itself and and 1. An integer x is **divisible** by an integer y if there is another integer z such x = y*z. The Greek mathematician Erathosthenes (pronounced: Er-ah-**tos**-thin-eeze) gave an algorithm for finding all prime numbers less than some integer N. This algorithm is call the S*ieve of Erathosthenes.* It works like this: Beginning with a list of integers 2 through N. The number 2 is the first prime. (It is instructive to consider why this is true.) The *multiples* of 2 , that is, 4, 6, 8, etc., are *not prime.* We cross these off the list. Then the first number after 2 that was not crossed off is the next prime. This number is 3. The *multiples of 3 are not primes.* Cross these off the list. Note that 6 is already gone, cross off 9 , 12 is already gone, cross off 15, etc.. The first number not crossed off is the next prime. The algorithm continues on this fashion until we reach N. All the numbers not crossed off the list are primes.

   a. Write a program using this algorithm to find all primes less than a user supplied number N. Use a vector container for the integers. Use an array of bool initially set to all true to keep track of crossed off integers. Change the entry to false for integers that are crossed off the list.

   b. Test for N = 10, 30, 100, and 300.

   Improvements:

   c. Actually, we don't need to go all the way to N. You can stop at N/2. Try this and test your program. N/2 works and is better, but is not the smallest number we could use. Argue that to get all the primes between 1 and N the minimum limit is the square root of N.

   d. Modify your code from part a) to use the square root of N as an upper limit.

4. Suppose you have a collection of student records. The records are structures of the following type:

```
struct StudentInfo
{
    string name;
    int grade;
};
```

   The records are maintained in a vector<StudentInfo>. Write a program that prompts for and fetches data and builds a vector of student records, then sorts the vector by name, calculates the maximum and minimum grades, and the class average, then prints this summarizing data along with a class roll with grades. (We aren't interested in who had the maximum and minimum grade, though, just the maximum, minimum and average statistics.) Test your program.

5. Continuing Programming Project 4, write a function that separates the students in the vector of StudentInfo records into two vectors, one containing records of passing students and one containing records of failing students. (Use a grade of 60 or better for passing)

   You are asked to do this in two ways, and to give some runtime estimates.

   a. Consider continuing to use a vector. You could generate a second vector of passing students and a third vector of failing students. This keeps duplicate records for at least some of the time, so don't do it that way. You could create a vector of failing students and a test-for-failing function. Then you push_back failing student records, then erase (which is a member function) the failing student records from the original vector. Write the program this way.

b. Consider the efficiency of this solution. You are potentially erasing $O(N)$ members from the middle of a vector. You have to move a lot of members in this case. Erase from the middle of a vector is an $O(N)$ operation. Give a big O estimate of the running time for this program.

c. If you used a list<StudentInfo>, what are the run-time for the erase and insert functions? Consider how the time efficiency of erase for a list effects the runtime for the program. Rewrite this program using a list instead of a vector. Remember that a list provides neither indexing nor random access, and its iterators are only bidirectional, not random access.

20 CHAPTER

Patterns and UML

Patterns and UML

Einstein argued that there must be simplified explanations of nature, because God is not capricious or arbitrary. No such faith comforts the software engineer. Much of the complexity that he must master is arbitrary complexity.

F. Brooks, "No Silver Bullet: Essence and Accidents of Software Engineering," *IEEE Computer*, April 1987.

INTRODUCTION

Patterns and UML are two software design tools that apply no matter what programming language you are using, as long as the language provides for classes and related facilities for object-oriented programming. This chapter presents a very brief introduction to these two topics. It contains no new details about the C++ language.

A pattern in programming is very similar to a pattern in any other context. It is a kind of template or outline of a software task that can be realized as different code in different, but similar, applications.

UML is a graphical language that is used for designing and documenting software created within the object-oriented programming framework.

This chapter uses some material from all of the chapters that come before. However, if you have read most, but not all, of the previous chapters, you can still get all or most of the benefit from reading this chapter.

20.1 Patterns

I bid him look into the lives of men as though into a mirror, and from others to take an example for himself.

Terence (Publius Terentius Afer, 190–159 B.C.), *Adelphoe*

pattern

Patterns are design principles that apply across a variety of software applications. To be useful the pattern must apply across a variety of situations. To be substantive the pattern must make some assumptions about the domain of applications to which it applies. For example, the Iterator pattern applies to container classes of almost any kind. Recall that when we discussed iterators in Chapter 19, we first described them in the abstract as ways of cycling through a range of data in any kind of container. We then gave specific applications of the **Iterator pattern**, such as list iterator, constant list iterator, reverse list iterator, constant reverse list iterator, vector iterator, constant vector iterator, reverse vector iterator, constant reverse vector iterator, and so forth. Using the overriding pattern of an iterator allowed you to organize your knowledge about container manipulation so that you could easily understand and communicate about software that used the container and iterator classes of the STL.

Imagine the huge amount of detail you would have had to digest if we had presented each kind of container iterator separately, with different names for begin( ), end( ), and ++. Indeed, to make sense of that mountain of detail, you might have had to invent the Iterator pattern yourself. Now that you know about the Iterator pattern, you would surely see that pattern no matter how we presented iterators. However, until somebody had the insight to see and explain the pattern, the various iterators were a large number of different applications that seemed similar but were not organized by any overriding principles. Another related pattern we have been using is the Container pattern. In fact, the way patterns are usually organized, these would be seen as parts of a larger pattern known as the **Container-Iterator pattern**.

This brief chapter can give only a taste of what patterns are all about. In this section we will discuss a few sample patterns to let you see what patterns look like. There are many more known and used patterns and many more yet to be explicated. This is a new and still developing field of software engineering.

Iterator
pattern

Container-
Iterator
pattern

ADAPTER PATTERN

The **Adapter pattern** transforms one class into a different class without changing the underlying class, merely by adding a new interface. (The new interface replaces the old interface of the underlying class.) For example, in Chapter 19 we mentioned that the stack and queue template classes of the STL were adapter classes. We described both the stack and queue interfaces and said you could choose the underlying class that would actually store the data. For example, you can have a stack of ints with an underlying vector, stack<int, vector<int> > or a stack of ints with an underlying list, stack<int, list<int> > (or a stack with some other underlying container class, but two is enough for our point). In either case, list or vector, the underlying class is not changed. Only an interface is added.

How might the interface be added? That is an implementation detail that need not be part of the Adapter pattern. There are, however, at least two obvious ways to do it. For example, for a stack adapter the underlying container class could be a member variable of the stack class, or the stack class could be a derived class of the underlying container class.

Adapter
pattern

THE MODEL-VIEW-CONTROLLER PATTERN

The **Model-View-Controller pattern** is a way of dividing the I/O task of an application from the rest of the application. The Model part of the pattern performs the heart of the application. The View part is the output part; it displays a picture of the Model's

Model-
View-
Controller
pattern

state. The Controller is the input part; it relays commands from the user to the Model. Normally each of the three interacting parts is realized as an object with responsibilities for its own tasks. The Model-View-Controller pattern is an example of a divide-and-conquer strategy: One big task is divided into three smaller tasks with well-defined responsibilities. Display 20.1 diagrams the Model-View-Controller pattern.

As a very simple example, the Model might be a container class, such as a stack. The View might display the top of the stack. The Controller gives commands to push or pop data on the stack. The Model (the stack) notifies the View to display a new top-of-stack value whenever the stack contents change.

Any application can be made to fit the Model-View-Controller pattern, but it is particularly well suited to GUI (graphical user interface) design projects, where the View can indeed be a visualization of the state of the Model. (A GUI is simply a windowing interface of the form you find in most modern software applications, as opposed to the simple text I/O we have used in this book.) For example, the Model might be an object to represent your list of computer desktop object names. The View could then be a GUI object that produces a screen display of your desktop icons. The Controller relays commands to the Model (which is a desktop object) to add or delete names. The Model object notifies the View object when the screen needs to be updated.

We have presented the Model-View-Controller pattern as if the user were the Controller, primarily to simplify the example. The Controller need not be under the direct control of the user, but could be some other kind of software or hardware component.

Display 20.1 Model-View-Controller Pattern

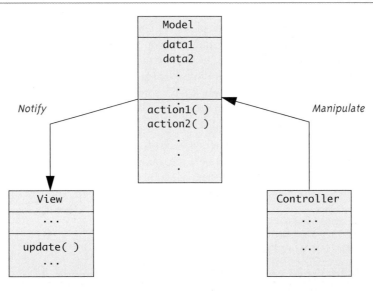

A SORTING PATTERN

The most efficient sorting algorithms all seem to follow a similar pattern. Expressed recursively, they divide the list of elements to be sorted into two smaller lists, recursively sort the two smaller lists, and then recombine the two sorted lists to obtain the final sorted list. In Display 20.2 this pattern is expressed as a template function to sort an array into increasing order using the < operator.

Our Sorting pattern uses a divide-and-conquer strategy. It divides the entire collection of elements to be sorted into two smaller collections, sorts the smaller collections by recursive calls, and then combines the two sorted collections to obtain the final sorted array. The following is the heart of our Sorting pattern:

```
int splitPt = split(a, begin, end);
sort(a, begin, splitPt);
sort(a, splitPt, end);
join(a, begin, splitPt, end);
```

Although the pattern imposes some minimum requirements on the functions split and join, the pattern does not say exactly how the functions split and join are defined. Different definitions of split and join will yield different sorting algorithms.

Array indexes are examples of iterators, and we will use the notation [begin, end) from Chapter 19 to comment the pattern and indeed to think about and derive the pattern.

The function split rearranges the elements in the interval [begin, end) and then divides the interval at a split point, splitPt. The two smaller intervals [begin, splitPt) and [splitPt, end) are then sorted by a recursive call to the function sort. Note that the split function both rearranges the elements in the array interval [begin, end) and returns the index splitPt that divides the interval [begin, end). After the two smaller intervals are sorted, the function join then combines the two sorted intervals to obtain the final sorted version of the entire larger interval.

The pattern says nothing about how the function split rearranges and divides the interval [begin, end). In a simple case, split might simply choose a value splitPt between begin and end and divide the interval into the points before splitPt and the points after splitPt, with no rearranging. We will see an example that realizes the Sorting pattern by defining split this way. On the other hand, the function split could do something more elaborate, such as moving all the "small" elements to the front of the array and all the "large" elements toward the end of the array. This would be a step on the way to fully sorting the values. We will also see an example that realizes the Sorting pattern in this second way.

The simplest realization of this Sorting pattern is the **merge sort** realization given in Display 20.3. A test program is given in Display 20.4. The merge sort is an example in which the definition of split is very simple. It divides the array into two intervals with no rearranging of elements. The join function is more complicated. After the two subintervals are sorted, it merges the two sorted subintervals, copying elements from the array to a temporary array. The merging starts by comparing the smallest elements in each smaller sorted interval. The smaller of these two ele-

merge sort

Display 20.2   Divide-and-Conquer Sorting Pattern

```
1   //This is the file sortpattern.cpp.
2   template <class T>
3   int split(T a[], int begin, int end);
4   //Rearranges elements [begin, end) of array a into two intervals
5   //[begin, splitPt) and [splitPt, end), such that the Sorting pattern works.
6   //Returns splitPt.

7   template <class T>
8   void join(T a[], int begin, int splitPt, int end);
9   //Combines the elements in the two intervals [begin, split) and
10  //[splitPt, end) in such a way that the Sorting pattern works.

11  template <class T>
12  void sort(T a[], int begin, int end)
13  //Precondition: Interval [begin, end) of a has elements.
14  //Postcondition: The values in the interval [begin, end) have
15  //been rearranged so that a[0] <= a[1] <= ... <= a[(end - begin) - 1].
16  {
17      if ((end - begin) > 1)
18      {
19          int splitPt = split(a, begin, end);
20          sort(a, begin, splitPt);
21          sort(a, splitPt, end);
22          join(a, begin, splitPt, end);
23      }//else sorting one (or fewer) elements, so do nothing.
24  }

25  template <class T>
26  void sort(T a[], int numberUsed)
27  //Precondition: numberUsed <= declared size of the array a.
28  //The array elements a[0] through a[numberUsed - 1] have values.
29  //Postcondition: The values of a[0] through a[numberUsed - 1] have
30  //been rearranged so that a[0] <= a[1] <= ... <= a[numberUsed - 1].
31  {
32      sort(a, 0, numberUsed);
33  }
```

Display 20.3   Merge Sort Realization of Sort Pattern (part 1 of 2)

```
1   //File mergesort.cpp: the merge sort realization of the Sorting pattern.
2   template <class T>
3   int split(T a[], int begin, int end)
4   {
5       return ((begin + end)/2);
6   }
```

Display 20.3   Merge Sort Realization of Sort Pattern *(part 2 of 2)*

```
7    template <class T>
8    void join(T a[], int begin, int splitPt, int end)
9    {
10       T *temp;
11       int intervalSize = (end - begin);
12       temp = new T[intervalSize];
13       int nextLeft = begin; //index for first chunk
14       int nextRight = splitPt; //index for second chunk
15       int i = 0; //index for temp

16       //Merge till one side is exhausted:
17       while ((nextLeft < splitPt) && (nextRight < end))
18       {
19           if (a[nextLeft] < a[nextRight])
20           {
21               temp[i] = a[nextLeft];
22               i++; nextLeft++;
23           }
24           else
25           {
26               temp[i] = a[nextRight];
27               i++; nextRight++;
28           }
29       }

30
31       while (nextLeft < splitPt)//Copy rest of left chunk, if any.
32       {
33           temp[i] = a[nextLeft];
34           i++; nextLeft++;
35       }

36       while (nextRight < end) //Copy rest of right chunk, if any.
37       {
38           temp[i] = a[nextRight];
39           i++; nextRight++;
40       }

41       for (i = 0; i < intervalSize; i++)
42           a[begin + i] = temp[i];
43   }
```

Display 20.4   Demonstrating the Sorting Pattern

```
1   //Tests the Divide–and–Conquer Sorting pattern.
2   #include <iostream>
3   using std::cout;
4   using std::cin;
5   using std::endl;
6   #include "sortpattern.cpp"
7   #include "mergesort.cpp"

8   void fillArray(int a[], int size, int& numberUsed);
9   //Precondition: size is the declared size of the array a.
10  //Postcondition: numberUsed is the number of values stored in a.
11  //a[0] through a[numberUsed – 1] have been filled with
12  //nonnegative integers read from the keyboard.
13

14  int main( )
15  {
16      cout << "This program sorts numbers from lowest to highest.\n";
17      int sampleArray[10], numberUsed;
18      fillArray(sampleArray, 10, numberUsed);
19      sort(sampleArray, numberUsed);

20      cout << "In sorted order the numbers are:\n";
21      for (int index = 0; index < numberUsed; index++)
22          cout << sampleArray[index] << " ";
23      cout << endl;

24      return 0;
25  }

26  void fillArray(int a[], int size, int& numberUsed)
27              <The rest of the definition of fillArray is given in Display 5.5.>
```

SAMPLE DIALOGUE

```
This program sorts numbers from lowest to highest.
Enter up to 10 nonnegative whole numbers.
Mark the end of the list with a negative number.
80 30 50 70 60 90 20 30 40 –1
In sorted order the numbers are:
20 30 30 40 50 60 70 80 90
```

ments is the smallest of all the elements in either subinterval, and so it is moved to the first position in the temporary array. The process is then repeated with the remaining elements in the two smaller sorted intervals to find the next smallest element, and so forth.

There is a trade-off between the complexity of the functions `split` and `join`. You can make either of them simple at the expense of making the other more complicated. For the merge sort, `split` was simple and `join` was complicated. We next give a realization in which `split` is complicated and `join` is simple.

Display 20.5 gives the **quick-sort** realization of our Sorting pattern. If the line

```
#include "mergesort.cpp"
```

in Display 20.4 is replaced by the following:

```
#include "quicksort.cpp"
```

then the program will give the same input and output. The files `mergesort.cpp` and `quicksort.cpp` give two different realizations of the same Sorting pattern.

In the quick-sort realization, the definition of `split` is quite sophisticated. An arbitrary value in the array is chosen; this value is called the **splitting value**. In our realization we chose `a[begin]`, as the splitting value, but any value will do equally well. The elements in the array are rearranged so that all those elements that are less than or equal to the splitting value are at the front of the array and all the values that are greater than the splitting value are at the other end of the array; the splitting value is placed so that it divides the entire array into these smaller and larger elements. Note that the smaller elements are not sorted and the larger elements are not sorted, but all the elements before the splitting value are smaller than any of the elements after the splitting value. The smaller elements are sorted by a recursive call, the larger elements are sorted by another recursive call, and then these two sorted segments are combined with the `join` function. In this case the `join` function is as simple as it possibly could be: It does nothing. Since the sorted smaller elements all preceed the sorted larger elements, the entire array is sorted.

(The quick-sort realization can be done without the use of a second temporary array (`temp`). However, that detail would only distract from the message of this example. In a real application, you may or may not, depending on details, want to consider the possibility of using the quick sort realization without a temporary array.)

quick sort

splitting value

EFFICIENCY OF THE SORTING PATTERN

Essentially any sorting algorithm can be realized using this Sorting pattern. However, the most efficient implementations are those for which the `split` function divides the array into two substantial chunks, such as half and half, or one-fourth and three-fourths. A realization of `split` that divides the array into one, or a very few, elements and the rest of the array will not be very efficient.

Display 20.5   Quick-Sort Realization of Sorting Pattern *(part 1 of 2)*

```
1    //File quicksort.cpp: the quick-sort realization of the Sorting pattern.
2    #include <algorithm>
3    using std::swap;

4    template <class T>
5    int split(T a[], int begin, int end)
6    {
7        T *temp;
8        int size = (end - begin);
9        temp = new T[size];

10       T splitV = a[begin];
11       int up = 0;
12       int down = size - 1;
13       //Note that a[begin] = splitV is skipped.
14       for (int i = begin + 1; i < end; i++)
15       {
16           if (a[i] <= splitV)
17           {
18               temp[up] = a[i];
19               up++;
20           }
21           else
22           {
23               temp[down] = a[i];
24               down--;
25           }
26       }
27       //0 <= up = down < size

28       temp[up] = a[begin]; //Positions the split value, splitV.

29       //temp[i] <= splitV for i < up; temp[up] = splitV; temp[i] > splitV for
30       //i > up. So, temp[i] <= temp[j] for i in [0, up) and j in [up, end).

31       for (i = 0; i < size; i++)
32           a[begin + i] = temp[i];

33
34       if (up > 0)
35           return (begin + up);
36       else
37           return (begin + 1); //Ensures that both pieces are nonempty.
38   }
```

Display 20.5   Quick-Sort Realization of Sorting Pattern *(part 2 of 2)*

```
39   template <class T>
40   void join(T a[], int begin, int splitPt, int end)
41   {
42       //Nothing to do.
43   }
44
```

For example, the merge sort realization of `split` divides the array into two roughly equal parts, and a merge sort is indeed very efficient. It can be shown, although we will not do so here, that the merge sort runs in time $O(N \log N)$ and that any sorting algorithm (that meets some minimal and reasonable constraints) cannot be faster than $O(N \log N)$. So, a merge sort is, in some sense, optimal.

The quick-sort realization of `split` divides the array into two portions that might be almost equal or might be very different in size depending on the choice of a splitting value. Since in extremely unfortunate cases the split might be very uneven, the worst-case running time for a quick sort is $O(N^2)$, which is much slower than the $O(N \log N)$ we obtained for the merge sort. However, for an array that is filled with randomly chosen values, most splitting values will produce a division that is close enough to an even division. So, under a suitable definition of *average case*, the quick sort has an average-case running time that is $O(N \log N)$. In practice, the quick sort is one of the best-performing sorting algorithms.

The selection sort algorithm, which we discussed in Chapter 5, divides the array into two pieces, one with a single element and one with the rest of the array interval (see Self-Test Exercise 2). Because of this uneven division, the selection sort has a worst-case, and even average-case, running time that is $O(N^2)$. In practice, the selection sort is not a very fast sorting algorithm, although it does have the virtue of simplicity.

We do not have room to provide proof of these running times in this book, but you can find such results in almost any data structures or analysis of algorithms text.

Tip   PRAGMATICS AND PATTERNS

You should not feel compelled to follow all the fine details of a pattern. Patterns are guides, not requirements. For example, we did the quick-sort implementation by exactly following the pattern in order to have a clean example. In practice, we would have taken some liberties. Notice that, with a quick sort, the `join` function does nothing. In practice, we would simply eliminate the calls to `join`. These calls incur overhead and accomplish nothing.

The Divide-and-Conquer Sorting pattern must divide the interval being sorted into two smaller intervals. If there were cases in which the `split` function divided the interval into an empty interval and the rest, then one subinterval would be the same as the original interval being divided, and infinite recursion would result. In the quick-sort realization we avoided this infinite recursion with the following lines from the definition of `split`:

```
if (up > 0)
    return (begin + up);
else
    return (begin + 1); //Ensures that both pieces are nonempty.
```

Without this extra adjustment, the function `split` could compute 0 as the value of up and so divide the interval into two intervals with one of the two being empty. That would produce infinite recursion. The way this is usually avoided with a quick-sort realization (and the way that produces the nicest code) is to separate out the split point and divide only the remaining element, so that the array interval is divided into three pieces: the split point, the subinterval before the split point, and the subinterval after the split point. This guarantees that even if one subinterval is empty, the other is shorter than the interval being divided. Thus, infinite recursion is avoided.

When these points are taken into consideration, you are likely to change the Sorting pattern to the following when you are designing the quick-sort realization:

```
if ((end - begin) > 1)
{
    int splitPt = split(a, begin, end);
    sort(a, begin, splitPt - 1);
    sort(a, splitPt + 1, end);
}//else sorting one (or fewer) elements, so do nothing.
```

Patterns are there to help you, not to provide an obstacle. Feel free to adjust them if need be.

PATTERN FORMALISM

A well-developed body of techniques exists for using patterns. We will not go into the details here. The UML discussed in Section 20.2 is one formalism used to express patterns. The place of patterns and any specific formalisms for patterns within the software design process is not yet clear. However, it is clear that basic patterns—as well as certain pattern names, such as *Model-View-Controller*—have become standard and useful tools for software design.

Self-Test Exercises

1. Is a template function definition a pattern?

2. Give the contents of a file named `selectionsort.cpp` that will realize the selection sort algorithm (see Display 5.8) for the Divide-and-Conquer Sorting pattern given in Display 20.2. (This is the selection sort analog of what was done for the quick sort in Display 20.5.)

3. Which of the following would give the fastest running time when an array is sorted using the quick-sort algorithm: a fully sorted array, an array of random values, or an array sorted from largest to smallest (that is, sorted backwards)? Assume that all arrays are of the same size and have the same base type.

20.2 UML

One picture is worth a thousand words.

Chinese proverb

People do not think in C++ or in any other programming language. As a result, computer scientists have always sought to produce more human-oriented ways of representing programs. One widely used representation is pseudocode, which is a mixture of a programming language such as C++ and a natural language such as English. To think about a programming problem without needing to worry about the syntax details of a language such as C++, you can simply relax the syntax rules and write in pseudocode.

Pseudocode has become a standard tool used by programmers, but it is a linear and algebraic representation of programming. Computer scientists have long sought to give software design a graphical representation. To this end, a number of graphical representation systems for program design have been proposed, used, and ultimately found to be wanting. Terms such as *flowchart*, *structure diagram*, and many other names of graphical program representations are today only recognized by those of the older generation. Today's candidate for a graphical representation formalism is the **Unified Modeling Language** (**UML**). The UML was designed to reflect and be used with the object-oriented programming philosophy. It is too early to say whether or not the UML will stand the test of time, but it is off to a good start. A number of companies have adopted the UML formalism for use in their software design projects.

Unified Modeling Language (UML)

HISTORY OF UML

UML developed along with object-oriented programming. As the OOP philosophy became more and more commonly used, different groups developed their own graphical or other representations for OOP design. In 1996 Grady Booch, Ivar Jacobson, and James Rumbaugh released an early version of UML. The UML was intended to bring together the various different graphical representation methods to produce a standardized graphical representation language for object-oriented design and documentation. Since that time the UML has been developed and revised in response to feedback from the OOP community. Today the UML standard is maintained and certified by the Object Management Group (OMG), a nonprofit organization that promotes the use of object-oriented techniques.

Display 20.6   A UML Class Diagram

Square
–side: double –topRtCorner: Pair<double, double>
+resize(double newSide): void +move(Pair<double, double> point): void #erase( ): void ...

UML CLASS DIAGRAMS

class diagram

Classes are central to OOP, and the **class diagram** is the easiest of the UML graphical representations to understand and use. Display 20.6 shows the class diagram for a class to represent a square. The diagram consists of a box divided into three sections. The top section has the class name, Square. The next section has the data specification for the class. In this example there are two pieces of data (two member variables): a value of type double giving the length of a side, and a value topRtCorner giving the location of the top-right corner of the square. (The value topRtCorner is given as a pair of numbers of type double, which specify a point in x,y-coordinates relative to some origin.) A minus sign indicates a private member. So, for the class Square, all data is private. The third section gives the actions (class member functions). A plus sign indicates a public member. A sharp sign, #, indicates a protected member. So for the class Square, the class diagram shows two public member functions and one protected member function. A class diagram need not give a complete description of the class. When you do not need all the members in a class for the analysis at hand, you do not list all the members in the class diagram. Missing members are indicated with an ellipsis (three dots).

CLASS INTERACTIONS

Class diagrams by themselves are of little value, since they simply repeat the class interface, possibly with ellipses. To understand a design, you need to indicate how objects of the various classes interact. The UML has various ways to indicate class interactions. Various sorts of annotated arrows indicate the information flow from one class object to another, for example, as in Display 20.1. The UML also has annotations for class groupings into library-like aggregates, for inheritance, and for other interactions. Moreover, the UML is extensible. If what you want and need is not in the UML, you can add it to the UML. Of course, this all takes place inside a prescribed framework so that different software developers can understand each other's UML.

This is just a hint of what the UML is all about. If you are interested in learning more, consult the references listed at the end of this book.

Self-Test Exercises

4. Draw a class diagram for a class whose objects represent circles. Use Display 20.6 as a model.

5. Draw a class diagram for the IntNode class presented in Display 17.4.

Chapter Summary

- Patterns are design principles that apply across a variety of software applications.
- The patterns discussed in this chapter are the Container-Iterator, Adapter, Model-View-Controller, and Divide-and-Conquer Sorting patterns.
- A pattern can give you a framework for comparing related algorithms for efficiency.
- The Unified Modeling Language (UML) is a graphical representation language for object-oriented software design.
- UML is one formalism that can and is used to express patterns.

ANSWERS TO SELF-TEST EXERCISES

1. Yes, a template function definition is a pattern, but the term *pattern* is much more general and encompasses more. Moreover, a useful pattern expressed as a template function would leave some details unimplemented. If the only variation possible is a type parameter, it is still a pattern but not likely to be usefully viewed as a pattern. (It can still be useful as a template function, but it might not be useful to view it as a *pattern* in the sense discussed in this chapter.)

2.
```
//File selectionsort.cpp: the selection sort realization
//of the Sorting pattern.
#include <algorithm>
using std::swap;

template <class T>
int indexOfSmallest(const T a[], int startIndex,
                                 int sentinelIndex)
{
    int min = a[startIndex],
        indexOfMin = startIndex;
    for (int index = startIndex + 1;
                 index < sentinelIndex; index++)
```

```
        if (a[index] < min)
        {
            min = a[index];
            indexOfMin = index;
            //min is the smallest of a[startIndex]
             //through a[index]
        }

    return indexOfMin;
}

template <class T>
int split(T a[], int begin, int end)
{
    int index = indexOfSmallest(a, begin, end);
    swap(a[begin], a[index]);
    return (begin + 1);
}

template <class T>
void join(T a[], int begin, int splitPt, int end)
{
    //Nothing to do.
}
```

3. An array of random values would have the fastest running time, since it would divide the array segments into approximately equal subarrays most of the time. The other two cases would give approximately the same running time, which would be the worst-case $O(N^2)$ running time because the algorithm would always divide an array segment into very unequal pieces, one piece with only one element and one piece with the rest of the elements. It is ironic but true that our version of the quick-sort algorithm has its worst behavior on an already sorted array. There are variations on the quick-sort algorithm that perform well on a sorted array. For example, choosing the middle element as the splitting value will give good performance on an already sorted array. But whatever splitting value you choose, there will always be a few cases with this worst-case running time.

4. There is no unique answer, but below is one suitable answer:

Circle
−radius: double −center: Pair<double, double>
+resize(double newRadius): void +move(Pair<double, double> point): void #erase( ): void ...

5.

IntNode
-data: int -link: IntNode*
+constructors +getLink( ): IntNode* +getData( ): int +setData(int theData): void +setLink(IntNode* pointer); void

PROGRAMMING PROJECTS

1. Recode the quick-sort implementation using the modified pattern given in the programming tip section entitled **Pragmatics and Patterns**.

2. Redo the Sorting pattern using classes. Define a template abstract class called Sort that has a constructor that takes an array argument. That array argument will be the array to be sorted. The class Sort will have member functions named the same and behaving the same as the functions in Display 20.2, except that they will not have an array argument. The array will be a member variable. Define the member function sort following the model of Display 20.2. The functions split and join will be pure virtual functions (Chapter 15). Then define derived classes called Mergesort and Quicksort that realize the Sorting pattern using the merge sort and quick-sort algorithms, respectively. The derived classes called Mergesort and Quicksort have definitions for the member functions split and join. Fully test all classes.

3. A vending machine accepts coins whose values sum to the price of a product or whose sum exceeds the purchase price by one coin of any denomination. The vending machine then accepts either a coin release button press that releases the inserted coins (for example, if the customer decides not to buy) or a button press to release the product and any required change, then resets the machine to a "start state." The vending machine owner can remove money, increase change in storage, or resupply the products on an as-needed basis. Write a design and code the corresponding program that models this situation.

4. In a two-story building a company has one elevator. We want to write a simulator for this elevator so that the building designers can study the elevator system.

   By each door on each floor there is a button to call the elevator. You decide what (if any) displays should be provided for the user. There are buttons in the car for door open, door close, and an alarm button. You will have to decide what outputs are needed from the simulator so that a user can see and understand what is happening in the simulation.

Identify the main objects in this situation. Identify the behavior of each object. Decide how the several objects interact. Then identify the classes and the member functions. Then identify the state that the class(es) must remember to be able to control the elevator.

We suggest a clock-driven simulation where everything happens on a clock tick (of say one second, but your program will not have any timing. A click will just be one execution of a loop.) You call a random-number generator to decide how many people arrive on each floor at each tick.

Design and code a simulation of the building's elevator.

This is not a hard exercise, but it requires clear thinking. It also requires that you supply some of the details we have left out such as the bell ringing on arrival at a floor, and the door opening, just to mention two things.

5. (Harder version of 4.) Generalize Programming Project 4 to simulate an elevator system where the number of elevators is greater than one and the number of floors is greater than two. In this version each floor will have two call buttons: one to call the elevator to go up and one to call the elevator to go down. For definiteness, use 2 elevators and 10 floors, but the principles will be the same regardless of the number. You have to decide on which of the elevators is called when the call button is pressed under several situations. For example suppose the elevator is called while one elevator is moving toward the caller's floor while the other is moving away. There are more than 4 such combinations, counting stopped elevators.

You will have to decide what additional controls and what display to provide for the users of the elevator. You will have to decide what outputs are needed from the simulator so that a user can see and understand what is happening in the simulation.

Appendix 1
C++ Keywords

The following keywords should not be used for anything other than their predefined purposes in the C++ language. In particular, do not use them for variable names or names for programmer-defined functions. In addition to the keywords listed below, identifiers containing a double underscore (_ _) are reserved for use by C++ implementations and standard libraries and should not be used in your code.

asm	do	inline	short	typeid
auto	double	int	signed	typename
bool	dynamic_cast	long	sizeof	union
break	else	mutable	static	unsigned
case	enum	namespace	static_cast	using
catch	explicit	new	struct	virtual
char	extern	operator	switch	void
class	false	private	template	volatile
const	float	protected	this	wchar_t
const_cast	for	public	throw	while
continue	friend	register	true	
default	goto	reinterpret_cast	try	
delete	if	return	typedef	

These alternative representations for operators and punctuation are reserved and also should not be used otherwise.

and	&&	and_eq	&=	bitand	&
not_eq	!=	or	||	or_eq	|=
bitor	|	compl	^	not	~
xor	^	xor_eq	^=		

Appendix 2
Precedence of Operators

All the operators in a given box have the same precedence. Operators in higher boxes have higher precedence than operators in lower boxes. Unary operators and the assignment operator are done right to left when operators have the same precedence. For example, x = y = z means x = (y = z). Other operators that have the same precedences are done left to right. For example, x+y+z means (x+y)+z.

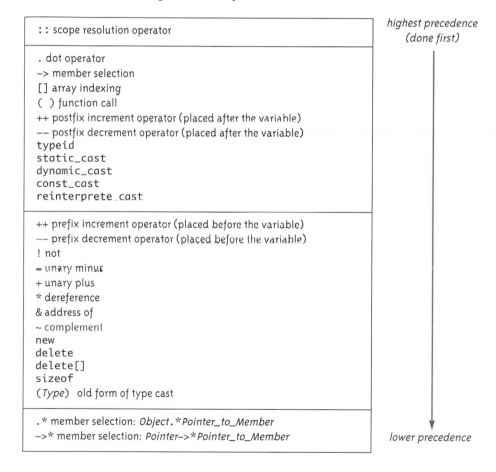

	highest precedence (done first)
:: scope resolution operator	
. dot operator -> member selection [] array indexing ( ) function call ++ postfix increment operator (placed after the variable) -- postfix decrement operator (placed after the variable) typeid static_cast dynamic_cast const_cast reinterprete_cast	
++ prefix increment operator (placed before the variable) -- prefix decrement operator (placed before the variable) ! not - unary minus + unary plus * dereference & address of ~ complement new delete delete[] sizeof (Type) old form of type cast	
.* member selection: Object.*Pointer_to_Member ->* member selection: Pointer->*Pointer_to_Member	lower precedence

* multiply / divide % remainder (modulo)
+ addition – subtraction
<< insertion operator (output), bitwise left shift >> extraction operator (input), bitwise right shift
< less than   <= less than or equal > greater than   >= greater than or equal
== equal != not equal
& bitwise and
^ bitwise exclusive or
| bitwise or
&& and
|| or
=   assignment +=   add and assign   –=   subtract and assign *=   multiply and assign   %=   modulo and assign <<=   << and assign   >>=   >> and assign &=   & and assign   ^=   ^ and assign |= | and assign
?: conditional operator
throw   throw exception
, comma

higher precedence

lowest precedence
(done last)

Appendix 3
The ASCII Character Set

Only the printable characters are shown. Character number 32 is the blank.

32		56	8	80	P	104	h
33	!	57	9	81	Q	105	i
34	"	58	:	82	R	106	j
35	#	59	;	83	S	107	k
36	$	60	<	84	T	108	l
37	%	61	=	85	U	109	m
38	&	62	>	86	V	110	n
39	'	63	?	87	W	111	o
40	(	64	@	88	X	112	p
41	)	65	A	89	Y	113	q
42	*	66	B	90	Z	114	r
43		67	C	91	[	115	s
44	,	68	D	92	\	116	t
45		69	[	93	]	117	
46	.	70	F	94	^	118	v
47	/	71	G	95	_	119	w
48	0	72	H	96	`	120	x
49	1	73	I	97	a	121	y
50	2	74	J	98	b	122	z
51	3	75	K	99	c	123	{
52	4	76	L	100	d	124		
53	5	77	M	101	e	125	}
54	6	78	N	102	f	126	~
55	7	79	O	103	g		

Appendix 4
Some Library Functions

The following lists are organized according to what the function is used for, rather than what library it is in.

ARITHMETIC FUNCTIONS

FUNCTION DECLARATION	DESCRIPTION	HEADER FILE
int abs(int);	Absolute value.	cstdlib
long labs(long);	Absolute value.	cstdlib
double fabs(double);	Absolute value.	cmath
double sqrt(double);	Square root.	cmath
double pow(double, double);	Returns the first argument raised to the power of the second argument.	cmath
double exp(double);	Returns e (base of the natural logarithm) to the power of its argument.	cmath
double log(double);	Natural logarithm (*ln*).	cmath
double log10(double);	Base 10 logarithm.	cmath
double ceil(double);	Returns the smallest integer that is greater than or equal to its argument.	cmath
double floor(double);	Returns the largest integer that is less than or equal to its argument.	cmath

■ INPUT AND OUTPUT MEMBER FUNCTIONS

FORM OF A FUNCTION CALL	DESCRIPTION	HEADER FILE
Stream_Var.open(*External_File_Name*);	Connects the file with the *External_File_Name* to the stream named by the *Stream_Var*. The *External_File_Name* is a C-string value.	fstream
Stream_Var.fail( );	Returns true if the previous operation (such as open) on the stream *Stream_Var* has failed.	fstream or iostream
Stream_Var.close( );	Disconnects the stream *Stream_Var* from file it is connected to.	fstream
Stream_Var.bad( );	Returns true if the stream *Stream_Var* is corrupted.	fstream or iostream
Stream_Var.eof( );	Returns true if the program has attempted to read beyond the last character in the file connected to the input stream *Stream_Var*. Otherwise, it returns false.	fstream or iostream
Stream_Var.get(*Char_Variable*);	Reads one character from the input stream *Stream_Var* and sets the *Char_Variable* equal to this character. Does *not* skip over whitespace.	fstream or iostream
Stream_Var.getline(*String_Var*, *Max_Characters* +1);	One line of input from the stream *Stream_Var* is read and the resulting string is placed in *String_Var*. If the line is more than *Max_Characters* long, only the first *Max_Characters* are read. The declared size of the *String_Var* should be *Max_Characters* +1 or larger.	fstream or iostream
Stream_Var.peek( );	Reads one character from the input stream *Stream_Var* and returns that character. But, the character read is *not* removed from the input stream; the next read will read the same character.	fstream or iostream
Stream_Var.put(*Char_Exp*);	Writes the value of the *Char_Exp* to the output stream *Stream_Var*.	fstream or iostream

FORM OF A FUNCTION CALL	DESCRIPTION	HEADER FILE
Stream_Var.putback(*Char_Exp*);	Places the value of *Char_Exp* in the input stream *Stream_Var* so that that value is the next input value read from the stream. The file connected to the stream is not changed.	fstream or iostream
Stream_Var.precision(*Int_Exp*);	Specifies the number of digits output after the decimal point for floating point values sent to the output stream *Stream_Var*.	fstream or iostream
Stream_Var.width(*Int_Exp*);	Sets the field width for the next value output to the stream *Stream_Var*.	fstream or iostream
Stream_Var.setf(*Flag*);	Sets flags for formatting output to the stream *Stream_Var*. See Display 12.5 for the list of possible flags.	fstream or iostream
Stream_Var.unsetf(*Flag*);	Unsets flags for formatting output to the stream *Stream_Var*. See Display 12.5 for the list of possible flags.	fstream or iostream

CHARACTER FUNCTIONS

For all of these the actual type of the argument is int, but for most purposes you can think of the argument type as char. For tolower and toupper, the type returned is truly an int. To use the value returned as a value of type char, you must perform an explicit or implicit typecast.

FUNCTION DECLARATION	DESCRIPTION	HEADER FILE
bool isalnum(char);	Returns true if its argument satisfies either isalpha or isdigit. Otherwise returns false.	cctype
bool isalpha(char);	Returns true if its argument is an upper- or lowercase letter. It may also return true for other arguments. The details are implementation dependent. Otherwise returns false.	cctype
bool isdigit(char);	Returns true if its argument is a digit. Otherwise returns false.	cctype

FUNCTION DECLARATION	DESCRIPTION	HEADER FILE
`bool ispunct(char);`	Returns `true` if its argument is a printable character that does not satisfy `isalnum` and that is not white space. (These characters are considered punctuation characters.) Otherwise returns `false`.	`cctype`
`bool isspace(char);`	Returns `true` if its argument is a white space character (e.g., blank, tab, newline). Otherwise returns `false`.	`cctype`
`bool iscntrl(char);`	Returns `true` if its argument is a control character. Otherwise returns `false`.	`cctype`
`bool islower(char);`	Returns `true` if its argument is a lowercase letter. Otherwise returns `false`.	`cctype`
`bool isupper(char);`	Returns `true` if its argument is an uppercase letter. Otherwise returns `false`.	`cctype`
`int tolower(char);`	Returns the lowercase version of its argument. If there is no lowercase versions, returns its argument unchanged.	`cctype`
`int toupper(char);`	Returns the uppercase version of its argument. If there is no uppercase versions, returns its argument unchanged.	`cctype`

C-STRING FUNCTIONS

FUNCTION DECLARATION	DESCRIPTION	HEADER FILE
`int atoi(const char a[]);`	Converts a C-string of characters to an integer.	`cstdlib`
`long atol(const char a[]);`	Converts a C-string of characters to a long integer.	`cstdlib`
`double atof(const char a[]);`	Converts a C-string of characters to a double.	`cstdlib`[a]

FUNCTION DECLARATION	DESCRIPTION	HEADER FILE
strcat(*C-String_Variable*, *C-String_Expression*);	Appends the value of the *C-String_Expression* to the end of the string in the *C-String_Variable*.	cstring
strcmp(*C-String_Exp1*, *C-String_Exp2*)	Returns true if the values of the two string expressions are different; otherwise, returns false.[b]	cstring
strcpy(*C-String_Variable*, *C-String_Expression*);	Changes the value of the *C-String_Variable* to the value of the *C-String_Expression*.	cstring
strlen(*C-String_Expression*)	Returns the length of the *C-String_Expression*.	cstring
strncat(*C-String_Variable*, *C-String_Expression*, *Limit*);	Same as strcat except that at most *Limit* characters are appended.	cstring
strncmp(*C-String_Exp1*, *C-String_Exp2*, *Limit*)	Same as strcmp except that at most *Limit* characters are compared.	cstring
strncpy(*C-String_Variable*, *C-String_Expression*, *Limit*);	Same as strcat except that at most *Limit* characters are copied.	cstring
strstr(*C-String_Expression*, *Pattern*)	Returns a pointer to the first occurrence of the string *Pattern* in *C-String_Expression*. Returns NULL if the *Pattern* is not found.	cstring
strchr(*C-String_Expression*, *Character*)	Returns a pointer to the first occurrence of the *Character* in *C-String_Expression*. Returns NULL if *Character* is not found.	cstring
strrchr(*C-String_Expression*, *Character*)	Returns a pointer to the last occurrence of the *Character* in *C-String_Expression*. Returns NULL if *Character* is not found.	cstring

a. Some implementations place it in cmath.

b. Returns an integer that is less than zero, zero, or greater than zero accordingly as *C-String_Exp1* is less than, equal to, or greater than *C-String_Exp2*, respectively. The ordering is lexicographic ordering.

string CLASS FUNCTIONS

In all cases the header file is string.

CONSTRUCTORS	
string *Variable_Name*;	Default constructor constructs an empty string.
string *Variable_Name*(*string_Object*);	Copy constructor
string *Variable_Name*(*C-String*);	C-string to string constructor
ELEMENT ACCESS	
string_Object[i]	Read/write access to character at index i.
string_Object.at(i)	Read/write access to character at index i.
string_Object.substr(*Position*, *Length*)	Returns the substring of the calling object starting at *Position* and having *Length* character.
ASSIGNMENT/MODIFIERS	
string_Object1 = *string_Object2*;	Allocates space and initializes it to *string_Object2*'s data, releases memory allocated for *string_Object1*, sets *string_Object1*'s size to that of *string_Object2*.
string_Object1 += *string_Object2*;	Character data of *string_Object2* is concatenated to the end of *string_Object1*; the size is set appropriately.
string_Object.empty( )	Returns true if *string_Object* is an empty string, false otherwise.
string_Object1 + *string_Object2*	Returns a string that has *string_Object2*'s data concatenated onto the end of *string_Object1*'s data. The size is set appropriately.
string_Object1.insert(*Position*, *string_Object2*);	Inserts *string_Object2* into *string_Object1* beginning at *Position*.
string_Object.remove(*Position*, *Length*);	Removes substring of size *Length* starting at *Position*.

COMPARISONS	
string_Object₁ == *string_Object₂* *string_Object₁*!= *string_Object₂*	Compare for equality or inequality; returns a Boolean value.
string_Object₁ < *string_Object₂* *string_Object₁* > *string_Object₂* *string_Object₁* <= *string_Object₂* *string_Object₁* >= *string_Object₂*	Lexicographical comparisons.
FINDS	
string_Object₁.find(*string_Object₂*)	Returns index of the first occurrence of *string_Object₂* in *string_Object₁*.
string_Object₁.find(*string_Object₂*, *Position*)	Returns index of the first occurrence of *string_Object₂* in *string_Object₁*; the search starts at *Position*.
string_Object₁.find_first(*string_Object₂*, *Position*)	Returns the index of the first instance in *string_Object₁* of any character in *string_Object₂*, starting the search at *Position*.
string_Object₁.find_first_not_of(*string_Object₂*, *Position*)	Returns the index of the first instance in *string_Object₁* of any character not in *string_Object₂*, starting the search at *Position*.

■ RANDOM NUMBER GENERATOR

FUNCTION DECLARATION	DESCRIPTION	HEADER FILE
int random(int);	The call random(n) returns a pseudorandom integer greater than or equal to 0 and less than or equal to n − 1. (Not available in all implementations. If not available, then you must use rand.)	cstdlib
int rand( );	The call rand( ) returns a pseudorandom integer greater than or equal to 0 and less than or equal to RAND_MAX. RAND_MAX is a predefined integer constant that is defined in cstdlib. The value of RAND_MAX is implementation dependent but will be at least 32767.	cstdlib
void srand(unsigned int); (The type unsigned int is an integer type that only allows nonnegative values. You can think of the argument type as int with the restriction that it must be nonnegative.)	Reinitializes the random number generator. The argument is the seed. Calling srand multiple times with the same argument will cause rand or random (whichever you use) to produce the same sequence of pseudorandom numbers. If rand or random is called without any previous call to srand, the sequence of numbers produced is the same as if there had been a call to srand with an argument of 1.	cstdlib

■ TRIGONOMETRIC FUNCTIONS

These functions use radians, not degrees.

FUNCTION DECLARATION	DESCRIPTION	HEADER FILE
double acos(double);	Arc cosine	cmath
double asin(double);	Arc sine	cmath
double atan(double);	Arc tangent	cmath
double cos(double);	Cosine	cmath
double cosh(double);	Hyperbolic cosine	cmath
double sin(double);	Sine	cmath
double sinh(double);	Hyperbolic sine	cmath
double tan(double);	Tangent	cmath
double tanh(double);	Hyperbolic tangent	cmath

Appendix 5
Old and New Header Files

In this book we have used the header files for standard libraries that are part of the new ANSI/ISO C++ standard. If you have an older compiler you may need to use the older header files. Below we list the new header file names that we have used in this book along with their corresponding older header file names. If the new header files do not work for you, then try the older header file names instead.

If your compiler requires the older header file names, then it also may not accommodate namespaces. In that case, you may have to eliminate all references to namespaces. If you have a compiler that requires the older header file names and/or does not support namespaces, you should consider obtaining a new compiler that comes closer to meeting the new standard.

NEW HEADER FILE	CORRESPONDING OLDER HEADER FILE
cassert	assert.h
cctype	ctype.h
cstddef	stddef.h
cstdlib	stdlib.h
cmath	math.h
cstring	string.h
fstream	fstream.h
iomanip	iomanip.h
iostream	iostream.h
string	string or no corresponding library

Further Reading

This is by no means a complete list of good C++ books available, but will get you started.

For some of the details about who and what influenced the development of the C++ language, and some of the reasons behind the decisions:

Bjarne Stroustrup, *The Design and Evolution of C++*, Addison Wesley, 1994.

For another basic C++ reference manual choose from the following:

Bruce Eckel, *Thinking in C++*, 2nd Edition, Volume One: *Introduction to Standard C++*, Prentice-Hall, 2000. Volume two was not yet out when this book went to press, but it can be expected to be as good as volume one. Volume one by itself is not as comprehensive as the other references, but is very understandable.

Margaret Ellis and Bjarne Stroustrup, *The Annotated C++ Reference Manual*, Addison Wesley, 1990. A definitive reference.

Bjarne Stroustrup, *The C++ Programming Language*, 3rd edition, Addison Wesley, 1997. Basically a shorter version Ellis and Stroustrup. If you only get one book in this group, this one would be a good choice. A new "Special Edition" is now available, which contains some additional material but appears to be basically the same book.

Stanley B. Lippman and Josée Lajoie, *C++ Primer*, 3rd Edition, Addison Wesley, 1998. Despite the title, this is not a beginner's book.

ISO/IEC FDIS 14882 *Information Technology—Programming Languages, Their Environments and System Software Interfaces—Programming Language C++*, available from ANSI, Attention: Customer Service, 11 W 42nd Street, New York, NY 10036. This is an International Standards Organization document, so it is quite expensive. There are essentially correct machine-readable copies of the December 1996 Draft Standard on the World Wide Web. Search with Altavista, for C++, ANSI, Standard. This is the definitive standards document, but one of the other choices would be less expensive and more readable.

For more on data structures in C++, any of the following would be good:

Frank M. Carrano, Paul Veroff, and Robert Helman, *Data Abstractions and Problem Solving with C++; Walls and Mirrors*, 3rd edition, Addison Wesley, 2002.

Michael Main and Walter Savitch, *Data Structures and Other Objects Using C++*, 2nd Edition, Addison Wesley, 2001.

Mark Allen Weiss, *Algorithms, Data Structures, and Problem Solving with C++*, Addison Wesley, 1996.

For more on the STL:

Graham Glass and Brett Schuschert, *The STL Primer,* Prentice Hall, 1996.

Nicolai M. Josuttis, *The C++ Standard Library, A Tutorial and Reference*, Addison Wesley, 1999.

David R. Musser, Gillmer J. Derge, and Atul Saini, *STL Tutorial and Reference Guide,* 2nd edition, Addison Wesley, 2001. This is the one I most often use in this group, but you may prefer one of the other excellent books in this group.

Mark Nelson, *A C++ Programmer's Guide to the Standard Template Library,* IDG Books, 1995.

P. J. Plauger, Alexander A. Stepanov, Meng Lee, and David R. Musser, *C++ The Standard Template Library,* Prentice Hall, 2001.

For the standard C++ libraries other than the STL:

Angelika Langer and Klaus Kreft, *Standard C++ IOStreams and Locales: Advanced Programmer's Guide and Reference* , Addison Wesley, 2000. A very detailed treatment of the iostream libraries.

P. J. Plauger, *The Draft Standard C++ Library,* Prentice Hall, 1995. A bit old but still a very good reference.

Object-Oriented Design:

Grady Booch, *Object-Oriented Design and Analysis with Applications,* 2nd edition, Benjamin-Cummings, 1994.

UML:

Grady Booch, James Rumbaugh, Ivar Jacobson, *The Unified Modeling Language User Guide,* Addison Wesley, 1999.

Index

Note to the Student

You should download Service Pack 5 for Visual C++ and install the service pack after you install Visual C++. It corrects some bugs in Vicusal C++. As we went to press the Microsoft URL for this download was:

http://msdn.microsoft.com/visualc/downloads/updates.asp